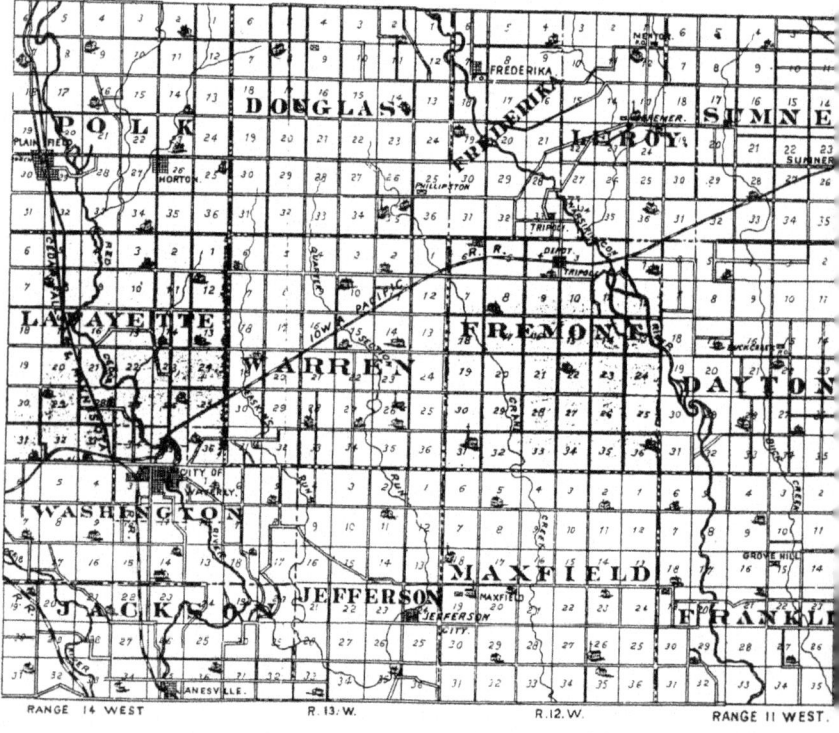

History of Bremer County Iowa

Union Publishing Company

HERITAGE BOOKS
2011

HERITAGE BOOKS
AN IMPRINT OF HERITAGE BOOKS, INC.

Books, CDs, and more—Worldwide

For our listing of thousands of titles see our website
at
www.HeritageBooks.com

A Facsimile Reprint
Published 2011 by
HERITAGE BOOKS, INC.
Publishing Division
100 Railroad Ave. #104
Westminster, Maryland 21157

Copyright © 1883 Union Publishing Company

Index Copyright © 1999 Heritage Books, Inc.

— Publisher's Notice —

Many of the pages in this book appear to be missing. The text and information is all there, the missing pages appear to be photographs that were missing from the original. The first half of this book is published in a separate volume titled *Butler Co., Iowa*.

In reprints such as this, it is often not possible to remove blemishes from the original. We feel the contents of this book warrant its reissue despite these blemishes and hope you will agree and read it with pleasure.

International Standard Book Numbers
Paperbound: 978-0-7884-1320-9
Clothbound: 978-0-7884-8824-5

TO THE PIONEERS

OF

BUTLER AND BREMER COUNTIES,

THIS VOLUME IS

RESPECTFULLY DEDICATED,

WITH THE HOPE THAT YOUR VIRTUES MAY BE EMULATED

AND YOUR TOILS AND SACRIFICES DULY APPRECIATED

BY COMING GENERATIONS.

TABLE OF CONTENTS.

HISTORY OF BREMER COUNTY.

CHAPTER I.
	PAGE
INTRODUCTORY	785

CHAPTER II.
	PAGE
EARLY SETTLEMENT	787
Historical Items	794
Organization of the County	796
The County's Name	800

CHAPTER III.
	PAGE
PIONEER LIFE	801
Early Manners and Customs	801
Character of the Pioneers	804

CHAPTER IV.
	PAGE
COUNTY GOVERNMENT	811
Acts of the County Court	811
Board of Supervisors	818

CHAPTER V.
	PAGE
OFFICIAL MATTERS	826
Bremer County Poor Farm	827
Civil Townships	828
Town Plats	828
Marriage Record	829
Abstract of Assessments	832
Other Items of Interest	835
Registry of Deeds	837

CHAPTER VI.
	PAGE
REMINISCENCES	838
By Chas. McCaffree	839
By M. Farrington	839
By Heman A. Miles	840
By S. F. Shepard	845

CHAPTER VII.
	PAGE
COURTS OF BREMER COUNTY	848
District Court	849
Circuit Court	853
County Court	854

CHAPTER VIII.
	PAGE
BAR OF BREMER COUNTY	854

CHAPTER IX.
	PAGE
THE MEDICAL PROFESSION	874
Bremer County Medical Society	883

CHAPTER X.
	PAGE
POLITICAL	884
Official Vote	897

CHAPTER XI.
	PAGE
NATIONAL, STATE AND COUNTY REPRESENTATION	913
Congressional	913
Members of General Assembly	914
Constitutional Convention	918
Auditor of State	918
Bank Examiners	918
Government Appointments	919
County Judge	920
County Auditor	921
Treasurer and Recorder	922
County Treasurer	925
County Recorder	926
Clerk of Courts	926
Sheriffs	928
County Attorneys	930
Surveyor	931
Coroners	932
Drainage Commissioners	933

CHAPTER XII.
	PAGE
THE PRESS	934
Bremer County Herald	935
Bremer County Argus	935
Waverly Republican	935
Democratic News	944
Bremer County Independent	945
Waverly Tribune	947
Sumner Gazette	948
Deutsche Volks-Zeitung	949
Janesville Clipper	949
Waverly Democrat	949

CHAPTER XIII.
	PAGE
THE WAR FOR THE UNION	950
Regimental Histories	955
Roll of Honor	971

TABLE OF CONTENTS.

CHAPTER XIV.
	PAGE
EDUCATIONAL	973
School Fund Commissioners	976
County Superintendents	979
The Development	981
Teachers' Institutes	985
Normal Institutes	986

CHAPTER XV.
TOPOGRAPHY, GEOLOGY AND AGRICULTURAL	987
Bremer County Agricultural Society	989
First Fair	991
Bremer County Farmer's Club	991
Bremer County Industrial Exposition	992
Farmers' Mutual Fire Insurance Company	992

CHAPTER XVI.
OLD SETTLERS' ASSOCIATION	997

CHAPTER XVII.
DOUGLAS TOWNSHIP	1013
Early Settlement	1013
Organic	1027
Religious	1029

CHAPTER XVIII.
DAYTON TOWNSHIP	1030
Organic	1034
Educational	1035
Religious	1035

CHAPTER XIX.
FRANKLIN TOWNSHIP	1037
Early Settlement	1037
Organic	1042

CHAPTER XX.
FREDERIKA TOWNSHIP	1044
Early Settlement	1044
Organic	1050
Educational	1051
Religious	1051
Village of Tripoli	1051
Village of Frederika	1052

CHAPTER XXI.
FREMONT TOWNSHIP	1052
Early Settlement	1052
Religious	1061
Educational	1062
Organic	1064
Town of Tripoli	1064

CHAPTER XXII.
JACKSON TOWNSHIP	1068
Early Settlement	1068
Organic	1083
Educational	1083
Town of Janesville	1083

CHAPTER XXIII.
	PAGE
JEFFERSON TOWNSHIP	1091
Early Settlement	1002
Organic	1094

CHAPTER XXIV.
LAFAYETTE TOWNSHIP	1106
Early Settlement	1106
Organic	1118
Educational	1122

CHAPTER XXV.
LEROY TOWNSHIP	1124
Early Settlement	1124
First Things	1127

CHAPTER XXVI.
MAXFIELD TOWNSHIP	1131
Early Settlement	1131
Educational	1132
Religious	1133

CHAPTER XXVII.
POLK TOWNSHIP	1136
Early Settlement	1136
Organic	1152
VILLAGE OF HORTON	1157
TOWN OF PLAINFIELD	1162

CHAPTER XXVIII.
SUMNER TOWNSHIP	1176
Early Settlement	1184
Organic	1188
TOWN OF SUMNER	1188

CHAPTER XXIX.
WARREN TOWNSHIP	1214
Organic	1223
Educational	1224
Religious	1225

CHAPTER XXX.
WASHINGTON TOWNSHIP	1226
Organic	1226
Early Settlement	1227

CHAPTER XXXI.
CITY OF WAVERLY	1242
Recorded Plats	1243
Early Days	1243
Incorporation	1252
Items Chronologically Arranged	1254
The Lost Child	1256
Business Development	1275
Industrial Enterprise	1281
Religious	1294
Educational	1296
Societies	1296

TABLE OF CONTENTS.

CHAPTER XXXII.

	PAGE
MISCELLANEOUS	1315
Bremer County of To-day	1323
Bremer County Bible Society	1315
Bremer County Temperance Society	1315
Bremer County in 1858	1319
Chapin, Jacob (dec.)	1316
Climate	1321
Elliott, John (dec.)	1318
Face of the County	1320
Faville, O. (dec.)	1316
Fruit	1321
Health	1321
Honored Dead	1316
Lands	1322
Lyman, James P. (dec.)	1318
Tyrrell, Edward (dec.)	1317
Morehouse, Henry (dec.)	1318
Products	1321
Settlement	1321
Society	1322
Soil	1321
Timber	1320
Towns	1322
Rivers	1319

BIOGRAPHICAL.

Name	PAGE
Adair, James	930
Ableqs, R. H.	1097
Alcock, Charles	1092
Alger, H. C.	1205
Allen, C. C.	860
Allen, A. D.	1022
Anderson, W. W.	861
Andrews, W. W.	863
Andrews, James	1112
Archer, Benj.	1241
Avery, O. F.	858
Annis, H. B.	1175
Austin, Albert	1154
Austin, C. A.	1195
Babcock, Orlando	1234
Baker, S. F.	925
Ballantine, Hugh	1083
Baskins, Abner	1227
Baskins, Joseph	1227
Baskins, Wm	1096
Barrick, Isaac	1068
Barrick, John T.	1084
Bartels, E. H.	1068–1097
Barnes, Eli	1048
Barrows, C. H	1312
Baumgartner, A	1201
Baumann, Hermann	1105
Bayer, Wm	1104
Beal, W. W	1040
Becker, Lewis	1105
Beck, Joseph	1019
Beebe, David	1114
Bennett, Benj	1114
Billings, N. B	865
Boardman, J. M	1173
Bodeker, C. L	1103
Bloker, John	1073
Bostwick, W. R.	1045
Bouckhouse, A	1067
Boylson, Patrick	1117
Boyd, H. B	1096
Boyer, M. L.	1049
Boys, Wm	877
Bowman, J. H.	1266
Bowen, Joseph	1118
Bradford, D. S.	882
Brandt, E. G.	1104
Braum, Heinrich	1105
Branch, L E	1144
Brainard, T. F	1027
Bredow, Paul	1135
Briden, Wm	1075
Briden, H. W	1102
Briden, H. T.	1101
Brodie, Robert	1125
Broadie, Adam	1262
Brown, James	1054
Brown, J. F	1307
Brown, A. F	868
Brodie, Charles	1127
Bryant, Z. A	877
Bryant, Z. Z	881
Byrnes, Patrick	1313
Bucknam, J. O.	1056
Buckins, Frank	1231
Bullock, Edward	1218
Bunth, H. S.	1147
Bunth, F. H.	1140
Burbank, Jerome	878
Burbank, Oscar	876
Burgess, Thomas	1151
Burke, John E	861
Burrington, H. H.	980
Bussey, E. I.	1233
Cadwallader, C	1081
Cagley, Jacob	1116
Calease, J. W	1104
Cass, O. A.	863
Carpenter, Chauncey	1194
Carey, John	1236
Carr, Ezra	862
Case, Louis	918
Case, Homer H.	1216
Case, A. J.	1301
Carpenter, Josiah	873
Carpenter, Philip	1020
Cass, E. M.	1033
Cass, S. F.	1195
Caswell, David	1182
Cavanaugh, N.	1228
Chamberlin, D. C.	981
Chapin, John	1056
Chandler, Willard	1234
Chambers, D. H.	1113
Chittenden, D.	1216
Christiern J. H.	1233
Clark, John	791
Clark, David	791
Clark, W. O.	879
Cleary, Timothy	1014
Clewell, R. W.	1082
Coan, D. W	861
Coddington, Frank	1073
Colton, Wm. R.	1112
Collins, C. P.	1174
Connon, James	1119
Conner, James A.	930
Converse, C. W	1023
Congdon, Myron	1197
Cooper, C. H.	928
Cooper, A. D.	1076
Cook, J. J	1057
Cool, D. W	876
Corlett, J. J	1137
Cruthers, James	1216
Cretzmeyer, Fred	1243
Cretzmeyer, W.	1243
Curtis, S. H	1258
Curtis, John	1114
Curtis, W. V	1031
Davis, W. M.	1145
Davis, B. F.	1074
Dawson, E. A.	867
Dawson, J.	1182
Dean, Geo. H.	979
Dean, Daniel	1303
Dean, E.	948
Dibble, R. V	1041
Dickinson, A. A	1027
Dunkelberg, R. A.	883
Dougherty, M. B.	866
Dougherty, E. C.	926
Dougherty, D. B.	1074
Dougherty, E. M.	1081
Downing, Thomas S	1257
Early, Wm	1024
Eckert, Henry	1175
Eggleston, Betsy	878
Eggleston, C. E.	1236
Eichler, F.	1295
Eisenhart, Eli	1046
Elvis, N. P.	1274
Ellsworth, R. J.	1246
Eldridge, J. R.	929
Emily, A. W	1145
Empson, J. W	1175
Emmons, T. P	1206
Eveland, Mason	1107
Eveland, Jacob M	1108
Eveland, Henry	1111
Farnsworth, Robert	1141
Farnsworth, Guy	1101
Farnsworth, John R.	1175
Farris, Jeremiah	920
Farrington, M.	1005
Farr, Wm	1145
Fitchthorn, Daniel	946
Fisher, Dr.	875
Fish, E. W	1073
Fletcher, James	944
Folks, Charles	1142
Forssman, Peter	1212
Fortner, A.	1265
Foster, Seth L.	1117
Foster, John R.	1117
Foutch, John J.	1097
Fox, D. B.	1116
Frank, F. H	1198
Fletcher, James	944
French, George H	1181
Freeman, Israel	1078
Freeman, J	1113
Pritcher, J. P	1140
Fulton, A. D.	1174
Fuller, W. W	857
Fuller, Harvey	1115
Furrow, J	1146
Gaines, Wm. N.	1075
Gardner, H. H.	1017
Garner, A.	1273
Garrod, Canfield	1041
George, W. H	1141
Gibson, D. T	867
Gillett, David	1046
Gillett, M. F.	927
Gleason, Alonzo	1098
Goodsell, H. W.	1237
Goodspeed, Seymour	1238
Gould, H. D.	1098
Gould, Nichols	1217
Gray, H. J.	873
Granger, E. A	1142
Gross, J. N	878
Grover, W.S.	1114
Haase, L. C	1313
Hamilton, W. B.	922
Hand, John C.	1078
Harker, John	1022
Hanner, John	1218
Harmon, W. P.	856
Harrington, Albert	1148
Harrington, O. C	916
Harris, Wm. P	1227
Hartman, H. B.	1297
Harwood, Wm	1042
Harris, Thomas	1141
Hastings, C. R.	1142
Hatch, D. R.	1178
Hanchett, L. S.	917
Hazlett, Hugh	1057
Hazlett, Wm. G	1058
Read, Amos	1163
Head, John K.	1141
Heine, Henry	1215
High, David	1074
Holt, D. P.	1273
Hoffman, H. J.	1258
Hoffman, S. E	861
Hoover, H. S	931
Homrighaus, John	1104
Howe, Chas. M.	1086
Hoyt, S. R. J.	1284
Hunter, John	922
Hurley, Wm	1308
Husband, Wm. C.	1183

TABLE OF CONTENTS.

	PAGE		PAGE		PAGE		PAGE
Ingersoll, W. B.	1214	McCumber, Albert	1031	Redeman, P.	882	Taber, E. F.	1303
Ingham, H. S.	1151	McCord, J. P.	1304	Reinler, C. F.	1197	Tanner, A. J.	864
Jackson, Alexis	1187	McDonald, R. G.	1014	Rice, W. A.	1221	Taft, Isaac	1187
Jarvis, A. H.	1204	McMeekin, Wm.	1206	Ried, C. D.	1024	Terry, Adin	1144
Jeffers, J. F.	1623	Meier, H. O.	1102	Rima, Levi	1045	Terry, Eri	1118
Jennings, Samuel	1073	Messenger, J. C.	1236	Roach, John	1118	Tibbitts, W. J.	1102
Jennings, W. H.	1211	Messenger, E. J.	1082	Roberts, C. B.	980	Tibbitts, O. O.	1188
Jolly, Robert	1056	Messenger, J. H.	730	Roberts, J. M.	1147	Thoren, Christian	1258
Jones, S. N.	1081	Mickley, Thomas	1078	Robinson, W. S.	1021	Thies, Henry	1258
Kasemeier, Henry	926	Miller, Anton	1183	Robinson, W. A.	1022	Thompson, Barnes	1143
Kelly, James	1116	Moehling, John	1054	Robinson, M. H.	862	Thull, Frank	1263
Kierchhoff, Diedrich	1021	Moehling, C. H.	1067	Robertson and Ladd	1217	Tower, Thomas W.	1187
Kingsley, S. H.	1221	Morse, Caleb	925	Rosencrans, John	1255	Trumbo, Israel	931
King, Wm.	1203	Moody, W. J.	889	Rowe, Albert	1178	Tyler, E. H.	1143
Kimbal, George	1053	Moody, Wm.	1057	Rowe, Charles	1177	Tyrrell, Clarence	1214
Kinnie, Eph.	864	Mooney, Wm.	1263	Rowen, W.	971	Tyrrell, Wm. H.	944
Kollock, Harriet M.	878	Mores, A. S.	1302	Ruddick, G. W.	856	Tyrrell, Thomas	1298
Knott, E.	1281	Mores, Wm. H.	1305	Runyard, Austin	1305	Tyrrell, N.	1296
Krause, Frederick	1183	Morehouse, Geo	975	Rust, Herman	921		
Krech, H. C.	1163	Moulton, A. K.	978	Russell, J. Q. A.	1301	Voight, John	1308
Krieger, S. C.	1112	McKee, John	1037				
Lay, Charles	1151	McRoberts, Thomas	1116	Sullivan, Harvey	1311	Wade, Abraham	1115
Lashbrook, Thomas	1231	Muffly, J. H.	1202	Stroune, O. A.	1277	Wagner, John	1205
Lawrence, A. S.	1303	Myers, Abraham	1072	Starr, A.	1262	Walker, R.	1021
Lease, Henry, Jr.	1181	Nafus, G. W.	1147	Sellsig, L.	1276	Walling, E. J.	1048
Leamon, J. S.	1014	Newcomb, E. S.	1224	Sewell, Allen	1306	Walling, D. P.	1049
Lee, F. A.	1314	Nicholson, W. J.	1221	Schlutsmeyer, F. H.	1311	Walker, P. N.	1174
Lehman, Daniel	928	Nichols, Gould	1217	Shoes, L. M.	1281	Walker, E. C.	1164
Lehman, Moses	1228	Nichols, Horace	879	Simmers, Abram	1268	Walker, Geo. E.	872
Lester, Hiram	1053	Norris, W. W.	922-679	Smillie, Francis	1305	Warn, H. L.	1257
Leverich, Charles	1232	Norris, Keeler	1301	Smith, Wm.	1305	Ward, Jesse	877
Leverich, Jesse	1237	Norton, Frances J.	1166	Spalding, M. S.	1303	Watts, Geo	1030
Linn, G. P.	949	Oberdorf, P.	1117	Swan, P. V.	856	Watenpaugh, E.	1126
Littell, D. R.	1198	O'Day, Patrick	1124	Shaver, Hiram	861	Watkins, M. M.	1055
Liebert, Charles	1041	Olney, J. B.	1020	Stowe, W. A.	868	Ward, Jacob	1040
Littlefield, M. S.	1017	Oitrogge, John	1163	Smalley, E. L.	875	Westcott, Orris	1194
Long, Nelson	1225	Orvis, S. N.	1182	Smith, J. G.	917	Wells, H. R.	1234
Long, D. A.	1022	Owen, C.	1205	Skitlin, James A.	929	Wente, H. C.	1135
Losee, L. E.	882	Owen, L. S.		Smith, N. M.	1137	Wheaton, George W.	1178
Loveland, J.	1076	Parker, Lucas	1108	Smith, Lloyd	1138	Whiting, Luther	1024
Loveland, C. K.	1114	Parsons, C. B.	863	Smith, Joseph	1138	Walker, Frank K.	1208
Loveland, D. E.	1237	Peck, N. C.	1638	Smith, J. L.	1145	Wilburm, U.	1066
Lucas, Parker	1272	Pelton, Wm. A.	1107	Spalding, J. F.	1152	Wilson, A. B.	1118
Lush, L. L.	1034	Perkins, Benj. F.	860	Sewell, Samuel	1019	Wilson, L. P.	1018
Lyon, Wm. T.	1146	Perkins, D. E.	878	Smith, C. O.	1019	Wile, John	1232
Lynes, W. W.	1648	Perry, M. B.	1040	Sinderson, Thomas	1025	Wilson, J. N.	880
Lytle, Henry	1304	Perry, E. N.	1233	Shirley, John W.	1032	Winner, A. M.	1233
LeValley, Geo		Pierce, N. E.	1278	Stephens, Alex	1057	Woodring, Peter	1201
Magee, John C.	1287	Pierce, Riley	1151	Sterling, W. P.	1058	Wood, J. W.	1307
Marsh, N. B.	1113	Pierce, Daniel	1071	Sweet, A. E.	1058	Wood, James W.	862
Martin, J. H.	1057	Pierson, W. J.	1157	Sweet, H. H.	1077	Woodring, J. F.	1204
Martin, A. T.	1655	Phillips, S. B.	1101	Schuknecht, C.	1006	Woodruff, E. A.	1304
Martin, Betsy	875	Potter, H.	1018	Shepard, S. F.	1105	Worden, John L.	1033
Martin, Asa T.	1047	Putter, Warren	1137	Shaw, Enos F.	1112	Wright, Gancelo C.	857
Maynard, J. K. L.	865	Pomroy, J. C.	878	Stears, John	1177	Wright, M. S.	1197
Maxfield, Geo. M.	928	Prue, Nelson	1215	Stufflebeam, J.	1215	Wynhoff, H. J.	1045
McCaffree, C.	788			Stevenson, A. L.	1229	Wyhm, Jasper	1238
McCormack, Charles	1228	Rand, J. C.	1207	Sturdevant, J. M.		Wuest, Mathias	1054
McCracken, Thomas	1023	Reeves, N. A.	1111	Simmons, John	1231	Yerton, J. H.	1032
McCracken, A. H	865	Reeves, B. M.	1311	Sewell, T. J.	1234	Youngs, Wm. H. H.	1077
				Stockwell, W. L.			

PORTRAITS.

	PAGE		PAGE		PAGE		PAGE
Barrick, Isaac	1069	Farrington, M	995	High, David	1189	Reeves, N. A.	1100
Boys, W. M. M. D.	1059	Fuller, Harvey	1129	Homrighaus, John	1199	Reeves, B. M.	1179
Briden, H. W.	1043					Rust, Herman	932
Brown, A. F.	1269	Gibson, D. T.	1309	Jennings, Samuel	1080	Shepard, S. F.	1079
Burr, H. S.	1259	Gleason, A.	1059			Stears, John	1160
		Gray, H. H.	1289	Knott, E.	1238		
Cadwallader, C.	1025	Gould, H. D.	977				
Case, Louis	1229			Lee, Frank A.	1249	Terry, Adin	1149
Coddington, F.	1115	Harmon, W. P.	959	Long, D. A.	1139	Tyrrell, Edward	1219
Colton, Wm. M.	1119	Harrington, O. C.	1129	Lush, L. L.	1150	Tyrrell, Nicholas	1299
Cooper, C. H.	1005	Heine, Henry	1209				

Certificates of Bremer County Committees.

Below is given a copy of the certificate, signed by the committee appointed by the Old Settlers' Society, to revise and correct the general History of Bremer County, and also committees from each township, to revise and correct the histories of the various townships, showing that the publishers have complied with their promises, and did their utmost to produce a reliable and complete history of the county. The general committee, in union meeting, unanimously appointed two additional members of the committee, to fill vacancies caused by others being unable to attend. The following is the certificate of the general committee:

"We, the undersigned, members of the general committee appointed by the Old Settlers' Society of Bremer County, to correct and revise the manuscript of the History of Bremer County, written and compiled by the Union Publishing Company, of Springfield, Illinois, do hereby certify that we did, to the best of our ability, examine said manuscript and made all the changes and additions that we in our judgment deemed necessary, and as corrected, approve the same:

O. C. Harrington,
C. R. Hastings,
V. B. Grinnell,
Oscar Burbank,   } Committee.
M. Farrington,
Louis Case,
David Clark.

Following is the certificate of the committees for the respective cities and townships:

"We, the committee appointed by the Old Settlers' Society, to revise and correct the history of [our respective townships] for the History of Bremer County, written and compiled by the Union Publishing Company, of Springfield, Illinois, do hereby certify that said manuscript was submitted to us, and that we did make all the changes, corrections and additions that we in our judgment deemed necessary, and as corrected, approve of the same."

George Watts,
J. B. Yerton,
—*Dayton Township.*

John McItea,
N. C. Peck,
—*Franklin Township.*

E. Watenpaugh,
Robert Brodie,
—*Leroy Township.*

H. H. Case,
James Sturtevant,
—*Warren Township.*

James Lennan,
Timothy Clary,
—*Douglas Township.*

Simeon Shepard,
Frank Coddington,
Isaac Barrick,
—*Jackson Township.*

Rev. P. Bredow,
—*Maxfield Township.*

Mark Gillett,
G. N. Bowers,
—*Frederika Township.*

Matthew Farrington,
J. J. Fontch,
—*Jefferson Township.*

O. C. Harrington,
C. R. Hastings,
—*Polk Township.*

David Clark,
D. A. Long,
Oscar Burbank,
Reuben J. Ellsworth,
Louis Case,

Asa Martin,
Andrew Carsteson,
—*Fremont Township.*

Mason Eveland,
James Andrews,
William Pelton,
—*Lafayette Township.*

S. F. Cass,
Myron Congdon,
D. R. Hutch,
—*Sumner Township.*

Mrs. Alma N. Wood,
—*Washington Township,*
and
City of Waverly.

Certificates of Butler County Committees.

"We, the undersigned, members of the general committee, appointed by the Old Settlers' Society of Butler County, to correct and revise the manuscript of the History of Butler County, written and compiled by the Union Publishing Company, of Springfield, Illinois, do hereby certify that said manuscript was submitted to us, and that we made all the changes and additions that we in our judgment deemed necessary, and as corrected, we are satisfied with and approve of the same:

J. J. Eichar,
J. M. Caldwell,
Jeremiah Perrin,   } Committee.
Milton Wilson,
James Griffith,
W. R. Jamison,

Following is the certificates of the committees for the respective townships and cities:

"We, the committee appointed by the Old Settlers' Society of Butler County, to correct and revise the history of [our respective five townships] for the History of Butler county, compiled and written by the Union Publishing Company, of Springfield, Illinois, do hereby certify that said manuscript was submitted to us, and that we made all the changes and additions that we in our judgment deemed necessary. As corrected, we are satisfied with and approve of the same."

P. P. Parker,
Richard Daniels,
Daniel Downey,
—*Albion Township.*

James Griffith,
Solomon Stintz,
—*Coldwater Township.*

Edward Coyle,
W. Watson,
—*Madison Township.*

John Leverich,
Mrs. Elizabeth Adair,
J. W. Stewart,
J. H. Carter,
J. L. Stewart,
W. A. Stewart,
—*Shell Rock Township.*

Charles Ensign,
James Collar,
G. E. Fitch,
—*Beaver Township.*

Hugh Thomas,
J. V. Boggs,
—*Dayton Township.*

James M. Caldwell,
W. F. Quinn,
—*Monroe Township.*

Milton Wilson,
Oliver Evans,
—*Bennezette Township.*

A. D. Young,
S. Bonwell,
—*Fremont Township.*

James Harlan,
M. S. Needham,
W. B. Jamison,
S. K. Dearmoun,
—*Pittsford Township.*

M. Parriott,
C. Stockdale,
—*Washington Township.*

J. P. ——,
Geo. W. Poisal,
J. J. Eichar,
—*Butler Township.*

Cyrus Doty,
M. S. Wensley,
—*Jackson Township.*

W. C. Thompson,
P. E. Dunson,
—*Jefferson Township.*

Henry Trotter,
James Hunter,
—*Ripley Township.*

C. L. Jones,
Frank S. Kelson,
—*West Point Township.*

HISTORY OF BREMER COUNTY, IOWA.

CHAPTER I.

INTRODUCTORY.

ONE of the most interesting, as well as the most useful, studies to the youthful mind, as well as the advanced thinker, is that of general and local history. Especially is this true when the historian treats of a country as it existed in its primitive state; tells how it was peopled, and enters somewhat into detail in relation to the manner and life of the pioneers. There is a peculiar fascination about the rude life of the early settlers of a new country. The freedom of action, the unconstrained manner with which he receives one and all, and the generous hospitality, is indeed commendable.

Less than a half century ago, that part of the State of Iowa comprising the county of Bremer was an unbroken wilderness, inhabited only by the wild beasts of the forests, wild birds of the air, and no less wild red men, who roamed at will over the broad prairies, fishing in the Cedar and Wapsipinecon rivers, or hunting the game that everywhere abounded, seemingly caring nothing for the morrow, and only living in the ever present. The thought of the "palefaces" penetrating this beautiful country had not yet disturbed them, and so they continued on in their daily life of hunting and fishing, with occasionally a short war between tribes, to relieve the monotony of their lives. But the time was soon to come when they would surrender up the lands and move on toward the setting sun. The time was soon to come when all nature must be changed; when the fair prairies, with their beautiful flowers, painted only by the hand of God, must be broken up by the husbandman, and grain fit for the use of civilized man sown therein.

Forty years ago, still all was a wilderness; the soil had been unvexed by the plow, and the woodman,s ax had never been heard; the cabin of the settler, with its smoke curling heavenward, with an air inviting the weary traveler to come and rest, was not to be seen, nor even the faintest trace of civilization, but, instead, boundless emerald seas and luxuriant grasses.

"These, the gardens of the deserts—these,
The unshorn fields, boundless and beautiful,
And fresh as the young earth ere man had sinned.
    Lo! they stretch,
In airy undulations, far away,
As though the ocean, in the gentlest swell,
Stood still, with all his rounded billows fixed,
And motionless forever."

The prairies, indeed, were a grand sight—in the summer, "clothed in verdure green;" in the fall, in that color that too well tells of the departing years. If a grand sight to see the prairies, as the tall grass waved to and fro, it was a magnificent sight, in the fall of the year, to see the annual prairie fire as it sweeps over all. A correspondent of an Eastern paper, in an early day, in traveling West, witnessed one of these fires, and thus describes it in a communication to his paper:

"Whilst enjoying the sublimity of the scene, night threw her mantle o'er the earth, and the sentinel stars set their watch in the skies, when suddenly the scene was lighted by a blaze of light, illuminating every object around. It was the prairie on fire. Language cannot convey, words cannot express to you the faintest idea of the grandeur and splendor of that mighty conflagration. Methought that the pale Queen of Night, disclaiming to take her accustomed place in the heavens, had dispatched ten thousand messengers to light their torches at the altar of the setting sun, and that now they were speeding on the wings of the wind to their appointed stations. As I gazed on that mighty conflagration, my thoughts recurred to you, immured in the walls of a city, and I exclaimed in the fullness of my heart:

'O fly to the prairie in wonder, and gaze,
As o'er the grass sweeps the magnificent blaze;
The world cannot boast so romantic a sight,
A continent flaming, 'mid oceans of light.'"

Behold, how changed the scene! Where the rude wigwam of the red man once stood, a palatial-like residence is seen; where once the sons of the forest gathered together for the worship of Manitou, the "Great Spirit," the handsome church edifice is erected in which assemble those of another race worshipping the God of their fathers. Change is written upon every hand. How this change was wrought, the various steps by which the wilderness has been transformed into habitations for civilized man, is the duty of the historian to show; and in the following pages the attempt is made, with the hope that his efforts will be appreciated, and that the facts contained therein may be of interest, and the lessons of the past may be instructive to each and every reader.

CHAPTER II.

EARLY SETTLEMENT.

To the readers of local history, the chapter pertaining to the early settlement of a country is of general interest, especially is this the case with pioneers themselves, those who have witnessed the changes that have been made, who have seen a trackless wilderness transformed into a beautiful country, and filled with an enterprising, happy people. He here reads, slowly and critically, every word, recalling memories of the past, which for a generation have been buried among a host of recollections, which now arise before him like a dream. His old associations, the deeds, the trials and battles against hunger and cold, while the settlers were few and far between, and wolves howled about the little log cabin, sending a chill to his heart; and the wind driving the sifting snow through the crevices—all now arise vividly before him. Often is it with pleasure, he can recall these recollections, viewing with satisfaction the thought that he has lived to see a thrifty and wealthy land, dotted with school houses and churches, villages and cities.

But again it will be, with sadness that the past is recalled, as thoughts spring up of the dark and painful side of early days. How a wife, whose virtues, bravery and simplicity will always be remembered, or a child, prattling in innocence, being called from earth to the eternal home, laid away under the cruel sod, in solemn quietude, by the rough but tender hands of hardy pioneers. Time had partially allayed the sting, but the wound is now uncovered by the allusion to days gone by, and the cases are not a few, where a tear of bitter sadness will course down the cheek in honor of the memory of those who have departed.

Notwithstanding the many disadvantages, and even sorrows attendant upon the first steps of civilization, the adversities to be encountered; the pioneers led a happy life. The absence of the aristocratic and domineering power of wealth and position, must have been a source of comfort and satisfaction. Merit alone insured equality, and this could not be suppressed by traditions. The brotherhood of man was illustrated in a sincere and practical way, and hospitality was not considered so much a christian trait as a duty to humanity.

Prior to 1845, the territory now comprising the county of Bremer was a vast expanse of prairie and timber, uninhabited by aught save Indians, and wild animals. The confines of civilization had not much more than crossed the Mississippi, and a journey through the territory west of the "Father of Waters," was a tedious, and justly considered a dangerous task.

This county, lying as it does in the Cedar and Wapsipinicon valleys, had no doubt been visited by white men, for these fertile valleys had long been the trail of the hunter and trapper before actual settlers made their appearance. . This part of the State was known as an Indian reservation, belonging to and occupied by various tribes. Those in actual possession, it is claimed, were the Winnebagos. Yet there were also members of the tribes of Musquaukees and Pottawatomies. There were about five hundred of the Winnebagoes who had quite a large village on sections 22 and 23, in Jefferson township. The Musquaukees numbered about one hundred, and the Pottawatomies about fifty. During the summer season they would leave their homes here and push northward for game and fish, leaving only their sap troughs, log shanties covered with bark, and their brass sugar kettles. The latter they buried where they would not be discovered by passers by; and it is not improbable that there are many of these brass utensils yet hid in the woods in Jefferson township.

The Indians did not, as is generally imagined, cultivate land, plant corn, or raise vegetables, but lived a life of indolence. The three tribes were intermixed and lived together in comparative harmony. The most notable chiefs were Womanokaker (often spelled Wananoker), Four Eyes, Pukatuk, Winnesheik, Hanahetaker, and Big Way (sometimes spelled Big Wave). Womanokaker (or Wananoker) was the great war chief; and the tradition has been handed down that he got his name from the fact that he had at one time stolen the woman of a white man—thus the name, "Woman-okaker." He is remembered as having the end of his nose shot off by a bullet. He lived on section 23, Jefferson township, near where H. C. Krech now resides, and his counsel had much weight among the Indians.

After the settlement of this county by whites began, the Indians became quite troublesome, stealing anything they could lay their hands upon. Finally, in the fall of 1848, two of the settlers made complaint to the government authorities, and, shortly afterward, the entire body of Indians were removed by a detachment of United States troops, from Fort Atkinson.

In the spring of 1845, the first settlement by white men was made in the territory now comprising Bremer county. Charles McCaffree was the first white man to locate, making claim to the whole of section 34, township 91, range 13, on what has since been known as Quarter Section Run, in Jefferson township. Mr. McCaffree is of Irish descent, born in Jefferson county, Kentucky, and during a portion of his early life was engaged as a boat hand on the Mississippi. After a few years of this life he went to southern Missouri, but in a short time turned his face northward, and settled in Lee county, Iowa.

In the spring of 1845, as stated, he came to Bremer county and located upon section 34, in what is now Jefferson township, put up a little log cabin in a small grove about fifty rods from the creek, on land now owned by Henry W. Briden, northeast of the present residence of Mr. Briden. During the first year of his residence, McCaffree broke about fifty acres, and raised considerable sod corn. Soon after McCaffree settled, there came to the county, Jerry O'Conner, an Irishman, who had for a time been making his home in Lee county, who took a claim embracing all of section 33, adjoining McCaffree's, and together they kept bachelor's hall. O'Conner broke and fenced about five acres and raised some corn, near where the house of H. D. Gould now stands. After this McCaffree and O'Conner went back to Lee county. The former soon returned, but the latter never came back. O'Conner during the season was accustomed to do but little clothes-washing; when his shirt became worn and dirty, he would tear off the sleeves and collar, and put on a new shirt. When he started for Lee county he had on the bodies of not less than five shirts. The weather being cold when they started, they wore their overcoats. O'Conner, having neither boots nor shoes, made a sorry appearance traveling bare-footed with an overcoat and five shirts on. The following year, McCaffree was married to Cynthia, a daughter of John H. and Mary Messinger, who were then residents of the county. They went to Independence to have the marriage ceremony performed. They had a family of ten children—Hardin, Floyd, Mary, Hannah, Laura, John, Hestina, Lewis, Owen and Elbert. Mr. McCaffree and wife remained in the county after marriage for about eight years, when they removed to Spring Creek, where they remained three years, then returning to Bremer county. In about one year he went to Missouri, where he lived nine years, until the rebellion drove him from that State, when he again settled in Bremer county, in 1862. He died about 1872, and was buried in the burial ground of Jefferson township. Mr. McCaffree was a man of good impulses, genial and social in disposition, and of much integrity. He made many friends among the pioneers. Mrs. Cynthia McCaffree, his wife, is still a resident of the county, living in Jackson township. She is the oldest female settler living in the county.

In the fall of 1845 Charles McCaffree brought his brother Isaac and their mother to Bremer county as permanent settlers. Isaac now lives somewhere in Missouri, having left Bremer county before the war. About the same time—September, 1845—Jacob Beelah and his family and son-in-law, Andrew Sample, moved into the county and took claims which, after the survey, turned out to be on section 35, township 91, range 13, now constituting Jefferson township. A log cabin was erected by them on the premises now owned by David Marquis. Not much is remembered of Beelah, as he did not remain long, removing to Floyd county. Andrew Semple, however, is remembered better, although he left about 1851. He is said to have been a disagreeable, quarrelsome fellow, nearly always in trouble with some of his neighbors. He moved into Chickasaw county, where he was a part owner in the town site of Nashua. He won a hard name there by his drinking, carousing and lawlessness, and finally left for Missouri, where he was when last heard from. Jacob Beelah has not been heard from since he left the county, but the grove he settled in, near the southern line of Floyd county, has since borne his name, though slightly corrupted, being called Beelar's Grove. Thus the first settlement in the county was made.

Early in the spring of 1846, a party came to the county from Marion county,

Indiana, consisting of J. H. Messinger, with a large family of girls and boys; George Tibbetts, with a like family; T. Fisher and P. Miller. They all came with ox-teams, spending a number of weeks in the journey.

J. H. Messinger took a farm on sections 35 and 36, township 91, range 13, and he and his wife lived there for twenty years, until called away by death. The family consisted of four boys and five girls. Elias J. was the oldest son, and now lives at Waterloo, where he owns a part of the mill power of the Cedar river. John was the second, and lives two miles north of Waterloo. Robert P., the third, still resides upon the old homestead, and is the earliest settler now living within the county. Henry M. C. was the youngest son. In 1878 he went to Oregon, where he still lives. Of the girls, two of them married the Tibbetts boys, one married Charles McCaffree, and one is now Mrs. H. B. Boyd, of Jefferson township. The youngest married Isaac Conner, and is now dead. Mr. Conner is in Kansas.

George Tibbetts located on section 24, —the present site of Jefferson City. His family consisted of four boys and four girls. About 1851 he ran away to Minnesota to avoid arrest. He has never returned, unless in secret. It is reported that he died a number of years since, with small-pox. His wife was a good woman, and much liked by all who knew her. For a number of years she lived with members of her family, finally going to Minnesota, where she died. Wesley Tibbetts, the oldest son, located on the north side of the Big Woods, on section 15, in what now constitutes Jefferson township, and the next son, Henry, took a place adjoining, on section 16. When the survey was made, the section line passed directly between their houses. Wesley sold his place, and now lives in Kansas. Henry also went to Kansas, but has since removed to California, where he yet lives, engaged in fruit culture. Jeremiah, the third son, removed to Minnesota, where he still remains, upon land given him by his brother Henry. Luther also lives in Minnesota. Jerry was peculiar in dress and actions, spending most of his time praying in fence corners. He never shook hands, his manner of salutation being a groan.

T. Fisher and P. Miller, who are mentioned as coming with this party, did not remain longer than the ensuing fall.

The year 1847 witnessed the addition of a number of pioneers to the little settlement in Bremer county. So far, nearly, if not all, had settled in and about the "Big Woods," of Jefferson township. The settlers had already commenced tilling the soil and were raising various products. Game of every description abounded, and much time was spent by the pioneers in hunting.

The arrivals of 1857 who can be recalled were, Charles Frady, Ezra G. Allen, Joseph and James Fee, each of whom made a claim.

Charles Frady was a son-in-law of George Tibbetts, and is supposed to have come from the same place. In a few years he moved to other parts. A son of his remained in the county a number of years but finally removed to Nebraska.

Ezra G. Allen settled upon the farm now owned by S. F. Shepard, on section 25, township 91, range 14, now Jackson township. Within half a dozen years he removed to Horton, and, in 1856, went to Kansas, where he has since died.

Joseph and James Fee were brothers, and were known as "Joe and Jim." Where they were from is not known. They settled near the Tibbetts family, and after remaining a short time, removed to Chickasaw county.

In the spring of 1849 John Clark came from Delaware county, Ohio, and made a claim on section 8, township 91, range 13, now a portion of Washington township. After selecting this claim he returned to Ohio, making the entire trip upon horseback. In the fall of 1849 he returned to Bremer county with his family, bringing the same horse which he had rode in the spring. Mr. Clark cut out the first wagon road from the north side of the Big Woods to Janesville. He was really a frontiersman—no one living north of him in this section of the State, nor west of him this side of Sioux City. Quasketon, forty miles distant, was the nearest grist mill, and Cedar Falls, then called Sturgis Rapids, was the nearest post office. At this time there was not a tradesman nor a professional man within the limits now constituting Bremer county. John Clark was born in Pennsylvania in February, 1796. At an early day, in company with his parents, he went to Delaware county, Ohio. He was brought up on a farm, and received a common-school education. He lived in Delaware county until 1849, when, in company with his wife and eight children, he came to Bremer county. There were but eleven families in the county when they arrived. The first spring, Mr. Clark and the boys tapped 400 maple trees and made 1,100 pounds of sugar, which they sold for six cents a pound. When they first came to the county they brought a little flour, which was soon borrowed by the neighbors, and Mr. Clark was obliged to go to Cedar Rapids for more. The family parched corn and ground it in a coffee mill, living upon this until his return, usually being about a week on the trip. Mr. Clark was one of the first justices elected in the county. He died at his home in December, 1855. His wife is still living at the advanced age of seventy-eight. Seven of the eight children are yet living. Mr. Clark was a man of grand impulses, upright and honest in all of his dealings, and when death removed him from among the pioneers, they lost one of their best and most respected members.

David Clark, son of John and Jane Clark, was born in Delaware county, Ohio, November 3, 1831. He came with his parents to Bremer county, in the fall of 1849. Mr. Clark received a liberal education and in the winter of 1853–54, taught school in Polk township, completing an unfinished term. This was the first school taught in Polk township. On coming to this county, he made a claim, but did not live upon it, remaining at home with his parents until 1858, when he located at Waverly, engaging in the boot and shoe trade, and operating a tannery at the same time. In this line of trade he continued about one year. From 1859 to 1869, he was in the real estate business, and subsequently, for about five years in the hardware trade. On account of failing health, he has not been very actively engaged for some years, spending much of his time in Nebraska. In 1860 he was united in marriage with Miss Mary C. Lyman, a native of Pennsylvania. They have five children, two girls and three boys—Mary, the oldest, living at home; John L., now at Eagle Grove, in the drug business; Ernest C., Grace and Arthur B. Mr. Clark has been assessor of the town, a member of the school board, deputy collector of internal revenue of this district, and has held various other offices of honor and trust. He has taken an active part in every enterprise looking to the advancement of the city of Waverly, and has sacrificed great personal interests for its benefit.

In 1850 the arrivals were numerous, among whom were, John T. Barrick, Heman A. Miles, William Payne, William Thorp, Samuel Armstrong, J. H. Martin, Jacob Hess, Charles N. Martin, J. H. McRoberts, William Hinton, and Frederick Cretzmeyer.

John T. Barrick made himself at home on section 35, township 91, range 14, where he subsequently erected a saw mill, and platted the town of Janesville, naming it in honor of his wife, Jane. Here he remained until late in the sixties, when he removed to Kansas, where he still lives. His son, Isaac T. Barrick, still lives near Janesville. Mr. Barrick was a genial and pleasant old gentleman, and made many warm friends among the old settlers.

Heman A. Miles, who was for many years identified with the progress of the county, located in Lafayette township. A letter from him, in connection with the chapter upon reminiscences, gives particulars of his early settlement.

William Payne came with Mr. Barrick, and also settled, with his family, near Janesville. He came from Indiana, and after making improvements, remained six or seven years, then moved to Dallas county, this State, where he still lives. He was an ardent Methodist, and was a man of good principles and many friends.

William Thorp, another pioneer of this year, settled with his family upon the place now occupied by Charles Thies in Jefferson township. In about four or five years he sold out and removed to Franklin county, this State. He was well-known among the early settlers; was a good kind of a man, but very passoniate, and when excited would commit acts that in his more sober moments he would sincerely regret. One little incident is recalled in which he figured conspicuously. On a certain occasion when his daughter—having just been married—came home, a party consisting of Matthew Farrington, the Messinger boys, Loren Gilbert, and some others made arrangements to serenade "the folks." Accordingly, a number of musical instruments, such as tin pans, shot horse-fiddles, etc. were obtained, and the party repaired to the scene of action. The performance began, and the din was almost unbearable. Thorp got angry, then mad, then wild, until, taking down his rifle, he swore the annihilation of the whole *posse*. Just as he was about to open the door preparatory to beginning his bloody work, the thought chanced to strike him that possibly the serenaders might object, and it might result in their "cleaning him out." The thought was enough, his courage failed, and putting up the rifle, decided to sit down quietly and listen to the balance of the "concert." When the entertainment was through the orchestra departed. During the cermonies M. Farrington mounted a stump, and in a spirited speech dwelt particularly upon the text that "anger rested only in the breast of fools."

Samuel Armstrong settled upon a farm on the south side of the Big Woods, in Jefferson township. He had a family and is remembered as a good neighbor and a conscientious man. He only remained upon his first farm a few years, then moved further up the river, and finally, in 1854, removed to Minnesota.

J. H. Martin and his brother came with their father, Rev. Charles N. Martin, and their good mother, Elizabeth. The old gentleman was a minister of the gospel, a man of much integrity and well esteemed by all who knew him. He settled upon the southwest quarter of section 13, of township 91, range 14, now Washington township. His wife, Elizabeth, was a great doctress, and rode all over this region healing the sick. The old folks went to Fayette county, where they have since died. John H. Martin located on section 26, on the road between Janesville and Waverly, in Jackson township. He was the first school fund commissioner of Bremer county.

Jacob Hess came with the Martins. He made his home on section 2, township 91, range 14, now a portion of the city of Waverly. His first log cabin was built near the site of the present stone house of G. R. Dean. He remained here for a number of years, but in 1864 went to Oregon.

J. H. McRoberts erected a log cabin upon the claim he made, on section 1, township 91, range 14, now a part of Washington township. A few years after his settlement, he was drowned in the Spring Branch. In company with Mace Eveland he had gone hunting, became fatigued and finally gave out all together. Mr. Eveland left him while he went for a conveyance to take him home. While he was gone it appeared that McRoberts had crawled to the edge of the brook for a drink, and, while in the act of drinking, fell forward on his face into the water. The water was only about six inches deep, but nevertheless, when Mr. Eveland returned, he found him cold in death.

In the fall of 1850, William Hinton and family came. Mr. Hinton made claim to a part of section 1, township 91, range 14, Washington township. After a number of years sojourn in Bremer county, the old folks moved to Kansas. Lorenzo and Shadrach, two of the sons, are yet residents of the county.

During the spring of 1850 quite a party arrived and were made welcome as valuable acquisitions to the settlement. The party consisted of Israel Trumbo and family, William Baskins, Joe Kerr and Aaron Dow; the latter bringing the family of Mr. Trumbo. All here secured homes. Israel Trumbo had a family of nine or ten children. He had previously visited the county, and made a claim on section 16, Jefferson township, where he remained until about 1861, when with his family, he removed to Dakota, where he and his wife have since died. He was a man of fair education, of good motives, genial and popular. He was one of the first justices of the peace in Bremer county, and was the first surveyor.

William Baskins was his nephew, and was a single man at the time of his arrival. He is still a resident of the county.

Joseph Kerr was a relative of the parties whom he accompanied. Being a young and single man, he soon began to look for a partner. He was soon afterward married to Martha Clark, and settled upon a place near the city of Waverly. He remained in the county until his death, which occurred in 1882. His wife is also dead, and the children scattered.

Aaron Dow, who came with the family of Israel Trumbo, like the rest, was a native of Ohio. Shortly after his arrival in Bremer county, he claimed a piece of land on section 5, in what now constitutes Washington township, erecting his log cabin in what has since been known as Sturdevant's Grove. He was an odd fellow, both in manner of speech and dress, but was honest and reliable in every respect. He was a nephew of Lorenzo Dow, and partook somewhat of the peculiarities of that good, though eccentric minister of the gospel. Aaron remained there until 1851, when he went south.

After this, the settlement became rapid. The details, as to the early settlement, will be found in connection with the histories of the various townships.

Among the early settlers of the county, who are still citizens, are the following: O. C. Harrington, C. R. Hastings, Abner Scott and brother, M. R. Flood, T. Clarey, P. Burgess, Watenpaugh, Adam Brodie and brother, M. F. Gillett, James Leaman, S. F. Cass, A. L. Stephenson, O. S. Hatch, J. B. Yerton, A. Macomber, George Watts, Isaac Barrick, Allen Sewell, Frank Coddington, S. F. Shepard, Joel Loveland, George Daniels, Matthew Farrington, John Foutch, John Stears, P. Bredow, Winne, Stumme, Fred Bruntz, N. C. Peck, R. V. Dibble, John McRae, Patrick O'Dea, Fred Hildebrand, G. N. Bowers, J. N. Johnson, Andrew Carstensen, Hiram Lester, Asa Martin, John Chapin, James Sturdevant, H. H. Case, W. B. Ingersoll, Moses Robinson, Mason Eveland, William Pelton, James Andrews, Stannard, R. J. Ellsworth, W. P. Harris, Moses Lehman, James Wood, and D. A. Long. These old settlers are mentioned merely as an index of what will be finished in the township histories.

HISTORICAL ITEMS.

The first white child born within the limits of what now comprises Bremer county was on the 15th day of January, 1848—Zachary T., a son of E. J. and Catherine Messinger. It is said that the Indians would sometimes get the boy and carry him off, and it was with difficulty that Mr. and Mrs. Messinger could keep them from claiming him as their own.

The first marriage in the county is described by a local writer as follows: "The first marriage among the young white settlers of the settlement was Isaac McCaffree to Rebecca Beelah, in 1847. The twain started for Linn county to have the ceremony performed. On their way they encamped at Spring Creek, in Black Hawk county, and were snow bound five days and nights. So it will be seen that it was under difficulties that they got to their destination. But, nothing daunted, they wended their way after the storm, and the ceremony was performed, though some days later than they had anticipated."

HISTORY OF BREMER COUNTY.

Charles McCaffree and Cynthia Messinger, who were the contracting parties in the second marriage, went to Independence, Buchanan county, to have the ceremony performed.

The first death in the county was that of Mrs. Fee, who was the mother of Joseph and James Fee, and her remains were carried to Linn county for burial.

The first burial and second death was an infant son of Isaac McCaffree. The child was buried upon the land which now constitutes a part of M. Farrington's farm in Jefferson township.

The first person naturalized in the county was William Gould, who on the 29th of June, 1854, renounced all allegiance to Great Britain, before Judge T. S. Wilson, now of Dubuque.

The first sermon preached in the county was by Rev. Mr. Collins, a Methodist Episcopal Divine, in the winter of 1850, at the house of E. J. Messinger in Jefferson township. The second minister to visit the county was a Rev. Mr. Vail, of the same faith.

The first frame house in Bremer county was erected in 1852, for a Methodist parsonage, on the farm of William Payne, near Janesville, lately owned by Judge M. Rowen.

The first marriage license issued in the county was by Judge Jeremiah Farris, and united Jonas Mishler and Sarah Michael. It bore the date of August 20, 1853. They were married the same day by the judge. The parties still live in Jefferson township.

The first deed upon record was dated October 4, 1853, and was given by John T. Barrick and wife, Jane, to Frank Codington, James M. and E. E. Moss. The acknowledgement was taken by John M. Bennett, justice of the peace.

The total amount of the first tax, levied in 1853, was $653.52. The following year it amounted to $1,194.75.

The first store opened in the county was by John H. Winter and Asbury Leverich, at Janesville.

The first probate proceeding of record in the county, related to the appointment of Simeon F. Shepard as administrator of the estate of James McRoberts, and bore the date of November 19, 1852. The Honorable O. H. P. Roszell, county judge of Buchanan county, required Mr. Shepard to give a bond in the sum of $2,000.

The first house in the county was erected by Jacob Beelah, in the fall of 1845, in Jefferson township.

Janesville was the first town laid out in the county, and the plat thereof was the first filed for record. The survey was made in the spring of 1853, and the plat recorded July 22, 1854.

The first school in the county was taught by Richard Miles, a brother of Herman A. Miles, in the winter of 1852-3, in a little log hut in Jefferson township, belonging to John Clark.

The first post office in the county "Neutral," is thus spoken of by a local writer: "The first post office in the county was established in 1850, J. H. Messinger, postmaster, the route being from Cedar Falls to Neutral. It is said that when the office was established, the way it received its name was as follows: The decision was to give the office a significant name, and as all the county was on what was known as "Neutral land," hence the name

Neutral. After a while Mr. Messinger became tired of the duties of the office (without pay), and, at his request, M. Farring took charge, and the name was changed.

Political partyism was becoming very strong, *neutral positions* therein were held in just contempt. Documents from Washington came plainly addressed to "Neutrille," and he favored the change and used the new name. After a while, reasonably enough, by mistaking *a* for *e*, it gradually assumed the present name "Nautrille," by which name it has since been known. The office was discontinued in 1879.

ORGANIZATION OF THE COUNTY.

For years prior to any thought of the existence of a Bremer county, all this territory of Iowa constituted a portion of the Winnebago Indian Reservation, and the territory particularly comprising Bremer, was occupied by various tribes, as stated elsewhere. The settlement began in 1845, and in 1847 the county was surveyed into congressional townships. Somewhat later it was sectionized, and in about 1851 the land came into market. Just prior to this the Indian reservation was purchased by the United States Government, and the Indians, who were yet inhabiting the county, numbering about three hundred, with the three chiefs who were left—Big Wave (or Way), Winneshiek, and Wananokaker (or Womanokaker)—were removed to Crow River, Minnesota, one hundred and fifty miles north of St. Paul. In the meantime —some time in 1850—the territory of Bremer was attached to Fayette for judicial purposes; but as there was hardly any intercourse between the two counties, and no road was broken connecting this settlement with Fayette, these relations were soon dissolved, and in the winter of 1850–1 Bremer was attached to Buchanan county for civil and judicial purposes. Preparations were made for a township organization, and the entire county was made a civil township. On the 29th day of April, 1851, the first election in the county was held at the house of John H. Messinger, in Jefferson township. The judges of this election were John Miles, George Tibbetts, and Elias J. Messinger; and the clerks were Heman A. Miles and Aaron Dow. The township officers elected were as follows: Israel Trumbo and Chas. N. Martin, justices of the peace; Heman A. Miles and John H. Martin, constables; George Tibbetts, John Clark, and John H. Messinger, trustees; Elias J. Messinger, treasurer; Aaron Dow, town clerk.

Fortunately the poll book is yet in existence, and is in the possession of Elias J. Messinger, of Waterloo. The following is a full list of the voters at this election: Israel Trumbo, William Payne, John H. Messinger, Joseph Kerr, Peter Hohyner. Wesley Tibbetts, Jacob Beelah, John Clark, William Hinton, John Miles, Samuel Beelah, Jacob Hess, William Thorp, Ezra G. Allen, Samuel Armstrong, John H. Martin, William Baskins, George Tibbetts, James H. McRoberts, John T. Barrick, Heman A. Miles, Elias J. Messinger, Henry Tibbetts, Charles N. Martin, and Aaron Dow.

This made a total of twenty-five voters, and of the entire number, only one is still a resident of the county—William Baskins, who resides just east of Waverly. Five of them are sleeping the last, long sleep in Bremer county soil, and the rest have been scattered. The five

HISTORY OF BREMER COUNTY.

buried here are, Charles McCaffree, John Clark, J. H. McRoberts, J. H. Messinger, and Joseph Kerr.

At this time O. H. P. Roszell was county judge of Buchanan county.

In April, 1853, the second election was held. This election was held at the house of Israel Trumbo, on section 16. Among the officers chosen was John Clark, justice of the peace. The clerks of the election were Matthew and Walter Farrington. The latter carried the returns to Independence, the county seat of Buchanan county. There were sixty-eight votes cast, an increase of twenty-seven over the former election.

It was now believed there were a sufficient number of inhabitants in the county to organize. Accordingly, in May, 1853, James W. Wood, John T. Barrick and O. H. P. Roszell, commissioners for that purpose, located the county seat at Waverly.

In July, 1853, a convention was held at the red cedar stake, which marked the location of the county seat, just north of where the court house in Waverly now stands, and candidates for the various offices were nominated. The convention was called regardless of party lines, and nearly all of the voters were present. When a party was proposed for any office, an opponent would also be named, and the mass would then separate, the friends of the two candidates ranging themselves upon opposite sides, and the "heaviest file" won the nomination. At this time the office of county surveyor was the most lucrative of any county office, and, after reviewing the field it was found that there was only one citizen of the county fully competent to discharge the duties. This was Matthew Farrington. But he was a "William Lloyd Garrison abolitionist," and declared he would not take the office. He mounted a wagon, and addressing the convention, stated that, as "the constitution of the United States upheld slavery, he could not take an oath to support it, and would accept no office conditional upon taking such an oath." Heman A. Miles and others who were prominent factors of the convention, assured him that it was not necessary for him to take such an oath, and he finally consented to accept the nomination. But before the day of the election he learned that the oath must be taken, and upon that day he again mounted the wagon and stated that he should not accept upon such a condition. He illuminated his house in honor of the occasion and invited all his abolition friends, within four or five miles, to take supper with him, at his home in Jefferson township.

In August, 1853, the organization of the county was made permanent by the election of county officers. At this election, which was held at the house of Fred Cretzmeyer; there were only eighty votes polled, and the following officers were elected: County judge, Jeremiah Farris; sheriff, Austin Farris; treasurer and recorder, John Hunter; clerk of courts, Heman A. Miles; school fund commissioner, John H. Martin; surveyor, Israel Trumbo. This brought Bremer county into official existence. At this time the property in the county listed for taxation amounted only to $43,437, which is a marked contrast to the $3,168,229 of property assessed in 1882.

The first court house in Bremer county was a little frame building that stood just north of the present fine court building. It was erected in 1854, and has long years since rotted to the ground. During the summer and fall of 1857, the present court house was erected in the eastern part of Waverly, upon a beautiful elevation overlooking the city, at a cost of about $23,000. It is constructed of brick, is forty-three by sixty-three, and is two stories in height above a stone basement. It is surmounted by a handsome dome, which adds much to its outward appearance. In the basement is contained the sheriff's apartments, and necessary cells for the confinement of prisoners. The court room in the second story is forty-one feet in width by fifty-one in depth.

On the first day of January, 1858, the erection of this building was celebrated within its walls by a "Bremer County Ball," at which about 150 persons of both sexes attended. The basement was appropriated to the purpose of a supper, the hall and offices on the first floor to the reception and seating of guests, the court room to dancing, and the offices connected therewith to dressing-rooms. For some years after its erection the court house was the scene of many gatherings, social, religious, political, literary and otherwise. In September, 1869, however, the board of supervisors directed the Sheriff to exclude from the building "all parties except political and county societies."

The fire-proof building constructed of brick and iron, 32x48 feet in size, and one story in height, is located upon the south side of the large square which incloses the court house, to which it is conveniently adjacent. It was erected at a cost of about $5,000, in the summer of 1870, for the better accommodation of county officers, and to ensure the safe preservation of the public records. Though unpretentious in style, it is a neat and commodious structure, and contains the offices of the county auditor, recorder, clerk of courts, and treasurer.

THE COUNTY'S NAME.

The territory comprising Bremer county was originally a part of the Winnebago reservation. It subsequently became a part of the "Neutral Land." On the passage of the act creating the counties in the northern part of the State, the name Bremer was bestowed upon this territory, at the suggestion of Governor Hempstead, in honor of Frederika Bremer, a noted Sweedish authoress.

CHAPTER III.

PIONEER LIFE.

One of the most interesting phases of national or local history, is that of the settlement of a new country. What was the original state in which the pioneer found the country, and how was it made to blossom as the rose?

Pioneer life in Bremer county finds its parallel in almost every county in the State, and throughout the entire West. While some of the customs here given may not be entirely applicable to pioneer life in Bremer, they are a truthful representation of pioneer life in general, and are thus worthy a place in this volume. When Charles McCaffree, Jacob Beelah, and others of that noble band of pioneers settled here, they found an unbroken wilderness. Wild beasts, and but little less wild savages, roamed at will over the prairie, through the forests, and along the waters of the Iowa river and its numerous tributaries. Forests were to be felled, cabins erected, mills built, and the river and creeks made to labor for the benefit of mankind. The beautiful prairies were to be robbed of their natural ornaments, and the hand of art was to assist in their decoration. Who was to undertake this work? Are they qualified for the task? What will be the effect of their labors upon future generations?

The Bremer county pioneers had many difficulties to contend with, not the least of which was the journey from civilization to the forest homes. The route lay for the most part through a rough country; swamps and marshes were crossed with great exertion and fatigue; rivers were forded with difficulty and danger; nights were passed on open prairies, with the sod for a couch and the heavens for a shelter; long, weary days and weeks of travel were endured, but finally the "promised land" was reached.

EARLY MANNERS AND CUSTOMS.

The young men and women of to-day have little conception of the mode of life among the early settlers of the country. One can hardly conceive how so great a change could take place in so short a time. The clothing, the dwellings, the diet, the social customs have undergone a total revolution, as though a new race had taken possession of the land.

In a new country far removed from the conveniences of civilization, where all are compelled to build their own houses, make their own clothing and procure for themselves the means of subsistence, it is to be expected that their dwellings and garments will be rude. These were matters controlled by surrounding circumstances and the means at their disposal. The earliest settlers constructed what were termed "three-faced camps," or, in other words, three walls, leaving one side open. They are described as follows: The walls were built seven feet high, when poles were laid across at a distance of about three feet apart, and on these a roof of clapboards was laid, which were kept in place by weight poles placed on them. The clapboards were about four feet in length and from eight inches to twelve inches in width, split out of white oak timber. No floor was laid in the "camp." The structure required neither door, window or chimney. The one side left out of the cabin answered all these purposes. In front of the open side was built a large log heap, which served for warmth in cold weather and for cooking purposes in all seasons. Of course there was an abundance of light, and, on either side of the fire, space to enter in and out. These "three-faced camps" were probably more easily constructed than the ordinary cabin, and was not the usual style of dwelling houses.

The cabin was considered a material advance for comfort and home life. This was, in almost every case, built of logs, the spaces between the logs being filled in with split sticks of wood, called "chinks," and then daubed over, both inside and outside, with mortar made of clay. The floor, sometimes, was nothing more than earth tramped hard and smooth, but commonly made of "puncheons," or split logs; with the split side turned upward. The roof was made by gradually drawing in the top to the ridgepole, and, on cross pieces, laying the "clapboards," which, being several feet in length, instead of being nailed, were held in place by poles laid on them, called "weight poles," reaching the length of the cabin. For a fireplace, a space was cut out of the logs on one side of the room, usually about six feet in length, and three sides were built up of logs, making an offset in the wall. This was lined with stone, if convenient; if not, then earth. The flue, or upper part of the chimney, was built of small split sticks, two and a half or three feet in length, carried a little space above the roof, and plastered over with clay, and when finished was called a "cat-and-clay" chimney. The door space was also made by cutting an aperture in one side of the room of the required size, the door itself being made of clapboards secured by wooden pins to two crosspieces. The hinges were also of wood, while the fastenings consisted of a wooden latch catching on a hook of the same material. To open the door from the outside, a strip of buckskin was tied to the latch and drawn through a hole a few inches above the latch-bar, so that on pulling the string the latch was lifted from the catch or hook, and the door was opened without further trouble. To lock the door, it was only necessary to pull the string through the hole to the inside. Here the family lived, and here the guest and wayfarer were made welcome. The living room was of good size, but to a large extent it was all—kitchen, bed-room, parlor and arsenal, with flitches of bacon and rings of dried pumpkin suspended from the rafters. In one corner were the loom and other implements used in the manufacture of clothing, and around the ample fireplace were collected the kitchen furniture. The clothing lined one side of the sleeping apartment, suspended from pegs driven in the logs. Hemp and flax were generally raised, and a few sheep kept. Out of these the clothing for the family and the sheets and coverlets were made by the females of the house. Over the door was placed the trusty rifle, and just back of it hung the powder horn and hunting pouch. In the well-to-do families, or when crowded on the ground floor, a loft was sometimes made to the cabin for a sleeping place and the storage of "traps" and articles not in common use. The loft was reached by a ladder secured to the wall. Generally the bedrooms were separated from the living-room by sheets and coverlets suspended from the rafters, but until the means of making these partition walls were ample, they lived and slept in the same room.

Familiarity with this mode of living did away with much of the discomfort, but as soon as the improvement could be made, there was added to the cabin an additional room, or a "double log cabin" being substantially a "three-faced camp," with a log room on each end and containing a loft. The furniture in the cabin corresponded with the house itself. The articles used in the kitchen were as few and simple as can be imagined. A "Dutch oven," or skillet, a long-handled frying pan, an iron pot or kettle, and sometimes a coffee pot, constituted the utensils of the best furnished kitchen. A little later, when a stone wall formed the base of the chimney, a long iron "crane" swung in the chimney place, which on its "pot-hook" carried the boiling kettle or heavy iron pot. The cooking was all done on the fire-place and at the fire, and the style of cooking was as simple as the utensils. Indian, or corn meal, was the common flour, which was made into "pone" or "corn-dodger," or "hoe-cake," as the occasion or variety demanded. The "pone" and the "dodger" were baked in the Dutch oven, which was first set on a bed of glowing coals. When the oven was filled with the dough, the lid, already heated on the fire, was placed on the oven and covered with hot embers and ashes. When the bread was done it was taken from the oven and placed near the fire to keep warm while some other food was being prepared in the same oven for the forthcoming meal. The "hoe-cake" was prepared in the same way as the dodger—that is, a stiff dough was made of the meal and water, and, taking as much as could conveniently be held in both hands, it was moulded into the desired shape by being tossed from hand to hand, then laid on a board or flat stone placed at an angle before the fire and patted down to the required thickness. In the fall and early winter, cooked pumpkin was added to the meal dough, giving a flavor and richness in the bread not attained by the modern methods. In the oven from which the bread was taken, the venison or ham was then fried, and, in winter, lye hominy, made from the unbroken grains of corn, added to the frugal meal. The woods abounded of honey, and of this the early settlers had an abundance the year round. For some years after settlements were made, the corn meal formed the staple commodity for bread.

These simple cabins were inhabited by a kind and true-hearted people. They were strangers to mock-modesty, and the traveler seeking lodgings for the night, or desirious of spending a few days in the community, if willing to accept the rude offerings, was always welcome, although how they were disposed of at night the reader may not easily imagine; for, as described, often a single room would be made to serve the purpose of a kitchen, dining-room, sitting-room and parlor, and many families consisted of six or eight persons.

CHARACTER OF THE PIONEERS.

The character of the pioneers of Bremer county falls properly within the range of the historian. They lived in a region of exuberance and fertility, where nature had scattered her blessings with a liberal hand. The inexhaustible forest supply, the fertile prairies, and the many improvements constantly going forward, with the bright prospect for a glorious future in everything that renders life pleasant, combined to deeply impress their character, to give them a spirit of enterprise, an independence of feeling, and a joyousness of hope. They were a thorough admixture of many nations, characters, languages, conditions and opinions. There was scarcely a State in the Union that was not represented among the early settlers. All the various religious sects had their advocates. All now form one society. Says an early writer: "Men must cleave to their kind, and must be dependent upon each other. Pride and jealousy give way to the natural yearnings of the human heart for society. They begin to rub off the neutral prejudices; one takes a step and then the other; they meet half way and embrace; and the society thus newly organized and constituted, is more liberal, enlarged, unprejudiced, and, of course, more affectionate, than a society of people of like birth and character, who bring all their early prejudices as a common stock, to be transmitted as an inheritance to posterity."

CLOTHING.

The clothing of the early pioneers was as plain and simple as their houses. Necessity compelled it to be in conformity to the strictest economy. The clothing taken to the new country was made to render a vast deal of service until a crop of flax or hemp could be grown, out of which to make the household apparel. The prairie wolves made it difficult to take sheep into the settlements, but after the sheep had been introduced, and flax and hemp raised in sufficient quantities, it still remained an arduous task to spin, weave and make the wearing apparel for an entire family. In summer, nearly all persons, both male and female, went barefooted. Buckskin moccasins were much worn. Boys of twelve and fifteen years of age never thought of wearing anything on their feet, except during three or four months of the coldest weather in winter. Boots were unknown until a later generation. After flax was raised in sufficient quantities, and sheep could be protected from the wolves, a better and more comfortable style of clothing prevailed. Flannel and linsey were woven and made into garments for the women and children, and jeans for the men. The wool for the jeans was colored from the bark of the walnut, and from this came the term "butternut," still common throughout the West. The black and white wool mixed, varied the color, and gave the name "pepper-and-salt." As a matter of course every family did its own spinning, weaving and sewing, and for years all the wool had to be carded by hand on cards from four inches broad to eight and ten inches long. The picking of the wool and carding was work to which the little folks could help, and at the proper season all the little hands were enlisted in the business. Every household had its big and little spinning wheels, winding-blades, reel, warping-bars and loom. The articles were indispensible in every family. In many of the households of Bremer county, stowed away in empty garrets and out-of-the-way places, may still be found some of these almost forgotten relics.

The preparations for the family clothing usually began in the early fall, and the work was continued on into the winter months, when the whirr of the wheels and the regular stroke of the loom could be heard until a late hour of the night. No scene can well be imagined so abounding in contentment and domestic happiness. Strips of bark, of the shell-bark hickory, thrown from time to time in the ample fire place, cast a ruddy, flickering light over the room. In one corner, within range of the reflected light, the father is cobbling a well-worn pair of shoes, or trying his skill at making new ones. Hard by, the young ones are shelling corn for the next grist. The oldest daughter whirls the large spinning wheel, and with its hum and whirr trips to the far side of the room, drawing out the thread, while the mother, with the click of the shuttle and the measured thump of the loom, fills up the hours—the whole a scene of domestic industry and happiness rarely elsewhere to be found.

It is well for "Young America" to look back on those early days. It involved a life of toil, hardship, and the lack of many comforts, but it was the life that made men of character. Bremer county to-day has no better men than the immediate descendants of those who built their cabins in the forest, and by patient endurance wrought out of the wilderness the landmarks for a prosperous commonwealth. One of these writes that "the boys were required to do their share of the hard labor of clearing up the farm, for much of the country now under the plow was at one time heavily timbered, or was covered with a dense thicket of hazel and young timber. Our visits were made with ox teams, and we walked or rode on horseback, or in wagons, to 'meeting.' The boys 'pulled,' 'broke' and 'hackled' flax, wore tow shirts, and indulged aristocratic feelings in fringed 'hunting-shirts' and 'coon-skin caps, 'picked' and 'carded' wool by hand, and 'spooled' and 'quilled' yarn for the weaving till the back ached."

Industry such as this, supported by an economy and frugality from which there was then no escape, necessarily brought its own reward. The hard toil made men old before their time, but beneath their sturdy blows they saw not only the forest pass away, but the fields white with the grain. Change and alterations were to be expected, but the reality has distanced the wildest conjecture, and, stranger still, multitudes are still living who witnessed not only the face of nature undergoing a change about them, but the manners, customs and industries of a whole people almost wholly changed. Many an old pioneer sits by his fireside in his easy chair, with closed eyes, and dreams of the scenes of the long ago.

"The voice of Nature's very self drops low,
As though she whispered of the long ago,
When down the wandering stream the rude canoe
Of some lone trapper glided into view,
And loitered down the watery path that led
Thro' forest depths, that only knew the tread
Of savage beasts and wild barbarians,
That skulked about with blood upon their hands
And murder in their hearts. The light of day
Might barely pierce the gloominess that lay
Like some dark pall across the water's face,
And folded all the land in its embrace;
The panther's screaming, and the bear's low
  growl,
The snake's sharp rattle, and the wolf's wild
  howl,
The owl's grim chuckle, as it rose and fell
In alternation with the Indian's yell,
Made fitting prelude for the gory plays
That were enacted in the early days.
"Now, o'er the vision, like a miracle, falls
The old log cabin with its dingy walls,
And crippled chimney, with the crutch-like prop
Beneath, a sagging shoulder at the top,
The 'coon-skin, battened fast on either side,
The whisps of leaf tobacco, cut and dried;
The yellow strands of quartered apples hung
In ricky festoons that tangled in among
The morning-glory vines that clambered o'er
The little clapboard roof above the door;
Again, thro' mists of memory arise
The simple scenes of home before the eyes;
The happy mother humming with her wheel
The dear old melodies that used to steal
So drowsily upon the summer air,
The house dog hid his bone, forgot his care,
And nestled at her feet, to dream, perchance,
Some cooling dream of winter-time romance.
The square of sunshine through the open door
That notched its edge across the puncheon floor,
And made a golden coverlet whereon
The god of slumber had a picture drawn
Of babyhood, in all the lovliness
Of dimpled cheek, and limb, and linsey dress.
The bough-filled fireplace and the mantle wide,
Its fire-scorched ankles stretched on either side,

Where, perchance upon its shoulders 'neath the
  joists,
The old clock hiccoughed, harsh and husky-
  voiced:
Tomatoes, red and yellow, in a row,
Preserved not then for diet, but for show:
The jars of jelly, with their dainty tops;
Bunches of pennyroyal and cordial drops,
The flask of camphor and vial of squills.
The box of buttons, garden seeds and pills.
And thus the pioneer and helpsome aged wife,
Reflectively reviews the scenes of early life.

WEDDINGS.

The wedding was an attractive feature of pioneer life. There was no distinction of life and very little of fortune. On these accounts the first impressions of love generally resulted in marriage. The family establishment cost but little labor—nothing more. The marriage was always celebrated at the house of the bride, and she was generally left to choose the officiating clergyman. A wedding, however, engaged the attention of the whole neighborhood. It was anticipated by both old and young with eager expectation. In the morning of the wedding day, the groom and his intimate friends assembled at the house of his father, and, after due preparation, departed *en massee* for the "mansion" of his bride. The journey was sometimes made on horseback, sometimes on foot, and sometimes in farm wagons and carts. It was always a merry journey; and to insure merriment, the bottle was always taken along. On reaching the house of the bride, the marriage cermony took place, and then dinner or supper was served. After the meal the dancing commenced, and generally lasted until the following morning. The figures of the dances were three and four-handed reels, or square sets and jigs. The commencement was always a square four, which was followed by what the pioneers called "jigging"—that is, two of the four would single out for a jig, and were followed by the remaining couple. The jigs were often accompanied with what was called "cutting out"—that is, when either of the parties became tired of the dance, on intimation, the place was supplied by some one of the company, without interruption of the dance. In this way the reel was often continued until the musician was exhausted. About 9 or 10 o'clock in the evening a deputation of young ladies stole off the bride and put her to bed. In doing this, they had to ascend a ladder from the kitchen to the upper floor, which was composed of loose boards. Here, in the pioneer bridal chamber, the young, simple-hearted girl was put to bed by her enthusiastic friends, This done, a deputation of young men escorted the groom to the same department, and placed him snugly by the side of his bride. The dance still continued, and if the seats were scarce, which was generally the case, says a local witness, every young man, when not engaged in the dance, was obliged to offer his lap as a seat for one of the girls; and the offer was sure to be accepted. During the night's festivities spirits were freely used, but seldom to excess. The infair was held on the following evening, where the same order of exercises was observed.

SHAKES.

Another feature of pioneer life, which every old settler will vividly recall, was the "chills and fever," "fever and ague," or "shakes,"·as it was variously called. It was a terror to new-comers, for in the fall of the year almost everybody was afflicted with it. It was no respecter of persons; everybody looked pale and sallow, as though frost-bitten. It was not contagious, but derived from impure water and air, which was always developed in the opening up of a new country of rank soil like that of Bremer county. The impurities continued to absorb from day to day, and from week to week, until the whole corporate body becomes saturated with it as with electricity, and then the shock came; and the shock was a regular shake, with a fixed beginning and ending, coming on, in some cases, each day, but generally on alternate days, with a regularity that was surprising. After the shakes came the fever, and this "last estate was worse than the first;" it was a burning hot fever, and lasted for hours. When you had the chill you couldn't get warm, and when you had the fever you couldn't get cool. It was exceedingly awkward in this respect—indeed it was. Nor would it stop for any contingency—not even a wedding in the family would stop it. It was imperative and tyranical. When the appointed time came around, everything else had to be stopped to attend to its demands. It didn't even have any Sundays or holidays. After the fever went down you still didn't feel much better, you felt as though you had gone through some sort of a collision, threshing machine, jarring machine, and came out not killed, but next thing to it. You felt weak, as though you had run too far after something, and then didn't catch it. You felt languid, stupid and sore, and was down in the mouth and heel and partially raveled out. Your back was out of fix, your head ached and your appetite crazy. Your eyes had too much white in them; your ears, especially after taking quinine, had too much roar in them, and your whole body and soul were entirely woe-begone, disconsolate, sad, poor and good for nothing. You didn't think much of yourself and didn't believe that other people did either, and you didn't care. You didn't quite make up your mind to commit suicide, but sometimes wished some accident would happen to knock either the malady or yourself out of existence. You imagined even the dogs looked at you with a sort of self-complacency. You thought the sun had a sort of sickly shine about it. About this time you came to the conclusion that you would not take the whole State as a gift; and if you had the strength and means you would pick up Hannah and the baby, and your traps, and go back "yander" to "Old Virginny," the "Jarseys," Maryland or Pennsylvania.

   "And to-day, the swallows flitting
   Round my cabin, see me sitting
   Moodily within the sunshine,
     Just within my silent door,
   Waiting for the "ager," seeming
   Like a man forever dreaming;
   And the sunlight on me streaming
   Throws no shadow on the floor;
   For I am too thin and sallow
   To make shadows on the floor—
     Nary shadow any more!"

The foregoing is not a mere picture of imagination. It is simply recounting in quaint phrase of what actually occurred in hundreds of cases. Whole families would sometimes be sick at one time, and not a member scarcely able to wait upon another. Labor or exercise always aggravated the malady, and it took General Laziness a long time to thrash the enemy out. These were the days for swallowing all sorts of roots and "yarbs" and whisky straight, with some faint hope of relief. Finally, when the case wore out, the last remedy got the credit of the cure.

WOLF HUNTING.

In early days more mischief was done by wolves than by any other wild animal, and no small part of their mischief consisted in their almost constant barking at night, which always seemed menacing and frightful to the settlers. Like mosquitos, the noise they made appeared to be about as dreadful as the real depredations they committed. The most effectual, as well as the most exciting, method of ridding the country of these hateful pests, was that known as the circular wolf hunt, by which all the men and boys would turn out on an appointed day, in a kind of circle comprising many square miles of territory, with horses and dogs, and then close up toward the center field of operation, gathering, not only wolves, but also deer and many smaller "varmint." Five, ten or more wolves, by this means, would be killed in a single day. The men would be organized with as much system as a small army, every one being posted in the meaning of every signal and the application of every rule. Guns were scarcely ever allowed to be brought on such occasions, as their use would be unavoidably dangerous. The dogs were depended upon for the final slaughter. The dogs, by the way, had all to be held in check by a cord in the hands of their keepers until the final signal was given to let them loose, when away they would all go to the center of battle, and a more exciting scene would follow than can easily be described.

BEE HUNTING.

This wild recreation was a peculiar one, and many sturdy backwoodsmen gloried in excelling in this art. He would carefully watch a bee as it filled itself with the product of some sweet flower or leaf bud, and notice particularly the direction taken by it as it struck a "bee-line" for its home, which, when found, would generally be high up in the hollow of some tree. The tree would be marked, and in the fall a party would go and cut down the tree and capture the honey as quick as they could before it wasted away through the broken walls in which it had been so carefully stowed by the busy little bee. Several gallons would often be taken from a single tree, and by a very little work, and pleasant at that, the early settlers could keep themselves in honey the year round. By the time the honey was a year old it would turn white and granulate, yet be as good and healthful as when fresh. This was called by some "candied" honey.

SNAKES.

In pioneer times snakes were numerous, such as the rattlesnake, viper, adder, bloodsnakes, and many varieties of large blue and green snakes, milksnakes, garter and watersnakes, and others. If, on meeting one of these, you would retreat, they would chase you very fiercely; but if you would turn and give them battle, they would immediately turn and crawl away with all possible speed, hide in the grass and weeds and wait for a "greener" customer. These really harmless snakes served to put people on their guard against the more dangerous and venomous kind. It was a common practice, in order to exterminate them, for the men to turn out in companies with spades, mattocks and crowbars, attack the principal snake dens and slay large numbers of them. In early spring the snakes were somewhat torpid, and easily captured. Scores of rattlesnakes were sometimes frightened out of a single den, which, as soon as they showed their heads through the crevices of the rocks, were dispatched, and left to be devoured by the numerous wild hogs of that day. Some of the fattest of these snakes were taken to the house and oil extracted from them, and their glittering skins were saved as a specific for rheumatism. Another method for their destruction was to fix a heavy stick over the door of their dens, with a long grapevine attached, so that one at a distance could plug the entrance to the den when the snakes were all out sunning themselves. Then a large company of citizens, on hand by appointment, could kill scores of the reptiles in a few minutes.

AGRICULTURE.

In the earlier settlements of this section, ponds, marshes and swamps abounded where to-day are found cultivated and fertile fields. The low and flat places were avoided for the higher grounds, not only on account of the wetness, but for sanitary reasons. Agricultural implements were necessarily rude, and the agriculture of a corresponding character. The plow used was called a "bar-share" plow, the iron point of which consisted of a bar of iron about two feet long, and a broad share of iron welded to it. At the extreme point was a coulter that passed through a beam six or seven feet long, to which was attached handles of corresponding length. The mold-board was a wooden one split out of winding timber, or hewed into a winding shape, in order to turn the soil over. In the springtime, when the ground was to be prepared for the seed, the father would take his post at the plow, and the daughter possession of the reins. This is a grand scene—one full of grace and beauty. The pioneer girl thinks but little of fine dress; knows less of the fashions; has probably heard of the opera, but does not understand its meaning; has been told of the piano but has never seen one; wears a dress "buttoned up behind;" has on "leather boots," and "drives plow" for father. In the planting of corn, which was always done by hand, the girls always took a part, usually dropping the corn, but many of them covering it with the hand-hoe.

In the cultivation of wheat, the land was plowed the same as for corn, and harrowed with a wooden-toothed harrow, or smoothed by dragging over the ground a heavy brush, weighed down, if necessary, with a stick of timber. It was then sown broadcast by hand at the rate of about a bushel and a quarter to the acre, and harrowed in with the brush. The implement used to cut the wheat was neither the sickle nor the cradle. The sickle was almost identical with the "grass hook" in use, and the cradle was a scythe fastened to a frame of wood with long, bending teeth or strips of wood, for cutting and laying the grain in swaths. There were few farmers who did not know how to swing the scythe or cradle, and there was no more pleasant picture on a farm than a gang of workmen in the harvest field, nor a more hilarious crowd. Three cradles would cut about ten acres a day. One binder was expected to keep up with the cradle. Barns for the storage of the unthreshed grain are comparatively a "modern invention," and as soon as the shock was supposed to be sufficiently cured, it was hauled to some place on the farm convenient for threshing, and there put in stack. The threshing was performed in one of two ways, by flail or tramping with horses, generally the later. The flail was used in stormy weather, on the sheltered floor, or when the farm work was not pressing; the threshing by tramping commonly in clear weather, on a level and well tramped clay floor. The bundles were piled in a circle of about fifteen to twenty feet in diameter, and four to six horses ridden over the straw. One or two hands turned over and kept the straw in place. When sufficiently tramped, the straw was thrown into a rick or stack, and the wheat cleared by a "fanning-mill, or sometimes, before fanning-mills were introduced, by letting it fall from the hight of ten or twelve feet, subjected to the action of the wind, when it was supposed to be ready for the mill or market.

RELIGION.

The religious element in the life of the pioneer was such as to attract the attention of those living in more favored places. The pioneer was no hypocrite. If he believed in horse-racing, whisky-drinking, card-playing, or anything of like character, he practiced them openly and above board.

If he was of a religious turn of mind he was not ashamed to own it. He could truthfully sing

"I'm not ashamed to own my Lord,
Or blush to speak His name."

But the pioneer clung to the faith of his fathers, for a time, at least. If he was a Presbyterian he was not ashamed of it, but rather prided himself on being one of the elect. If a Methodist, he was one to the fullest extent. He prayed long and loud if the spirit moved him, and cared nothing for the empty form of religion.

CHAPTER IV.

COUNTY GOVERNMENT.

As stated, on its creation Bremer was attached to Fayette for judicial purposes. It was subsequently attached to Black Hawk for the same purposes, and was duly organized in 1853. At this time the powers of the present board of supervisors was vested in the county court. This court consisted of a judge, a county prosecuting attorney and the sheriff. The judge had entire jurisdiction in all matters which could not properly be brought before the District court, and he was, therefore, to a certain extent, "supreme ruler" in local matters. The office was the most important one in the gift of the people of the county.

The records of the county court commence with the first session, held at Waverly, in the fall of 1853. The first court consisted of Jeremiah Farris, county judge; Austin Farris, sheriff; and Hon. W. P. Harmon, prosecuting attorney.

ACTS OF THE COUNTY COURT.

The first entries upon the records of the county court, were orders fixing the amount of bond required of the various county officers elected August, 1853. The date of the record is August 15, 1853. The bonds of the treasurer, recorder and sheriff, were each fixed at $5000.

The first regular session of the county court upon record, was held in December, 1853. The only business transacted was the issuing of several county warrants, the first being in favor of William Powell, for services rendered as judge of election, at the August election, 1853, for the sum of one dollar, and for making return of said election, for six dollars and forty cents. The second order was in favor of John S. Jenkins, for the sum of two dollars, for services rendered as judge of election. The third warrant was in favor of William Pattee, for the sum of $100.75, for furnishing books for the various county offices.

Various entries are made upon the first page of the record of the county court, of different dates, the order in which they are recorded going to show that they were not entered at the time specified.

On the 6th day of February, at a regular term of the county court, the county was divided into election precincts, as follows:

Township 91, 92, 93, range 11, and townships 91, 92, 93; range 12 constituting the first precinct, and known as Bremer precinct.

Township 93, range 13, and township 93; range 14 constituting the second precinct to be known as Polk precinct.

Township 92, range 13, and township 92, range 14, constituting the third precinct, to be known as Washington precinct.

Township 91, range 13, constituting the fourth precinct, to be known as Jefferson precinct.

Township 91, range 14, constituting the fifth precinct, to be known as Jackson precinct.

On the sixth day of March, 1854, the county court being in session, the name of Bremer precinct was changed to Frederika.

At this time, the county court issued an order for the regular April election.

The county seat having been located at Waverly, by the commissioners appointed for that purpose on the 29th of June, 1854, the first record is made of the county court being held at that place.

The county judge, at this time appointed Phineas V. Swan prosecuting attorney, *pro tem.*, for the district court then in session.

On the 3d of July, 1854, court being in session, an order was drawn upon the county treasurer, for the sum of $147.60, in favor of Richard Miles "for building and completing the court house in Waverly." Mr. Miles was also allowed $1.25, "for services in clearing the ground, and furnishing seats for court room."

On the 15th day of June, an order was made that lots 1, 2, 3, 4, 5, 6, and 7 be sold at public auction on Tuesday, July 4, 1854, in block 25, in the town of Waverly.

On the 4th, court was convened, and the following record was made:

"Ordered by the court that Edward Tyrrell sell at public auction, lots No. 1, 2, 3, 4, 5, 6, and 7, in block No. 25, in the town of Waverly, in the county of Bremer, Iowa.

Lot No. 1 was sold to Moses Layman for the sum of $40; lot No. 2 to Silas Walters for $24; lot No. 3 to Moses Layman for $26; lot No. 4 to P. W. Koukle for $53; lot No. 5 to Daniel Layman for $76; lot No. 6 to Edward Tyrrell for $50; lot No. 7 to Moses Layman for 57. Mr. Koukle, failing to pay according to terms of sale, his bid was declared null and void by the court.

On the 15th of July, 1854, the following order was entered upon the records:

"Comes into court, Edward Tyrrell, one of the trustees of Washington township, in Bremer county, Iowa, and stated that on the 15th day of July, 1854, Sarah Ingersoll, a resident of Washington township, made application to him, the said Tyrrell, for a portion of Hiram Ingersoll's property to be secured for the support of Catherine Ingersoll, a daughter of the said Hiram Ingersoll, which from sickness and disease is unable to contribute or provide for her support, and that the said Hiram Ingersoll is about to abscond and leave the said Catherine Ingersoll without leaving any means for her support; the said Tyrrell therefore requests that the court issue a warrant authorizing the trustees of said township to sieze the property of said Ingersoll. Due proof being made to the court that the said Ingersoll was about to abscond and leave his family, or a portion of them, in such condition that they would be likely to become chargeable upon the public, the court therefore ordered that a warrant issue authorizing the trustees of said township to sieze the aforesaid property. The warrant was accordingly issued."

On the 17th of July, Hiram Ingersoll and his wife, Sarah, appeared before the court, when the latter made statement that if the former would pay to her the sum of $60, she would give bond to the county, that Catherine Ingersoll should not become a charge to the county. The court thereupon ordered that when the sum of $60 was paid to Sarah Ingersoll, and the execution of her bond, the property of Hiram Ingersoll be released.

On the first day of August, 1854, the following record was made by the court:

"The amount of fees received by the judge, treasurer and clerk of Bremer county, from the 15th day of August, 1853, up to the 1st day of August, 1854, as allowed by law, amounts to $143.50, of which $112.60 was paid to the treasurer, and $30.90 paid to the clerk, which was divided between the aforesaid officers as provided by law, paying to each of said officers the sum of $47.83."

This was certainly a small amount received to enable the officers to sport the dignity of their respective offices.

On the 19th day of December, 1854, an order was issued for advertising the letting of a contract to build a county jail, and on the 26th of December, the contract was awarded to James W. Wood for the sum of $1194.

On the 25th day of August, 1855, the following record was made:

"Ordered by the county court, that Michael Currier, of Jackson township, Bremer county, Iowa, be and is hereby appointed county agent, to sell intoxicating liquors, for said county, for medicinal, mechanical and sacramental purposes, and no other purpose, from the 25th of August, 1855, till the first day of May, 1856, and that the said Currier give bond in the sum of one thousand dollars, and to purchase liquors to the amount of $211.31."

Jonathan N. Fowler, of Le Roy township, was also made county agent for the same purpose, and required to give bond to the same amount. He was permitted to purchase a bill amounting to $69.66.

It would appear from the foregoing that the citizens of Jackson township were not in as healthy a state as those in Le Roy township, or else they were of a scientific turn of mind, and required a large amount of liquor for mechanical purposes.

G. C. Wright, ex-officio county judge, on the first day of April, 1857, issued a proclamation, calling an election in the various townships, on the 4th day of May, 1857, for the purpose of voting upon the question whether the county of Bremer should vote the sum of $100,000 to aid in the construction of the Chicago, Iowa and Nebraska Railroad.

The election was duly held, resulting in favor of issuing the bonds by a vote of 385 for, and 234 against.

The same ex-officio judge, on the 4th of March, 1857, issued a proclamation to the qualified voters; that an election would be held, in April, of that year, for the purpose of voting upon the question as to whether hogs should be allowed to run at large. The election was duly held on the 6th of April, 1857, and resulted in adopting a law whereby hogs were to be restrained, the vote standing 429, to 108. The canvass of votes was signed by George W. Ruddick, prosecuting attorney of the county.

Under the date of May 13, 1857, appears the following entry:

Now comes into court B. F. Perkins and makes the following as his report as liquor agent of Bremer county, which report is accepted:
Paid out for liquor and handling...... $417.05.
Twenty-five per cent. of which is..... 145.05.
Remaining on hand of said liquor..... 200.00.
Twenty-five per cent. of which is...... 50.00.

Which said $50.00 substracted from $145.05, leaves $95.05; salary allowed agent by judge, $30.00; leaving a balance of $65.00 to be paid to the county treasurer by me.

[Signed] B. F. PERKINS.

Immediately following this is the record of a new license issued to Perkins as agent of the county, to sell liquor for medicinal and mechanical purposes, in Washington township, and states that he shall not dispose of liquor except for the purposes mentioned. Perkins was a lawyer who had located at Waverly.

On the 24th of September, 1857, county warrant No. 884 was issued to I. M. Preston for the sum of $7,000, to be paid in one year, for services rendered in securing to the county the title to the swamp or overflowed land, according to a contract which had been made. On the same date an additional amount of $500, was issued in warrant No. 885. There is some mystery as to the date of this, as it bears two dates, i. e., August 24, 1856, and August 24, 1857; both appearing in connection with the same paragraph. The matter evidently gave rise to some trouble, as two pages further on, in record, appears the entry, under the date of August 24, 1857, in which it culminates as follows:

"Ordered by the county court that warrant No. 884, for the sum of $7,000, and warrant 885, for the sum of $500, that were issued to I. M. Preston, on the county treasurer, on the 10th of August, 1857, be and the same are hereby declared null and void, on the ground that no services have been rendered the county by the said I. M. Preston, and that said warrants have been issued without Bremer county having received any value therefor."

It was also ordered that the treasurer be notified not to pay any money on the warrants, and the contract made with Preston was annulled. A few days later the warrants were presented and cancelled by the county judge, George W. Maxfield.

In 1858, the taxes levied on the taxable property of Bremer county, was as follows: For county, state, school, road and bridge purposes, ten mills on the dollar; road tax; one dollar; county poll tax, fifty cents.

On the sixth day of June, 1859, applications were made to the county judge, by J. J. Smith and Miles P. Comstock, for licenses to operate a ferry across the Cedar river, at Waverly, the former on Ellsworth street and the latter on Jefferson street. The proper notices having been posted, Judge George W. Maxfield ordered that licenses be granted to the parties. The following is a copy of the license:

STATE OF IOWA,
BREMER COUNTY.

To M. P. Comstock:

You are hereby licensed to run a ferry boat for the transportation of persons, teams, goods, wares, merchandise, etc., across the Cedar river, at the foot of Jefferson street in the town of Waverly. The rates of toll hereby allowed are as follows:

Trip for double team, same day........25 cents.
Trip for one horse and carriage, same day..15 cents.
Trip for man and horse, same day.....10 cents.
Transient person trip, same day....... 5 cents.
Persons in the habit of crossing may commute at the rate of from...15 to 50 cents.
For crossing cattle over five in number per head............................ 2 cents.
Less than five in number.............. 3 cents.
Ferry to be run from 6 o'clock A. M., to 9 o'clock a: night.

[Signed]   GEORGE W. MAXFIELD,
County Judge.

Several petitions were presented to the judge shortly after this, for a license to run a ferry across the Cedar river at Janesville. Asbury Leverich and R. Morehouse were among the applicants, and Asbury Leverich was successful. It later appears, however, that the case was appealed, and the application of the Morehouse petition was allowed.

On the 1st day of September, 1859, Judge G. W. Maxfield issued a proclamation to the effect that at the October election the question would be submitted to the people as to whether the county of Bremer should use the Swamp Land Fund, then in the county treasury, and apply it to the following purposes, viz:

$250 on the road and bridge in Franklin township, where the road leading from Waverly to Fairbanks crosses the Wapsipinicon river, in said township. $150 on the road on bridge known as Titcomb's bridge in Fremont township. $200 on the road and bridges leading from Martinsburgh, in Frederika township, to Bremer in LeRoy township. $291.25 towards the construction of a bridge in the town of Waverly.

The election was duly held and resulted in a majority favoring such use of the Swamp Fund, the vote standing 599 for, to 145 against the proposition.

Under the date of October 1, 1860, appears the following entry upon the records of the county court, and it was undoubtedly hailed with feelings of gratification by the county officials:

"The amount of salary allowed the county officers has been increased by the taking of the United States census, from five hundred dollars per year to five hundred and fifty dollars, the number of inhabitants of the county exceeding five thousand.

GEO. W. MAXFIELD,
County Judge."

On the 24th of October, 1860, a case came before Judge Maxfield, in which Rhoda Harmon was charged with insanity by her husband, J. W. Harmon. Sheriff Ellis was directed to bring the accused before the court, and Dr. O. Burbank, J. W. Harmon, Mary Jane Harmon and D. Mills were subpœnied as witnesses. Evidence was taken which all went to substantiate the charge, and the testimony of Dr. Burbank was to the effect that Mrs. Harmon was laboring under temporary insanity and that with medical treatment, suitable care and attention, she would soon recover. The judge then says, that—

"Having taken the testimony of W. W. Norris, J. G. Ellis and J. W. Harmon, in regard to the value of the property of J. W. Harmon, the husband of the said Rhoda Harmon, after deducting what is exempt from execution, which said testimony established the fact that the property of said J. W. Harmon was worth less than one thousand dollars. It is therefore ordered by the county judge that the cost and expense growing out of the charge of insanity of the said Rhoda Harmon be paid by the county, and, inasmuch as there is no poor house in said county, and further as the county jail is not in a suitable condition for keeping the said Rhoda Harmon, that she be taken in charge by the said J. W. Harmon, and kept by him until further order of the court, or until information shall be received that the Insane Asylum is open for the reception of patients; and that while she remains in the charge of said J. W. Harmon, he receive such an amount as is allowed by law, not to exceed the sum of $50 per year, and that she also receive such medical attendance as may be necessary for her speedy recovery."

What finally became of the case the record does not state.

During the winter of 1859–60 an act was passed by the General Assembly, which was approved by the Governor, changing the mode of local government, and creating the board of supervisors of the county. This board took charge, and had all the powers formerly vested in the county court, excepting the issuance of marriage licenses, probate matters, and civil cases.

The county court still held its sessions, and continued so to do until 1869, when it was abolished by law; but nothing of interest transpired, as the time was all spent in routine matters. (See chapter on county representation.)

The board of county supervisors consisted of one member from each township. The election for members occurred at the general election, in November, 1860.

The first meeting of the board was held on the 7th day of January, 1861, at the auditor's office, in the court house, at Waverly. The members were all present and took their oaths of office before Louis Case, clerk of the district court, who, by virtue of his office, was also clerk of the board. Mr Case filed his bond, in the sum of $1,000, for the correct performance of his duties. The board then effected an organization by electing L. J. Curtis president. Ballots were then drawn to ascertain the length of term to be served by the various supervisors, resulting as follows:

B. M. Reeves, two years............Washington
Barnes Thompson, one year..........,....Polk
T. V. Axtell, one year.................Jackson
David Marquis, two years............Jefferson
N. M. Smith, one year.................Warren
John Aken, two years.............. ....Douglas
E. J. Walling, one year............Frederika
P. H. Wilson, two years.................LeRoy
Otis Clark, two years..................Fremont
William Mathias, one year............Maxfield
Ichabod Richmond, two years.........Franklin
L. J. Curtis, two years... .... Dayton
L. M. Sholes, one year.................Sumner
R. J. Stevenson, one year...........Lafayette

After attending to a few preliminary matters, the board adjourned until the following day, when rules and regulations were adopted.

On the third day of this session, the bond of the clerk of the board was increased to $5,000.

On the 10th of January, from the report of the committee on school funds and lands, it appears that the funds for school purposes were in bad shape. Their report says that they "find a large proportion of the school fund, notes and mortgages, confined to a small portion of the county, and indifferently secured by irresponsible persons, and secured by real estate of but little value, and of a perishable nature, and recommend that the district attorney commence prosecution against all delinquents at the earliest practicable period, and that the district clerk and board of supervisors distribute the loans hereafter made as much as possible through the county, and place every possible safeguard about our school fund."

About the same time the matter of the bond of the clerk of the board was again brought up, and it was reduced to $1,000.

On the 11th day of January, 1861, a report from the committee appointed for the purpose, states that they find a large deficiency in the accounts of the ex-county treasurer and recorder, and recommend that the district attorney be requested to collect the same at once.

This, apparently, had the desired effect, for, under the date of the 3d of April, the following entry appears:

"In reply to the representations made of the delinquency of W. B. Hamilton, late treasurer of Bremer county, the district attorney is of the opinion that Hamilton paid over to the county the amount named in the indictment as found against him by the grand jury, and hence the prosecution was discontinued. But if anything further remains due the county he will attend to it at once."

Everything was satisfactory, and the matter was accordingly dropped. During the same session a committee which had been appointed at a previous meeting to investigate as to whether the court house had been erected according to contract, reported finding considerable fault with the way it had been built, and setting forth that G. W. LeValley and H. F. Beebe had not complied with the plans and specifications which were a part of the contract. This committee was composed of N. M. Smith, E. J. Walling and P. H. Wilson.

At a meeting on the day following, a compromise was presented by the contractors in question, which was accepted and the matter was dropped.

On the 3d of April, 1861, the following entry appears:

Resolved, That hereafter no bills presented for tobacco furnished paupers will be allowed by this board.

It is to be supposed that since that date Bremer county paupers have paid for their own chewing and smoking tobacco.

On Thursday, June 6, 1861, the board of supervisors unanimously passed the following preamble and resolution:

WHEREAS, Certain patriotic citizens of the county of Bremer have volunteered their services to maintain the constitution and Union of our common country, and as there is a possibility that families thus deprived of their natural protectors may suffer for the need of succor and protection; therefore,

Resolved, That the county of Bremer take all such families under their especial care and protection, and for the purpose of carrying this resolution into effect, the chairman of this board is instructed to appoint a committee of three (who in all cases shall serve without compensation) whose especial duty it shall be to look after such families and see that they are supplied with all the necessary comforts of life, while their fathers and husbands are in the service of the United States.

O. C. Harrington, of Horton; J. T. Barrick, of Janesville; L. J. Curtis, of Dayton; E. J. Walling, of Frederika; and B. M. Reeves, of Waverly, were appointed as a committee to carry into effect the foregoing resolutions. The following resolution was also adopted:

Resolved, That the board of supervisors of Bremer county appropriate the sum of $500, or so much thereof as may be necessary, for the benefit of families of volunteers who have enlisted or may enlist in the service of our country; that we also request those persons having paid subscriptions for the benefit of volunteers, and who wish the county should reimburse them, in whole or in part, shall make out and present their bills therefore, at the next meeting of the board for action at that time.

On the 15th of October, the following appears as entered upon the record:

"Motion by John Acken, that the committee on volunteer fund report, how, when, where, and to whom the volunteer fund had been expended, and that the same be published. Whereupon there was considerable discussion among the members, it being the understanding of a majority that the names of the recipients of said fund were not to be published, and that when said committee report, they report the amounts distributed, having taken receipts therefor."

The vote on the matter was as follows: ayes — Acken, Mathias and Stephenson; nayes — Thompson, Richmond, Axtell, Marquis, Sholes, Reeves, Walling, Clark, Curtis.

At a session on the 21st of August, 1862, the board of supervisors passed a resolution to the effect that the clerk of the board should be authorized to issue a warrant for the sum of $50.00 to each volunteer that had or should thereafter enlist from Bremer county, "under the present call of the Governor of Iowa, as soon as they have been received and mustered into the service." The vote on the resolution was close, being decided by a majority of one.

This gave rise to the following resolution, which was at once adopted:

"Resolved, that the county of Bremer, through its board of supervisors, will levy a tax two mills additional, at its September meeting, to cover ordinary and extraordinary expenses incurred by reason of the present rebellion and ask the Legislature to legalize the same."

Shortly afterward the record says that warrants were issued to the following named volunteers, viz:

H. F. Beebe	$50
E. C. Dougherty	50
E. L. Brown	50
S. Kinyon	50
T. Orthmann	50
Ellis Shaw	50
H. H. Bartlett	50
W. O. Butler	50
P. H. Smith	50
Jacob T. Renn	50
Geo. A. Michael	50
Samuel Downs	50
Francis Henston	50
J. O. Jones	50
Henry Smith	50
J. M. Farris	50
Adam Fleisher	50
Geo. A. Brown	50
Samuel Wilson	50
S. F. Beebe	50
Richard Currier	50
E. M. Dougherty	50
S. S. Reynolds	50
Fred. Leege	50
Casill Sharp	50
Geo. W. Baskins	50
H. McHenry	50
L. H. Lowe	50

W. M. Baskins	$50
T. A. Stearns	50
J. F. Messinger	50
Charles E. Smith	50
William Ogden	50
Francis Kerr	50
Cyrus Robbins	50
Shadrach Hinton	50

Others followed in rapid succession. The above list includes many of the first warrants issued for war purposes.

In 1864, the board first met on the 4th of January, and organized by the re-election of L. J. Curtis as chairman. The new members who were present and took their seats were:

Eri Terry	Polk
P. Ingersoll	Lafayette
W. C. Dove	Jackson
L. C. Prince	Frederika
Wm. S. Detrick	Maxfield
D. R. Hatch	Sumner
D. Wenrick	Warren

One of their first official acts this year was to grant a license, for twenty years, to J. Ackerson Taylor, permitting him to build a toll bridge across the Cedar river at Janesville.

At the January session, this year, the following resolution was adopted:

Resolved, that a county bounty of $100 be given to every volunteer who shall enlist from Bremer county to fill the present call for 300,000 men.

This carried by a vote of eleven to three.

At the June term, in 1864, this resolution was amended as follows:

Resolved, that the record of the action of this board at the January session, A. D., 1864, for granting bounties of $100 to volunteers to fill the President's call for 300,000 volunteers, be so amended to give or grant the same bounties to soldiers that have enlisted in the three years service since that call, whether veterns or new recruits, provided that they are accredited to this county, and that the county warrants be delivered to the families of said soldiers; or if they have no families to the order of the volunteer.

It was also resolved that the members of the board mutually "pledge themselves to levy a tax of three mills on the dollar, for the benefit of soldiers' families." This was to be done at the September session.

The following apportionments of the Relief Fund to the several townships was made at the June term, viz:

Polk	$200 00
Douglas	25 00
Frederika	25 00
LeRoy	100 00
Sumner	125 00
Dayton	100 00
Fremont	150 00
Maxfield	75 00
Warren	50 00
Lafayette	150 00
Washington	400 00
Jackson	350 00
Jefferson	550 00
Franklin	150 00

In 1865 the board commenced their work on the 2d of January, with all the members present save John Troy, of Douglas township. The board then proceeded to organize, by the election of William C. Dove, of Jackson, as chairman. The newly elected members were as follows:

E. J. Messinger	Jefferson
John Buckmaster	Warren
John Chapin	Fremont
David Chadwick	Dayton
Ichabod Richmond	Franklin
B. M. Reeves	Washington
A. Brodie	LeRoy

In June, 1865, $250 was appropriated to repair the bridges over the Cedar river at Janesville.

At the September session, in 1865, of the board, the recompense to those who had served in the war was made more general and more liberal. The resolution was presented by D. C. Hatch, and was adopted, as follows:

Resolved, That the county issue orders, at the rate of $100, for three year-enlistment soldiers, who have enlisted or been drafted, and served from Bremer county: *Provided,* said soldiers have not received a bounty from another county, and that such sum or sums as have been paid to soldiers as bounty by this county be deducted from said $100, and the balance be paid in the following manner, to-wit: In three equal annual payments of thirty-three and one-third per cent. of the whole amount due The clerk of this board shall issue said bounty to said soldiers, or their heirs or their legal representatives, on proof presented from the Adjutant General's reports, certificates of Provost Marshal, discharge papers, and other legal evidence; and the clerk shall commence paying the said bounties on and after the 20th of this month.

At the October session, Mr. Dove vacated the chair, and tendered his resignation as supervisor from Jackson township. The resignation was accepted, and Mr. Reeves took the chair.

On New Year's Day, 1866, the board of supervisors convened at Waverly, and the following members elect, appeared, qualified and took their seats:

Elias Congdon..........................Sumner
N. A. Reeves........................Lafayette
W. S. Dietrich.......................Maxfield
John K. Head ... .Polk
W. C. Dove..........................Jackson
John Henry........................ Frederika
B. F. Call...........................Franklin

On ballot being taken, N. A. Reeves was chosen chairman for the ensuing year.

For the year 1867, the board of supervisors first convened on the first Monday of January, and commenced routine business. The following members elect from their respective townships, qualified and took their seats:

N. J. Moore .. ..Douglas
George Parker....................... Dayton
John Bingham.... ... .LeRoy
Thomas Fountain.....................Jefferson
B. F. Call ... .Franklin
John Mohling........................Maxfield
C. Morse.........................Washington

W. C. Dove took the chair *pro tem* and the matter of electing a chairman for the ensuing year was taken up. Six ballots were taken before a choice was arrived at, but finally the election of W. C. Dove was made unanimous.

At the June session, this year, a resolution was presented, proposing to submit to a vote the question of purchasing a poor farm. The resolution was defeated. It was then resolved that a committee be appointed to purchase a poor farm for Bremer county. Accordingly the committee was appointed, consisting of C. Morse, J. K. Mead, N. J. Moore, Thomas Fountain and D. R. Hatch, who were instructed to purchase the farm. But before the board adjourned, one of the committee moved that the last resolution be reconsidered, and upon vote, the former was adopted, submitting the matter to the people and a committee was appointed to inquire the price of suitable farms. This matter is treated elsewhere in this volume.

During the session a petition was presented to the board, praying that the boundaries of Sumner township be changed, and sections 6 and 7 be annexed to LeRoy township. It was soon followed by a remonstrance and the matter was laid upon the table.

During 1868, the matter was again taken up and it was decided to make the west half of section 7, and the southwest quarter of section 6, a part of LeRoy township.

The years' work of 1868, was inaugurated by the board at a session on the 6th of January. N. J. Moore was elected chairman for the ensuing year, and the following members-elect appeared and qualified:

F. Coddington.......................Jackson
M. F. Gillette.....................Frederika
John Mohling.......................Maxfield
A. Gerry...............................Polk
G. C. Stephenson..................Lafayette

John Smalley appeared and presented his appointment as supervisor from Warren township, which was duly approved.

It was also stated that Sumner was not represented. Henry Lease, Jr. was elected but resigned.

The first meeting in 1869, was held on the 4th of January, and A. J. Tanner was elected chairman for the ensuing year. The following members took their seats:

N. J. Moore........................Douglas
A. J. Tanner, chairman.........Washington
John D. Woodruff..................Warren
Patrick O'Dea ....LeRoy
Hiram Lester.......................Fremont
C. S. Wellman....................Jefferson
Jocob Ward.........................Franklin
John Kehe.........................Maxfield
George Parker......................Dayton

Mr. Tanner presented the credentials of appointment of J. N. Johnston, as supervisor of Frederika township, and he was accordingly sworn in.

During this year the name of Louis Case as clerk of the board of supervisors drops from sight and again appears signing the records as "county auditor," that office in the meantime having been created.

At the June term the committee appointed to confer with the officers of Bremer county in reference to the safe keeping of public records reported—

That after making examination, and advising with said officers, we have come to the unanimous conclusion that it would be unwise to attempt a reconstruction of the court house for that purpose. We therefore recommend a separate building from the court house to be erected on the court house square, and we would further recommend that a committee of one be appointed to apply to a good architect to draw a plan for said building and make a probable estimate of the cost of the same to be submitted to this board at its next session, all of which is most respectfully submitted.

[Signed.]   N. J. MOORE,
                ADIN TERRY,
                J. N. JOHNSTON,
                Committee.

The report was accepted, and Louis Case appointed as committee of one, to attend to the matter.

The members-elect of the board for the year 1870, were as follows, and appeared at the January session, and duly qualified:

Otis Clark........................Lafayette
John Kehe.........................Maxfield
R. Morehouse......................Jackson
A. L. Stephenson..................Sumner
J. N. Johnston..................Frederika
Adin Terry...........................Polk

A. J. Tanner was elected chairman for the ensuing year.

This was the last meeting of the board of supervisors, represented by a member from each township, as the General Assembly passed an act changing the system, and providing that the board should consist of three members, elected at large, instead of one member from each township.

The first meeting of the new board was held on the 2d day of January, 1871, at Waverly, and the members-elect—S. P. Curtis, M. Farrington, and John Chapin—were duly qualified. John Chapin was elected chairman for the ensuing year.

The board for 1872 consisted of John Chapin, S. H. Curtis, and M. Farrington. Mr. Chapin had been re-elected, and qualified by taking the usual oath. The board first met on the 1st of January, and proceeded to the election of a chairman for the ensuing year, which resulted in the choice of S. H. Curtis.

During this session the auditor of the county was directed to issue orders on the iron bridge fund, in payment for the King iron bridge, which had been erected at Waverly, in amounts as follows:

One due January 4th, 1873	$200 00
One due March 1st, 1873	3,466 00
One due March 1st, 1874	3,667 00
One due March 1st, 1875	3,667 00
Total	$11,000 00

The whole to bear interest at the rate of ten per cent.

The board evidently did not propose to have the county come out behind, passed the following resolution at the same session:

Resolved, That Messrs. Ellis, Slimmer, Ridgeway, and Gillette are released from their bond for the cribbing of the Stockwell bridge piers, on condition that the stone got out by them for that purpose be donated to the county.

The salary of the county auditor was fixed at $1,200 and the fees of the office, he to pay the necessary clerk hire.

It was also resolved that the delinquent tax lists for 1861, 1862, and 1863, be cancelled, as it was deemed that all had been collected that could be.

At the September session, the following was presented by Mr. Farrington which was adopted:

WHEREAS, The census board of the State of Iowa, in accordance with chapter 26, of the General and Public Laws of the Fourteenth General Assembly, have filed with this board the following statement, viz:

STATEMENT

Showing the length in miles of the several railroads in Bremer county, Iowa, on December 31, 1871, and the assessed value thereof per mile, as fixed by the census board on July 31, 1872.

The Cedar Falls and Minnesota Railroad, operated by the Illinois Central Company, has 19.47 miles of road in Bremer county, which is assessed at $3,000 per mile.

The Burlington, Cedar Rapids and Minnesota Railroad has 4.5 miles of road in the county, assessed at $3,800 per mile.

Therefore, it was resolved by the board that the total assessed value for all purposes of the former road should be for the year 1872, $58,410; of the latter, $17,100.

For the year 1873, the board comprised the same gentlemen as of the year before, Messrs. S. H. Curtis, M. Farrington and John Chapin, the first named having been re-elected. He was also chosen chairman for the ensuing year.

In 1874 the board consisted of S. H. Curtis, John Chapin and Marvin Potter,

HISTORY OF BREMER COUNTY.

The chairman chosen for the year was S. H. Curtis. Routine business occupied the attention of the board during this year.

At the June session, in 1874, the board of supervisors divided the county into supervisor's districts, by passing the following resolution:

Resolved, That Bremer county is hereby divided into supervisor's districts, comprising territory as follows:

District No. 1, to embrace Washington and Jackson townships, having a population of 4,251.

District No. 2, to embrace Polk, Douglas, Warren, Lafayette and Jefferson townships; population, 4,214.

District No. 3, to embrace Frederika, LeRoy, Sumner, Dayton, Fremont, Maxfield and Franklin townships; population, 4,052.

This division of the county is still in force.

The board held a session on the fourth of January, 1875. S. H. Curtis and Marvin Potter answered to their names and A. L. Stevenson, the new member, qualified and took his seat. The chairman this year was S. H. Curtis.

The board of supervisors was the same during the year 1876, S. H. Curtis being re-elected and again chosen chairman.

By the report of the county auditor to the board, at its January session, it was shown that during the year just closed $20,051 worth of county warrants had been issued, and the assets and liabilities of the county, balanced.

In 1877, the new member was Barnes Thompson, of Polk township, who qualified and took his seat. S. H. Curtis and A. L. Stevenson, answered to their names. Mr. Curtis was re-elected chairman.

During this year, a resolution was passed offering, as an inducement for residents to plant trees and hedges along public highways, an exemption of $300 from assessed value of taxation for each mile of hedge or shade trees.

At the September session, in 1877, the following was adopted and entered upon the records:

Resolved, that a vote of thanks is hereby tendered to the retiring member of this board, Mr. A. L. Stevenson, for the uniform courtesy he has always shown during the sessions of this board, and for the very efficient and prompt manner in which he has attended to all official business entrusted to him during his term of office as county supervisor.

In 1878 the board first met on the 7th of January, when the old members, S. H. Curtis and Barnes Thompson, took their seats and the member elected in place of Mr. Stevenson, Andrew Carstensen, qualified and took his seat. The same chairman was elected for this year that served the year previous.

During the January session a vote of thanks was tendered to the retiring county treasurer, George Morehouse, for his courtesy, carefulness and efficiency.

The following resolution was also presented and adopted at the October session of the board:

Resolved, That the thanks of the people of Bremer county are due S. H. Curtis, the retiring member of this board, for the very able and tireless manner in which he has discharged the duties of his office during his long term of service, and that the remaining members will miss his genial good nature and guiding counsel.

The members of the board for 1879 were, Barnes Thompson, Andrew Carstensen and C. Cadwallader, the latter being the new member. Barnes Thompson was elected chairman for the year.

In 1880 the board consisted of Andrew Carstensen, C. Cadwallader, and T. P. Wilson. Andrew Carstensen was chosen chairman.

The following report from Mr. Rice, steward of the poor house, was presented for the year 1880:

Total number of paupers at poor house during year............................. 12
Greatest number at any one time............ 8
Number on January 1, 1881.................. 6
Average number kept....................... 6
Health good.

In 1881 the board was the same as in 1880, Mr. Carstensen being re-elected chairman.

For the term commencing in 1882, James S. Conner was elected in place of Mr. Cadwallader, and Andrew Carstensen was again chosen chairman.

The only change for the year 1883, is that John Homrighaus takes the place of T. P. Wilson. This makes the present board of supervisors as follows: Andrew Carstensen, chairman; James S. Conner and John Homrighaus.

Andrew Cartstensen, the present chairman of the board of supervisors, was born in Germany, on the 14th day of August, 1823. He came to America in 1852, and soon after his arrival, settled on a farm in Will county, Illinois, and there lived until 1869, when he came to Iowa, and settled on a farm on section 15, Fremont township, where he now owns 340 acres of land. In 1881, he removed from his farm into the village of Tripoli, and is now engaged as a stock dealer and farmer. In 1878, he was elected to the office of county supervisor, and in 1881, was re-elected. In 1854, he was united in marriage to Miss Elizabeth Butler, a native of Germany, who bore him six children, of whom five are now living—George Peter, John, Andrew and Ella. Mrs. Carstensen died in 1866. Mr. Carstensen was again married, in 1868, to Miss Mary Johnson, and they have four children—Reka, Matilda, Henry and Herman.

CHAPTER V.

OFFICIAL MATTERS.

In this chapter are presented various matters gathered from the county records and other sources.

POPULATION.

In 1845 the population of Bremer county was about four. In 1850 this had increased to probably twenty-five, although in the census of these two years no notice was taken of this region. In 1860, just prior to the breaking out of the rebellion, the census gave this county a population of 4,915. By the census of 1870—ten years later—this had increased to 12,528. By the last census taken, in 1880, it had 14,081 inhabitants, which has probably been increased to 15,000. Its American and foreign population is almost equally divided, the German element predominating among those of foreign birth or descent. The American inhabitants emigrated mostly from New York, New England, Pennsylvania, Ohio, Indiana and Illinois, and they are as a whole, an enterprising people. The German inhabitants emigrated almost exclusively from the northern part of the German Empire. As a class they came poor, bought land at low rates on long time, making small payments and by industry and frugality have since become thrifty and substantial farmers. Comparatively few of the Germans in the county are engaged in trade or mercantile pursuits, the various departments of which are conducted principally by Americans.

BREMER COUNTY POOR FARM.

After the close of the war it became evident that the county was in need of a place for the care of its poor, and at the June session of the board of supervisors, in 1866, it was resolved to submit the matter to a vote of the electors of the county, to ascertain if they would vote to authorize the purchase of a poor farm in the county. It was shown that during the last preceding six months, $1,698.77 had been expended for the support of the poor. Nothing resulted from this action. The matter again came up in 1867, and the board appointed a committee "to purchase a poor farm for the county." A re-consideration of this action was taken at the same session, and it was resolved to have the matter submitted to a vote of the people. At the same time a committee was appointed to procure information respecting the price of farms suitable for a poor farm, the cost of maintaining the poor of the county, and any other information important in the premises. At the September session of the board, in the same year, the committee orally reported, re-committing the general subject to the board, but reporting the cost of maintaining the poor for the years named, to have been as follows: In 1860, $780.75; 1861, $1,256.38; 1862, $967.48; 1863, $810.87; 1864, $944.96; 1865, $891.66; 1866, $1,347.67; 1866, up to the 19th of June of that year, $1,841.95; grand total, $8,841.72. At the latter session, also, a committee was appointed to draft and submit, in its proper form, to the legal voters of the county, a proposition to purchase a poor farm at a cost not exceeding $5,000. The proposition was so submitted at the next ensuing election, and was carried by a vote of 944 in the affirmative, to 261 in the negative. Accordingly, at the meeting of the board in October, 1867, immediately succeeding the election, still another committee was appointed to seek a location suitable for a poor farm, and ascertain the prices thereof, with instructions to report at the following January meeting. At the time directed, the committee reported that they were unable to agree, and asked to be discharged, adding the recommendation that another committee be appointed, to examine improved and unimproved lands within five miles of the geographical center of the county, and report at the next June meeting. The report and recommendation were accepted. Nothing further was done in the matter until the meeting of the board in January,

1869, when, the committee last appointed having failed to report, another committee was appointed, for the like purpose of examining lands within the limits mentioned, with instructions to report at the next meeting of the board. The last committee, consisting of N. J. Moore, A. L. Stevenson and J. D. Woodruff, faithfully and promptly discharged their duties. In June, 1869, they reported in favor of purchasing the southeast quarter and the south half of the northeast quarter of section 24, township 92, range 13, Warren township, comprising 240 acres of land, at the price of ten dollars an acre. The report was adopted, but nothing was done regarding it. The next action was taken in 1872, when, in June of that year, a committee was appointed to have the poor farm surveyed, stones set at corners, forty acres on the south side broken, and a strip eight feet wide, around the farm on the fence line, also broken for the purpose of planting trees thereon. At the January meeting of the board, in 1873, 1,400 seasoned fence posts and 15,000 feet of lumber were ordered for fencing the farm. At the same session another committee was appointed, to let the farm for that year; also, to procure plans, receive proposals, and to contract for building a house upon the farm; for which latter purpose the sum of $1,500, or so much thereof as should be necessary, was appropriated. Pursuant to this action, the present tenement house was erected.

CIVIL TOWNSHIPS.

The fourteen civil townships in the county were organized upon the following dates, viz:

Jackson township, on the 9th of March, 1857.

Dayton township, on the 10th of February, 1858.

Jefferson township, on the 17th of February, 1858.

Douglas township, on the 22d of May, 1858.

Frederika township, on the 22d of May, 1858.

Sumner township, on the 27th of July, 1858.

LeRoy township, on the 27th of July, 1858.

Maxfield township, on the 6th of September, 1858.

Franklin township, on the 6th of September, 1858.

Lafayette township, on the 6th of December, 1858.

Polk township, on the 6th of December, 1858.

Warren township, on the 21st of February, 1859.

Washington township, on the 21st of February, 1859.

Fremont township, on the 21st of February, 1859.

TOWN PLATS.

The plats of the several towns in Bremer county were filed for record upon the following dates, viz:

Janesville was the first, and was filed on the 22d of July, 1854. The second plat of it was filed on the 20th of January, 1857.

Waverly—the original plat—bore the date of April 14, 1855. The last of several subsequent additions was filed February 29, 1860.

Horton was filed on the 6th of December, 1856.

Jefferson City was filed on the 20th of March, 1856.

Tripoli was filed on the 27th of December, 1865.

Deanville was filed on the 16th of June, 1868.

Plainfield was filed on the 18th of June, 1868.

Sumner was filed on the first of July, 1873.

Frederika was filed on the 29th of July, 1873.

These matters are treated at length in the township and village histories.

MARRIAGE RECORD.

Marriage licenses have always been required in this State and the greater portion of the facts here found were taken from the clerk's record of certificates issued.

The first license issued in Bremer county bore date of August 20, 1853, and authorized the proper person to legally unite Jonas Mishler and Sarah Michael. This ceremony was performed on the same day by Jeremiah Farris, county judge.

The second license was issued on the 23d of August, 1853, to Joel Bartlett and Miss Mary H. Dean. They were married by Judge Farris on the 25th of the same month.

Licenses, during the year 1853, were issued to the following persons:

Johnson Ovelerug and Debby Farris, August 23. They were married on the same day, by Judge Jeremiah Farris.

George W. Baskin and Mahala McHenry, November 9. They were married on the following day by Israel Trumbo, a justice of the peace.

John Powell and Rebecca Thorp, November, 14. They were married on the 17th by Jeremiah Farris.

This comprises all the licenses issued during the year 1853. During the year 1854 the list increased materially:

James Elliot and Eleanor Buckmaster, February 6. Married February 16, by by Judge Farris.

Pyront McGee and Mary Webster, February 6. Married on the 9th, by Judge Farris.

Frederick Cretzmeyer and Julia Bellkerrys, February 20. Married on the 23d, by Israel Trumbo, justice of the peace.

James Moore and Eliza Blockey, March 25. Married by Rev. Elias Pattee, on the 26th.

Phelix Cretzmeyer and Jemima Scott, May 28. Married on the same day by Rev. S. W. Ingham.

David Dewey and Ann Dudgeon, July 24. Married on the following day by Judge Farris.

Peter Heery and Abigail J. Gibson, July 22. Married by Judge Farris, July 23.

Jehial Hamory and Rhoda Boardmore, August 10. Married August 13, by Stephen D. Jackson, Esq.

Spencer W. Jackson and Margaret A. Pool, September 18. Married by Stephen D. Jackson, Esq., on the 20th of the same month.

Henry B. Boyd and Lucinda Carberry, December 23. Married on the 24th of the same month, by Rev. Isaac Waterhouse.

Lafayette Sturdevant and Sarah A. Ogden, December 23. Married on the 25th by Judge Farris.

Robert Messinger and Sarah Michael, January 2, 1855.

J. N. Fowle and Ann Page, February 5, 1855.

Burlin Stephens and Juliann Hinton, March 3, 1855.

Jonathan H. Goforth and Celia A. Webster, March 15, 1855.

Henry Deckmeyer and Sophia Bockhert, April 25, 1855.

James Edgington and Elizabeth Null, April 30, 1855.

Arial Rimon and Harriett P. Freeman, May 5, 1855.

Marquis F. Gillett and Olive A. Wolling, March, 1855.

Eron E. Herdy and Emma Smith, May, 1855.

Henry J. White and Elizabeth Richmond, April, 1855.

James Wells and Caroline Beath, July, 1855.

Daniel Hutchinson and Mary Buckmaster, August, 1855.

George A. Michael and Elizabeth Trumbo, December, 1854.

Henry Messinger and Mary Buckmaster, August, 1855.

LeRoy Shippy and Susanna Mishler, July, 1855.

Cristopher Frink and Mary Ebey, August, 1855.

Daniel Clayton and Cyrena Moore, October, 1855.

Henry Griffing and Lydia A. Thorp, August, 1855.

Henry Stears and Hannah Thurston, September, 1855.

John T. Dicken and Aldine Auney, March, 1856.

N. A. Reeves and Rhoda A. Willey, March, 1856.

Samuel Henderson and Beda Goforth, August, 1854. This license was never returned.

William Rowen and Mary Cleavey, September, 1854. Immediately following this entry are written, in a scrawling hand, the words, "backed out;" so it is to be presumed the parties changed their minds.

Richard Miles and Adaline Phelps, September, 1854. This license was never returned.

Solomon Belden and Maria Buckmaster, March, 1855. Never returned.

Francis M. Codner and Armeldo McHenry, August, 1855. Never returned.

Norman Miller and Mary Rengory. Never returned.

Henry P. Moore and Clarinda Bussy, November, 1855.

W. E. Andrews and Frances Briggs, November, 1855.

Amos Hurst and Samantha J. Clayton, November, 1855.

James Hunter and Elizabeth Koop, November, 1855.

Essex Farris and Catherine Mishler, November, 1855.

Seymore Ayers and Margaret Hinton, January 1856.

John Johnson and Jane Creyton, January, 1856.

David Down and Patience Luther, February, 1856.

Thomas R. Ponde and Emeline Bennett, February, 1856.

W. J. Michael and Miss Campbell, April, 1856.

William Mullin and Orvilla Boyed, May, 1856.

HISTORY OF BREMER COUNTY.

George Meeder and Barbara Snider, 1856.

Nelson Lockeber and Lucinda Reddington, S. H. Curtis and Sarah Couse, June 30, 1856. Married on the same day by Rev. E. D. Lamb.

G. R. Baskins and Harriett Page, June 30, 1856.

H. F. Kline and Hannah Wright, June, 1856.

Lavinus Phelps, and Mary E. Eldridge, July, 1856.

But this is sufficient. Many of the names will be recognized by the settlers of later years.

The following table will show how the number of marriages, per year, has varied, and how the matrimonial market is affected by the state of the times.

Year	Marriages	Year	Marriages
1853	5	1868	130
1854	15	1869	123
1855	26	1870	111
1856	30	1871	118
1857	43	1872	100
1858	33	1873	136
1859	28	1874	108
1860	32	1875	134
1861	33	1876	144
1862	49	1877	118
1863	43	1878	112
1864	49	1879	108
1865	62	1880	120
1866	97	1881	128
1867	103	1882	130

MARRIAGE UNDER DIFFICULTIES.

A local paper in Waverly is responsible for the following:

"A couple of children, aged fourteen and eighteen years, came over from Butler county Tuesday, with matrimonial intentions. The would be head of the family walked up to the clerk's office with all the gravity of an old man, and called for a 'pair of license.' Charley Cooper asked him who wanted them. The young man from Butler answered, 'Me and Sary Ann wants them.'

"Charley looked at him with the steady gaze of a granger, and at the same time gave him the sign of 'distress.' But the work was lost, for the young man had never crossed the 'rubicon.' Says Charles, 'young man, you are not old enough to marry. Go back to Butler county and tarry there until your mustache has grown out, then come and I will see what I can do for you.' The young chap said: 'Look here, mister, I am a man. I have chawed tobacker and swore for more than two years. Now none of your fooling; give 'em to me.' But it would not answer, and Charley told them they must have a guardian appointed before they could slip under the same blanket. They marched down town and Hi Brown made out the necessary papers and they went back to Butler County to get a stick for guardian timber. They came back and Charley issued the papers and they were joined in wedlock, and such Poetry has no echo more sonorious and prolonged than the heart of youth in which it is fresh born(?)."

ABSTRACT OF ASSESSMENTS
FOR THE YEAR 1882.

TOWNSHIPS.	CATTLE.			HORSES.			MULES AND ASSES.			SHEEP.		
	Number.	Total assessed value.	Per head.	Number.	Average value.	Assessed value.	Number.	Value.	Per head.	Number.	Value.	Per head.
Dayton	1,935	$17,500	$9 04	522	$28 68	$14,970	2	$80	$40 00	48	$48	$1 00
Douglas	1,910	17,576	9 20	638	30 50	19,450	18	625	34 72	86	86	1 00
Franklin	1,739	14,590	8 45	509	31 70	16,133	9	322	37 33	73	73	.....
Frederika	789	7,881	10 00	232	28 30	6,561	14	420	30 00	7	7	.....
Fremont	2,322	19,542	8 41	617	21 60	13,325	2	50	25 00	99	102	.....
Jackson	959	9,424	10 14	414	19 80	8,178	8	142	17 75	100	100	.....
Jefferson	1,466	13,887	9 47	450	21 30	9,767	....	....	....	108	125	.....
Lafayette	1,805	13,078	7 25	492	17 60	8,612	10	160	16 00	5	5	.....
LeRoy	1,234	10,792	8 75	269	18 30	4,916	....	....	....	88	88	.....
Maxfield	2,609	22,317	8 55	637	19 60	12,510	....	....	....	92	92	.....
Polk	1,999	19,399	9 70	734	27 15	19,932	22	780	35 50	108	108	.....
Sumner	1,609	15,376	9 56	548	25 75	14,113	4	95	23 75	29	29	.....
Warren	2,258	18,652	8 26	629	21 23	13,352	3	85	28 33	120	120	.....
Washington	1,211	12,812	10 58	409	26 00	10,582	6	110	18 33	12	12	.....
Waverly	333	2,572	7 72	423	23 50	9,910	8	155	19 37	17	17	.....
Average	....	....	$8 92	....	$24 20	....	....	....	$28 53	....	....	$1,02
Totals	24,176	$215,698	....	7,582	....	$182,311	106	$3,024	....	992	$1,012	.....

Abstract of Assessments—Continued.

TOWNSHIPS.	SWINE.			VEHICLES.			MERCHANDISE—Value of.	MANUFACTURING CAPITAL.	MONEYS AND CREDITS.	TAXABLE HOUSEHOLD PROP'TY
	Number.	Average value.	Assessed value.	Number.	Average value.	Assessed value.				
Dayton	2,146	$2 00	$4,450	35		$1 50	$2 25	$10	$700	
Douglas	1,805	1 42	2,561	9		2 20	2 00		3,700	
Franklin	1,783	1 45	2,580	44		6 51			5,199	$1 92
Frederika	670	1 67	1,120	17		3 20	1,000		800	
Fremont	2,299	99	2,281	30		4 65	8,900		2,760	
Jackson	11,10	1 72	1,911	51		8 38	5,270		4,112	4 65
Jefferson	1,728	1 83	3,149	62		1,146	2 05	1 30	35,949	5 13
Lafayette	1,472	1 80	2,658	8		202			4,525	
LeRoy	501	1,88	9 42	5		1 05			2,300	
Maxfield	2,739	1 96	5,371	43		6 15		6 45	23,472	1 70
Polk	2,169	1 74	3,772	69		1,226	2,055	1 25	15,421	367
Sumner	1,281	1 41	1,806	90		1,386	10,675	50	3,500	
Warren	3,533	1 73	6,270	42		840			11,272	135
Washington	873	1 77	1,546	21		270			5,650	65
Waverly	138	1 50	2 01	2 28		4,735	36,090	2,670	67,381	3,285
Average		1 68			$10 82					
Totals	24,247		$40,618	7 54		$13,769	64,620	3,630	$186,741	$5,192

Abstract of Assessments—Continued.

Townships.	Corporations Stocks.	Taxable Farm Utensils.	Other Taxable Property.	Total Value Assessed.	Lands [Assessment of 1881].			Value of Town Property 1881.
					No. of acres.	Average value.	Value.	
Dayton			$637	$39,370	22,821	$6 37	$164,943	
Douglas		$50	50	44,518	23,309	5 98	139,300	
Franklin			543	40,283	22,856	6 31	163,784	
Frederika		50	390	18,549	11,703	4 98	58,226	$3,556
Fremont			2,555	49,980	23,130	7 22	185,414	8,491
Jackson	$150		315	31,205	14,997	8 51	141,692	13,501
Jefferson		155	131	65,157	15,124	9 67	146,248	1,670
Lafayette		225	88	29,553	19,457	9 15	178,659	
LeRoy				19,143	13,713	4 58	57,206	
Maxfield		210		65,402	22,514	8 73	144,223	
Polk			1,354	64,530	23,019	8 63	197,694	15,799
Sumner			320	47,350	20,192	7 41	118,152	15,200
Warren			160	50,886	23,121	8 17	188,918	
Washington			60	31,107	16,711	9 19	153,584	
Waverly	1,300		2,800	131,116	1,959	19 94	33,966	129,780
Average						$7 56		
Total	$1,450	$690	$9,403	$728,158	276,726	$7 56	$2,077,059	$187,997

HISTORY OF BREMER COUNTY.

OTHER ITEMS OF INTEREST.

In addition to the abstract, a number of other items taken from the auditor's reports, are here given:

Lands, exclusive of town property, in acres	272,385
Total exemptions for trees planted	17,050
Valuation of above, after deducting exemptions	$2,098,474

The value of realty in the towns of the county, as per assessment of 1882, is as follows:

Frederika and Tripoli	$3,416
Tripoli	7,647
Janesville	12,162
Jefferson	1,670
Bremer	77
Plainfield and Horton	15,499
Sumner	18,489
Waverly	150,706
Aggregate	$210,666
Total value of railroad property	134,689
Total value of personal property, including horses, cattle, etc.	728,158
Total valuation of the county	$3,166,987

LIVE STOCK.

	Number.	Valuation
Cattle assessed in the county	24,176	$215,698
Horses " " "	7,532	182,311
Mules " " "	106	3,024
Sheep " " "	902	1,012
Swine " " "	24,247	40,618
Valuation of live stock		$442,663

TAX LEVIED.

The total tax levied in the county, in 1882, was $75,453.73.

FINANCIAL.

The following items shows the value of taxable property, and tax levied each year, from 1863 to 1882:

1863.

Value of lands in the county	$927,987
Value of town lots	78,234
Value of personal property	182,469
Total as'es'd value of all property	$1,188,690
Total tax levied	$22,874

1864.

Total value of lands	$933,573
Total value of town lots	78,881
Total value of personal property	254,683
Total assessed value of county	$1,267,187
Total tax levied	$30,408

1865.

Value of lands	$973,939
Value of lots	88,034
Value of personal property	340,834
Total valuation	$1,402,807
Total tax levied	$47,019

1866.

Value of lands	$976,954
Value of lots	87,779
Value of personal property	380,037
Total assessed value	$1,444,770
Total tax levied	$51,179

1867

Number of acres	$269,658
Value of lands	$1,398,909
Value of lots	210,511
Value of personal property	374,718
Total assessed value	$1,984,188
Tax levied	$76,797

1868

Number of acres assessed in the county	271,012
Assessed value of land	$1,399,031
Assessed value town lots	211,761
Assessed value personal property	411,663
Total valuation	$2,022,455
Total tax levied	$60,990

HISTORY OF BREMER COUNTY.

1869.
Value of land	$1,446,933
Value of town lots	221,913
Value of personal property	427,146
Total value all property	$2,125,992
Total tax levied	71,923

1870.
Value of land	$1,452,996
Value of town lots	221,873
Value of personal property	479,996
Total value of all property	$2,154,865
Total tax levied	61,197 25

1871.
Value of lands	$1,736,119
Value of town lots	246,282
Value of personal property	395,471
Total value of all property	$2,377,872
Total tax levied	$139,356

(This includes the railroad tax which was collected in 1872, of $50,000.)

1872.
Total value of lands	$1,735,211
Total value of town lots	246,526
Value of personal property	476,585
Total value of all property	$2,458,322
Total tax levied	$92,956

The following was the way in which the total value was divided among the various townships:

	Total value.
Dayton township	$ 95,092
Douglas	113,387
Franklin	114,902
Frederika	59,352
Fremont	124,718
Jackson	243,711
Jefferson	160,638
Lafayette	209,956
Le Roy	67,413
Maxfield	154,018
Polk	260,084

Sumner	$102,369
Warren	180,547
Washington	218,676
Waverly City	353,509

1873.
Value of land	$1,846,781
Value of lots	188,143
Value of personal property	516,013
Total value of all property	$2,550,937
Total tax levied	$77,015

1874.
Value of land	$1,843,238
Value of lots	188,254
Value of personal property	504,909
Total value of all property	$2,536,401
Total tax levied in 1874	$84,546

1875.
Value of land	$1,974,795
Value of lots	214,612
Value of personal property	564,218
Total value	$2,753,625
Total tax levied	$74,714

1876.
Value of land	$1,969,722
Value of lots	214,704
Value of personal property	588,146
Total value of all property	$2,772,572
Total tax levied	$82,957

1877.
Value of lands	$2,093,042
Value of lots	209,514
Value of personal property	587,689
Total value of property	$2,890,245
Total tax levied	$81,558

1878.
Value of land	$2,090,429
Value of lots	210,764
Value of personal property	608,437
Total value	$2,909,630
Total tax levied	$85,202

HISTORY OF BREMER COUNTY.

1879.

Value of lands	$2,007,739
Value of lots	210,997
Value of personal property	645,369
Total value	$2,864,105
Total tax levied	$67,665

1880.

Value of lands	$2,005,700
Total value of lots	210,702
Value of personal property	688,804
Total value of property	$2,905,206
Total tax levied	$78,982

1881.

Value of lands	$2,092,999
Value of lots	208,916
Value of personal property	815,183
Total value of property	$3,117,098
Total tax levied	70,050

1882.

Value of lands	$2,089,747
Value of lots	208,826
Value of personal property	869,656
Total valuation	$3,168,229
Total tax levied	$75,453 73

The different townships show total value of all property as follows:

Dayton	$ 186,510
Douglas	182,817
Franklin	186,764
Frederika	80,201
Fremont	236,501
Jackson	209,525
Jefferson	212,929
Lafayette	222,895
LeRoy	84,385
Maxfield	267,467
Polk	296,790
Sumner	221,444
Warren	252,202
Washington	198,904
Waverly	328,895
Total	$3,168,229

TREASURER'S REPORT.

By the last report of the county treasurer, S. F. Baker, the following is a summary of cash on hand for the county, and credited to the various funds, as follows:

SUMMARY OF CASH ON HAND.

State revenue	$ 581 20
County	850 87
County school	188 72
Bridge	2,724 20
Insane	373 09
Incorporation	384 81
Dubuque & Dakota Railroad	439 47
Penal Fines	32 51
Institute	133 50
Sanitary	5 41
Road	326 87
Teachers	2,116 99
Contingent	798 86
School house	206 19
Permanent school fund	4,068 62
School fund interest	1,435 37
School fund apportionment	720 76
Total cash on hand	$15,387 44

REGISTRY OF DEEDS.

As has already been stated, before its organization, Bremer county was attached to Buchanan county. The first transfers of land therefore were recorded in the books of Buchanan county, and were afterward transcribed into Bremer county books.

The first entry affecting land in Bremer county was recorded as being filed March 13, 1852, and conveyed from Samuel and Tabitha Armstrong to William Thorp, the east half of the northwest quarter of section 34, in township 90, north of range 13 west, for the consideration of $100. This was witnessed by Israel Trumbo, justice of the peace for Bremer township, on the 25th of February, 1852.

After Bremer county was organized, books were procured and records kept at Waverly, William Hunter being the first recorder of deeds. These differ very much from those now in use in the county. As a fair sample, the first record is here given as it appears upon the books, the original spelling retained:

"Know All men by these presantz, that i, William Thorp, of the County of Breemer and State of iowa, am held and firmly Bound unto Richard Holtom, Henry Stears and John Stears, of the County of S. T. Irsep, State of Mishigan, in the Sum of five hundred Dollarz, lawful money of the United states, to Bee paid to the Said Richard Holtom, Henry Stears and John Stears, their Executors, Administrators or assigns, for which payment well and truly to Bee made, i Bind My Self, my heirs, Executors, Administrators and Each of them, firmly by these Presants. sealed with my Seal, this 20 day August, A. D., 1853."

The document then goes on to state the conditions, which, as the record says are "as fowloing."

There are now thirty-five books of deed records, the recorder now using No. 35, having run through the alphabet and then taken numbers.

The first mortgage recorded bears the date of March 20, 1856, in Book A, of Mortgages. In the sum of $400, Philander and Cornelia Olmstead mortgaged certain lots in the city of Janesville, to William McHenry. This was recorded March 27, 1856, by W. B. Hamilton, and was satisfied in October of the same year.

There are now twenty-four books of mortgages, being nineteen of real estate and five of town lots.

The following is a list of the various plats that have been recorded in the plat books of the office:

Waverly proper, Cretzmeyer's addition, Gothard's addition, Hess' addition, incorporation of Harmon and LeValleys, Wm. Sturdevant's addition, Bremer, Horton, Janesville, Jefferson City, Monroe, Syracuse, Tripoli, Deanville, Plainfield, Sumner and Frederika.

Particulars of each appear in their proper places,

The whole number of record books in the office at present is 122.

CHAPTER VI.

REMINISCENCES OF PIONEERS.

In this chapter are given the personal experiences of the pioneers of Bremer County. These articles are written or related by the pioneers, and when written, the compiler has in no case attempted to change the style of the writer, it being

HISTORY OF BREMER COUNTY.

the design to show the peculiarity of the writer as well as to record the facts narrated. The expressions of an individual in writing show his character and peculiarities, as much as his features painted upon canvass, or printed from steel or stone. These reminiscences are interesting and well worthy of perusal.

By Charles McCaffre.

The following from the first settler of Bremer county—Charles McCaffre— to a Waverly paper, explains itself:

MR. EDITOR.—Seeing a Historical Sketch of the early settlements of Bremer county in the *Bremer County Independent* of January 5th, 1871, and, as it was incorrect in many particulars I, the undersigned, thought I would endeavor to make a few corrections through the columns of your paper for the information of the present inhabitants of Bremer county. I commenced work in Bremer county about the 5th day of May, 1845, followed shortly after by brother Isaac September following, Jacob Beelah moved to the county. Early spring of 1846, Calvin Frady, Goliver Fisher, John H. Messinger, accompanied by his son, E. J. Messinger, George Tibbits, accompanied by his sons Wesley and Henry, settled in this county, and between then and the time that John T. Barrick and A. H. Miles settled in the county, the following named persons came in: Joseph and James Fee, Aaron Dow, Ezra Allen, Philip Miller, Andrew Samples, Harry McRoberts, John James, Collier and Israel Trimbo. Although it is an acknowledged fact that some of these named above did not remain in the county very long, but they made claims, erected cabins, consequently were actual settlers. And it was also asserted in the *Independent* that John T. Barrick and H. A. Miles are the only one of the settlers that are present residents of the county which is incorrect, for the widow of said John H. Messinger, although quite young when they came here, is still a resident of the county.

Also John Clark's widow is a present resident of the County, and also David Clark's son is a citizen of Waverly. Besides there are several others I could mention.

The first birth and death in the county occured in the Fee family. The first marriage was Isaac McCaffre and Rebeca Buler.

CHARLES McCAFFRE.

INDIAN HISTORY.
M. Farrington.

There were three tribes of Indians represented in this township at the time the whites began to settle therein—the Winnebagos, the Misquakees and Pottawatomies. The Winnebagoes were about 500 in number, and their town was mostly in sections 22 and 23. The Misquakees were about 100 in number, and about 50 of the Pottawatomies. During the summer season they went north and west for sap-troughs, and leaving nothing here but their log shanties, covered with bark, and their brass sugar kettles, which they buried. There are probably many of their kettles still buried in the timber. They cultivated no corn nor anything else, and their ponies were subject to browsing for their living in winter. The three different tribes were considerable intermixed and lived much together. Womanokaker, Four Eyes, Pukatuk, Hanahetakes, and Big Way were the five chiefs here. Womanokaker lived on the west side of the creek, in section 23, near where H. H. Ketch now lives. He was the great war chief and had the end of his nose shot off by a bullet.

The Indians were quite troublesome to the whites in stealing things which they might want, but never in the night, as they were too great cowards to sally out in the night for any such purpose. They were removed from here by a detachment of U. S. troups from Fort Atkinson, in the fall of 1848. They took the Indians by surprise and disarmed and drove them off like so many cattle. The white settlers had secretly informed the government authorities that they wished the Indians removed, and the soldiers came without the knowledge of the unsuspecting Indians. Had they known whom of the whites had carried the information against them, their blood would doubtless have atoned for the act. Two of the settlers went one night and returned the next, and the Indians were entirely ignorant of the matter.

By Heman A. Miles.
LERADO, TEXAS, Dec. 15, 1882.
Sister Elector:

For the past three weeks I have not been able to use my right arm at all, and can just barely write now by resting on the table and moving the paper to and fro to suit my hand, and dipping the pen in the ink with my left hand. I should be pleased to answer all your questions in detail, and give in full the incidents of my civil and military life, which as Mr. N. C. Deering once remarked to me, as I gave him a brief sketch of my life, that it would make a history of itself that would interest any one and surprise my acquaintances, and if I could see the man who is getting up the history of Bremer and Butler counties, with its early pioneers, I could give him many important and interesting points, but as it is I shall have to be very brief, as I can only write a few moments at a time, having to stop and rest my arm. In many instances I shall have to leave dates blank as I cannot remember them.

My mothers maiden name was Mary Jennings. She died in Sheffield, Vermont, in 1831, aged 37 years and 6 months. My father's name was Mastain Miles. He died October 12, 1863, in Owatonin, Minnesota, aged 66 years, 1 month

I was born in Sheffield, Vermont, on the 6th of September, 1825, and was married on the 29th of December, 1844, to Jane Hall. My wife's father's name was William Hall. His mother's maiden name was Jane Crocker, both were born in England. He died at Pike's Peak in 1859, aged 55 years. Her mother died in Milville, Massachusetts, Nov. 1872, aged 67 years. I emigrated to Iowa in 1847. I resided in Linn county for upwards of two years, and then went to Bremer county in March, 1850. I moved my family there in September, 1850, at which time there were only fifteen families in the county, consisting of the Messingers, Tibbetts, Fees, Samples, Colliers, Beelers, Dows, Trumbos and J. Clark, all of whom are now dead, if I am correctly informed, except Henry Tibbets, Wesley Tibbets and Elias Messinger, and I am informed that they have all left and sought homes in other parts like myself. Many of the children of these early pioneers are now living in Bremer county, married there and have raised families. Our nearest post office was Cedar Falls, sixteen or seventeen miles distance away. Our nearest flouring mill was at Quasqueton, a distance of forty miles. Quite a number of Indians infested what was known as the Big Woods, for a time, but were not in any way hostile. They only stole a few chickens and pigs occasionally, from the settlers. In the spring of 1851, it rained, more or less, for thirty-nine days in succession. The whole county was flooded and it was almost impossible to get to a neighbor's, much less to mill, and the result was that many of us got almost entirely out of provisions. I remember very distinctly that myself and family lived on hulled corn alone, for nearly three weeks The first two years of my stay in Bremer county, I run a breaking team. I have broken prairie from the fork of the Shell Rock and Cedar River, on nearly every farm along and adjoining the Big Woods on the south and east sides to nearly the north line of the county.

I was appointed assessor, and made the first assessment of property that was ever made in Butler and Bremer counties. I taught the first school that was taught in Bremer county. I built the first house that was built from sawed lumber in the county. I was elected the first constable and first clerk of the district and county court, one of the first school directors, one of the first law graduates, started and published the first newspaper, called together the citizens and organized the republican party, and have had the honor of filling the only county office in the county that has never been filled by a democrat. I have acted as justice of the peace, mayor, constable, road supervisor, town trustee, school director, secretary of the school board, postmaster, schoolmaster, sheriff, auctioneer, farmer and lawyer. I had charge of building the first school-house in the town of Waverly, which was built of stone. I built the piers and abutments for the second bridge across the Cedar River at Waverly. I done more to break up and close the whisky shops and gambling dens in Waverly, than any other man, for which my life was sought and threatened, my office gutted, books, records, and everything burnt up and thrown into the river.

I have two children, both young men, of whom I feel proud. The oldest one's name is Mostoin William—named after his two grandfathers. He was born in Linn county, Iowa, on the 14th day of June, 1859. The youngest one's name is Charles Sheridan—named after my oldest brother and General Sheridan. He was born in Waverly, Bremer county, Iowa, on the 20th day of July, 1860.

For two years I was law partner of the Hon. G. W. Ruddick, who came to Waverly a young man, seeking out a place to establish himself in his profession. When he arrived in Waverly, and made known his purpose, he was referred to me. I at once formed a very favorable opinion of him, and took him into my family, and furnished an office for him. He remained in my family until he married. The longer I knew him the more I loved and esteemed him. To-day he is one of Bremer's most noble men. In the fall of 1861 I sold out to him, and enlisted in the Union army, to sustain the flag of my country. I enlisted first on the 1st of October, 1861, and by false representations and fraud, the Governor of Iowa consented and permitted the company I enlisted in to be taken to St. Louis, Missouri, to make up a regiment, to be called the Lyon Regiment, said to have been organized by permission of the War Department, at the request of General Fremont, in memory of General Lyon. It was represented that General Fremont had secured the organization of this regiment, to be composed of one company from each of the western States in his department, and one company from Connecticut, General Lyon's native State, to be armed and equipped with extra arms, and each company to be credited to the State from which they enlisted. After reaching St. Louis, the place designated as the headquarters for organizing said regiment, we were held in quarters for a time, and then mustered into the Third Missouri, at which we all demurred, but in vain. Governor Kirkwood, Governor Gamble and the Secretary of War were appealed to by a resolution passed by the Legislature of the State of Iowa, to have us transferred to an Iowa regiment, but it was all to no purpose.

We left St. Louis, I think, in March, 1862, and under Gen. Curtiss took up our march down through Arkansas. Landing at Helena, we were not provided with any tents, and the weather for some time was quite cold, rainy with slight snow. This was quite severe on the soldiers. Before we reached Helena our supplies were cut off and we suffered much for want of proper rations. On this march, near Red River, Arkansas, in crossing a small stream of water on a log, while the Company was on a forced march to relieve a party that had been attacked by the enemy; the log broke and I fell on the rocks at the water's edge, dislocating my shoulder, elbow and fracturing my collar-bone. From here I was taken to Helena in an ambulance and after a short time discharged on account of my injuries. I returned home to Waverly and, as soon as I sufficiently recovered I recruited another Company and went into the Fourteenth Iowa Infantry. When we were taken out on the Meridian raid, under Gen. Sherman, from there back to Memphis, then up the Red River to join Gen. Banks. On the march up Red River I was not able to go with my Company, but remained in the hospital at Memphis, with chronic diarrhœa contracted on the Meridian raid. On the return of the Regiment to Memphis I joined them when we were taken to Jefferson Barracks, Mo., from there my Company, Capt. Lucas, and Company H., accompanied Gen. Ewing, as an escort, to Pilot Knob. Soon after our arrival we were notified of a raid made by the enemy into Ironton, about two miles distant from the Fort. We pursued the enemy with our little force consisting of about 400, with 60 mounted men and two pieces of artillery. Just about dark our mounted men run into Price's army, estimated at from 15,000 to 20,000 men, which caused us to fall back to Ironton, where we remained during the night. At daybreak the next morning the enemy moved forward and caused our hasty retreat. We held the enemy for some time in the pass between the Sheperd and Knob mountains, distributing our forces along the sides of the mountains on each side of the pass, as the enemy advanced along the pass we fired into them from the sides of the mountains, when they became panic-stricken and confused. Soon, however the enemy sent forces along two sides of the mountains and forced us to retreat to the Fort. Major Williams and some of his men were captured from the Sheperd Mountain in their attempt to retreat and were delivered over by Gen. Price to one Jeffreys, who took them out and in cold blood shot them down. They made several assaults upon the Fort, meeting with continuous repulses and severe losses. Their attacks upon the fort continued until dusk, when they fell back and went into camp, being surrounded by a force of fifteen or twenty thousand men, with our communications and supplies cut off, having only six or seven hundred men, we determined to make good our retreat and took up march about 1 o'clock at night, when we quietly left the Fort and made our way through the enemy's lines undiscovered. Next day we were pursued by about 5,000 of the enemy's cavalry and when overtaken were in heavy timber, where, for one whole day we fought the enemy on a retreat. Reaching Leesburgh, a point on the Railroad, about dusk, fortifying ourselves the best we could and dispatching a messenger to Rolla for reinforcements. The last charge made upon us by the enemy before reaching Leesburgh was a very determined one and we lost several men in wounded and killed. My First Lieutenant, John Broclan, was mortally wounded in this charge. I was slightly wounded at the Knob in retreating to the Fort so that I was compelled to ride most of the way on our retreat from the Knob to Leesburgh.

Just after our arrival at Leesburgh there was a heavy train of cars come in from St. Louis loaded with quartermasters and company stores for the post at Rolla, which were soon unloaded and put in a position to burn, except the liquors, which were emptied out on the railroad track; it was thought that the small force we had there could be put aboard the cars and escape to St. Louis, but before everything was aboard, a fire was discovered down the track. The engine run down and found the enemy had sent a force around and fired the railroad bridge. Not having sufficient headway to prevent the engine from crossing, it run across and went on to St. Louis; so we returned to our post determined to do the best we could to defend our lives, expecting every moment the enemy would take us in. It being very dark, and in order to prevent the enemy from marching upon us in the darkness of the night, one of the boys from Captain Lucas's Company, Jerome Sampson, volunteered to go out near the enemy's lines and fire a hay stack and a log building, which lit up the whole line of the enemy, and burned nearly all night. This gave us an opportunity to see if the enemy attempted to advance upon us during the night. The next morning, about 9 or 10 o'clock, we received reinforcements from Rolla, of about 600 cavalry, who soon after their arrival charged on the enemy's lines, and to our surprise, found that the enemy had retreated early that evening, in double quick haste, the cause of which was soon learned that a good Union man residing at Leesburgh, had gone over into the enemy's lines early in the evening, and represented himself to be a full fledged rebel, whereupon some of the rebel officers inquired of him what the train of cars that just arrived brought in, when he replied, that it brought in seven or eight thousand more of them Lincoln hirelings and damned Yankies; this saved us from being captured, also all the stores that were intended to be burned we moved from there to Rolla, thence to St. Louis. While at St. Louis I was detailed as officer of the guard to take out a certain number of rebel prisoners a short distance from the city, to be shot in retaliation of the men that were shot by Jeffries, who were captured at Pilot Knob.

My company was mustered out in 1864, at Davenport, Iowa. When I returned home to Waverly, I then served one term as mayor of the city of Waverly, after which I received the appointment as postmaster at Waverly, and on account of poor health resigned the place and came to Texas, in September, 1873, during which time I have enjoyed the best of health. I should be pleased to give in detail the incidents of my pioneer life, also of my military life, together with a complete detailed account of the incidents connected with the early settlement of Bremer county, but I am hardly able to write at all, and doubt very much whether you can read half I have written. Remember us to our friends; we are as well as usual. Love to all.

Yours truly,
H. A. MILES.

P. S. If any further questions you wish answered, let me know.

INCIDENTS OF EARLY DAYS IN BREMER COUNTY.

By S. F Shepard.

On the 20th of March, 1851, William Hale, Orrin O. Pitcher, John H. Shepard and myself left DuPage county, Illinois, for Iowa, to look for homes for our families. We arrived at Janesville, as it is now called, the last of March, and stopped with John T. Barrick some two or three weeks, while looking the country over. We found Mr. and Mrs. Barrick very agreeable folks to stop with. Mr. Barrick offered to give Mr. Hale the water power in Janesville, if he would come there and improve it. Mr. Hale said it was too far from land, and the country would never be settled to any great extent. My brother and I bought a claim—one half section—of Ezra G. Allen, on which I now reside. Forty acres of it were broke and fenced, on which was a log cabin 18x20 feet. We paid for the whole $250. In October, 1851, I moved to the claim with my family, and went into the house with Mr. Allen's family of seven, which, with my family of four, made a house full. Only one room, and a very low chamber, and not one light of glass in two sash, six lights, each filled with greased paper. Some time in January, 1852, Mr. Allen moved up to Horton, six miles above Waverly, on the east side of the Cedar river, and was the first settler in Horton. Mrs. Allen said in the winter of 1849-50, they ground three bushels of corn and fourteen bushels of buckwheat in their coffee mill, there being no grist mill nearer than Quasqueton, ten miles below Independence, in Buchanan county, and forty-five miles distant from Janesville. In 1852 the snow commenced falling on the 9th of November, snowing for three days, in succession, the snow being about twelve inches deep. On the 13th, two of my neighbors, Mason Eveland and James McRoberts, went out hunting deer. They soon came upon a fresh track, and followed it nearly all day before they killed the deer, fording or wading through the Cedar river twice during the day, and after dressing the deer and hanging it up they started for home, but McRoberts complained of being faint and hungry, and after traveling something like a mile, he became so much exhausted that he fell behind, unable to keep up with Mr. Eveland. Mr. Eveland took his gun, and carried it for him, and took him by the arm, and led him, until they came down near the mouth of Spring Branch, where it empties into the Cedar river, when McRoberts said he could walk no farther, and sat down on a log. Eveland said, "Now, stay right here until I send some one for you." Eveland got down to my house about dark, and said he wanted me to go after McRoberts. I said that I never had been up the river to that point yet, and did not know the way, "but," I said to Eveland, "you go over to McRoberts' house, and have one of his boys go with me." I harnessed my team, and in the course of a half an hour his oldest son, Thomas McRoberts, was at my house, and we started with the team around the road, a distance of five or six miles to the creek. We hitched the team and started with a lantern and finally came to the track where they crossed the creek. We followed their tracks until we came to the log where Mr. McRoberts had been left. He was not there, he had tried to follow Mr. Eveland's trail, but was unable to walk only a few steps without falling down and wallowing around in the snow; he got along in this way some twenty or thirty rods, and, as the ground was descending toward the creek, he naturally took that direction until he reached the water. He left his rifle on the bank of the creek and made his way to about the middle and lying, or falling, on his back was drowned. This was at the mouth of the creek, where it empties into the Cedar River. I said to Thomas McRoberts, "there is your father out there in the creek and drowned." I waded out to him, took him up and brought him to the shore. I found him lifeless and cold. I cut a pole and we thought we could carry him to where we left the team. We laid him across the pole and his rifle to carry him, but we could not carry him and the light, and I carried him back again to where I found him, so that the wolves could not find him, and we started for home again, getting home about 1 a. m., the next morning. I went with my team and three of the neighbors and brought him home to his children, five in all (no wife living). November, 1852, a gentleman farmer, living near Anamosa, Jones county, by the name of Berry, followed the Waubesipenican river up, doing the threshing for the farmers as he came to them along the river, until he came into Bremer county, and then came down through the Big Woods to S. F. Shepard's farm to do his threshing and other jobs. While he was threshing for S. F. Shepard it commenced snowing and in the course of two or three days the snow fell to the depth of about thirty inches. Mr. Berry and his hands shoveled away the snow, finished S. F. Shepard's threshing and then moved the threshing machine to Mr. John T. Barrick's. While there he sold the threshing machine to John H. Martin and S. F. Shepard, and they finished the threshing for that winter.

The next season Martin and Shepard done all the threshing in the west half of Bremer county, and all the threshing that was done in Black Hawk and Butler counties, when Shepard bought out Martin's interest and done the threshing in the west half of Bremer, and all in Black Hawk and Butler county, until the fall of 1856. The price for threshing was four cents for oats and six cents for wheat. I have had a threshing machine, or an interest in one ever since, and threshing, more or less, every year since, until 1876. From 1852 to 1855, we had to go to Dubuque for repairs and heavy blacksmith work. In the fall of 1853, the Overman Brothers, at Cedar Falls, got a pair of burr mill stones, and put them into a part of their saw mill; then we could get our grinding done there. But there was no gearing to run the bolt and those who brought wheat to grind had to turn the bolt by hand, at least it was so in my case. Andrew Mullarkey had a small stock of dry goods, in a room about twelve feet square, at Cedar Falls, and the only store for three or four years at Cedar Falls. In 1851 there was only six or seven houses in this place, not a house in Waterloo, not one in Waverly, not one at Shell Rock and not one at Clarksville. All of these towns have grown to their present size in the course of thirty-one years.

In the fall of 1853, there was a great scare and fright among the white settlers and Winnebago Indians, near Clear Lake. A man by the name of Hewitt lived there; he harbored some Winnebagoes about him and some of the Sioux Indians came to his (Hewitt's) house one morning and wanted a Winnebago Indian boy to go out with them to hunt the Sioux Indians' ponies. The boy started out with one of the Sioux Indians, and when they had got out a short distance from the house the report of a gun was heard. The Sioux Indian had shot down the Winnebago boy. This was the first of the fright. Several of the Sioux Indians went to Mr. Hewitt's house looking for the rest of the Winnebago Indians. They searched Hewitt's house all over, up-stairs and down, but could not find them, for they had fled. They came down the Shell Rock River and frightened the whites as they came along, saying the Sioux Indians were after them and would kill all the whites. It made a general stampede of what few settlers there were from Cerro Gordo county, until they reached Janesville. They took their household goods, what they could carry, with their families and started, driving what live stock they had with them; stopping with friends and neighbors. The excitement by this time was at its highest pitch, and about ten o'clock in the evening, after most of the families had come to Janesville, I heard some one galop up near the house. My dog began to bark; I got up and went out to see what was up. Squire Rowen had sent his hired man, Mr. Rumsey, to my house to warn me of my danger. He said the Indians were coming down the river, that they had divided their band some ten or twelve miles northwest of Janesville, and some were coming down the Cedar River and some down the Shell Rock, and would be upon us before morning. He wanted me to go out east to William McHenry's and to Samuel Jennings and let them know, and after he had given his orders like a major-general, he galloped off to headquarters at Janesville, and I went back into the house and went to bed. My wife asked me what was the matter. I said to her that Mr. Rowen had sent his hired man here on an errand; she soon dropped to sleep again.

The next morning found all in my family alive and well, no depredations or massacres committed. The next day my brother, then living in a small cabin on McHenry's place, came to my house to see whether we were all alive, and in the afternoon we went down to Janesville to see what the conclusion was. We found them building trenches, hauling slabs from the saw mill, setting them up endways and filling in the dirt again to hold them there. We went to work with them, until nearly sundown, and then went home; and Henry Moore and wife came home with us, to stay until the scare was over. Three families of us, nine in number, in one cabin, 18x20 feet square, and only one room below and a very low chamber above.

When the Winnebago Indians came down to Janesville, they wanted to stop and have the whites protect them, but the whites said, no, you must go on to Cedar Rapids. Mr. James Moss and family, with an infant child, only two days old, left Janesville with his team to go to Cedar Rapids, his wife caught cold and only lived a short time. Some families below Janesville, and some at Waterloo went down to Cedar Rapids, and some on the road moving into the country, turned around and went back to Independence, and stopped there until the scare was over. While the excitement was up to fever heat, John F. Barrick started out with his team and a load of men, guns and amunition to meet the foe. Captain Eads started out with a squad of men from Cedar Rapids to the seat of war. They went up to Clear Lake, or near there, and finding no enemy to fight, turned the opportunity into a jolification and a social dance at Mr. Hewitt's.

CHAPTER VII.

THE COURTS OF BREMER COUNTY.

Man is an imperfect being, and as such, requires that laws shall be enacted for his government. When the Almighty placed Adam and Eve in the garden of Eden, he gave laws for their observance, with penalties attached for their violation. The children of Israel, after leaving the Egyptian land, were given the "ten commandments," the principles underlying which have probably been the basis of all laws from that time to the present. The existence of laws necessarily implies the existence of courts wherein all questions of law shall be determined. This fact being determined, the framers of the State constitution instituted certain courts of justice with well defined powers. Changes have been made in the jurisdiction of these courts from time to time, but the rights of every citizen of high or low degree have ever been maintained.

DISTRICT COURT.

When Bremer county was organized it became a part of the Second Judicial District, composed then of the counties of Buchanan, Cedar, Clayton, Clinton, Delaware, Dubuque, Fayette, Jackson, Jones, Muscatine, Scott, Allamakee, Winneshiek, Black Hawk, Butler, Grundy and Bremer. Chickasaw and Howard were subsequently added, and various counties were taken from it, so that in 1858, when the district was abolished under the new constitution, it consisted of the counties of Black Hawk, Bremer, Buchanan, Delaware and Dubuque.

The first term of the district court held in Bremer county was in June, 1854, and presided over by Thomas S. Wilson, Judge of the Second Judicial District. There were present besides the judge, Austin Farris, sheriff, and H. A. Miles, clerk of the court. Among the attorneys present, were P. U. Sevan, I. M. Preston, B. W. Poor and Older Lee.

The sheriff returned the following named who composed the first grand jury in the county: T. J. Sewell, J. Queen, James Michael, Jacob Benard, Lafayette Sturdevant, Ira Earl, John S. Jenkins, George K. Baskins, Culver Tuttle, Chandler Eveland, William Powell, Claudius Albee, Alexis Jackson, James Null and William Baskins.

The first petit jury was composed of the following named: J. D. Jackson, William Edgington, Enos Lewis, George Kerr, William Westerveldt, Samuel Jennings, Washington Thorp, W. P. Harmon, George Cagley, Nathan Payton, G. W. Baskins, Westley Tibbetts, John Pattee, Elijah Kendall and Loren Rima.

The first case upon the docket was a petition for divorce filed by William Baskins against his wife, Mary Baskins. It is presumed that William repented of his rash act in asking the court to sever the marriage tie, and therefore by his attorneys, asked leave to withdraw his petition. The request was granted, and the costs of the suit were entered against him, which it is presumed he willingly paid

There were eight civil cases on the docket at this term of court.

The grand jury found one bill of indictment against Calvin Tuttle, for selling intoxicating liquors, whereupon the accused was brought before his honor, Judge Wilson, who required him to give bond in the sum of $200 for his appearance at the next term of the court. Tuttle was a member of the grand jury which indicted him.

Tuttle's case being continued, and there being no further business requiring the aid of a petit jury, it was discharged. Before time for trial the defendant escaped, so the matter was dropped.

On motion of I. M. Preston, Esq., Phineas N. Swan, Esq., an attorney from Vermont, was admitted as an attorney, and Mr. Swan appeared and took the necessary oath. This was the first admission to the bar.

Nothing further appearing court adjourned.

On May 1, 1854, William Gough, an Englishman, was granted naturalization papers by Heman A. Miles, clerk of court.

The second term was held in September, 1855, and was presided over by the same officials. One of the first acts was the admission of John B. Wyle to the bar, on motion of B. W. Poor.

James Shaultz was indicted at this term for murder. The case was never tried, the prisoner escaping. An account of this murder is found in connection with the history of the city of Waverly.

The third term of the district court was held at Waverly, in June, 1856. A few naturalization papers were issued, and, for some reason, the attorneys aggreed that all legal matters which had come up for this term should be postponed. This agreement was signed by L. L. Ainsworth, I. M. Preston, Smith, McKinly & Poor, J. T. Lovell, Adams & Lovell, D. S. Lee, A. F. Brown, P. V. Swan, and G. C. Wright. Judge Samuel Murdock, of the Tenth District, presided.

At the September term, in 1856, Judge T. S. Wilson was on the bench; J. G. Ellis, sheriff, and Heman A. Miles, clerk. A number of minor suits came up at this term. The record states "as P. V. Swan, the prosecuting attorney, is sick, and unable to attend, B. F. Perkins is appointed in his stead for this term."

The next term was held in March, 1857, and was presided over by Thomas S. Wilson, judge of the Second District; J. G. Ellis, sheriff, and Heman A. Miles, clerk.

In 1858, Bremer county became a part of the Tenth Judicial District, which was composed of Alamakee, Bremer, Butler, Clayton, Chickasaw, Fayette, Floyd, Howard, Mitchell, and Winneshiek counties. At the October election, of 1858, Elias H. Williams was elected judge; was re-elected in 1862, and served until 1865.

On the 4th of July, 1864, the Twelfth Judicial District was created, and comprised the counties of Bremer, Butler, Cerro Gordo, Floyd, Hancock, Mitchell, Winnebago, and Worth. The counties composing the district, however, remained connected with their former districts, the Tenth and Eleventh, for the purpose of holding court, until January, 1865. On the 8th of November, 1864, William B. Fairfield, of Floyd county, was elected district judge, and John E. Burke, of Waverly, district attorney. Judge Fairfield was re-elected in 1868, and I. W. Card was elected district attorney. In 1870 Judge Fairfield resigned, and George W. Ruddick, of Waverly, was elected to fill the vacancy. Since that time he has been elected as his own successor at the end of each term, and is the present judge.

Hon. George W. Ruddick was born in Sullivan county, New York, May 13, 1835. Until fourteen years of age he remained at home upon his father's farm, his time being spent alternately at work and in attendance upon the district school. On leaving home he went to Chester, Ohio, where he attended a seminary for one year. He then went to Kingsville, Ohio, where he remained two years, then removed to Monticello, New York. After remaining in Monticello one year, he entered the law office of A. C. Niven, reading law with him two years and a half. In the fall of 1855 he entered the Albany Law School, graduating therefrom in April, 1856. He was then admitted to the

HISTORY OF BREMER COUNTY.

bar. In July, 1856, he started West. After stopping a few days at Delphi, Iowa, he came to Waverly, arriving here on the 18th day of August, 1856, and at once entering upon the practice of his profession. In 1858 he formed a partnership with Heman A. Miles, which partnership continued about two years, when it was dissolved and Mr. Ruddick continued practice alone until 1865, when the firm of Ruddick & Avery was formed. This partnership continued until Mr. Ruddick was elected Judge of the Circuit Court in November, 1868. Before the expiration of his term, Judge Ruddick was elected Judge of the District Court, a well deserved compliment to his legal ability. He still discharges the duties of the office. Judge Ruddick is a man of fine legal ability, with a thorough understanding of the law, and has made an acceptable Judge. He has frequently been honored by his fellow citizens with offices of honor and trust. He was a member of the Legislature in 1860-1. He has also held the offices of County Judge and County Attorney. In politics he is a Republican. On the 15th day of December, 1859, Judge Ruddick was united in marriage with Mary E. Strickland, of Andover, Ashtabula county, Ohio. Five children have been born unto them, two of whom are now living—Julia, book-keeper in the Bank of Waverly; and Berosus, a student in the Iowa College.

CIRCUIT COURT.

By an act of the General Assembly, passed and approved April 3, 1868, circuit courts were established in this State, and each judicial district was divided into two circuits, in each of which, at the general election, in November, 1868, and every four years thereafter, a circuit judge shall be elected. Four terms of court were provided per year in each county in the circuits. By this act the office of county judge was abolished, and all business pertaining to that office was transferred to the circuit court, which was to have concurrent jurisdiction with the district court in all civil actions at law, and exclusive jurisdiction of all appeals and writs of error from justices' courts, mayors' courts, and all other inferior tribunals, either in civil or criminal cases.

Bremer county, together with other counties, made a circuit of the Twelfth Judicial District.

George W. Ruddick, of Waverly, was the first circuit judge, being elected at the November election, in 1868. He served from January, 1869, until October, 1870, when, having been elected judge of the district court, he assumed his higher duties.

Robert G. Reiniger was appointed to fill the vacancy occasioned by Judge Ruddick's resignation, and has since been elected his own successor, being the present judge of circuit court.

The first term of circuit court for Bremer county was held at Waverly, commencing February 5, 1869. George W. Ruddick presided as judge, Charles M. Kingsley was sheriff, and Marquis F. Gillett, clerk. The following petit jury was summoned, and all the members appeared, viz: Edward Hubbell, Daniel Chambers, James Sturdevant, Hartwell C. Hamblin, Adin Terry, Warren Kellogg, S. D. Comins, David Clark, William F. Barker, James McCormick, and Cyrus Clark. The first case tried was entitled, "William Young vs. J. H. Eldridge. Appeal from justice court." The same day the jury found a verdict for the plaintiff, and assessed the damages at one hundred and sixty-eight cents. The defendant thereupon filed a motion for a new trial, which was overruled by the court. To this ruling the defendant excepted.

COUNTY COURT.

In 1851, by an act of the General Assembly, County Courts were established and the office of County Judge was created. By the same act the office of Probate Judge was abolished as were the offices of County Commissioners; the duties of the Commissioners and Probate Judge, devolving upon the County Judge. The county of Bremer, not being organized until 1853, it had no Probate Judges or County Commissioners. The first County Judge was Jeremiah Farris, one of the early settlers of the county. Upon him devolved the duty of perfecting the organization of the county, dividing it into townships, and such other work as was necessary to perfect a system of County government. Judge Farris' successors were George W. Maxfield, Matthew Rowen, George W. Ruddick, D. F. Avery and Louis Case. During 1861 the offices of County Supervisors were created, which relieved the County Judge of much of the business which had previously devolved upon him.

In the chapter under the title of National, State and County Representation, this office is treated in detail, and personal sketches of many of the Judges will be found.

CHAPTER VIII.

THE BAR OF BREMER COUNTY.

There is no subject connected with the history of the county of more general interest than a faithful record of its Bar. In reviewing the history of the Bar, it must be borne in mind that as the prosperity and well being of every community depends upon the wise interpretation as well as the judicious framing of its laws, therefore it must follow that a record of the members of the Bar must form no unimportant part in the county's history. Upon a few principles of natural justice is erected the whole superstructure of civil laws, tending to meet the desires and relieve the wants of all alike. The business of the lawyer is not to make the laws, but to apply them to the daily affairs of men. But the interests of men are diversified; and where so many interests and counter interests are to be protected and adjusted, to the lawyer and judge are presented many interesting and complex problems.

Change is everywhere imminent. The laws of yesterday do not meet the wants and necessities of the people of to-day, for the old relations do not exist. New and satisfactory laws must be established. The discoveries in the arts and sciences, the invention of new contrivances for labor, the enlargement of industrial pursuits, and the increase and development of commerce, are without precedence, and the science of law must keep pace with them all; nay, it must even forecast the event, and so frame its laws as will most adequately subserve the wants and provide for the necessities of the new conditions. Hence, the lawyer is a man of to-day. The exigencies he must meet are those of his own time. As has been often said, his capital is his ability and his individuality. He cannot bequeath to his successors the characteristics that distinguish him, and at his going, as a general thing, the very evidences of his work disappear.

Anthony Thornton, president of the Illinois State Bar Association; in 1878, in an address before the Association, thus speaks of the lawyer:

"In the American State, the great and good lawyer must always be prominent, for he is one of the forces which move and control society. Public confidence has generally been reposed in the legal profession. It has ever been the defender of popular rights, the champion of freedom, regulated by law, the firm support of good government. In times of danger it has stood like a rock and breasted the mad passions of the hour, and firmly resisted tumult and faction. No political preferment, no mere place, can add to the power or increase the honor which belong to the pure and educated lawyer. The fame of Mansfield and Marshall and Story, can never die. 'Time's iron feet can print no ruin trace' upon their character. Their learning and luminous exposition of our jurisprudence will always light our pathway. It is our duty to perserve the prestige of the profession. The past, at least, secure; the present and future summon us to action. With the progress of society and the increase of population, wealth and trade, varied interests arise, and novel questions requiring more thought confront us. A disregard of the law has been developed, crime meets us unabashed, and corruption stands unmasked in the high places of the land. It is no fancy picture that the law has, to some extent, lost its authority, and it is only the shade of that which was great. Hence new duties are imposed and a firmer courage is required. * * *

The exaltation is a duty enjoined upon us. It is a death that only death can discharge. Lord Bacon has said: 'Every man is a debtor to his profession; from the which, as men of force do seek to receive countenance and profit, so ought they of duty, to endeavor themselves, by ways of amends, to be a help and ornament thereto.' Every lawyer is a debtor to his profession. If worthy, it gives him an honorable character and position. The lawyer should prize and love his profession. He should value its past renown and cherish the memory of great men, whose gigantic shadows walk by us still. He should love it for the intrinsic worth and innate truth of the fundamental truths which adorn it."

The Bar of Bremer county has numbered among its members some who have been an honor, not only to the county, but to the profession and State as well. So far as material was accessible sketches are given of each attorney who has practiced before the courts of the county. None are omitted intentionally, and of some, more would gladly have been said if more were known of the parties by those now living in the county. The peculiarities and personalities which form so pleasing and interesting a part of the lives of the members of the Bar, and which, indeed, constitute the charm of local history, are in a great measure wanting. Unlike the fair plaintiff in famous Bardell vs. Pickwick, we have no painstaking "sergeant to relate the facts and circumstances of the case."

Among those who have practiced before the courts of Bremer county, and who have been resident lawyers, were the following: Phineas V. Swan, George W. Ruddick, G. C. Wright, Benjamin F. Perkins, C. C. Allen, Samuel E. Hoffman, W. W. Fuller, Hiram Shaver, W. A. Stowe, John E. Burke, O. A. Call, Robinson & Ladd, H. P. Brown, W. W. Andrews, —. —. Turner, Ezra Carr, Charles B. Parsons, B. F. Thorp, H. A. Miles, Judge O. F. Avery, Wm. P. Harmon, M. W. Anderson, and D. W. Coan.

Of those attorneys who resided in the county at one time and are now either dead, or have quit practice, or gone, we will speak first. Later, of the present Bar.

Phenias V. Swan was undoubtedly the first attorney to locate in Bremer county, and was the first here admitted to the Bar. He came from Vermont, where he had been engaged in the practice of law, and upon arriving here, at the first term of court held in the county, was, upon motion of I. M. Preston, admitted to the Bar of this State, upon the presentation of his certificate. Swan located with his family at Janesville, and there opened his office. He had a good library, and was a well-read lawyer; an excellent office worker, and a very fair debator; rather prepossessing in appearance, with a gentlemanly address, he worked up what would be termed an extensive practice, considering the newness of the country. He was, as to religious belief, an outspoken infidel, and would not hesitate to let anyone know his belief. On the 4th of August, 1856, he was elected prosecuting attorney of the county, but died before the expiration of the first year of his term. As will be seen, by a glance at the press chapter, he was interested in the first paper published in Bremer county. After his death, his little property was disposed of, and his family returned to Vermont, their native State.

William P. Harmon was born in St. Stephens, New Brunswick. His youth was spent at Calias, Maine, where he received a good common school education, or rather, educating himself, for he was in every respect a self-made man. He read law at Calias, Maine, which borough he represented in the State Legislature. Seeking his fortune in the western world, he tried his luck with indifferent success in various places, and finally came to this State and settled at Cedar Rapids, where he remained a few years, and then went to Independence, Iowa, where he remained until 1853; there he married Alzina E., a daughter of Manassah Reeves, Esq., and immediately removed to Waverly, where he remained until the time of his death. He was the proprietor of the town, and it was mainly through his energies and perseverance that it owes its present prosperity. In every enterprise of a philanthropic or patriotic nature he was ever foremost, and his private charities were almost without number. He devoted his energies entirely to his business, and never would accept a public office, except when convinced the public good and his duty required it. He held the office of prosecuting attorney for the county when that office was one of the most important in the county. He also represented his district in the State Legislature. He labored long and ardently to give Waverly the benefits of railroad communication, and lived to see from his chamber window, just before his death, the cars arrive at Bremer Avenue. He was buried Monday, the 12th day of December, 1864, by the Masonic Fraternity, of which he was a member. In his death, Waverly lost one of its best men, a loss hard to replace. He left a wife, three daughters and one son to mourn his loss, together with a large circle of friends.

On the 18th of August, 1856, George W. Ruddick located at Waverly, and became a prominent member of the Bar of this portion of the State. He was for many years at the head of the Bar of Bremer county, and continued his practice until chosen to the circuit bench of this district in 1869. Two years later he was elected judge of the district court and still acts in that capacity. He is treated at length in that chapter.

H. A. Miles was another of the early lawyers of Bremer county. An interesting letter from him, presented in connection with the chapter upon Reminiscences of Pioneers, gives particulars of his locating here, and his practice.

Gancelo C. Wright was born in Lewiston, Maine, in 1828. He there read law and was admitted to the Bar in January, 1856. On his admission to the Bar, he came west, arriving in Bremer county in March, 1856, where he at once commenced practice. He continued practice until 1879, when he went into the newspaper business and has since been engaged in that profession. He was successful as a lawyer, and was well posted in matters pertaining to the legal profession. He has always been a democrat and has twice been a delegate to the National Conventions. He says he was always a democrat but "did not vote for Jim Buchanan." He was at one time prosecuting attorney for Bremer county. He was a charter member of the Masonic Lodge, of Waverly, both Tyrrell Lodge and Jethro Chapter, and was for a number of years, Master of the Lodge.

About the same time, in 1856, W. W. Fuller came to Bremer county and located at Janesville. He had been admitted to the Bar in Vermont, but, it is thought, had never practiced. In a short time he opened an office with J. K. L. Maynard, and remained for a few years, when he removed to Monona county, Iowa. He was a single man, and being a hard student and a man of good sense, he had a brilliant prospect for becoming distinguished and influential, and after his removal to Monona did win an enviable reputation throughout the western part of the State; while here, he was rather quiet and of a retiring disposition. When the war broke out he enlisted and died in the service. When the news of his decease reached Waverly, the following article was published in the *Republican* regarding him :

"Capt. W. W. Fuller, who died near Vicksburg, Mississippi, March 14, 1863, was born in Montgomery, Vermont, and came to this State in 1856, and engaged in the practice of law at Janesville. In 1858, he removed to Magnolia, Harrison county, Iowa, where he continued in the practice of his profession up to the time of his enlistment, in the fall of 1862. Captain Fuller was of a retiring disposition, but a young man of superior talents; and every one who knew him, saw in his extraordinary intellect a certain promise of future distinction and extensive influence. He was fast securing an extensive and lucrative practice, and was honored by, and an honor to his profession. He was elected a member of the Ninth General Assembly, in the fall of 1861, by a large and unprecedented majority. He was a fast friend and a sociable and agreeable companion."

Orrin Frank Avery was born in Auburn, Pennsylvania, May 1, 1831. His parents emigrated in an early day from Puritan New England, and maintained that high-toned, moral and Christian character and conduct that distinguished the old Puritan stock. They moved from Pennsylvania to Illinois in 1843. The next year his father died when Orrin was but thirteen years old. His mother was spared to him until he was twenty years old. After the death of his father, his uncle, Jeremiah Meachan, generously took a father's care of him, furnishing him means for a liberal education. He accordingly went to Montrose, Pennsylvania, prepared himself for college, matriculated at Yale College in 1853 and graduated with the class of 1857. On leaving college he studied law with Mr. Fuller, at Belvidere, Illinois, and with Poor & Co., at Dubuque, Iowa. After completing the prescribed course, he was admitted to the Bar, and in a few years came to Bremer county. Mr. Avery was married to Miss Jennie Gardner, of Elgin, Illinois, September 17, 1867. He died May 26, 1870.

At a meeting of the members of the Bar of Bremer county, held on Saturday evening, May 28, 1870, for the purpose of expressing the sense of the Bar with reference to the decease of Hon. O. F. Avery, the following resolutions were adopted:

WHEREAS, Intelligence has been received, that the Hon. O. F. Avery, a member of the Bar of Bremer county, departed this life on the 26th day of May, A. D. 1870; therefore, be it

Resolved, That we, the members of the Bar of Bremer county, have learned with profound regret of the decease of our esteemed professional brother and personal friend, Hon. O. F. Avery, whose exalted character as a citizen, thorough knowledge of the law, uniform courtesy and honor as a practitioner, have long since won our esteem and endearing regards, and placed him high in the ranks of his chosen profession.

Resolved, That we tender to the family of the deceased, our sincere sympathy in their bereavement.

Resolved, That a copy of these resolutions be presented to the family of the deceased, and also to the Waverly *Republican* and *News* for publication, and we ask that the same shall be spread upon the records of the circuit court of Bremer county, now in session.

H. H. GRAY,
JOHN E. BURKE, } Com.
G. C. WRIGHT,

On the passage of the above resolutions, G. W. Ruddick said:

"This is the first time in the history of the Bar of Bremer county that we have been called together as such, to give expression to our sorrow at the loss of one of our active members; for fifteen years, past, in fact, ever since there has been a Bar in this county, no active prosecuting member has been called away by death.

"At the last term of this court, our professional brother was with us in this room, attending to the ordinary business of the profession, among us. We all knew he was in failing health, but none of us thought he would be called from among us so soon. It is only one week ago that his partners received from him a letter, which was, on the whole, hopeful; hardly had it been read and its contents talked over by his friends, when the telegraph informs us that his dead body is on its way to its last resting place among us, and that in a day or two we will be called to follow it to the grave. It has been my fortune to know the deceased for nearly eleven years. I think it was in the fall of 1859 that he first came to this place. He had just completed his studies and was about to commence the practice of law, in partnership with Mr. G. C. Wright, when I first knew him; from then until, as a volunteer, he became a soldier of the United States. His rise in his profession was rapid, and when he then left us, he had no superior among us as counsellor and office lawyer. His universal attention to business and his peculiar fitness for the place, procured for him, almost immediately upon entering the United States service, the honorable and responsible position of Judge Advocate, which he filled creditably for a large part of the term of enlistment. When he joined his regiment toward the close of the war he was put into active service, and it was probably from exposure during that time that the disease of which he died was fastened upon him. But I do not intend to speak of him as a soldier. It was as a lawyer and a man that we knew him, and, as such, he always commanded our respect and very often our admiration. As a lawyer he brought to bear upon every legal question that thorough and downright common sense which is the foundation of every correct legal principle; he was not content to know what one another said upon a subject, but he would search the whole library for days together upon any question of doubt, and before coming into court he knew what had been written on all sides of the question, and hence was never taken by surprise. He did not profess to be an advocate, but as a lawyer he took rank among the very first of this Bar.

"In his business, his first thoughts were to know that his client's cause was just, and when assured of this, he was the most untiring among you in the preparation of it for trial, and in presenting the law to enforce it before the court.

"I never in my life have known a more conscientious, hard-working or better office lawyer. As a man, he was strictly honest —above even the breath of suspicion—

strongly attached to his friends, slow to think evil of them, prompt and generous in rendering them assistance when needed —a thoroughly good man.

"On his return from the army, in 1865, I offered him a partnership with me, which was accepted, and for the last five years I have known him very intimately. While you met him in this court room and upon the streets, and in social life, I had the privilege of a more intimate relation with him, for three years, during which our partnership existed, from morning until night, on nearly every day, I was with him in the office. I have had opportunities of knowing the man, that none of you have had. I worked with him at the law table, over the same cases, day after day, for three years, and since then I have been with him until he left here almost daily; in his intercourse it is but natural that stronger ties would be formed between us than existed with his other business associates, and in his loss I feel that I have a more peculiar and exclusive sorrow than you. We had been accustomed for the last five years to consult together about our private business, and as I now go into the office and see the chair and table he used to occupy, vacant, and know that I shall never see him there again, I realize most keenly that the pleasant relations which have existed are now broken forever, that his work is done, that mine must be continued for how long or short a time I know not, without his friendly advice or assistance. With all the mementoes I see around me every day to remind me of him and that he is now dead, I feel that death has come very near me.

"Gentlemen, his place among us from this time will be vacant. We will not feel his honest, hearty grasp of hand or hear his pleasant words of cheer, or see his kindly smiles again, and in paying this tribute of respect and love to his memory, I feel how poor and inexpressive are all words to show the grief that fills the heart, and moistens the eye, and chokes the utterance."

About the fall of 1855, Benjamin F. Perkins located at Waverly, and commenced the practice of law. He was a native of Vermont, where he had graduated from a law school. He was a young man, and is remembered as having a very pretty wife. As a lawyer he was not a success. He was a good fellow, and his actions were always prompted by good motives; but being a little inclined to take his ease, he was never blessed with much business. As a counsellor he was, probably, above the average, but as an orator he was not a success, stammering considerably. In about 1857, he removed to Kansas.

C. C. Allen was another of Bremer county's lawyers. He came to Waverly, from Illinois, in 1858, and being a printer by trade, commenced work in the *Republican* office. He studied law with Gancelo C. Wright, now editor of the *Democrat*, and in 1860 was admitted to the Bar. He opened an office, but did not succeed in getting much business, and when the war broke out, in 1861, he enlisted and served during its continuance, most of the time as Provost Marshal. At the close of the rebellion he returned to Waverly, and was engaged, at various times, in the livery and hardware business. About 1868, he removed to Jasper county, Missouri, and has served one term as State Senator. He has been the candidate, on the republican ticket, for Lieutenant-Governor, but was defeated, and is now serving his second term as United States Marshal, for the Western District, with headquarters at Independence, although his family live at Carthage, Missouri.

W. W. Anderson came to Bremer county from Polo, Illinois, in 1863, and located at Waverly. He opened a law office and remained here for several years. He was a native of Upper Canada, where he was born in 1819. He was a small man, noisy, a great talker and a fair lawyer. He is still practicing law at Iowa Falls.

D. W. Coan was another member of the Bremer county Bar. He came here from Illinois early in the sixties and remained about two years. He was a pleasant fellow, but did not meet with much success at law. He went back to Illinois where he still remains.

S. E. Hoffman came to Waverly from Monroe, Wisconsin, about 1853, and engaged in the general merchandise business in company with his brother, S. J. Hoffman. In a few years he read law with G. C. Wright and was here admitted to the Bar, but did not open an office. He left about 1857, and spent a number of years of his life in Neosha Falls and Topeka, Kansas, and is now in St. Louis, Missouri, where he is engaged in the banking business, and is a very prominent and influential man. He is president of a bank in that city.

Hiram Shaver came to Waverly, from Wisconsin, in 1869, and engaged in teaching school. He commenced reading law with G. C. Wright, and in about 1871, was admitted to practice. He did not open an office here, and soon left, locating in Chickasaw county, where he began practice. He was a single man, full of energy and of natural, as well as acquired ability. In his practice he has been eminently successful, having for a number of years been considered at the head of the Bar of Chickasaw county.

W. A. Stowe was a native of Vermont, and came west with his mother, settling in Clayton county. In 1863 he came to Waverly, soon went into the army, and served about a year and a half. Returning, he read law with G. C. Wright, was admitted, and became a partner of Mr. Wright, continuing thus for three years. He finally removed to Hamburg, Fremont county, where he has been twice elected a member of the Lower House of the General Assembly, and has been a trustee of the Iowa State Normal School. Stowe was far above the average lawyer, was well-posted, sharp, shrewd, and a fine orator. He was a democrat, and an enthusiastic stump speaker; was very sarcastic, and called things by their right names. A few years since he removed to Omaha, where he now lives.

John E. Burke, was a very prominent member of the Bar of Bremer county. He came to Waverly, in 1858, from Dubuque, where he had been engaged as clerk in a bank. He at once opened an office and commenced practice. His business grew rapidly, as he was an excellent orator, a hard worker and full of energy. He was elected district attorney and has served one term each as a member of the State Senate and House of Representatives. He remained in Waverly about eighteen years, when he removed to Chicago, where he still lives and follows his profession. While here he accumulated a fortune. Burke was a man of good address and had long, curly, auburn hair, on which he rather prided himself, which gave him the title of "Man of the Ambrosial Locks." One little incident is remembered about Burke which is worth relating. He knew nothing of farming, but his tendencies rather ran in that direction. In the spring of 1859, he put in a lot of "garden truck," which he took good care of and worked zealously over. Among the vegetables planted, was a lot of beans. When he thought they had been in the ground long enough, he made up his mind that something was wrong, or the beans would come up. He opened a hill to see what was the matter and saw that the bean as he thought was growing downward, taking the root for the stock. After worrying over the matter, he called in Father Harris and wanted to know if beans "must be planted with a certain end up, that he guessed he had made a mistake, as his was sprouting downward." Harris smiled and told him to "put some manure over it to coax up the sprouts." It is said that Burke went to work and turned some of the plants upside down. But, notwithstanding he knew less about farming than Horace Greeley, he was a good lawyer.

Robertson & Ladd were a firm of attorneys that opened an office in Waverly in 1866. They came from Wisconsin, where they had been in practice. Their office was on the west side of the river, where they remained about one year; not getting much business. Robertson was the main member of the firm, and was a brilliant young man, a good orator, and with fair prospects; he returned to Illinois, his native State. Ladd was a good counselor; he removed to Clarion, Wright county, where he still lives.

H. P. Brown came to Waverly in 1864, from Junietta county, Wisconsin, and remained for nearly ten years. He was a fine orator, a good lawyer, and had a first-rate practice. He was also a preacher of the Latter Day Saints. He removed to Oakland, California, where he still lives.

A Mr. Turner came in 1865, from Wisconsin, and began practice. He had been admitted to the Bar prior to his coming here, and had also been in practice. He was not much of a lawyer, either in office work or before the courts. He left for parts unknown.

Colonel James W. Wood located in Waverly in 1868, and became a member of the Bar of Bremer county, remaining for a number of years. He is now located at Steamboat Rock, in Hardin county. He is one of the oldest settlers and the oldest practicing attorney in the State of Iowa. He was born in Middlesex county, Massachusetts, April 30, 1800. He was admitted to the Bar at Lewisburg, Virginia, in March, 1827, and immediately came west and located in Illinois, where he practiced law for some years, and was contemporaneous with Lincoln, Douglas, Baker, Shields, Trumbull, Browning, Walker and others of the most prominent men of that State. In 1863, in company with five others, he crossed the Mississippi near where Burlington now stands, and built a cabin, but did not make a permanent settlement until 1834. In 1837, he was appointed the first city solicitor of Burlington, and was secre-

HISTORY OF BREMER COUNTY. 863

tary of the first senate, in 1846-7. From 1847 to 1854, he was clerk of the Supreme Court of Iowa. The Colonel has always taken a part in the politics of the State, and has been a democrat in the strictest sense.

Ezra Carr came from Wisconsin about 1874, and became a member of the Bremer county Bar, locating at Waverly. He was a young man, and a hard working office lawyer. He returned to Warren, Wisconsin, after a two years residence in Waverly.

Charles B. Parsons was a native of New York, and came to Waverly early in the decade between 1850 and 1860. He was a married man. He remained until the time of his death, which occurred a few years ago. Mr. Parsons was a good lawyer, an honorable man, and had a very lucrative practice. He was very popular and witty, and Judge Ruddick says he had one of the finest legal minds that he ever met with; a man of great discernment and preception, but he was much more in his place in the office than in the court room.

O. A. Call came to Bremer county at an early day, with his parents, and grew to manhood here. About 1870 he commenced reading law with H. P. Brown, finishing up with G. C. Wright, and was admitted to the Bar in 1877. He was a young man of rare prospects, and while he remained had a good practice. He was well-posted in law, a good pleader, and a very hard student. A few years ago he started for Florida, for the benefit of his health, and died on the way, of consumption.

B. F. Thorpe came here in 1878, from Wisconsin, and opened an office, but did not remain long. He was said to be a good lawyer.

W. W. Andrews came here from Ohio, in 1879, and was admitted to the Bar here. He was for six months a law partner of A. F. Brown. He had been a school teacher, was well educated, but too timid, with not enough self reliance for a successful lawyer. He is now in Dakota.

THE PRESENT BAR.

The members of the Bar of Bremer county, now in active practice, are recognized throughout the State as able representatives of the legal profession. The following named constitute the Bar: J. K. L. Maynard, A. J. Tanner, Eph. Kinnie, A. H. McCracken, Col. M. E. Billings, E. L. Smalley, H. H. Gray, M. B. Dougherty, D. T. Gibson, Edward A. Dawson, Alfred A. Brown, George E. Walker and Josiah Carpenter.

J. K. L. Maynard, a son of Jesse K. and Lucy (Taylor) Maynard, was born July 26, 1829, in Bakersfield, Vermont. His grandfather was a native of Massachusetts. When he emigrated to Bakersfield, he found his way there by trees which had been marked by previous emigrants. His marriage was the first ever celebrated in that town. J. K. L. was reared on a farm, and obtained a part of his education at the Bakersfield Academy, which was one of the first institutions of that kind in the State of Vermont. When nineteen years of age, he began studying preparatory to entering college. During 1852, he entered the Vermont University, at Burlington, but at the end of two years his health failed to such an extent that he had to abandon his studies. He then returned home, and after regaining his health, entered the law office of Judge Wilson.

In 1855, he attended the law school at Albany, New York, being in the class with Judge Ruddick, of Waverly; John T. Stoneman, of Cedar Rapids, and A. J. Case, President of the National Bank of Charles City. During the fall of 1855, he was admitted to the Bar, and the following spring came to Bremer county, Iowa, locating in Janesville, where he practiced law two years. In 1858, he formed a partnership with W. W. Fuller, of Harrison county. After a short time he sold his interest to his partner and returned to Vermont, where, in 1853, he was married to Maria J. Kimpton—a daughter of Rev. Orville Kimpton—who was born June 11, 1836, in Franklin county, Vermont. They immediately returned to the west, and Mr. Maynard, in company with Louis Case, purchased the *Republican*, at Waverly. In a few months time he bought Mr. Case's interest, and continued to edit the paper alone. In June of 1861, he was appointed postmaster of Waverly, and held the office for ten years. During his residence in that city, he held the office of mayor and other local offices. He was trustee of the Methodist Episcopal Church at the time their present house of worship was erected. Mr. Maynard settled on his farm in Jackson township, in March, 1873. In 1877, he was elected a member of the State Legislature, and filled that office with honor to himself and to his constituents. Mr. and Mrs. Maynard have five children living—Orville K., J. Dana, J. Wilbert, Loret M. and A. Howard.

A. J. Tanner was born in Wyoming county, New York, February 11, 1825. He is a son of Able and Electa (Foot) Tanner, who, in May, 1839, left western New York, in wagons, for Boone county, Illinois, where they took up government land, A. J. working out by the month to pay for it, his father being poor, having only seven shillings in his pocket when he landed in the county. A. J. was educated in the common schools and Academy at Belvidere, and also attended Knox College. After leaving Knox College he taught school, and, in the meantime read law. In 1848 he was admitted to the Bar. In 1850 he was appointed clerk by the county court of Boone county, and the same fall elected to the office. In January, 1854, he emigrated to Buchanan county, Iowa, where he practiced his profession. Losing his health, he returned to Belvidere. In 1855 he went to Dubuque, and opened a land office. In 1856 he removed to Fairbault, Minnesota, and while there, Seabeary University was organized, he acting as attorney for the corporation. In 1862 he went to the Rocky Mountains, making the trip on foot, returning the same fall. In July, 1863, he came to Waverly, Iowa, where he has since resided. In January, 1869, he was appointed justice of the peace, which office he holds at the present time. He married Miss Ellen A. Mallory, in August, 1854. Mr. and Mrs. Tanner are the parents of one son, who was drowned in the Cedar river, at the age of ten years.

Eph. Kinnie, attorney at law, and mayor of Waverly, Iowa, was born in Seneca county, New York, on the 22d day of June, 1842. He is a son of Silas M. and Lufanny (Halsey) Kinnie. He commenced reading law in Minnesota, afterward attended the law school at Albany, New York, and was admitted to the Bar, in New York, in 1867, and in Iowa, in 1868. In December, 1867, he emigrated to Bremer county, Iowa, where he engaged in his profession. In politics he is a republican, and in the spring of 1882, was elected mayor of the city of Waverly. In November, 1871, he was married to Miss Emma C. Halt, formerly of Savannah, Illinois, where she was born in August, 1852. They have two children—Lufanny and Morris. Mr. Kinnie is a member of the K. P. of Waverly.

A. H. McCracken was born in Monroe, Green county, Wis., February 15th, 1839. His father was Joseph McCracken, a native of Washington County, N. Y., whose parents, in 1825, moved to Edgar County, Ill., traveling all the distance with teams, being among the earliest settlers of that county. In 1837 he removed to Green county, Wis., where he engaged in farming, remaining there until his death in 1870. He was married in Onondago county, N. Y., to Ruth Sutherland by whom he had ten children. She died in Green county, Wis. A. H. McCracken was reared on his father's farm, receiving the education afforded in the common schools of that day. In 1858 he attended Madison University, remaining there until the breaking out of the war, when he enlisted in Company G, Twenty-Second, Wisconsin Volunteer Infantry, remaining in that regiment until May, 1864, when he was transferred to the Thirty-Eighth Wisconsin Infantry, and commissioned Adjutant. He was mustered out at the close of the war at Washington, D. C., and discharged at Madison, Wis. After which he returned to Monroe, where he taught school for two years, when he emigrated to Bremer county, Ia., locating in Waverly. In the fall of 1872, he was elected District Clerk, filling the office for six years. In the meantime, reading law, and in April, 1879, admitted to the Bar. May 22, 1864, he was married to Miss Sarah Hoffman, a daughter of John Hoffman. They have four children, Edward G., Ruth, Guy, Edith and Merritt.

Mr. McCracken is a member of the Masonic fraternity and Legion of Honor.

Colonel N. E. Billings, one of the attorney's of Waverly, Iowa, was born in Booneville, Oneida county, New York, July 8, 1837. His father was Jarvis Billings, formerly of Tolland, Connecticut; his mother, Almira Partridge, of Wilbraham, Massachusetts. They were married in Chenango county, New York, where eight children were born to them. In 1845, he emigrated with his family to Boone county, Illinois, where he engaged in farming until 1855. That year he removed to Fillmore county, Minnesota, where he laid out Preston, the county seat of that county, and where he still resides at the advanced age of ninety-three. The subject of this sketch was reared on a farm, receiving his early education in the common schools, spending two years and eight months at Notre Dame, South Bend, Indiana, where he studied the languages and law, and fitted himself for a civil engineer. He was admitted to the Bar of the United States Courts in 1865, by the United States District Court of Kentucky. In the spring of 1861, he entered in the First United States Sharp Shooters, participating in the engagements with the Army of the Potomac. He was wounded at the battle of Antietam, by the explosion of a shell, and for this cause discharged January 7, 1863. He then returned to Minnesota, where he raised a company and joined the Second

Minnesota Cavalry. He was commissioned First Lieutenant of the company. After a time he resigned and enlisted as a private in Company L, of the Fifth Iowa Cavalry. He was promoted to Second Lieutenant of the One Hundred and Fifteenth United States Veterans, and still later promoted to Captain of the One Hundred and Twentieth United States Veterans. He was in front of Petersburg and Richmond, when the Rebel army surrendered, at which time he was promoted to Lieutenant-Colonel of the One Hundred and Twenty-fifth United States Veterans. At the close of the war he returned to Minnesota. In 1867, was appointed as assistant United States District Attorney, at Russellville, Kentucky; also appointed agent in the Freedman's Bureau. In 1869, he went to Kansas as civil engineer on the L. & G. R. R.; then to northwestern Missouri, where he was engaged on the Chicago and Southwestern Railroad; then to the Central Iowa Railroad. In the fall of 1869, Mr. Billings came to Waverly, where he has since followed his profession, and is one of Waverly's most studious and energetic attorneys. He has built up a lucrative practice. Aside from his practice here, he has an extensive real estate interest in Fillmore county, Minnesota. He is an active member of the Legion of Honor of this place.

E. L. Smalley is also among the prominent members of the Bar of Bremer county. He was born in Muncy, Lycoming county, Penn., January 23d, 1847, a son of John Smalley, a Presbyterian minister, who for many years filled the pulpit for that denomination, and was proprietor and principal of the Muncy Female Seminary. In 1855 the family removed to Butler county, Pa., and two years later they came to Bremer county, Ia., locating at Waverly, where Mr. Smalley, senior, was instrumental in raising funds for the erection of the Presbyterian Church of Waverly, filling the pulpit there for ten years. In 1865 he purchased a farm in Warren township, where he removed and remained until his death, which occurred in 1879. He was a man of culture, broad intellect, and much esteemed by all who knew him. He was a republican in politics, and for a number of years represented his township in the county board.

The subject of this sketch was educated in the Muncy and at Weatherspoon Institutes. In 1869, and 1870, he attended Hanover College at Hanover, Ind., in the meantime reading law, and on Nov. 17th, 1874, was admitted to the Bar. In 1871 he was married to Miss Louisa Gasaway, of Madison, Jefferson county, Ind. Mr. and Mrs. Smalley are members of the Methodist Church. Mr. Smalley does abstract real estate and a law business. He is a successful lawyer, well-read, a good orator and a hard worker.

M. B. Dougherty, of Waverly, Iowa, was born in Beaver county, Pennsylvania, on the 1st day of February, 1844. He is a son of D. B. Dougherty, who emigrated to Bremer county, Iowa, locating at Janesville, Jackson township, where he engaged in farming being among the earliest settlers of the county. His mother was Eliza Crail. Mr. and Mrs. Dougherty were the parents of five children—Eli M., merchant at Janesville; Edward C., secretary and treasurer of the Spanish-American Curled Hair Company, of Chicago; Sarah, wife of Dr. Bradford, of Janesville; Eliza J., wife of A. S. McMullen, editor of the Vandale *Journal*, of Minnesota. M. B. received an academacal education. January 1, 1867, when twenty-two years of age, he entered the office of Judge Ruddick & Judge Avery to study law. He was admitted to the Bar in September, 1869. January 1, 1870, he entered into partnership with Judge Avery and H. H. Gray, and the firm was Avery, Dougherty & Gray. This partnership lasted until the 1st day of June, of the same year, when Judge Avery died, and the firm was changed to Gray & Dougherty. In 1873 they took into partnership with them Mr. Gibson, when the style of the firm became Gray, Dougherty & Gibson. In February, 1881, Gibson retired from the firm. In October, 1871, M. B. Dougherty was married to Miss Mary E. Caldwell, by whom he has two children — Amy L., and Mary E. C. Mrs. Dougherty died in April, 1876. She was a consistent member of the M. E. Church, loved and respected by all who knew her. Mr. Dougherty is a member of the Masonic fraternity, and Ancient Order of United Workmen.

D. T. Gibson, of the law firm of Gibson & Dawson, was born in Chautauqua county, New York, May 1844; the son of S. C. and Martha (Hall) Gibson. His father is a leading physician of that county, still in practice, having been in constant service there for over forty years; his mother died when he was quite young. His early life was spent in his native county, where he received an academic education, spending three years at Oxford Academy and for some time taught by a private tutor. When about eighteen years of age, having developed a taste for the legal profession, he entered the law office of Henry R. Mygatt, of Oxford, for the purpose of fitting himself for the practice of law, where he continued some time. Subsequently he emigrated to Wisconsin, where in 1868 he was admitted to the bar, before Judge Stewart He followed his profession in Madison until the spring of 1870, when he moved to Mason City, Iowa, where he continued his practice for two years, then, in 1872, coming to Waverly, where he associated himself with John E. Burke, under the firm name of Burke & Gibson. After one year the partnership was disolved, Mr. Gibson associating himself with Gray & Dougherty. Here he continued for eight years, when he withdrew and formed a partnership with E. A. Dawson, under the name of Gibson & Dawson. It may be said that this firm has the most extended law practice of any firm in the county. Both are men of great popularity, having hosts of friends. Mr. Gibson, although an ardent republican, has never entered the field as a politician, yet some of the minor offices have been crowded upon him. He served during the war, as a Union soldier, in the Ninetieth New York Volunteer Infantry, enlisting soon after arriving at the age of twenty-one years. In 1873 he was married to Miss Elizabeth A. Hazelton, a native of the State of New York.

E. A. Dawson, of the law firm of Gibson & Dawson, is the son of Edward and Catherine Dawson, who were pioneers of Albion township, Butler county, having settled there in 1856. He was born in Trumbull county, Ohio, March 22, 1853. When about one year old his parents emigrated to Delaware county, Iowa, remaining until 1856, when they removed to Butler county and settled in Albion township. There, on his father's farm, the early life of young Dawson was spent. He worked on his father's farm, attending the comman schools. Early in his boyhood days he developed a taste for books. He was encouraged by his parents, who furnished him such books as would benefit him both morally and intellectually. In 1872, he entered the University of Upper Iowa, at Fayette, where he completed his education in 1874, excepting a business course at Bailey's Commercial College, at Dubuque. Previous to this he aspired to the legal profession, and had from time to time made a study of law books. In 1875, he determined to make the legal profession his life work, and that year came to Waverly and entered the law office of Gray, Dougherty and Gibson, where he diligently applied his time in the study of the law, until the fall of 1877, when he was admitted to the Bar, before Hon. G. W. Ruddick. He continued in this office until January 1, 1878, when he formed a partnership with A. O. Call and E. R. Carr, under the firm name of Call, Carr & Dawson; later the firm became Call & Dawson, and in the fall of 1879, Mr. Dawson succeeded to the entire business, continuing alone until March, 1881, when he formed a partnership with D. F. Gibson, which partnership still continues. This firm stands at the head of the legal profession in Bremer county. Their suite of rooms and library are the finest in the city, and would be a credit to a larger town than Waverly. Mr. Dawson is a rising young man, and if health does not fail him, is sure to distinguish himself in his profession. He has been employed on one side of every important criminal case, in the county, since admitted to the Bar; he is a careful and conscientious counselor, an able and eloquent advocate; always pleasant and agreeable, and when he forms the acquaintance of a man, he makes that man his friend; and it has often been remarked in the presence of the writer, that "Ed. Dawson has more warm friends than any other man in Bremer county."

Alfred F. Brown was born December 8, 1828, near Zanesville, Muskingum county, Ohio. His paternal grandparents emigrated to and established their home at the place of his birth while that State was a territory. After their death the farm was purchased by his father, who continued to reside there until his death. The names of the parents of the subject of this sketch, were Parley and Rachel (Evans) Brown; both died upon the old farm. They raised a family of thirteen children —Elizabeth, Lucretia, Amasa, Mary, James, Harriet, Henry, Parley, Rachel, Ann, Alfred F., Hiram and Robert Franklin. It is a subject of pleasurable pride to the surviving members of the family, that the old homestead on which all the family were born, still remains family property. Industrious, prudent and frugal as his parents were, it was impossible for them to do more than to give to each of so large a family, anything more than a common school education, each one being required to do a share of the farm labor. Notwithstanding this limitation upon the opportunity of acquiring knowledge, Amasa and James succeeded in fitting for an honorable and successful practice of medicine, the latter becoming an M. D.

At an early age, Alfred developed a fondness for books. This desire for the acquisition of knowledge, made him dissatisfied with the order of business on the farm, and to form a plan for independent action. A plan he immediately matured and executed in March, 1842. He left the home of his parents at the age of fourteen years and traveled on foot to the city of Columbus, a distance of sixty miles. The writer has often heard him relate, that during that lonely "march," he ate but one meal, and this at the close of the first day, at the house of a friend of the family with whom he spent the night. So anxious was he for the success of his plan, and fearing a "hot pursuit" from home, that he renewed his walk without waiting to be refreshed with a breakfast. One incident of this day's walk is worthy to be presented. The weary march had been continued until about noon, when the demand for dinner had become imperative. Too poor to buy a dinner and too proud to beg, was a situation in the highest degree perplexing. Arriving opposite a large brick farm house, he approached the woman of the house and told his errand. To his utter confusion she replied in a language unintelligible to him. At this juncture the farmer came in, who, understanding the request, spoke to his wife, who thereupon cut from a loaf of bread a "chunk," which she unceremoniously handed the traveler. Reaching the road with his dinner in his hand, he made several attempts to bite the bread, finally concluding that the process of eating it would be more exhausting than the hard bread would be refreshing. The chunk was thrown upon the roadside and the journey continued, reaching Columbus before sunset. Obtaining the situation of "devil" in the office of the *Herald*, the next day he began to learn the art of type-setting. After about six weeks he returned home at the urgent call of his mother, who had devised another plan of life for him. Yielding to her desire, he entered a select school at Chandlersville, in his native county. In the fall of 1844 he began teaching a district school near home, and from this time until the completion of his study of the law, and his admission to the Bar, he taught school frequently. He was admitted to practice law, in the spring of 1848, by the supreme court of Ohio, after studying for two years with Hon. Richard Stilwell and Judge Seal at Zanesville, Ohio. Whatever educational attainments he has acquired is due to his own efforts, aided by the advice and limited patronage of a noble mother. Soon after his admission to the Bar, he emigrated to Iowa, where he has continued to reside. In 1852 and 1853 he edited a newspaper, called *The News Letter*, at Rochester, in Cedar county. At that time Rochester was competing with Tipton for the county seat. Upon the termination of that question in favor of Tipton, *The News Letter* office was purchased by parties residing at Cedar Falls, in Black Hawk county, and moved, in the summer of 1854. Upon severing his connection with the paper, in the spring of 1855, Mr. Brown devoted his time exclusively to the practice of his profession, soon acquiring a large and lucrative business. Having been raised in a whig family, he remained such until the organization of the republican party, to which he allied himself. In 1856 his friends presented his name as a candidate for delegate to the constitutional convention of Iowa, but was beaten by one vote, by James Trayner, of Vinton. In 1859 he received the nomination and was elected to the State Senate, in the district composed of the counties of Black Hawk, Butler, Franklin and Grundy. In this body he held honorable rank, in which his compeers were able and distinguished. During the session of 1862, the bill to grant certain lands to the DesMoines River Improvement Company was considered. He delivered a speech in the Senate chamber, in defense of the settlers upon these lands, which was highly commended for the clear and forcible manner in which the objections to the bill were stated. The estimation in which he was held, may be realized by reference to the following extract from the correspondent of the Dubuque *Times:* "That plump, rather stout gentleman, who has just risen to speak on the supervisors' bill, is Hon. A. F. Brown, the efficient and able Senator from Black Hawk county. He is, perhaps, thirty years of age, weight 150 pounds, and is the least trifle below the medium height. He dresses rather neatly, presents a smoothly shaven phiz., a fine blue eye, and is, decidedly, a good-looking man. He has pursued a most judicious course during the present session, speaking seldom, but laboring hard in committees. when he does speak, however, he is clear, able and eloquent, and always commands the attention of the Senate." In 1860 he he was a delegate from Iowa to the republican national convention at Chicago, when Lincoln was nominated. The following testimonial, from the pen of Judge Bogg, of Waterloo, in *Commercial Law Register,* 1876, will be recognized as just by those who know him: "As a lawyer he is more than ordinarily efficient, intelligent, and learned; true and faithful to the contracts of his clients, and as an advocate he has few superiors in this vicinity; ready, earnest and convincing as an associate or opponent, and to the bench uniformly courteous and obliging." In the spring of 1877, Mr. Brown removed from Cedar Falls to Waverly, where he has resided since, devoting his time and talent to his profession with eminent success. Since his residence here he has been twice elected city solicitor of Waverly, an office which he now fills. In the fall of 1867, he married Miss Jennie McCall, who has since that time presided over his home.

George E. Walker, attorney-at-law, was born in New York city, October 14th, 1837. He graduated from the law department of Columbia College in 1863. During the year of 1878 he removed to Dubuque, Ia., where he remained two years and then settled in Waverly, Bremer county, where he has since practiced his profession. In 1866 he was joined in marriage to Miss Jeannette E. White, a grand-daughter of Gen. Whitney, whose father was the founder of Burmingham, New York. Six children bless this marriage; Llewellyn J., Gerald G., Catherine A., Cecil L., Rhoda J. and Constance E. His father, Thomas E. Walker, was one of the directors of several of the early Iowa railroads, and for many years Vice-President of the Illinois Central Railroad, furnishing the capital for building a great portion of the lines which now traverse this part of the State. His grandfather, Phillip E. Thomas, of Baltimore, Md., was the first President of the Baltimore and Ohio Railroad, and held the position for many years. This was the first great railroad in America.

Josiah Carpenter was born in Bradford county, Pennsylvania, in 1826. When he was eleven years of age his parents moved to DuPage county, Illinois, where he lived until he was twenty-five; then he went to Will county, Illinois, where he was justice of the peace for nineteen years, during four of which he was also associate county probate judge. He taught school seventeen winters in Will county, Illinois, and for six years was deputy school commissioner. In 1868, he came to Iowa and bought a farm of 360 acres in Sumner township. His brother, Washington, came to this place in 1861, and located near the present site of Sumner. He died in September, 1882. His brother, Chancey, platted the village of Sumner. Their father died in DuPage county, Illinois, in 1848; also three brothers. After locating his farm, Mr. Carpenter returned to Will county, and remained there until 1875. In the year 1871, he was admitted to the Bar by the Supreme Court of Illinois, and practiced there until his return to Sumner, in 1875, where he settled and continued in the practice of law. At the same time he was busy in improving his farm. From 1861 to 1875, he was in the bounty and pension business, in connection with real estate and insurance; dealing in real estate in Chicago, Joliet and other places. He was also deputy provost marshal during the war of 1861 and 1865. Mr. Carpenter was married in 1852, to Miss Francis M. Hanadon, a native of Vermont. They have had four children—Sarah, who married the Rev. C. A. Hilton, now of East Kendall county, New York, where he has been located as pastor for seven years; Loren H., Chester H. and Willie I. Loren has been for seven years in Cass' store, he has also taught school for a number of years; was at the Fayette College one term. All of the boys have taught school more or less. Chester has taught several terms. Willie is now employed in the extensive lumber yard of James C. Garner. When Mr. Carpenter came to Iowa he anticipated that his three sons would find it pleasant to go with him on to the farm and improve and cultivate it for future use; but after attending school a few winters, they caught the "idea" of teaching school, and hence engaged in that business.

H. H. Gray was born on the 22d of November, 1842, at Marion, in the Territory of Iowa, a son of Thomas and Pricilla Moore Gray, who was a farmer in Linn county, Iowa, his father a native of Pennsylvania and his mother of Kentucky. His father died in 1842 and his mother in 1852, leaving two children. Thomas is in the hardware business at Shellsburg, Ia., and Henry Harrison, who is the subject of this sketch. Henry H. received his education at Cornell College, at Mount Vernon, Iowa; enlisted in Company K, of the Ninth Iowa Infantry, serving as private for six months, when he was promoted to Quartermaster's Sergeant. Two years later he received his commission as Quartermaster and served as such until discharged at Louisville, Ky., in July, 1865. He took an active part in the battle at Pea Ridge. Upon returning from the army he commenced reading law, entered the Law School at Ann Arbor, Mich., in 1867, where he took one term, returned to Linn county and was admitted to the Bar at Marion, Ia., in 1866. He practiced at Cedar Rapids one year, coming to Waverly in 1869, where he has been engaged in the practice of law ever since. First forming a partnership with O. F. Avery and after the death of his partner in 1870, formed a partnership with M. B. Dougherty, under the firm name of Gray, Dougherty & Gibson, from 1873 to 1881, when Mr. Gibson went out of the firm, leaving Gray & Dougherty, who dissolved March, 1883. He is a republican in politics, and acted as Chairman of the County Republican Committee several years and held the office of Mayor of Waverly one term. He is a member of Tyrrell Lodge, No. 116, A. F. and A. M.; he is also a member of the A. O. U. W. In 1870 he was married to Miss Marie E. Matthews, daughter of John and Anna Spencer Matthews, of Jackson county, Iowa. By this union there are two children, both living—Alice Maud, born Nov. 22, 1873, and Harry William, born Feb. 25, 1879.

CHAPTER IX.

THE MEDICAL PROFESSION OF BREMER COUNTY.

In all ages of the world among civilized and uncivilized people, the medical profession has been held in high esteem. Whether it be the learned professor, who has studied the science of medicine in all its branches, or the "great medicine man" of the untutored savages, who from actual experience has made discoveries of the healing powers of herbs and roots, honor awaits them on every hand, while the life and death of every human being is virtually placed in their keeping. The weary patient lying upon a bed of pain, and the no less weary watcher, wait anxiously for the coming of the "good doctor," and, on his arrival, note his every movement and every expression of countenance for a ray of hope.

The medical fraternity of Bremer county have, with few exceptions, been an honor to the profession. They have ever been ready to respond to the call of duty. The winter's cold, the summer's heat, or the rains of spring and autumn, could not keep them back when the cry of distress reached their ears. They have been compelled to cross trackless prairies, to face blizzards from the north, often with no hope of fee or reward, but only to relieve, if possible, those who plead for their case. All this has been done by the physicians of Bremer county without complaint. If the good deeds of the profession are not now remembered by those who have received aid, a time will come when they will be. When the names of these pioneer doctors are recalled to mind, it is hoped the hearts of the old settlers will be touched, and all will respond, "May God bless them."

For a number of years after the first ingress of settlers, Bremer county did without doctors, as well as lawyers. Early in the spring of 1850, a dentist located among the pioneers, who with his turnkeys, could bring a tooth at every clatter. This was William Baskins, who yet lives upon his farm, east of Waverly. For a number of years he did quite a business, but finally, as the new arrangements for extracting teeth became known and used, the old turnkeys were laid upon the shelf. By many, these instruments of torture, in the hands of Mr. Baskins—or as he was termed for short, 'Bill'—are too well remembered, for when once set upon a tooth, something had to come. However, Mr. Baskin was skilled in their use and says he cannot remember of ever "breaking a jaw or jerking anyone's head off."

The honor is due to Mrs. Betsey Martin for being the first in Bremer county to make a business of healing and administering to the wants of the sick. She was the wife of Rev. C. N. Martin, who, in 1850, located upon a farm on section thirteen of what is now Washington township. Mrs. Martin's right name was Elizabeth, but she was known far and wide over this region as "Aunt Betsy." Her practice was more of the nature of "womanish common sense;" the ingredients in her prescriptions usually consisted of a few roots and herbs. Her rides extended all over this portion of the county, and her success was very good. She continued practice for about eight or ten years, when she, with her husband, removed to Fayette county, where she died. Her son, John H. Martin, was the first school fund commissioner of Bremer county. It should be stated that during the time of her practice, Mrs. Martin became a homœopathist.

PHYSICIANS OF WAVERLY.

Those who have been heretofore mentioned could very properly be classed under this head, as they both lived within a short distance of Waverly. The first physician in the city, after it had been projected and platted, was Dr. Fisher. The first regular graduate in medicine was Dr. O. Burbank. Since that time the medical profession of Waverly has been represented by Drs. D. M. McCool, Butler Jesse Ward, Z. A. Bryant, J. C. Pomeroy, J. G. Smith, Jerome Burbank, Mrs. Betsey Egleston, William Boys, Miss Harriet M. Kallock and sister, and others whose names are not recalled.

The present representatives of this profession are Drs. Oscar Burbank, William Boys, J. C. Pomeroy, W. M. Barber, W. O. Clark, Carl Dermenden and D. M. Cool.

Dr. Fisher, who was the first physician to locate in Waverly, came to this place in the spring of 1854, and remained for about two years, when he went to some point not far from Dubuque, where, it is supposed, he still resides. Dr. Fisher was an odd looking genius, but a man of good motives; had never received much training in the profession, but gathered by observation what he knew of it. His practice was all alopathic.

Dr. Oscar Burbank was the next physician in Waverly, and was undoubtedly the first regular graduate of medicine in the county. He arrived on the 8th of September, 1854, at once commenced practice, which he has continued; is still an esteemed citizen of Waverly, and as a physician enjoys a lucrative practice. A sketch of the Doctor's life is here presented, as he is the oldest practicing physician in Bremer and several surrounding counties:

Oscar Burbank, M. D., was born in York county, Maine, on the 25th day of September, 1819. He is a son of Samuel and Lydia (Parks) Burbank. The Doctor was reared on a farm, and received his education in his native State. When about nineteen years of age he learned the trade of stair-building. Not liking the business, he entered the office of Dr. William Cornell, of Boston, Massachusetts, remaining in the same for three years, and, in 1848, graduated at Harvard University. From there he went to Lowell, where he commenced the practice of his profession. In 1849 he took a trip to the gold fields of California. A portion of the time he spent in the mines, and the balance practicing his profession. In the fall of 1851 he returned to Lowell, attending another course of lectures. In 1852 he went to Calias, Maine. In August, 1853, he emigrated to Cedar Rapid, Iowa, then a village of about 600 inhabitants. In September, 1854, he came to Bremer county, Iowa, locating in Waverly, where he has followed his profession since. At that time there was only twenty-one roofs in the town, counting sheds, dwelling houses, shops, etc. The Doctor is a member of the County Medical Society, and of the United States Association. In 1843 he married Miss Caroline E. Wait, a daughter of Amos Wait, of Western Vermont. Mr. and Mrs. Burbank are the parents of three children, two of whom are living—Carrie L., wife of Frank A. Lee, and Aldis W.

D. W. Cool, M. D., was born in Hamilton, Canada, on the 6th day of August, 1822, and is a son of Benjamin R. Cool, of Massachusetts, and Lois (Maxon) Cool, of Rhode Island. When four years of age, his parents emigrated to Erie county, Pennsylvania, remaining a short time, being engaged in hotel keeping, when he removed to Ashtabula county, Ohio, where he purchased a farm and embarked in farming. In the spring of 1841, he went to Cook county, Illinois, and located near Blue Island, where he took up a large tract of land. While on a trip to St. Louis, he was taken sick, and died in 1848. His mother died in Cook county, Illinois, 1876. The Doctor's early education was received in the common schools of Cook county. When eighteen years of age he commenced reading medicine with Dr. J. F. Daggett at Lockport, Illinois, remaining with him for one year. He then entered the office of Dr. David Brainard, of Chicago, where he remained seven years. His first course of lectures was at Rush Medical College in 1845 and 1846. In 1851 he graduated. The same year he commenced the practice of his profession, at Marengo, Illinois. The Doctor started out under difficulties to gain his professional education, working for his tuition and board, and for three years, with the exception of one week, never eat a warm meal. After leaving Marengo he went to a small town called

Franklinville, Illinois, where he stuck out his shingle, and engaged in his profession. Here he became acquainted with Miss Lydia Couse, a daughter of H. H. Couse, a native of New York. In the summer of 1855 he came to Waverly, then a wilderness, where he followed his profession until 1861, when he was appointed as assistant surgeon in the Third Iowa Volunteer Infantry. In April, 1862 he was commissioned as surgeon of the same. Having lost his health in active service, he was sent to Benton Barracks, St. Louis, where he remained for one year and a half, until the expiration of his term of service. After leaving the army he returned to Waverly, where he made an attempt to practice, but his health failed, and he went to Boston, where he regained his health. He returned to Chicago in 1870, where he followed his profession for twelve years. The Doctor is a member of the State Microscopical Society, of Illinois. He was, for a time, teacher of diseases of children, in the Chicago Medical College, of Chicago, Illinois.

About the latter part of the year 1855, a Doctor Butler arrived at Waverly and hung out his shingle as physician and surgeon. He was a young man, of ability, and his education was very fair. Business did not come to him, and after trying for six months he gave it up and left for Illinois.

Dr. Jesse Ward came from Independence, Buchanan county, a short time prior to the war, and after remaining a few months—but long enough to be convinced that waiting for practice was not earning a living—returned to his former home, and his whereabouts at present are unknown. He was an alopath in his practice, but was not a regular graduate.

The Rev. Z. A. Bryant next put in his appearance, his advent dating about 1865. He was a preacher of the Baptist faith; in medicine he followed the homœopathic faith, and came here from Bradford, in Chickasaw county, where he had been following his dual profession. In the ministry he made an earnest and sincere worker, but he only filled the pulpit occasionally, after he came here. He was the first homœopathic practitioner in Waverly, and at that time, the only one; he worked up quite an extensive practice. Dr. Bryant succeeded well in his profession, and made many friends throughout Bremer county. He left a couple of years since, removing to Mahaska county, Iowa, where he still resides.

William Boys, M. D., one of Waverly's prominent physicians, was born in Monroe county, Pennsylvania, April 28, 1843. He was the seventh son of Robert and Amora E. (Musch) Boys, there being eight children. When sixteen years of age he commenced reading medicine in the office of Dr. A. Reeves Jackson, now president of the Chicago Medical College of Physicians and Surgeons, where he studied for five years, spending two years in the University of Pennsylvania, where he graduated in the spring of 1864. In the same year he settled in Earlville, Delaware county, Iowa, and one year later, or, in 1865, came to Waverly, where he has followed his profession ever since. He has a very extended practice, and is considered one of the most successful physicians in the county. The Doctor is a member of the Bremer county, Iowa, State and American Medical Society; has been United States examining surgeon for pensions at Waverly, and is at this time president of the board of examining surgeons. In 1865, he married Miss Arabella Parker, of Bremer county. Dr. and Mrs. Boys are the parents of four children.

J. C. Pomroy, M. D., one of the enterprising business men of Waverly, embarked in the drug business in 1867. He carries a full line of drugs, medicines, paints and oils. In fact everything that is carried in a first class drug store. He was born in Franklin county, Vermont, and educated at the University at Burlington, Vermont. In 1857, he commenced reading medicine with Dr. George M. Hull. In 1859, he emigrated to Madison, Wisconsin, where he followed his profession for one year. In 1860, he came to Waverly, where he has followed his profession since. He was married in Waverly, in 1863, to Miss Clarrissa Dement. By this union there were two daughters—Martha and Maria. The Doctor is a member of the Iowa State Medical and County Societies. He is also a member of the Blue Lodge and Chapter of Masonry.

Dr. J. G. Smith was a native of New York and a medical graduate of Bellevue, where he had held positions which gained for him a large experience in the various branches of the profession. Socially he was a clever man, but drink proved his ruin. He married a daughter of Norman Clark and removed to DesMoines, where his wife died, and he returned to Waverly. He then married the widow of Judge Avery. She became deranged in mind and is now deceased. He is at present at Des Moines and has an extensive practice.

Dr. Jerome Burbank came to Waverly from Wisconsin just after the close of the rebellion, and commenced practice as a physician. For a time he enjoyed a very fair practice, and having been an army surgeon, his experience warranted it. He remained in Waverly about seventeen years, when he removed to Allison, in Butler county, where he is engaged in practice and running a drug store. A sketch of him appears in connection with the medical chapter of that county.

Dr. Betsey Egleston ranks among Waverly's doctors. She is a wife of C. E. Egleston and lives a short distance southwest of the city. She is a Botanic physician and has had thirty years' experience in her profession.

About 1875, Dr. Harriett M. Kollock came to Waverly from Illinois, and commenced, practice which she continued for two or three years. She was a regular physician and a graduate of the Medical Department of Ann Arbor. A sister, who was married, assisted Miss Kollock, and she also was a graduate of the same school. The former returned to Illinois.

Dr. J. N. Gross, dentist, is a native of Brighton, Canada West, and was born Aug. 21st, 1837. He is a son of Pitkin and Rebecca (Cory) Gross. The Doctor received his preparatory education at his home, and in 1862 began reading medicine with his father, who was a graduate of Dartmouth College, N. H. During the winter of 1862-3 he attended lectures at the Buffalo Medical College and graduated from that institution in 1865. The same year he began practicing at Brighton and there remained for nearly two years. In October of 1866 he located in Charles City, Iowa.

Abandoning the practice of medicine, he entered the office of Dr. A. H. Marsh, a brother-in-law, and began practicing dentistry. During the spring of 1869, Mr. Gross removed from Charles City to Osage, Mitchell county, where he remained about two years, and thence to Waverly, Bremer county, where he now resides, and is the oldest established dentist in the city. In 1872 he was united in marriage with Miss Mary E. Smith, daughter of John Smith, who is a pioneer of Bremer county. The Doctor is a member of the Masonic fraternity—the Blue Lodge and Chapter.

Wesley O. Clark, M. D., a practicing physician of Waverly, was born September 22d, 1858, in Clinton county, Ia. He is a son of Orlando B. and Amanda Wright Clark, who are natives of the State of Massachusetts. They settled in Clinton county during 1855 or '56. Wesley O. began the study of medicine at his home and in 1880 entered the office of Dr. M. H. Chamberlin, a brother in-law. February 23d, 1882, he graduated from the Hahnemann Medical College of Chicago, and soon after began the practice of his profession in Waverly. The Doctor is a young man, but being thoroughly versed in the art of medicine, is meeting with marked success. He is a member of the V. A. S. fraternity.

PHYSICIANS OF PLAINFIELD.

Among those who have represented the medical fraternity in Plainfield, are: Drs. Horace Nichols, L. S. Osborne, D. M. Lowell, and the present physician, Dr. W. J. Moody.

Dr. Horace Nichols was the first to locate here. He came in 1869, and hanging out his shingle, continued practicing until November, 1882, when he sold his good will to Dr. W. J. Moody.

Dr. L. S. Osborn practiced here six months in 1879.

Dr. D. M. Lowell came to Plainfield in 1877, and remained for one year, following his profession. He then removed to the Pacific coast.

Dr. W. J. Moody came to Plainfield in November, 1882, and purchased the good will of Dr. Nichols, as stated. Dr. Moody is still practicing, and is the only physician in the village.

Horace Nichols, M. D., a native of Burlington, Vermont, was born in 1832. When he was quite young his parents moved to Kane county, Illinois, and here the son passed his youth—helping his father on the farm in the summer time, and attending the district school during the winter season. Upon attaining his majority he began life for himself, and started out with the determination of obtaining an education to fit himself for the profession he has since so successfully followed. When twenty-two years of age, he began fulfilling that determination, by attending, for six months, a literary school at Aurora. During the winter of 1864 he attended the medical department of the Michigan State University, one term, and afterward entered Rush Medical College, of Chicago, graduating from that institution in the class of 1855-6. Previous to graduating, Dr. Nichols practiced medicine with Dr. McAlester, of Kingston, and after receiving his diploma he returned to that town, and continued practicing with Dr. McAlester until 1869, when he came to Bremer county, and began practice at Plainfield. From 1872 until

1876, the subject of this sketch held the office of county coroner, and at the present time is director and secretary of the school board. During the year 1855, Dr. Nichols was married to Miss Sarah J. Robinson, who died, November 15, 1878, leaving her husband and three children to mourn her loss. In 1879 he was joined in wedlock with Miss Nannie C. Nichols, a native of Kentucky. They are members of the Baptist Church, and are highly respected by all.

[NOTE.—Since the above was written it is learned that Dr. Nichols has left the county.]

W. J. Moody, a prominent physician of Bremer county, was born in Orleans county, New York, on the 4th of July, 1829. His father graduated at Dartmouth College in the class of 1822, and studied law with Judge Miller, father-in-law of William H. Seward. In 1833 he went to Detroit, Michigan, and was a member of the legislature when that territory was admitted as a State. He afterward moved to the town of Jackson, and during his residence there was judge of the circuit court. W. J. Moody entered the University of Michigan at Ann Arbor in 1852, graduating in the spring of 1854. In 1847 he entered the literary department of the University, but in his senior year was compelled to leave the college on account of ill health. Some time afterward, he went to Chicago and followed his profession for two years. However, at the end of that time he had a severe attack of hemorrhage of the lungs, and was obliged to give up his practice. Dr. Moody was in Chicago during the cholera epidemic of 1854-55, and that winter became an orphan—his father and mother dying of that dreadful disease, on the same day. Upon leaving Chicago he formed a co-partnership with Dr. John A. Kennecott, president of the Illinois State Horticultural Society and editor of the Horticultural Department of the *Prairie Farmer*, and in January of the year 1862, came to Bremer county, Iowa, and began the practice of his profession; since that time he has resided here and has enjoyed an extended patronage. He was married, November 4, 1857, to Miss U. C. Williams, a native of Orleans county, New York. Six children have been born to them, five of whom are now living.

PHYSICIANS OF SUMNER.

The medical profession in Sumner is represented by Drs. J. N. Wilson and Z. Z. Byrant, who are both also engaged in the drug business.

Dr. J. N. Wilson was born in Wyandotte county, Ohio, February 17, 1838. He was the son of N. W. Wilson, who was engaged in the practice of medicine until his death, at the age of eighty-seven years. Dr. J. N. Wilson has a brother who is the leading physician in Linn county. He remained in Ohio until he was thirteen years of age, when his parents moved to Linn county, Iowa, staying there two years, and then went to Buchanan county, same State. His literary education was received in the University of Iowa, and his medical education at the University of Iowa and the College of Physicians and Surgeons in Keokuk, Iowa, graduating in 1872. Previous to this he commenced the study of medicine, in 1858, under his father, and practiced some with his brother, of Troy Mills, Iowa. After attending one year in college he came to Sumner and located. Dr. Wilson was the first regular physician to locate in this place. He was for two years engaged in the drug business, here, having erected a building for that purpose, but his practice became so extensive, that in order to give it his entire attention, he disposed of his interest in the store, and devoted his whole time to his chosen profession. He was largely instrumental in organizing Lookout Masonic Lodge, of which he was one of the charter members, also first Master; he also assisted in organizing the A. O. U. W., of which he was first trustee, and has been the examing physician since its organization. He is the present county coroner, and has held the office for two terms. Dr. Wilson is one of those jovial, good-natured men that always make friends and rarely ever an enemy. He was married September 1, 1872, to Miss C. M. West, a native of Ohio.

Dr. Z. Z. Bryant was born in Courtland county, New York, April 7th, 1839; was the son of Z. A. and M. A. Bryant, his father was a native of Pennsylvania; his mother, of Massachusetts. The father has been a physician for the past 45 years and is still practicing at Eddyville, Ia., where his mother died in October, 1882, at the age of 61 years. When he was about 15 years old his parents moved to Illinois, where they remained one year and then went to Bradford, Ia. In 1857, at the age of 18, he commenced the study of medicine, having received an academical education. In 1861 he went into the army in Company B, Seventh Iowa Infantry; while in the army he took a course of lectures in the Holmboldt Medical College at St. Louis. Retiring from the army in December, 1863, he became associated with his father in the practice of medicine. About 1867, he went into the drug business for one and a half years, in connection with his practice. Soon after, he came to Waverly, remaining, however, but a short time, when he went to Clarksville, Butler county, and engaged in the drug business, besides following his profession. There he continued until he was burned out, losing all he had. In 1872 he came to Sumner, where he has been in the practice of medicine ever since, with the exception of the time spent in attending lectures. In 1878-9-80-1, his medical education not being completed, he entered the Hahnemann Medical College in Chicago, graduating in the class of '79 and '80. He is a member of the Iowa State Medical Society, also of the Third District Medical Association. He is also a registered pharmacist, by the Iowa Pharmacy Asoociation. Dr. Bryant has been Chairman of the Township Central Republican Committee, also Captain of the militia, Company G, Iowa National Guards. Is one of the charter members of Lookout Lodge 395, A. F. & A. M., and took an active part in establishing the lodge in Sumner, and is the present Master. In the spring of 1882 he engaged in the drug business in company with Martin Robish. He is local correspondent for the *Waverly Independent*, *Waverly Republican*, *Dubuque Daily Times*, and *West-Union Gazette*. He was married in 1870 to Miss Margaret H. Hairiman, a native of New Hampshire. They have four children—Gracie M., Charles Z., Mabel H., and Roy H.

PHYSICIANS IN JANESVILLE.

The first physician to locate in Janesville was Dr. Joel Loveland. At present the profession is represented by Drs. Joel Loveland, D. S. Bradford, S. B. Tompkins and C. B. Davis.

Dr. J. Loveland, one of the oldest physicians in Bremer county, is a native of St. Lawrence county, New York, and was born June 13, 1827. He is a son of R. and Lucy (Shaw) Loveland. His father died in St. Lawrence county, in 1844, and his mother in Janesville, Iowa, twenty years later. The doctor was reared on a farm and obtained his early education in the common schools of his native State. At the age of twenty-two he entered the office of Dr. Z. B. Bridges, of Ogdensburg, New York, and there spent eighteen months. He then attended the Michigan University at Ann Arbor. In the spring of 1853, he located in Dubuque, Iowa, and during the fall of the same year, settled in Janesville, Bremer county, where he has since followed his profession. For many years his practice extended over a large section of country. He was married, January 13, 1859, to Miss Lucy J. King, a daughter of Elias King, of St. Lawrence county, New York. They have had five children, three of whom are now living— Fannie, Casper and Wilbert. The wife and mother died in 1875. She was a member of the Presbyterian church, and her death was deeply mourned.

Dr. D. S. Bradford, a practicing physician of Janesville, was born in Schoharie county, New York, December 4th, 1840. He is a son of Sylvester and Polly (Schofield) Bradford. His father was a minister of the gospel. The Doctor is the oldest of nine children, and was reared and educated in his native State. At the age of twenty-three he began reading medicine, and at the same time, working to educate himself. In 1864 he entered the Albany University, graduating from there in 1866. After receiving his diploma, he began practice at Rock City, and there remained until 1869. In the spring of that year he came to Bremer county, Iowa, locating in Janesville, where he now enjoys an extended practice. Dr. Bradford is a charter member of the Bremer county Medical Association. He is a Master Mason, being a member of Equity Lodge, No. 131, Janesville.

Dr. S. B. Tompkins is a homœopathic physician and surgeon.

Dr. C. B. Davis is a physician and veterinary surgeon.

TRIPOLI PHYSICIANS.

Here the profession is represented by Dr. Phil. Redeman. He was born in Germany, February 24, 1835. He received a good education in his native country, and when twenty-one years of age, came to America, and settled in Gutenburg, Clayton county, Iowa. In 1862 he began the study of medicine with Doctor Winter. In September, of that year, he enlisted in Company E, Ninth Wisconsin Volunteers, but was transferred, at Fort Scott, Kansas, to the Army Medical Corps, and worked at the general hospital, at Leavenworth, and the post hospital at Fort Leavenworth. He was honorably discharged at the last named place, in 1864, and returning to Clayton county, he continued the study of medicine. During the winter of 1855-6, he graduated at Rush Medical College, Chicago. Upon receiving his diploma he located at Gutenburg, and in 1870, came to Bremer county. After practicing four years in Waverly, he moved to Tripoli, where he has since enjoyed an extended practice. In 1860 he was married to Miss E. Seaman, who bore him three children— William, Augusta, and David—and died in 1867. In 1869 he was married to Matilda Bithner. They have three children —Bertha, Robert and Charles.

DENVER, OR JEFFERSON CITY.

The only physician in this place is Dr. R. A. Dunkelberg. He is a native of Germany; but some years ago came to America and graduated as a physician and surgeon, from the Ann Arbor Medical College, in 1881. He is a member of the Bremer County Medical Society.

BREMER COUNTY MEDICAL SOCIETY

During the summer of 1880, a number of meetings were held among the representatives of the profession, with the object of forming an association of this kind. Finally a meeting was held at the office of Dr. O. Burbank, in Waverly, on the 6th of October, 1880, at which the society by the above name was organized. The following gentlemen were present at this meeting, viz: Oscar Burbank, J. C. Pomeroy, William Boys, J. N. Wilson, Horace Nichols, William M. Barber, C. B. Thompson, D. S. Bradford and W. J. Moody. The officers elected were as follows: Dr. O. Burbank, president; J. N. Wilson, vice-president; W. J. Moody, secretary. This resulted in the permanent organization of the society.

The rules and regulations adopted, fixed the time of meeting on the first Wednesday of every month. The officers for the second year were as follows: W. M. Barber, president; Horace Nichols, vice-president, and Oscar Burbank, secretary. At the third annual meeting these officers were re-chosen.

The object of the society was declared to be "the advancement of medical knowledge, the uniformity of medical ethics, the promotion of harmony and fraternity in the profession, the protection of the interest of its members, the promotion of all measures adapted to the relief of suffering." The society is auxilary to the State Medical Society, and is governed by the national code of medical ethics. The condition of membership, as fixed by this code, is that the applicant has graduated from some recognized medical college. At each meeting of the society, a paper upon some suitable subject is always read and discussed.

The present members of the Bremer County Society, together with the place and date of their graduation, are as follows:

Oscar Burbank, M. D., graduated from Harvard, in 1848.

Jesse N. Wilson, Keokuk Medical College, 1875.

W. J. Moody, Ann Arbor, 1874.

William M. Barber, Ann Aarbor, 1864.

Daniel S. Bradford, Albany Medical College, 1866.

William Boys, University of Pennsylvania, 1864.

J. C. Pomeroy, Castleton Medical College, 1860.

Daniel M. Cool, Rush Medical College, 1861.

W. E. Whitney, Rush Medical College, 1881.

R. A. Dunkelberg, Ann Arbor, 1881.

Three who were members of the society have left the county, namely: Jerome Burbank, who is now in Allison, Iowa; Horace Nichols and C. B. Thompson. Of the present members of this society, the following named are also members of the State Medical Society: Oscar Burbank, Jesse N. Wilson, William Boys, and J. C. Pomeroy. Two of whom are also members of the American Medical Association, William Boys and Oscar Burbank.

CHAPTER X.

POLITICAL.

The political history of a Nation, State or county is always one of great interest. Especially is this true of a free land, where, in the eyes of the law, all are equal, and the most lowly—even the rail-splitter or the treader of the tow-path—can attain the highest honor that can be bestowed upon an American citizen. It is only a question of merit, and where this exists it must, sooner or later, push aside the chaff and rise to the top, where it will be respected and rewarded. How many instances of this have occurred in the political history of America? The greatest men who have graced the halls of Congress, from the time of Washington to the present, are examples of it, and this must continue through time to come, so long as equality and democratic principles are supported by the masses. The policy of the nation justly encourages political ambition, and we watch with satisfaction those in the arena, as, step by step, they pass from the humble walks of life, and ascend the ladder of fame. Much as it may be denied, nearly every true citizen has a political ambition, and even if he does not reach the highest pinnacle, the possibility exists that he or his children may.

There is an excitement about a political campaign which all enjoy, and although personalities are often indulged in, yet as a general thing, all yield gracefully to the verdict of the people, as represented by the majority vote, and submit to "the power behind the throne." There are always issues which arise, affecting the country, and which often lead to bitter struggles for supremacy. In this chapter is sketched a synopsis of the issues as far as possible, and the local complexion of the various campaigns since the organization of the county, is given. Following this is presented the official vote of every general election.

Bremer county was organized in 1853, but as already stated it had been connected with Buchanan county for judicial purposes, and had a township organization. The first election was held in 1851, at the residence of John H. Messinger, in Jefferson township, all the citizens of the county going there to vote. Only township officers were elected. In those days there was not visible in political campaigns the excitement or eagerness to win at the expense of others, but it seemed that more of the feeling of the brotherhood of man existed, and while contests may have been sharp and pointed the enmity and bitterness of to-day was unknown.

In 1853, Bremer county proper, came into existence, H. A. Miles being a prominent worker in effecting the organization. The first election of county officers was held at the house of Frederick Cretzmeyer in August, 1853. There was not much excitement in regard to the election, nor could there well be, as there was only eighty votes polled in the county.

Another election was held on the 3d of April, 1854. At this election the records show that only three officers were voted for—State Superintendent, School Fund Commissioner and Drainage Commissioner. The candidates for School Fund Commissioner were John H. Martin, and George W. Baskins, the former receiving 95 votes and the latter 84; John Wright also receiving two votes. Edward Tyrrell received 53 votes and was declared elected Drainage Commissioner.

At the fall election of this year, more interest was wrought up. The offices to be filled were of greater importance. Heman A. Miles, and Edward Tyrrell were candidates for Clerk of Court, the former whig and the latter democrat. Mr. Miles was elected by a majority of 24. There were two candidates for County Attorney, W. P. Harmon and Phineas V. Swan. Mr. Harmon came off victorious. A. A. Case and J. Stufflebeam were candidates for the honor of being the first coroner. The former recieved a majority of 53. From the appearance of the vote it would seem that there were no party lines drawn. At this time the republican party had no existence, and the field was left to the whigs and democrats, the latter usually coming out victorious.

The August election in 1855, was, in reality, the first election in which political questions were considered, and was the greatest contest yet experienced by the new county. The candidates for county judge were Jeremiah Farris on the democratic ticket, and Henry Morehouse on the whig. Farris had the advantage of being the incumbent and was elected, after a decisive struggle, by a majority of nine. Morehouse was a Methodist preacher and was the largest man in the county, weighing three-hundred pounds, but this did not save him. William B. Hamilton and James Queen were candidates for treasurer and recorder, the former whig and latter democrat. Hamilton ran ahead of his ticket and was elected by a majority of fifty. Joseph G. Ellis, a democrat, was elected to the office of sheriff over Nelson M. Smith. Richard Titcomb was elected coroner without much opposition, Moses

Lehman and J. G. Ellis each receiving one vote. Israel Trumbo was elected surveyor. The highest vote polled was for the office of county judge—348—a gratifying increase.

Former issues dividing political parties had disappeared in 1856, and new issues were rapidly arising. The whig party had ceased to exist, and on its ruins had been erected, two other parties, one having for its central truth, opposition to the further extension of African slavery, and the other that American born citizens must rule America. These parties embraced, of course, many of the members of the old democratic party. The American party, not being opposed to slavery, or at least, making no opposition to it, either in the States in which it existed or the newly formed territories, where it had been made subject to admission by the repeal of the Missouri Compromise, had become a powerful body in the South, with many adherents in the North.

The republican party, basing its claims upon its advocacy of freedom in the territories, was not permitted to exist in the Southern States, and was of necessity, confined to the Northern States.

The first convention of the newly-organized republican party, in this State, was held at Iowa City, February 22, 1856, placing a ticket in the field for State officers, and adopting a platform in accordance with the principles of equal rights to all men, and a firm opposition to any further extension of human slavery. The democratic convention met at the State Capitol, June 26, and nominated a ticket, and adopted a platform in harmony with that adopted by the national convention, at Cincinnati, the same year. The nominations made at the national convention of James Buchanan, for President, and John G. Breckenridge, for Vice-President of the United States, were enthusiastically endorsed. In Bremer county the newly-organized republican and democratic parties had regular tickets in the field, to be voted on at the August election. The republicans won by a majority of from fifty to seventy-five. H. A. Miles was re-elected clerk of the courts, over G. S. Matthews, by a small majority; Phineas V. Swan was elected prosecuting attorney over G. C. Wright. The proposition for holding a constitutional convention carried by a majority of twenty-six.

For the campaign of April, 1857, the democrats rallied all their forces, and the election was very close. The office of county assessor, which had been created to take the place of the same offices in the townships, was the only important office to be filled. The republicans again carried, by a very slight majority. Simeon F. Shepard was elected over O. P. Haughawout, by one vote. George W. Ruddick, was elected prosecuting attorney, over G. C. Wright, by a majority of fifty-five.

The election held in the fall of 1857, was also very close, and followed an exciting campaign. The candidates for county judge were, George W. Maxfield and Thomas Downing; the former a democrat and the latter a republican. One incident connected with the campaign is worthy of relating. The Germans at that time, as at the present, held the balance of power, and were much opposed to extravagance, and the taxation that must follow. One of the active workers in the democratic party was John C. Hazlett, a merchant of Waverly. In the heat of the canvas, he went into the wealthy and thickly settled German localities of Maxfield and Franklin townships, and spread the report that it was the intention of Thomas Downing, in case he was elected, to build, for the county, a solid marble court house. This story spread among the Germans, who exagerated it to a "solid marble court house, with silver-plated doors, knobs and window sills," etc. The election passed off, the returns from Franklin came in slowly, and for several days it was supposed that Downing was elected; but finally the returns from Franklin were received, throwing the majority on the other side, and Maxfield was declared elected. Shortly afterward the township by that name was organized, and named in honor of the Judge.

The October election, in 1857, was for Governor, Lieutenant-Governor, and Representative. Ralph P. Lowe, republican candidate for Governor, received a majority of seventy-nine votes, over Benjamin M. Samuels, democratic candidate. Orrin Faville, republican candidate for Lieutenant-Governor, received a majority of 83, over George Gillaspie. W. P. Harmon was elected Representative.

The office of county superintendent was created by the new constitution, adopted in 1857, and candidates were voted for at the April election. A. K. Moulton, republican, and G. C. Wright, democrat, were in the field for the office, and the former elected by a majority of 112. He had the honor of being the first superintendent of common schools of Bremer county.

It should have been stated that at the April election in 1857, the question of giving the right of suffrage to negroes was voted upon, and was defeated by a majority of 138, the vote standing 114 for, to 252 against. It would seem from this vote that there were 327 voters in the county who were non-committal upon the subject. The proposition was defeated in both the county and State.

At the October election in 1858, only two officers were to be elected—clerk of courts and coroner. Louis Case was elected clerk, and W. W. Norris, coroner, without much of a fight.

In the fall of 1859, there were both State and county officers to be elected, and the contest was sharp in Bremer county. S. J. Kirkwood, afterward known as the "War Governor," of Iowa, was the republican, and A. C. Dodge, the democratic candidate for Governor. Mr. Dodge received a majority of twenty-one in the county, out of a total vote of 855. The democrats carried the county by a small majority, electing their entire county ticket. This left Louis Case, clerk of courts, the only republican officer in the court house.

The country was now becoming deeply moved over questions which stirred the popular heart as none had ever before. The storm had been gathering ever since the repeal of the Missouri compromise; the struggles in Kansas had deeply intensified the feelings of the people of the North, and John Brown's attempt upon Harper's Ferry had been skillfully managed, so as to arouse the fury of the people of the South. That the Territories of the United States should be forever consecrated to freedom was the solemn determination of a large majority of the people of the North and that the boundaries of the institution of slavery should not be further enlarged. The South seeking the perpetuation of the institution of slavery, by means of enlarged political power, determined that its territory should not be restricted, but should be extended. The questions dividing parties were chiefly sectional, and pointed directly to war. At this stage of public sentiment, the republican party met in national convention at Chicago, for the purpose of placing in the field candidates for the office of President and Vice-President. The names of Seward, Lincoln, Chase, Blair, and Bates were proposed for the chief office. In the convention it was plain to see who was the favorite of the lookers-on. Every mention of Lincoln's name was received with cheer after cheer. Three ballots were taken. On the last Mr. Lincoln received a majority of the whole number of votes, and was made the unanimous choice of the convention, amidst the most intense excitement. Hannibal Hamlin, of Maine, was selected as the candidate for Vice-President.

The Democratic National Convention met at Charleston, South Carolina, April 23, 1861. The friends of Stephen A. Douglas were active in urging his claims to the nomination for the presidency, the delegates from the Northern States being instructed to use all honorable means to attain that end. His claims were stoutly contested by the leaders of the democracy of the South, and it was evident some time before the convention assembled, that it would be difficult to come to an agreement, especially as the rule of the democratic national conventions required a two-thirds vote to nominate. The convention remained in session ten days, at the expiration of which time no nominations were made. After taking fifty-seven ballots, it was found impossible for any candidate to receive a two-thirds vote of the entire body, as many Southern delegates had withdrawn. An adjournment to Baltimore, June 19th, was agreed upon. The convention met pursuant to adjournment; but even here no agreement could be reached between the factions. After a six days' meeting, Stephen A. Douglas was nominated for President, and Benjamin Fitzpatrick, of Alabama, for Vice-President. The nomination of Douglas was received with great enthusiasm in the North. Mr. Fitzpatrick declining, Herschel V. Johnson, of Georgia, was substituted, and he accepted the nomination.

That portion of the democratic convention which seceded, held a convention, June 23d, and nominated John C. Breckenridge, of Kentucky, for President, and Joseph Lane, of Oregon, for Vice-President. A "Union" convention was also held, at which John Bell, of Tennessee, was nominated for President, and Edward Everett, of Massachusetts, for Vice-President.

With four Presidential candidates in the field, the exciting questions growing out of the institution of slavery, and the threats of secession by a portion of the South, in the event of the election of Lincoln, tended to make the campaign one of great excitement. "Wide-Awake" clubs, on the part of the republicans, and organizations of "Hickory Boys" on the part of Douglas democrats, tended to increase the excitement. Large and enthusiastic meetings were held by each party, in all the leading towns and cities throughout the land, and n many of the smaller villages. The names of the "Rail-Splitter, and the "Little Giant" became household words, and evoked the greatest enthusiasm.

The Republican State Convention of Iowa met in Iowa City, May 23d, nominated a State ticket, adopted a platform in harmony with the action of the national convention at Chicago, endorsed its nominations, and favored rigid economy in State matters. The democratic convention met at Des Moines, July 12th, nominated a State ticket and passed resolutions endorsing Douglas and Johnson. The "Union" ticket was strongly condemned.

In Bremer county the fight was waged as earnestly as in any county in the State, and political feeling ran high on all sides. There was only one county officer to be elected—clerk of the courts—consequently there was little to detract from the great national questions. The year before the county had gone democratic, but this year Lincoln received a majority of ninety-two, and the whole republican ticket ranged about the same. The total vote was 1,017. The candidates for the county office mentioned were Louis Case, republican, and William Pattee, democrat, the former was re-elected by a majority of 115.

The war for the Union was in progress during the political campaign of 1861, and issues, growing out of the war, were forming. The republicans were first to meet in convention, assembling at Des Moines in July, they put in nomination a State ticket and adopted a platform heartily supporting the government in its assertion of the right to coerce, denouncing the doctrine of secession, maintaining the supremacy of the Constitution, and declaring in the most forcible language, that the Rebellion should be put down at any cost.

The Democratic State Convention passed resolutions also unequivocally condemning the action of the seceding States, but declaring it to be the legitimate results of the teaching of the "irrepressible conflict," and also denying *in toto* the right of the government to perpetuate the Union by force of arms. State sovereignty was endorsed, and the opposite doctrine declared to be fraught with disastrous consequences. The campaign in this county afforded but little interest, the all-exciting questions of the war filling the mind of every voter. A light vote was polled but party lines were drawn very close, and the republicans elected their entire ticket.

The Union army had met with several reverses during the year 1862, and a gloomy feeling pervaded the minds of the people, having its effect upon the canvass for State officers. The democrats met in convention at Des Moines, and adopted a platform in which they declared in favor of using all constitutional means for the suppression of the rebellion, and opposed to any scheme of confiscation and emancipation; opposed to a suspension of the writ of *habeas corpus*, declaring the superiority of the white over the black race, and opposed to the purchase of the slaves. The republicans, in their platform adopted at Des Moines, resolved that it was the duty of every man to help maintain the government; condemned the course of secession sympathizers, and asked all favorable to giving the national administration honest support, to co-operate with them. In this county the vote was lighter than the year previous, but this was somewhat increased by the "soldiers' vote," the soldiers being allowed to vote in the field and send the returns home. Henry C. Moore, republican, was elected clerk of the court over H. W. Perry, democrat, by a majority of 195. This was the average majority for the republican ticket.

The democracy of the State met in convention at Des Moines, July 8, 1863, and nominated a ticket for State offices. Questions growing out of the war still afforded issues between parties. The writ of *habeas corpus* had been suspended by the President, martial law had been declared in some of the States not in rebellion, and the Proclamation of Emancipation had been issued. These measures the democracy in convention, by resolution opposed, while the republican convention, which convened June 17, favored.

In Bremer county both republicans and democrats had full county tickets and a soldiers' ticket was in the field with D. F. Goodwin for county judge; and Barnes Thompson for treasurer and recorder, making three candidates for both of those offices. A fair vote was polled and the entire republican ticket elected by majorities ranging above 300.

In 1864 Abraham Lincoln was re-nominated by the republicans, and associated with him on the ticket was Andrew Johnson, the Union Governor of Tennessee.

The democrats put in nomination, Gen. George B. McClellan, for the Presidency and George H. Pendleton, of Ohio, for the Vice-Presidency.

The republicans of Iowa held a convention at Des Moines, July 7, and adopted a platform endorsing the re-nomination of Abraham Lincoln, and paying high tributes of praise to the loyal soldiers and soldiers' wives, who were daily making sacrifices that the Union might be saved. The Democratic State Convention met at Des Moines, July 16, selected a State ticket, but adopted no platform.

A peace convention, however, was held at Iowa City, August 24, which adopted resolutions denouncing the war and its further support, and denying the equality of the negro with the white man. In this county both parties had a full county ticket in the field and the republicans elected every officer, by majorities ranging from 480 to 500, about 1,000 being the total vote.

In 1865 the republicans were first in the field, meeting in convention at Des Moines, June 14th, nominating a ticket and adopting a platform. The Union Anti-Negro Suffrage party met at the capital, August 23d, and nominated a ticket and adopted a platform, in which they resolved to sustain the administration of Andrew Johnson; that they were opposed to negro suffrage, that the soldiers of the late war deserved well the sympathies of their countrymen. The democrats met in convention the same day, but made no nominations, the party supporting the "Soldiers' Ticket," as it was known. In this county the parties were somewhat divided on local issues. The democrats made no nominations, but after the republican convention had been held, some of the dissatisfied called a soldiers' convention and nominated a soldiers' ticket, endorsing all the nominees of the republicans, except for county treasurer and surveyor. For the first, they placed W. V. Lucas against William P. Reeves, the regular nominee, and the former was elected. For surveyor they placed M. F. Gillett against H. S. Hoover, and the latter was elected. N. M. Smith for sheriff, and C. B. Roberts for county superintendent, had no opposition. Allen Holmes, soldiers' candidate, was elected representative over M. Farrington, the republican nominee.

The campaign of 1866 was fought on the issue of reconstruction in the southern States. The republicans in convention resolved that the people who subdued the rebellion, and their representatives in Congress, had the right to re-organize the States that had been in the rebellion. This was denied by some of the republicans, and the entire democratic party. The conservative republicans, or those who were opposed to congressional action, met in convention and nominated a State ticket. The democratic convention adopted a platform, nominated two candidates, and resolved to support the ticket of the conservatives. The republican State officers received a majority of about 715 in this county. The republican county ticket was also elected by a trifle larger majority. The total vote was about 1,400. The general issues dividing the parties in 1867 were about the same as in 1866. In this county the republicans were victorious.

The year 1868 brought with it another presidential campaign. The Republican National Convention met in Chicago, and placed in nomination Ulysses S. Grant, the victorious Union General, associating with him, Schuyler Colfax, of Indiana. The Democratic National Convention nominated Horatio Seymour and Francis P. Blair, Jr., for President and Vice-President. The financial question began to be a leading issue, especially with reference to the payment of the bonds in coin or greenbacks, the republicans favoring the payment in coin, the democrats opposing. The latter also, by resolution, favored the abolition of the national banking system, and the substitution of United States notes for those of national banks. This was opposed by the republicans.

The campaigns of 1869, 1870, and 1871, were devoid of much interest, and were but repetitions of the results of previous years, as a glance at the official vote in this chapter will show.

In 1872, the movement known as the liberal republican had a large influence, politically, having virtually dictated the democratic nomination for the presidency, and the platform of principles on which the campaign against the republican party was dictated. The liberal republicans were those connected with the republican party who were opposed to any extreme measures in the reconstruction of the Southern States, and who believed the time had come when past issues should be forgotten and new issues formed, that the hand of reconciliation should be offered to the South, and a united country working together to build up the waste places in the South. Many of the most able men in the republican party, including Horace Greeley, Charles Sumner, Lyman Trumbull, John M. Palmer, and others, united in the movement. In May, a National Republican Convention was held in Cincinnati, which nominated Horace Greeley for President, and B. Gratz Brown for Vice-President. The democracy in convention ratified the nominations of Greeley and Brown, and adopted the same platform. The republicans re-nominated President Grant, and associated with him on the ticket, Henry Wilson, of Massachusetts, for Vice-President.

The disaffection among the democrats in consequence of the nomination of Horace Greeley, a life-long enemy, politically, was so great that a third ticket was nominated at the head of which was Charles O'Conner, the distinguished lawyer of New York. The democrats and liberal republicans met in State convention and nominated a State ticket composed of two democrats and three liberal republicans, and passed resolutions endorsing Greeley. The liberal ticket in this county did not meet with much encouragement, the vote given it being only that number usually polled by democratic nominees. The presidential vote stood: Grant 1,490; Horace Greeley 463; Charles O'Connor 7. The total vote was about 1,960, and the republican majority was about 1,080, on an average.

The question of capital *vs.* labor, engaged the attention of the people in 1873. The Republican State Convention met at Des Moines, June 25th, and after nominating candidates, adopted resolutions declaring against monopolies, and urging that the several States should carefully restrict the powers of railroad companies and other monopolies. Class legislation was also demanded. The democratic party of the State made no regular nomination this year but generally supported the anti-monopoly ticket. A convention was held at Des Moines, August 12th, nominated candidates and adopted resolutions declaring that the old party organizations were no longer useful, denouncing corruption in government affairs, and urging the necessity of political honesty. In this county the general aspect of affairs remained unchanged, the republicans electing their whole ticket by slightly decreased majorities, averaging about 900; the total vote was about 1734.

A convention was called to meet at Des Moines, June 24, 1875, to be composed of democrats, anti-monopolists and liberal republicans. Assembling, a ticket was nominated, headed by Shepherd Lefler for Governor, and a platform of principles adopted covering the principal ground of belief of the three elements represented. The republicans met in convention and nominated S. J. Kirkwood for Governor. A temperance convention was also held, and Rev. John H. Lozier nominated for Governor. The latter received three votes in this county. The republicans elected all local officers except one. There were three tickets in the field—republican, democratic and people's. Amon Fortner, candidate for sheriff, was opposed by many farmers on account of his connection with the board of trade, and the people's candidate, L. S. Hanchett, was elected by a majority of 148. Joseph G. Ellis was the democratic candidate for sheriff. For county superintendent, there were three candidates, Sadie E. Martin, E. C. Bennett, and H. H. Burrington, and the latter, the republican nominee, was elected.

The election in 1876 was for National, State and county officers. Rutherford B. Hayes and William A. Wheeler were the republican candidates for President and Vice-President, while Samuel J. Tilden and Thomas A. Hendricks received the nomination of the democratic party for the same offices. Peter Cooper was the nominee of the independent party, or greenbackers, for President. The hard times which began in 1873 had a perceptible effect upon this campaign. The democratic party, which for some years had been acting upon the defensive, when not allied with some other political body, now assumed the aggressive, and under the banner of "Tilden and Reform," forced the republicans in defensive. On the part of the democrats, the campaign was boldly conducted, and the result is well known. The greenbackers held two conventions in Iowa, at the first of which they adopted a platform containing their principal tenets, and nominated a State ticket. In this county the republican State ticket was carried by a majority of 978. The presidential candidates received: Hayes, 1,737; Tilden, 757; Cooper, 51. The county ticket carried by about the same majority as did the State ticket. The total vote was 2,546.

In 1877 State tickets were nominated by democrats, republicans, greenbackers and prohibitionists. Bremer county, as usual, elected the republican ticket by a majority ranging from six hundred, down.

Greenbackers, democrats and republicans nominated State tickets in 1878. Subsequently a fusion was effected between the democrats and greenbackers, and a portion of the nominees of each of their State tickets were chosen as the candidates of both parties. There were two local tickets in the county, fusion and republican, and the latter carried the entire ticket except for recorder, for which Henry Kasemeier, the fusion candidate, was elected. The majorities were all close as will be seen by the official vote, the fusion candidates making a hard fight for supremacy. M. Farrington was this year a candidate for register of State land office on the fusion ticket, and received 1,136 votes in this county.

The campaign of 1879 was opened on the 12th of May, by the democrats meeting in convention and nominating a State ticket headed by H. H. Trimble for Governor. A lengthy platform was adopted. The greenbackers were next in the field, their ticket being headed by Daniel Campbell for Governor. The republicans met and nominated John H. Gear for Governor, together with a full State ticket. Lastly, the prohibitionists met and placed in nomination, George T. Carpenter, of Mahaska, for Governor. Mr. Carpenter declining, D. R. Dungan, of Eldora, was substituted. The Republicans nominated a straight ticket, while the opposition combined upon a "People's State Ticket," composed of independent republicans, greenbackers and democrats.

In county affairs this was one of the most remarkable campaigns in the political history of the State. Upon the State ticket, the republicans were successful by a majority of about 774, but local issues split the county ticket in a manner never before equalled. There were three tickets for the county offices, in the field, and an independent candidate for representative. L. S. Hanchett was elected sheriff, Herman Rust, auditor, and D. C. Chamberlin, county superintendent on the republican ticket, and E. J. Dean was elected representative, independent, The latter's candidacy and election was remarkable. He had been pushed to the wall financially, had been tried for perjury, kept in jail for about 200 days, and then sent to the lunatic asylum. He had been a resident of Bremer county for twenty years, and was, therefore, well known. After being discharged from the lunatic asylum, Mr. Dean came back to the county, and it 1877 ran for representative, without success. When the campaign of 1879 opened, he began work early, and as he was without money he was obliged to conduct the canvass alone and in the best way he could. He began lecturing in all the school houses, on the street corners, and anywhere he could get an audience. Not being able to afford a conveyance, he walked from place to place, and foot-sore and hungry, he would stop by the way-side and partake of his meager fare of cheese and crackers. His campaign, unlike the one of 1877, was aggressive, his theme being almost wholly the persecution he claimed he had undergone. There were three other candidates in the field, J. K. L. Maynard, the republican nominee; Allen Sewell, the democratic nominee; and Isaac High, the greenback nominee; but Dean came out independent in the strictest sense, nominated by no party, and, at the beginning, supported by but few friends. No one feared his candidacy; the other parties did not notice him; the press ridiculed him and often he was roundly abused in his own political meetings. But he persevered, usually answering a sneer with the calm statement: "*I will carry eleven out of the fifteen townships.*" The election day drew near, and "Crazy" Dean, as he had been dubbed in ridicule, preserved his same placid appearance. Tickets were to be printed, and this threw a damper, for a time upon even Dean.

He finally went to Daniel Fichthorn of the *Independent*, and laid the case before him, and that gentleman generously, with no thought of pay, ordered them struck off. A livery was then hired and Dean was told to get in and get the tickets into the various townships, the donor never imagining anything more than a joke could come from it. The night before election a public demonstration was made in honor of "Crazy" Dean, by the working men of Waverly and vicinity, and three bands, torch-light procession, cheers, speeches, etc., enlivened the occasion. But even then the opposing parties considered the matter as a huge joke. Election day passed off, and the returns disclosed the astonishing fact that Dean—"Crazy" Dean, whom everyone had ridiculed, and laughed at, had been elected representative over the head of the three other candidates by a majority of 358. It is not for the historian to speculate as to the astonishment, these are the facts. Mr. Dean is now publisher of the *Waverly Tribune*, and a biography of him appears in that connection.

The general campaign for 1880 began quite early, especially among the aspirants for office and their friends. The preliminary canvass for the nomination grew quite warm, as both republicans and democrats were alike confident that they would succeed in the national struggle. James A. Garfield received the Republican nomination for President. Winfield S. Hancock was chosen to lead the democracy. Gen. James B. Weaver was nominated by the greenbackers. The canvass was pushed with vigor, the democratic and republican parties using their utmost endeavors to be successful. The national party, under the lead of Weaver, also endeavored to increase its votes, Mr. Weaver making speeches in more than half the States of the Union. The first State convention held in Iowa this year was by the republicans, at Des Moines, April 7th. The platform adopted consisted of three resolutions, the first demanding that the candidates nominated at Chicago by the National Republican Convention, should be of national reputation for ability; second, that James G. Blaine be the choice of the republicans of the State, and third, instructing the delegates to the national convention to vote for Blaine. The greenbackers met at Des Moines, May 11, and adopted a platform re-asserting their demands for the abolition of the national banks, the reduction of the army, the limitation of Chinese immigration, the reduction of salaries, and the payment of the national debt in greenbacks. The democrats met at Des Moines, September 2, nominated a ticket, and adopted a platform endorsing Hancock and English, and the national platform adopted at Cincinnati. In this county the republicans carried the State ticket by a majority of about 800. The entire vote polled was about 2,574.

The election of 1881 was for State and county officers, and the three leading parties had tickets in the field. In this county the republicans elected their entire ticket except representative and sheriff, James Adair, democrat, being elected sheriff by a majority of 302. The total vote polled was 2,264. L. S. Hanchett, people's ticket, was elected representative over J. M. Roberts, republican, and E. J. Dean, independent.

In the campaign of 1882, the republicans were successful. (See official vote of that year.)

OFFICIAL VOTE.

The following is the official vote of Bremer county for every general election from 1854 to the present time, so far as could be ascertained from the records in the auditor's office. It will be appreciated as a means of reference:

Election, April 3, 1854.

State Superintendent.
James D. Eads, Dem..................160—145
I. I. Stewart, Whig................... 15

School Fund Commissioner.
John H. Martin....................... 95—11
George W. Baskins.................... 84
John Wright.......... 2

Drainage Commissioner.
Edward Tyrrell....................... 56

Election, August 7, 1854.

Clerk of the District Court.
H. A. Miles........................... 98—24
Edward Tyrrell...................... 74

Prosecuting Attorney.
W. P. Harmon........................ 102—36
P. V. Swan........... 66

Coroner.
A. A. Case........................... 89—53
J. Stufflebeam....................... 36

Election, April 2, 1855.

Drainage Commissioner.
Rufus C. Gates................. ....61—50
E. M. Wright...........................11
A. Gaines 1

Election, August 6, 1855.

County Judge.
Jeremiah Farris, Dem..................178— 9
Henry Moorehouse, Whig............169
Samuel Moorehouse.................... 1

Treasurer and Recorder.
William B. Hamilton, Rep.............190—50
James Queen, Dem......................140

Sheriff.
Joseph G. Ellis, Dem..................187—29
Nelson M. Smith, Rep..................158

Coroner.
Richard D. Titcomb, Rep..............279
Moses Lehman, Dem.................... 1
J. G. Ellis............................... 1

Surveyor.
Israel Trumbo, Rep...................206—76
Joel Loveland, Dem...................130
John H. Messinger..................... 2
Henry Morehouse....................... 1

Election, August 4, 1856.

Clerk of the District Court.
H. A. Miles, Rep......................248—46
G. S. Matthews, Dem..................202

Prosecuting Attorney.
P. V. Swan............................236—77
G. C Wright...........................159

Coroner.
A. T. Owen, Rep......................259—69
Isaac H. Goodenow, Dem..............190

Secretary of State.
Elijah Sells, Rep.....................262—66
George Snyder, Dem..................196

Auditor of State.
John Pattee, Rep.....................260—67
James Pollard, Dem..................193

State Treasurer.
M. L. Morris, Rep....................263—58
George Paul, Dem....................195

Attorney-General.
Samuel H. Rice, Rep.................260—65
James Baker, Dem...................195

Congress.
Timothy Davis, Rep..................258—59
Stephen Lefler, Dem................199

State Senator.
Aaron Brown, Rep...................266—62
G. A. Kellogg, Dem.................194

Representative.
E. R. Gillett, Rep..................266—57
William Pattee, Dem................199

Constitutional Convention.
For convention......................122—26
Against convention.................. 96

Election, April 6, 1857.

Prosecuting Attorney.
G. W. Ruddick, Rep.................334—55
G. C. Wright, Dem..................279

County Assessor.
Simeon F. Shepard, Rep.............317—1
O. P. Haughawout, Dem.............311

Drainage Commissioner.
Lafayette Walker, Dem.............318—10
Matthew Rowen, Rep...............308

Coroner.
H. F. Beebe, Rep...................325—25
L. B. Ostrander, Dem..............300

Election, August 3, 1857.

County Judge.
George W. Maxfield, Dem...........358—17
Thomas Downing, Rep..............341

Sheriff.
Joseph G. Ellis, Dem..............379—68
W. R Bostwick, Rep...............311

Recorder and Treasurer.
William B. Hamilton, Rep.........366—38
C. C. Allen, Dem..................328

Surveyor
H. S. Hoover......................376

Coroner.
John Acken........................357—21
Andrew Daily.....................336

HISTORY OF BREMER COUNTY.

Constitution.
For.................................338—47
Against.............................291
Against striking out word white......352—138
For striking out word white..........114

Election, October 13, 1857.
Governor.
Ralph P. Lowe, Rep.................307—79
Ben M. Samuels, Dem................228

Lieutenant-Governor.
Orrin Faville, Rep..................309—83
George Gillaspie, Dem...............226

Representative.
W. P. Harmon, Rep..................305—82
A. G. Case, Dem....................223

Election, April 5, 1858.
County Superintendent.
A. K Moulton, Rep..................307—112
G. C Wright, Dem...................195

Election, October 12, 1858.
Clerk of the District Court.
Louis Case, Rep....................378—55
George S. Matthews, Dem............323

Coroner.
B F. Goodwin, Rep..................367—44
W. W. Norris, Dem..................323

Election, October 11, 1859.
County Judge.
George W. Maxfield, Dem............512—176
Thomas Downing, Rep................336

Recorder and Treasurer.
W. W. Norris, Dem..................485—120
L. J. Curtiss, Rep.................365

Sheriff.
J. G. Ellis, Dem...................481—113
N. M. Smith, Rep...................368

County Superintendent.
G. Y. Sayles, Dem..................456—75
H. H. Burrington, Rep..............382

Surveyor.
A. S. Funston, Dem.................435—22
H S. Hoover, Rep...................413

Coroner.
John Mohling, Dem..................438—37
T. V. Axtell, Rep..................401

Drainage Commissioner.
J. N. Bemis, Dem...................458—80
H. W. Griffith, Rep................378

Governor.
Augustus C. Dodge, Dem.............438—21
Samuel J. Kirkwood, Rep............417

Lieutenant-Governor
L. W. Babbit, Dem..................438—22
N. J. Rusch, Rep...................416

Judge of Supreme Court.
T. S. Wilson, Dem..................443
Charles Mason, Dem.................440
C. C. Cole, Rep....................440
R. J. Lowe.........................412

State Senator.
L. L. Ainsworth, Dem...............447—45
Aaron Brown, Rep...................402

Representative.
W. C. Mitchell, Dem................469—92
George W. Ruddick, Rep.............377

Election, November 6, 1860.
President.
Abraham Lincoln, Rep...............544—92
Stephen A. Douglas, Dem............452
John C. Breckenridge, Dem..........18

Congress.
William Vandevere, Rep.............541—67
Ben M. Samuels, Dem................474

Secretary of State.
Elijah Sells, Rep..................539—64
J. M. Corse, Dem...................475

State Auditor.
George W. Maxfield, Dem............508—2
J. W. Cattell, Rep.................506

State Treasurer.
J. W. Jones, Rep...................540—65
J. W. Ellis........................475

Register Land Office.
A. B. Miller, Rep ....541—66
Patrick Robb, Dem....................475

Attorney-General.
C. C. Nourse, Rep....................540—112
William McClintock, Dem............428

Judge Supreme Court.
G. G. Wright.........................542—67
J. M. Elwood........................475

Clerk of District Court.
Louis Case, Rep......................563—115
William Pattee, Dem.................448

Election, October 8, 1861.

Governor.
Samuel J. Kirkwood, Rep............562—222
William H. Merritt, Dem.............340

Lieutenant Governor.
J. R. Needham, Rep.................560—220
Lauren Dewey, Dem..................340

Judge Supreme Court.
Ralph P. Lowe......................566—233
J. M. Elwood.......................333

Representative.
J. O. Hudnutt, Rep..................621—341
Thomas Lashbrook, Dem 280

County Judge.
Matthew Rowen, Rep ....563—266
G. C. Wright, Dem..................297

Treasurer and Recorder.
Caleb Morse, Rep...................519—134
George W. Maxfield, Dem...........385

Sheriff.
J. H. Eldridge, Rep.................560—236
J. H. Haughawout, Dem.............324

County Superintendent.
George R. Dean, Rep................607—410
H. D. Perry, Dem...................297

Surveyor.
H. S. Hoover.......................641—372
A. S. Funston......................269

Coroner.
J. S. Jenkins, Rep..................580—253
Devillo Holmes, Dem................327

Drainage Commissioner.
W. P. Harmon.......................574—250
J. W. Matthews.....................324

Election, October 14, 1862.

Secretary of State.
James Wright, Rep..................472—181
Richard Sylvester, Dem.............291

State Auditor.
J. W. Cattell, Rep..................472—181
John Browne, Dem...................291

State Treasurer.
William H. Holmes, Rep.............472—181
Samuel L. Larah, Dem...............291

Attorney-General.
Charles C. Nourse, Rep.............472—181
Benton J. Hall, Dem................291

Register Land Office.
J. H. Harvey, Rep..................472—183
Frederick Gottschalk, Dem..........289

Congress.
William B. Allison, Rep............477—219
Dennis A. Mahoney, Dem............258

Judge District Court.
Elias H. Williams..................477—476
C. L. Miller....................... 1

District Attorney.
Milo McGlathery....................478—471
G. C. Wright....................... 7

Member Board of Education.
George H. Stevens, Rep.............478—477
W. W. Griffith..................... 1

Clerk District Court.
H. C. Moore, Rep...................474—195
Horace W. Perry, Dem..............279

Soldiers' Vote.
H. C. Moore Rep.................... 93
Louis Case, Rep.................... 18
H. W Perry, Dem................... 5

HISTORY OF BREMER COUNTY.

Election, October 13, 1863.

Governor.
William M Stone, Rep .... 669—360
James M. Tuttle, Dem 309

Lieutenant-Governor.
Enoch W. Eastman, Rep .... 673—364
John F. Duncomb, Dem 309

Judge Supreme Court.
John F. Dillon, Rep .... 670—361
Charles Mason, Dem 309

State Senator
L. W Hunt, Rep .... 673—363
John Acken, Dem 310

Representative
John E. Burke, Rep .... 637—321
G. C. Wright, Dem 316

County Judge.
George W. Ruddick, Rep .... 536—223
Devillo Holmes, Dem 313
D. F. Goodwin 119

Treasurer and Recorder.
Caleb Morse, Rep Nominee .... 506—228
A. S. Funston, Dem 278
Barnes Thompson, Rep 157

Sheriff
N. M. Smith, Rep .... 558—226
J. G. Ellis, Dem 332

County Superintendent.
George R. Dean, Rep .... 561—248
Y. A. Acken, Dem 313

Surveyor.
H. S. Hoover, Rep .... 666—282
Porter Bement, Dem 382

Coroner.
Matthew Rowen, Rep .... 656—341
J. W. Matthews, Dem 315

Soldiers' Vote.
John E. Burke 72
G. C Wright 4
A. S. Smith 1

Soldiers' Vote.
George W. Ruddick 63
Louis Case 7

L. F. Godwin 5
David Maxfield 4
John E. Burke 1

Soldiers' Vote.
Caleb M. Cole 70
B. Thompson 6
Old Man Geddes 1

Soldiers' Vote.
N. M. Smith 77
Joseph Ellis 5

Soldiers' Vote.
H. S. Hoover 74
Norman Miller 1

Soldiers' Vote.
George R. Dean 59
G. C. Wright 1

Soldiers' Vote.
Matthew Rowen 59
Elias Grove 1

Election, November 4, 1864.

President.
Abraham Lincoln, Rep .... 738—481
George B. McClellan, Dem 257

Supreme Judge.
Chester C. Cole, Rep .... 738—479
Thomas M. Monroe, Dem 259

Secretary of State.
James Wright, Rep .... 740—482
John H. Wallace, Dem 258

State Auditor.
John A. Elliott, Rep .... 739—481
E. C. Hendershott, Dem 258

State Treasurer.
William H. Holmes, Rep .... 739—481
J. B. Lash, Dem 258

Attorney-General.
Isaac L. Allen, Rep .... 740—482
Charles M. Dunbar, Dem 258

Congress.
William B. Allison, Rep .... 737—477
B. B. Richards, Dem 260

HISTORY OF BREMER COUNTY.

District Judge.
William B. Fairfield, Rep.............703—444
C. W. Foreman, Dem..................259

District Attorney.
John E. Burke, Rep....................693—441
M. P. Rosecrans, Dem.................252

Clerk District Court.
H. C. Moore, Rep.....................749—508
William Smith, Dem...................241

Recorder.
Louis Case, Rep......................737—499
Charles C. Moulton, Dem 238

Soldiers' Vote.
H. C. Moore..........................110
N. B. Gardner........................ 1
J. C. Williams....................... 1

Soldiers' Vote.
Louis Case...........................110
R. F. Little......................... 1
Asbury Collins....................... 1

Election, October 10, 1865.
Governor.
William M. Stone, Rep................775—558
Thomas H. Benton, Jr., Dem...........217

Lieutenant-Governor.
Benjamin F. Gue, Rep.................790—635
W. W. Hamilton, Dem..................155

Supreme Judge.
George G. Wright, Rep................794—646
H. H. Trimble, Dem...................148

State Superintendent.
Orrin Faville, Rep...................797—653
J. W. Sennett, Dem...................146

Representative.
Allen E. Holmes......................491—89
Matthew Farrington...................452

County Judge.
O. F. Avery..........................922—921
Matthew Rowen........................ 1

County Treasurer.
W. V. Lucas, Ind. Rep................528—138
William P. Reeves, regular nominee...390

Sheriff.
N. M. Smith..........................904

County Superintendent.
C. B. Roberts........................904

Surveyor.
H. S. Hoover.........................565—181
M. F. Gillett........................384

Coroner.
J. J. Merrill........................486—72
J. H. Eldridge.......................414
G. M. Harker......................... 2

Drainage Commissioners.
E. J. Messinger......................884—883
John Mischler........................ 1

Election, October 8, 1866.
Secretary of State.
Ed. Wright, Rep......................1,059—715
S. G. Vananda, Dem................... 344

State Treasurer.
S. E. Rankin, Rep....................1,060—716
George W. Stone, Dem................. 344

State Auditor.
James A. Elliott, Rep................1,060—716
Robert W. Cross, Dem................. 344

Register Land Office.
C. C. Carpenter, Rep.................1,021—680
Linus P. McKinnie, Dem............... 341

Attorney-General.
F. E. Bissell, Rep...................1,060—715
W. Ballinger, Dem.................... 345

Supreme Court Reporter.
E. H. Styles, Rep....................1,059—715
A. Stoddard, Dem..................... 344

Clerk Supreme Court.
C. Lindeman, Rep.....................1,057—710
Fred Gottschalk, Dem................. 347
H. C. Moore..........................   1

Congress.
William B. Allison, Rep..............1,049—694
Reuben Noble, Dem.................... 355

HISTORY OF BREMER COUNTY.

Clerk District Court.
H. C. Moore, Rep. .... 1,077—755
B. F. McCormack, Dem. 322

Sheriff.
D. W. Cowen, Rep. .... 1,078—757
C. Runyan, Dem. 321

Recorder.
E. C. Dougherty, Rep. .... 1,027—675
F. W. Foster, Dem. 352

Election, October, 1867.

Governor.
Samuel Merrill .... 1,000—520
Charles Mason 480

Lieutenant-Governor.
D. M. Harris 999
John Scott 482

Judge of the Supreme Court.
Joseph M. Beck, Rep. .... 999—513
John H. Craig, Dem. 483

Attorney-General.
Henry O'Conner, Rep. .... 996—510
W. T. Barker, Dem. 486

Superintendent of Instruction.
D. Franklin Wells, Rep. .... 1,000—516
M. L. Fisher, Dem. 484

Senator, Thirty-sixth District.
W. G. Donan, Rep. .... 957—436
George Lindley, Dem. 521

Representative.
D. P. Walling, Rep. .... 994—508
William Smith 486

County Judge.
O. F. Avery .... 1,016—553
A. Whitcomb 463

County Treasurer.
W. V. Lucas, Rep. .... 986—510
George S. Mathews, Dem. 476

Surveyor.
H. S. Hoover .... 1,003—525
A. S. Funston 478

Sheriff.
C. M. Kingsley .... 944—427
G. D. Lamb 517

Superintendent.
J. R. Hall .... 1,000—519
Mark Hunt 481

Coroner.
G. W. Nash .... 991—812
Hugh Hill 179

For poor farm, to cost $5,000 944
Against   "   "   " 261

Election, November 3, 1868.

Ulysses S. Grant, Rep. .... 1,470—912
Horatio Seymour, Dem. 538

Secretary of State.
Ed. Wright, Rep. .... 1,468—928
David Hammer, Dem. 540

State Auditor.
John A. Elliott, Rep. .... 1,468—928
H. Dunkavey, Dem. 540

State Treasurer.
Samuel E. Rankin, Rep. .... 1,467—927
L. McCarty, Dem. 540

Register Land Office.
Cyrus C. Carpenter, Rep. .... 1,468—928
A. D. Anderson, Dem. 540

Attorney-General.
Henry O'Conner, Rep. .... 1,467—927
J. E. Williams, Dem. 540

Congress.
William B. Allison, Rep. .... 1,450—900
William Mills, Dem. 550
Lewis Thomas 4

District Judge.
William B. Fairfield, Rep. .... 1,448—891
Cyrus Foreman, Dem. 557

District Attorney.
Irving W. Card, Rep. .... 1,449—899
W. A. Stowe, Dem. 550

Circuit Judge.
G. W. Ruddick, Rep..................1,449--903
Robert N. Matthews, Dem.......... 546

Clerk District Court.
Marquis F. Gillett, Rep..............1,411--825
J. E. Busby, Dem.................... 586

Recorder.
E. C. Dougherty, Rep................1,453--913
H. D. Perry, Dem................... 540

Election, November, 1869.

Governor.
Samuel Merrill, Rep.......................970
George Gillaspie, Dem....................325

Lieutenant-Governor.
M. M. Walden, Rep.......................971
A. P. Richardson, Dem....................324

Supreme Judge.
John F. Dillon............................971
W. F. Brennan............................325

State Superintendent.
A. S. Kissell..............................948
H. O. Dayton.............................175

Senator, Forty-fourth District.
R. B. Clarke..............................886
William Pattee............................400

Representative.
O. C. Harrington, Rep......................943
William Smith, Dem........................328

Auditor.
Louis Case, Rep...........................941
John Warring, Dem.........................346

Treasurer.
W. V. Lucas, Rep..........................908
Levi Nichols, Dem.........................372

Sheriff.
C. M. Kingsley, Rep........................864
A. Whitcomb, Dem..........................244

Superintendent.
C. S. Harwood, Rep........................936
H. Shaver, Dem............................347

Surveyor.
S. H. Wallace, Rep.........................869
A. S. Funston, Dem.........................320

Coroner.
C. O. Paquin, Rep..........................974
J. Biederman, Dem..........................320

Election, October, 1870.

Secretary of State.
Ed. Wright, Rep.........................1,128
Charles W. Doerr, Dem..................... 383

State Auditor.
John Russell, Rep........................1,127
W. W. Garner, Dem......................... 383

State Treasurer.
S. E. Rankin, Rep........................1,076
W. C. James, Dem.......................... 361

Attorney-General.
Henry O'Conner, Rep.....................1,128
H. M. Martin, Dem......................... 383

Register Land Office.
Aaron Brown, Rep........................1,128
D. F. Ellsworth, Dem...................... 382

Reporter Supreme Court.
E. H. Stiles, Rep........................1,127
C. H. Bane, Dem........................... 383

Revising the Constitution.
For 492
Against................................... 524

Congress, Third District.
W. G. Donan, Rep........................1,124
J. T. Stoneman, Dem....................... 387

District Judge.
George W. Ruddick, Rep..................1,493

Clerk Courts.
M. F. Gillett, Rep....................... 1,115
George Stephenson, Dem.................... 375

Recorder.
John Rowray, Rep........................1,485

Supervisors.
S. H. Curtis, Rep.......................1,040
M. Farrington, Rep........................ 918

HISTORY OF BREMER COUNTY.

John Chapin, Rep...................1,104
R. Morehouse, Rep...................591
Hiram Lester, Dem...................418
N. Johnston, Dem....................305

Shall there be Five Supervisors.
For................................361
Against............................811

Election, October, 1871.

Governor.
C. C. Carpenter, Rep..............1,212
J. C. Knapp, Dem....................403

Lieutenant-Governor.
H. C. Bulis, Rep..................1,215
M. M. Ham, Dem......................400

Supreme Judge.
J. G. Day, Rep....................1,212
J. F. Duncombe, Dem.................400

State Superintendent.
Alonzo Abernethy, Rep.............1,214
Ed. Mumm, Dem.......................400

State Senator.
J. E. Burke.......................1,110
L. H. Weller........................367

Representative.
O. C. Harrington....................633
James A. Skillen....................963

Circuit Judge.
R. G. Reiniger, Rep...............1,219
C. A. L. Roszell, Dem...............401

Auditor.
S. H. Morse, Rep..................1,065
Henry Lease, Jr., Dem...............540

Treasurer.
L. L. Lush, Rep.....................648
George Morehouse, Ind...............970

Sheriff.
Jas. S. Conner, Rep.................959
H. S. Halbert, Dem..................632

Surveyor.
H. S. Hoover, Rep.................1,565

Superintendent.
H. H. Burrington, Rep...............986
E. C. Bennett, Dem..................624

Coroner.
Dr. J. M. Ball, Rep.................959
J. M. Deyoe, Dem....................634

Supervisor.
John Chapin, Rep....................912
John Kehe, Rep......................702

Election, November 5, 1872.

President.
Ulysses S. Grant, Rep.........1,490—1,028
Horace Greeley, Lib.................462
Charles O'Conner, Dem.................7

Secretary of State.
Josiah T. Young, Rep..........1,500—1,032
E. A. Guilbert, Lib.................468
Charles Baker, Dem....................1

State Auditor.
John Russell, Rep.............1,499—1,030
J. P. Cassady, Lib..................468

State Treasurer.
William Christy, Rep..........1,499—1,031
M. J. Rohlfe, Lib...................438
D. B. Bears, Dem......................1

Register Land Office.
Aaron Brown, Rep..............1,500—1,031
Jacob Butler, Lib...................469
David Sheward, Dem....................1

Attorney-General.
M. E. Cutts, Rep..............1,482—994
A. G. Case, Lib.....................488

Congress.
H. O. Pratt, Rep..............1,476—973
A. T. Lush, Lib.....................503

District Judge.
G. W. Ruddick, Rep............1,506—1,029
William A. Lathrop, Dem.............477

Circuit Judge.
R. G. Reiniger, Rep...........1,502—1,023
W. C. Stansbury, Dem................479

District Attorney.
L. S. Butler, Rep.................1,480—978
J. W. Woods, Dem................ 502

Clerk District Court.
A. H. McCracken, Rep............1,507—1,485
W. P. Reeves..................... 22
Scattering........................ 9

Recorder.
J. W. Rouray, Rep................1,984—1,983
William Lashbrook................ 1

County Supervisor.
S. H. Curtiss, Rep ....1,378—800
James Adair, Dem.................. 578
E. Ferry.......................... 13

Coroner.
Horace Nicholls, Rep.............1,492—1,000
P. H. Redeman, Dem............... 492

Election, October 14, 1873.

Governor.
Cyrus C. Carpenter, Rep..........1,365—968
J. G. Vale........................ 397

Lieutenant-Governor.
Joseph Dysart, Rep...............1,370—952
C. E. Whiting..................... 418

Judge Supreme Court.
J. M. Beck, Rep..................1,368—947
B. J. Hall, Dem................... 421

State Superintendent.
Alonzo Abernethy, Rep............1,374—1,317
D. W. Prindle..................... 57

State Senator.
A. J. Felt.......................1,002—241
Hiram Bailey...................... 761

Representative.
Louis Case, Rep...................1,222
David High, Dem................... 556

County Auditor.
S. H. Morse, Rep..................1,301
Louis Oberdorf, Dem............... 468

County Treasurer.
George Morehouse, Rep.............1,790

Sheriff.
James S. Conner, Rep.............1,120—460
Joseph G. Ellis, Dem.............. 660

County Superintendent.
H. H. Burrington, Rep............1,127—582
James Harwood, Dem................ 545

Surveyor.
H. S. Hoover, Rep................1,728—1,722
William Lashbrook, Dem............ 6

Coroner.
Horace Nicholls, Rep.............1,408—1,050
James Hooker, Dem................. 358

Board of Supervisors.
Marvin Potter, Rep................ 895—18
Adin Terry, Rep. on Dem. ticket... 879

Election, October, 1874.

Secretary of State.
Josiah T. Young, Rep.............1,078—745
David Morgan...................... 331

State Auditor.
Buren R. Sherman, Rep............1,080—347
Joseph M. King.................... 333

State Treasurer.
William Christy, Rep.............1,080—772
Henry C. Harges................... 308
J. W. Barnes...................... 22

Register State Land Office.
David Secor, Rep.................1,081—752
Robert H. Rodeamal................ 329

Attorney General.
M. E. Cutts, Rep ....1,029—648
John H. Keatly.................... 381

Clerk Supreme Court.
Edward Holmes, Rep...............1,080—752
George W. Ball.................... 328

Reporter Supreme Court.
John S. Runnells, Rep............1,079—750
James M. Weart.................... 329

Congress.
H. O. Pratt, Rep.................. 793—251
John Bowman....................... 542
Fred Neidert...................... 28

HISTORY OF BREMER COUNTY.

Clerk District Court.
A. H. McCracken, Rep............1,401—1,398
H. S. Munger...................... 3

County Recorder.
H. S. Munger, Rep................ 822—243
Floyd J. McCaffree, Dem.......... 579

Board of Supervisors.
A. L. Stevenson................... 221
Robert Brodie..................... 135

Election, October, 1875.

Governor.
Samuel J. Kirkwood, Rep..........1,493—806
Shepherd Lefler, Fusion............ 687
John H. Lozier, Temp............. 3
D. W. Lyons...................... 2

Lieutenant-Governor.
Joshua G. Newbold, Rep....1,520—848
Emmett B. Woodward............ 672

Judge Supreme Court.
Austin Adams....................1,526—860
William J. Knight 666

Superintendent Public Instruction.
Alonzo Abernethy, Rep............1,525—858
Isaiah Doane..................... 669
Sadie E. Martin................... 1

Representative.
Louis Case, Rep..................1,645—1,112
Andrew J. Lowe.................. 533

County Auditor.
Herman Rust, Rep................2,132—2,121
S. H. Morse...................... 11

County Treasurer.
George Morehouse, Rep...........2,170—2,168
H. Brandenburg.................. 2

Sheriff.
L. S. Hanchett, People's Ticket.... 818—148
Amon Fortner, Rep............... 670
Joseph G. Ellis, Dem 659

County Superintendent.
H. H. Burrington................. 860—104
E. C. Bennett..................... 756
Sadie E. Martin 494

County Surveyor.
H. S. Hoover, Rep................1,530—895
Andrew S. Funston, Dem.......... 635

Coroner.
Horace Nichols, Rep..............1,537—901
Philip Reideman, Dem............ 636

Election, November, 1876.

President.
Rutherford B. Hayes, Rep........ 1,737—980
Samuel J. Tilden, Dem............ 757
Peter Cooper, Gr.................. 51

Secretary of State.
Josiah T. Young, Rep ....1,738—976
John Stubenrauch, Dem........... 762
A. McCready, Gr.................. 51

State Treasurer.
George W. Bemis, Rep...........1,739—978
Wesley Jones, Dem............... 761
George C. Fry, Gr................. 51

State Auditor.
Buren R. Sherman, Rep...........1,738—976
William Gronewig, Dem........... 762
Leonard Brown, Gr............... 51

Register Land Office.
David Secor, Rep.................1,738—976
N. C. Ridenour, Dem.............. 762

Attorney-General.
John F. McJunkins, Rep..........1,728—976
J. C. Cole, Dem................... 752

Judge Supreme Court.
William H. Severs, Rep ....1,738—977
Walter S. Hayes, Dem............. 661
Charles Negus, Gr................. 22
O. Jones, Gr...................... 38

Superintendent Public Instruction.
C. W. VonCoelin, Rep............1,739—1,688
J. A. Nash, Gr.................... 51

Congress.
N. C. Deering, Rep...............1,741—937
Cyrus Foreman, Dem............. 804

HISTORY OF BREMER COUNTY.

District Judge.
George W. Ruddick, Rep........1,501—512
C. A. L. Roszell, Dem............ 980

Circuit Judge.
R. G. Reineger, Rep..............1,732—930
James M. Elder, Dem............. 802

District Attorney.
J. B. Cleland, Rep...............1,739—932
John J. Cliggett, Dem............ 807

Clerk of the Courts.
A. H. McCracken, Rep.........1,556—985
J. H. Mickel, Dem................ 385
J. B. Barber, People's 571

County Recorder.
H. S. Munger, Rep..............1,468—390
H. C. Kasemeier, Dem 1,078

Election, October. 1877.

Governor.
John H. Geer, Rep..............1,180—598
J. P. Irish, Dem.................. 582
David P. Stubbs, Gr.............. 195
Elias Jessup, Tem................ 1

Lieutenant-Governor.
Frank T. Campbell, Rep..........1,199—628
W. C. James, Dem................ 571
A. H. McCready, Gr.............. 194

Judge Supreme Court.
James G. Day, Rep..............1,205
H. E. J. Boardman, Dem......... 567
John Porter, Gr................... 195

Superintendent Public Instruction.
Carl W. VanCoelin, Rep.........1,203—635
G. D. Culleson, Dem............. 568
S. T. Ballard, Gr................. 194

Senator.
Aaron Kimball, Rep..............1,013—87
L. H. Weller, Dem................ 926

Representative.
J. K. L. Maynard................. 859—262
Thomas Fountain.................. 597
Benjamin Archer.................. 364
E. J. Dean....................... 121

County Treasurer.
G. W. Nash......................1,124—364
James Skillen.................... 760

Sheriff.
L. S. Hanchett, Rep.............1,261—611
A. T. Thull...................... 650

County Auditor.
Herman Rust, Rep...............1,940—1,938
E. R. Carr....................... 2

County Superintendent.
D. C. Chamberlin, Rep..........1,050—157
Isaac High....................... 893

Surveyor.
H. S. Hoover, Rep..............1,182—582
L. E. Goodwin, Dem.............. 600

Coroner.
Horace Nichols, Dem............1,107—1,097
P. H. Rideman................... 10

Election, October 8, 1878.

Secretary of State.
J. A. T. Hull, Rep..............1,275—107
E. M. Farnsworth................1,168
T. O. Walker, Dem............... 35

State Auditor.
B. R. Sherman, Rep..............1,278—78
Joseph Eiboeck, Fusion..........1,200

State Treasurer.
George W. Bemis, Rep...........1,275—107
M. L. Devin, Fusion.............1,168
E. D. Ferris, Dem................ 36

Register Land Office.
J. K. Powers, Rep..............1,274—138
M. Farrington, Fusion...........1,136
F. S. Bardwell, Dem.............. 33

Attorney-General.
J. F. McJunkin, Rep............1,276—235
John Gibbons, Fusion............1,041

Judge Supreme Court.
J. H. Rathrock, Rep............1,275—113
Joseph Knapp, Fusion............1,162

Reporter Supreme Court.
J. S. Rummel's, Rep..............1,275—72
J. B. Elliott, Fusion...............1,203

Clerk Supreme Court.
E. J. Holmes, Rep................1,304—139
Alex Runyon, Fusion..............1,165

Congress.
N. C. Deering, Rep...............1,225—417
L. H. Weller, Fusion................ 808
W. V. Allen, Dem................... 393

Clerk of the Courts.
C. H. Cooper, Rep................1,289—167
J. B. Barber, Fusion..............1,122

County Recorder.
Henry Kasemeier, Fusion..........1,390—322
H. S. Munger, Rep................1,068

Election, October 14, 1879.

Governor.
John H. Gear, Rep................1,382—721
H. H. Trimble, Dem................. 661
Dan Campbell, Gr................... 509
D. R. Dungan, Pr................... 75

Lieutenant-Governor.
Frank T. Campbell, Rep...........1,472—827
J. A. O. Yeoman, Dem............... 645
M. H. Moore, Gr.................... 511

Judge Supreme Court.
J. M. Beck, Rep..................1,446—769
Reuben Noble, Dem.................. 677
M. H. Jones, Gr.................... 502

Superintendent Public Instruction.
C. W. VanCoellin, Rep............1,430—782
Irwin Baker, Dem................... 648
J. A. Nash, Gr..................... 549

Representative.
E. J. Dean, Ind..................1,251—378
J. K. L. Maynard, Rep.............. 873
Allen Sewell, Dem.................. 260
Isaac High, Gr..................... 186

County Auditor.
Herman Rust, Rep................1,763—1,066
William Glattley, Gr............... 691

County Treasurer.
G. W. Nash, Rep..................1,225—284
M. S. Wright, Dem.................. 941
Jonathan Freeman, Gr............... 411
M. S. B Wright, Dem................ 58

Sheriff.
L. S. Hanchett, Rep..............1,296—104
James Adair, Dem.................1,192
E. F. Temple, Gr................... 98

County Superintendent.
D. C. Chamberlin, Rep............1,310—490
L. C. Oberdorf, Gr................. 820
I. Bice, Dem....................... 371
L. Oberdorf........................ 102

Surveyor.
H. S. Hoover, Rep................1,407—497
L L. Goodwin, Gr................... 910

Coroner.
W. S. Mickle, Rep................1,335—709
Hugh Hill, Dem..................... 626
J. N. Wilson, Gr................... 550

Election, November 2, 1880.

President.
James A. Garfield, Rep...........1,548—840
Winfield S. Hancock, Dem........... 708
James B. Weaver, Gr................ 212
Neal Dow, Pr....................... 5

Secretary of State.
John A. T. Hull, Rep.............1,551—846
A. B. Keath, Dem................... 705
George M. Walker, Gr............... 312

State Auditor.
W. V. Lucas, Rep.................1,512—797
Charles J. Baker................... 715
G. V. Swearingen, Gr............... 317

State Treasurer.
Edwin H. Conger, Rep.............1,547—840
Martin B. Blim..................... 707
M. Farrington, Gr.................. 308

Register Land Office.
James K. Powers, Rep.............1,549—843
Daniel Dougherty, Dem.............. 706
Thomas Hooker, Gr.................. 305

HISTORY OF BREMER COUNTY.

Attorney-General.
Smith McPherson, Rep............1,549—843
Charles A. Clark, Dem..........706
W. A. Spurrier, Gr..............306

District Judge.
George W. Ruddick, Rep..........1,425—336
John Cliggett, Dem..............1,089

Circuit Judge.
Robert G. Reineger, Rep..........1,547—564
C. Foreman, Dem................983

District Attorney.
John B. Cleland, Rep............1,572—624
A. C. Ripley, Dem..............948

Congress.
N. C. Deering, Rep.............1,373—848
J. S. Roqt, Dem................625
E. J. Dean, Independent..........513
William B. Doolittle............135

Clerk of the Courts.
Charles H. Cooper, Rep..........1,668—779
J. H. Muffly, Dem..............889

County Recorder.
Henry Kasemeier, Rep..........1,864—1,172
Henry Rathe, Dem..............692

Coroner.
J. N. Wilson....................2,529

Election, October, 11, 1881.
Governor.
Buren R. Sherman, Rep..........1,426—886
L. G. Kinne, Dem..............540
D. M. Clark, Gr................301

Lieutenant-Governor.
O. H. Manning, Rep............1,431—893
J. M. Walker, Dem..............538
J. H. Holland, Gr..............306

Judge Supreme Court.
Austin Adams, Rep..............1,432—892
H. P. Hendershott, Dem..........540
H. W. Williamson, Gr............305

Superintendent of Public Instruction.
John W. Akers, Rep............1,427—924
Walter H. Butler, Dem...........503
Mrs A. M. Swain, Gr.............303

State Senator.
C. A. Marshall.................1,205—146
M. F. Gillett..................1,059

Representative.
L S. Hauchett, People's..........921—187
J. M. Roberts, Rep.............734
E. J. Dean, Ind................575

County Treasurer.
S. F. Baker, Rep...............1,541—825
M. M. Watkins, Dem.............716

County Auditor.
Herman Rust, Rep...............1,488—745
L. C. Haase, Dem...............743

Sheriff.
James Adair, Dem...............1,275—302
J.L. Leonard, Rep..............973

County Superintendent.
D. C. Chamberlin...............1,158—83
G.P. Linn, Dem.................1,075

County Surveyor.
H. S. Hoover, Rep..............1,133—15
George Watts, Dem..............1,118

Coroner.
J. N. Wilson, Rep..............1,460—657
Z. Z. Bryant, Dem..............803

Election, June 27, 1882.
Prohibition.
For...........................1,268
Against.......................1,302—34

Election, November 7, 1882.
Secretary of State.
J. A. T. Hull..................1,434—646
T. O. Walker...................788
W. G. Gaston...................152

State Auditor.
J. L. Brown....................1,399—571
W. Thompson....................828
G. A. Wyant....................239

State Treasurer.
E. H. Conger......................1,396—566
John Foley........................ 830
George Dere...................... 239

Attorney General.
S. G. McPherson..................1,395—564
J. H. Bemerman 831
J. H. Rice 213

Supreme Judge
William Seevers..................1,397—567
C. E. Bronson.................... 830
M. A. Jones...................... 239

Congress.
D. B Henderson...................1,510—859
C. M. Durham..................... 651
R. Foster........................ 238

Clerk of Courts.
C. H. Cooper.....................1,406—359
J. B. Barber.....................1,047

Recorder.
Henry Kasemeier..................2,445

Supervisor.
J. Homrighaus.................... 466—186
William Boyer.................... 286

CHAPTER XI.

NATIONAL, STATE AND COUNTY REPRESENTATION.

The truly representative citizen of a Nation, State or county, is the public office holder. He stands in the relation of a representative of the people, and, as such, demands in his individual capacity the respect we owe to the people as a body. In this connection are presented sketches of many who have served Bremer county in official capacity. The sketches in some instances are short, and do not do full justice to those represented, but in no case is it the fault of the historian. The material was not accessible for more extended sketches.

CONGRESSIONAL.

Upon its organization, Bremer county became a part of the Second Congressional District, which then embraced about one half of the State, there being but two districts. At that time, Hon. John P. Cook of Davenport, was representing the district in the Thirty-third Congress, and remained the length of his term. Cook was a native of the State of New York, coming west and locating at Davenport in 1836. He was elected to Congress as a whig, and held to the views of that party until its dissolution, when he affiliated with the democratic party, the principles of which he labored earnestly to sustain and promulgate, even to the end of his days. He died at Davenport on the 17th day of April, 1872.

At the April election in 1854, James Thorington of Davenport, was elected to succeed Mr. Cook. His term commenced in March, 1855, and expired in the same month in 1857. He was not a man of great ability, but an active politician and a good wire-puller. He is now Consul to one of the South American States.

Timothy Davis succeeded Thorington, and took his seat March, 1857. Davis was from Elkader, Clayton county, and served through the Thirty-fifth Congress.

The district was represented in the Thirty-sixth Congress by William Vandever, of Dubuque, who was re-elected to the Thirty-seventh, serving until March, 1863. In connection with this chapter in the history of Butler county, appears an extended sketch of Mr. Vandever.

By the census of 1862, Iowa was entitled to six Representatives, and on the State being re-districted, Bremer county was made a part of the Third Congressional District, which was first represented by William B. Allison, of Dubuque. He was first elected in October, 1862, and was elected his own successor twice, serving until March, 1871. He is now United States Senator.

In the Forty-second Congress, the Third District was represented by William G. Donan, of Independence.

In 1872, Bremer county was a part of the Fourth Congressional District, and H. O. Pratt, of Charles City, was elected. He was re-elected and served through the Forty-third and Forty-fourth Congress.

Nathaniel C. Deering, of Osage, was successor to Mr. Pratt, was re-elected and served through the Forty-fifth, Forth-sixth and Forty-seventh Congress.

In 1882, on the State being re-districted, Bremer county was continued a part of the Fourth Congressional District, and David B. Henderson, of Dubuque, was elected for the Forty-eighth Congress. Mr. Henderson is a prominent lawyer, and will doubtless make an able legislator. This is usually known as the Dubuque district.

MEMBERS OF THE GENERAL ASSEMBLY.

The Fourth General Assembly convened at Iowa City, December 6, 1852, and adjourned January 24th, 1853. At this time, Bremer county, though unorganized, with Dubuque, Delaware, Buchanan, Black Hawk, Grundy, Butler, Clayton, Fayette, Allamakee, Winneshiek, Howard, Mitchell, Floyd and Chickasaw counties constituted one Senatorial District, and was represented by John G. Shields, Warner Lewis and Maturin L. Fisher.

The Fifth General Assembly convened at the same place on the 4th of December, 1854, and adjourned January 26th, 1855. The extra session convened in July, 1856. In this assembly, Bremer county, associated with the same counties, was represented by J. G. Shields, M. L. Fisher and W. W. Hamilton, in the Senate; in the House, by Reuben Noble and Lafayette Bigelow, the Representative District comprising the counties of Bremer, Fayette, Chickasaw, Butler, Black Hawk, Grundy, Franklin, Cerro Gordo, Floyd, Howard, Mitchell and Worth, as No. 3. The Sixth General Assembly convened at Iowa City, on the 1st of December, 1856, and adjourned January 29th, 1857. Bremer county was at this time in the Thirty-third Senatorial District and was represented by Aaron Brown, of Fayette county, who was elected for four years and served his full term. Bremer was in the Forty-eighth Representative District, and was represented by Edwin R. Gillett, of Chickasaw county. He was a farmer and a brother of M. F. Gillett, a prominent old settler of Bremer county.

The Seventh General Assembly convened on January 11th, 1858, at Des Moines, and adjourned on March 23d, 1858. Aaron Brown was still in the Senate. In the House, William P. Harmon, of Waverly, was Representative, the district being Number 11, embracing the counties of Howard, Chickasaw and Bremer.

The Eighth General Assembly convened at Des Moines, January 8, 1860, and adjourned April 3, 1860. An extra session convened May 15, 1861, and adjourned on the 29th. At this time the counties of Fayette and Bremer constituted the Thirty-eighth Senatorial District, and were represented by Lucian L. Ainsworth, of Fayette county, who had been elected for the full term of four years. Ainsworth was a practicing lawyer at West Union, a democrat, and was subsequently a member of Congress. Bremer was associated with Chickasaw county as the Fifty-Fourth Representative District and was represented by George W. Ruddick, of Waverly, now Judge of the District Court.

The Ninth General Assembly convened at Des Moines, January 13, 1862; and adjourned April 5, 1862. It also convened in extra session, September 3d, 1862, and adjourned September 11, 1862, L. L. Ainsworth was still in the Senate. Bremer county alone, constituted the Forty-Ninth Representative District, with Joseph O. Hudnut as representative. Mr. Hudnut was a civil engineer by profession, and some years prior to his election had settled at Sumner, in Bremer county. Immediately after this session he enlisted for the war, and was promoted to Colonel. After the close of the war he came back to Bremer county, but soon left again, this time for Texas.

The Tenth General Assembly convened at Des Moines, January 11, 1864, and adjourned March 29, 1864. L. W. Hart, a lawyer residing at Independence, represented the Thirty-ninth Senatorial District, of which Bremer formed a part, having been elected for the term of four years. John E. Burke represented Bremer county in the House. He was an attorney, located at Waverly, and is noted at length in the history of the Bar of the county.

The Eleventh General Assembly convened at Des Moines, January 8, 1866, and adjourned April 3, 1866. L. W. Hart was still in the Senate. Bremer county constituted the Forty-eighth Representative District, with Allen E. Holmes as Representative. Mr. Holmes was from Jefferson township, and was a democrat, although elected upon what was termed a "soldiers' ticket." He had been a Lieutenant in the late war, and having returned in safety, was engaged in working in a mill, for his brother. Shortly after the expiration of his term of office, he removed to Mitchell county.

The Twelfth General Assembly convened at Des Moines, in January, 1868. Bremer county was a part of the Thirty-sixth Senatorial District, and was represented by G. W. Donan, an attorney of Independence, who was afterwards a member of Congress. The county still constituted the Fourty-eighth Representative

District, and was served by D. P. Walling, of Frederika township.

The Thirteenth General Assembly convened at Des Moines, in January, 1870. R. B. Clark had been elected as Senator from this, the Forty-Fourth District, but died before taking his seat. Emmons Johnson was elected to fill the vacancy. Mr. Clark was from Jackson township, and his wife is still in the county. Emmons Johnson is now a banker in Waterloo. He only served ten days in the Senate. In the House, O. C. Harrington represented this county, which was the Forty-Eighth Representative District. He was one of the pioneers of Polk township, and a native of Onondago county, New York, born August 30, 1828. At the age of eighteen he accompanied his father and sisters to Ogle county, Illinois, his mother having died in New York in 1842, and engaged with his father in farming. There they continued to live until 1846, at which time, having sold their place, Mr. Harrington came to Iowa, and, after looking over the State for a suitable location in which to make for himself a new home, determined to settle in Polk township, Bremer county. He purchased land on section 23 and now owns there a well improved farm of 330 acres, valued at $30 per acre. Since coming to this county Harrington has held a number of local offices and in the fall of 1869 was elected on the republican ticket, a member of the General Assembly. The people of Bremer county have honored him by conferring upon him the presidency of the Old Settlers' Society, by virtue of his being one of the oldest and most respected men in the county. On the 16th day of December, 1855, he was joined in wedlock with Miss Ellen Du Bois, who was born in New York State, but in the spring of 1855 moved with her parents to Illinois, where she was afterwards married. Eleven children have been born to them, eight of whom are now living—Emma (now Mrs. G. A. Pierson) Henrietta, Ellen, William S., Oliver, Anna, Sarah and Jennie. Mr. Harrington's father died in Illinois, in 1880, at the advanced age of nearly ninety years.

Mr. Harrington has been identified with nearly all the public enterprises and improvements of his township, having been the largest contributor to the erection of the church and parsonage at Horton; also taking an active part in the formation of the school district at Horton. He took a deep interest in the erection of the bridge across the Cedar between Horton and Plainfield, personally securing the right of way for a new road on the east side of the river to the bridge. Mr. Harrington is a man that never sits straddle of the fence, asking how the crowd or majority are going upon any great question of the day; but after thorough investigation takes off his coat and works with a vim for principles and measures which he thinks will do the greatest good to the greatest number. In politics, he is independent, or an anti-monopolist, believing that a confederation of monopolists have got complete control of the government, the railroads and land corporations, telegraph corporations, banking corporations and high protective monopoly, and that the press, pulpit and courts nearly all are subsidized in their interest. Mr. Harrington formerly acted with the republican party, voting for Fremont and Lincoln.

HISTORY OF BREMER COUNTY.

In the last presidential election he voted for General J. B. Weaver.

The Fourteenth General Assembly convened at Des Moines in January, 1872, and the Forty-fourth Senatorial District was represented by John E. Burke, of Waverly. James A. Skillen, of Tripoli, represented Bremer county, which comprised the Forty-eighth Representative District, in the House.

James A. Skillin was born in Otsego county, N. Y., February 26, 1832. He is a son Hugh and Grace (Maxwell) Skillin. When four years old, his parents removed to Chenango county, New York, where he grew to manhood on his father's farm. In the fall of 1856 he came to Bremer county, and in the following year bought his present farm from his brother, who had preceded him. In June, 1858, he returned to Chenango county, New York, and there resided until 1862, and was married, October 2d, of that year, to Miss Lucinda Adams, daughter of Moses B. and Anna (Webb) Adams. Her father was a native of Duchess county, New York, and her mother was a native of Great Barrington, Massachusetts. They have had two children—Mary Ellen, born July 15, 1863; died August 6, 1865; and Grace Anna, born October 4, 1865. In the fall of 1870, Mr. Skillin was elected to represent Bremer county, for a term of two years in the Fourteenth General Assembly of Iowa, and worthily filled the office. Mr. Skillin is a democrat, and his election to the office just mentioned, is noteworthy, in that his personal qualities alone could have earned the honor for him in a county so strongly republican.

The Fifteenth General Assembly convened at Des Moines, in January, 1874. Bremer county, in the Forty-eighth Senatorial District, was represented by Hiram Bailey, a farmer and a very good man, from Chickasaw county. Louis Case, of Waverly, represented Bremer county in the House, this term, and ably performed his duties. The district was No. 62.

The Sixteenth General Assembly convened in January, 1876, at Des Moines, in which Bremer county was represented in the State Senate by Aaron Kimball, of Cresco, Howard county. He was a banker, and is now president of the State Temperance Association. In the House, Hon. Louis Case having been re-elected, again represented Bremer county.

The Seventeeth General Assembly convened at Des Moines in January, 1878, with Aaron Kimball representing the Senatorial Disrtrict of which Bremer county formed a part. J. K. L. Maynard represented Bremer county in the Lower House of the General Assembly. He is a resident of Janesville, and is a member of the Bar, in which chapter he is noted at length.

The Eighteenth General Assembly convened at Des Moines January, 1880. In the Senate, this district was represented by C. A. Marshall, who is a Congregational minister in Nashua. In the House, E. J. Dean, represented Bremer county.

The Nineteenth General Assembly convened at the Capitol, in January, 1882, and Bremer county was served in the Senate by C. A. Marshall. L. S. Hanchett was Representative of the county in the Lower House.

L. S. Hanchett was born in Chautauqua county, New York, on the 14th day of July,

1843. He is the son of Joseph C., and Sabrina (Howard) Hanchett. L. S. was reared on a farm, and received a liberal education. In 1861 he enlisted in the Forty-ninth New York Volunteer Infantry, and participated in the following engagements: Yorktown, May 3, 1862; Williamsburg, May 5, 1862; Mechanicsville, May 5, 1862; South Mountain, September 14, 1862; Antietam, September 17, 1862; first and second battles at Fredericksburg and Gettysburg, July 3, 1863. He was taken prisoner near Spotsylvania court house, and was thrown into prison at Andersonville, where he remained six months, when he was exchanged, and returned to his regiment. He participated with Grant before Petersburg, and at the surrender of Lee. The company left Buffalo eighty strong, but only eight returned with the regiment. In January, 1865, Mr. Hanchett came to Bremer county, Iowa, and embarked in the mercantile business. In the fall of 1875 he was elected sheriff of the county, which office he filled for three terms. In the fall of 1881, he was elected to the State Legislature. In 1878 he was married to Miss Kate Wuest, a native of Germany. By this union there are two children—Ray, and Lou.

CONSTITUTIONAL CONVENTION.

The Third Constitutional Convention convened at Iowa City, on the 19th of January, 1857, and adjourned on March 5, 1857. Bremer county was associated with the counties of Fayette, Butler, Franklin, Grundy, Hardin, Wright, Webster, Boone, Story, Greene, Allamakee, Winnesheik and Humboldt as District No. 33, and was represented by Sheldon Greenleaf Winchester, of Eldora, Hardin county, where he is yet one of the most prominent early settlers.

AUDITOR OF STATE.

Before its organization Bremer county was represented in this office by William Pattee, who was elected August 5, 1850, and re-elected August 2, 1852, serving two terms. He was a Democrat.

John Pattee was appointed by the Governor, September 13, 1855, to fill the vacancy caused by the resignation of Andrew J. Stevens. After filling out the term he was elected by the people, August 4, 1856, and served until January 3, 1859. John Pattee was a republican in politics.

W. V. Lucas was elected Auditor of State at the November election, 1880, and served during 1881 and 1882. He was for many years a resident of this county, and was for six years county treasurer, but was not a resident when elected, having removed to Mason City where he yet resides, and is engaged in the newspaper business.

BANK EXAMINER OF IOWA.

Hon. Louis Case, of Waverly, is the only citizen of Bremer county that has filled this position, having been appointed in March, 1877. As he has for many years been in public life, and been prominent in official matters, a sketch of his life is here presented:

Hon. Louis Case, one of the early settlers of Bremer county, was born in Harmony, Chautauqua county, New York, July 6, 1834. He was the twelfth of fourteen children, of George E. and Sally (Alexander) Case, natives of New York; thirteen of the children lived to be adults, and ten are living at the present time. The united ages of those living are 574 years. In 1854 the parents of Mr. Case left New York emigrating to Bremer county, where his father died, January 30, 1867, and his mother died March 5, 1877. His father was a soldier in the War of 1812. He was wounded and taken prisoner at the battle of Queenstown Heights, and received a pension until his death. The subject of this sketch was reared upon a farm. He attended one term at Maysville Academy, and a term at the Jamestown Academy, a prominent educational institute in Chautauqua county; with these exceptions his education was obtained at the district school. In 1857, when in his twenty-first year, Mr. Case resolved to seek fame and fortune in the west, and accordingly emigrated to Illinois, locating in DeKalb county. There he remained one year, engaged in teaching school. In March, 1855, he again emigrated westward, locating at Delhi, Delaware county, Iowa, where he was employed in the office of the recorder of deeds. This position he retained until August of the same year, when he settled at Waverly, Bremer county, where he has since resided. Entering the office of recorder as clerk soon after his arrival. Mr. Case continued there until June, 1858. In August of that year, he was elected clerk of the district court. In October, 1860, he was re-elected to the same office, having received a unanimous nomination in the republican county convention. In October, 1864, he was elected recorder of deeds for Bremer county, continuing in that office the two succeeding years. In January, 1869, he was appointed by the board of supervisors of Bremer county, to fill the vacancy caused by the resignation of Hon. O. F. Avery, county judge. In October following, he was elected the first county auditor, serving the full term. He was next elected Representative of Bremer county, in the State Legislature, in October, 1873, and was re-elected Representative in October, 1875; besides several more important offices not named. Mr. Case was on the school board of the city of Waverly in the years 1873-74-75, and three times elected assessor of the same city. He was joint proprietor of the Waverly *Republican*. He has been notary public of Bremer county, during eighteen successive years, and has profitably conducted an extensive land and conveyance business, when not officially engaged. In his political life he has been invariably a republican. While not an office seeker, Mr. Case has served the county more years that any other person mentioned in this work. His official work has been valuable to the county, and he is one of those men who believe that honesty and purity are as essential in public as in private life. Efficient, accommodating and honorable, he is one of the most popular men in this part of the State.

GOVERNMENT APPOINTMENTS.

In 1881, W. B. Wilcox was appointed assistant paymaster of the navy, and is now on duty. He was reared in Bremer county, and learned his trade—printing—in the Waverly newspaper offices. He is an intelligent and capable young man.

Lesley Fisk received an appointment in the military service of the government, and is now in charge of an engineering force somewhere in the south. He is a graduate of West Point, and ranked high in his class on graduating.

COUNTY JUDGE.

As stated in connection with the chapter devoted to the "Courts of Bremer County," this office was created by an act of the General Assembly, in 1851. It was the most important office in the gift of the people of the county. This official, assisted by a county prosecuting attorney and a sheriff, held what was termed county court, and transacted almost all the business now devolving upon the auditor, board of supervisors, circuit court, and clerk of courts. It will thus be seen that a county judge in those days had abundant opportunity to earn the little pay he received.

Jeremiah Farris was the first county judge of Bremer county, being unanimously elected in August, 1853, at which election there were eighty votes polled. Judge Farris' duties began immediately after his election. He was re-elected in 1855, and served until August, 1857. Jeremiah Farris came to Bremer county, with his family, at an early day, from Fulton county, Illinois, and settled on a farm upon which the town plat of Jefferson City was subsequently located. He was a "hard-shell" democrat, but in early days, party lines were not very rigidly drawn. When he was elected to office he removed to Waverly, leaving a son upon the place. One of his sons yet remains in Jefferson township.

After the expiration of his term, Judge Farris engaged in the mercantile trade at Waverly, with John H. Martin. About the time the war broke out he moved to Burton county, Kansas, where he died a few years ago. Judge Farris was not a man of much education, but he was a man of good, common sense, and of honest motives. His sociability made him popular, and he was well liked by all. It was a failure of his that he could not, or would not resist the temptation to now and then take a glass of something for the stomach's sake; but he always knew just how far he was going with it, and when he reached that certain point, he quit. It is told, by way of a joke, that on one occasion a facetious correspondent addressed him as "Jerry Farris, Esq., County Jug." However, the Judge is now dead and gone; but he will always be remembered by those who knew him as a man who never betrayed a trust, and whose impulses were always honorable.

George W. Maxfield succeeded Mr. Farris, assuming his duties in August, 1857. In 1859 he was re-elected, and served until January, 1862. He was born in Herkimer county, New York. In 1854 he came west, and after some time spent in prospecting in Iowa and Minnesota, he located at Janesville, where he engaged in mercantile pursuits. At the election, in 1856, he was elected justice of the peace, the duties of which office he performed with ability until the fall of 1857, when he was elected to the responsible office of county judge. He discharged the duties of judge in so acceptable a manner to the citizens of Bremer county, that in 1859 he was re-elected. His election and re-election both attest the estimation in which he was held by his fellow citizens, for when party strife ran high he was elected on the democratic ticket in a strongly republican county. As a financier he was seldom equaled. In the man-

HISTORY OF BREMER COUNTY.

agement of his affairs, both public and private, he bent his every energy, and crowded into his short life what many men need three score and ten years to accomplish. In 1860 he was the democratic candidate for State Auditor. He died shortly after the expiration of his second term. He was buried by Tyrrell Lodge, No. 116, of Free and Accepted Masons, (of which lodge he was an active and honored member), in due and ancient form; assisted by the brethren from Cedar Falls and Janesville. He left a wife and two small daughters to mourn the loss of a kind husband and affectionate father. In the death of Judge Maxfield Bremer county lost one of its best citizens.

At the October election in 1861 Matthew Rowen was elected to succeed Mr. Maxfield to the judgeship. In the meantime the board of supervisors had been created and it took much of the business out of the judge's hands. Judge Rowen was also elected from Janesville, where he was an early settler. He was a farmer and a Republican. One of his sons still resides at or near Janesville.

In October, 1863, George W. Ruddick was elected county judge and served from January, 1864, to January, 1866. He is now judge of the district court.

Orrin F. Avery succeeded Judge Ruddick and was re-elected, serving until January, 1869. He was a prominent lawyer in Bremer county and is mentioned at length in connection with the Bar chapter.

Louis Case was appointed county judge in January, 1869, serving in that capacity one year when the office was abolished by law, and that of

COUNTY AUDITOR,

was created, the judge being made ex-officio county auditor. Louis Case was by these means made first county auditor. In October, 1869, he was elected and served from January, 1869, to January, 1872.

S. H. Morse was elected to succeed Mr. Case, was re-elected and served from January, 1872, to January, 1876.

The present auditor of Bremer county, Herman Rust, was next elected. He is a native of Du Page county, Illinois, and was born on the 6th day of October, 1851. He is a son of Louis and Louisa (Hanebuth) Rust, who were born in Germany, and there lived until 1848, when they immigrated to America, and settled in Du Page county, Illinois, and there, as stated above, their son of whom we write, was born. In 1863 he came with his parents to Bremer county, and settled on a farm in Jefferson township. His parents now reside in Warren township. In the spring of 1866 he came to Waverly, and entered the store of George Evans, deceased, as clerk. In the spring of 1867, he entered the grocery store of T. C. Aldrich, as clerk, in whose employ he remained until January 1, 1876. In 1875 he was elected to the office of county auditor for the term beginning January 1, 1876, and has since been re-elected three times, the last time in 1881. Mr. Rust makes an efficient officer, gentlemanly and accommodating. He is popular among his constituents. He is principally a self-educated man, not having had the opportunities of any schooling since his fifteenth year. In 1879 he was married to Miss Belle Acken, a daughter of John Acken, and a native of Bremer county. She was born in Douglas township in 1856. In 1870 she came with her parents to Waverly and entered the schools, and was a member of the first class which graduated from the Waverly high school. She is at present, deputy auditor, and the first lady official the county has ever had.

TREASURER AND RECORDER.

This office was created when the county was organized. The first treasurer and recorder was John Hunter, who was elected August, 1853, receiving 80 votes—all that were polled. He served until his successor qualified in August, 1855. Hunter was from Fulton county, Illinois, and came to Bremer county at a very early day, settling in Janesville, where he lived at the time of his election, engaged in merchandising. He remained here for a number of years, but finally removed to Louisa county, Iowa, where he died some years ago. Not much is remembered of him, more than that he was a jovial, good-natured fellow, and attended to the little business of the office with fair efficiency.

William B. Hamilton, the next treasurer and recorder, was first elected in August, 1855, and re-elected and served from August, 1855, to January, 1860. He was one of the first settlers in Waverly, where he was engaged in mercantile business. He came here from Independence, and in the spring of 1861 started for California, with his wife and children, for the benefit of his health. He was then quite feeble. While en route, and when near Fort Laramie, he was seized with a fit of coughing and strangulation, on the evening of July 3, 1861, and died in a few moments. His last words were, "Here I go! here I go! here I go!" Mr. Hamilton left many friends in Bremer county. His wife went on to California, but has returned to Iowa, married again, and now lives in Waterloo.

W. W. Norris was successor to Mr. Hamilton, and served from January, 1860, until January, 1862. Norris was a democrat politically, and a native of Illinois. He was fairly educated, had a good allowance of common sense, and endowed by nature with a genial disposition, which makes a man popular. He had already served one term as school superintendent and is noted in that connection. A few years after serving, he returned to Illinois and his whereabouts at present are unknown.

On the 2d of January, 1862, an iron safe in a vault in the office of the county treasurer, in the court house, was feloniously opened by (it is supposed) one Knowles, a professional cracksman, who first burglariously entered the house of W. W. Norris and procured the necessary keys for the purpose. About $7,000 in money, about $2,000 of which were funds belonging to the State, besides many valuable papers were abstracted. R. J. Stephenson, a former supervisor of the county, and a third person named Bemis, were (then supposed to be) confederates in the robbery. After a long protracted and persistent pursuit, all the parties implicated in the affair were arrested, each in a different and remote part of the country. For want of sufficient testimony, however, to secure their conviction, they were finally acquitted. About $1,100 was recovered but fully this much was expended in pursuit and prosecution.

At the October election, in 1861, Caleb Morse was elected to succeed Norris. At the expiration of his first term he was re-elected, and served from January, 1862, to January, 1866. During his term the General Assembly passed an act separating the two offices, and defining the duties of each. Caleb Morse was the last treasurer and recorder. He is still a much esteemed citizen of Waverly, and a pioneer of Bremer county. He was born in Salisbury, Massachusetts, August 19, 1808. He received an excellent common school education in his native State, and continued to reside there for a number of years. In 1846, he left his native State, in company with two other families, emigrated to St. Croix, Wisconsin. There he was employed by a Boston firm in the lumber interest —the company consisting of such men as Caleb Cushing, Robert Rantoun and B. F. Cheever. At that date there were but few settlements on the banks of the Mississippi river, and no educational advantages, therefore Mr. Morse, having a family of small children, whom he desired to have well educated, left that section of the country. He returned by river to Galena, Illinois, and thence to Monroe, Wisconsin, where he continued to live until 1856, and then came with his family to Waverly, Bremer county, where he purchased land and soon had a comfortable home. In 1861, he was elected to the office of county treasurer and recorder, and four years later was elected one of the county supervisors. Mr. Morse has also held the office of mayor of Waverly, and in 1876, received the honor of being commissioned one of the committee to visit the Centennial. The family are members of the Congregational Church.

COUNTY TREASURER.

In October, 1865, W. V. Lucas was elected to this office, and was first to serve exclusively as county treasurer. In January, 1866, he assumed his duties, and in the fall of 1867 was re-elected, and again re-elected in the fall of 1869, serving six years in all. Mr. Lucas now lives at Mason City, Cerro Gordo county, and has since served one term as Auditor of State, in which connection more will be found regarding him.

George Morehouse succeeded Mr. Lucas, and being re-elected served four years, from January, 1872, until January, 1876. Mr. Morehouse had settled at Janesville at an early day with his family, consisting of a wife and one child. He was a good business man, and well qualified to discharge the duties of the office. He made an accommodating and efficient officer. After his term expired, he was for some time cashier of the Bremer County Bank, and finally, a few years ago, went to Brookings, Dakota Territory, where he is engaged in the banking business.

George W. Nash was successor to Mr. Morehouse, and served all of one term and a portion of another. Upon his resignation he went to Dakota, and the present county treasurer, S. F. Baker, was appointed.

In the fall of 1881, Mr. Baker was elected his own successor, and is the present incumbent.

The present treasurer of Bremer county, S. F. Baker, was born on the 29th day of October, 1846, in Putnam county, Illinois. He is a son of Amanda A. (Rose) and Flaville Baker. The latter was a native of Vermont, and emigrated to Putnam county in 1842. He was a mechanical genius, and constructed the first reaper propably that was ever used in the United States. While preparing the model, he was taken sick, and soon after died, leaving others to reap the harvest of his labors. The only survivor of six children (three sons and three daughters) is S. F., of whom we write. He received a collegiate education at Dexter, Maine, and in 1864 enlisted in company B, 146th Illinois Infantry, serving until mustered out at the close of the rebellion. During the spring of 1865, he came to Bremer county, Iowa, locating in Waverly, where he continues to reside. In 1881 Mr. Baker was appointed county treasurer, to fill the vacancy left by G. W. Nash, and the following fall was elected to the office. In 1871 he was married, choosing for a helpmeet Miss Eve J. LeVally, daughter of G. W. LeVally, an early settler of Bremer county. She was born in 1852. Two children have blessed the union—Bertrand E. and Clyde N.

COUNTY RECORDER.

This office was formerly connected with that of treasurer, but, as stated, was separated by an act of the General Assembly in 1863-64. Louis Case was the first recorder after the division. He was elected in the fall of 1864, and served through the years 1865 and 1866.

E. C. Dougherty succeeded Mr. Case—was re-elected in 1868, and served four years, from January, 1867, to January 1871. He subsequently went to the Mountains, where he was engaged in some mining enterprise. He is now in Chicago engaged in the manufacture of hair mattresses.

John W. Rowray was the next recorder, and also served four years. He made an accommodating and capable officer. His term began January 1, 1871, and expired in January, 1875.

In the fall of 1874, H. S. Munger was elected recorder, and two years later was re-elected serving until January 1879. Mr. Munger is still a much esteemed and prominent citizen of Waverly. He made an efficient officer.

Henry Kasemeier was Mr. Munger's successor, and is the present recorder. He was first elected in the fall of 1878, was re-elected in the fall of 1880, and again in the fall of 1882. He was born July 5, 1855, in Bremer county, Iowa, and is a son of Elizabeth (Ebel) and John Kasemeier, natives of Germany. His father emigrated to the United States in 1847, and first located in Cook county, Illinois, where he remained about six years. At the expiration of that time he removed to Bremer county, Iowa, settling in Fremont township, where he entered a number of acres of wild prairie land, which he immediately began cultivating. The subject of this sketch was educated principally in the common schools, he however, attended the State Normal School at Cedar Falls, two terms.

CLERK OF COURTS.

This office was in existence at the time the county was organized. At the first election, in August, 1853, Heman A. Miles was elected clerk of the courts, for Bremer county. He made a good officer, and was re-elected in 1854 and 1856, serving until January, 1859. Mr. Miles is now in Larado, Texas, having left Bremer county in 1873. In the chapter entitled "Reminiscences" will be found a very interesting letter from him, to which the reader is referred.

In October, 1858, Louis Case was elected clerk of the courts, to succeed Mr. Miles. He served his first term and was re-elected for a second, turning over the office to his successor, H. C. Moore, in January, 1863.

H. C. Moore was re-elected two successive terms, in 1864 and 1866, serving six years. At the time of his election Mr. Moore was a farmer, living in Leroy township; but moved into Waverly when elected. He now resides in Oscaloosa.

M. F. Gillett, of Frederika township, was the next clerk, being elected in the fall of 1868, and re-elected in 1870, serving until January, 1873. He is still a resident of the county.

Marquis F. Gillett now lives on section 29, Frederika township, within a few miles of Tripoli. He was born in Ontario county, New York, March 20, 1824, and is the son of David B. and Sylvania T. (Moon) Gillett. His father was a native of Hartford, Connecticut, and his mother of the State of New York. In 1837, he removed from his native county with his parents, to Ashtabula county Ohio, where they remained until 1840, in which year his parents moved to Stephenson county, Illinois, leaving Mr. Gillett behind them to learn the trade of tanner and currier. Five years later he followed them, taught school two years, and then returned to Ohio, settling in Summit County, where he followed his trade for about four years, and then rejoined his family in Stephenson county, Illinois, upon his twenty-eighth birthday. Remaining there until June of the following year (1851), he started alone for the west, in search of a home for himself, and during the next year wandered around among the then thinly settled Western States, finally making selection of his present home, and entering it at the United States Land Office at Dubuque. Being a single man, he for the next two years, and while he was breaking and fencing his farm, boarded with L. C. Rima and W. R. Bostwick. In 1854, he began getting lumber together to build a dwelling; hauling much of it from a saw-mill at Chickasaw, Chickasaw county, and in the following year, upon his thirty-second birthday, he married Miss Olivia A. Walling, a daughter of Peter and Esther (Bigelow) Walling. The ceremony was performed by Squire Rima, who was the first settler in the township, and its first justice of the peace, and they were the first couple which he was called upon to unite, and the first to be married within the township. The children of this union, with the dates of their births, are as follows: Lois, December 20, 1855; Edwin R., December 27, 1856; Frank W., March 23, 1858; Norman W., September 11, 1859; Albert L., August 4, 1862; Leversee M., January 4, 1864; Likum S., August 2, 1867; Nettie M., December 22, 1869; Fayette M., September 16, 1871. On May 27, 1861, Mr. Gillett enlisted at Cedar Falls, in Company K, Third Iowa Infantry, and served one year, taking part in the various encounters of the army of the Tennessee, up to the battle of Shiloh, where he was injured so severely as to necessitate his discharge. Mr. Gillett has filled a long roll of county and township offices. He was from 1868 to 1873, clerk of the courts. He has been township assessor and supervisor, and also for the past four years, township clerk. He owns and farms 390 acres—10 acres under timber. He is a member of the Liberal League of Northern Iowa, and is politically an out and out greenbacker.

In the fall of 1872, A. H. McCracken was elected clerk of courts, and served so acceptably that he was twice re-elected, serving six years, from January, 1873, to January, 1879. He is a lawyer, living at Waverly, and is noted at length in the chapter upon the Bar of Bremer county.

C. H. Cooper, the present incumbent, succeeded Mr. McCracken as clerk of the courts. He was first elected in October, 1878; re-elected in 1880, and 1882; and is now serving his third term, making one of the most accommodating and competent officials the county has ever had.

C. H. Cooper was born in Shoreham, Addison county, Vermont, on the 4th day of November, 1833. He is the son of Asa and Lydia (Rehern) Cooper. When C. H. was four years old his parents emigrated to Bridgeport, in the same county, remaining there until he was twelve years old, when they moved to Stephenson county, Illinois, where he grew to manhood. In 1848 his mother died, and in 1849 his father removed to Racine county, Wisconsin. The subject of this sketch was married, March 23, 1856, to Miss Esther E. Harwood, a daughter of François and Sophronia Harwood, natives of New York. In June, 1861, he enlisted in an Illinois Regiment, from Tazewell county, as a private; but before the company left the State, was promoted to Orderly Sergeant. Among some of the principal engagements he participated in were: Fort Donalson, Fort Henry, Shiloh, siege and capture of Vicksburg, first and second battles of Corinth, Missionary Ridge, and Atlanta. The regiment was discharged at Nashville, and he proceeded to Bremer county, where his family had preceeded him. In Bremer county he turned his attention to farming, which he followed up to 1873, when he entered the office of the clerk of district court, as deputy. Mr. and Mrs. Cooper are the parents of four children, two sons and two daughters —Ernest, now filling the office of deputy clerk; Julia E., Mary S., and George C.

SHERIFFS.

The first sheriff Bremer county ever had was Austin Farris, who was elected in August, 1853. He moved to Kansas and remained there until about 1879, when he came back to Bremer and died in Jefferson township.

Farris resigned before his term was out and Daniel Lehman was appointed sheriff, and filled out the term. Daniel Lehman, an early settler of Bremer county, was born July 12th, 1829, in Dauphin county, Pennsylvania. At the age of fourteen he began learning the trade of a mason, and followed that occupation for thirty years. In 1851 he emigrated to Stephenson county, Illinois, and while there became acquainted with and married Miss Martha Wilson, a native of Kentucky, born in 1830. In 1855 he removed to Bremer county, Iowa, locating in Waverly. Mr. Lehman settled here when this county was one rough, unbroken waste of land, and has seen it develop into one of the finest farming counties in the northwest. In 1859 he settled on his beautiful farm in

Jackson township. It consists of 102 acres of cultivated land, valued at $50.00 per acre.

In August, 1855, Joseph G. Ellis was elected sheriff, and was twice thereafter re-elected, serving from August, 1855, until January, 1862. He was elected as a democrat, and still holds to that faith.

J. H. Eldridge was the next sheriff of Bremer county, and served from January, 1862, until January, 1864. He still lives in Horton, where he did at the time of his election.

J. H. Eldridge, a pioneer of Bremer county and one of the enterprising men of Polk township, was born in Washington county, New York, October 21, 1810. He is a son of James D. and Nancy (Woodworth) Eldridge, who were also natives of New York State. About two years after his birth, the family moved to Madison county in the same State, where the son grew to manhood. His last school days were passed at Hamilton Academy, but at the early age of fifteen he was obliged to cease his studies and begin life for himself. In 1822 his mother died, and he, being one of the eldest of eight children, was compelled, a few years after, to earn his own living. Therefore, upon leaving school, he began learning the fullers' trade and subsequently worked in wollen manufactories in different parts of the State, until nearly forty years of age; after which he followed farming a short time, and was also engaged in the grocery trade. During the year 1833 he was married to Miss Sarah Youmans, who was born in Oneida county, New York, but was reared in Madison county. In 1853 he turned his steps westward, and, after spending about two years in Lake county, Illinois, came to Bremer county, Iowa, and first located on a farm in Douglas township where he lived five years, and then came to Horton. It is said of him that he knew nearly every man in the county. In 1864, he returned to Horton and turned his attention to farming and general merchandising. However, for several years past he has lived a retired life. Mr. Eldridge has been one of the leading, and is also one of the most respected men in Bremer county. Thirteen children have been born to them, eleven of whom are now living—Nancy Madaline (wife of Adelbert G. Lawrence, a lumber dealer of Motley, Minnesota); Lydia Louisa, (wife of Adrian Nutting, of Sioux Falls, Dakota); J. R., who now lives in Kokomo, Colorado; Mary E., (wife of Lavinus Phelps, and living at Appleton, Minnesota); John W., now living at Horton: Frances Eugene, now living in Dakota; Sarah E.; (wife of Albert G. Lawrence, of Nashua, Iowa); William Y., now in business at Horton; Helen Annette, (wife of E. B. Hayes, of Dallas, Texas); Herbey, now living at Horton; Emma D., (wife of James McDonald, and now living in Dakota).

N. M. Smith succeeded Eldridge, and served two terms, from January, 1864, to January, 1867. Mr. Smith was a republican, and was an early settler of Warren township. He only remained in the county a few years after the expiration of his term of office. He went to Missouri.

D. W. Cown, the next sheriff, was a son-in-law of Mr. Smith; he served one term and went to Missouri with Smith.

In October, 1867, C. M. Kingsley was elected sheriff. In 1869, he was re-elected, and served until 1872. He was a staunch republican, and was quite an early settler in Washington township, where he lived at the time of his election. He now lives in Verndale, Minnesota, but has a brother living in Lafayette township, Bremer county.

James A. Conner, who succeeded Mr. Kingsley, was born in Clark county, Kentucky, May 25, 1832. He is the second son of James and Pauline (Sharp) Conner, both natives of that State. In 1851, his parents removed to Will county, Illinois, and in 1856, to Lafayette township, Bremer county, where James entered 240 acres of land on section 19, which he improved and sold in January, 1872, when he took possession of the office of sheriff of Bremer county. In 1876, he settled on his present farm of 80 acres, one mile west of Waverly, In 1881, he was elected county supervisor. In politics he is a republican, and cast his first presidential vote for Abraham Lincoln. Mr. Conner is a Master Mason, and a member of Tyrrell Lodge, No. 116, of Waverly. He is also a member of Jethro Chapter R. A. M. of Waverly. In 1862 he was married to Miss Jane A. Tyrrell. They have been blessed with six children, five of whom are still living— Edith, Elizabeth J., Earl, Ruth and Edna P. His father died in March, 1863, and his mother in 1874.

L. S. Hanchett was the next sheriff, being elected in the fall of 1877. In 1879 he was re-elected, and served until January, 1882. He was then elected a member of the lower house of the General Assembly, and is noted at length in that connection.

The present sheriff, James Adair, succeeded Hanchett, having been elected in the fall of 1881. He makes an efficient and careful officer. Politically he is a democrat. James Adair was born in Ireland, where he was educated partly in his native country, and in Chenango county, New York. When twenty years of age he emigrated to New York, and located in Chenango county, where he turned his attention to farming, which occupation he followed for eight years. He was married to Miss Eliza Stewart, by whom there were six children born, four of whom are living —Maggie, Jennie, Stewart and James. In December, 1856, he settled in Bremer county, Iowa, purchasing eighty acres of land in Washington township, and made a farm. Mrs. Adair died in Bremer county May 29, 1871. He again married in 1874 Miss Sarah Clark. She was born April 18, 1850. One child blessed this union— Reane. In politics, Mr. Adair is a democrat, and is the first county officer elected by that party for twenty years, overcoming a republican majority of 300 votes. Mr. Adair came to Bremer county a poor man, but by close application to business has accumulated a comfortable property and home; has 91 acres of land under cultivation, valued at $40 per acre.

SCHOOL SUPERINTENDENTS.

The various gentlemen who have officiated in this capacity and also that of school fund commissioner, are treated at length in the chapter upon educational matters, to which the reader is referred.

COUNTY ATTORNEY.

A short time prior to the organization of Bremer county, this office was created by an act of the General Assembly. The first to fill it was William P. Harmon, founder of the city of Waverly. He was elected in August, 1854, and served until August, 1856.

Phineas V. Swan succeeded Mr. Harmon, but for some reason only served for a few months, when G. C. Wright, the present proprietor of the Waverly *Democrat*, was appointed to fill the vacancy, and served until April, 1857.

At this time George W. Ruddick was elected, and served until the office was abolished by law, and that of district attorney taking its place.

SURVEYOR.

The first surveyor of Bremer county was Israel Trumbo, who was elected in August, 1853. Mr. Trumbo came from Morrow county, Ohio, in company with his family, William Baskins, and Joseph Kerr, in 1850. He was a man of moderate education, and good, common sense; having that social, genial disposition which makes men popular. He is well remembered by the old settlers as a man of much integrity and honor. He held the office of surveyor from August, 1853, until August, 1857, and was also one of the first justices of the peace in the county. About the time the war broke out he went to Dakota, and died a few years later.

H. S. Hoover was the next county surveyor, and served at this time one term.

He was succeeded by A. S. Funston, who also served one term, from January, 1860, to January, 1862. He was a democrat, and lived in Leroy township at the time of his election. He is noted in the Bar chapter.

Succeeding him, H. S. Hoover was again elected, and re-elected for four successive terms, serving from January, 1862, until January, 1870.

In 1869, S. H. Wallace was elected surveyor, and served part of a term. He had been teaching school in the county, but has now gone to parts unknown. He was a very conscientious man, in fact it is stated that his delicately framed conscience would not allow him to survey the grounds of a church which in creed opposed the one of which he was a member. M. E. Billings was appointed to fill the unexpired term. In October, 1871, H. S. Hoover was again elected, and, having been re-elected from time to time, is the present incumbent.

H. S. Hoover was born in Fayette county, Pennsylvania, on the 17th day of December, 1827. He is the son of J. Hoover, who in early life learned the trade of a blacksmith, which he followed for some time, afterwards turning his attention to farming. In politics he was an old line whig, and was an active worker in the campaign of General Harrison. He married Miss Catherine Stouffer, by whom there was four children, three sons and one daughter, all of which are living at the present time. They were married in 1819, and lived together for sixty years, save a few months. Mr. Hoover being the first death in the family. The sons are all living, married, and but two deaths have occurred in all the families. Mr. Hoover died December 18, 1878, at the advanced age of eighty, Mrs. Hoover following April 30, 1879. The subject of this sketch was reared on a farm, receiving his education principally in his native county. When seventeen years of age he commenced teaching school, which he followed for a number of years. In the fall of 1856, he left his home in Pennsylvania and came to Iowa, locating in Waverly, where he was soon after employed in book-keeping for the firm of Hazlett & Company. In 1856, he was appointed a deputy county surveyor. In August, 1857, was elected to the office which he has held since with the exception of four years. In the fall of 1859, he returned to his native State, when he married Cecilia Child, a daughter of Wm. and Susan Child. By this union there are three children, one son and two daughters—Elmer E., Miriam C., and Kate. In politics Mr. Hoover is a republican, taking an active interest in all the issues of the day. He is also an ardent supporter of the temperance cause. The family are members of the Episcopal Church.

CORONERS.

While this office was already in existence, at the time Bremer county was organized, for some reason it was not filled at the first election. In August, 1854, the second election was held, and A. A. Case was elected the first coroner of Bremer county, receiving 89 of the 125 votes polled. He served just one year, when his successor qualified. Mr. Case was a native of New York and was a brother of Louis Case, well known in Bremer county. He came to the county in the fall of 1853 from Monroe, Wisconsin, where he had stopped on his westward march for several years. He brought his family with him and settling, erected the first house on the west side of the river in Waverly. About the time the war broke out, he moved to Missouri, and was there pressed into the Rebel service, but escaped and made his way to Bremer county, this time remaining three or four years. He finally returned to Carthage, Missouri. He was a cabinet maker by trade, and was a man of honor and integrity.

Robert D. Titcomb was the second county coroner, and served from August, 1855 to 1856. He was an early settler in Fremont township, and was elected as a republican. He left the county years ago, and now lives in Waterloo.

A. T. Owen succeeded Titcomb, and served from August, 1856, to 1857. He was a native of Vermont, and settled in Waverly at an early day, engaging in the mercantile trade. He only remained three or four years.

In April, 1857, H. F. Beebe was elected coroner, but almost immediately resigned. He was a contractor and builder, and settled in Waverly about 1855, remaining until 1866, when he followed his brother-in-law, A. A. Case, to Carthage, Missouri. When the the war of the rebellion broke out, Mr. Beebe raised a company and went into the army as a lieutenant. He was soon promoted to captain, and before the close, he was honored with the promotion to major.

L. B. Ostrander was appointed to fill the vacancy in the coroner's office, occasioned by Mr. Beebe's resignation, and served from May until August, 1857. He was a democrat and resided in Lafayette township, but has long since left for parts unknown.

John Acken, who still lives at Waverly, next filled the office, serving from August, 1857, until January, 1859.

Herman Rust

L. F. Goodwin was next elected, but not qualifying, W. W. Norris was appointed to fill the vacancy, and served until August, 1860.

At this time, John Mohling, of Fremont township, was elected and served until January, 1862.

John S. Jenkins succeeded Mr. Mohling to the coronership, and served until January, 1864. He was a citizen of Jefferson township, where he had been justice of the peace for many years. He died three years ago.

Matthew Rowen was next elected; his term expiring in January, 1866.

J. J. Merrill came next, and held the office two years. He was a republican and a citizen of Polk township.

G. W. Nash succeeded Mr. Merrill, his term commencing January, 1868, and expiring January, 1870.

Dr. C. O. Paquin came next, and held the office for two years.

Dr. J. M. Ball was elected to succeed Paquin, and held it during 1872. He is now at Waterloo, Iowa.

Dr. Horace Nichols was elected in the fall of 1872, and re-elected his own successor in 1873, 1875 and 1877. He is noted at length in the medical chapter.

W. S. Mickle succeeded Dr. Nichols, and served for one year.

The present coroner, Dr. J. N. Wilson, was elected in 1880 to fill the unexpired term. In 1881 he was re-elected for the term he is at present serving.

DRAINAGE COMMISSIONER.

This office is a very unimportant one in this county, and has not been filled by an officer much more than half the time.

Edward Tyrrell was the first drainage commissioner. He was elected in April, 1854, and served for one year.

Rufus C. Gates, then of Jefferson township, was next qualified, and served until April, 1857.

Lafayette Walker succeeded Gates. He was at the time a resident of Fremont township, and served from April, 1857, till January, 1860.

J. N. Bemis came next, and served two years.

He was succeeded by William P. Harmon, of Waverly, who filled the office until 1864.

Allen Smith, of Polk township, was elected in the fall of 1863, and served till January, 1866.

E. J. Messinger succeeded Mr. Smith, and served until January, 1868. He was the last drainage commissioner Bremer county has ever had.

CHAPTER XII.

THE PRESS.

There is no instrumentality, not even excepting the Pulpit and the Bar, which exerts such an influence upon society as the Press of the land. It is the Archimedian lever that moves the world. The talented minister of the gospel on the Sabbath day, preaches to a few hundred people; on the following morning his thoughts are reproduced more than a thousand fold, and are read and discussed throughout the length and breadth of the land. The attorney at the bar, in thrilling tones, pleads either for or against the criminal arraigned for trial, often causing the jury to bring in a verdict against the law and the testimony in the case. His words are reproduced in every daily that is reached by the telegraphic wire, and his arguments are calmly weighed by unprejudiced men and accepted for what they are worth. The politician takes the stand and addresses a handful of men upon the political questions of the day; his speech is reported, and read by a thousand men for every one that heard the address. Suddenly the waters of one of our mighty rivers rise, overflowing the land for miles and miles, rendering thousands of people homeless, and without means to secure their daily bread. The news is flashed over the wire, taken up by the Press, and known and read of all men. No time is lost in sending to their relief; the Press has made known their wants, and they are instantly supplied. "Chicago is on fire! Two hundred millions worth of property destroyed! Fifty thousand people rendered homeless!" Such is the dread intelligence proclaimed by the Press. Food and clothing are hastily gathered, trains are chartered, and the immediate wants of the sufferers are in a measure relieved.

The power for good or evil, of the Press, is to-day unlimited. The short-comings of the politician are made known through its columns; the dark deeds of the wicked are exposed, and each fear it alike. The controlling influence of a Nation, State or county, is its Press; and the Press of Bremer county is no exception to the rule.

The local Press is justly considered among the most important institutions of every city, town and village. The people of every community regard their particular newspaper or newspapers as of peculiar value, and this not merely on account of the fact already alluded to, but because these papers are the repositories wherein are stored the facts and the events, the deeds and the sayings, the undertakings and the achievements, that go to make up final history. One by one these things are gathered and placed in type; one by one the papers are issued; one by one these

HISTORY OF BREMER COUNTY.

papers are gathered together and bound, and another volume of local, general and individual history is laid away imperishable. The volumes thus collected are sifted by the historian, and the book for the library is ready. The people of each city or town naturally have a pride in their home paper. The local Press, as a rule, reflects the business enterprise of a place. Judging from this standard, the enterprise of the citizens of Bremer county is indeed commendable. Its papers are well filled each week with advertisements of home merchants, and of its business enterprises. No paper can exist without these advertisements, and no community can flourish that does not use the advertising columns of its local Press. Each must sustain the other.

BREMER COUNTY HERALD.

The first newspaper in Bremer county was entitled the *Bremer County Herald*. It was established upon a very doubtful foundation, at Janesville, in 1855, by Phineas V. Swan. It soon ceased to exist. In November, 1856, it was revived by D. P. Daniels, but again lived only a few weeks. Mr. Swan, the first editor in the county, was a practicing attorney from Vermont, and was the first lawyer admitted to the Bar in Bremer county.

BREMER COUNTY ARGUS.

This was the name of a paper established at Waverly, in January, 1860, by Colonel William Pattee, which advocated and labored to advance the democratic doctrines. Mr. Pattee was an able writer, and in those days a man of considerable note, having been Auditor of the State of Iowa, and holding other prominent positions. Prior to this time the politics of the county had been largely democratic, but this was just on the eve of the war, and the sentiments were undergoing a radical change. For a few months the *Argus* prospered; but then the retrograde set in, and after a year of gradual decline the publication was permanently abandoned.

THE WAVERLY REPUBLICAN.

This is the oldest established newspaper in Bremer county, and in fact, in this part of the State, and its many years of useful existence has placed it among the foremost republican newspapers. Its founder was Heman A. Miles, who, although not being a practical printer, saw the need of a newspaper in Waverly, and took steps to fill that need. He had been the most prominent man in arranging and perfecting the organization of the county, and was at the time, one of the best informed men in this part of the State. The first issue of the paper made its appearance, March 5, 1856. Mr. Miles in this issue made the following remarks, embracing a short history of the county:

Salutatory.

In commencing the publication of our sheet, we frankly acknowledge that we have enlisted in an enterprise of which we have had little experience, but hope that by close application, dilligence and perseverence, we shall become more and better acquainted with the business in which we have engaged, and thereby be enabled to conduct it in a manner that will add credit to the young and flourishing town in which it is published, and deserve merit ourselves.

We shall labor under some inconveniencies at present, as we have but one mail per week, and are entirely dependant upon that for news, but we hope for a speedy increase of mail facilities, as the interest of this, as well as other northern counties of Iowa much demand it; and by diligence and perseverance we hope soon to obtain it. We shall spare no pains in endeavoring to make the *Republican* a useful and interesting sheet, hoping that the citizens of this and adjoining counties may contribute liberally to its support, and that we may succeed in our undertaking.

We shall be confined to no party or clique, whatever, but express our views calmly and independently upon all topics of the day, ever aiming to advance the interests of this and adjoining counties.

Having been one of the early settlers of Bremer county, we have experienced many of the hardships and privations which are attendant to the settling of a new country. We have also had the pleasure of turning over the sod of many acres of its rich and beautiful prairies, while we have at the same time witnessed its rapid growth in population and wealth, which has far exceeded our most sanguine anticipations. We do not wonder at the rapidity with which it has settled up with enterprising and intelligent inhabitants when we look around and see its rich and beautiful prairies, interspersed with the choicest groves of timber and beautiful streams of water unequalled in the State of Iowa. In the spring of 1851, it had about twenty log cabins, destitute of stores and mills of all kinds and description, and the settlers were compelled to go from forty to fifty miles to mill, and fifteen miles to a store. The first store was established here by Messrs Hunter & Leverick, in the spring of 1852, at Janesville, a new town there just laid out by John T. Barrick, Esq.

The county was organized in August, 1853, at which time it had some eighty voters, and the amount of property listed for taxation was $43,437. In August, 1854, the number of voters was one hundred and eighty, the amount of property listed for taxation $285,056

In August, 1855, the number of votes was three hundred and thirty, and the amount of property listed for taxation was upwards of $600,000; since which time there has been erected and put in operation five steam saw-mills, one water saw-mill, one large and splendid flouring mill with two run of burrs, and two other water saw-mills, and one steam saw-mill nearly ready for operation. At present there are laid out in this county seven towns, the oldest of which is Janesville, which was laid out in the spring of 1852, by John T. Barrick, Esq., when the first store was established.

This is a flourishing little town, pleasantly situated on the east side of the Cedar river, some two or three miles above the junction of the Cedar and Shell Rock. It contains at this time, some two hundred and fifty intelligent and enterprising inhabitants, with two stores, a steam and water saw-mill, one hotel, a fine stone school house, 24x36 feet, and a printing office. Next comes the flourishing town of Waverly, the county seat, which was laid out in the fall of 1853, by W. P. Harmon, Frederick Cretzmeyer and William Sturdevant, when was erected and put in the first saw-mill in the county, by W. P. Harmon. The town is pleasantly situated on both sides of the Cedar river, about six miles above Janesville, on the west side of the well-known Big Woods of Cedar, which contain about forty sections of the choicest timber in this part of Iowa, and is one of the most flourishing towns of its age in the Cedar Valley. There are at present four hundred and fifty inhabitants of an enterprising and intelligent character, with nine dry goods stores, three groceries, two hardware stores, a tin shop, drug store, saddle and harness shop, two shoemakers, two blacksmiths, one flouring mill, two hotels, fanning mill manufactory, two shingle machines, printing office, two physicians, two lawyers and a jail.

H. A. Miles, the first editor, was a man of considerable ability and integrity. His education, although somewhat limited was backed by sound common sense. He was the first clerk of courts

HISTORY OF BREMER COUNTY.   937

and was otherwise officially prominent in the early history of the county. His home is now in Texas. He continued in charge of the *Republican* until the 26th of November, 1856, when C. T. Smeed purchased and took editorial control. Mr. Miles in stepping down from the editorial tripod said:

With this number of the paper we transfer the editorship to C. T. Smeed who has purchased one-half of the *Republican* office and will hereafter conduct the paper.

It has now been about eighteen months since we commenced the publication of our paper and it was only the interest that we felt for our town and county that induced us to engage in a business with which we were wholly unacquainted, and owing to our inexperience and the pressure of other business, our paper has been very much neglected and it is with the greatest pleasure that we deliver it into able hands, hoping a continuation of the liberal patronage and support it has ever received from the citizens of our adjoining counties. Our patrons will please accept our sincere thanks and best wishes for unmerited favors.

In the same issue C. T. Smeed assumed the duties, and published a lengthy "Salutatory," setting forth the position he should occupy relating to various questions then rankling the public mind. The article is presented in full:

Salutatory.

Having taken an interest in the Waverly *Republican*, and assumed the care and responsibility of editing and publishing it, it is but due to its patrons that we indicate the course we intend to pursue.

Large promises are of no avail unless fully redeemed, and it is somewhat difficult from unforseen contingencies to redeem such promises, we therefore, deem it best to make but few. We have, however, marked a general course we intend to pursue as far as in us lies, which will yet be subject to the mutability of all human calculations.

We intend to have our say upon all and every topic that may arise through any discussion, and in so doing, we intend to be independent of the control of any party, faction or clique. There is nothing neutral in our composition and character. Therefore, whatever eminates from us will be of a positive character. While we are positive, we shall endeavor not to be dogmatic, but weigh carefully and give due consideration to the opinions of everyone, and ask only the same from others in regard to our own.

We deem almost every subject that may arise, benefitted by discussion, if it be conducted in the proper spirit, and the fact that fanatics exist and many times damage the cause they espouse, is no good reason that discussions should be forgone. Our opinions are liable to change, and we hope they may ever be so, for we do not desire to become a fossil.

On some subjects it is but right that we should at this time declare our views, and in such a manner that no one can mistake them.

Politically, we have labored long and earnestly to organize a party entertaining and advocating the principles laid down in the platform of the republican party, which we aided in erecting. We are emphatically opposed to the extension of the area of bondage, by force or fraud, or even by the enactment of the general government.

We do not believe the Constitution grants to Congress the power to make such enactments. The party which proposes the most active and efficient means to compass the end of a complete divorce of the general government from the thrall and meshes of the slave power, will get our sympathies and support.

Now, therefore, if said party shall honestly redeem the professions made north of Mason & Dixon's Line, and dedicate Kansas to freedom and free labor, it will so far, merit and receive our support, otherwise it will meet our decided opposition.

This is the great political question of the day. Is this continent to be overrun with slavery, or is the fundamental principles of the Declaration of Independence to be carried out in good faith, as was intended by the illustrious penman of that important document?

This is the question that prevailed during the canvass just passed, which has for the next Presidential Olympiad, put the power of the government into the hands of the aristocratic or slave power—not by a majority of the free and thinking people, but by the undue influence given the slave power through the cumberous machinery of the electoral college; and we believe that ere the end of that period is reached, slavery will be theoretically, as far as enactments and decisions of court can do it, rendered national, or, in other words, established wherever the American Congress has jurisdiction over the Territory including, all the now miscalled slave States. It will be extended to all territory outside of organized States, by actual enactment, either of Congress direct or through Territorial legislation, by procurement of the executive sustained by congressional enactment. In the States the constitutions and State enactments will be over borne by the decisions of the courts, and slave-holders will be allowed to drive their slaves where and when they please. Toombs will be supported by the United States Army, to put his threats into execution, of calling the roll of his slaves on Bunker Hill.

We wish to be understood. We do not say that Toombs will do that, but we do say that it is our prediction, that ere the end of the incoming Olympiad is reached, the powers of the government would be exerted to that end, if Toombs should ask it. Our present position is, no more slave territory, no recognition of slavery outside of the present organized slave States, no political interference with slavery within these bounds.

If the powers that be, thrust slavery into Kansas, or in any other unorganized Territory, and organizes it into slavery States, then our position must change and we shall insist upon its being expelled from such Territory. We shall not hold ourselves accountable for the consequences, if the slave power compel us to change from the defensive position we now occupy to the aggresive one—of thrusting back slavery from territory thus invaded. Upon this point we believe we are now understood, and we will pass to the consideration of other matters. The farming interests of Iowa shall receive our special attention, and we ask the aid, counsel and assistance of the farming community in collecting statistics and usuful information in regard to that interest.

To local matters we intend to allot a large space, and ask the public to make this office the connecting point of local intelligence, that we may be able to disseminate the same through the ramifications of the postoffice, to the end of the earth. C. T. SMEED.

On the 17th of April, 1857, H. A. Miles sold his interest in the *Republican* to J. O. Stewart, and the firm became Smeed & Stewart.

In June, 1861, Mr. Smeed disposed of his interest in the *Republican* to J. K. L. Maynard and Louis Case. The first number under the new management bore date June 26, 1861. The new editors in defining their position stated that they were for "the Union, the Constitution, and the enforcement of the laws," and added:

We are now in favor of a complete and perfect vindication of the ability of the General Government to maintain its authority over every foot of Federal territory, and for our own part, we should rejoice to see each and every patriot united as one man, for its speedy accomplishment, even to the extinction of party lines; but the persistent efforts of certain democratic leaders will doubtless compel the republican party of Iowa to maintain a separate and distinct organization, in which case we should labor for the advancement of the interests of the republican party, believing in so doing we shall advance

HISTORY OF BREMER COUNTY.

the welfare and happiness of the citizens of our county and State. We believe that in politics the question of right should be considered; that politics and morals are not divorced, and we shall use all honorable means to maintain the right while we denounce the wrong.

The political department of the *Republican* was placed under charge of Mr. Maynard, while the local and miscellaneous columns were under charge of Mr. Case. The issue of June 19, 1861, contained Mr. Smeed's valedictory. He said:

This step has been somewhat suddenly resolved upon. Duties to my country calls, and such duties are paramount to all personal or private consideration. It is with many regrets that I break up the numerous pleasant associations formed with the readers of my humble journal; and let my lot be cast in pleasant places or otherwise, my remembrances will ever recur to my many friends in this county and State, and my best wishes and constant prayers for their well being will be a part of my very existence. In my intercourse of years with the people, harsh things may have been wrongfully said, such I most sincerely regret. No ascerbity of feeling is now entertained by me toward any one; and whatever of harshness has ever been manifested toward me, is forgotten, to be remembered no more forever. Thanks, and thanks only, have I to tender to the citizens of Iowa, and more particularly to those of Waverly and vicinity, for the thousand manifestations of kind consideration that I have received at their hands. * * * * Next week I expect to leave Iowa, perhaps never to return, to go where my country's service call. Once ere this, at her call I sped to the scene of conflict. It may call me there again. If so, the call will be obeyed.

Mr. Smeed—or, as he was always called "Tarbox" Smeed—went into the army and never returned to Bremer county. A few years later, while in Washington city, he committed suicide.

On the 31st of December, 1871, the *Republican* suspended publication, the office having been consumed by fire, and for four months, Bremer county was without a paper. The cause of the suspension was want of support and destroyal by fire. Mr. Maynard had, for a short time previous been running the paper alone, Mr. Case having retired from the concern in November. On the 26th day of April, 1862, the paper was revived under the name of the *Bremer County Phœnix*, J. K. L. Maynard, editor and proprietor. Mr. Maynard, under the head of "Our County Paper," said that it was the universal remark that the county must have a paper, but he gave the people to understand that he would not publish and lose money. He promised to do his part if the citizens would give substantial encouragement to the enterprise. In regard to its name, the editor says that when he first purchased the office he thought of changing the name of the paper, for the reason there were a number of papers published in the State by the name, *Republican*. The office having been burned, and the new paper arising, as it were, from its ashes suggested "*Phœnix*."

In October, 1864, H. L. Halbert became joint partner with Maynard, but subsequently withdrew, leaving Maynard alone again. Sometime in the summer of 1866, Maynard sold to James O. Stewart, a former proprietor of the paper and Ezra C. Moulton, who assumed the editorship. At this time the name of *Bremer County Phœnix* was discarded and that of

THE WAVERLY REPUBLICAN

again placed at the mast-head. Van E. Butler and C. F. Mallahan, were successors to the above firm, the change taking place in the spring of 1868. Butler is now in some of the Western States, in the newspaper business. Mallahan was a very practical man and a good printer. He is now running a paper at Elk Point, D. T., and has served one term as clerk of the Territorial legislature.

On the 25th of November, 1869, the office was purchased by Daniel Fichthorn and J. B. Scott—the latter remaining in connection only a short time. In mounting the editorial platform, Mr. Fichthorn presented the following as his salutatory:

In making our bow to the readers of the *Weekly Republican*, as editor and publisher thereof, we would remind them that we take upon ourselves no small responsibility

We expect to pass through many trials, troubles and vexations, which generally follow in the walks of those who launch their bark upon the waves of editorial felicity. We are well aware of the difficulties an editor has in pleasing everybody, and are also perfectly acquainted with the fact that an editor's work is never done. He is drained incessantly, and no wonder in many instances he dries up prematurely. Other people can attend banquets, weddings, and the gay and festive halls of amusement, where bright eyes sparkle and hearts made glad, but the editor can not—he must be on hand to answer the cry of "copy," and attend to the hundred and one things essential to a well regulated printing office. The press, like a sick baby, must not be left alone for a moment. If it is delayed a single day, or the paper a few hours behind time, some inhuman subscriber indignantly orders the carrier boy to stop bringing that infernal paper,—there is nothing in it,—I wouldn't have it in the house. These are a few of the perplexities that editors have to put up with. So all can see that it requires a great deal of patience to stand the pressure.

In politics, the *Republican* as heretofore, will be radically conducted in the interests of the republican party—that party which relies for success upon its record in the past the promises which it presents for the future, while the democratic party relies for its success upon having its past record forgotten, and being taken entirely upon faith for the future, or, as the patriot and statesman, Senator Morton, of Indiana, has said: "The democratic party does not invoke the pleasure of memory but invites the blessings of oblivion."

It is our intention to devote as much of our space as possible to general and local news. Hoping that our efforts in giving to the citizens of Bremer county a paper worthy of their patronage, may prove a success, we trust our hopes for the future, to our energies and the liberality of the citizens of the county in sustaining us in our new enterprise. DANIEL FICHTHORN.

Mr. Fichthorn continued in charge of the *Republican* for about five years. Sometime in 1873, an interest was purchased by C. F. Case, and until April, 1874, the firm remained Fichthorn & Case. About the last of 1874, Daniel Fichthorn closed his connection with the paper and Mr. Case assumed entire control. In this shape the management continued until the 24th of of September, 1874, when he sold to W. H. Tyrrell, and went to Minnesota. He is now editor of the *Statesman* in Marshall, Minnesota. Case was not a man of much ability, and a poor newspaper man, yet he was a good financial manager, and would make money in spite of hard times.

In bidding good-bye, he said that "Having sold to W. H. Tyrrell, late senior editor of the *Independent*, he left the paper in a prosperous condition, over a hundred subscribers having been added since last May, and he was glad to leave the *Republican* in such good hands."

H. W. Briden

HISTORY OF BREMER COUNTY. 943

In taking charge, Mr. Tyrrell rather infringed upon the time honored and worn custom of devoting a column of space to a salutatory, but tersely says:

As Mr. Case bids you good-bye, and introduces me, not entirely a stranger to most of you, I will only say, that it will be my earnest endeavor to make the *Republican* worthy of your patronage.
W. H. TYRRELL.

But Mr. Tyrrell did not long continue the management of the *Republican* alone. In October he sold a half interest to Capt. W. V. Lucas, and the firm became Lucas & Tyrrell, they having been prior to this, in partnership in the management of the *Independent*. This made a strong journalistic company. This co-partnership continued until January, 1876, when Capt. Lucas withdrew, James Fletcher having purchased his interest in the paper. The Captain soon afterward removed to Mason City, Cerro Gordo county, where he engaged in another newspaper enterprise. He has served one term as Auditor of the State of Iowa, and was prominent officially during his many years residence in Bremer county. In the chapter upon National, State and County Representation, he is noticed more at length.

James Fletcher, who purchased Lucas' interest, soon took charge of the *Republican* and the firm has since remained Fletcher & Tyrrell—James Fletcher and W. H. Tyrrell. Upon taking the editorial chair, Mr. Fletcher, in a plain, practical talk with his readers, said:

I enter upon a new field of duty—that of editor of this paper. It was not my design to take part in the duties till the new year, but for private reasons of the retiring editor, Captain W. V. Lucas (justifiable to himself, and on the whole, satisfactory to me), I assumed the place so ably filled by him, on the 18th inst. And now that I am installed in the editor's chair, grave question rise in my mind, foremost of which is, how to conduct the *Republican* so as to give the best satisfaction to its many readers. I see on its long list of patrons, many familar names, and withal personal friends of mine; friends whose kind patronage in years gone by has helped to place me in position to purchase this interest in our county paper. It is on those friends' account, as well as many others, whose names I hope to see on the subscription list by-and-by, that the above question arose. The near future will decide whether I anticipated their wants or not.

In this social chat with my friends I beg leave to state that the *Republican* will remain true in politics to the name it bears. This paper will not, however, be a shield for any one in their wrong doings, no matter what political banner they sail under. It has been too much the custom of newspapers—and deplorably so—to defend the official corruption of their political party. This is wholly wrong. A newspaper should be fearless in exposing villany, no matter on whose head the axe falls. Public exposure by the Press will soon cleanse all offices of rascals. It shall be the creed of the *Republican* to perform this duty, should occasion require it, at home or elsewhere.

Friendly criticisms will undoubtedly occur at times, but nothing of that nature shall be written in anger.

Sensation of all kinds will be carefully avoided, and facts only, instead of fancy, will find place in these colums.

Finally, I propose to meet the wants of our patrons by giving them, as far as lies in my power, the worth of their money, and to do this (having the hearty concurrence of my partner, Mr. Tyrrell), I announce that about the commencement of the new year, the *Republican* will be enlarged from its present size to a six column quarto. This change will incur just double the expense for material that it costs now. I hope our friends will appreciate our effort, and recognize them in the manner always so acceptable to newspaper men.

Respectfully,
JAMES FLETCHER.

The *Republican* has always rested solely upon its merits, and stood for its intrinsic worth; with what success is shown by their present condition, as it to-day has undoubtedly as large a permanent circulation and as much influence as any paper in the county. At various times it has been enlarged, growing from a six page folio—the size of its first issue—to its present size, a seven column quarto, the largest in the county, the last enlargement being made in 1878. The last given salutatory, was written, it is but justice to state, by Mr. Fletcher, just after his return from a tour to the Old World, and finding one of his children dead, it is no wonder that his mind was in no condition to enter upon editorial duties, yet it is well and tersely written.

James Fletcher was born in Berkshire, England, in 1840. When five or six years of age he came to America and lived with relatives in Lawrence, Mass. There he remained until twelve years of age, when he removed to Vermont. His youthful days were spent in school and at work, preparing himself for college, and working for his board. When twenty years of age he enlisted in one of the first regiments which left Vermont for the war, and served three years. His health failing him, he was honorably discharged and soon afterward came to Waverly, arriving in November, 1865. He was deputy treasurer of the county for two years, and then purchased an interest in the book store, which, with the exception of a few months he has since owned. In November he purchased his interest in the *Republican*. Mr. Fletcher is an able and tasty writer, and is well adapted to the profession he has chosen.

William H. Tyrrel, Mr. Fletcher's partner, is a native of McHenry county, Ill., where he was born on the 26th of December, 1848. His father was a farmer and stone mason. When five years of age his parents removed to Bremer county, Iowa, where Mr. Tyrrell has since lived. In 1864 he commenced work at his trade, printing, and still continues it. His connection as to ownership, dates from 1872. He is a thorough printer and a gentleman.

THE DEMOCRATIC NEWS.

This newspaper was started at Waverly, in 1867, by Wright & Stow—Gancelo C. Wright and W. A. Stow. It first made its appearance on the 27th of June, 1867, as a six-column folio, all printed at their office, one door east of the Bremer House. The paper was pretty well filled with advertisements, and presented a very neat appearance. In accordance with the immemorial custom of the craft, upon presenting a new paper, the publishers made a formal introduction of the *News* to the reading public, in which, after a brief reference to local matters, they said:

Ours is a business enterprise and not a political scheme, and is identified with the business interests of the place. As its name would indicate, the *News* takes its stand in the political field upon the side of democracy, and, planting its standard upon a platform of *principles*, will never be found beating the "policy" role. We shall raise at our mast-head the candidates only of regular democratic conventions, and shall advocate such healthy democratic doctrines as:

Equal taxation and representation; The sovereignty of States and the supremacy of civil law; The Union of the States under the old constitution; And *white* men for rulers.

* * * We will seek to avoid giving needless offense, and endeavor at all times to show that courtesy and respect due an honest opponent. With these its objects, aims and principles, the *News* presents itself as a candidate for public favor.

In about six months the *News* was purchased by George Lindley. He ran it for about three years, when it was finally changed to the

BREMER COUNTY INDEPENDENT,

having been purchased by Maynard & Lord, in 1870. In about a year and a half it was purchased by Daniel Fichthorn, who was then proprietor of the Waverly *Republican*. Through his influence Capt. W. V. Lucas was induced to go into the newspaper business, and assume management of the *Independent*.

In January, 1872, Capt. W. V. Lucas purchased the *Independent* and in its issue of January 12th, assumed full control. He says in his salutatory:

In entering upon the management of the *Independent* we do so with many misgivings, knowing something of the difficulties that surround a country newspaper. But we are willing to work, provided we can make a living by doing so. It is not the notoriety or fame we seek, but the public good and our own interest. We have been a resident of Bremer county for seventeen years; we have seen it transposed from a vast plain to a well cultivated and prosperous community; we have seen the growth and wealth of our city accumulate from year to year; we have seen them in times of war and in times of peace, always the same industrious people. * * * *

We do not undertake the publication of *The Independent* for the purpose of breaking down or crippling the interests of any like enterprise, but simply to continue its existence as long as it pays for the time and money used in furnishing it to our patrons.

In politics *The Independent* will be straight republican. advocating the doctrine as enunciated by the last National Republican Convention, not hesitating to denounce corruption wherever found, believing that to be the correct way to preserve the integrity of any party * * To the public we now make our bow and say, "Walk up to the captain's office and subscribe for *The Independent* for the year 1872."

This was the beginning of Captain Lucas' editorial career. He was very prominent in the political history of the State.

At this time *The Independent* was a six-column quarto, well printed, ably edited and its columns well filled with advertisements. In the issue of January 26th, 1872, the form of the paper was changed, it coming out as a seven-column folio. Before the close of the year, however, the old form was resumed.

In the fall of 1873, the management of the *Independent* underwent a change—W. H. Tyrrell purchasing an interest, the firm became Lucas & Tyrrell, and in a short time it again changed, becoming Fitchthorn & Tyrrell. The latter partnership continued for about six months, when in 1873, Tyrrell became connected with the *Republican*, and Daniel Fitchthorn assumed full management of the *Independent*, which he has since continued. The *Independent* has varied somewhat as to form, for a time being a seven-column quarto, but is now back to the convenient size of six-column quarto. A few years since Mr. Fichthorn inaugurated a system of drawings, giving every paid up subscriber a chance to win various valuable articles, among which, at the 1883 drawing, were a piano and wagon. This has proved a success, and "the *Independent* offering day" has become one of the gala occurrences of Bremer county.

In the issue of the 15th of June, 1882, the *Independent* closed its fifteenth volume, and in making a few remarks regarding it, Mr. Fichthorn said:

With this number we close the fifteenth volume of the *Independent*. We have stood by it in storm and in sunshine, and we are glad to announce that never in its existence has it enjoyed a more healthy patronage than at the present time. With a paying list of 1,350 subscribers, and a healthy advertising and job patronage, we have reason to be thankful, and we start on the new year with renewed vigor and a determination to leave nothing undone to maintain the confidence manifested us in giving to our large family of readers a paper worthy of their support.

The circulation of the paper has now grown to 1,550, which is a healthy and paying list. It is a valuable medium for advertising.

Daniel Fichthorn, editor and proprietor of the *Independent*, was born in Lewistown, Pennsylvania, on the 16th of November, 1836. His father was engaged in various occupations, and Daniel was brought up attending school and at odd times working at "mighty hard work." He spent several years in the Lewistown Academy, and finally, when about seventeen years of age, his father wishing to educate him for a Lutheran minister, tried to persuade him to go to one of the noted colleges, although the matter was left to Daniel to choose a life calling for himself. This he did by deciding to follow the printing business, and accordingly commenced his apprenticeship in an old time democrat office in his native town. After working for one year for $40 per year, and boarding himself, his employer, William McKay, died, thus releasing him from two years of his apprenticeship. He next went to Altoona, Pennsylvania, then a little village of 1500, and commenced work upon the first paper established in the place. After working a short time there, and being swindled out of small and hard earnings, he returned to his native place, and for a time drove boat on the canal, and occupied his time in various ways. He was yet a young man, or rather a boy, and having expressed a desire to go west, his father, who was then worth about $40,000, asked him if he really wished to go. This was entirely unexpected to Dan, for, although he had expressed a desire to go, the thought of leaving home for a land which was supposed to be inhabited by Indians and "half animal pioneers," had never once really entered his head. But he did not hesitate and at once answered, "yes." His father then told him that he would supply him with enough money to get him to the point to which he wanted to go, but no more, as he did not propose to give him a chance for squandering. Thus it was settled, and much against the wishes of his mother, Daniel started for Indiana, which was then considered as being "way out west." He arrived at Lafayette, in that State, one Saturday night, with only a five franc in his pocket, and at once proceeded to the *Daily Journal* office, where he applied for a place, which he obtained. He was told that his wages would be $9 per week until they knew what he could do. This made him feel pretty good, as he had never received more than $40 per year for his services, boarding himself. The result was that, as he was a very rapid "typesticker," he was soon getting $15 per week. He remained at this place about a year and a half, and then went to Delphi, Indiana. Here he remained in the employ of James B. Scott for about fourteen years, acting in the capacity of foreman, editor-in-chief and pressman, in fact doing about all the work on the paper. During the war, he took an active stand against the rebellion, and was an abolitionist in the strictest sense. He won a reputation throughout the entire State from the bitter and telling articles he wrote upon the subject. Upon one occasion, while defending himself against a rebel sympathizer who was going to kill him for some article which had appeared in his paper, he was shot through the wrist. In November, 1869, through the influence of Capt. Lucas, he and his old employer, Mr. J. B. Scott, were induced to come to Waverly, and purchase the *Republican*. After the purchase had been made, and notes given, Scott backed out, leaving Mr. Fichthorn alone to stand the brunt of the battle, with but little means to do it. This involved him in debt to the amount of $3,200. However he went to work and by industry and perseverance soon cleared himself of it. In January, 1864, he was married to Miss Jennie McClure. Mr. Fichthorn was postmaster of Waverly for nearly four years, and has also held other positions of trust. He is a man of good natural as well as acquired ability. As a writer he is pungent and to the point, wasting no time trying to display what he could do. Gentlemanly and accommodating, he is popular and esteemed in Waverly circles. It should have been stated in connection with the foregoing, that Mr. Fichthorn served his country in the war of the rebellion.

THE WAVERLY TRIBUNE.

This representative of the Press of Bremer county, was established in 1882, by E. J. Dean, the first issue making its appearance on Friday, the 17th day of February, as a seven-column folio, well printed, and the editorials showing the mark of a mind well stored with reading and education. There is probably a good deal of interesting history connected with the foundation of this paper, and from what the project sprung. In taking the editorial pen, Mr. Dean, in his salutatory, addresses his readers as follows:

In this, the first number of the *Tribune*, it may be well enough to outline, to some extent, its character. I propose to publish, during the ensuing year, a newspaper devoted to such interests as will conduce to the public weal—local notices, general news boiled down to a minimum, accurate market reports, facts rather than opinions. Fairness and impartiality will characterize its treatment of men and events. Personalities will be excluded, but principles affecting the public welfare, and reflecting shades of opinion, however diverse, will be welcomed to its columns. To interpret the spirit that ought to actuate an American, will be my aim, and to reflect it will be my object. The Press is the greatest power in the land; it helps to mould or reflect public opinion, which, right or wrong, when chrystalized, is irresistable. A blessing or a scourge, it is always something of a force in society. It exposes the sophistries of demagogues, turns the

HISTORY OF BREMER COUNTY.

calcium light of truth upon the dark recesses of depravity; it helps to eliminate error, and to hold up that for emulation which is only worthy of it. To tell the truth, defend the right, expose the wrong, convey the news, and to do what it can to make one better in the world for having lived in it, gives some idea of the scope and object of the *Tribune*.
E. J. DEAN.

The *Tribune* is still thriving, and has worked up the largest circulation of any newspaper between Dubuque and Ackley in the counties of Bremer, Chickasaw, Howard and Butler, amounting in all to 1,920; and Mr. Dean declared upon affidavit, that 1,094 of them were in Bremer county.

Hon. E. J. Dean, editor and proprietor of the *Tribune*, was born in New York State, in April, 1833. His early life was spent upon a farm and in teaching school several winters. When nineteen years of age he went to Kentucky, and after remaining in the west for a few years, went back to New York, where he prepared for and entered the Central College, in that State, from which he graduated June 23, 1858, at which the degree of Bachelor of Arts was conferred upon him, and later the degree of Master of Arts. He then came west and spent several years in teaching school in Kentucky, Indiana, Illinois and Iowa. In 1863, he came to Bremer county for the purpose of making it his home, having previously been here and purchased about 500 acres of land. He has been here ever since, and was for many years one of the most wealthy men of the county. He was Representative of this district in the Lower House of the General Assembly, and made one of the best Representatives the county has ever had. He is also noted in connection with the chapter upon National, State and County Representation.

THE PRESS AT SUMNER.

The history of Press matters in Sumner does not extend as far back as in other towns in Bremer county, but it is now ably represented by the *Gazette*. The pioneer journalist was R. W. Lee, now attorney-at-law, DesMoines, Iowa. His paper was called *The Sumner Camera*. He took typographical pictures of the town and vicinity during 1875, but turned off the light in a few months and left the whole scene in editorial darkness. Nothing more was done in this direction until the railroad came, upon which arrived J. O. Stewart and Ed Madigan. They were pleased with the town and opened a subscription-list for a paper to be called the *Sumner Review*. Arrangements were quite well perfected for its issue, when E. H. Yarger bought up the prospect, and the paper appeared on January 5th, 1881, as

THE SUMNER GAZETTE.

Mr. Yager continued its publication a short, time when he sold to S. F. Case and T. W. Tower and a son of the latter, assumed editorial charge. He was a young man of much promise, but for some unaccountable reason, committed suicide before the first issue was published—his salutatory and obituary appearing in the same paper. While the second issue under this management was in course of preparation the *Gazette* was transferred to G. P. Linn & Co., the present owners. Since which time it has appeared with G. P. Linn as editor and C. S. Linn as business manager. It seems to have a healthy growth. G. P. Linn, the editor, is a young man of ability and well calculated for the work in hand. He was for some time principal of the school here, but the increasing business of the *Gazette* compelled him to give his whole attention to the paper.

G. P. Linn, editor of the *Gazette*, was born in Winnebago county, Illinois, August 30, 1849. His father, George Linn, died in 1868, at the age of fifty years; but his mother, Adeline, is living in Sumner. In 1853, Mr. Linn, with his parents, came to Iowa, and settled in Fayette county, Banks township, being the third family to settle there. He was educated at the Upper Iowa University, Fayette county, graduating in 1876, teaching winters in order to carry him through college. After graduating he went to New Hartford and taught the high school, continuing to teach in Butler county until September, 1881, when he was engaged to take charge of the high school in Sumner, which position he held until the 30th of November, 1882, when he resigned to take full charge of his paper which he purchased in 1881. Mr. Linn now owns the building where his paper is published, and by strict integrity and attention to business, has won for himself many warm-hearted friends. He is a member of the Masonic Fraternity. He was married August 7, 1878, to Miss Grace E. Paulger, of Butler county. They have one son—Louis P.

DEUTSCHE VOLKS-ZEITUNG.

This was the first representative of the German Press of Bremer county. It was established at Waverly, as a weekly, in 1874, by Tyrrell & Fichthorn; the first issue making its appearance on the 20th of May. On the 31st of July following, it was purchased by John Weidmann. For a number of years he continued as proprietor, the paper being a seven-column folio, and published in the *Republican* office.

Within the past few months it came into the hands of Dr. Carl Dermenden, Mr. Dryer and the Hilmer brothers, who are yet proprietors. It is a neatly printed seven-column folio, and is printed upon a press which the new managers have lately purchased.

The name of the paper has been changed to the "*Volks-Blatt.*"

THE JANESVILLE CLIPPER.

This was a journalistic venture attempted by O. J. Smith, in Janesville, in 1874. It existed but two months.

WAVERLY DEMOCRAT.

The *Waverly Democrat* was started in 1880 by G. C. Wright and his son James W. The first number made its appearance on the 27th of February, the paper being an eight column folio, the same size as at present. The publishers, in their inaugural address, said:

It being customary and proper to announce in the first issue of a newspaper the course intended to be pursued by the editors in future issues, we, in accordance with such custom, state that we intend to publish a democratic newspaper, one that will support the nominees of the democratic conventions, when regularly expressed by the properly constituted delegates of such convention, national, State and county, and will advocate democratic principles as defined by such conventions; that it will be independent at all times; that it will treat all subjects and persons fairly, and we shall endeavor

950   HISTORY OF BREMER COUNTY.

to the best of our ability to make it a lively and readable paper, one worthy the support of the citizens of Bremer county.

The *Democrat* has moved along very successfully, and is still under the original management, as G. C. Wright & Son. In February, 1883, it closed its third volume, not having missed a single issue, and in making some general remarks regarding it, the publishers say:

Our subscription list has been steadily upon the increase, being now about 900, and we have reduced the price 25 per cent. if paid in advance, hoping thereby to save the expense of collections, upon which basis we enter next week upon the fourth volume with renewed assurance and confidence that we shall meet the approval of the reading people, and that they will sustain us in the future, as in the past, in our endeavors to furnish the latest, most accurate, general and local news, and to our subscribers and advertisers we return our heartfelt thanks for past favors, and hope and believe that as friendly relations will continue to exist in the future.

Gancelo C. Wright, one of the proprietors of the *Democrat*, for a number of years practiced law in Bremer county, and is noted at length in the chapter upon the Bar. His son, James W. Wright, who has charge of the mechanical and local departments, is a native of Bremer county, is a thorough printer, and is a young man of much promise.

CHAPTER XIII.

THE WAR FOR THE UNION.

The institution of slavery was always a source of trouble between the free and slave-holding States. The latter were always troubled with the thought that the former would encroach upon their rights, and nothing could be done to shake this belief. Compromise measures were adopted from time to time to settle the vexed question of slavery, but the fears of the slaveholders were only allayed for a short time. Threats of secession were often made by the slave-holding States, but as some measures of a conciliatory character were passed, no attempt was made to carry their threats into execution. Finally came the repeal of the Missouri Compromise and the adoption of a measure known as the Kansas-Nebraska bill. This bill opened certain territory to slavery, which, under the former act, was forever to be free. About the time of the passage of this act, the whig party was in a state of dissolution, and the great body of that party, together with certain democrats who were opposed to the Kansas-Nebraska bill, united, thus forming a new party, to which was given the name of Republican, having for its object the prevention of the

HISTORY OF BREMER COUNTY.

further extension of slavery. The people of the South imagined they saw in this new party, not only an organized effort to prevent the extension of slavery, but one that would eventually be used to destroy slavery in those States in which it already existed.

In 1860 four Presidential tickets were in the field. Abraham Lincoln was the candidate of the republicans, Stephen A. Douglas of the national democrat, John C. Breckenridge of the pro-slavery interests, and John Bell of the Union. The Union party was composed principally of those who had previously affiliated with the American or know-nothing party. Early in the campaign there were threats of secession and disunion in case of the election of Abraham Lincoln, but the people were so accustomed to Southern bravado that little heed was given to the bluster.

On the 20th of December, 1860, South Carolina, by a convention of delegates, declared, "That the Union now existing between South Carolina and the other States of North America is dissolved, and that the State of South Carolina has resumed her position among the Nations of the earth, as a free, sovereign and independent State, with full power to levy war and conclude peace, contract alliances, establish commerce, and do all other acts and things which independent States may of right, do."

On the 24th Gov. Pickens issued a proclamation declaring that "South Carolina is, and has a right to be, a free and independent State, and as such has a right to levy war, conclude peace, and do all acts whatever that rightfully appertain to a free and independent State."

On the 26th, Major Anderson evacuated Fort Moultrie and occupied Fort Sumter, Two days previously he wrote President Buchanan's Secretary of War, John B. Floyd, as follows:

"When I inform you that my garrison consists of only sixty effective men, and that we are in very indifferent works, the walls of which are only fourteen feet high; and that we have, within one hundred and sixty yards of our walls, sand hills which command our works, and which afford admirable sites for batteries and the finest coverts for sharp-shooters; and that besides this there are numerous houses, some of them within pistol shot, and you will at once see that, if attacked in force, headed by any one but a simpleton, there is scarcely a possibility of our being able to hold out long enough for our friends to come to our succor."

His appeal for re-inforcements were seconded by Gen. Scott, but unheeded by President Buchanan, and entirely ignored by John B. Floyd, Secretary of War.

On the 28th, South Carolina troops occupied Fort Moultrie and Castle Pinckney, and hoisted the palmetto flag on the ramparts. On the 29th John B. Floyd resigned his place in Buchanan's cabinet, charging that the President, in refusing to remove Major Anderson from Charleston Harbor, designed to plunge the country into civil war, and added: "I cannot consent to be the agent of such a calamity." On the same day the South Carolina commissioners presented their official credentials at Washington, which, on the next day were declined.

On the second day of January, 1861, Georgia declared for secession, and Georgia troops took possession of the United States arsenal in Augusta, and Forts Pulaski and Jackson.

Gov. Ellis, of North Carolina, seized the forts at Beaufort and Wilmington and the arsenal at Fayetteville. On the evening of the 4th, the Alabama and Mississipppi delegations in Congress telegraphed the conventions of their respective States to secede, telling them there was no prospect of a satisfactory adjustment. On the 7th, the conventions of Alabama, Mississippi and Tennessee met in secret conclave. On the 9th, Secretary Thompson resigned his seat in the Cabinet on the ground that, contrary to promises, troops had been sent to Major Anderson. On the 9th, the "Star of the West," carrying supplies and re-inforcements to Major Anderson, was fired into from Morris Island, and turned homeward, leaving Fort Sumter and its gallant little band, to the mercy of the rebels. On the same day, the ordinance of secession passed the Mississippi Convention. Florida adopted an ordinance of secession on the 10th, and Alabama on the 11th. The same day (the 11th) Thomas, Secretary of the Treasury, resigned, and the rebels seized the arsenal at Baton Rouge, and Forts Jackson and St. Philip, at the mouth of the Mississippi river, and Fort Pike at the entrance to Lake Pontchartrain. Pensacola navy yard and Fort Barrancas were surrendered to rebel troops by Colonel Armstrong on the 13th. Lieutenant Slemmer, who had withdrawn his command from Fort McRae to Fort Pickens, defied Armstrong's orders, and announced his intention to "hold the fort" at all hazards.

The Georgia Convention adopted an ordinance of secession on the 19th. On the 20th, Lieutenant Slemmer was besieged by a thousand "allied troops" at Fort Pickens. Louisiana adopted an ordinance of secession on the 25th. On the 1st of February the rebels seized the United States Mint and custom house at New Orleans. The Peace Convention assembled at Washington on the 4th, but adjourned without doing anything to quiet the disturbed elements. On the 9th, a provisional constitution was adopted at Montgomery, Alabama, it being the Constitution of the United States "re-constructed" to suit their purpose. Jefferson Davis, of Mississippi, was chosen President, and Alexander H. Stevens, of Georgia, Vice-President of the "Confederate States of North America." Jeff. Davis was inaugurated on the 18th, and on the 25th it was learned that General Twiggs, commanding the Department of Texas, had basely betrayed his trust, and that he had surrendered all the military posts, munitions and arms to the authorities of Texas.

Mr. Lincoln was inaugurated March 4, 1861, in front of the capitol, the inauguration ceremonies being witnessed by a vast concourse of people. Before taking the oath, Mr. Lincoln pronounced in a clear, ringing voice, his inaugural address, to hear which, there was an almost painful solicitude, to read which the whole American people and the civilized world awaited with irrepressible anxiety. With that address, and the administration of the oath of office, the people were assured. All doubt, if any had previously existed, was removed. In the hands of Abraham Lincoln, the people's President, and himself of the people, the government was safe.

Traitors were still busy, plotting and planning. Troops were mustering in all the seceded States. On Friday, April 12, the surrender of Fort Sumter, with its garrison of sixty effective men, was demanded and bravely refused by the gallant Major Anderson. Fire was at once opened on the helpless garrison by the rebel forces, numbered by thousands. Resistance was useless, and at last the National colors were hauled down, and by traitor hands were trailed in the dust. On Sunday morning, the 14th, the news of the surrender was received in all the principal cities of the Union. That was all, but that was enough. A day later, when the news was confirmed and spread through the country, the patriotic people of the North were startled from their dreams of the future—from undertakings half completed—and made to realize that behind that mob there was a dark, deep, and well organized purpose to destroy the government, rend the Union in twain, and out of its ruins erect a slave oligarchy, wherein no one would dare question their right to hold in bondage the sons and daughters of men whose skins were black. Their dreams of the future—their plans for the establishment of an independent confederacy—were doomed from their inception to sad and bitter disappointment. Everywhere north of Mason and Dixon's line, the voice of Providence was heard:

> "Draw forth your million blades as one;
> Complete the battle now begun;
> God fights with ye, and overhead
> Floats the dear banner of your dead.
> They, and the glories of the past,
> The future, dawning dim and vast,
> And all the holiest hopes of man,
> Are beaming triumphant in your van."
>
> "Slow to resolve, be swift to do!
> Teach ye the False, how fights the True!
> How buckled Perfidy shall feel,
> In her black heart the Patriot's steel;
> How sure the bolt that Justice wings;
> How weak the arm a traitor brings;
> How mighty they who steadfast stand,
> For Freedom's flag and Freedom's land."

On Monday, April 15th, President Lincoln issued the following proclamation:

"WHEREAS, The laws of the United States have for some time past, and are now, opposed, and the execution thereof obstructed, in the States of South Carolina, Alabama, Florida, Mississippi, Louisiana and Texas, by combinations too powerful to be suppressed by the ordinary course of judicial proceedings, or by the powers vested in the marshals; now therefore, I, Abraham Lincoln, President of the United States, by virtue of the power in me vested by the Constitution and the laws, have thought to call forth, and hereby do call forth, the militia of the several States of the Union, to the number of 75,000, in order to suppress said combinations, and to cause the laws to be duly executed.

The details for this subject will be immediately communicated to the State authorities through the War Department. I appeal to all loyal citizens to favor, facilitate, and to aid this effort to maintain the honor, the integrity, and existence of our National Union, and the perpetuity of popular government, and to redress wrongs already long endured. I deem it proper to say that the first service assigned to the forces hereby called forth will probably be to repossess the forts, places and property which have been seized from the Union; and in every event the utmost care will be observed, consistently with the object aforesaid, to avoid any devastation, any destruction of, or interference with property, or any disturbance of peaceful citizens in any part of the country; and I hereby command the persons composing the combinations aforesaid, to disperse and retire peaceably to their respective abodes, within twenty days from this date.

Deeming that the present condition of public affairs present an extraordinary occasion, I do hereby, in virtue of the power in me vested by the Constitution, convene both Houses of Congress. The Senators and Representatives are therefore summoned to assemble at their respective chambers at 12 o'clock, noon, on Thursday, the fourth day of July next, then and there to consider and determine such measures as in their wisdom the public safety and interest may seem to demand.

In witness thereof, I have hereunto set my hand and caused the seal of the United States to be affixed.

Done at the city of Washington, the fifteenth day of April, in the year of our Lord one thousand eight hundred and sixty-one, and of the independence of the United States the eighty-fifth.

By the President.
    ABRAHAM LINCOLN.
W. H. SEWARD, *Secretary of State.*"

The last word of this proclamation had scarcely been taken from the electric wire before the call was filled. Men and money were counted out by hundreds and thousands. The people who loved their whole country, could not give enough. Patriotism thrilled and vibrated and pulsated through every heart. The farm, the workshop, the office, the pulpit, the bar, the bench, the college, the school-house—every calling offered its best men, their lives and fortunes, in defense of the Government's honor and unity. Party lines were for a time ignored. Bitter words, spoken in moments of political heat, were forgotten and forgiven, and, joining hands in a common cause, they repeated the oath of America's soldier statesman: "*By the Great Eternal, the Union must and shall be preserved!*"

Seventy-five thousand men were not enough to subdue the rebellion. Nor were ten times that number. The war went on, and call followed call, until it seemed as if there were not men enough in all the free States to crush out the rebellion. But to every call for either men or money, there was a willing and ready response. The gauntlet thrown down by the traitors of the South, was accepted; not, however, in the spirit which insolence meets insolence, but with a firm, determined spirit of patriotism and love of country. The duty of the President was plain under the Constitution and laws, and, above and beyond all, the people, from whom all political power is derived, demanded the suppression of the rebellion, and stood ready to sustain the authority of their representative and executive officers, to the utmost extremity.

While other portions of the State and Nation were manifesting, in words and deeds, their patriotism, the citizens of Bremer county were not idle. A large and enthusiastic meeting was held in Waverly, on the evening of April 22d, in which strong resolutions were passed, breathing intense loyalty, and in favor of sustaining the government. A military company was formed at the time numbering forty men, which completed its organization by electing G. W. Ruddick, Captain; H. F. Beebe, First Lieutenant, and C. C. Allen Second Lieutenant, with a full compliment of non-commissioned officers. The citizens of Horton held a meeting the

HISTORY OF BREMER COUNTY.

same evening, passed strong resolutions, and instituted measures for raising a company, which, the Waverly *Republican*, of the 29th, said would be ready to go to the front at the "drop of a hat." The Horton company was organized by electing H. A. Tinkham, Captain; C. A. Brown, First Lieutenant; M. L. Marsh, Second Lieutenant; W. W. Gray, Orderly Sergeant. Flags were thrown to the breeze from nearly every business house, and from many of the private residences of the citizens of the entire county.

The first meeting held to raise funds for the benefit of the volunteers or their families, was on the evening of May 21, 1861. There was raised on that occasion $365.50, in addition to which W. P. Harmon gave to each volunteer in the company known as the Pioneer Greys, a town lot in Waverly, and also a lot to the wife of each volunteer.

Bremer county was behind no county in the State in the exhibition of sublime patriotism. Being without railroad or telegraph facilities, the news did not reach the people of the county in time to be numbered in the first call of the President for 75,000 men, but in the second and every succeeding call, it responded with its noblest and best men, some of whom went forth never to return. The record of the county at home or in the field, is a noble one. By referring to the chapter containing the action of the Board of Supervisors, it will be seen what was done in an official way. In an unofficial way the people took hold of the work, aided enlistments, and furnished a large amount of sanitary supplies.

In this connection has been compiled from the Adjutant-General's report, the name of every soldier from Bremer county. If any are omitted, it is not intentional, for great care has been exercised in the compilation, and none have more veneration for the brave soldier than the author of this volume. So far as it could be done, mistakes in spelling names have been corrected.

Bremer county was first represented in the Third Infantry, but those names were not credited to the county, having gone to Cedar Falls and there enlisted. The following is the record:

THIRD INFANTRY.

COMPANY K.

George W. Briggs,
W. W. Wood.
Pat Burke,
G. E. Ellsworth,
Samuel Grove,
M. F. Gillett,
W. E. Gosting,
S. C. Hammond,
Albert G. Lawrence,
John McRoberts,
C. C. Moulton
William Peyton,
John W. Pattee,
J. A. Ross,
F. M. Tyrell,
G. H. Watson,
C. E. Wemple,
A. H. Wemple.

SIXTH INFANTRY.

COMPANY G.

Privates.
Jones, Robert J.,
Richardson, Wm. A.,
Hudson. William H.
Richardson, George S.,
Wait, John.

NINTH INFANTRY.

COMPANY F.

Corporal:
Alfred C. Gunsabris.

HISTORY OF BREMER COUNTY.

COMPANY G.

First Lieutenants:
Hinkley F. Beebe,   Edward Tyrell.

Second Lieutenant:
Asbery Leverich.

Sergeants:
Andrew J. Strow,   Silas D. Tabor,
Orran A. Beebe.

Corporals:
Cyrus D. Neff,   Asahel Thornsbree,
Charles W. Mallory,   Samuel W. True,
Nathan S. Harwood,   David Vankleck,
Caleb J. Sturdevant,   William A. Pelton.

Musician:
James R. Eldridge.

Wagoner:
James T. Fowler.

Privates:
Brown, Thomas W.,   Lucus, Alexander,
Buckmaster, James F.,   Lampson, James H.,
Barrick, John,   Myers, Phillip B.,
Baskeins, Clark J.,   Morton, Franklin A.,
Cutts, Levi,   McRoberts, Alonzo,
Cave, Philip,   More, Robert,
Ellis, George W.,   Risden, Daniel,
Figg, Lewis M.,   Reum, Benjamin F.,
Green, Abijah B.,   Sewell, Sylvester,
Jordan, Michael L.,   St. John, Johnnie G.,
Kinsey, James M.,   St. John, James W.,
Karker, John,   Sturdevant, Cabel J.,
Linsey, James S.,   Tyrrell, Edward.

VETERANS:

First Lieutenant:
Floyd W. Foster.

Sergeants:
Cyrenius D. Neff,   Silas D. Taber.

Corporals:
William A. Pelton,   Asahel Thornbrue,
David Vankleck.

Privates:
Cave, Philip,   Green, Abijah B.,
Ellis, George W.,   Sewell, Sylvester,
Figg, Lewis M.,   Tanner, William.

COMPANY H.
Hinkley, Albert.

COMPANY I.
Axile, Frances.

UNASSIGNED.
Chambers, William.

NINTH IOWA INFANTRY.

The Ninth Iowa Infantry was organized by Hon. William Vandevere, early in August, 1861, and went into rendezvous at Dubuque, and was mustered into service on the 24th of September, with the following organization: William Vandevere, Colonel; Frank J. Herron, Lieutenant-Colonel; William H. Coyle, Major; William Scott, Adjutant; F. S. Winslow, Quartermaster; Benjamin McClure, Surgeon; H. W. Hart, Assistant Surgeon; Rev. A. B. Kendig, Chaplain.

The regiment remained at Dubuque but a few days after being sworn in, proceeded to Benton Barracks and went into camp, where it remained until the middle of October, when it was sent to guard the southwestern branch of the Pacific Railway between Franklin and Rolla; they remained here three months.

On the 22d of January they went to Rolla and joined the army of the southwest, under Brigader-General Samuel R. Curtis. They then marched to Lebanon and stayed a week. Colonel Vandevere had command of the Second Brigade, and the Iowa troops participating in the campaign were in Colonel Carr's Division.

The army marched after the Rebel Price, and it was on one of these marches that the Ninth was first under fire, during which they behaved more like veterans than raw recruits, charging and driving before them a force fully three times as strong as their own.

The Ninth Iowa took quite an active part in the battle of Pea Ridge, after a most laborious march (through a snow storm) of forty-one miles, and reached the scene of action in good time; and during the two days hard fighting they never flinched, although they lost very heavily, and had not a field officer fit for duty.

Having buried the dead and cared for the wounded, the army moved from Pea Ridge through part of Missouri and Arkansas, to Helena, where the regiment had its first and last permanent encampment.

The regiment commenced the new year with the Campaign of Arkansas Post, which resulted in the capture of a large number of prisoners, and an immense quantity of supplies and arms. Remaining a few days at Arkansas Post, they next went to Young's Point, and were here encamped many weary weeks, in a vast swamp, while death held high carnival, and vast acres of grave yards were seen in all directions.

Meantime Colonel Vandevere had been promoted a Brigadier-General, and Captain David Carkaddon was elected and commissioned in his place.

The first active campaign in which the regiment engaged after he took command, was the expedition of General Steele into central Mississippi. Returning, the command encamped for a short time at Milliken's Bend, and then joined in the grand campaign of Vicksburg, which they commenced on the 2d of May. Rapidly marching by Richmond, they took part in the capture of Jackson. Then, facing about, it moved in the direction of Vicksburg, and, on the 18th took position on the right of our lines, before the enemy's works. On the 19th, there was an irregular assault in which the Ninth lost a number in killed and wounded. It was on the front line in the unsuccessful assault of the 22d, and on that day alone lost nearly one hundred men in killed and wounded. The regiment lost, during the siege, one hundred and twenty-one.

The next day after the capitulation, the army, under Sherman, moved after Joe Johnson and followed him to Jackson, during which campaign the Ninth fully participated, after which they went into camp to enjoy a rest, so well earned.

Their next move was toward Chattanooga, which was begun on the 22d of September, and on the 22d of November, after a march of three hundred miles, the regiment pitched its tent at the foot of Lookout Mountain. Twenty four hours later it was taking a gallant part in the "battle above the clouds," under General Hooker. The enemy encamped on Lookout Mountain on the night of the 24th, and on the following day the battle of Missionary Ridge took place, the rebels running to escape and our troops running to catch them. Thus they had a running fight for miles. The regiment continued in pursuit, under Hooker, to Ringold, where they had an engagement with the enemy. The loss in these three engagements was three killed and sixteen wounded.

From Ringold they marched to rejoin Sherman; and went into winter quarters but a few days before the close of the year.

HISTORY OF BREMER COUNTY.

New Year's day was spent by the regiment in re-enlisting. By this time the number of men had been reduced to about five hundred, of whom all were not eligible as veterans under the rules of the War Department. Nearly three hundred re-enlisted, and the Ninth became a veteran regiment, and all went home on a furlough the following month, and stayed thirty days. They then, with many recruits, went to the rendezvous at Davenport, and, under command of Major George Granger, moved to Nashville, from thence to Woodville, where they arrived April 10th.

On the 1st of May, Colonel Carksadden, just returned from sick-leave, in command, took up line of march for Chattanooga, and at once entered upon the campaign of Atlanta. For the next four months the regiment took part in all the labors, marches, skirmishes, battles and sieges of this great campaign. The losses of the regiment were fourteen killed and seventy wounded and six captured.

They next started in pursuit of Hood, making, in one month, a march and countermarch of three hundred and fifty miles.

After a few weeks halt at Savannah the regiment sailed to Beaufort, South Carolina, where it remained a short time awaiting the complete readiness of General Sherman to march through the Carolinas.

The march northward began on the 26th of January. After taking part in the grand review, they proceeded to Louisville and were mustered out. From there they moved by rail to Clinton, Iowa, for final payment and home.

ELEVENTH INFANTRY.

COMPANY F.

Sergeant:
Isaac N. Carr.
Privates:
Capen, Alexander,   Hitchcock, Jabez,
Layton, Stephen,   Morrow, Thomas A.

TWELFTH INFANTRY.

FIELD AND STAFF OFFICERS.
Com. Sergt.—Rich, Andrew J.

COMPANY C.
Corporal:
Henry C. Curtis.

COMPANY E.
Corporals:
Joseph W. Rich,   M. V. B. Sunderlin
Privates:
Sharp, Oliver,   West, David F.
[For history see War Chapter of Butler county.]

THIRTEENTH INFANTRY.

UNASSIGNED:
Converse, Charles.

FOURTEENTH INFANTRY.

COMPANY B.

Captain:
Richard Currier.

First Lieutenant:
William V. Lucas.

Second Lieutenant:
A. J. Allen.

Sergeants:
Allen E. Holmes,   William Parmenter,
Harris G. Wells,   Thaddeus W. Kelley,
J. L. Scott.

HON. Wᴍ P. HARMON.

Corporals:
Alfred Robinson,
Carl J. Lamson,
Charles Runyon,
Alexander F. Nichol,
Edwin H. Tyler,
Joshua Gilmore.

Musicians:
Sayles B. Phillips.

Privates:
Auner, Hiram,
Bevard, Darius
Bevend, James M.,
Beeker, Charles,
Churchill, Elias A.,
Carberry, Amos M.,
Chadwick, John J.,
Dildine, William H.,
Dutcher, Albert W.,
Gars, Henry,
Graves, Cyrus B.,
Haun, George
Kerr, John B ,
Lucas, James B.,
Meeker, Joshua,
Mohling, Christain,
Messinger, John F. 2d,
Nergo, John,
Parker, Sidney J.,
Rockwood, James B.,
Severine, John,
Sleeper, Stephen,
Shoemaker, Joseph,
Winklepleck, Noah,
Winklepleck, Seth,
Webb, Albert,

Arnal, James,
Barclay, William H.,
Bodecker, August,
Baseley, George W.,
Conner, Sanford E.,
Clark, Maroni,
Dean, James W.,
Dicken, Stephen M.,
Farnsworth, Guy ,
Griever, Robert,
Higgins, Hubert R.,
Hall, Levi,
Legge, Frederick,
Moser, John,
Meier, Henry,
Messinger, John F. 1st,
Mabb. William D.,
O'Brien, Edward,
Richman, John,
Smith, Elijah,
Sowers, John,
Shivley, Stephen A.,
Thorp, Charles J.,
Winklepleck, Abram,
Westervelt, Lewis R.,
Zoler, John R.

COMPANY C.
First Lieutenant:
Heman A. Miles,

Sergeant:
Roswell Keith.

Corporal:
Barney W. Robbins.

Musician:
William Morgan.

Privates:
Buckmaster, Frederick,
Davidson, C. F.,
Brown, Richard,
Harmon, Abner,

Lashbrook, Royal,
Tenaure, Charles H.
Streeter, Henry W.,
Walling, James P.,
Wright, Philander D.

RESIDUARY BATTALION OF THE FOURTEENTH.

COMPANY A.

Meeir, Henry, Nergo, John.

COMPANY B.
Stewart, Charles.

Before going to the field, a sword was presented to Captain Currier. The following account of the affair is from the Waverly *Republican:*

"On Thuesday evening, December 9, 1862, the ladies of Bremer county presented a fine Damascus Blade to Captain R. Currier, of Company B, Fourteenth Regiment, Iowa Infantry. The presentation speech made by the Hon. G. W. Ruddick, was neat and appropriate.

"The Captain's reply shows that he has the true mettle, and we are sure he will not disappoint the hopes of his numerous friends. Below we give the presentation speech and reply:

" 'Captain Currier, we meet together this evening under peculiar and solemn circumstances. The country that has given us a home, and the government that has protected us in our lives, our liberties and our accumulations of property, formed by the wisdom of our fathers, and transmitted to us with all its blessings and obligations, is now in danger; its existence is threatened by a conspiracy in magnitude, extent of its ramifications, and black-hearted treachery, has never been paralleled. Traitors have been and now are waging a war which they design shall put a period to our existence as a Nation; a war that has drenched our fair land with blood of our brothers; has sent death and mourning into every family; has been so destructive of human life that our dead armies now almost equal our living ones; has burned our cities, ravaged and destroyed the wealth and improvement of a large section of our country, and the soldiers see instead of happy homes and fruitful fields, mouldering heaps of ashes and barren waste. They have not struck at the life of this Nation, but they have struck at the great principle of civil liberty all over the earth. In this dark hour of the Nation's trials, she has called her sons to the rescue, and they come—the sturdy farmers of New England; the stalwart lumbermen of Maine, Michigan and Wisconsin; the hardy frontiersmen of Minnesota, Iowa and Kansas. Even the gold diggers of California have cast aside their picks and shovels for the sabre and musket; the Middle States pour fourth their teeming thousands, until the land resounds with the thundering tramp of a million of men in arms. But in the embattled ranks no hearts are braver, no arms are stronger, none can more bravely dare or nobly do, than the brave sons of Iowa; first in the charge and last in the retreat, they have gained for our noble State a reputation that cannot be surpassed.

" 'You have heard this call, you have marshalled your band and gone forth to do the noblest duty of a freeman; we honor your resolution, and hope for your success. It will be your privilege to defend that flag that we delight to honor, and which must never trail in the dust; to emulate the deeds of those brave men who have gone before, and to defend, if need be with your life, the principles of free government.

" 'In the full belief you will do your part in this great struggle manfully, and never shrink in that hour which tries men's souls; and wishing to convey to you a testimonial of the confidence and esteem, the ladies of Bremer county have purchased this sword, and have requested me to present it to you, together with their best wishes for your success.

" 'Those fair ones, whose only privilege it is to cheer and comfort the living, and mourn the dead, have an interest in this contest surpassed by none, and when you draw the sword in battle, think that you are defending the rights of those who can not defend themselves; think the prayers of your loyal and patriotic friends and neighbors go with you, and it will lend a double force to your arm and a courage to your heart.

" 'Accept this as the offering of true and loyal hearts; guard it as you would guard your life; never suffer a stain of dishonor to tarnish the brightness of its steel, draw it valiantly in defense of all that is sacred and just, and sheath it not except in the bosom of our enemies, until our country is triumphant over all her foes.

" 'Be vigilant and faithful and brave, and when the war clouds which now darken our land shall have been borne away, and a brighter sun than has ever shown upon America, shall be shedding its golden light over a united land, smiling in its abundant fields and happy homes, we will welcome back to the paths of peace, you and your brave companions in arms, with hearts filled with gratitude and pride for the services you shall have done us and our common country.'

"In reply, Captain Currier said:

"'Ladies of Bremer county: I thank you for so beautiful a token of your confidence and esteem, promising you that its blade in my hands, and myself, shall never be separated from the cause of our country, and that when called upon to use it, I shall never disgrace it. I have volunteered to serve my country in this war. Of about twelve hundred thousand men who have taken the field, nearly all are volunteers; a proud proof to the world of the strength of our free government and the patriotism of its citizens. The war in which we are engaged is a holy and just one; treason has taken up arms to destroy; a powerful and brave enemy is waging war with desperate fury; many thousand of our comrades have given their lives to their country; duty may require of us the same sacrifice.

"'The regiment with which I am associated is composed of brave men and true; they have been recently released from Rebel prisons, will be nerved by the thought that they are sustaining a righteous cause, and consoled by the assurance that a Just Being will crown them with success, and when I return to you I will continue to treasure this token as a pleasing memento to the donors and citizens of Waverly.'"

The Fourteenth Infantry, Colonel William T. Shaw, was re-organized under somewhat peculiar circumstances, in the fall of 1861, being enrolled under the President's proclamation of October of that year. Before the regiment was organized, three companies recruited therefor, designated as Companies A, B, C, were sent to the western frontier on special service, and remained ever afterward detached from the regiment.

Though these companies continued *pro forma*, to constitute a part of the Fourteenth Regiment for a considerable period, they were never under command of the commanding officer of the regiment, and never did, except by the merest technicality, make a part of it. They were afterward, by order of the War Department, permanently detached from the regiment, and for a time constituted the First Battalion of the Forty-first Infantry. But the formation of that regiment not being completed, they were left out in the cold again until they became, at last, an integral part of one of the Cavalry regiments. It will suffice here to state that, until they were thus assigned, they were in the performance of garrison duty at the fort before named.

As a matter of fact, the Fourteenth Iowa, during the first year of its service, consisted of only seven companies.

The regiment was organized at Camp McClellan, near Davenport, November 6, 1861, with the following officers: William T. Shaw, Colonel; Edward W. Lucas, Lieutenant-Colonel; Hiram Leonard, Major; Noah N. Tyner, Adjutant; C. C. Buell, Quartermaster; George N. Staples, Surgeon; S. N. Pierce, Assistant.

At this time, not counting those companies who never served with the main body, there were more than six hundred officers and enlisted men in the regiment.

After remaining at Camp McClellan a few weeks, they were moved to Benton

HISTORY OF BREMER COUNTY.

Barracks, near St. Louis, where a great many were stricken down with pneumonia and measles, and quite a number died.

On the 5th of February, they embarked on steamers for the theater of war, and went into camp at Fort Henry, just after its surrender. On the morning of the 12th it took up line of march, with the army moving on the enemy's works at Donelson, and on the first day of the battle, was in position on the left wing, Gen. Percifer F. Smith commanding. In the battle which followed, the Fourteenth was conspicuous for its gallantry, fighting with that immortal brigade, under command of Colonel J. G. Lauman, Seventh Iowa, which first forced its way into the rebel works, and won the brightest laurels among all the bright wreathes which were here won by the army under Grant. The regiment, in its first battle, lost three killed and twenty-one wounded.

It remained at Fort Donelson about three weeks after the capitulation. It then embarked on steamers for Pittsburg Landing and went into camp here on the 18th of March. In the battle of Shiloh, the Fourteenth formed part of that self-constituted, forlorn-hope, which, fighting the live-long day against fearful odds, and staying the rebel advance, by its own heroic immolation, saved the army and made the victory of the 7th of April, possible. Just as the sun was setting, Colonel Shaw, seeing further fighting useless, surrendered his command prisoners of war.

The losses up to this time in killed and wounded had been heavy, but the sacrifice of these and of the principal command in captivity, practically closed the career of the Fourteenth, for many months. They were held as prisoners of war at the south until late the following fall. They were then sent to Benton Barracks, Missouri, and exchanged on the 19th of November. They remained here all winter for re-organization. Those who had not been captured rejoined the regiment, also two new companies that had been organized—A and B—in lieu of two of those that had been sent to Fort Randall; many new recruits were received.

On the 10th of April, the re-organized command took steamer for Cairo, where they went into camp, and were joined by Company C. Thus was the "bloody old Fourteenth," for the first time, organized with a full complement of companies. This was in June, 1863.

In the latter part of June they were sent to Columbus, Kentucky, where they remained on garrison duty for seven months. The men became very dissatisfied at this action, and longed to be taking part in the siege of Vicksburg. Colonel Shaw, and the officers, made such good use of this long period of inactivity that when they left Columbus for active service they were one of the best drilled and disciplined regiments in the volunteer army.

On the 24th of January, 1864, the regiment started for Vicksburg. Here it was assigned to the Second Brigade, with Colonel Shaw, who retained the command until he left the service, nine months after. His brigade, by its endurance of fatigue and its firmness in battle, acquired the *sobriquet* of the "Iron Brigade," and its commander that of "Grim Fighting Old Shaw." Soon after its arrival at Vicksburg, the Fourteenth took up the line of march with Major-General Sherman, on his famous Meridian raid.

On the return of the regiment to Vicksburg they at once proceeded to the mouth of Red River, where they took a prominent part in the charge and capture of Fort De Russey. Marching part of the way and moving part of the way by steamer, it proceeded with the force under General Smith, to and beyond Grand Ecore.

On the 8th of April, Banks fought and was defeated in the battle of Mansfield. On the next day General Smith saved the army by the victory of Pleasant Hill. In this severe engagement Colonel Shaw's Iron Brigade long stood the brunt of battle, fighting against fearful odds, till night put an end to the contest. His losses were very heavy. The Fourteenth fought with great bravery and effect, and did as much toward saving the army from defeat as any of the gallant regiments of the little band. The regiment here lost its commanding officer, several other officers of great merit, and many men, killed and wounded.

On the retreat of Banks from Pleasant Hill, the army were continually harrassed by the rebels, and had a skirmish at Clantierville, April 23d, and at Moore's Plantation, May 5, 6, 7; Marksville on the 16th, and had a severe engagement at Yellow Bayou on the 18th, and here ended its contests in the Department of the Gulf. On the next day they reached Atchafalaya, where they had disembarked two months before, and crossed to Morganza, from whence they proceeded by river to Vicksburg. From here they proceeded to Memphis, and from there marched into Mississippi, having a number of skirmishes, then returned to Memphis. General Smith then moved to Cairo, from thence was ordered into Missouri to help repel Price. They first went to St. Louis, then to Pilot Knob to reinforce General Thomas Ewing, Jr., where they had an engagement with the enemy, and fought against fearful odds. General Ewing, after a severe struggle, evacuated and blew up his magazine, scattering the fort in ruins, and retreated to Rolla, cutting his way through the rebel lines, which he did in good style, fighting all the way for four days, with only about one hour's rest in the twenty-four; their feet were covered with blisters, but they had done their duty under a General who had done his, and they marched into Rolla with feelings of pride.

The regiment proceeded to Davenport and going into Camp Kinsman, near by, was mustered out of service on the 16th of November. Those recruits and companies whose time had not expired, were formed into an organization called the "Residuary Battalion," and consisted of two companies.

FIFTEENTH VETERAN INFANTRY.

COMPANY H.

Fairbrother, Hiram.   Wade, Abraham.

TWENTY-FIRST INFANTRY.

COMPANY F.

Patterson, Flavins J.   Patterson, Osbra.

COMPANY K.

Potter, George.

COMPANIES UNKOWN.

Andrews, Ralph.   Blake, Calvin B.
Bowstitch, Elisha.   Brown, James F.
Root, Elisha R.

TWENTY-SEVENTH INFANTRY.

COMPANY B.
Ashline Lewis.

COMPANY C.
Hale, William A. Celsey, John W.
Kelsey, Eastman. Lashbrook, Edgar
Martin, Charles J. Ober, Elijah S.
Watkins, David.

COMPANY E.
Ashland, Lewis.

THIRTY-SECOND INFANTRY.

COMPANY E.
Robbins, Alfred.

THIRTY-EIGHTH INFANTRY.

COMPANY A.
Dixey, Thomas L.

COMPANY B.
Captain:
Hinkley F. Beebe.

First Lieutenant:
Asbury Leverick,

Second Lieutenant:
Orrin F. Avery.

Sergeants:
Ed. C. Daugherty, John H. Brooks.
Abel M. Crail. John D. Garrrison.
Joseph A. J. Nichols.

Corporal:
Henry Schaffer, Hiram Queen,
Leander L. Reynolds, George W. Baskins,
George A. Michael, Cyrus Robbins,
Philander H. Smith, Lorin L. Curtis.

Musician:
Norman E. Dodge.

Wagoner:
George W. Baskins.

Privates:
Baskins, David W. Baskins, Francis M.
Benjamin, William S., Bell, Elisha,
Beebe, Jerod J., Beebe, Charles,
Brown, George A., Baskins, William,
Blocker, George. Brower, Erastus L.,
Bacher, James A., Barrick, Isaac,
Baum, Yenger, Bartlett, William H. H,
Butler, William O., Burke, David C.,
Beebe, Sherman F., Chesley, John H,
Downs, Samuel, Dudgeon, Hugh,
Dougherty, Martin, Davis, George W.,
Dodge, Levi, Farris, James M.,
Farris, Joseph B, Fleisher, Adam,
Freeman, Alzathan S, Gardner, George N.,
Griffin, James S, Garner, James,
Huston, Francis, Hinton, Shadrick,
Hursh, John A., Jeffers, Thomas C.,
Jones, John O., Jones, John G.,
Jeffers, James G., Keller, Henry,
Kern, Samuel, Kenyon, Sanford,
Kerr, Francis, Lowe, Lewis H.,
Leslie, Thomas H., Lewis, Isaac M.,
Mattix, Jacob, Moore, Aaron, Jr.,
Michael, Jacob B., McHenry, William H.,
McRoberts, Sanford, Norris, Edward F.,
Newell, Marion, Osthman, Thomas,
Ogden, William H., Rose, William E.
Rodgers, George, Ren), Jacob T.,
Smith, Charles E., Stearns, Thomas A.,
Sewell, Samuel, Shepard, Lambert P.,
Sharp, Coswill, Smith, Harvey D.,
Sturdevant, William, Sewell, Thomas J.,
Shores, William, Shane, Ellis,
Taylor, William S., Taylor, Arthur S.,
Wilson, Samuel, West, David F.,
Wilson, William.

ADDITIONAL:
Smith, P. H., Barrick, William N.,
St. John, David J.

COMPANY C.
Captain:
Henry A. Tinkham.

Sergeant:
James F. Luman.

Corporal:
Edgar J. Nutting.

Wagoner:
Hiram King.

HISTORY OF BREMER COUNTY.

Privates:
Beebe, Chester A., Edgington, William O.,
Buckmaster, F. M., Glass, James A.,
Brant, John H., Harwood, George F.,
Brant, Nimrod, Henry, John,
Blackwell, Wm. H. E., Knott, John,
Cook, George G., Lewis, Enos,
Colby, Smith, Phelps, Lavenus,
Wilson, James.

COMPANY F.

Miller, Hiram, Obenchain, William F.
Obenchain, Philip B., Russett, Joseph,

THIRTY-FOURTH INFANTRY.
[Consolidated with Thirty-eighth Infantry.]

COMPANY G.

Brant, Nimrod, Gates, Emory J.,
Brant, John H., Harwood, George F.,
Blackwell, James F., Harwood, Childs S.,
Blackwell, Wm. H. C., Knott, John,
Downer, John L., Phelps, Lavinus,
Evans, Alson, Phelps, John S.,
Wilson, James.

COMPANY I.

Captain:
Orrin F. Avery.

First Lieutenant:
Edward E. Dougherty.

Sergeants:
Able M. Crail, George N. Gardner.
Martin Dougherty.

Corporals:
George A. Michael, William E. Rose,
Hugh Dudgeon, George A. Brown,
Isaac Barrick, James Gardner.

Privates:
Beebe, Jerard J., Lowe, Lewis H.,
Brower, Erastus L., Mattix, Jacob,
Bicher, James A., McHenry, William H.,
Blocker, George, McRoberts, John,
Burke, David C., Mallery, John N.,
Barrick, William N, Moore, Samuel S.,

Bogart, Nelson, Miller, Nathan R.,
Burlingame, Seymour, Newell, Marion,
Colby, Smith, Renn, Jacob T.,
Davis, George W., Sharp, Caswell,
Dodge, Levi, St. John, David J.,
Davis, Amasa W., Smith, Charles E.,
Dingman, Jacob, Sewell, Samuel,
Flesher, Adam, Smith, Harvey D.,
Farris, James M, Shane, Ellis,
Gilbert, Joseph F., Shores, William,
Hinton, Shadrack, Shaw, Enos F.,
Houghton, John C., Sharp, Levi,
Jeffero, Thomas C., Sleeper, Edgar N.,
Jeffero, James G., Sturdevant, William,
Kerr, Francis, Wilson, Samuel,
Lewis, Isaac M., West, David F.,
Wilson, Charles A.

THIRTY-EIGHTH.

The companies of the Thirty-eighth Regiment, Iowa Volunteer Infantry, were enrolled in five counties—Fayette, Winneshiek, Bremer, Chickasaw and Howard, Bremer furnishing two.

They went into rendezvous at "Camp Franklin," near Dubuque, and were mustered into service on the 4th of November, numbering about nine hundred strong, with David H. Hughes, Colonel; Joseph O. Hudnott, Lieutenant-Colonel; and Charles Chadwick, Major.

Having remained in Camp Franklin several weeks for drill and discipline, Colonel Hughes moved to St. Louis, and went into quarters at Benton Barracks. The regiment remained there a few days, during which time Colonel Hughes procured complete equipments for the field. During the holidays he was ordered by General Curtis to report with his command at Helena, Arkansas.

At Columbus, Kentucky, the order was countermanded, and he was ordered to proceed to New Madrid, which had recently been evacuated. He reached New Madrid, January 2, 1863, and proceeded at once to re-garrison the fort, re-build the barracks, unspike the guns, and in all ways put the place in a state of defense. They remained here entirely undisturbed until June.

On the 7th of June, they left New Madrid, for Vicksburg, joining Major-General Herron's troops on the way thither; on the 15th they took position on the left of the investing army, and from that time until the capitulation, was engaged in the duties of the siege.

The encampment of the regiment was on the border of a cypress swamp, whose baleful influences brought many officers and men to beds of sickness, and finally to the grave.

On the 12th of July, the regiment embarked for Port Hudson, but went instead to Yazoo City, with General Herron's forces, they took part in the severe march which followed, in the direction of Jackson. General Herron returned to Vicksburg on the 21st, and a few days after moved to Port Hudson, where they stayed about three weeks. It was here that their unfavorable position in the investment of Vicksburg, and its severe labors, became most painfully evident. The command was almost entirely prostrate, there being at one time only eight officers and twenty enlisted men fit for duty. The encampment was a hospital, filled with the sick and dying. Colonel Hughes died here, also Captain Henry A. Tinkham and Lieutenant George H. Stevens, all valuable and gallant officers, which the Thirty-eighth never ceased to lament. Lieutenant-Colonel Hodnett being sick, the command of the regiment devolved on Major Chadwick.

The regiment moved from Port Hudson and went into convalescent camp at Carrollton, Louisiana, about the middle of August, where they remained two months. When Banks started on his expedition to Texas, the Thirty-eighth joined Herron, and on the 23d of October sailed for Brazos Santiago; thence it joined in the march to Brownsville, where it arrived November 9th, and remained there on garrison duty till the latter part of July, 1864, when the town was evacuated by the Unionists. On the last day of July they embarked at Brazos Santiago for New Orleans. In a few days it embarked for Fort Morgan, and went into camp on Mobile Point, in the rear of that work, now besieged, on the 9th of August. Here the command remained until the work fell into Union hands, when it returned to New Orleans.

On the 12th of December, Major-General Canby issued an order for the consolidation of the Thirty-fourth and Thirty-eighth Iowa regiments into the Thirty-fourth Iowa Volunteers. This was consummated on the 1st of January, 1865. Thus the Thirty-eighth Iowa Volunteers passed out of being. Its members formed a goodly portion of the Thirty-fourth.

The history of the Thirty-eighth is the saddest of all the Iowa regiments. It had not been in the service two years when more than three hundred of its enlisted men and a number of its officers had died of disease. More than one hundred men and a score of officers during the same period had been discharged on account of ill-health. There were long weary weeks when there were not enough well men to take care of the sick, not even enough to bury the dead. The Thirty-eighth was composed of as gallant men as any who went to the war, and if it did not have an opportunity to achieve brilliant renown in the field, it did all that men could do—it gave itself entirely up for the good of the service, and is fairly entitled to the honor of being called Iowa's Martyr Regiment.

FORTY-FIRST INFANTRY.

FIELD AND STAFF OFFICERS:
Hospital Steward—John M. Peebles.

COMPANY A.

Second Lieutenant:
Wallace Patter.

Musician:
William C. Morton.

Privates:
Collins, Alfred,
Pitcher, Luther S.
Green, James S.,
Roop, Amos,
Watts, Levi F.

FORTY-FOURTH INFANTRY.

COMPANY C.

First Lieutenant:
Lyman L. Smith.

Second Lieutenant:
George W. Wood.

Corporals:
Lafayette J. Sturdevant, John W. Eldredge.

Privates:
Allen, Lorenzo C.,
Bowman, Jonas E.,
Case, Oscar,
DeCamp, John A.,
Jefferson, William,
Screbner, John W.,
Bryans, Andrew,
Belt, Aaron J.,
Dyre, George F.,
Farnum, Zuriah L.,
Smith, Oliver J.,
Sturdevant, Harvey,
Tibbles, James.

FORTY-SIXTH INFANTRY.

COMPANY D.

Mallory, William.

FORTY-SEVENTH INFANTRY.

COMPANY D.

Adams, James A.,   Loftus, Robert.

COMPANY H.

Smith, Herbert F.

SECOND CAVALRY.

COMPANY C.

Funston, Charles R.,   Goodenow, Martin,
Hall, James,   Hurd, James.

THIRD CAVALRY.

COMPANY D.

Beard, William.

FOURTH CAVALRY.

FIELD AND STAFF OFFICERS:
3 B. S. M.—Henry A. Tinkham.

COMPANY G.

Noble, Jacob B.

COMPANY H.

Corporal:
Luther P. Chandler.

Privates:
Fairbanks, John,
Gates, George W.,
Johnson, Lockwood,
Fox, James H.,
Hopkins, Leman S.,
Lovejoy, Abija,
McDonald, William G.

ADDITIONAL ENLISTMENTS.
Campbell, Dennis,
Fish, Earnest,
Horton L., Jackson,
Dodge Henry,
Harker, George M.,
Morse, John.

VETERANS.

Corporals:
Luther P. Chandler, Leman S. Hopkins.

Trumpeter:
Harvey W. Case.

FIFTH CAVALRY.

VETERAN.
Seward, Daniel E.

SIXTH CAVALRY.

COMPANY B.
Harker, John D.

COMPANY C.
Bingham, Charles W., Moon, Whitcomb,
Powell, Arthur J.

COMPANY H.
Bywater, Adelbert.

SEVENTH CAVALRY.

COMPANY K.
Second Lieutenant.
Wallace Pattee.

Sergeant:
Edward C. Bristol.

Corporal:
Campbell McLane.

Trumpeter:
William C. Morton.

Farrier:
Jacob H. Fordney.

Privates:
Barnhouse, John, Brant, Michael,
Collins, Alfred, Graham, John W.,
Green, James F, Morton, Robert L.,
Roop, Amos, Watts, Levi F.,

COMPANY UNKNOWN.
Sherwin, Lewis P.

VETERANS OF COMPANY K.

Second Lieutenant:
Wallace Pattee.

Quartermaster Sergeant:
James R. Mitchel.

Farrier:
Jacob H. Fordney.

Trumpeter:
William C. Morton.

Privates:
Barnhouse, John, Brant, Michael,
Green, James S., Roop, Amos,
Shepherd, William H., Smith, Philip,

EIGHTH CAVALRY.

COMPANY G.
Hamilton, Thomas D., Hursh, Samuel,
Hursh, Daniel, Lashbrook, William,
Lovejoy, Marshall.

FIRST BATTERY IOWA LIGHT ARTILLERY.
Fortner, Church, Moody, Charles D.,

IOWA SOLDIERS IN MISSOURI REGIMENTS.

ENGINEER REGIMENT OF THE WEST.
COMPANY F.
Payson, Louis B.

THIRD MISSOURI INFANTRY.

COMPANY I.
Sergeants.
William F. Peck, Charles C. Allen.

Privates:
Burris, John W., Chettenden, F. C.,
Fisher, William, Freeman, John H.,

HISTORY OF BREMER COUNTY.

Johnson, William,
McGinnis, Orville,
Pound, Orange,
Keer, James L.,
Morrille, George W.,
Wise, George.

Total number furnished from Bremer county, 477; including those in every position.

ROLL OF HONOR.

"It is sweet and honorable to die for one's country." The following is a list of those who lost their lives in the service of the government:

Lieutenant Edward Tyrrell, killed in battle, at Vicksburg, Mississippi, May 22, 1863.
Lieutenant Leverich, died April 6, 1863, at New Madrid, Missouri.
Adams, James A., died of typho-malarial fever, September 18, 1864.
Bloker, George, died February 10, 1864, at Janesville.
Baum, Yeager, died July 24, 1863, at Vicksburg, Mississippi.
Butler, William O., died September 4, 1863, at Vicksburg, Mississippi.
Beebe, Chester A., died February 17, 1863, at Horton.
Baskins, George W., died August 20, 1863, at Memphis, Tennessee.
Baskins, David W., died August 19, 1863, on steamer City of Memphis.
Baskins, Francis M., died August 14, 1863, at Fort Hudson.
Benjamin, William S., died September 27, 1863, at Dubuque, Iowa.
Bell, Elisha, died September 3, 1863, at New Orleans, Louisiana.
Bingham, Charles W., died October 20, 1863, at Byron's Hills, D. T.
Brown, Thomas W., died June 25, 1863, at Memphis, Tennessee, of wounds.
Bevend, James M., died November 29, 1862, at Davenport, Iowa.
Bogart, Nelson, died July 13, 1865, at Galveston, Texas.
Beebee, Charles, died October 27, 1863, at Janesville.
Baskins, William, died November 25, 1863, at New Orleans, Louisiana.
Clark, Meroni, died July 15, 1862, at Tyler, Tex., while prisoner of war.
Chandler, Luther P., died February 4, 1864, near Bolton, Mississippi.
Case, Harvey W., died May 18, 1865, at Eastport, Mississippi.
Davidson, Christopher F., died September 6, 1863, at Columbus, Kentucky.
Dodge, Norman E., died August 25, 1863, at St. Louis, Missouri.
Downs, Samuel, died August 26, 1863, at Carrollton, Louisiana.
Evans, Alson, died April 15, 1865, at Barrancas, Florida.
Edgington, William O., died August 16, 1863, at Vicksburg, Mississippi.
Funston, Charles R., died in March, 1864, at Columbus, Mississippi.
Freeman, Alzathan S., died August 25, 1863, at New Orleans, Louisiana.
Goodenow, Martin, died March —, 1864, at Camp Dennison, Ohio.
Gilmore, Joshua, died August 2, 1863, at Centralia, Illinois.
Graves, Cyrus B., died July 24, 1862, at Columbus, Kentucky.
Gates, George W., died October 8, 1862, at St. Louis, Missouri.
Gars, Henry, died December 1, 1862, at Davenport, Iowa.
Griffith, James S., died August 30, 1863, at Memphis, Tennessee.
Hurd, James, died of typhoid fever, at Davenport, Iowa, January 25, 1863.
Higgins, Hubert, died August 18, 1863, at Denver.
Hursh, John A., died December 31, 1863, at New Orleans, Louisiana.
Henry, John, died December 24, 1862, at Dubuque, Iowa.

Jones, John G., died August 28, 1863, at New Orleans, Louisiana.
Karker, John, killed in battle at Pea Ridge.
King, Hiram, died at New Madrid, Missouri, February 2d, 1862.
Kern, Samuel, died Nov. 8, 1862, at New Orleans, Louisiana.
King, Hiram, February 2, 1863, at New Madrid, Missouri.
Keith, Roswell, died July 16, 1864, at Waverly.
Kelsey, John W., died May 13, 1865, at Montgomery, Alabama.
Linsey, James S., died of fever at Springfield, Missouri, June 25, 1862.
Leverick, Willard, killed in battle at Pea Ridge.
Lucas, Alexander, J., died March 30, 1862, at Vicksburg.
Leslie, Thomas H., died July 18, 1863, at Vicksburg, Mississippi.
Lewis, Issaac M., died November 10, 1863, at Janesville.
Lyman, James F., died October 1, 1863, at New Orleans, Louisiana.
Lewis, Enos C., died Oct. 8, 1863, at Cairo, Illinois.
Myers, John M., killed in battle at Pea Ridge.
Morrille, George W., died of pneumonia, at Benton Barricks, February 16, 1862.
McDonald, William G., died September 12, 1862, at Helena, Arkansas.
McRoberts, Alonzo, died April 21, 1863, at Vicksburg, Mississippi.
Messinger, John F., died January 15, 1863, at Davenport, Iowa.
Moore, Aaron, Died August 28, 1864, at New Orleans, Louisiana.
McRoberts, Sanford, died November 30, 1863, at Point Isabell, Texas.
Morrill, George W., died February 16, 1862, at Benton Barricks, Missouri.
Nutting, Edgar J., died May 20, 1863, at New Madrid, Missouri.
Ogden, William H., died of Measles at Waverly, Iowa, November 13, 1862.

Olenchain, Philip B., died April 19, 1864, at Barrick Hospital, New Orleans.
O'Brien, Edward, killed, April 9, 1864, in battle at Pleasant Hill.
Ober, Elijah S., died April 9, 1864, at Helena, Arkansas.
Osthman, Thomas, died August 24, 1863, at Port Hudson, Louisiana.
Parker, Sidney J., killed April 9, 1864, in battle at Pleasant Hill.
Payson, Louis B., died at Sedalia, Missouri, March 8, 1862.
Robbins, Barney, died of pneumonia at Columbus, Kentucky, November 1, 1863.
Russett, Joseph, died June 7, 1864, at Jefferson Barracks, Missouri.
Richardson, William A., died December 24, 1863, at Chattanooga, Tennessee, of wounds.
Reynolds, Leander S, died October, 30, 1863, at New Orleans, Louisiana.
Robbins, Cyrus, died December 27, 1863, on Steamer Crescent.
Rodgers, George, died November 19, 1863, at New Orleans, Louisiana.
Smith, Philander H., died in hospital, January 23, 1863.
Sturdevant, Harvey B., died at Keokuk, Iowa, August 30, 1864.
Smith, Isaac A., died March 10, 1865, at Spirit Lake.
Sturdevant, Caleb J., died January 26, 1863, at Vicksburg, Mississippi.
Shepard, Lambert P., died July 14, 1853, at Vicksburg, Mississippi.
Thorp, Charles I., died September 27, 1864, at Pilot Knob, Missouri, of wounds.
Taylor, Authur S., died March 5, 1863, at Horton.
Taylor, William S., died July 26, 1863, at Vicksburg, Mississippi.
Watkins, David, died May 15, 1864, at Columbus, Kentucky.

CHAPTER XIV.

EDUCATIONAL.

The educational history of Bremer county is one of interest, and the zeal displayed by many in the interests of good schools, is indeed commendable. The common schools of our country are now regarded by many as essential to the safety of the Republic. The first settlers in the territory showed in their works, their faith in the public schools. Governor Robert Lucas, in his message to the first legislative assembly of Iowa Territory, which convened at Burlington, November 12th, 1838, says in reference to schools:

"The 12th section of the act of Congress establishing our Territory, declares, 'that the citizens of Iowa shall enjoy all the rights, privileges and immunities heretofore granted and secured to the Territory of Wisconsin and its inhabitants.' This extends to us all the rights, privileges and immunities specified in the ordinance of Congress of the 13th of July, 1787.

"The 3d article of this ordinance declares, 'that religion, morality and knowledge being necessary to good government and the happiness of mankind, schools and all means of education shall be forever encouraged.'

"Congress, to carry out this declaration, has granted one section of land in each township, to the inhabitants of such township for the purposes of schools therein.

"There is no subject to which I wish to call your attention more emphatically than the subject of establishing, at the commencement of our political existence, a well digested system of common schools."

This assembly addressed itself early to the task of providing for a system of common schools, and enacted a law providing for the formation of districts, the establishing of schools, and authorized the voters of each district, when lawfully assembled, to levy and collect the necessary taxes, "either in cash or good merchantable property, at cash price, upon the inhabitants of their respective districts, not exceeding one-half per centum, nor amounting to more than $10 on any one person, to do all and everything necessary to the establishment and support of schools within the same."

The second legislative assembly enacted January 16, 1840, a much more comprehensive law to establish a system of common schools—a law containing many excellent features. Its provisions were, however, in advance of the existing public sentiment, on the subject of education making ample provision as it did for free public schools. Even the people of Iowa were scarcely ready for such a law.

In the United States Census of 1840, very few schools, either private or public, were reported. One academy in Scott county, with twenty-five scholars, and in the State, sixty-three primary and common schools with 1,500 scholars, being the whole number reported.

The first section of the act of 1839, for the establishment of common schools, provided, that, "there shall be established a common school or schools, in each of the counties of this territory, which shall be open and free for every class of white citizens between the ages of five and twenty-one years;" the second section providing that "the county board shall, from time to time, form such districts in their respective counties, whenever a petition may be presented for that purpose by a majority of the voters resident within such contemplated district." These districts were governed by a board of three trustees, whose duties were to examine and employ teachers, superintend the schools, and collect and disburse the taxes voted by the collectors, for school purposes.

Among the earlier enactments of the Territorial Legislature, were those requiring that each district maintain at least three months school every year, and that the expenses of the same be raised by taxes levied upon the property of said district. Among the latter enactments was that providing for a county school tax to be levied to pay teachers, and that whatever additional sum might be required for this purpose should be assessed upon the parents sending, in proportion to the lenght of time sent. The rate bill system was thus adopted near the close of the territorial period.

When Iowa was admitted into the Union, as a State, December 28, 1846, with a population of 100,000, and a reported school population of 20,000, about four hundred districts had been organized. From this time the number of districts rapidly increased, reaching 1,000 in 1849, and 1,200 in 1850. In 1857, the number of organized school districts had increased to 3,265. The Hon. Maturin L. Fisher, who then so ably filled the office of superintendent of public instructions, in his report, dated November, 1857, urged the revision of the school law, and of the reduction in the number of school districts.

The seventh General Assembly again took up the subject of the revision of the school laws, and on the 12th day of March, 1858, passed "An Act for the Public Instruction of the State of Iowa," the first section of which provided that "each civil township in the several counties of this State is hereby declared a school district, for all the purposes of this act, the boundaries of said township being the boundaries of said school district; and each district as at present organized, shall become a sub-district for the purpose hereinafter provided: *Provided*, that each incorporated city or town, including the territory annexed thereto, for school purposes, and which contains not less than 1,000 inhabitants, shall be, and is hereby created a school district." This law took effect March 20th, 1858, and reduced the number of districts from about 3,500 to less than 900.

In December, 1858, a law was enacted providing that any city or incorporated town, including the territory annexed thereto for school purposes, may constitute a school district by vote of the majority of electors residing upon the territory of such contemplated district. In 1860 the provisions of this act were extended to the unincorporated towns and villages containing not less than 300 inhabitants.

By an act passed April 3d, 1866, this privilege was further extended to any city or sub-district containing not less than 200 inhabitants, and certain territory contiguous thereto. It soon became evident that by this amendment a serious innovation would be made in the district township system, by the formation of independent districts in the more thickly settled and wealthier portions of the townships. The amendment was repealed early in the session of the following General Assembly.

Hon. D. F. Wells, in his report, dated December, 1867, says that, "the advantages of the district township system are so numerous and apparent that prominent educators in other States where it is not yet introduced, are laboring earnestly for its adoption."

Hon. A. S. Kissell labored assiduously to secure such a change as would remove the sub-district feature of our system, which has proved a fruitful source of discord and dissatisfaction, and was every year making the system more unpopular as it became more difficult of administration. He desired to abolish the sub-district meeting and the office of sub-director, and make each township a single school district, to be governed by a board of directors elected at the annual district township meeting for the term of three years. In his report, dated January 1st, 1872, he says:

In this system every township becomes a shool district, and all sub-district boundaries are abandoned; and if this plan were carried into effect in this State, it would allow no other school divisions than those of the independent and township districts.

The most experienced educators of the country have advocated this system. Among these are such men as Horace Mann, United States Commissioner Barnard, ex-Governor Boutwell, Dr. Newton Bateman, of Illinois, Dr. Gregory, late Superintendent, of Michigan, and the County and State Superintendents of one third of the States in the Union. The arguments advanced by many of these experienced school men are unanswerable. Massachusetts and Pennsylvania have tested the system practically for several years; it is pronounced by these States as a success, and this successful experiment of three or four years should have greater weight with us in this young and growing commonwealth than any theoretical arguments that could be advanced."

Notwithstanding the efforts and array of argument, and the conviction on the part of those who had made a special study of this subject, the General Assembly, which convened January 8, 1872, enacted a law providing for the formation of independent districts from the sub-districts of a district township. This law has ever been a plague to county superintendents, and several efforts have been made to effect its repeal, but without avail.

Every Governor that Iowa has had has given his warmest approval of the common school system. Governor James W. Grimes, in his inaugural message, December 9, 1854, displays broad statemanship, advanced and liberal views and eminently sound philosophy in the following language:

"Government is established for the protection of the governed. But that protection does not consist merely in the enforcement of laws against injury to the person and property. Men do not make a voluntary abnegation of their natural rights, simply that those rights may be protected by the body politic. It reaches more vital interests than those of property. Its greatest object is to elevate and ennoble the citizen. It would fall far short of its design if it did not disseminate intelligence and build up the moral energies of the people. It is organized to establish justice, promote the public welfare and secure the blessings of liberty. It is designed to foster the instincts of truth, justice and philanthropy, that are implanted in our very natures, and from which all constitutions and laws derive their validity and value. It should afford moral as well as physical protection, by educating the rising generation, by encouraging industry and sobriety; by steadfastly adhering to the right; and by being ever true to the instincts of freedom and humanity.

"To accomplish these high aims of government, the first requisite is ample provision for the education of the youth of the State. The common school fund of the State should be scrupulously preserved, and a more efficient system of common schools than we now have should be adopted. The State should see to it that the elements of education, like the elements of universal nature, are above, around, and beneath all.

"It is agreed that the safety and perpetuity of our republican institutions depend upon the diffusion of intelligence among the masses of the people. The statistics of the penitentiaries and alms-houses throughout the country abundantly show that education is the best preventative of pauperism and crime. They show, also, that the prevention of those evils is much less expensive than the punishment of the one, and the relief of the other. Education, too, is the great equalizer of human conditions. It places the poor on an equality with the rich. It subjects the appetites and passions of the rich to the restraints of reason and conscience, and thus prepares each for a career of usefulness and honor. Every consideration, therefore, of duty and policy impels us to sustain the schools of the State in the highest possible efficiency."

SCHOOL FUND COMMISSIONER.

When Bremer county came into existence, in 1853, the office of superintendent had not been created. The only school officer was the school fund commissioner who merely had charge of the school funds, to a certain extent the same as has the board of supervisors of to-day. He had authority to make loans of the school funds to private parties upon liberal security, and most of the mortgages recorded as made in early days were made to him in consideration of the school funds. So far as educational matters were concerned, he had about the same authority as the supervisors now have. In those days, the directors hiring teachers, examined those whom they wished to employ, and public examinations were unknown.

The first school fund commissioner was John H. Martin, who was elected in April, 1854, receiving ninety-five out of the one hundred and eighty-one votes cast in the county. His term of office commenced

H. D. Gould.

HISTORY OF BREMER COUNTY.

immediately after the election and expired when his successor qualified, two years later. Mr. Martin came to Bremer county direct from Illinois, about 1841, and located upon a farm north of Janesville. He was a good man socially, and was well liked by his neighbors. As to education he was somewhat wanting, it being said that he learned to write his name after being elected, and when he did place his signature to a document, it was only by "much sighting and bending." After his term of office expired, he lived in the city for a time, meeting with some misfortune, finally left for Oregon, in which State he now lives. It might be of interest in this connection to state that Martin was denominated a "Hard Shell Baptist," and it was his father who erected the "little stone" Baptist church, which is now used as a dwelling, southeast of Waverly.

Thomas Downing was the successor to J. H. Martin as school fund commissioner, his term commencing in April, 1856, and expiring in August, 1858.

In 1858, the office of school fund commissioner was abolished, the duties devolving mostly upon the board of supervisors, and the

COUNTY SUPERINTENDENT OF SCHOOLS,

which office at this time was created. The duties and work of the office was then the same as at the present day, visiting schools, holding examinations, and looking after the interests of educational matters in general.

The first to fill this office was A. K. Moulton, whose term of office began when he was elected, in April, 1858. Moulton was from Great Falls, New Hampshire, but did not come to Bremer county direct from that place. He brought his family and settled in Sumner township early in the fifties. He was a man of good education; was a Free Will Baptist preacher, and had, prior to his coming here, filled the pulpit of his church in Lowell, Massachusetts. He was considered by all who knew him an honorable upright citizen. For some reason he did not fill out his term as superintendent, only holding until May, 1859.

The vacancy so caused was filled by the appointment of W. W. Norris as superintendent of schools, who served during the balance of the term. Norris was very popular, a democrat in politics. It is an evidence of his popularity that he was subsequently elected as county treasurer. He was a man of good education and marked ability. Some years ago he went to Illinois, where he has had softening of the brain.

At the October election, in 1858, G. T. Sayles was elected superintendent, receiving 456 of the 838 votes polled. His term of office commenced January, 1860, and continued two years. He has left the county.

George R. Dean was Mr. Sayles' successor, and entered upon his duties on the 1st of January, 1862. In 1863, he was reelected, and served until January, 1866, making a most capable and satisfactory officer.

George R. Dean is a native of Saratoga county, New York, and was born April 18, 1832. He is a son of George and Phœbe (Hooker) Dean, who immigrated to the United States about 1825, settling in Saratoga county. When George R. was a child the family removed to Otsego county, where he received his early education. Subsequently he graduated from the State Normal School at Albany. During the spring of 1856 he was united in marriage with Mrs. Helen V. Chamberlin, who was born in Otsego county, New York, October 24, 1837, and is a daughter of Henry and Emily (Edson) Chamberlin. In the spring of 1857 he, with his family, removed to Bremer county, Iowa, and settled in Waverly. In 1863 he was elected mayor of Waverly and has also held other offices of trust.

The next superintendent of schools was Charles B. Roberts, who was elected in the fall of 1865, and took up his duties with the following year, serving two years. He came to Waverly just before the war, and was a school teacher by profession. He had lost one arm through a threshing machine accident. After serving his time as superintendent, for a time he ran the Bremer Hotel at Waverly, and finally removed with his family to West Union. As an official he was accomodating and efficient. His successor was J. R. Hall, who was elected in the fall of 1867 and began to discharge the duties of the office in January, 1868. He was a son of the Rev. Dr. Hall, of Michigan, and, upon coming to Bremer county, located upon a farm within two miles of the geographical center of the county, and followed agricultural pursuits, until elected to office. After his term had expired he went into the patent right business, peddling various patented articles. In six or seven years he left for parts unknown.

C. S. Harwood was the next superintendent, serving from January, 1870, to January, 1872. He had come to the county some years prior to this, in company with his father and several brothers, settling in Franklin township. A few years ago he returned to Illinois. Mr. Harwood had a very good education, and was endowed by nature with excellent talents. He was a good teacher—as were all of his brothers and sisters, who made that branch, a business—a hard worker, and an enthusiastic as well as competent and thorough superintendent.

H. H. Burrington succeeded Harwood, and was re-elected his own successor, serving from January, 1872, until January, 1876. Rev. H. H. Burrington was born in Washington county, New York, on the 8th day of May, 1826. He is the son of Henry H., Sr., and Betsy (Wait) Burrington. Henry H., the oldest of five children, was educated in the common schools. He received his preparative education at Poultney Seminary, Vermont. He graduated at Brown's University, Rhode Island, and in 1853 he spent two years at Rochester Theological Seminary, where he graduated. He was ordained in Burlington, Vermont, December 27, 1855, where he occupied the pulpit for two years. In 1859 he came to Waverly. In 1872 he was elected to the office of county superintendent of public schools of Bremer county, serving the county faithfully for six years. In September, 1855, he was married to Miss Hannah M. Faville, a daughter of Thomas Faville. She was born in Herkimer county, New York, October 8, 1830. Five children blessed this union, four of whom are living—Carrie, Charlie, Mary and Stella. Mr. Burrington was the first regular pastor of the Baptist church of Wa-

HISTORY OF BREMER COUNTY.

verly, and has always taken an active interest in the welfare of the same.

D. C. Chamberlin, the present county superintendent of schools of Bremer county, was born in Otsego county, New York, on the 3d day of November, 1839. He was a son of Heman and Drusilla (Davis) Chamberlin. There was a family of six children — three sons and three daughters — four of whom lived to be adults. The subject of this sketch was reared on his father's farm, receiving an academic education, completing the same in 1860, after which he engaged in farming in his native county, working by the month until he went into the army, in 1861. He enlisted in the Third New York Artillery, under Colonel Stewart, serving nineteen months, eight months of the time he was military postmaster of the regiment, and for six months, city hospital clerk and steward. At the end of the nineteen months he was mustered out on account of physical disability. He returned to his home in New York, where he remained until 1863. He received an appointment as clerk in one of the military departments at Washington, but after three weeks' trial, was again obliged to give up on account of poor health, and return home. On the 4th of May, 1864, he was married to Miss Delila Hummell, a daughter of Peter Hummell, who died in defense of the Union, in the hospital, at Newton, North Carolina, in the spring of 1863. Mr. and Mrs. Chamberlin have one son — George R. Chamberlin. Mr. Chamberlin taught school in his native county, one term, during the winter of 1864-5. On the 13th of March, 1865, they left their home in New York, and emigrated to Bremer county, Iowa, locating on a farm in Warren township, where, however, he remained but a short time, when he removed to Waverly. At that time he became connected with the public schools in Waverly, as teacher, which occupation he followed until 1877, having taught twenty-nine terms without losing a day. This made thirty-four terms that he has taught in all. In the year 1877 he was elected to the office of county superintendent of schools, which office he was well-qualified to fill, and the fact that he has continued in the possession of this office, term after term, is sufficient evidence that he has filled it with credit to himself, and the entire satisfaction of his constituents. And to say that by industry, hard work, and a close application to his duties he has greatly improved the school system, is drawing the picture mildly. Indeed, too much credit cannot be given Mr. Chamberlin for the active interest he has taken in bringing the schools of Bremer county to their high standard. He has 125 teachers under his charge, visiting them every term, when he thinks it advisable. In politics he is a strong republican; he was city assessor of Waverly for one year, when he resigned; was city superintendent of schools for four years, from 1872 to 1876. He has been a member of the Baptist Church since 1868. He is a member of the A. F. & A. M. Lodge, No. 116; also a member of the Chapter, No. 24. He was made a Mason, in Waverly, in 1873, and has occupied all the principal offices in the lodge, filling the chair for one year.

THE DEVELOPEMENT.

From the time of the first settlement of the county, and the time of organization of the first district, the number of school districts increased very rapidly, and educational facilities became more and more efficient. Every decade that passed showed a marked contrast to the preceding one.

In 1870, there were between the ages of five and twenty-one, 2,502 males and 2,118 females. There were ninety-five schools in the county, with one graded. There were three brick, eight stone, one log, and seventy-eight frame school houses. Male teachers received an average of $8.01 per week, and females teachers, $5.72. In speaking of educational progress at this time, C. S. Harwood, county superintendent, says:

"We have ten per cent. less teachers than when two years ago, or nearly two years, I took charge of these schools; and we are able to-day to pay upon a written examination a very much higher per cent. on a much more severe examination. I think I can safely say that our average qualification has advanced not less than ten per cent.

The most interesting feature of improvement is the fact that teachers are more fully awake in a common-sense manner, viz: that their pecuniary interests demand better qualification. That demand is ever regulated by supply, and that the world is not indifferent to the results of skilled labor. And the interest that parents and school officers are evincing in our school work, is increasing; where one year ago last spring, a director said to me: "She will do to teach our summer school; we can get her cheap," the same man said to me this spring: "Send us a good teacher, money is no object." And I am fully convinced that in many districts of this county, a known poor teacher cannot get employment at any price, while a known good and faithful one will be secured regardless of cost. This is progress. The laborer is worthy of his hire, and in no department more so than in ours."

With respect to educational work done, the superintendent in his report says:

"I have given almost every moment of my time, and all of my interest to this work. I have visited every school, or very nearly every school, in the county *twice*, and many more frequently, and have kindly yet firmly, almost invariably, corrected all the errors noticed; have encouraged and commended all the good, and discouraged all the bad; have in fact made school my trade and "worked at my trade." I have held about a dozen Teachers' Associations in the county—primary object to teach method. Yet in order to teach method, facts must be taught. Results, method, and fact, or fact and method. I cannot tell how much work I have done. I can truly say this: never in my life time did I ever do more hours of work or work more diligently and earnestly, and all my life has been toil. And as regards the work done by other agencies, I can say this: We have fully a score of the ablest, most conscientious, working teachers in the world, and several men on our school boards will do all in their power to fix and sustain a standard of education that is an honor to our State. With the aid of these we have been enabled to work up in several parts of our county a genuine enthusiasm, and poor work will not be tolerated, and good work will be well compensated."

HISTORY OF BREMER COUNTY.

In 1877 the number between the ages of five and twenty-one had increased to 2,883 males and 2,681 females. The old log school house had ceased to be reported. There were then seven stone, eleven brick and eighty-nine frame schoolhouses. H. H. Burrington, in his report to the State Superintendent, has the following:

"Having been county superintendent six years, my position has enabled me to watch the practical workings of our school system. We may justly feel proud of our common schools. They are the surety and defense of our national life, and the efficient means of our national prosperity. We ought to do all that we can to sustain them and to increase their efficiency.

"My experience has suggested some improvements in our school work, and some amendments to our school laws.

"It must be confessed by those that are acquainted with school reports, that there is a painful waste of school money, or rather, a loose and careless way of keeping account of school money. School boards, and especially district treasurers, fail in many cases, to keep and give a correct account of school money that comes into their hands. To remedy this, the county superintendent should be made the guardian of all school money.

"It seems to me that some changes might be profitably made in the duties of the county superintendent, both in examining teachers and in visiting schools. As the law now stands, one day in every month, and only one, is provided for examination of teachers. In the spring and in the fall, more time is needed for this work than in mid-winter and mid-summer. Further, the law requires the superintendent to visit every school in the county, large or small, whether doing well or not. More discretion should be given him in this matter.

"My work has been to me exceedingly pleasant in every department of my labor—in examining teachers—in visiting schools—in talking to children—in visiting with their parents—in counseling with school directors—in gathering up the statistics and keeping a record of the schools—in working out the various reports, and in conducting the extensive correspondence of the office. Teachers have been uniformly kind and courteous to me in my official work, and school directors and other officers have been always ready to carry out my plans or to engage in any work that promises to increase the efficiency of our schools.

"In visiting schools, I have necessarily been much from home, but have always found a pleasant home among the friends of the schools. I have traveled over the county a great many times, and have found the hospitality of teachers and patrons peculiarly generous and cordial. I owe a debt of gratitude to the people of Bremer county that I can never repay. I shall ever hold them in grateful remembrance."

PRESENT CONDITION.

From the last statistical report available, a number of items have been collected, which will show conclusively the present condition of educational matters in Bremer county:

REPORT OF 1880.

Number of district townships in the county	6
Number of independent districts	59
Number of sub-districts	43

Total number of districts.................. 108
Number of ungraded schools in the county................................. 100
Number of rooms in the graded schools.. 19
Average term of schools in the county... 7.40
Number of male teachers employed in the county................................. 51
Number of female teachers.............. 151
Total number of teachers 202
Average monthly compensation to male teachers........................... $28.04
Female teachers.......................$22.00
Total number of children in county between ages of five and twenty-one years. 5,255
Total number of pupils enrolled in the schools of the county................. 3,935
Total average attendance................ 2,310
Average cost of tuition per month, per pupil................................ $1.30
Number of school houses in the county— frame, 91; brick, 9; stone, 8; total....... 108
Total value of houses...................$81,090
Total value of apparatus................ $2,309
Total number of certificates issued during 1880 130
Of which were professional.............. 24
First grade............................ 40
Second grade........................... 110
Number of applicants rejected.......... 56
Average age of female applicants........ 19
Average age of male applicants.......... 24

As to the financial condition of school matters, below is presented the account of the county treasurer, with the various funds pertaining to it, for the year ending December 31, 1882:

TEACHERS' TAX.

To balance from last report..........	$1,653 90
To amount of tax collected..........	18,221 59
	$19,875 49
Contra.	
By amount paid school treasurers....	$17,758 50
By balance on hand.................	2,116 99
	$19,875 49

CONTINGENT SCHOOL TAX.

To balance from last report..........	$ 583 92
To amount of tax collected..........	7,119 05
	$7,702 97
Contra.	
By amount paid school treasurers....	$6,904 11
By balance on hand.................	798 86
	$7,702 97

SCHOOL HOUSE TAX.

To balance from last report..........	$ 336 62
To amount of tax collected..........	3,695 56
	$4,032 18
Contra.	
By amount paid school treasurer....	$3,825 99
By balance on hand.................	206 19
	$4,032 18

PERMANENT SCHOOL FUND.

To balance from last report..........	$1,788 62
By amount received on notes........	8,940 00
	$10,728 62
Contra.	
By amount re-loaned................	$6,660 00
By balance on hand................	4,068 62
	$10,728 62

SCHOOL FUND INTEREST.

To balance from last report..........	$3,214 12
To amount of interest collected......	4,191 57
	$7,405 69
Contra.	
By transfer to State Revenue........	$932 38
By apportioned to schools...........	2,037 94
By transfer to county fund..........	3,000 00
By balance on hand.................	1,435 37
	$7,405 69

SCHOOL FUND APPORTIONMENT.

To balance from last report..........	$877 66
To amount received from tax levy....	3,003 28
To amount received from penal fines.	160 89
To amount received from interest....	2,037 94
	$6,079 87

HISTORY OF BREMER COUNTY.

Contra.
By paid school treasurers............ $5,359 01
By balance on hand................. 720 76
$6,079 87

COUNTY SCHOOL TAX.
To amount from last report.......... 89
To amount of tax collected.......... $3,191 11
$3,192 00

Contra.
By amount apportioned to school.... $3,003 28
By balance on hand................. 188 72
$3,192 00

FIRST TEACHERS' INSTITUTE.

At a meeting of the friends of education, held at Waverly, October 7, 1858, it was unanimously resolved that it was expedient to hold a teachers' institute in said village, and the first week in November, was selected as the time for holding the same.

The first issue of the *Waverly Republican*, published after the meeting, gave the following account of the proceedings:

The first Teachers' Institute was held in Waverly, November 1st, 1858, at which some fifty teachers were in attendance. We desire to say here, however, that the Institute was a very pleasant and profitable occasion, not only to the teachers themselves, but to many outsiders. The ordinary exercises were conducted with much spirit and ability by the Rev. A. K. Moulton, as principal; Isaac High, of Janesville, E. C. Moulton, of Waverly, and L. F. Goodwin, of Douglas, as assistants. The exercises embraced all the branches ordinarily brought within the scope of the common schools.

Resolutions adopted by the teachers of the common schools of Bremer county, at the session of the Teachers' Institute held at Waverly during the week, ending on Saturday, the 6th inst.:

Resolved, That we, the members of the Teachers' Institute, tender our sincere thanks to the citizens of Waverly for the hospitality so magnificently extended to us while attending said Institute; to our efficient superintendent, A. K. Moulton, for the apposite suggestions he presented upon the subject of school government; to those other gentlemen who addressed us with so much ability on several occasions, and Mrs. L. W. Thickstun, and those assisting her, for music executed in the highest style of that exquisite science, with which they gratuitously favored the Institute.

Resolved, That all teachers who absent themselves from the Teachers' Institute, either from an egotistical selfishness, or from a consciousness of inefficiency, are not deemed by us as sufficiently progressive to teach school in the State of Iowa.

Resolved, That we earnestly desire to assemble annually in the capacity of a Teachers' Institute, and to this end we hereby solicit the County Superintendent to convene another Institute on the last Monday of October, A. D. 1859, at such place in this county as to him shall seem most expedient.

Resolved, That as teachers we will endeavor to elevate the standard of common school instruction in Bremer county, by qualifying ourselves to the full extent of our opportunities, for the more perfect discharge of those grave duties and responsibilities which our profession imposes upon us.

Resolved, That the present superintendent and his successors in office, be requested to require of all candidates for certificates as thorough a knowledge of the branches required by law to be taught in common schools, as he or they can do, and yet supply the schools of the county with resident teachers.

Resolved, That we concur in the sentiments expressed by Dr. Burbank, that the use of tobacco is a filthy and injurious habit, and hold that it should be discontinued and abandoned by all teachers.

Signed, E. C. MOULTON,
Chairman of Committee.

NORMAL INSTITUTES.

Under an act passed by the General Assembly in 1873, it was made a part of the duty of county superintendents to hold each year, a normal institute in their respective counties, for the purpose of instructing teachers, and thus elevating the efficiency of the county schools. The funds for carrying on the institute are raised in various ways—partly by the teacher's examination fee, and the institute fee. This fund is under the direct control of the county superintendent, and is paid out by the county treasurer upon his order.

The first normal institute of Bremer county was held at the high school building in Waverly, commencing August 24th and lasting until September 5th, 1874. There were 124 teachers present and the institute passed off very satisfactorily. The officers were as follows: Manager, H. H. Burrington, superintendent; instructors, Prof. Irwin Shepard, D. C. Chamberlin and Miss Elie M. Washburn; treasurer, D. C. Chamberlin; secretaries, Delia J. Farrington and Emma J. Chamberlin.

Since this time an institute has been held each year, with increasing interest and success; demonstrating beyond a doubt, the success of the system. Each year they have grown in attendance and the effect is plainly visible in the records of examination.

The last normal institute was held at Waverly, in 1882, commencing on August 14th, and lasting until August 27th. There were 126 members. The officers were as follows: Conductor, county superintendent, D. C. Chamberlin; secretary, Jennie Benton Dean; instructors, A. W. Stewart, R. S. Holway, G. G. Lampson, and E. C. Bennett. State Superintendent Akers delivered the lecture upon the occasion, and in regard to him the following entry is made upon the record books of the institute:

"The session was made memorable by the presence of our State Superintendent, whom, having never seen, we were desirous to welcome. Mr. Akers was weary from traveling and much speaking, but said that the presence of such a body of teachers inspired him, so that he forgot his weariness. The words he uttered will not soon be forgotten, and we are sure he gained many warm friends among the teachers. His lecture in the evening was excellent, and well attended."

BREMER COUNTY TEACHERS' ASSOCIATION.

This association was organized in 1878. The constitution declared the object to be, "the improvement of its members in the science of teaching, and in the most approved practice; the diffusing of information upon the system of common school education among the people, and promoting harmony of feeling; and the greatest possible advancement in scientific and general information." Meetings were to be held on the third Saturday in each month, at places decided upon by the association.

The first meeting entered upon the records of the association was held in the school house at Tripoli, on the 18th of October, 1878, with D. C. Chamberlin,

HISTORY OF BREMER COUNTY. 987

president of the association, in the chair; Mary Kenny, acting secretary. A. H. Beals was elected vice-president.

For several years meetings were held quite regularly, but at present the active work of the association has ceased.

CHAPTER XV.

TOPOGRAPHY, GEOLOGY AND AGRICULTURAL.

The county of Bremer lies in the northeastern portion of the State of Iowa, three tiers of counties from both the north and east State lines. It is surrounded by the counties of Chickasaw, Fayette, Black Hawk and Butler, respectively on the north, east, south and west. Bremer is among the smallest counties in the State, embracing only twelve congressional townships. The territory comprised are townships 91, 92 and 93, north of ranges 11, 12, 13 and 14, west of the fifth principal meridian. Thus making it 18 miles across from north to south, by 24 miles from east to west containing, 276,-480 acres, or 432 square miles. This territory is divided into civil townships as follows: Sumner, Dayton, Franklin, Leroy, Fremont, Maxfield, Frederika, Douglas, Warren, Jefferson, Polk, Lafayette, Washington and Jackson.

The surface of Bremer county is beautifully diversified with prairie and timber land. It is generally level with the graceful undulations so common to prairie countries. This, of course, is somewhat different in the vicinity of the streams, where the rolling tendency is increased to a sufficient extent to be termed hilly. But the locations are few where there are breaks in the surface sufficiently abrupt to be detrimental to agriculture. This whole region of Iowa has long borne the reputation of being one of the finest in all the great State. The "Valley of the Cedar" has a wide renown as the "garden spot of Iowa," and the "Gem of Iowa Waters" is a term very frequently applied to the Cedar. As to the soil and geological formation of this region, an alluvial deposit, averaging about three feet deep, resting upon a bed of blue clay, varying in depth from ten to one hundred feet, below which limestone rock is invariably found, forms the general geological structure of the county. The soil is for the most part a rich, dark, adhesive loam, underlaid by a mixed clay and gravel subsoil. Limestone rock, of excellent quality, easily quarried and wrought, abounds, and has for many years received the attention of a good deal of energy and capital. It admits of a fine polish, and endures the action of the weather without deterioration in color or texture; makes good lime, and possesses strong hydraulic properties. Choice corals of manifold formations are found in great number near the Cedar river, in the vicinity of Waverly. Very fine chrystalizations and petrifactions are likewise obtained, from twelve to seventy feet below the surface, all over the county. Brick-clay and sand exist in abundance.

The county is well watered, and in all parts of it excellent well water can be obtained in abundance at various depths ranging from eighteen to eighty feet. Several streams, each pursuing a more or less southeasterly course, intersect every township, without exception. Cedar River, the principal stream, finds its source in Minnesota, and enters the county in the northwestern corner and traversing the townships of Polk, LaFayette, Washington and Jackson—the western tier—it crosses the line and passes into Black Hawk county, at about midway of the southern line of the township last mentioned. The transparently clear waters of the Cedar have a rapid flow over a limestone bed, between banks that, although high, are seldom precipitous.

Its bottom lands have a general elevation above the highest rise of freshets, and the stream furnishes a water power sufficient to propel a vast amount of machinery, which does not fail, even at the lowest stage of water.

The next stream in importance is the main Wapsipinicon, which also rises in Minnesota. It likewise enters the county from the north, at nearly the center of the northern boundary, running thence through the townships of Donglas, Frederika, Fremont, Dayton and Franklin, and crosses into Black Hawk county, at a distance west from the southeast corner of Bremer county about three miles. It has sufficient fall to render it valuable for mill power, with a constant and steady flow over a sandy and pebbled bottom. Unlike those of the Cedar, the bottom lands of the Wapsipinicon, are low, extending a good distance back from the stream and are subject to overflow. Next to the main Wapsipinicon ranks the Little Wapsipinicon. Rising in Chickasaw county, it crosses the northeastern corner of Bremer on its way to Fayette county. Returning, it enters Bremer and crosses portions of Sumner and Dayton townships, and again enters Fayette county, pursuing a southerly course near the Bremer county line, and finally empties into the main Wapsipinicon in Buchanan county.

The Shell Rock River, scarcely inferior in size and beauty to the Cedar, crosses the southwestern corner of the county. Its mill power is abundant and its beauty renowned. Its confluence with the Cedar takes place in the northwestern part of Black Hawk county.

Originally, about one-sixth of the entire surface of Bremer county was covered with variously large and small bodies of excellent timber, well distributed. Twenty-six thousand acres of heavy oak, ash, maple, elm, locust, black walnut, and other varieties, each variety of the largest growth and of the best quality were comprised in the lower Big Woods, lying wholly within the county, on the east side of the Cedar river near the southern boundary. North of this body, large groves skirted the Cedar, on either side, nearly to the north line of the county. The main Wapsipinicon was also skirted with timber, extending in places to several miles in width. On Crane creek, and elsewhere in many parts of the county, were other large and fine groves, at distances convenient to every settler. But, while greater or smaller portions of these once larger bodies of timber yet remain, there is less than one-half the amount originally existing.

As to the products of the county, wheat, corn and oats are the staples, varying relatively in amount from year to year. Barley, hay and potatoes rank next as important productions. Rye, sorghum and grass-seed are also largely cultivated. Vegetables and fruit, common to this latitude, grow here to perfection, and there are now many fine and profitable fruit orchards in Bremer county. Years ago about the whole attention of agriculturalists was devoted to raising wheat, but that day has gone by. The wheat belt seems, from its history, to be always moving westward, and, while it hovered over this portion of America, it was well improved, thirty, forty and even forty-five bushels to the acre being raised, and all farmers considering it the staple product. Of late years, however, farmers are turning their attention more toward raising stock. Their success in this line has been marked and rapid, and few counties in Iowa can boast of the amount and quality of blooded stock that can Bremer. On the whole, Bremer county ranks high among its sister counties of the great State, and its resources not having all been developed, its promise is indeed flattering.

BREMER COUNTY AGRICULTURAL SOCIETY.

In the fall of 1856, there were a number of unsuccessful attempts made to organize this society. Finally, these attempts being renewed in the spring of 1857, a meeting was called and adjourned until May 5th, 1857, and a "loud" call for attendance issued.

Pursuant to adjournment, the friends of agricultural improvements met on the 5th day of May, 1857, at the school house in Waverly, and perfected an organization by adopting a constitution and electing the officers herein provided for, as follows: President, W. P. Harmon, Waverly; Vice-Presidents, W. Pattee, Janesville, and M. F. Gillett, Frederika; Recording Secretary, G. C. Wright, Waverly; Corresponding Secretary, D. P. Walling, Frederika; Treasurer, B. F. Gass, Waverly; Board of Managers, N. M. Smith, Giles Mabee, J. H. Eldridge, Matthew Rowen and C. C. Allen.

The newly elected officers assumed their positions and duties, and the following named gentlemen were appointed as the committee provided for in the constitution: W. H. Jay, of Washington; N. J. Perry, of LeRoy; James Quinn, of Jackson; James Bevard, of Jefferson; R. D. Titcomb, of Fremont; J. Richmond, of Franklin; Silas Furr, of Polk.

The treasurer was requested to procure the necessary books for the use of the officers, at the expense of the Society.

The board of Managers were constituted a committee to report to the next regular meeting a code of by-laws for the government of the Society.

The publishers of the *Waverly Republican* were requested to publish the proceedings of this meeting and the constitution adopted by it.

The proceedings were signed by

W. P. HARMON, President.
G. C. WRIGHT, Secretary.

CONSTITUTION.
Preamble.

The name of this society shall be the Bremer County Agricultural Society; its object shall be improvements in the character and operations of agriculture, horticulture, mechanical and household arts.

SECTION 1. The society shall consist of such citizens of the county as shall signify their wishes to become members by signing their names to this constitution and paying one dollar on subscribing, and one dollar annually thereafter, on or before the first Monday in June, or by paying at one time, ten dollars, which payment shall constitute them life members and exempt them from all annual payments thereafter.

SEC. 2. The officers of the society shall consist of a president, two vice-presidents, to be located in different townships in the county, a recording secretary, a corresponding secretary, a treasurer, and a board of managers, consisting of five, who, with the president and recording secretary shall constitute the board of managers, and a general committee composed of one member from each organized township in which there is a member of the society. Five members of the board shall constitute a quorum for the transaction of business.

SEC. 3. The President shall preside over the deliberations of the meetings of the society, or in his absence, one of the vice-presidents shall preside. The president shall, by virtue of his office, be chairman of the board of managers.

SEC. 4. It shall be the duty of the recording secretary to keep the minutes and records of the society and read the minutes of the last meeting as the first order of business after the meeting is duly organized. It shall be his duty, also, to make out a certificate of the sum actually raised by the society, and the precise application of all money for the past year, and transmit the same to the Auditor of State, in accordance with the act for the encouragement of agriculture, approved February 5, 1857, on or before the third Wednesday in June, of each year.

SEC. 5. It shall be the duty of the corresponding secretary to answer all communications of the society, and shall arrange and publish all communications that are designed for publication, as he may think will best promote the interest of the society, and to communicate with other societies when necessary for the improvement of this society.

SEC. 6. It shall be the duty of the treasurer to hold the funds of the society and disburse them on the order of the president, countersigned by the recording secretary, and shall make a full report of his receipts and disbursements, at the annual meetings, as the second business in order, and he shall give bonds for the sum of twice the amount of money that is likely to come into his hands by virtue of his office, with two sufficient sureties to be approved by the president; and it shall be his duty on or before the second Monday in June, to file with the recording secretary, a full statement of all the moneys received from the State, and from members and individuals, annually.

SEC. 7. The board of managers shall take charge of and preserve, or distribute (as shall be proper), all seeds, plants, books, implements, models and other property which may be transmitted to or ordered by the society, and they shall make their report at the annual meetings previous to the election of officers. It shall be the duty of the board to select suitable persons to deliver addresses at the annual fairs, upon the general prospects of the matters which the secretary designs to foster and encourage; they also shall have power to fill any and all vacancies, which may occur in offices before the annual meeting of the society.

SEC. 8. The general committee are expected to look after the affairs and interests of the society in towns in which they reside, and will be regarded as useful mediums of communication between the board of managers and different portions of the county.

SEC. 9. The society shall hold their meetings on the third Wednesday of December, of each year, at the county seat, at which time the president, vice-president, recording secretary, corresponding secretary and treasurer shall be elected; and a semi annual meeting on the first Monday in June, in each year, at which time the board of managers shall be elected, the voting to be by ballot, and a plurality of votes cast electing the candidates. The committee shall be appointed by the president at the semi-annual meeting of the society: *Provided*, In case a general attendance of members at either of said meetings is prevented by some unavoidable obstacle, then such members as may be present may adjourn the meeting and election to some future time, at their discretion; but not exceeding three weeks, in which event they shall immediately publish the same in one or more newspapers, if any be published in the county, and at which adjourned meeting the usual and appropriate business shall be performed.

SEC. 10. The society shall hold annually, on the first Wednesday and Thursday of October, a cattle show and general fair. The place of holding said fair to be designated by the board of managers.

The board of managers shall have power to call extra or special meetings, by publishing notice of the time and place of said meeting in the newspapers of the county, for at least two successive weeks previous to the time of holding of such meetings. Seven members shall constitute a quorum for the transaction of business.

SEC. 11. The board of managers shall have annually, a meeting on the first Monday of July, for the purpose of appointing committees on premiums.

SEC. 12. The fiscal year of this society shall commence on the first day of January, and close on the last day of December, of each year, at which time the terms and duties of all the officers elected at the annual elections shall close; and the officers elect shall take their place, at which time also the books, records, papers and other property of the society shall be transferred in proper order, by the out-going officers, to their successors, and the terms and duties of the officers elected at the semi-annual election shall close on the last day of June, and the officers elect shall commence on the first day of July, each year; provided that all officers shall hold their places until their successors are elected

SEC. 13. This constitution may be amended by a vote of two-thirds of the members present, at any annual meeting of the society, provided that notice has been given at a previous regular meeting, that said proposed amendments will be presented.

FIRST FAIR.

The first County Agricultural Fair was held at Waverly, on the 7th and 8th days of October, 1857. The premiums consisted mostly of diplomas, several copies of the *Northwestern Farmer*, and of cash of different amounts, ranging from fifty cents up to $3.00. Chinese sugar-cane and superior blooded stock were especially noticeable entries.

BREMER COUNTY FARMERS' CLUB.

This association was organized on the 16th of March, 1870, at Waverly. W. H. Jay was elected president, and Jonathan Freeman, secretary. The object of this association was also to advance the members in agricultural pursuits and enlighten ment as to farm knowledge. Others who were interested in founding it, beside the officers named, were W. H. Jordan, B. M. Reeves, W. P. Harris, Norman Reeves, and others. Meetings were held once each month at Lashbrook's Hall, in Waverly, and for a time, quite an interest was manifested in its welfare; quite a library was accumulated, but finally the novelty wore off, and its members did not evince interest sufficient to support it, and the library was turned over to the Grange, or Patrons of Husbandry, and the organization cased to exist. The Grange has since turned the collection of books over to the city of Waverly.

BREMER COUNTY INDUSTRIAL ASSOCIATION.

This association was organized and incorporated at Waverly, on the 21st of June, 1875. Among the incorporators were C. C. Keeney, W. H. Smith, Ed Knott, H. S. Burr, J. B. Barber, Frank Bulckens and Peter Fosselmann. The articles adopted declared that the corporation should continue for the space of twenty years, but should have the right to perpetual succession; it should have a common seal and have the right to sue and be sued. The capital was fixed at $10,000, but the power was left that it might be increased at any regular meeting of the stockholders. The first officers chosen were as follows: Edward Knott, president; G. W. Nash, secretary; N. B. Ridgway, first vice-president; Henry Heine, second vice-president; directors, J. B. Barber, Amon Fortner, Peter Fosselmann, Clark Fairfield, M. M. Watkins, R. S. Bentley. The secretary and treasurer were required to give bonds in the sum of $3,000, to be approved by the president.

Section nine of the by-laws adopted, declared that "the capital stock should be divided into shares of $100 each, and the certificates issued therefor should be transferable by endorsement, when recorded by the secretary.

The first fair of the association was held in the fall of 1875, at Waverly, and was in every sense, a decided success. The officers named managed this exhibition. Every year since that time a fair has been held with like success.

The Eighth Annual Fair of the association was held at Waverly on the 19th, 20th, 21st and 22d days of September, 1882. An extensive and liberal premium list was prepared and the fair was largely attended and interesting.

The officers at the time—who are the present ones—are as follows:

President, Ed Knott; vice-president, J. H. Bowman; vice-president, W. L. Stockwell; secretary, W. R. Bowman; treasurer, H. S. Burr; directors, Ed Knott, George Stephenson, S. R. Hunt, Henry Heine, L. L. Lush, J. C. Garner and E. Taylor.

THE BREMER COUNTY FARMERS' MUTUAL FIRE INSURANCE COMPANY.

By Matthew Farrington.

At a county meeting of the Granges in Bremer county, held sometime during the fall of 1874, M. Farrington, of Maple Grange, spoke upon the subject of fire and lightning insurance. He insisted that there should be in this county, a Farmers' Mutual Insurance Company. He declared that he had paid his last dollar to enrich a stockholding insurance company and that when his present policy expired, if no farmers' company was organized, he should be an insurance company by himself, that he would be the president and his wife the treasurer. David High, of

Janesville Grange, and C. R. Hastings, of White Oak Grange, endorsed the sentiment uttered.

His remarks resulted in the appointment by the meeting, of a committee of three, consisting of M. Farrington, of Maple Grange, David High, of Janesville Grange, and Charles R. Hastings, of White Oak Grange, to draft and report a plan for a Farmers' Mutual Insurance Company. The committee was so widely scattered that there was not opportunity for conference, and therefore that labor was performed by the first named.

At a future meeting of the Granges, held during the winter of 1874-5, the report, signed by all the committee, was read by the chairman, and, after discussion, was endorsed by the meeting. This meeting, on motion, authorized M. Farrington to call a public meeting for the purpose of organizing such a company.

A meeting for the purpose of organizing a Farmers' Mutual Insurance Company was called at Tripoli, Martinsburg, March 9, 1875. At this meeting, Hon. John Chapin was chosen chairman, and M. Farrington, secretary. The plan drawn up was discussed, but, owing to the unfavorable weather and the few in attendance, it was judged not proper to organize, and the meeting adjourned to meet at 10 o'clock, A. M., March 23d, 1875, at school house No. 9, in Warren Township.

Again the weather was not propitious, still the attendance was better than at the previous meeting. Truman Churchill was chosen chairman, and M. Farrington secretary. The articles of association and by-laws, reported by M. Farrington were discussed and adopted separately. The meeting then proceeded to the election of officers for the first year with the following result: M. Farrington, president; Isaac Trumbauer, vice-president; Israel Freeman, secretary; Jonathan Freeman, treasurer; W. W. Beal, T. Churchill and C. A. Mohling, directors.

The two last named were not members of the Grange. The vice-president was a member of Palm Grange; the secretary and treasurer were members of Waverly Grange, and W. W. Beal was a member of Franklin Grange.

The articles provided that the company should not be responsible for any losses until $100,000 worth of property was insured. It required some time to be prepared with the necessary books, and blanks before policies could be obtained. The secretary and vice-president were put to work to survey and insure, and on the 5th of the following May, the risks exceeded $100,000. On that day the officers published a proclamation stating, that from that day, the company would be responsible for loss or damage by fire or lightning, to any member of the association. After this the surveys were made by the secretary. The amount of risks were continually increasing as farmers became aware of the existence of the organization.

The first annual meeting was held at school house No. 8, in Warren, March 4, 1876. The officers elected were: M. Farrington, president; C. A. Mohling, vice-president; Jonathan Freeman, secretary; Benjamin Archer, treasurer; John Mohling, W. W. Beal, Henry Klages, directors.

On October 24, 1876, the risks of the Company amounted to $491,600.

On March 3, 1877, the second annual meeting was held. The officers elected were as follows: M. Farrington, president; C. A. Mohling, vice-president; Jonathan Freeman, secretary; B. Archer, treasurer; John Mohling, Henry Lehmann, W. W. Beal, directors.

At this meeting the Articles were amended so as to hold the annual meeting on the first Saturday in October.

On October 6, 1877, the third annual meeting was held. The officers elected were: M. Farrington, president: C. A. Mohling, vice-president; Jonathan Freeman, secretary; Wm. Cornforth, Treasurer; W. P. Sterling, A. Carstensen, C. R. Hastings, directors.

On January 1, 1878, the risks amounted to $777,440.

The fourth annual meeting, (October 5, 1878,) elected the following officers, viz:— M. Farrington, president; C. A. Mohling, vice-president; Jonathan Freeman, secretary; W. Cornforth, treasurer; A. Carstensen, J. Kasemeier, C. R. Hastings, directors.

On January 1, 1879, the risks in force amounted to $1,015,690.

The fifth annual meeting (October 4, 1879,) elected the following officers, viz:— M. Farrington, president; C. A. Mohling, vice-president; Jonathan Freeman, secretary; Benjamin Archer, treasurer; A. Carstensen, John McRae, C. R. Hastings, directors.

Risks in force January 1, 1880, amounted to $1,254,935.

The sixth annual meeting (October 2, 1880,) was without the required quorum, and by the Articles of Association the same officers held for the ensuing year.

Risks in force January 1, 1881, amounted to $1,322,545.

The seventh annual meeting (October 1, 1881,) elected: M. Farrington, president; C. A. Mohling, vice-president; Jonathan Freeman, secretary; Thomas Lashbrook, treasurer; A. Carstensen, John McRae, C. R. Hastings, directors.

Risks in force, January 1, 1882, amounted to $1,375,095, and exceeded the amount of any similar company in the State.

On the 6th day of March following, Mr. Freeman, in consequence of severe and protracted illness, tendered his resignation to the board of directors, of the office of secretary. He had long, faithfully and acceptably performed the duties, being annually and unanimously elected. The board, though regretting the necessity, felt compelled to accept; looking about for some one to fill the vacancy, they desired the president to take that position. He therefore tendered his resignation which was accepted, and he was at once chosen secretary for the remainder of the term. Mr. Freeman was then chosen president for the remainder of the term, but his health not permitting him to discharge the duties, they were performed by the vice-president.

The seventh annual meeting (October 7, 1882), elected the following officers, viz: C. R. Hastings, president; C. A. Mohlings, vice-president; M. Farrington, secretary; Thomas Lashbrook, treasurer; S. F. Shepard, O. C. Harrington and A. Carstensen, directors.

The company, still leading all similar insurance companies in the State of Iowa, carried risks on January 1, 1883, amounting to $1,510,830.

CHAPTER XVI

OLD SETTLERS' ASSOCIATION.

One of the most enjoyable affairs is the re-union of the pioneers of any given locality. For the purpose of providing for stated re-unions, associations of old settlers are formed in almost every county throughout the length and breadth of the land; especially is this true in all the States west of the Allegheny mountains—States that have been settled during the present century. These associations have done and are doing much for the preservation of historical events, and as such are surely commendable. The lessons of the past teach us the duties pertaining to the future. The fires of patriotism, the love of country or of home, is strengthened by a narration of such important events as tend to stir the blood or quicken to life those divine affections in man. Many a youth has chosen the life of a soldier from reading the accounts of the great battles and glorious deeds of an Alexander, a Hannibal, a Napoleon, a Wellington, or our own brave and noble Washington. The lists of statesmen have been augmented by the example of a Pitt, a Webster, a Clay, or Calhoun. Patriotism and love of country have been awakened by reading the sublime utterances of Patrick Henry, John Adams, Thomas Jefferson, Abraham Lincoln and Stephen A. Douglas. The love of home, love of parents and kindred have been strengthened by oft-told tales of aged fathers or mothers, especially of that pioneer father or mother, who toiled early and late, hard and long, in order to give their descendants the priceless boon of a home of plenty and of peace, of refinement and love for God and humanity.

The pioneers, in gathering together in these annual re-unions, seem to live over again the early days. Their eyes sparkle and they grow young as the fading reminiscences of other days are recalled. As well stated by a speaker—himself a pioneer—at a meeting in a neighboring county:

"You come together with varied emotions. Some of you, almost at the foot of life's hill, look back and upward at the path you have trod, while others, who have just reached life's summit, gaze down into the valley of tears with many a hope and fear. You, gray-headed fathers, have done your work; you have done it well; and now, as the sunset of life is closing around you, you are given the rare boon of enjoyment, the fruits of your own labor. You can see the land won by your own right arm from its wilderness state, and from a savage foe, pass to your children, and your children's children—literally 'a land flowing with milk and honey;' a land over which hovers the white-robed angels of religion and peace; a land fairer and brighter and more glorious than any other land beneath the blue arch of Heaven. You have done your work well, and when the time of rest shall come, you will sink to the dreamless repose with the calm consciousness of duty done.

"In this hour let memory assert her strongest sway; tear aside the thin veil that shrouds in gloom the misty past; call up before you the long-forgotten scenes of years ago; live over once again the toils, the struggles, the hopes and fears of other days. Let this day be a day sacred to the memory of the olden time. In that olden time there are, no doubt, scenes of sadness, as well as of joy. Perhaps you remember standing by the bedside of a loved and cherished, but dying wife—one who, in the days of her youth and beauty, when you proposed to her to seek a home in a new, wild land, took your hand in hers and spoke to you in words like this: 'Whither thou goest, I will go, and where thou lodgest, I will lodge; thy people shall be my people, and thy God my God; when thou diest I will die, and there will I be buried; the Lord do so to me, and more also, if aught but death part me and thee.' Or, perhaps, some brave boy, stricken down in the pride of his strength; or some gentle daughter, fading away in her glorious beauty; or some little prattling babe, folding its weary eyes in the 'dreamless sleep.' If so—if there are memories like these, and the unbidden tear wells up to the eye, let it come, and to-day one and all shed a tear or two to the memory of the 'loved and lost.' "

FIRST MEETING.

Pursuant to notice published in the county papers, about one hundred of the old settlers of Bremer county met at Lashbrook's Hall, in Waverly, on the 29th of March, 1873, for the purpose of renewing acquaintances, talking over old times, and organizing an Old Settlers' Association for Bremer county.

The meeting being called to order, G. C. Wright was called to the chair, and W. V. Lucas elected secretary.

Many interesting reminiscences were related, the speakers being G. C. Wright, W. V. Lucas, Louis Case, Nicholas Cavanaugh, B. M. Reeves, Dr. Burbanks, J. K. Head and David Clark. Among the stories told were one or two at the expense of Ezekiel Ladd, who was the butt of many jokes in the early days of Bremer county. Ladd was deeply in love with one of the fair damsels of Waverly, who did not return his passion. The boys understood how matters stood, and determined to have a little sport at poor Ladd's expense. Word was sent Ladd that the object of his heart's devotion was ready to wed him, and would meet him at a certain place, where they could proceed together to the court house, and there be "solemnly united in the holy bonds of wedlock." By some means some of the lady's clothes were obtained and donned by some of the boys, and he then proceeded to the appointed rendezvous. Ladd was overjoyed, and the couple hurriedly went to the court house, where the ceremony was duly performed, witnessed by a number of spectators. The poor fellow's disappointment was great indeed, when he discovered the joke that had been played upon him.

A committee was appointed to prepare a constitution and by-laws and report at an adjourned meeting.

Everything at this first meeting passed off pleasantly, and all present were happy.

SECOND ANNUAL MEETING.

On the 18th of July, 1874, was held the second annual meeting of the Old Settlers' Association of Bremer county, Iowa. The meeting was held in the grove near the Presbyterian Church, in Waverly. At the hour of 12 o'clock, G. C. Wright, president, called the association to order, and invited Elder H. H. Berrington to offer prayer to the Giver of all good things, which he did in a very feeling and fervent manner. The second order of business was an address by President Wright, setting forth the object and claim of the association.

Dinner was served to all of the old settlers and invited guests. After dinner the election of officers took place, which resulted in the choice of the following: M. F. Gillett, president; John M. Ellis, first vice-president; John K. Head, second vice-president; W. V. Lucas, secretary; William O. Smith, treasurer.

The president read several toasts. "The old settlers of Iowa" was responded to by Colonel James W. Woods in an earnest and interesting manner. Following these exercises was a social and genial time. The association voted to hold the next annual meeting at Tripoli, in June, 1875. The following persons were present, and herewith we give the time when and place from which they came to Bremer county:

George Kerr, came May 6, 1852, from Monroe county, Ohio.

Pat Bagiston, came June 8, 1855, from Butler county, Ohio.

Adam Boodie, came November, 1855, from Rockford, Illinois.

Alfred Boodie, came May 6, 1856, born in Bremer county, Iowa.

James L. Kerr, came May 21, 1852, from De Kalb county, Illinois.

Joseph Wade, came August, 1854, from London, England.

Mrs. Joseph Wade, came August, 1854, from London, England.

A. S. Morse, came March 4, 1855, from Oneida county, New York.

Mrs. A. S. Morse, came June 8, 1855, from Columbus, Ohio.

Dr. O. Burbank, came September 12, 1854, from Linn county, Iowa.

Mrs. O Burbank, came September 12, 1854, from Linn county, Iowa.

Rachael Hoffman, came July, 1854, from Freeport, Illinois.

Leonia Lee, came July, 1854, from Freeport, Illinois.

James Skillen, came April 3, 1853, from Shelby county, Ohio.

Mrs. James Skillen, came October, 1855, from Linn county, Iowa.

H. H. Burrington, came September, 1858, from Washington county, New York.

F. A. Rowen, came October 23, 1853, from St. Joseph, Michgan.

M. Rowen, came October 23, 1853, from St. Joseph, Michigan.

Mrs. M. Rowen, came October 23, 1853, from St. Joseph, Michigan.

Miss Rowen, came October 23, 1853, from St. Joseph, Michigan.

James M. Sturdevant, came September 10, 1854, from McHenry county, Illinois.

Mrs. J. M. Sturdevant, came September 10, 1854, from McHenry county, Illinois.

David Hugh, came October 20, 1854, from Clinton county, Iowa.

Henry Hurmon, came March 10, 1854, from Calias, Maine.

Mrs. Henry Hurmon, came February, 1857, from Calias, Maine.

M. F. Gillett, came May 7, 1852, from Sumerset county, Ohio.

Mrs. M. F. Gillett, came November 1, 1853, from Steuben county, New York.

Isaac Barrick, came May 7, 1850, from Muscatine county, Iowa.

Mrs. Isaac Barrick, came December, 1865, from La Porte county, Indiana.

Robert Boodie, came October 15, 1855, from Cataragus county, N. Y.

Mrs. Robert Boodie, came May 15, 1855, from Chautauqua county, New York.

B. M. Reeves, came September 30, 1856, from Delaware county, Iowa.

G. W. Ruddick, came August 18, 1856, from Sullivan county, New York.

Mrs. G. W. Ruddick, came June 1, 1860, from Ashtabula county, Ohio.

James A. Sankey, November 16, 1854, from Holmes county, Ohio.

Mrs. James A. Sankey, came November 16, 1854, from Holmes county, Ohio.

David Clark, came, October 15, 1849, from Delaware county, Ohio.

Mrs. David Clark came in 1357, from Bradford county, Pennsylvania.

John Acken, came May 30 1855, from Sauk county, Wisconsin

B. Chittenden, came October 3, 1855, from St. Joseph, Michigan.

Miss Tina, came May 7, 1856, born in Bremer county, Iowa.

Spencer Lee, came September 10, 1857, from Kane county, Illinois.

Mrs. Spencer Lee, came September 10, 1857, from Kane county Illinois.

John McRea, came October 17, 1854, from De Kalb county, Illinois.

Dexter Beal, came June, 1855, from Pittsford, Vermont.

J. M. Ellis, came April 27, 1855, from Alleghany county, New York.

Mrs. J. M. Ellis, came April 27, 1855, from Alleghany county, New York.

Miss Rosetta Ellis, came April 27, 1855, from Alleghany county, New York.

Mrs. Margaret Fortun, came October, 1855, from Alleghany county, New York.

Ann Fortun, came October, 1855, from Alleghany county, New York.

Mrs. Fortun, came July, 1856, from Alleghany county, New York.

Daniel Chittenden, came November 1, 1855, from St. Joseph, Michigan.

Mrs. D. Chittenden, came March 1, 1855, from St. Joseph, Michigan.

John Elliott, came June 23, 1854, from Knox county, Ohio.

Mrs. John Elliott, came June 23, 1854, from Knox county, Ohio.

H. H. Case, came November 17, 1856, from Cataraugas county, New York.

Mrs. H. H. Case, came November 17, 1856, from Cataraugas county, New York,

Miss Hattie Case, came November 17, 1856, from Cataraugas county, New York.

Barney Ingersoll, came October, 1854, from DuPage county, Illinois.

Miss Best Baskins, came June, 1852, from Richland county, Ohio.

Mrs. Shaffer, came June, 1852, from Richland county, Ohio.

Felix Cretzmeier, came November 28, 1853, from Columbia, New York.

Mrs. F. Cretzmeier, came November 28, 1853, from McHenry county, New York.

G. C. Wright, came March 17, 1856, from Androscoggin county, Maine.

Mrs. G. C. Wright, came February 12, 1857, from Chestertown, Maryland.

W. V. Lucas, came April 26, 1855, from Carroll county, Indiana.

Mrs. M. V. Lucas, came May 8, 1857, from Marshall county, Illinois.

Bernhardt Berie, came May, 1854, from Tuscarawas county, Ohio.

Miss Berie, came May, 1854, from Tuscarawas county, Ohio.

HISTORY OF BREMER COUNTY.

J. K. Head, came September 9, 1855, from Kane county, Illinois.

Mrs. W H. Cook, came November, 1857, from Tioga county, New York.

Daniel Watters, came ———, 1853, from Columbiana county, Ohio.

Geo. A. Michael, came October 7, 1853, from Carroll county, Indiana.

Mrs. A. N. Wood, came November, 1853, from Enfield, New Hampshire.

Stell Terry, came June 3, 1853, from McHenry county, Illinois.

John W. Head, came September 9, 1855, from Kane county, Illinois.

THIRD ANNUAL MEETING.

The third annual meeting was held at Tripoli in June, 1875.

The exercises were opened with music by the Nashua Cornet Band. Prayer by Rev. H. H. Burrington.

The president, M. F. Gillett, made a few remarks, welcoming the people to the hospitalities of the citizens of Tripoli. Being disappointed in getting a speaker, the president announced that short addresses would be made by persons on the ground.

G. C. Wright, W. V. Lucas and H. H. Burrington each made a short speech, with which the audience seemed to be well pleased.

A very appropriate piece was sung by the Tripoli glee club followed, by music by the Sumner martial band, after which an elegant dinner was served. An hour or two was then spent in social chat and a renewal of acquaintances by old settlers.

The following named persons became members by paying $1,00 each:

Eli Eisenhart,
Adin Terry,
E. Wattenpaugh,
J O. Buckman,
J. L. Kerr,
W. H. Cook,
John Aiken,
John McRea,
James A Skillen,
W. R. Bostwick,
C. C. Cook,
S H. Curtis,
George Kimball,
A. T. Martin,
J. M. Gross,
Robert Brodie,
John Franklin,
Henry Reddington,
G. W. Ruddick,
John E Brown,
Bernhart Brin,
James Adair,
John Elliott,
D. P. Waiting,
Henry Harmon,
C. R. Hastings,
Louis Case,
Thomas Downu,
David Beebe,
J. B. Kerr,
O. C. Harrington,
J. M. Elles,
J S. Conner,
Henry Laso, Jr.,
S. W. Kung,
Elmer Flood,
George F. Harwood,
John Swale,
J. M. Sturdevant,
A. S. Funston,
George Watts, Jr.,
C. M. Kingsley,
Daniel Chittenden.

The following named were elected officers for the ensuing year:—M. F. Gillett, president; J. O. Buckingham, first vice-president; John McRea, second vice-president; W. V. Lucas, secretary; James A. Skillen, treasurer.

W. V. Lucas, G. C. Wright and O. C. Harrington, were appointed a committee to prepare constitution and by-laws to govern the association.

The following preamble and resolution was presented, on the death of Daniel Walters:

WHEREAS, since our last annual meeting, the hand of death was laid upon our esteemed and valued friend, Daniel Walters; therefore

Resolved That we recognize in his death the loss of one of Bremer county's old pioneers, an honest man and good citizen; but in submission to the will of the Ruler of the Universe, we offer this tribute of honor to his memory, and sympathy to his family.

FOURTH ANNUAL MEETING.

This meeting was held at Tripoli, June 24, 1876, and was called to order by the president. Music by the Tripoli glee club, and prayer by Norris Felt.

Short addresses were made by Hon. Louis Case, James Fletcher, of the Waverly *Tribune*, Hon. D. P. Walling, and Dr. Oscar Burbanks.

On motion, the former committee on constitution and by-laws was discharged, and the following named appointed: Louis Case, O. C. Harrington, and D. P. Walling.

On motion, the time of membership was extended to July 4, 1857.

The following officers were then chosen: J. K. Head, president; O. C. Harrington, first vice-president; D. P. Walling, second vice-president; Louis Case, secretary; Charles Hastings, treasurer.

FIFTH ANNUAL MEETING.

The fifth annual meeting was held at Horton, June 16, 1877.

After being called to order, and an address of welcome made by J. K. Head, president, the Horton glee club sang "America." Invocation by Rev. S. George.

The following named were added to the membership:

J. H. Eldridge, came November, 1855, from Madison county, New York.

Simon George, came November, 1856, from Richland county, Ohio.

Allen Sewell, came August, 1852, from Hamilton county, Ohio.

Allen Showalter, came October, 1856, from Preble county, Ohio.

Robert Skillen, came January, 1855, from Chenango county, New York.

John Runyon, came June, 1853, from Chenango county, New York.

George R. Dean, came June, 1857, from Saratoga county, New York.

Mrs. G. R. Dean, came June, 1857, from Otsego county, New York.

J. K Head, came September, 1855, from Pembroke, New York.

Mrs. J. K. Head, came September, 1855, from Pembroke, New York.

David Beebe, came June, 1857, from Brown county, New York.

Martin Hurlbut, came October, 1856, from Chautauqua county, New York.

J. P Peape, came August, 1856, from Catarangus county, New York.

John Crane, came May, 1857, from Isle of Man, England.

Felix Cook, came May, 1855, from Berks county, Pennsylvania.

F. Coddington, came September, 1853, from Chautauqua county, New York.

The following constitution was adopted:

CONSTITUTION.

ARTICLE I. This society shall be known as the Old Settlers' Association of Bremer County.

ART. II. The object of this association shall be to obtain and keep a record of all the old settlers of Bremer county, that we may know who the first settlers were; also those that are still spared to meet together annually from time to time, may know who the old settlers are that still remain.

ART. III. It shall be the duty of every member of this society to attend all the annual meetings of this association for a social visit, and to become better acquainted.

ART. IV. It shall be the duty of all members of this society to attend the funeral of those who will be called from our number, so far as convenient to attend, and form in procession and follow the remains of our departed ones to their last resting place.

HISTORY OF BREMER COUNTY.

ART. V. The officers of this association shall consist of a president, vice-president, secretary and treasurer.

ART. VI. It shall be the duty of the president to preside at all meetings of the association, to preserve order, to perform all duties appertaining to such office, and to sign all orders drawn on the treasury.

ART. VII. It shall be the duty of the vice-president, in the absence of the president, to preside at the meetings, and to perform all duties of that office; also to assist on all occasions.

ART. VIII. It shall be the duty of the secretary to keep the minutes of all the meetings of this association; register the names of the members in a book kept for that purpose, and to record deaths of members and date of same; to issue all notices required; to do such correspondence as may be necessary; sign all orders, and at the end of his term of office turn over all papers and books in his possession, belonging to the society, to his successor in office.

ART. IX. It shall be the duty of the treasurer to keep an account of all monies, from what source received and for what expended, and report the same to the association at its annual meeting; to turn over to his successor in office, all monies and effects belonging to the association.

ART. X. Each of the above officers shall hold his office for the term of one year, and until his successor is elected.

ART. XI. This constitution can be changed or amended at any annual meeting of the association by a majority vote of the members of the society.

The regular address was delivered by Hon. George W. Ruddick, followed by remarks from Hon. E. J. Dean and Allen Sewell.

After the speeches were made, the following named were elected officers for the ensuing year: Allen Sewell, president; George R. Dean, vice-president; Oscar Burbank, secretary; William P. Harris, treasurer.

Thanks were tendered Judge Ruddick for his address; W. M. Davis for the use of his park and for the pains taken by him to prepare it for the occasion; the musicians and the officers of the association, and citizens of Horton, who did so much for the entertainment of all.

SIXTH ANNUAL MEETING.

The sixth annual meeting of the association was held June 15, 1878, at Moore's Woods, near Waverly. The secretary in his report said:

"Good roads, sunshine over head, and sunshine in the hearts of the old settlers, made this one of the largest and pleasantest meetings ever held by the society.

After the meeting was called to order, prayer was offered by Rev. James Skillen, an early settler, and eighty years of age.

An invitation was then given for membership, and the following named were added:

James and Lorinda Milburn, 1853; from Cedar Rapids.

Thomas J. and Margaret Sewell, 1853; from Boone county, Indiana.

A. J. and Julia A. Case, 1855; from DeKalb county, Illinois.

Sally M. Daily, 1854; from Boone county, Illinois.

Mrs. Margaret Starr, 1855; from Lycoming county, Pennsylvania

Edwin H. Tyler, 1868; from Ogle county, Illinois.

Mary M. Tyler, 1855; from Richland county, Ohio.

Mrs. S. Diana Merrill, 1853; from Boone county, Iowa.

Joseph and Mary Wade, 1855; from London, England.

Abram Wade, 1854; from Huntingtonshire, England.

Martha Ann Wade, 1854; from Cook county, Illinois.

George A. and Sarah Brown, 1854; from Washington county Maine.

James and Sarah E. Andrews, 1856; from McHenry county, Illinois.

S. F. Sheppard, 1850; from Madison county, New York.

Mrs. S. W. Sheppard, 1851; from Boone county, New York.

Harriet C. Coddington.

After all had signed the constitution who desired, David Clark, one of the earliest settlers of the county, took the stand and delivered the regular address. When the speaker came to this county there were not a road or bridge, store or postoffice, mill or mechanic, lawyer or minister, teacher or doctor. Log cabins of one room capacity were the fashion. They were shelters from the rains and the storms, but were unfavorable for sparking. Mails came from Cedar Rapids; flour and meal from Anamosa, or Cedar Falls.

The following named were elected officers for the ensuing year: Matthew Farrington, president; Henry Boyd, vice-president; H. S. Hoover, secretary; W. P. Harris, treasurer.

James M. Sturdevant exhibited a pitchfork, jug, cup and saucer, and tomahawk, family heirlooms over one hundred years old.

Mrs. Daniel Chittenden exhibited her mother's finger ring, eighty years old.

John Miller exhibited cup and saucer one hundred and seventy years old.

A seventy year old blue ribbon jug also invited attention.

Oscar Burbank, who signed himself "de facto Secretary," in his report of the occasion, said:

"The president gave notice that the dinner was ready. Under the trees on the green sward, family after family, group after group, with invited friends and strangers, exhibited and strongly contrasted camping out thirty years ago, with to-day.

"All things have an end, so did our dinner. We naturaly gravitated around the speaker's stand, when, on being many times called, Father Skillen went on the stand and gave a little of his personal experience. He was over eighty years old; emigrated here when the country was new, eat his corn bread, broke the prairie, preached the gospel, Sundays, mauled rails week days, had done what he could to convert sinners, and had been bitten by mad dogs; yet he was alive and here, and hoped to meet us all again on this earth, if not, in the one to come.

"After much calling, Matthew Farrington took the stand. He wished to speak of one of the earliest settlers, who came here thirty-three years ago. He referred to Charles McCaffree. At that time three-hundred Indians lived in the big wood on section 22. None of Charles McCaffree's descendants are with us to-day. Mr. Farrington now spoke of the change that the last thirty years had wrought—a change that hard working men and women had made, a change that had filled our houses with plenty and with happiness, a change

whose basis was not capital or education, but hard work.

"William Jay, E. J. Dean, Silas Bryant and some others, gave short speeches.

"On motion, a vote of thanks was tendered Alpheus Moore for the use of his beautiful grounds; to David Clark for his able address, and to the band."

SEVENTH ANNUAL MEETING.

This meeting was held in the grove of Mr. Blazier, in Jefferson township, on Saturday, June 21, 1879. The following is the report of the secretary, Dr. Burbanks:

"The day was warm and fair. The grateful shade of this old forest was all that heart could desire. The committee of arrangements had bountifully provided everything to make the meeting a success.

"The president, Matthew Farrington, called the meeting to order, when the exercises of the day commenced with music by the Janesville cornet band, followed by a song by native young men and maidens, with organ accompaniment. Invocation by Rev. James Skillen, eighty-one years of age.

"O. C. Harrington, in a short address, told us that he did not belong to the kid-gloved aristocracy, but was a good sample of that class upon whom the curse had been pronounced, 'In the sweat of thy face shalt thou eat bread till thou return unto the ground, for out of it thou wast taken; for dust thou art and unto dust shalt thou return.' He suggested that the curse might be so amended as to except the untaxed bond-holders. He then gave us some of his personal history for the twenty-three years he had been here, of the improvement made, of fishing in the Wapsie, of the grand jury of 1858, when he first made the acquaintance of those old settlers, Judge Favies, Jenkins, Harris, Tyrrel, Blackwell and others; also the political campaign of 1856, where and when William P. Harmon and G. C. Wright worked side by side in the know-nothing party. The defeat of that party sent Harmon into the Republican party and Wright into the democratic party."

The following named were added to the membership of the society: Mrs. Maria Repp, 1858; Alonzo and Lydia O. Gleason, 1854; Abram and Mary Starr, 1855; A. G. and Maddie Lawrence, 1856.

Matthew Farrington exhibited the record of the first election ever held in Bremer county, which was held at the house of John Messinger.

The following officers were elected for the ensuing year: David High, president; Isaac Barrick, vice-president; Oscar Burbanks, secretary; William P. Harris, treasurer.

After the election of officers, C. Krech was loudly called for. He prefaced his remarks by singing "Pat Malloy" in German, and then relating one of his inimitable stories.

Elias Messinger, John Messinger, Allen Sewell and Rev. James Skillen related their experiences of pioneer life. B. W. Johnson also amused the audience with a relation of his early exploits and efforts.

Mrs. Charles McCaffree came upon the stand and was introduced by the president as the first white woman in Bremer county.

The meeting was largely attended, and one of the most enjoyable ever held in Bremer county.

EIGHTH ANNUAL MEETING.

The meeting was held June 19, 1880. From the minutes of the secretary, Dr. Burbanks, the following extracts are taken:

"The week was unfavorable for business. Terrible wind and rainstorms, with great disturbance of the electrical element, had done much damage to property and life. In many fields of corn, the rainy weather had kept the corn plows idle, so that the hope of a fair day for the old settlers' meeting, was a faint hope in the hearts of many.

"At last, Saturday, June the 19th, came. We were looking for it in the spirit of scientific prophecy, as it had been foretold by the wise men, the magi of our day, the scientist who had foretold the very second when it should be ushered in.

"It came in glory, and found us in peace and plenty. No cloud obscured the sky. The morning was cool and fresh. Peace and happiness seemed over all, as if a grand benediction from the Infinite Father had come down upon the whole earth, without respect to persons, or things, or previous condition of servitude, or poverty, or riches, or election, or free grace.

"The grounds at Janesville, where we assembled under the direction and inspiration of the president, David High, was just a splendid sylvan bower of old trees, and grass and sodded earth, that neither time, nor caprice, nor want had been able to induce the owner to efface, but stands to-day a memento of the early settlers of Bremer county. Here, in this delightful, cool and shady spot, on June 19, 1880, at 10:30 o'clock, A. M., the Old Settlers' meeting was called to order by the president.

"Music by the Janesville band, and invocation by Rev. James Skillen.

"The annual address, by Hon. Matthew Farrington, met expectations.

"After the transaction of some necessary business, dinner was next in order. In the shade, under the trees of the old forest, as the dew in the morning upon the broad oak leaves, from the attractions of its particles, resolves itself into drops greater or smaller, so this vast, moving, floating audience, by affinity, by natural attraction, divided, separated, dissolved into groups of near acquaintances, of friends and families to partake of a picnic dinner beyond measure or need, illustrating the wisdom and forethought of those early settlers who had the true grit and sand to hold on and hold out. Here we hunted up old friends, and renewed the acquaintance of those who belong to us by the grace of blood or matrimony, or the descendants of those who came with William the Conqueror, to subdue the prairies, improve the water powers, and build the towns for the use of men, according to the civilization of to-day; men and women who had staying qualities, and in whose veins flowed the bluest blood of man's nobility.

"Shaking hands, greeting and being greeted, swiftly wore away the time, when the sound of music and of song suggested that half past one o'clock was here and waiting. Coming to order at the call of the president, we had the pleasure of listening to a solo entitled, "Olden Days," by Miss Florence Rowen.

"Balloting for officers for the ensuing year resulted in the election of the following named: James M. Sturdevant, president; William Basking, vice-president;

Oscar Burbanks, secretary; William P. Harris, treasurer.

"The president gave notice to all who wished to join the association. The following named were added:

"Frank A. Lee, came to the county Sept. 10, 1857, from Kane county, Illinois.

"Carrie L. Lee, came to Waverly in 1854.

"O. C. Harrington exhibited some Continental money about one hundred years old, which he said was a regular old settler in the money line, of these United States. This was fiat money which the United States promised to redeem in Spanish milled silver dollars, but owing to the poverty of the country, the money was never redeemed, but the government allowed those of its citizens who had given their property for it, to bear the whole burden of its depreciation.

"Professor McIntyre, of Janesville, being called on for a speech said that, having a big voice, some people were simple enough to suppose that his big voice had a patent attachment of big ideas, and of course he could talk at any time, and upon any subject, just as easy as nothing. He said this was a mistake—he had been over estimated. He had always been in sympathy with the hardy pioneers of civilization, for they were the ones who laid the foundations of society, and a large debt of gratitude was due them for the enterprise, toil and suffering that had made such a day as this a possibility in this new fair land.

"Parker Lucas came upon the stand after much calling, and said that he would not make a speech, that he had never learned to sing in the scientific way, but he could sing a little by rote; so he sang an old war song entitled 'General Jackson,' which was loudly applauded.

"Being called for, Father Skillen said that he was neither an orator or a politician, but many years ago while he was on his way to Cedar Falls with a load of wheat, he met a man on horseback who inquired the way to Fort Barrick. Then he told us how a body of armed men marched up the Shell Rock river to exterminate the scalping red skins, and how they saw a smoke by the side of the river where an emigrant's wife was doing her washing quietly by the river's side, and fearing an ambush from the Indians, retreated to a safe place, where, instead of shedding their blood for home and loved ones, they shed something out of a jug.

"This allusion to the Indian scare brought upon the stand many of the actors, spectators and frightened ones of that time. A diversity of views was expressed among the speakers, but only one sentiment prevailed relative to the protection of loved ones and home.

"Mrs. Jennie Maxfield said that twenty-four years ago, the 4th of July was celebrated here upon these very grounds, and that the officers and singers and the orator were all alive save one, whom we understood to mean her husband, Judge Maxfield.

"Robert Nussinger said that he had been here thirty-three years. He was a boy then, and the first public gathering that he went to was at his father's house, July 4, 1850. He had seen no one here to-day, save Isaac Barrick, who was present that day.

"William Mickle being loudly called for, came forward and said that he was not an old settler, but he felt thankful to the men who had endured the hardships necessary to redeem this fair land from the useless and superfluous Indian, to culture and to civilization. Its fertile soil, with its bubbling springs and crystal streams; its green prairies and sylvan groves, were all dotted over with happy homes—farm houses and villages, where peace and plenty reign. The school-house was everywhere by law, and the church where faith and love, plants it. Where we need railroads and carriage roads, there they are. Bridges of iron or of wood are over every river and every brook. Cities and villages where commerce and manufactures flourish, and where art and science build enduring homes. Who has done this great thing—who has made this thing possible? The pioneers of Bremer county."

NINTH ANNUAL MEETING.

The old settlers of Bremer county held their ninth annual meeting June 23, 1881, in the grove on the grounds and near the residence of James M. Sturdevant, in Warren township.

The meeting was called to order by the president, James M. Sturdevant, and Rev. James Skillen addressed the Throne of Grace, returning thanks for meeting so many old friends and familiar faces, and thanks for that living faith that triumphs over the ills of this life, and when all is over, opens to us a life of immortal glory.

The principal address was by H. H. Grey. The secretary says of this address:

"Mr. Grey discussed man as a social being, asserting that if there was only two people on the face of the globe, they would manage some how to get together, and he thought this idea was sustained by the history of the race. Mr. Grey being a native and to the manor born, gave advice, history, suggestions, poetry and anecdote, illustrating the struggles of the early settlers.

The following named were elected officers for the ensuing year:—D. P. Walling, president; Marcus Gillett, vice-president; Frank A. Lee, secretary; William P. Harris, treasurer.

From the secretary's report the following extracts are taken:

"Matthew Farrington being called upon, said he thought it was against the rules to explode small fire-crackers in that crowd, and so he must be excused for attempting to make a speech.

"Rev. James Skillen said there was no speech in him, but he would show them a fool thing; it was how Ohio people made bull-frogs. They were solid as iron, and warranted to wear. But he would lay the fool thing aside, and say that he had a pleasant visit in Ohio; visited Columbus, saw two of his brothers, and had a pleasant time with relatives and friends. He was thankful that at 84 he could stand before his old friends once more before he passed over the rolling stream of time. He wanted them all to do well, and to do well was to be prepared to pass safely through the valley of the shadow of death.

"A unanimous vote of thanks was tendered James M. Sturdevant and family for the great labor and pains taken by them to prepare the grounds; for the use of their house for the aged and infirm; and for the many courtesies and kindnesses shown to all."

TENTH ANNUAL MEETING.

The tenth annual meeting of the Old Settlers' Association of Bremer county, was held at Tripoli, on Saturday, June 24, 1882. The following is the report of the secretary:

"The uncertainty which had attended the weather, and the frequency and severity of storms during the whole month of June, had caused it to be next to impossible to select a day for the occasion with any encouraging prospect of escaping the disturbance of the elements. Arrangements had, however, been made with the D. & D. Railroad Company for excursions from Waverly and from Sumner, to the place of meeting, and all thought that if God and nature were only on our side, the meeting would still prove to be a success.

"The morning of the 24th dawned upon us with that sultry, oppressive heat, which so surely and peculiarly indicates the approach of the storm king, while the black ominous clouds hung like a pall in the northwest; their slow but certain approach being heralded by the roar and deep-toned groanings of the distant thunder.

"The terrible and heart-rending details of the cyclone which had visited the State but one short week before, which with its mighty and resistless power, had nearly destroyed the beautiful city of Grinnell, with its costly residences, its churches and colleges, together with the sacrifice of over fifty human lives, were still fresh in the minds of all. Besides this, a cyclone of like nature, but made fearful by its proximity, only two days previous to the meeting—so recently that full particulars had not yet reached us—had passed through our neighboring city of Independence, unroofing houses, tearing bridges, etc., with three or four human lives lost.

"With this record of devastation and destruction to contemplate, it was but natural that there should be some hesitancy on the part of nearly all of us in starting out in the face of such a storm as was threatened. Notwithstanding all this, however, about one hundred people, including about thirty-five ladies, started from Waverly, and although for a few minutes a hard wind and rain storm prevailed, by the time we reached Tripoli all was pleasant and serene, and every one felt that it was good to be there. Soon old settlers from the surrounding country began to arrive, and by the time the train was in from Sumner, a goodly number had assembled, and hearty hand-shakes, and cheerful salutations gave no trace of the difficulties of the morning. The rain had caused the grounds, which had been prepared, to be unfit for use; therefore the Free Will Baptist Society kindly threw open the doors of their new church, in which the exercises of the association were held.

The association was called to order by the president, Hon. D. P. Walling, who made a few appropriate remarks. The following officers were elected for the ensuing year: O. C. Harrington, president; Charles Hastings, vice-president: Frank A. Lee, secretary; William P. Harris, treasurer.

The president introduced as the speaker of the day, V. B. Grinnell. Mr. Grinnell said that in an unguarded moment he had promised the president that he would make a few minutes' speech after dinner, but did not know he was to be *the* speaker of the occasion. He then gave an interesting account of his early experience in the county. How he took the hack at Dubuque and came to Independence, and from there walked to Dayton Township; stopped on the way at a hotel where he had some bread that would make E. C. Bennett's red hog squeal; stopped in Franklin township where a lady got dinner for him; never had a dinner that tasted so good in his life. The house in which the lady lived was built of logs, and had augur holes bored in the sides, in which stakes were driven, and upon these were laid rails and some hay, which constituted the bed. The chamber floor was made of rails and hay also, and fourteen slept in one bed up there. In speaking of the Wapsipinicon, Mr. Grinnell said that the traditions were that the bed of the river was made by a large serpent crawling through the mud.

"Mr. Sewell made a motion that all who came to the county before July 1, 1872, be considered old settlers, and eligible for membership in this association. After considerable discussion the motion was laid on the table until the next annual meeting.

"John Chapin and wife; V. B. Grinnell and wife, and E. J. Dean became members of the association, by paying the membership fee of $1.00.

"After dinner V. B. Grinnell was called on for his five minutes' speech, and responded in a few humorous remarks. He was followed by O. C. Harrington, E. J. Dean, Allen Sewell and Dan Fitchthorn.

"On motion of Dr. Burbanks, and as amended by V. B. Grinnell, all old settlers were required to have their photographs, as well as photographs of settlers, deceased, so far as possible, in the hands of the secretary before the next annual meeting, and that the secretary be empowered to procure a suitable frame therefor.

"On motion of the secretary the following resolution was unanimously adopted:

"*Resolved*, That a vote of thanks be tendered the Baptist Society for the use of their church; to Rev. R. Norton for his efficient services as chaplain; to the martial band and glee club for their excellent music; to V. B. Grinnell for his happy speech; to A. T. Martin for his superior coffee; to D. P. Walling for his interest and services as president; to E J. Dean and family, and other citizens of Tripoli for the kindness shown to the members of this association."

CHAPTER XVII.

DOUGLAS TOWNSHIP.

This territory lies in the northern tier of townships in Bremer county, and is bounded by Chicasaw county, Polk, Warren and Frederika townships, respectively on the north, west, south, and east. It is an agricultural township, having no village or railroad within its boundaries. The Wapsipinicon river runs through a portion of section 1, when it flows into Frederika township, then entering again on section 12, makes a short curve, and leaves on the same quarter. Three creeks flow toward the south that have their source in the southern part of the township—Erskine run, Quarter-section run, and Crane creek.

The soil is a dark, sandy loam, with clay sub-soil, very rich and productive, but inclined, in places, to be flat. Much of this land, that years ago was considered swampy, and not desirable for cultivation, now comprises rich and productive farms. This is a prairie township, having very little natural timber, excepting about five hundred acres on sections 1 and 12. The population consists mainly of Germans, although other nationalities are represented.

EARLY SETTLEMENT.

Albert Stannard, the first settler of this township, came from Battle Creek, Michigan, with a son and daughter—the former, sixteen years old, the latter two years younger. They came in the fall of 1852. Mr. Stannard cut hay to supply his oxen for the winter and to cover a rude hut which he constructed of logs and poles, on the bank of the Wapsipinicon, in which they lived during the winter. He was followed next summer by Crawford Thoroughman and Andy Gulen, his son-in-law. Albert Stannard, Asa Adams and Louis Branch left the township in May, 1861, bound for California. Stannard died on the way—Adams changed his route and went to Oregon, where he has since lived, and Branch went on to his destination.

John Mitchell was a settler of 1855, and located on section one.

John Acken selected a home the same season on section 12.

James H. Eldridge also came in 1855, and located on section 18.

William Blackwell run his lines the same year, around a farm on section 31, and Simon George established himself on section 30. Then followed Frank Goodwin, who died in May, 1881, and Benjamin Goodwin, now living in the north part of the township, on section four—Thomas Lashbrook, now living in Waverly; R. G. McDonald, Malcomb Fisher, Robert McCracken, who went to Ireland, last April; Jack McCracken, also an early settler, and went to Ireland a number of years ago; James Leaman, Timothy Cleary, Chauncy Brooks, and others, followed in rapid succession—a number of which are mentioned—George Sailes came in 1855, and settled on section 24, he sold out and went to Kane county, Illinois.

J. S. Leaman, a son of Isaac and Rebecca (Spencer) Leaman, was born in Boone county, Illinois, on the 17th day of September, 1837. He remained in his native county until nineteen years of age when he, with his parents, emigrated west. Isaac Leaman, father of J. S., who is now living in Charles City, Iowa, was born near Lancaster, Pennsylvania, in the year 1809. His youth, and the first years of his manhood were passed in the State of Ohio. In the spring of 1837 he moved to Illinois, and for eighteen years lived in Boone and DeKalb counties. Here he formed one of the early pioneers, and had Indians as neighbors for several years after his arrival. He witnessed and took no small part in the developments of that section of the country. In the year 1855 he made another move westward, and took up his abode in the township of Frederika, in Bremer county. Mr. Leamon has raised a family of ten children, six boys and four girls, all of whom are now living, with the exception of the second daughter. James S. is the second eldest child of his father's family, and is the oldest son. In the spring of 1859 he moved to the township of Douglas, where he has since lived, always taking an active part in the growth and development of his township, and a lively interest in public affairs. His farm contains 160 acres of prairie and 10 acres of timber land. August 19, 1858, he was married to Miss C. M. Goodwin, a daughter of J. P. Goodwin, an old settler of this township. Mrs. Leaman is a native of Essex county, New York, born the 2nd day of July, 1838. She moved to Illinois at the age of ten years, and in 1856 came to Iowa, Ten children have been born to them, eight of whom are now living—four boys and four girls.

Timothy Cleary, a native of Tipperary, Ireland, was born in 1822. In May, 1851, he came to America, and upon his arrival worked for one year in the State of New York, and then moved to Illinois, where he remained until the spring of 1855, when he came to Bremer county Iowa, and made a claim in Douglas township. He then worked in Minnesota and Illinois for the three following years, and in the fall of 1858, settled on his claim. His farm contains 420 acres on section 24. He was married in White Hall, New York, in 1853, to Miss Mary McCormick, also a native of Ireland. They have had eleven children, nine of whom are now living—Mary A., Martin, Thomas (deceased,) Katie, Sarah J., John, Emma, Tim, George and Thomas (twins,) Jessie (deceased.)

R. G. McDonald, a native of county Antrim, Ireland, was born January 4, 1833, and there his life was passed on a farm until he was eighteen years of age. At this period he emigrated to America, and landing in New York State, worked there one year, and then moved westward, locating at Racine, Wisconsin, where he remained one year. He then went south, remaining there one and one-half years, when he returned to Racine, where he passed another year. In October, 1855,

he came to this township, and in company with a cousin, whose name also was Robert McDonald, purchased 240 acres of land on section 1. Shortly after, his cousin moved to Minnesota, and the subject of this sketch bought a part of his land. Mr. McDonald is one of the oldest living settlers of this town. He came here a poor man, and has, by persevering toil and good management, acquired a competence. He, with his four sons, are the possessors of eleven hundred acres of excellent land. The farm is located on sections 1, 2, 11 and 12, and is drained and watered by the Wapsipinicon river, which runs through it, and which is skirted with timber in abundant supply for fuel. He was married in Racine, Wisconsin, February 14, 1855, to Miss Ann McDonald, a native of his own county. She came to America with her parents at the age of three, and grew to womanhood in Racine. They were the parents of twelve children, eleven of whom are living. Mrs. McDonald died at their home, October 1, 1881. The children are all living at home with the exception of the eldest son, who is married and lives on an adjoining farm. The children were born as follows: John William, born March 24, 1856; Samuel, March 3, 1858; David, January 29, 1862; Mary Ann, April 20, 1864; Margaret E., January 24, 1866, Agnes in 1868; Sarah Elizabeth, October 1, 1870; Robert, March 29, 1873; Julia, July 23, 1875; Emily, July 4, 1877; Liddie, September 21, 1879.

B. H. Gardner, a native of Stephentown, Rensselaer county, New York, was born on the 25th day of September, 1828 When twelve years of age, his parents moved to Orleans county, and in 1843 came west, and settled in Rock county, Wisconsin, near where Broadhead now stands. Here B. H. passed his early life, attending the district schools, and helping his father about the farm. After reaching his majority, he returned to Orleans county, New York, and for two years worked as engineer in a saw mill, after which he moved back to Wisconsin, and followed the same occupation for two or three years. He next engaged in farming for a few years, and in May, 1863, came to Bremer county, and worked a rented farm in Lafayette township, for two years. In 1865 he purchased a farm on section 31, Douglas township, where he has ever since resided. His land consists of eighty-two and one-half acres in Douglas, and ten acres of timber land in Lafayette township. His sons, Charles and Francis, each also own and manage eighty acres of land in this township. Mr. Gardner has been a member of the board of trustees for several terms, and has held the office of secretary in his school district for ten years. He was married, in Green county, Wisconsin, June 13, 1858, to Miss Harriet Lampson, a native of Ohio, born in 1839. While she was quite young her parents moved to Wisconsin, where she grew to womanhood. Six children have been born to them—Francis, born November 22, 1860; Harley and Charley, (twins), born May 30, 1862; Edith, born November 5, 1866; Mattie, born August 19, 1870, and Ernest, born March 4, 1875.

M. S. Littlefield, a son of D. K. and Dollie (Sawyer) Littlefield, was born in Piscataquis county, Maine, on the 7th of December, 1833. He received his education in the common schools, and, when grown, helped his father on the farm. The family remained in that section of the country until 1855, when they emigrated to Kenosha county, Wisconsin, where they remained eight years, and M. S. employed his time for five years, during the winter months, teaching school. In the fall of 1863, they came to Iowa, purchased a farm in Polk township, Bremer county, which they opened up, improved and afterward sold. In October, 1878, Mr. Littlefield bought a farm in Douglas township, where he has since resided. He now owns one hundred acres here, and also seven acres of timber in Polk township. He has held the office of clerk of Polk township for six years, and has held school offices in that township and Douglas, at various periods, and is now secretary of Independent School District No. 3. He was married, in Polk township, on the 31st day of October, 1872, to Miss E. A. Collins, a native of Orange county, Vermont, born August 22, 1852. Mr. Littlefield's mother died in Piscataquis county while he was still a babe, and his father married Miss Polly Buck, a native of Maine. The second wife died in Polk township, August 31, 1878, and was buried in the Horton cemetery. M. S. Littlefield's father was born in New Gloucester, Cumberland county, Maine.

M. Potter was born May 5, 1833, in Franklin county, New York, where he grew to manhood on a farm. He received a common school education, and when old enough learned the mason's trade, which occupation he has since followed, in connection with farming, until the last few years. In August of the second year of our great rebellion, he enlisted in company F, 142d New York Volunteers, and served until honorably discharged at the close of the war. Upon returning from the army he sold his farm in New York, and in August of the same year, came to Iowa. Here he purchased a farm of 80 acres on section 19, in the township of Douglas, and has there since resided. Mr. Potter has held the position of county supervisor for three years, and has also held other town offices at different times. He was married in his native county, November 3, 1859, to Miss Orville Clarke, of the same place, who was born July 25, 1838. They have two children—twins—Harmon and Herman, who were born August 15, 1861.

L. P. Wilson was born in Clarion county, Pennsylvania, on the 22d of June, 1837. Here he received his education in the common school, and remained with his parents on their farm until he reached the age of twenty-five. In the spring of 1855, the family moved west and settled in Buchanan county, Iowa, where L. P. farmed until 1864, when he came to Bremer county. He first settled in Franklin township, living there until the spring of 1872. He then came to Douglas township, and settled on the farm where he now lives, and which he had purchased the year previous. Mr. Wilson takes great interest in stock raising, hogs being a specialty with him. He has from seventy-five to one hundred of the celebrated Poland-China breed, and owns seventeen full-blooded animals of that breed. Around the buildings, is a fine grove of shade trees of his own planting, which lessens the excessive heat of summer and breaks the coldest winds of our northern winters. On his farm is also an orchard of seventy-five thrifty trees. He was married in Buchanan county on the 12th of March, to Miss Olive Lucinda Tucker, who is a native of Tompkins county, New York, born October 20, 1842. Three children have been born to them—Samuel Parks, born March 2d, 1863, in Buchanan county; Mary Jane, born August 29, 1864, in Bremer county; Perry Ulysses, born October 6, 1865, in this county.

James Connor was born in Ireland in 1820. He continued to reside in his native country until about thirty years of age, when he emigrated to America, locating in Cleveland, Ohio. He made that city his home until 1864, when he came to Bremer county and settled in Douglas township, where he now owns 120 acres of land on section 14. He was married in Cleveland, Ohio, in December, 1855, to Miss Mary Costello, of that city. She is a native of Ireland. They have seven children living—James Edward, Patrick John, Elizabeth Ann, Thomas William, Mary Ellen, Margareta and Robert Henry.

Thomas Sinderson, a native of Lincolnshire, England, was born December 22d, 1819, and grew to manhood on a farm in his native place. When grown, he served as a groom until 1858, at which time, he emigrated to America, and located in Belvidere, Illinois, where he lived for seven years. In April, 1865, he came to Bremer county, Iowa, and settled in Douglas township, where he purchased 120 acres of land on section 14. He also owned ten acres of timber in the township of Frederika. Since Mr. Sinderson's first settlement in this county he has resided on his farm, on section 14. He was married in England in 1850, to Miss D. Smith, born February 19, 1826, and who is also a native of Lincolnshire. Eight children have been born to them, six of whom are now living. Charles, born September 28, 1853; Arthur, born November 1, 1855; Emma, born July 8, 1857, died February 1, 1859; Alice, born July 7, 1859, died March 7, 1879; Ellen, born September 24, 1861; Keziah, February 28, 1865; Sarah, July 13, 1866; Emma, May 30, 1869.

Joseph Beck was born in Gros de ching, France, on the 22d day of May, 1830. At the age of sixteen, he emigrated to America, and located in Rensselaer county, New York, where he lived for ten years. He then moved to DuPage county, Illinois, where he farmed for twelve years. In the spring of 1866, he came to Bremer county, and lived in Polk township for three years. In the fall of 1869 he purchased and moved on the place where he still lives. His farm is located on sections 29 and 30, and consists of 160 acres. He was married in Chicago on the 22d day of November, 1855, to Miss Mary Jamieson, born in Ireland March 16, 1836. When ten years of age, she came to America with her parents, and grew to womanhood in Albany, New York. In the spring of 1855, she moved west, to DuPage county, Illinois. Nine children have been born to them, six of whom are now living. The names of said children are—Libbie, Perry, Emma, Ida, Roy, Charles, and Mary, Samuel, Josephine, deceased.

John W. Shirley, was born in LaPorte county, Indiana, on the 3d day of October, 1836. When he was five years of age his parents moved to Winnebago county, Illinois, where John was reared on his father's farm, and received an education in the common schools. In the spring of 1864, he left his home, and for nearly two years engaged in mining in Nevada. Returning to his former home, he passed a short time, and in 1866 came to Iowa, locating in Douglas township, Bremer county, and the year following his arrival bought the farm on which he has since lived. This land comprises 240 acres on section 10, and three, and ten acres of timber in the township of Frederika. Mr. Shirley has held the office of trustee for two terms, as well as other town and school offices, and is present chairman of the board of trustees. He was married in Schenectady county, New York, in 1859, to Mary A. Rainbow, a native of New York, who died in Illinois, in the spring of 1864. On the 19th day of November, 1868, Mr. Shirley married Miss Elizabeth E. Felt, who was born September 21, 1843, and who is a native of Madison county, New York. Two children have been born to them—Mary Delia, born September 26, 1869, Raymond Felt, born August 13, 1882.

J. B. Olney, a native of Chenango county, New York, was born May 31, 1837. When seven years of age, his parents moved to DeKalb county, Illinois, and settled on a farm, where he remained until twenty-seven years of age. February 25, 1864, he enlisted in Company I, Ninth Illinois Cavalry, and served until honorably discharged at the close of the rebellion. Upon leaving the army, he passed the following winter at his former home; and in the spring of 1866, came to Iowa, locating in Warren township, Bremer county, where he stayed one year, and then came to his present home in Douglas township. He owns 160 acres on section 36, and also some land in the township adjoining. Mr. Olney has held the office of justice of the peace for the past four years; has been assessor for two terms, and has held other local offices. He was married in DeKalb county, Illinois, February 25, 1858 to Miss Fidelia A. Barringer, a native of New York, born December 1, 1842. They have two children living—Florice Edward, born April 3, 1862; and Volney, born August 17, 1870. Mary Ann died in the spring of 1862, aged three years and two months.

Philip Carpenter was born in Montgomery county, New York, on the 10th day of June, 1830. When he was about six years of age his parents moved to Jefferson county, and four years later, to St. Lawrence county, where his father died. Here Philip remained until about eighteen years of age, and then spent six years in other counties of the State, first going to Oswego county, thence to Onondago county, and, lastly, moving to Rensselaer county, where he remained until the spring of 1854. He then removed to Waukesha county, Wisconsin, where he lived one year, and then located in Fon du Lac county, where he engaged in farming for twelve years. He then farmed for three years in an adjoining part of Sheboygan county. In the fall of 1867, he came to Iowa and settled on the place where he has since resided. His farm consists of 120 acres of prairie land, on sections 30 and 31, and ten acres of timber land in Polk township. He was married in Rensselaer county, New York, on the 7th day of January, 1854, to Miss Catherine Miller, a native of that county, born on the 25th day of March, 1836. They have six children living, and one deceased. —Ida J., born November 22, 1854, in the town of Vernon, Waukesha county, Wisconsin; Mary A., born February 11, 1858, in the town of Marshfield, Fon du Lac county, Wisconsin; Ella, born January 16, 1860, in the same place; Alice O., born August 28, 1864, in the same place; Wesley M., born April 11, 1866, in Greenbush, Sheboygan county, Wisconsin; Vernie E., born May 30, 1869, in Douglas township; Avery D., born February 17, 1871, in Douglas township. Ella A. died May 1, 1863.

W. S. Robinson was born in Piscataquis county, Maine, on the 26th day of November, 1837. He remained in his native county until seven years of age, when, with his parents, he moved to Boone county, Illinois, where he lived until within three years of his majority. At this time his parents located in Crawford county, Wisconsin, and here their son lived with them two years, then returned to Boone county and purchased a farm where he lived until September, 1867, when he came to Iowa and settled in Douglas township, Bremer county. Here he bought a farm of excellent land located on section 9. Mr. Robinson has held the office of assessor for one year, and at different periods has held other town and school offices. In February, 1882, he was commissioned postmaster of Pony postoffice, which was established at his residence in Boone county, Illinois. He was married in Boone county, Illinois, January 1, 1864, to Miss Mary E. Vaughan, born in Ogle county, Illinois, March 10, 1843. They have two children living—Ertie E., born December 26, 1866; Bertha M., born June 18, 1878.

Diedrich Kierchhoff, was born in Hanover, Germany, on the 13th day of December, 1834. He remained in his native country until he was twenty-one years of age, when he emigrated to America, and settled in the State of Illinois, where, for the greater share of the time, he pursued the carpenter's trade, working in Chicago, Elgin, Freeport, and other points. In the fall of 1868, he moved to Iowa, and located on a rented farm, situated in the northeastern part of this township. Here he remained for one year, and then purchased his farm of 160 acres, on section 27, where he has since resided. Mr. Kierchhoff was elected a member of the board of trustees in the fall of 1879, and still fills that position; he has also been road supervisor for three terms. He was married in Chicago on the 20th day of March, 1866, to Miss Dora Mummealtie, a native of Prussia, born May 26, 1841. Nine children have been born to them, six of whom are living—Emma, born October 28, 1868; Dora, born January 17, 1872; Mary B., born May 24, 1874; Diedrich, born July 15, 1875; William, born December 5, 1878; Wilhelmina, born September 17, 1880; Frederick, born January 25, 1867, and died when fifteen months old; Alvina, born May 19, 1870, and died, aged nine months; Bertha, born July 30, 1882, and died when twenty-five days old.

R. Walker was born in Cleveland, Ohio, on the 9th of September, 1848. While he was quite young, his parents moved to Columbia county, Wisconsin, where he remained on a farm until nineteen years of age. In March, 1868, he came to Iowa, and located near Tripoli. Here he lived for a year and a half, after which he lived for a short time at Clermont, Iowa, then went on a visit to his old home in Wisconsin. He soon returned to this county, where he has since lived. In the fall of 1874, he purchased a farm of forty acres on section 8, in Douglas township, where he moved his family. Mr. Walker was married in Portage City, Wisconsin, March 19, 1868, to Miss Mary Ann Elizabeth Diffee, a native of Utica, New York, born on the 25th of January, 1849. Three children have been born to them—Myrtie, Ione, Gertie May and Guy Prentiss. Mr. Walker opened a store in December, 1880, and has since kept a good assortment of general merchandise.

W. A. Robinson was born in Boone county, Illinois, on the 6th of September, 1846. He there received a common school education, and grew to manhood's estate. In October, 1868, he came to Bremer county, Iowa, and settled in Douglas township. He first purchased a farm on section 4, where he spent a year and a half, and then bought 80 acres in section 5, where he now resides. He was married in Horton county, on the 4th of July, 1870, to Miss Margaret Ann Reed, of Douglas township. She is a native of Washington county, Missouri, born on the 15th of October, 1856. They have had three children two of whom are now living—Mary Ellen, born November 29, 1871; Leon Ray, born November 23, 1878; Elizabeth A. was born October 7, 1875, and died August 15, 1877.

John Harker, a native of Yorkshire, England, was born June 10, 1842. When he was about two years of age, his parents emigrated to America and settled in Grant county, Wisconsin, where John grew to manhood and received a common school education. He engaged in farming in Grant county until the spring of 1869, when he came to Bremer county and purchased a farm on section 23, Douglas township. Here he lived until the winter of 1878–9, when he moved to the farm on which he now resides, located on section 14. He was elected a member of the board of trustees in the fall of 1881, and still serves in that capacity. He was married in Grant county, Wisconsin, April 7, 1866, to Miss Ruth Slack, of that county. They have been blessed with three children—George William, born January 11, 1867; James Louis, born January 24, 1872, and Lydia Ann, born April 13, 1877.

Charles Alcock was born in Yorkshire, England, on the 27th day of October, 1819. He there passed his youth, and four years of manhood, and then came to America, locating in Grant county, Wisconsin, where he engaged in mining until the spring of 1869. At this period he came to Bremer county, Iowa, and purchased the farm on which he has since resided. His land lies in sections 14 and 23, and consists of 240 acres. He was married in Yorkshire, England, on the 20th day of March, 1845, to Miss Elizabeth Peacock, who was born in 1826, and is a native of that place. Mrs. Alcock died at their home on the 3d of November, 1870, and was buried in what is known as the "Alcock Cemetery." She had borne him nine children, eight of whom are living. Their daughter, Hannah L., died November 21, 1870, aged nineteen years, four months and twenty-one days.

L. E. Losee, a native of DeKalb county, Illinois, was born July 1, 1845. He there received a common school education, and when old enough, learned the carpenter's trade, which occupation he has since followed in connection with farming. In May, 1872, he came to Bremer county, Iowa, and bought a farm in Douglas township, upon which he has since resided. He has been assessor of the town for one term, and also secretary of school district number two, for three years. Mr. Losee was married in Boone county, Illinois, September 15, 1870, to Miss Fannie A. Jones, a native of Hillsdale county, Michigan, born on the 6th day of September, 1845. When she was eight years of age her parents moved to DeKalb county, Illinois, where she grew to womanhood. They have been blessed with four children—Clayton, born August 6, 1871; Harry, born August 4, 1874; Edith, born October 17, 1877; Lyndes, born April 22, 1879.

Thomas McCracken, a native of county Down, Ireland, was born in August, 1853. He grew to manhood's estate in the country of his birth, continuing to reside there until the fall of 1877, when he came to America, and took possession of his father's farm, in Douglas township, Bremer county. Thomas' father, John McCracken, came to America soon after the former's birth. He first spent one or two years in Pennsylvania, then came west to Iowa, and settled in Douglas township, Bremer county. Here he lived with his brother Robert, who had come to America a year or two earlier, and located in the northeastern part of the township. The brothers—Robert and John McCracken—were among the early settlers of Douglas township, and together owned about 700 acres of valuable land, which they held until Robert sold his farm one year ago. Thomas now owns 240 acres of land on sections 12 and 14, and 140 acres in the township of Frederika.

The Wapsipinicon river runs through his farm, and along its banks is a valuable supply of timber.

J. F. Jeffers was born in Seneca county, New York, on the 14th day of May, 1814. While a child his parents moved to Wayne county, where he received a common school education. When grown, he farmed in this county until 1850, when he moved to Will county, Illinois, where he lived for five years. In 1855 he came to Iowa, locating in Blackhawk county, being one of the early settlers. He remained there until 1871, when he came to Douglas township, and purchased a farm lying on section 9, upon which he has since lived. Mr. Jeffers was married in Wayne county, New York, February 19, 1833, to Miss Hannah Rinehart, born July 13, 1813, in Columbia county, Pennsylvania. They have had twelve children born to them, eight of whom are now living; have married and formed homes of their own.

Alexander Stephens was born in Cornwall, England, on the 4th day of March, 1842. When about seven years of age he came, with his parents, to America. The family located in Lafayette county, Wisconsin, where Alexander grew to manhood, on a farm. In his youth he attended the district schools of Lafayette county. In the spring of 1879 he came to Bremer county, and purchased the farm in Douglas township, where he has since lived. He was married, in Platteville, Grant county, Wisconsin, on the 8th day of February, 1868, to Miss Mary Ann Alton, of that county. She is a native of England, born in 1841. Nine children have been born to them, eight of whom are now living.

William Early, a native of the county of Essex, Canada, was born on the 13th day of January, 1823, and there grew to manhood on a farm, about twenty-five miles east of Detroit. In 1846, in company with his parents, he moved to Boone county, Illinois, where he followed agricultural pursuits untill 1880. In October of that year he came to Douglas township, Bremer county, and purchased his farm of 80 acres lying in section 4, where, with his family, he resides. Mr. Early was born in Boone county, Illinois, September 25, 1850, to Miss Sarah Jane Whiting, a native of Maine, born on the 9th day of December, 1830. Four children have been born to them—Edward, born December 19, 1851; Horace, born July 4th, 1861; George, born February 8, 1866; Effie, born December 25, 1870.

C. D. Ried was born in Scotland on the 18th day of March, 1831. When he was eighteen years of age, he left his home in the old country and crossed the waters to America. Upon his arrival, he settled in Ogdensburg, New York, where he remained for five years, and then removed to Chicago, Illinois, which city he made his home until the fall of 1876, when he came to Douglas township and purchased the place on which he has since lived. His farm is located on section 5, and consists of 72 acres of good land. He was married in Lake county, Illinois, July 4, 1857, to Miss Margaret Steele of that county, born December 25, 1839. While a resident of Chicago Mr. Ried was foreman of a lumber-yard for Swan, Clark & Co., furniture manufacturers, for nine years.

D. E. Perkins was born in Courtland county, New York, on the 25th of October, 1840. He there lived with an uncle (his mother having died in his infancy) until he was ten years of age, when he removed with the family to Waukesha county, Wisconsin. On the 2d of November, 1861, he enlisted in Company H, Thirteenth Wisconsin Infantry, and served until honorably discharged, December 27, 1865. At the close of the war, he came to Iowa and located in Buchanan county, where he lived four years. He then came to Douglas township, Bremer county, locating on the farm where he now resides. His land lies on section 6 and consists of seventy-five acres. He was married in Douglas township, on the 7th of May, 1871, to Miss Martha Marsh, of Polk township, but whose birth place is DeKalb county, Illinois, where she was born July 4th, 1850. Seven children have been born to them—Lucia E., born March 10, 1872; Marcia L., born May 10, 1873; Carrie I., born August 9, 1874; Grace M., born May 31, 1876; Edna J., born June 3, 1878; Sholto M., born February 29, 1880; Olive M., born December 13, 1881.

Luther Whiting was born in Boone county, Illinois, on the 28th of November, 1841. He received a common school education and grew to manhood's estate in that county. In his 19th year he entered the army, enlisting at Belvidere, on the 15th day of September, 1861, in Company A, Twelfth Illinois Infantry. He served the Nation faithfully for four years and three days. At the close of the rebellion he was mustered out of service, at Benton Barracks, Missouri, on the 8th of September, 1865. Upon returning to civil life,

Yours Truly
C. Cadwallader

he followed farming in his native county until the fall of 1880, at which time he came to Bremer county, Iowa, locating in Douglas township, where he purchased a farm of 240 acres on section 8, and ten acres of timber land in sections 1 and 5. Mr. Whiting was married in Winnebago county, Illinois, May 28, 1866, to Miss Mary E. Sabin, a native of Schenectady county, New York, born on the 28th of May, 1846. Four children have been born to them—Nellie, born May 2d, 1868; John H., born October 24, 1870; Ira, born August, 18, 1875; Frank, born May 22, 1882.

A. A. Dickinson was born in Orange county, Vermont, on the 19th day of December, 1840, and grew to manhood on a farm in his native place. In 1862, he enlisted in Company B, Sixth Vermont Volunteers, and served until the close of the war. After returning to civil life, he conducted his farm at his former home for seven years. In November, 1872, he came to Bremer county and settled in Douglas township, on section 8, where he lived for a short time, and then purchased 80 acres of land on section 30, where he has since resided. Mr. Dickinson was married in Williamstown, Orange county, Vermont, on the 7th day of September, 1862, to Alice A. Briggs, who is a native of that place. This couple have one adopted child—Mary D., born on the 14th day of July, 1869.

T. H. Brainard was born in Lower Canada, on the 8th day of August, 1837. When he was two years of age his parents moved to Massachusetts, and in that State he passed ten years of his life. The two years following he lived in the State of Vermont, and in Canada. In 1851, his family moved to Wisconsin, and located in Black Earth, Dane county, which place was his home until 1870. In the fall of 1861, he enlisted in Company A, Eleventh Wisconsin Infantry, commanded by Captain D. E. Hough. He served until the close of the war; and among other engagements in which he took part, was the siege of Vicksburg and the fall of Mobile. In the fall of 1870, he came to Bremer county, Iowa, and made Horton village his home for two years. He then returned to Wisconsin where he remained until 1879. In the fall of this year he returned to this county. He was married in Dane county, on the 21st day of August, 1866, to Miss Hannah Hollis, of the town of Black Earth. Mr. and Mrs. Brainard have had four children, two are now living—Alice M., deceased; Edna J., Edgar, deceased, and David R.

ORGANIC.

The first election in Douglas township was held at the house of Asa Adams, June 28, 1858. John Acken, James P. Goodwin and Albert Stannard were chosen judges of election; G. T. Sayles and L. F. Goodwin, clerks. The following persons were elected: Township clerk, L. F. Goodwin; justice of the peace, G. F. Sayles, and William Blackwell; trustees, A. Stannard, N. A. Sanford, and Simon George; constables, Thomas Lashbrook, and Horace Spaulding. Whole number of ballots cast, twenty-three.

The officers for 1882, were: John Sherlie, John Harker, and Diedrick Kierchhoff, trustees; James Ayres and R. C. Link, justices of the peace; N. G. Moore, clerk; Fred. Scheuam and J. Jeffers, constables.

The officers for 1883 are: Trustees, J. W. Shirley, John Harker, and Augustus Hoppinworth; clerk, Marvin Potter; constables, A. Hoppinworth, and L. Bergman; Justices of the peace, L. Whiting and Fred Scheuam; assessor, Jacob Alney.

FIRST THINGS.

The first death in the township was that of Stephen D. Goodwin, a son of James P. Goodwin. He was a lad ten years of age. Seventeen days after the arrival of the family, and while they were still living in their wagons, he attempted to get a rifle from the wagon to shoot some chickens. Reaching in he caught the gun by the muzzle, and drawing it toward him it was accidentally discharged, the ball entering his chest, and lodging under the skin on the back of his neck. Death was almost instantaneous. This occurred on Friday, June 20, 1856. He was buried, the Sabbath following, in the township of Frederika.

The first marriage was that of Orvile McGinnis to Miss Mary Goodwin, October 4, 1854, at the residence of the bride's father, James P. Goodwin, by Elder Terry, of Polk township.

The first birth was that of Walter Goodwin, son of Benjamin Goodwin, on section 4, in March, 1857.

POSTOFFICES.

Phillipston postoffice was established on section 25 in January, 1880. Philip Burgess was commissioned postmaster. It was discontinued in May, 1881.

Pony postoffice was established February 15, 1882. W. S. Robinson being the postmaster. It is located at his place on section 9. Mail is received three times each week.

MERCANTILE.

In 1879-80 Philip Burgess opened a small store in connection with the Philipston postoffice. He only continued in the business a short time. Mrs. A. E. Walker established a store on section 8, with a stock of general merchandise. This store is still in operation.

CEMETERIES.

There are three cemeteries in the township, one on section 14, called "Alcock Cemetery" and one on each of the church lots in the southeast part of the township. The first burial in Alcock cemetery was the remains of Mrs. Charles Alcock, during the fall of 1871.

EDUCATIONAL.

Helen J. Acken, daughter of John Acken, taught the first term of school in a log house formerly used as a dwelling by the Acken family, on section 12. There are now eight public schools and two denominational schools in the township.

TERPSICHOREAN.

Lovers of the dance have good opportunity in this township to trip the "light fantastic." Not only this township but the surrounding country attend in large numbers at "Leaman's Hall," located on section 8, which is the scene of frequent gatherings of this description, adding much to the good social feeling that generally prevails in this community.

RELIGIOUS.

The first services of a religious character were conducted by Mr. Newell, a freewill Baptist, in the spring of 1856, at what was then known as the Acken school house, on section 12. These meetings were conducted regularly for about three months, when they were discontinued. In June, 1857, Elder Terry, of Polk township, who is now living in Waverly, a regular Baptist, began to hold meetings at the residence of James P. Goodwin. These meetings were continued at that place for about one year. The first regular religious organization was effected, however, by the German Lutherans in the southeast part of the township. This society, called St. Paul's Evangelical Lutheran Church, was organized in 1872, the Rev. August Engelke officiating, with a membership of about thirty-two. The first officers of this church were—Fred. Hildebrand, Charles Hoppenworth and Henry Hopper. The pastors who have been successively in charge are Rev. Baumibach, Rev. Frederick Kuthe and Rev. August Albert, the present pastor, who has been in charge since the fall of 1878. The present officers of the church are—Trustees, Fred Schenam and Henry Hopper; secretary, August Hoppenworth; treasurer, Wm. Schwartz; sextons, Adolph Hoppenworth and Charles Miller. Until 1878 services were held in the schoolhouse in district No. 6. In June of that year, their church building was erected at a cost of about $1,050, not including a large amount of work furnished gratuitously. The structure is 24x36 feet. There is also a parsonage which was erected in the fall of 1870, at a cost of $300, to which an addition has been made costing $250. Here the pastor teaches a day school during five months of each year, having an average attendance of about twenty-five. Rev. August Albert, the present pastor, organized a Sabbath School in July, 1881, which is still continued and has an attendance of about twenty-two families.

St. John's Evangelical Lutheran Church was organized by Rev. G. Hageman, of Amboy, Lee county, Illinois, in April, 1874, with a membership of twenty-two families. Rev. David Kurz was the first pastor, and remained in charge until October, 1880; he is now located at Sigourney, Keokuk county, Iowa. He was formerly from Freeport, Illinois. Rev. G. Becker succeeded Mr. Kurz, he came from Princeton, Illinois, and remained a little more than one year. The present pastor, Rev. John M. Rosenthal came in January, 1872. The parish building is 30x45 feet, and was built in 1874, at a cost of $2,000. It is used for church, school and parsonage. The pastor teaches a six months term of school each year, and has an average attendance of about forty. Rev. Rosenthal organized a Sabbath School in June, 1882. This school is now in a prosperous condition with a membership of forty. The church is in a flourishing condition—nearly out of debt—and has a membership of thirty-seven families. The first officers were Henry Berzman, John Shanneman, D. Kierchhoff, Henry Moller and Joe Buls. The present officers are Fred Bergman, John Prop, William Knolte, Fred Gerbert and William Kappinyer.

The Methodist Episcopal Church, under the direction of Rev. Isaac Barnard, effected an organization in the fall of 1876, at the Lehman School House. Mr. Barnard remained one year, and was followed by Rev. Bailey, from Frederika township; he in turn by J. M. Beall, who conducted the services for three years. In September, 1881, the meetings were discontinued. There had been about sixty members.

CHAPTER XVIII.

DAYTON TOWNSHIP.

Dayton is the center of the eastern tier of townships, and was first settled in 1854. In the spring of that year, Isaac Brandt, John Book and Mr. Alshouse, located on the east side of the Wapsipinicon river, Brandt entering the southeast quarter of section 32, and Book the southeast corner of section 29. By mistake Brandt erected his shanty on the southeast corner of the northeast quarter of the southwest quarter of section 32.

During the summer and fall of 1854, several other families came in, among whom were Isaac Guard, Simeon Peck and his sons William M. and A. S., and William Gibbs. The latter together with Mr. Peck and sons, located on section 33. Isaac Brandt remained but a short time when he sold out to William M. Peck. His present whereabouts are unknown.

Mr. Alshouse, who also located on section 32, subsequently sold his farm to Elijah Grinnell, and left the country.

John Book remained here about fifteen years and then removed to Missouri. His farm was purchased by Fred Mohlis, who is still the owner. Samuel Peck died here in 1855.

Another settler of this year was George Watts, Jr. He is the son of George and Elizabeth Watts, and was born in Somersetshire, England, May 27, 1823. When about twenty-six years of age, he decided to come to America, leaving the country of his birth; on the 1st of May, 1849, he landed in New York City, Immediately after his arrival he started west, first locating in Lake county, Illinois, where he remained five years, then removing to Iowa and locating on section 2, in Fremont township. He there entered eighty acres of land on which he lived about two years, and partially improved it. He then settled on section 31, Dayton township, where he has since resided (with the exception of twelve years passed in Frederika township, in the old town of Tripoli.) Mr. Watts now owns 300 acres of land in the county. He has filled nearly every township office, and has also held a number of school offices. In the year 1853, he was married to Miss Rebecca Orledge, who was also born in England. They have had five children, four of whom are now living—Robert O., Susan, Martha, (now the wife of William McCumber,) and Hattie.

Among those who settled in the township in 1855 were John Develin, Jacob Glattley, Albert McCumber, John Zimmerman, John Koch, Theodore Link, John Hill, Ira Allen, H. N. Miller and A. Dallen.

John Develin located on the north half of the northwest quarter of section 28.

Jacob Glattley on the south half of the southwest quarter of section 27.

John Zimmerman made claim to the northwest quarter of the soutwest quarter of section 28.

John Koch selected the east half of the southwest quarter of section 28.

Theodore Link located on the northwest quarter of the northwest quarter of section 28.

W. V. Curtis was another settler of '55, a son of Newman and Ann Maria (Van Bergen) Curtis and was born in the town of Dalton, Berkshire county, Massachusetts, August 7, 1825. Shortly after his birth the family settled in Orleans county, New York, where he received his education and grew to manhood. When twenty-six years of age he came west and located in Rock county, Wisconsin, and in the spring of 1855 came to Bremer county and settled on a farm on section 36, Dayton township, where he now resides, and owns 120 acres of land; he also owns 30 acres in Fayette county. Mr. Curtis has held the office of trustee and also several minor offices. He was married in the fall of 1852 to Miss Salena Dodge, who was born in New York State. They have four children—Herman, Harriett, Ann Maria and Newman.

Albert McCumber, already mentioned, was born in Ellisburg, Jefferson county, New York, September 1, 1818. He is the son of James and Mercy (Pool) McCumber, who, also were born in New York State. He received his education in the district schools of his native county, where he remained on his father's farm until twenty-seven years old. On the first day of May, 1845, he was married in the town of Levi, Jefferson county, New York, to Miss Achsa M. Peck, daughter of Simeon Peck, who was one of the first settlers of Dayton township. After their marriage the couple came west and located in Belvidere, Illinois, where they lived two and one-half years and then returned to Jefferson county and remained there until 1855, when they came to Dayton township and located on the northeast quarter of section 33, where they lived for fifteen years. They then moved to section 31, where they now reside and own 160 acres of land. Mr. McCumber has held nearly all of the township offices and has held the one office of trustee for about ten years. Nine children have been born to them, seven of whom are now living—Orin A., who now lives in Dayton township; Marquis C., who lives at home; William Henry, who lives in Dayton township; Ida Jane, wife of William M. Robins of Douglas county, Minnesota; Albert, E., Charles and Mary.

John Hill erected his cabin on the northeast quarter of the southeast quarter of section 20.

J. G. Williamson, James H. Yerton, B. J. Allen, Elijah Grinnell and George White became residents in 1856.

James H. Yerton was born in the town of Howard, Steuben county, New York, on the 23d day of November, 1818. He is a son of Henry N., and Catherine (McDowell) Yerton. His father was born in Germany, and his mother in New York State. When James was ten years old the family moved to Oswego county, New York, and one year later to Madison county, in the same State. During the year 1838 James returned to Steuben county, and there married. He engaged in farming until 1854, when he moved to Marion, Lee county, Illinois. In the spring of 1856 he came to Dayton township, and located on section 16. He built a small cabin upon what he supposed to be section 16; but on surveying his farm found the house to be on section 9. Nine years after his settlement he sold his farm, and then moved to his present location, on section 15, where he now owns 165 acres. Mr. Yerton has held the office of trustee several years, and also the office of justice of the peace, two years. On the 10th day of March, 1846, he was married to Miss L. M. Smith. They have one child living—Eveline, wife of R. L. Dibble.

A. D. Allen was born in Steuben county, New York, on the 1st day of October, 1848, and is a son of B. J. and Irene (Maydole) Allen, who were also natives of the same State. When the son was seven years old the family came to Dayton township, Bremer county, and settled on section 22. A. D. remained at home until twenty-two years of age, and then began life for himself. He first purchased and settled on a farm on section 16; but some time afterward also bought one on section 12, and has since lived on both places. He now owns 160 acres, all of which is under cultivation. Mr. Allen has held the office of township clerk five terms. On the 1st day of January, 1872, he was married to Miss Estella Yerton, a daughter of John B., and Phœbe Jane (Smith) Yerton; who came to Dayton township in 1863, and are now living in Crawford county, Iowa. Mr. Allen's father and mother are living in Sumner. Mr. and Mrs. A. D. Allen have one child—Lillian May.

W. P. Sterling was born in the town of Brooklyn, Susquehanna county, Pennsylvania, January 21, 1827, and is a son of James W. and Betsy (Tooksbury) Sterling. His father was born in Connecticut and his mother in Massachusetts. He received a common school education, and grew to manhood on a farm. During the year 1852, he came west, and after remaining in Will county, Illinois, three years, removed to Fayette county, Iowa, and settled on a farm in Orin township. In 1863, he moved to Franklin township, and there bought a farm of wild prairie. In June, 1872, he purchased his present farm on section 34, of Dayton township, and three years later, settled there. The last farm bought was also wild prairie land, but since his settlement Mr. Sterling has cultivated and improved it. He now owns 240 acres in the county. He has held the office of justice of the peace four years, and was re-elected to that office in 1882. During the year 1850, he was united in marriage to Miss Caroline C. Robinson, who is a native of Wyoming county, Pennsylvania. Four children have blessed this union, three of whom are now living—Elizabeth M., Catherine and John G.

John L. Worden was born in the town of Lloyd, Ulster county, New York, March 10, 1833, and is a son of John and Hannah (Dubois) Worden, who were also natives of New York State. He remained in the county of his birth until seventeen years old, and then went to Wyoming county, New York and settled in Castile. In 1861, he came to Bremer county, Iowa, and settled on section 24, Dayton township, and at the present date owns 200 acres of land in this and Fayette counties. Mr. Worden has held the offices of assessor, justice of the peace and trustee. In the year 1857, he was united in marriage to Miss Sarah A. Fuller, who was born in Wyoming county, New York. They have two children—Fuller D. and Hannah A.

C. W. Converse, a son of Winthrop and Laura (Wentworth) Converse was born in Portage county, Ohio, on the 8th day of November, 1836. Two years after his birth the family moved to Richland county, Ohio, and some time afterward, to Western Pennsylvania. In 1862 C. W. enlisted in the army, but four months later was honorably discharged, because of disability. During the year 1864 he came to Iowa, and immediately upon his arrival, again enlisted, and served until the close of the rebellion. Upon returning to civil life, he went to Dubuque, and in the spring of 1866 returned to Pennsylvania. After a six months' visit, he came back to Iowa, and located in Leroy township, where he lived for five years. He then settled on section 24, Dayton township, where he now resides. Mr. Converse was married in the spring of 1875, to Miss Mary A. Hazen. They are the parents of one child. Mr. Converse's father died in August, 1868, and his mother followed September 1, 1882.

E. M. Cass was born in Canada West, July 31, 1823. He is a son of Stephen and Jerusha (Abbey) Cass. His mother was born in New York State, and his father in Canada. He received a common school education, and, when of sufficient years, learned the carpenter's trade, which occupation he followed in Canada until twenty-one years old. He then came to the United States and worked at his trade, in the eastern section of the country, until 1856, when he removed to Lake county, Illinois, where he remained one year, and then moved to Vernon county, Wisconsin, where he lived for eleven years. During the latter years of his residence there he followed farming. In February, 1868, he came to Iowa, and located on a farm in Sumner township, Bremer county; but after remaining there one year, moved to section 15, Dayton township. In 1870 he opened a store on his farm, and there sold goods for seven years. He was postmaster of Buck Creek Postoffice seven years. While living in Vernon county, Wisconsin, Mr. Cass was a member of the county board, besides holding several of the township offices, and at the time of his departure from that county, was chairman of the town board and clerk of the school board. In Dayton township he has held the office of secretary of the school board ever since his residence there, and has, also, been township trustee four terms. In politics he is a staunch republican. During the year 1850 Mr. Cass was united in marriage to Miss Elvira Jane Packard, a native of Vermont. They have nine children—Stephen Arthur, Linda Amelia, Elvira Jane, Frank E., Frederick M., Charles E., William N., Earl M., and Martha A.

William T. Lyon was born in the town of Hartford, Susquehanna county, Pennsylvania, September 12, 1830, and is a son of Isaac and Sally (Blodgett) Lyon, who were born in the State of Massachusetts. He remained in his native town engaged in farming, until twenty-four years old, and while there received an excellent common school education, completed by an attendance at a seminary. Since that time he has spent about eighteen years teaching. During the year 1854, he moved to Greene county, Wisconsin, and after engaging in mercantile pursuits for three years, went to Pike county, Illinois, and was employed in teaching. On the 20th of April, 1861, he enlisted in Company G, Eighth Illinois, as a private, under Colonel Oglesby, in the three months service. At the expiration of this time, he returned home and shortly afterwards, in company with Captain Lawton, raised Company I, Thirty-third Illinois, and entered that company as first lieutenant, on the 18th of August, 1861, they were mustered into service. Mr. Lyon served in that capacity until August 15, 1863, when he was promoted to the captaincy of the company. He was honorably discharged at Springfield, Illinois, December 6, 1865. Upon returning to civil life, he removed to Buchanan county, Iowa, and engaged in buying wheat, at Independence, where he suffered a severe loss from fire. In the year 1869, he settled on section 24, Dayton township, Bremer county, where he owns ninety acres of land. Capt. Lyon has held the offices of justice of the peace and trustee. He was married in April, 1861, to Miss Louise J. Farner, born in Adams county, Illinois. They have had four children—Fred F., Frank M., Percy I., and Winnie O.

ORGANIC.

The first election was held at the house of William Peck, April, 1858. The judges of this election were Elijah Grinnell, Albert McCumber and John Williamson. The clerks were William M. Peck and John Zimmerman. The following named were elected:

James H. Yerton and Lyman J. Curtiss, justices of the peace; W. M. Peck, Albert McCumber and J. J. Williamson, trustees; Lyman J. Curtiss, clerk; A. S. Peck, W. V. Curtis, constables; William Gibbs, James H. Yerton and W. V. Curtis, supervisors.

The following named comprise the officers for 1883:

Trustees, Jake Ambrose, A. Frauhm and W. H. Triplett; clerk, Albert Glattley; assessor, Ambrose Allen; justices, C. H. Brooks, W. P. Sterling; constable, Leroy Triplett.

FIRST BIRTH.

Ida Frances, daughter of Mr. and Mrs. William Gibbs, born August, 1854, was the first white child born in the township. She was born at the house of the Widow Peck, on section 33. Ida Frances is now the wife of Romain Fuller, and resides, with her husband, on section 24, Dayton township.

FIRST DEATH.

Simeon Peck died April 15, 1855, of congestive chills, aged 61 years, 6 months and 14 days. This was the first death in the township. He was buried in Grove Hill Cemetery, in Franklin township. This was the first burial in that cemetery.

FIRST MARRIAGE.

The first couple united in marriage were V. B. Grinnell and Amanda Harwood, the ceremony being performed at the house of Lyman J. Curtiss, by Mr. Curtiss, who was a justice of the peace. They were married in November, 1858. Mr. and Mrs. Grinnell now reside in Waverly.

EDUCATIONAL.

The first school taught in the township was in a log building erected by John Book, for a residence, by Maggie Harwood, in the summer of 1858. The first building erected for school purposes was on section 28. It was built by L. J. Curtiss; it is now known as No. 4. The following named were the scholars in attendance at Miss Harwood's school:—Elijah E. Grinnell, Orin McCumber, Marquis McCumber, Jacob Williamson, Elijah Williamson, Falton Link, Mary Zimmerman, Elizabeth Cook, Jacob Ambrose, and Ellen Ambrose. Miss Harwood subsequently married Mr. Waite, and, with her husband, now resides in Waverly.

Another school was taught during the summer of 1857, at the residence of J. H. Yerton, by Maggie Dickey. On account of sickness Miss Dickey did not complete the term—it was finished by Jane Crane. Among those who attended this school were—Isabel Yerton, Olive Yerton, Evaline Yerton, A. D. Allen, Miss H. A. Allen, Francis White, Albert White, Ann Chadwick, Lulu Chadwick, Gilbert Chadwick, John Chadwick and Jason Chadwick.

The second school building was erected on section 20—it is now known as No. 2.

RELIGIOUS.

The first discourse delivered in Dayton township was on the occasion of the death of Simeon Peck, in the fall of 1855. No regular services were held from that time until the completion of the school house, already spoken of as being erected by L. J. Curtiss. When completed it was first occupied for religious services by Elder Reardon, a Baptist divine. During the first meeting held, he baptized several persons in Buck creek, among whom were John McCray and wife, Mrs. N. Porter, Mrs. Alfred Robinson, Mrs. Fred Hamilton. This was in the spring of 1862. During the next year J. H. Yerton and wife, B. J. Allen and wife, and Nettie Parker were also baptized.

The German Evangelical Lutheran Church is located on section 27, on land donated by Louis Buhr. It was built in 1876. Among the first members of the society were Fred Pohler and wife, Louis Buhr and wife, Henry Thies and wife, William Buhr and wife, G. Wolf and wife. Rev. William Adicks was the first pastor in charge, and yet continues to minister to the spiritual wants of the congregation, which now has a membership of one hundred and sixty. The church building is 36x70, and cost $800. A day school, with an attendance of fifty scholars, is taught by the minister. A Sunday School is held during the summer.

A Presbyterian society was organized at the Union School House, District No. 3, on section 25, in 1877. The first members were Jacob Glattley and wife, Henry Wisner and wife, W. T. Lyon and wife. Rev. John Sayers was the first pastor. He was succeeded by Rev. Mr. Jennings. Services are held every two weeks. During the summer, Sunday School is held. The first superintendent of the school was W. T. Lyon. It has an average attendance of twenty.

MERCANTILE.

In 1866, Robert R. Davis opened a small store at his residence on section 15, the place now owned by C. H. Moehling. He remained in business about two years. E. M. Cass then started a small store which he ran four years. Louis Mohlis, in 1874, commenced business about a quarter of a mile east of the river, on section 32. He also opened a shoe shop at the same time, and still continues both branches of the business. In 1877, W. W. Bezold opened a store on section 32, on the east side of the river. He ran it until November, 1880, when he sold to Orrin McCumber, who yet continues the business.

GRIST MILL.

A grist mill was erected on the east side of the Wapsie, on section 32, in 1876, by Cornelius Miller, who operated it about three years, when he sold to Jacob Minkler, who is still the owner.

Around this mill a small collection of houses was built, and the embryo village was nicknamed by the people "Smoketown," on account of the miller's family being inveterate smokers.

BLACKSMITHING.

In 1878 August Meier started blacksmithing, near Mohlis' store, on section 32, and still continues the business.

POSTOFFICES.

A postoffice was established in the township, under the name of Bremer, in 1858. For some time previous, efforts had been made to have an office, but without avail. J. H. Yerton finally came to the conclusion that he would make a personal application. He accordingly wrote the department, stating the distance those in his neighborhood were from an office, and how many would be accommodated by one being established here. Having some influence with "the powers that be," he soon received an appointment and a commission was duly forwarded him as the first postmaster of Bremer postoffice. The mail was first carried by Mr. Yerton from the mill postoffice in Fayette county, but the office was finally placed on the route between Independence and Chickasaw. Mr. Yerton continued as postmaster about three years, and was succeeded by B. J. Allen. The name of the office was changed to Buck Creek, and it was removed to the residence of Mr. Allen, on section 25. George Parker succeeded Mr. Allen, and removed the office to his residence, on section 15. E. M. Cass was the next appointee. He also resided on section 15, the office being kept at his residence. William Adicks succeeded Mr. Cass, and removed the office to his residence, on section 28. Mr. Adicks was succeeded by C. Brooks, the present incumbent, who resides and keeps the office on section 26. The mail is now received from Sumner three times a week.

Dayton postoffice was established in 1861, with Burrell Rood as postmaster. Mr. Rood kept the office at his residence on section 9. Dr. S. S. Marvin, residing on section 4, was Mr. Rood's successor. The office was kept at his residence until 1870, when it was discontinued.

CHAPTER XIX.

FRANKLIN TOWNSHIP.

This territory lies in the extreme southeast corner of Bremer county, and is a full Congressional township, comprising about 23,040 acres. There are within its limits, two streams of water. The Wapsipinicon river enters on section five and flowing toward the south passes through sections 8, 17, 20, 29, 28 and makes final exit on 33. Buck creek enters from the north on section, 3 and, passing through sections 10, 15, 22, 23, 26 and 35, leaves on 36.

The soil is a dark, sandy loam. The surface is rolling and timber is found in limited quantities along the river. The land is nearly all occupied, and in the township are many desirable farms, well improved and under a good state of cultivation.

EARLY SETTLEMENT.

The first settler in the township was Melton Harrington, who selected a home on the south half of the northwest quarter of section 3, in the spring of 1854. He at once built a log house, the first residence in the township. Ichabod Richmond and family arrived in the township May 21, 1854, and located on the north half of the northwest quarter of section 15. Noah Porter came about the same time and established a home on the northeast quarter of section 16. A man by the name of Kerr arrived about this time, and moved into the Harrington house. He died soon afterward. This was the second death in the township. In July, H. Buckholt and H. Kniffken were numbered among the settlers of the township. Buckholt located on the southwest quarter of section 26 and erected a log house. Kniffken built a house on the north half of the northeast quarter of section 33.

John McRae was also one of the settlers of 1854. He was born November 14, 1826, in Canada East. There he passed his youth, and obtained a common school education. In 1845 he moved to Kane county, Illinois, where he engaged in farming, and three years later, located in Chicago. He located upon the south side of the river, and there broke 130 acres of wild prairie land, which now lies in the center of the great city. In 1850 he returned to Canada, and was married April 18, to Miss Phœbe Robinson, a native of Canada East. During that year he returned, with his young wife, to Kane county, and thence, after one year's sojourn, to DeKalb county, where he purchased a farm. October 7, 1854, he left that State for Iowa, arriving in Franklin township, Bremer county, on the 17th day of the same month, and settling on section 10, where he now has a very comfortable home. Four children—George, Albert (deceased), Frank Almas and Fred Ellis—have been born to them. Mr. McRae is an enthusiastic republican, and has held several of the local offices; he also built the first school house in the county. During his first winter here, deer were so plenty that they kept the family in meat the entire season. However, the second winter there was a very deep snow, which had a crust so solid and thick that it would bear up men and dogs when on their hunting expeditions; either because of the depth of the snow or on account of the country's becoming more settled, deer have scarcely been seen since that time.

Another early settler of Franklin township, was N. C. Peck. He was born in Albany, New York, in 1831. His parents were natives of the State of Connecticut. His father was born in 1791, and during his life, followed the trade of black-smithing. He died in 1856. Mr. Peck's mother was born in 1793, and died in 1859. Four years after his birth, the family removed to the State of Connecticut. and there the son continued to reside until he had reached his majority. During the year 1852, he was married to Miss Clarisa Bolter, a native of New York City, born in 1832. In 1864 he enlisted in Company D, Fourth Iowa Infantry, and served one year. He formed one in Gen. Sherman's great army in its famous "March to the Sea," and was in the battle of Fayettsville, North Carolina. Mr. Peck is a republican and has held several of the local offices. He came to Bremer county, in June, 1855, and is the present postmaster of Grove Hill, Franklin township.

S. K. Davis came from Michigan in 1854, and lived with I. Richmond, the first winter. He entered a claim on section 14, in the spring of 1855, and then went back to Michigan. He returned again in the fall of 1855, and built a log house on his land; here he remained about a year and then removed to Fairbanks. The land is now owned by Jacob Minkler.

During the fall of 1854, also came James D. Sankey, who settled on section 35. At the same time W. H. Taylor, selected a place on section 4, and built a log house; this place was afterward known as the Meir property.

William F. Peck, an early settler, built a log house on section 15, in January, 1855.

Albert Dexter and W. W. Beal came in 1855, with their father, and settled on sections 30 and 31, where W. W. Beal still remains, and where his father died.

Section 26 was occupied this season by Mr. Bellows, from Illinois; he built a sod house which was considered very remarkable, as timber was plenty in this county at that time, yet a sod house he must have, it being as he thought, cheaper, warmer,

HISTORY OF BREMER COUNTY.

and more comfortable. It was the only house ever built in the township of such material. Notwithstanding these extraordinary comforts, he remained but one winter, and then returned to the good old "Sucker" State.

This same season, Frank Everett came from Michigan and located on section 4, remained a number of years, and then moved to Fairbank, Buchanan county, where he now lives.

Clarence Bacon, from the same State, settled on the same sections; he likewise moved away in a few years and went to New York.

Pennsylvania was also represented this season, among the settlers. J. Brechner and George Haun, coming from that State, settled on section 19. Brechner remained on his original claim about fifteen years, and then moved to another quarter of the same section, where he yet remains. Haun, who was a brother-in-law of Brechner, lived with him for some time, building a blacksmith shop near by, where he may yet be found. J. M. Ellis came from Illinois and made a home on section 22, where he remained until 1881, when he moved to Waverly. His father-in-law, F. Fortner, came with him and occupied some land on the same section where he subsequently died. A. Fortner, a son, came in October and lived with his father. He followed farming a number of years, and in 1865, removed to Waverly, where he is now keeping the "Bremer House." Another son, C. Fortner, came in the spring, and also left the farm in 1865, and is now a resident of Sumner in the same county.

Bernhardt Berry and Nicholas Berger came together this season and located on section 7, where the former died. The latter moved to Independence about 1876.

Thomas Day was from Ohio, and during this year settled on section 11, where he lived several years; moved to Illinois, and thence to his native State, where he died in 1882. The next year—1856—Joseph McKinley arrived from Indiana and made his home on section 34, where he remained about ten years, and then moved to the western part of the State. Joseph McCray from Virginia, settled on section 34. He remained until about 1870, when he moved to Southern Iowa, and died there soon after.

Section 31 this year received a settler, Horace Butler, from Illinois. Mr. Butler remained only about two years, and then tried his chances elsewhere. He returned, however, after a few years and settled near his old home, but in Black Hawk county, where he now lives. Rufus West, also from the "Sucker State," located on this same section and remained about seven years, when he moved to Missouri. During this year, Hugh Patterson and his son John, came from Ohio and bought the Davis place on section 14. Hugh, after a number of years, removed to Fairbanks.

Two brothers, William and A. S. Bentley, the same season located on section 26, where A. S. still remains. William starved out during the season of 1857 and left, but soon returned again and remained until about 1879, when he went to Oelwein, Fayette county. In 1856 or 1857 Francis Harwood, from Illinois, occupied a portion of section 3, where he died, after the war. Mr. Harwood kept "Grove Hill"

HISTORY OF BREMER COUNTY.

postoffice at this point and was the first postmaster. Among others who came on this and the year following, were: A. J. Torrence, Henry Jones, William Copeland, James Neal, Robert Hutchinson, James Cavern, Robert Cavern, Andrew Gardner, Joseph and John Wright, William Coleman, George Bond, David Freeland, John Conway, Edward McGowan, Edward McHue, John Richards, and his sons Joseph, Jerry and John, John Link, B. F. Nute, and Henry Jones and family. The biographies of a few other settlers and representative men, who came at a later date, are here annexed.

W. W. Beal, one of the pioneers of Franklin township, was born in Pittsford, Rutland county, Vermont, November 29, 1829. After receiving a common school education, he attended the Vermont Literary Seminary, and then taught two terms of school. However, finding that profession not suited to his taste, he gave up teaching and turned his attention to carpentering and millwrighting. In 1855 he left Vermont for Waukesha county, Wisconsin, and in August, of the same year, came, with two of his brothers, to Bremer county, Iowa, where he settled on his present farm, and immediately began improving it. February 23, 1862, he was married to Miss Fannie Hill, a native of Albany, New York, born June 8, 1842. They have had eight children, three of whom are now living—Bell A., John H. and Willard W. Mr. Beal is a republican and has held several offices of trust. He took an active interest in the organization of the Bremer County Fire Insurance Company, and was elected one of its first directors.

Marvin E. Perry, a native of New York, was born in 1832. His father, Ozias Perry, was born in Plymouth, Vermont, in 1802. When twenty-one years of age, he was married to Miss Eliza Merchant, a native of New York, born in 1806. At an early day they settled in Winnebago county, Illinois, and there the wife and mother died, April 7, 1875. Her husband still survives her, and continues to reside on the old homestead, in Winnebago county. Seven children were born to them, five of whom are now living. Their fifth child, Marvin E., as stated, was born in New York. When a child, he removed with his parents to Illinois, and there obtained a common school education, and grew to manhood. In 1857 he came to Bremer county, Iowa, settling on his farm in Franklin township, where he now resides. April 8, 1860, he was joined in wedlock with Miss Sarah Johnson, a native of Clinton county, Pennsylvania, born in 1841. When she was thirteen years old she came, with her parents, to Iowa. Three children—Arthur M., Alice E., and John S.—have been born to them, and they have, also, one adopted child—Minnie M. Mr. Perry has identified himself with the republican party, holding the office of justice of the peace, and constable. Both himself and wife are members of the Baptist Church, of Lester, Black Hawk county.

Jacob Ward was born March 1, 1833, in Licking county, Ohio. Three years after his birth, the family removed to De Kalb county, Illinois, where he passed his time until grown to manhood's estate, working on his father's farm and attending the district school. In the fall of 1864, he came to Bremer county, Iowa, settling on a farm in Franklin township, where he has since resided. On the 1st day of March, 1855, he was joined in wedlock with Miss Margaret C. Perry, a native of New York, and born in 1831. Three children have blessed this marriage—Leonard Adolph (deceased) Rosalia J. and Ambrose Perry. Mr. Ward is a republican, and has held political offices.

One of the early settlers of Bremer county—Canfield Garrod—was born in Tioga county, New York, on the 13th day of September, 1823. Five years after his birth, the family forsook their old home for a new one in Loraine county, Ohio. Ten years later they removed to Sangamon county, Illinois, thence, seven years after, to Walworth county, Wisconsin, where they remained but two years, and then came to Iowa, locating in Jones county, where Mr. Garrod entered some land. Afterward he entered the land in Franklin township where he now resides, but did not settle on it until three years later. November 24, 1856, he was joined in wedlock with Miss Elizabeth Everson, a native of Norway, born December 22, 1833. While she was a child, the family emigrated to the United States, settling in Wisconsin, where Elizabeth grew to womanhood. Six children have been born to them—Jeremiah, Ancel, Andrew (deceased); Mary, Milo and Elsie. Mr. Garrod is at present justice of the peace of Franklin township. He is a republican in politics.

Charles Liebert, a native of Prussia, was born in 1835. While in that country he obtained a common school education, followed by an academic course, and some years later he attended a medical school in Berlin, Prussia, where he studied veterinary surgery. In 1855 he came to the United States, and after spending some time in New York City, removed to Pennsylvania, where he continued to reside until 1865. At that time he came west to Bremer county, Iowa, settling in Franklin township, where he has since lived, practicing veterinary surgery in connection with farming. He was married in 1858 to Miss Catherine Herbert, also a native of Prussia; she died in 1880. They have had four children. Mr. Leibert was again married February 7, 1881, to Miss Carolina Ernst, a native of Illinois. In politics, he is an independent. He has held the office of constable. He and his wife are members of the German Methodist church.

R. V. Dibble, a native of Schoharie county, New York, was born in 1814. When he was thirteen years old, his parents removed to Oneida county, where Richard grew to manhood on a farm. His marriage with Miss Fanny Barnes, a native of New York State, occurred on the 11th of January, 1837. They have had five children—Francis, Elmora (deceased,) Ira, Luzette and Herbert. Mrs. Dibble died March 2, 1858. Five years previous to his wife's death, Mr. Dibble located in Stephenson county, Illinois, where he continued to live until 1862. At that time he came to Bremer county, Iowa, settling on his present farm in Franklin township. Mr. Dibble was again married, October 2, 1858, to Amanda Rathburn, who was born in Herkimer county, New York, in 1836. They have had two children—Fanny and Floyd. Mr. Dibble is a staunch republican and has held several offices of trust.

He and his wife are members of the M. E. church.

William Harwood was born in Herkimer county, New York, May 29, 1828. He obtained a "district school" education, and passed his youth on a farm. He also learned the carpenter's trade in his native State. Subsequently he removed to Wisconsin, where, in 1852, he was joined in matrimony with Miss Lucia Sabin, a native of Burlington, Vermont, born July 18, 1828. After his marriage, Mr. Harwood removed to Stephenson county, Illinois, where he continued to reside until 1856, at which time he made a year's visit to Bremer county, Ia., and then returned to Illinois, where he lived until January, 1863. At that date, he enlisted as corporal in Company E, One Hundred and Forty-seventh Illinois Infantry. While in service he was taken sick, and upon his way home, grew so much worse that he was placed in a hospital at Jeffersonville, Indiana, and there died, August 5, 1863, leaving a wife and four children—Lewis C., William H., Frank N. and Lillian S.—to mourn him. In 1866, Mrs. Harwood, with her children, came to Bremer county, Iowa, and has since, with her own and her sons' exertions, supported the family. Her son, L. C., was born in Stephenson county, Illinois, in 1853. He obtained a good common school education, and since reaching his majority, has identified himself with the republican party. He has held several of the local offices, and is at present, clerk of Franklin township.

ORGANIC.

Upon the second day of April, 1855, an election was held at the house of Ichabod Richmond. The officers appointed to hold this election were: Judges, I. Richmond, Wm. F. Peck and Ormel Clark; clerks, Wm. P. Sanders and Wm. F. Peck. The persons voting at that election were the above named, and John McRea, Theodore Link, Wm. Taylor, H. Kniffken, H. Buckholt, H. Drunkenmoller, John Koch, Isaac Guard, John Barker, J. Book, Simeon Peck and Noah Porter—in all 17. The following officers were elected: Justices of the peace, Ichabod Richmond, Simeon Peck; constables, Noah Porter and Wm. M. Peck; trustees, J. F. Barker, Wm. H. Taylor and John McRea; town clerk, Ormel Clark; assessor, Wm. M. Peck. The following named are the officers of this township for 1883: Trustees, Geo. Neal, John Knittle, Henry Wermacher; clerk, L. C. Harwood; assessor, John Knittle; justices, E. W. Leonard, G. Vanderwalker; constables, Wm. Brechner, J. Richards.

FIRST THINGS.

The first house built in the township was on the south half of the northwest quarter of section three, in the spring of 1854; it was constructed of logs, and was built by Melton Harrington.

The first marriage in the township was that of Henry White, of Buchanan county, Iowa, to Miss Elizabeth Richmond, in 1856, Ichabod Richmond, her father, performing the ceremony.

The first white child born in the township was Frank McCrea, a son of John and Phœba McCrea.

The first death was that of Mary Ellen Kerr, daughter of Francis Kerr, September 27, 1854, and in eight days thereafter the father was numbered among the dead.

HISTORY OF BREMER COUNTY.

The first school was taught by widow Greeley, in the winter of 1855, in the house of Ichabod Richmond.

The second school was taught in the house of J. M. Ellis, in the winter of 1856, by Mrs. J. M. Ellis.

The first school house was built on the northwest quarter of section 10, during the fall of 1857. It was constructed of logs, 16x20 feet; inverted slabs with wooden pins for legs, constituting the furniture.

The first religious service was held in the house of Mrs. Elizabeth Kerr, by Rev. Mr. Abbott.

The first election was held in the house of I. Richmond, in August, 1855.

The first bridge built across Buck creek was on the public road east of Ellis and Fortners, in the winter of 1857-8. The bridge across the Wapsie—known as Taylor's bridge—was built in the early spring of 1859, at the point where an iron bridge has since been erected.

The first postoffice established was "Eagle," on section 22, at the house of Thomas Fortner, and Fortner was the first postmaster and W. O. Walker, the mail carrier.

POSTOFFICE.

As stated, the first postoffice was "Eagle." The next, "Grove Hill," was established in the summer of 1859, Francis Harwood being the first postmaster; after a short time this office was also discontinued, but was re-established in 1869, with H. C. Peck as postmaster, who has since remained in charge, and keeps the office in his residence on section 15. Mail is received three times each week. There is another postoffice in this township called "Key," which was established about 1876 or 1877. George Vanderwalker was the first postmaster. He was succeeded by F. H. Page, who is the present incumbent. It is on the same route with Grove Hill, and has mail four times each week.

MERCANTILE.

There is one store within the limits of this township, kept by Howard Page, who established the business in 1882. There is also a blacksmith shop on section 21 which has been in operation since 1856; the proprietor is George Kaun.

CEMETERY.

There is but one cemetery in the township, located on section 4.

The first burial here was the remains of Simeon Peck, in 1855.

FLOWING WELLS.

This township has four flowing wells. One situated on the farm of B. F. Call, on the southwest corner of section 15, furnishes about sixty gallons of water per minute. This well is ninety-two feet deep, and is strongly impregnated with iron.

The other wells are on the farms of George Smeltzer, on section 22; Joseph Collier, on section 19, and Marvin Perry, on section 32. The quantity of water flowing from the first two is small, but the latter furnishes an abundant supply. Other wells in this township are bored through the blue clay to this sub-strata of water, and varying in depth from 75, to 140 feet. The water rises to within a few feet of the surface, and remains in undiminished quantity.

EDUCATIONAL.

School matters have not been neglected in this territory, and early in the settlement schools were held at different places, until such time as houses could be built, and districts organized. There are nine buildings in the township, valued at $700 each. They are in good repair, and well furnished. The character of teachers employed has been such as generally to give satisfaction, the schools being in fairly good condition.

CHAPTER XX.

FREDERIKA TOWNSHIP.

Frederika township is one of the five townships comprising the northern boundary of the county, being bounded on the west by Polk and Douglas townships, and on the east by Leroy and Sumner. At this date it consists of eighteen and one-half sections, and had at the census of 1880, a population of 514. It contains much good land but at least one third of it is still unimproved.

Bremer county and Frederika township were so named after Frederika Bremer, a very popular Swedish novelist. This township is watered by the Wapsipinicon river, which passes diagonally through it from northeast to southwest, entering on section 6, passing thence into Douglas township, it returns on section 7, then runs through sections 18, 19, 20, 29, 28 and makes its exit on the west half of 34. The soil is generally a dark, sandy loam. The surface of the land is slightly rolling. When first settled, about one-third of this territory was timber, but the quantity has now been reduced to about one quarter. The inhabitants are mostly American and principally from New York State.

EARLY SETTLEMENT.

Levi Rima, with his family and his father, Loren Rima, were the first settlers and came to the township September 20, 1852, locating on section 18. Loren Rima returned to Illinois in the spring of 1853, but came back to Bremer county in the fall of the same year, accompanied by two other sons—Ariel and Gideon, and a daughter—Lucinda. George Rima, a brother of Loren, came to the township, while Loren was in Illinois arranging for the removal of the rest of the family.

William R. Bostwick and family came in August, 1853, and also M. F. Gillett, during the next September.

Crawford Thoroman and Andrew Gillilan came to the township in June, 1853.

HISTORY OF BREMER COUNTY.   1045

Albert Walling and mother, with his sisters, came in October, 1853, from Steuben county, New York, and settled on section 19. The mother died in 1856. Albert removed to Illinois in 1857.

Jeremiah Turk came at the same time from the same State, with his family, locating on section 32. He removed to Missouri where he yet lives. His place was purchased in 1863 by D. P. Walling, who now occupies it.

William R. Bostwick, resides on section 29, Frederika township, was born in Montgomery county, New York, November 30, 1814, and is the son of Daniel and Elizabeth Brewer Bostwick, both of whom were native Americans of Dutch extraction. When sixteen years old he came with his parents to Rochester, New York, where they remained for about two years, and then removed to Cayuga county, Ohio. Four years later he came alone to the west, and spent about five years working on farms in LaPorte county, Indiana. Returning home he stayed with his parents for the next four years, and then again came west, and began to make a farm upon land which he had previously bought in McHenry county, Illinois. On February 26, 1846, he married in LaPorte, Indiana, Miss Margaret Jane Finley, daughter of Samuel Finley, and niece of Rev. James B. Finley, then a very well known Methodist preacher, of the west. He brought his wife to his farm in McHenry county, and after seven years, sold out and came to his present location August 3, 1853, where he has ever since resided. He was the second settler in the township, only Levi Rima and family being before him. Mr. Bostwick has had three children, two now surviving—Sylvester D., born January 29, 1847; William E., born April 26, 1850, died April 12, 1872, and Arthur L., born April 13, 1858. Together with his eldest son, Mr. Bostwick owns and farms 440 acres of land, 80 acres being timber. He has taken his full share of duty in the administration of the affairs of the township, having filled the offices of supervisor, clerk, and other offices. In politics he is a republican. He started in his battle for a home with nothing to aid him but a stout heart and his bare hands, and all he now owns and enjoys, he owes to his own efforts and the efficient assistance of his wife and family.

Levi Rima was born in the State of New York, September, 1816, and was the son of Loren and Katherine Rima, natives of the same State. When very young he came with his parents to Ohio, and after a few years removed with them to Stephenson county, Illinois, where he grew to manhood and married January 4, 1844, to Miss Juliet Jane Gillett, eldest daughter of David and Chloe Gillett, by whom he had two children, one dying in infancy, and the other, Charles L. Rima, born November 12, 1848, in Stephenson county, Illinois, now the oldest living settler in Frederika township. Levi Rima came to this township September 20, 1852, with his family and his father, Loren Rima, settling on section 18. They built a little log cabin, 14x16, which remained standing for a number of years. They were the first settlers in Frederika township, and had no neighbors nearer than Horton, in Polk township, nine miles distant. He had made entry of 120 acres at the government land office at Dubuque, and with a stout heart, entered upon the task of making of it a farm. He was possessed of those sterling and undaunted qualifications necessary to a pioneer settler, and struggled manfully under all the disadvantages to which he was exposed till he had accomplished his object. He died February 2, 1874, at the old homestead, and was buried in the cemetery on Mr. Alcock's land in Douglas township. He was a strictly honest, quiet, orderly, peaceable man, of few words, slow but sure in his undertakings, and strictly temperate. In a word he was a good man, and his worth was recognized by his neighbors. He was the first justice of the peace in the township, and held the office till his death. He also held many other offices of trust and honor in the administration of its affairs, and all of them with credit to himself. His death was deeply mourned, especially by the old settlers to whom his sterling qualities had endeared him. His son still resides at the old homestead. He married January 20, 1875, Miss Mary E. Walters, daughter of John Walters and Lucy Dick. He owns 235 acres of land in Frederika township, and 80 acres in Douglas township.

David Gillett came to the township of Frederika July 10, 1855. He was born in Ontario county, New York, in 1812, moved to Geauga county, Ohio, about 1830, to Stephenson county, Illinois, in 1839, to McHenry county, Illinois, in 1843, and came from thence to Frederika township, as stated. He married in Geauga county, Ohio, Chloe Canfield, a native of New York, by whom he had seven children, six now living—Julia F., (deceased) married L. C. Rima; Lois married D. P. Walling; Eliza Ann married Chauncey Brooks; Susan married Robert Skillen; Orrin married Elmira Nettloch; Kate married William Fairburn; Eudora married Al. Pickett. Gillett was among the earliest settlers in the township and built the first frame barn, and the first house with a shingle roof, within its bounds. He was an honest man and a good neighbor, contracted few debts and none that he was unable to meet, thrifty and economical, both of his words and his means. He died in the latter part of December, 1868, and his wife followed him in September, 1877.

William W. Gillett arrived here from Chickasaw county in March, 1854, and purchased land on section 29, where he remained about one year and then returned to Chickasaw county. The place is now owned by L. N. Walling.

In July, 1855, D. P. Walling and David Gillett, with their families, came, and Walling bought land in section 18, Gillett in 29.

D. P. Walling went to Pike's Peak in 1858, returned in 1863, and now occupies the Turk place.

Isaac Lehman and Eli Eisenhart came in March 1856, from Illinois. Lehman settled on section 7, where he remained until 1864, when he purchased land in Douglas township, section 14, and moved onto it. He left Douglas twelve years ago and now lives in Charles City.

Eli Eisenhart was born, September 28, 1830, in York county, Pennsylvania. He is the son of John and Catherine Eisenhart, natives of that State. He grew up on the farm, and learned his father's trade—carpentering. In 1849, in company with a brother and sister, he removed to Cherry Valley, Winnebago county, Illinois, where he worked at his trade for a little over three years. Being smitten with the California fever, he organized a company of eight, and crossed the plains, the journey occupying nearly five months. On arriving, he started a grocery and butcher shop, at Placerville, Eldorado county; but sold out after three months, and turned his attention to mining and lumbering. He then determined, after a stay of twenty-two months, to return home by water, and on his way was detained six weeks on the Isthmus, doing military duty, during the occurrence of some local difficulty, until the arrival of regular troops released him, and he continued his journey. He reached his native village in July, 1854. In September, of the same year, he returned to Cherry Valley, Illinois, and on the 19th of the next month married Miss Mary Lehman daughter of Isaac Lehman, a native of Ohio, raised in Illinois, by whom he had five children—Arthur A., born March 1, 1856; Melvina L., born July 7, 1858; Alice Louisa, born March 3, 1861; Nettie E., born July 4, 1863, and Carrie R., born September 23, 1865. In May, 1855, he removed with his wife to Bremer county, Iowa, and bought land in Frederika township, and then, following the bent of his inclination for an active business life, rented out his land, and opened a general country store in the village of Tripoli. As the district became populous, his business increased, and grew, under his careful and shrewd management, to be a large and profitable one. After fourteen years of merchandising, he gave it up, and bought the homestead now occupied by his widow and family. He owned and ran a saw mill for almost two years at this time, and afterward turned his attention, as a capitalist, to what ever enterprises presented themselves in course of the development of the county. Mr. Eisenhart was sick one and one-half years, with inflamatory rheumatism, and died September 8, 1877. He was buried in Harlington Cemetery, at Waverly. He was a member of the Free-Will Baptist Church, to which body his widow and family also belong. During his life he held, for about three years, the commission of justice of the peace, and, in general, took an active and prominent part in the administration of township affairs and in everything calculated to promote the welfare and prosperity of the district. He was a man of fine business ability, of keen perception, great natural shrewdness, and of strict integrity. His death was a serious loss to the county, and he was missed and mourned by many outside the circle of his more intimate friends.

Another settler of 1855 was Asa T. Martin, who came from Illinois with his family and selected a home on section 33, where he remained until 1863, when he removed to Fremont township, section 4. He now lives in Tripoli. His original farm in this township was purchased by Eli Eisenhart. Mr. Martin erected the first steam saw-mill in the township, on section 33. It was a twelve-horse power. He run this mill until about 1863, when he sold it to William A. Carmack, who conducted the business a number of years and then sold to Eisenhart and Klingemsmith. The mill was removed in 1873.

In 1856 Thomas Lashbrook came from Illinois and selected a place on section 10, where he remained about two years, when he removed to Douglas township and purchased a farm on section 13. From there he returned to Waverly in 1865, where he yet lives. John Ronco, also, was a settler of this year. He came from Illinois and made his selection on section 30, where he remained until 1862, when he removed to Fremont township, and thence to Fayette county. He returned in 1864 and again located in this township on section 19. In 1867 he removed to Cerro Gordo county, and thence to Minnesota, where he yet lives.

E. J. Walling and family arrived the same year and settled on section 19, where he remained until 1866, then moved to Waverly and thence to Mason City, Cerro Gordo county, where he now lives. The year following, 1857, John Henry came from York State with his family and purchased some land on section 7. He there built a grist-mill in connection with the Rima saw-mill, which is now in running order and owned by William Smith. John Henry and wife are now dead. Mr. Henry died in 1869 and Mrs. Henry about a year earlier.

BIOGRAPHICAL.

Eli Barnes was born in Broome county, New York, February 2, 1826, and is the son of Daniel Barnes and Ruth Finch, natives of the New England States. When 18 years old he removed, with his parents, to Wayne county, Pennsylvania, where they remained but a short time, and then settled in McHenry county, Illinois. In the spring of 1861, he came, with his family to his present location in Bremer county, where he has ever since remained. His father died in the fall of 1862, and his mother in the spring of 1864. He married in McHenry county, Illinois, July 22, 1858, Miss Mary Ellen Mulock, daughter of Amsey and Elizabeth (Wyant) Mulock, natives of Orange county, New York, by whom he has had three children, two now alive—Rexford E., born November 10, 1856, and Oscar E., born July 26, 1850. During the war, Mr. Barnes took no active part in the ranks, being debarred from service by a physical disability, but he took an active part in upholding the righteousness of the issue then at stake. He owns 200 acres of prairie in Frederika township, and 20 acres of timber in Leroy township, worth thirty-five dollars per acre. He is at present treasurer of Central school district, of Frederika township, and has borne his share of the administration of township affairs; belongs to the "Church of Humanity," and tries to show his religion by his life and acts. He is politically impartial, but in monetary matters inclines to give adherence to the principles of the Greenback party, believing that through their adoption great good would be wrought to our moneyed system and to the Nation at large.

Henry Lytle was born in St. Lawrence county, New York, July 29, 1839, the son of Samuel Lytle, a native of Massachusetts, and Harriett Ross, a native of Canada. When four years old, he removed with his parents to Wisconsin, settling in Walworth county, where he grew to manhood on the home farm. His father died there a year after his arrival. In 1862 Mr. Lytle enlisted in Company C, Twenty-second Wisconsin, and served with it in the army of the Cumberland, under General Rosecrans. He took part in the defense of Fort Donelson and in the fight at Thompson's Station, where he was taken prisoner and sent to Libby Prison. After ninety days he was sent to parole camp at Annapolis, Maryland, and was regularly exchanged in July, 1863. He was discharged from service in December of the same year for disability, consequent upon diseases contracted at Libby Prison, and thereupon returned home. He was married, September 28, 1865, to Miss Julia Potter, born March 4, 1841, daughter of Richard and Lucinda (Shaw) Potter. They have had had three children—Louise, born June 18, 1868, Georgie, born December 12, 1870; and Mary Grace, born February 19, 1873. He removed to his present home in April, 1874, where he owns and farms eighty acres of land. He has ten acres of timber. He has been road supervisor and school secretary of the central district of the township. On national questions he votes the greenback ticket. Is a member of Lodge No. 77, A. F. and A. M., at Elkhorn, Wisconsin. Mrs. Lytle is a member of the Baptist Church.

D. P. Walling was born in Tompkins county, New York, July 10, 1820, and is the son of Peter and Esther (Bigelow) Walling, both native Americans. He lived at home, working on the farm and teaching school winters, until 23 years of age, when he removed with his sister and settled in McHenry county, Illinois. While there he worked rented land and taught school winters, and was married, May 11, 1848, to Miss Lois J. Gillett, daughter of David and Chloe Gillett. They have had eight children, seven of whom are now living—Leroy N., born March 19, 1849; Zurie L., born June 7, 1850; Everett P., born December 28, 1851; Lula May, born November 26, 1863; David G., born March 16, 1865; Lillian J., born April 25, 1867; and Vinnie Ream, born February 12, 1871. In 1855 he came to this township, and after a short stay went to Waterloo, where he farmed for two years. In 1859 he went with his family to Pike's Peak, and engaged in the dairy business, and built the first house erected on South Boulder River. He returned to the township in 1863, and bought his present farm from Jeremiah Turk. He owns 280 acres of land in the township, sixty acres under timber and worth an average of $30 per acre. In 1868 he was elected to the State Legislature from the Forty-eighth Representative District. He has been town trustee and town clerk, and has held other offices. He is in religious matters a spiritualist, and is politically a republican.

M. L. Boyer, wagon-maker, Frederika, was born in Montour county, Pennsylvania, October 4, 1847, and is the son of Christopher and Mary (Haynes) Boyer, natives of that State. In 1863 he went to Hillside, Dubuque county, Iowa, and began to learn his trade with an elder brother. He came to Frederika in 1867, and started, on his own account, the business which he has since profitably conducted. He was married November 5, 1871, to Miss Caroline Johnson, daughter of S. M. Johnson. They have had six children, four of whom are living—William S., Benjamin F., Martin L., and Caroline E. Having a thorough knowledge of his trade, and being its only representative in the township, Mr. Boyer finds plenty of work to do, and shares in the prosperity of the district.

HISTORY OF BREMER COUNTY.

ORGANIC.

The township was organized in April, 1854, and the election for officers was held at the house of William R. Bostwick, the names of the voters being, Loren Rima, Crawford Thoroman, Silas Watrous, L. C. Rima, William R. Bostwick, M. F. Gillett, Charles Edwards, Andrew Gillilan, and Ariel Rima.

The first officers were: L. C. Rima, justice; Ariel Rima, constable; M. F. Gillett, clerk; William R. Bostwick, Loren Rima and Crawford Thoroman, trustees.

The present township officers are as follows: Dr. L. S. Boyce, Alonzo E. Johnston, justices; M. F. Gillett, clerk; J. W. Johnston, assessor; Nelson Felt, Christian Kuhrt, H. M. Pickel, trustees.

FIRST THINGS.

The first death was a child of a settler named Robinson—who lived on what is now section 3, of Fremont township, but was then in Frederika township—in November, 1853. M. F. Gillett and William R. Bostwick arranged for the funeral, and dug the grave. Charles Edwards made the coffin.

The first marriage was that of M. F. Gillett and Olivia Walling, March 20, 1855. They were married by Levi C. Rima, who was the first justice, and they were the first couple he was called upon to unite.

The first birth was a child of Jeremiah Turk, who lived on section 32.

The first sermon preached in the township was by Rev. Father Jenkins, at the house of William R. Bostwick, in April, 1854.

The first school was taught by D. P. Walling in his own house on section 19, during the winter of 1855-6.

The first school was commenced in the summer of 1858, on section 19, and was occupied as such the following winter. Porter Bement was the first teacher.

The first saw-mill was built by Loren Rima in the village of Frederika. It was in running order in June, 1855. Water was the motive power.

A steam power saw-mill was built by A. F. Martin in the village of Tripoli, in the fall of 1853.

The first cluster of houses in the township was called Martinsburg, after A. T. Martin who located it. Its name was afterwards changed to Tripoli upon its being made a postoffice. A. T. Martin was the first postmaster.

The first officers of the township were as follows: L. C. Rima, justice; Ariel Rima, constable; M. F. Gillett, clerk; Wm. R. Bostwick, Loren Rima and Crawford Thoroman, trustees.

The first house in the township was built by L. C. Rima, on section 18, in 1852. It was constructed of logs, and has since been torn down.

The first frame house was built in Tripoli, in 1855, by A. T. Martin; it still stands on section 33, its original location.

The first frame barn was erected by David Gillett, in 1857, on section 29. It was 30x40 feet, 16 feet posts, and is still standing. This barn was considered at that time a remarkable building, and was a land mark for years. Such and such a direction, or distance, from the "big red barn," was a frequent instruction given to persons inquiring for different locations.

EDUCATIONAL.

As stated, the first school was taught by D. P. Walling, and the first school house was built on section 19. There are now five districts and six school houses within the limits of the township. The buildings are all frame, and cost about $500 each, on an average. All are well furnished and supplied, and the educational facilities of this township will compare favorably with other sections. Wages paid are from twenty to forty-five dollars per month.

RELIGIOUS.

The Methodist Episcopal Church of Lime Rock was organized about 1858, with the following named members: John Henry and wife, Norton Henry, Mary Henry and John Austin. Mr. Spencer was the first class leader. Among those who have served as pastors were Elders Webb, Zimmerman, Dorson, Hayward, Borp, and then Dorson again; afterward Barnard, Bailey, Bell and Hewett. Services were held at the Rima school house for a number of years. Afterward in a building located on section 7, which was erected for general purposes, and had a board of management consisting of G. M. Bowers, N. C. Baxter, William Hinkley and John Ager. This building was acquired by the church in May, 1878, and on the 28th of that month the following board of trustees were elected: G. N. Bowers, N. C. Baxter, William O. Service, J. H. Michner and N. J. Henry. The condition of the church at the present time is not very prosperous.

Prior to the organization of this class, a Sabbath School was organized with Norton Henry as superintendent. At the present time, Mary Hinkley is superintendent. There is an average attendance of about 25.

CEMETERY.

There is one cemetery in this township, located on section 19. It consists of one acre of ground and is owned by Mrs. Olive Gillett. The first interment here was the remains of a son of Mr. Robinson, during the fall of 1853. The next was a daughter of D. P. Walling, in the fall of 1855. Then in February, 1856, all that was mortal of Nathan Main was here consigned to the grave. Esther Walling was also here buried in March, 1856.

POSTOFFICE.

Frederika postoffice was established on section 14, in what is now Douglas township. It remained there about four years with G. F. Sayles as postmaster, when it was moved to section 13, same township, and John Mitchell was commissioned postmaster. There it remained about four years; then L. C. Rima was made postmaster and it was removed to his residence on section 18. In 1874 it was removed to the village of Frederika and J. M. Johnston received the appointment. He remained in charge of the office until his death in 1870. He was followed by Thomas Taylor, the present incumbent. Mail is received three times each week.

VILLAGE OF TRIPOLI.

The land on which was platted this village, was owned by A. T. Martin, who had the place laid out in 1856—it was located on section 33. Different branches of trade were represented here for a number of

1052   HISTORY OF BREMER COUNTY.

years, until 1880-81, when the place was literally moved, so far as buildings were concerned, to the railroad in Fremont township, one and one-quarter mile distant.

VILLAGE OF FREDERIKA.

The land on which this place was platted was owned by John Henry. It is located near the center of section 7, and was surveyed by H. S. Hoover, county surveyor, in 1868, at the instance of John Henry. This is now the only village in the township, and the different lines of trade are represented by William Smith, proprietor of Frederika mill, which has three run of stone, water-power with a capacity of about sixty barrels a day—a most excellent quality of flour is manufactured here. Seth Adams, dealer in general merchandise; G. N. Bowers, dealer in general store, conducted by his wife and children; Charles Matthews, blacksmith shop; Louis Butts, blacksmith shop; M. L. Boyer, wagon shop; James Howell, hotel and saloon; Dr. L. S. Boyce, physician; Thos. Taylor, shoemaker.

CHAPTER XXI.

FREMONT TOWNSHIP.

The township of Fremont comprises Congressional township 92, range 12, west of the 5th principal meridian.

EARLY SETTLEMENT.

George Kimbal made a claim of 240 acres on sections 10, 11, 12 and 13, in November, 1853, and settled thereon in 1854. He yet resides on the old homestead.

R. D. Titcomb made a claim on sections 10 and 11, at the same time with Mr. Kimbal, and also settled on the claim in 1854. He remained here until 1863, when he removed to Waterloo, Black Hawk county.

These men were among the first permanent settlers of the township, but were preceded by three men who made squatter's claims in the fall of 1853. One of these men was named Butler. The three squatted in the southwestern part of the township, on Crane creek, in a grove which was given the name, and was long known as Butler's Grove. It is now known as Tegmeier's Grove. They only remained here until the spring of 1854. Butler sold his claim to Russell and Fletcher, who came from Maine. Butler was a character in his way, and cared but little for the laws of his country. While in this township he lived with two wives, taking them with him on his removal to Butler county. There the authorities took notice of his mormonish proclivities, and compelled him to abandon one of his wives. He became disgusted with such interference and left for parts unknown.

Another settlement was made in the fall of 1853. Two hunters and trappers—Robinson and Carter—located on the northwest quarter of section 3, where they remained until March, 1854, when they sold their claim to Hiram and Henry Lester for $100. They laid claim at this time to over five hundred acres.

The Lester brothers settled on their claims in May, 1854, where Hiram still resides, the oldest living settler in the township. Henry, in May, 1864, removed to California, where he yet remains.

John Franklin settled on section 14, August, 1854. He died in 1860, his widow surviving him until 1876. Several of the family yet reside in the township.

Matthias Wuest settled on section 14, in 1855, and yet resides on the old homestead.

Mr. Sattersfield came in 1855, and located on section 23, where he remained until 1856. Mr. Adkins also settled in the township in 1855, locating on section 24, where he remained until the following year.

The first ground broken in the township was on the 25th of May, 1854, on the Titcomb farm, section 10, by R. D. Titcomb and George Kimbal. During that season a crop of sod corn was raised by R. D. Titcomb, Hiram Lester, Henry Lester, Mr. Russell and Mr. Fletcher.

George Kimbal, the first mentioned, was born in Germany, June 15, 1832, and came to America, with his parents, in 1847. Upon their arrival in this country, they settled in Bloomfield, Walworth county, Wisconsin. In 1853 George made a claim of 240 acres in Fremont township, Bremer county, Iowa, and the year following made a trip here, but after a few months' sojourn returned to Wisconsin. In 1856 he came with his family, and settled on his claim, where he has since resided. He now owns 195 acres, all of which are under improvement. Mr. Kimbal has held the offices of constable, road supervisor, and school director. In 1855 he was united in marriage to Miss Emma Pranty, who was born in the State of New York; she bore him three children—Eva Adella, William P. and Carrie B.—and died in the fall of 1876. He was married the second time in 1878, to Mary E. Wilson, who has borne him one child—George.

Hiram Lester, one of the oldest settlers living in this township, is the eldest son of Charles and Lydia (Pixley) Lester. He was born in the town of Whitehall, Washington county, New York, February 25, 1820. He received his education in his native county, and passed his youth there, on his father's farm. When 22 years of age he came west to Kenosha county, Wisconsin, and afterwards lived in that and Lake county, Illinois, twelve years, engaged in farming. In February, 1854, he, in company with his brother Henry, made a trip through the State of Iowa, and in May, purchased and settled on a claim in Fremont township, Bremer county, where he has since resided. Although Mr. Lester has seldom taken an active part in politics, he has always used his influence to keep the right men at the head of affairs. He has held the office of county supervisor two years; in politics he is a democrat, and cast his first presidential vote for Martin Van Buren. December 10, 1860, Mr. Lester was married to Miss Frances H. Markell. They have two children—Laura and Charles H.

Matthias Wuest was born in Rhine Province, Prussia, near Cologne, August 24, 1813. He learned to read under his father's instruction, then attended the high school until he was eighteen years of age. His English education has been acquired at odd moments. Until he was seventeen years old, his life was passed on his father's farm, except the time spent at school. At that age he began learning the carpenters' trade, and at nineteen, volunteered in the army and served three years. Upon returning to civil life, he followed his trade, and in 1837 was married to Miss Mary Kopp, who also was born near Cologne. During the last five years spent in his native country, Mr. Wuest was engaged exclusively in stair-making. In 1848 —during the Revolution—he became a Liberal and was chosen a delegate to elect a representative. About this time he read a book descriptive of America, and thinking he would like the country, decided to cross the ocean and settle here. Accordingly in 1852, he, with his family, came and located first in Chicago, but one month after his arrival, left because of cholera becoming an epidemic. Upon quitting that city he settled in Freeport, Illinois, where he remained, working at his trade until the summer of 1855, when he came to Bremer county, Iowa, and entered eighty acres of land on section 14, Fremont township, where he has since resided. Since his settlement here, he has added one hundred acres to his original eighty.

Mr. Wuest has held the office of trustee several terms, besides being assessor and holding other minor offices. He belongs to no political party, but believes in "equal rights to all," and his religion is the "Golden Rule." They have had nine children, seven of whom are now living—Peter, who now lives in Nevada; Frank, now living in Nashua, Iowa; Christina, wife of David Bessemar, of Waverly; Kate, wife of Hon. Louis Hanchett; Sabella, wife of Leroy Walling; Mary, wife of Sanford Ferror; and Albert who now owns a drug store in Tripoli.

James Brown was born in Somersetshire, England, May 27, 1816. He received his education in England, and was reared on a farm, and, when old enough, followed that occupation. In 1850 he came to America, and settled in Kenosha, Wisconsin, where he engaged in farming for five years. In the fall of 1855 he came to Fremont township, Bremer county, Iowa, and entered 200 acres of land; he now owns 320 acres, besides 20 acres of timber. The year following his arrival here, he brought his family and began the improvement of his farm. Mr. Brown has held the offices of trustee and road supervisor, several times. He was married in England, in 1850, to Elizabeth Watts. They have six children living—John E., Frederick G., Seth H., Edgar Herbert, Albert J., and Mary E.

John Moehling was born in Germany, October 13, 1830. When he was twenty-one years of age he came to America, and after spending one year in Cook county, went to DuPage county, Illinois, where he lived three years. In 1855 he came to Bremer county, Iowa, locating in Maxfield

HISTORY OF BREMER COUNTY.

township, where he entered 77 acres of land. He also entered 40 acres of timber in Jefferson township. In 1869 he came to Fremont township and settled on section 10, where he now owns a farm of 338 acres. Mr. Moehling was the first justice of the peace of Maxfield township, and was afterwards clerk of that township. The latter office he has also held in Fremont township. In September, 1855, he was united in marriage to Miss Sophia Wehrmacher. Six children have been born to them, three of whom are now living—Henry, Sophia and Annie.

A. T. Martin, a son of Ira and Ann (Thompson) Martin, was born in Washington county, New York, October 8, 1818. When twenty years of age he came west, and, after remaining two years in La Porte, Indiana, moved to McHenry county, Illinois, where he lived for about fifteen years, engaged in farming the greater part of the time. In the fall of 1855 he came to Bremer county, and first located in Frederika, where he started a steam saw-mill and had the honor of sawing the first lumber in this part of the county. Mr. Martin purchased his farm in Frederika two years previous to his settlement here. The first sermon in the old town of Tripoli, was preached in his house and the first Sabbath School was also held at his house and conducted by his wife. He remained in that township eight years and then settled on section 4, Fremont township, where he lived until his removal into the village of Tripoli, in February, 1882. Mr. Martin now owns 107 acres of land. He was the first postmaster of the old Tripoli postoffice, and has held the office of justice of the peace. He was married in 1840 to Miss Harriet Branch, who was born in the State of Vermont. Seven children have been born to them, of whom six are now living—Charles I., now living in Fremont township; Emma C., now the wife of T. O'Bryan; Mary, now the wife of H. W. Lobdell; Asa, who is now living in Kansas; Ella, wife of E. L. Starbuck, of New York city, and Hattie, who is teaching in Illinois. Sidney, the second son, was killed by a saw-log falling on him, August 15, 1856. Of Mr. Martin's early life in this county, much can be said. His house, which was known far and near as the "big" house (it was 18x24) was a home for all, and many an early settler will cherish a warm place in his heart for A. T. Martin and wife; remembering their hospitality when starvation stared them in the face, and must surely have come, had not the "latch-string" ever been out at Martin's.

M. M. Watkins is a son of Emanuel Miner and Anna (Barr) Watkins, and was born in Windsor county, Vermont, May 19, 1829. When he was ten years of age, the family moved to St. Lawrence county, New York, where he remained until 1845. At this time he went to Rock county, and afterward to Walworth county, Wisconsin, where he followed the trade of a carpenter. Some time after, he moved to McHenry county, Illinois, and was engaged for five years in wagon-making. In the spring of 1855, he came to Bremer county, Iowa, and settled near Horton, on a farm. There he lived eleven years and then returned to Aurora, Illinois, and engaged in manufacturing doors, windows, sashes and blinds, and also engaged in the lumber trade for five years. Upon leaving Aurora, he returned to Bremer county and turned his attention to farming, in Lafayette township. In February, 1880, he moved to Tripoli, and again engaged in the lumber business. Mr. Watkins was married to Miss Lorica Terry, in 1852. They have had four children—May, wife of C. A. Austin, of Sumner; Ralph R., who is now in business in Waverly; Frank W., who died in 1874; and Mary, who died in 1876. Mrs. Watkins died in 1862, and in 1871 Mr. Watkins married Miss S. Dette Terry, who is a sister of the first wife. They have one child—E. Ray.

John Chapin was born in the town of Heath, Franklin county, Massachusetts, August 16, 1817. He is a son of John and Clarissa (Patterson) Chapin, who were born in Massachusetts, and were descendants of Deacon Samuel Chapin, who settled in that State in 1634, and was one of the founders of Springfield, in 1642. When John was eleven years of age the family moved to Alleghany county, New York, where he remained until 1837. At that time he came west to Geneva, Wisconsin, and, as soon as land came into market, purchased a farm. In June, 1856, he came to Iowa and settled on his farm—which he had purchased the year previous—on section 27, Fremont township, Bremer county, and now own 120 acres of fine land. Mr. Chapin has held nearly all of the town offices; has been a member of the board of supervisors eight years. He was married in 1847, to Miss Elizabeth Ann Williams, who was born in Easton, Washington county, New York. They have seven children—Angeline, Juliette, wife of G. W. Price, and now living in Wisconsin; John, who lives in Washington Territory; Rhoda, Elizabeth, Clementine, wife of Henry Rausch, and Carrie D.

J. O. Bucknam was born in Otsego county, New York, November 10, 1822. He remained in his native county until twenty-three years of age, then came west and settled in Walworth county, Wisconsin, and engaged in farming. In 1856, he came to Bremer county, Iowa, and settled on a farm on section 11, Fremont township, which land he had entered in 1854. From Mr. Bucknam's settlement here until his death, November 8, 1878, he took an active part in both the town and county politics. He was married August 23, 1849, to Miss Diantha Chapin, who bore him four children—Alletta, now the wife of Frank Williams; Ella, now the wife of Charles Nafus; Clara and Elbert—and died in 1862. He was married in March, 1863, to Miss A. J. Southwick, who was born in Wayne county, New York, and came to Bremer county, with his mother, in 1861.

Robert Jolly was born in London, England, on the 15th day of August, 1824. Shortly after his birth the family moved to Somersetshire, where Robert grew to manhood. In 1847 he left his native land for America, and, soon after his arrival, located in Kenosha, Wisconsin, where he engaged in farming. In June, 1856, he came to Bremer county, Iowa, and bought a farm of forty acres, on section 11, Fremont township, where he now lives, and at present owns 120 acres. Mr. Jolly was married, in 1855, to Sarah Ford, a native of England. They have had three children—Sidney, Edwin, and Mary. Mrs. Jolly died March 13, 1864. In October, 1864, he was again married, chosing as a wife

Julia Sherman, who was born in the State of Ohio. She has borne him three children—Albert, Grace, and Ervin.

After the year 1856, others came in; but the township did not rapidly fill up. A few sketches are here presented of some of the representative citizens.

Hugh Hazlett, a son of John and Elizabeth (McIntyre) Hazlett, was born in County Antrim, Ireland, May 25, 1825. He came to America, with his parents, and settled in Utica, New York, where he remained until 1854. At that time he came west, and engaged in farming in Stephenson county, Illinois, for six years, then came to Bremer county, Iowa, and settled on section 24, Fremont township, where he now resides, and owns 200 acres of land. Mr. Hazlett is the present justice of the peace, and has filled that office for several years. He belongs to the democratic party, and cast his first presidential vote for Martin VanBuren, in 1848. He was married in December, 1849, to Miss Eliza Jane Young, who was also born in County Antrim, Ireland. Five children have blessed this union, three of whom are now living—James Young, who now occupies a position in the office of the Second Auditor of the Treasury, at Washington, D. C.; William G., who lives in Fremont township, and Louis C., who lives at home.

J. J. Cook, a son of Wyatt and Sophia (Root) Cook, was born in Huron county, Ohio, February 12, 1837. He received his education and grew to manhood in the county of his birth. In October, 1860, he came to Bremer county, and settled on section 1, Fremont township, where he now owns 400 acres of land, of which 300 are under cultivation. Mr. Cook has held the office of town trustee two terms. In 1869 he was united in marriage to Miss Julia Cormack, who was born in McHenry county, Illinois. Three children have been born to them—Ruth, Elma and Hattie.

J. H. Martin is a son of John and Mary (Patterson) Martin, and was born in Washington county, Ohio, November 30, 1842. Four years after his birth, the family came west, and settled in Winnebago county, Illinois, where the son received his education, and grew to manhood. In 1861 he came to Iowa, and settled on section 3, Fremont township, Bremer county. He now owns 560 acres of land in the townships of Fremont and Leroy. Mr. Martin has held nearly all the township offices of Fremont, and is at present a member of the school board. He was married in 1866 to Miss Elvira Mulock, who was born in New York State. They are the parents of two children—Eddie and Myra.

William Moody, a son of John and Mary (McKnown) Moody, was born in county Antrim, Ireland, November 22, 1829. He came to America in 1851, and settled in Herkimer county, New York, where he lived for thirteen years. In February, 1864, he came to Bremer county, Iowa, and two years later settled on section 10, Fremont township, where he now lives, and owns 80 acres of land. Mr. Moody was married in January, 1864, to Miss Rosetta J. Lobdell, who was born in New York State. They have seven children—Willis, Cora, Mary, Orin, Clara, Viola and Jennie.

A. E. Sweet is a son of Henry and Hannah (Graham) Sweet, and was born in Perry, Geauga county, Ohio, November

11, 1830. When he was four years old, the family moved to St. Joseph county, Michigan, and after remaining there about four years, moved to Cook county, Illinois, where his father died when he was fourteen years of age. Here the son grew to manhood and received his education. In 1853 he went to California, where he engaged in mining for eleven years, and was quite successful. Upon leaving there, he returned to Illinois, and in 1867 came to Bremer county, Iowa, and settled on section 10, Fremont township, where he now owns a farm of 320 acres, and also owns 100 acres in other parts of the township. Nearly all his land is under cultivation and contain buildings that have cost about $4,000. Mr. Sweet has held the office of town trustee and school director. In 1866 he was united in marriage to Miss Isabel Lyon. They have two children—Bertie E. and Eveline E.

H. H. Sweet is a son of H. H. and Lydia (Bates) Sweet, and was born in Will county, Illinois, January 7, 1842. He received his education in his native county and grew to manhood on his father's farm. In the spring of 1861, he enlisted in Company B, First Illinois Light Artillery, and served three months. September 12, 1861, he re-enlisted in Company I, Ninth Illinois Cavalry, and served until honorably discharged at Nashville, Tennessee, December 12, 1864. Upon receiving his discharge, he returned to his home and in March, 1865, again enlisted in Company D, Fourth United States Veteran Volunteers, and after serving one year was again honorably discharged. During the year 1867, he came to Iowa and settled on section 16, Fremont township, and now owns a fine farm of 120 acres. Mr. Sweet has held the office of school director. In 1868 he was married to Miss Adelle Chapin, a daughter of Jacob Chapin. They have had three children—Ethel I., Earl C. and Eugene A.

William G. Hazlett was born in county Antrim, Ireland, July 11, 1833. In 1842 the family came to America, and settled in Utica, New York. William remained at home, engaged in farming, until he attained his majority. In 1858 he came west and located in Stephenson county, Illinois, where he farmed for ten years, then moved to Iowa and settled on section 24, Fremont township, Bremer county, where he now resides and owns 160 acres of land. Mr. Hazlett has held the office of trustee and is, at present, a member of the town board. In 1856 he was united in marriage to Miss Philinda A. Snyder, who was born in New York State. They have six children living—John M., William G., Mary, George, Philinda and Hugh.

Christoph Schuknecht was born May 2, 1832, near Stralsund, Prussia, and is a son of Johann S., and Elizabeth (Wesemann) Schuknecht. After going through the public schools of his native village, he took up agricultural pursuits, remaining in his country until 1858, when he left for the United States, landing at Quebec in June of that year. From Quebec he came west and settled in Kane county, Illinois, where he engaged in farming about seven years, when he moved to Bremer county, Iowa, settling in Fremont township, where, one year after his arrival, he bought a farm and now owns 160 acres of land and five acres of timber. He

HISTORY OF BREMER COUNTY.

was married to Friederike Rahn, a daughter of Joachim and Friederike (Hemming) Rahn. By this union there are ten children, viz: Albert S., born October 21, 1860, now in the dry goods business at Greene, Iowa; Charles, born September 1, 1862; Louisa, born May 26, 1864; Wilhelm, born May 5, 1866; Theodore, born February 24, 1868; Hermann, born November 30, 1871; Emma, born November 8, 1873; Theresa, born November 28, 1876; Edward, born April 26, 1879; John, born April 12, 1882. In politics, Mr. Schuknecht is a Republican; by faith, a Lutheran and a member of the Evangelical Lutheran church, of Fremont township. He has served his township as trustee for about seven years.

RELIGIOUS.

The first religious services were held at the house of John Franklin, Sr., on section 14. This house is now owned by James C. Franklin. The services were held by Rev. Mr. Smith, a Methodist divine, in the fall of 1857. A class was organized at the same time. Among its first members were John Franklin, Sr. and wife; John Franklin, Jr. and wife, and Mrs. Erastus Warner. From that time till the present, services have occasionally been held in the neighborhood at private houses, and at the school house. The class at present numbers but few members.

St. John's Evangelical Lutheran Church is located on section 31. The first members were John Fritz and wife, Christopher Rohlwing and wife, Henry Wilkening and wife, Fred Everdeng and wife, Christ. Schuknecht and wife, and William Tegmayer and wife. The church has now a membership of about forty-two. The first building was erected in April, 1868, which was used both for a church and parsonage, until 1881, when the present church was built, at a cost of $1,639. The first pastor was the Rev. Wm. Beherent; then came Henry Hunsocker, Rev. Gustaf Blessin and Andrew Hahn. The church is now without a pastor. A day school is taught in the parsonage.

EDUCATIONAL.

The first school was taught in a log building erected for school purposes on section 23. Mr. Owen was the first teacher, and commenced a term in the winter of 1858-9. He did not remain, however, through the term. This school building was sold after the township was organized as a district township. The building was erected by the township, and was one of the first four built in the township. One was located on section 1; another on section 3, and one on section 32. There are now nine school houses in the township, all frame, costing about $600 each. The first four cost $100 each.

The second school was taught in the school house on the southeast corner of section 3, by Miss Emily Higgins, in the summer of 1859. She was married August 10, 1860, to Albert Sykes. They now live in Oswego, Kansas.

FIRST THINGS.

The first death in the township was a child of John Hall and wife, October 11, 1859, at the age of four months and seven days. The burial was on section 10.

The first birth was a daughter of Matthias Wuest and wife, was born August 25, 1855, on the farm which he now owns, southeast quarter of section 14. She was named Mary, and was married to Samuel Ferro, of Tripoli, in 1880. She was engaged, for some time previous to her marriage, teaching in different parts of the county.

The first marriage ceremony was performed September 22, 1857, the contracting parties being C. C. Cook, and Miss Ellen M. White, at the residence of the bride's parents, by her father, E. B. White, justice of the peace. These parties still live in the township, on section 1. They have two children—Mary Eva, and Clara C.

CEMETERY.

A cemetery was located on the southwest quarter of section 11, on land belonging to J. O. Bucknam. The first burial was John Franklin, Sr., who died in 1860. The cemetery location was afterward changed to the southeast quarter of the northeast quarter of section 10, in the fall of 1878.

ORGANIC.

The first election in Fremont township was held at the house of John Hale, on section 10, in 1856. The land is now owned by John Moehling.

The first officers elected were as follows: Henry Lester, and E. B. White, trustees; Sidney Booth, clerk; J. G. Closson, constable, and R. D. Titcomb, supervisor of Road District No. 1, that being the only road district in the township.

The officers since that time have been elected as follows:

April, 1857.—Henry Lester, John Chapin, and L. Walker, trustees; J. O. Bucknam, clerk; E. B. White, justice; John G. Closson, and George Kimbal, constables.

April 5, 1858—R. D. Titcomb, Erastus Warner, Samuel Snyder, trustees; R. D. Titcomb and John Closson, justices; E. A. Churchill and Robert Porch, constables; J. O. Bucknam, clerk; John Hale, township supervisor.

October, 1858—Lafayette Walker and John G. Closson, justices; C. C. Cook and Richard Churchill, constables; Moses W. Clark, Israel Trumbo, Hiram Lester, trustees; Otis Clark, clerk. Israel Trumbo afterward resigned, and Erastus Warner was appointed in his stead.

October 1859—Wm. B. Hale and E. A. Churchill, justices; M. W. Clark, Hiram Lester, Erastus Warner, trustees; Otis Clark, clerk; E. A. Churchill, assessor; Robert Porch, Chandler Fletcher, constables.

November, 1860—E. A. Churchill and Cyrus Fletcher, justices; John Hale, Jas. Skillen, James Brown, trustees; E. A. Churchill, clerk; J. W. Kelsey, assessor; Otis Clark, supervisor; E. A. Kelsey, John Fletcher, constables.

October, 1861—R. D. Titcomb, justice; Charles F. Davis, E. A. Kelsey, constables; E. A. Churchill, clerk; John Chapin, assessor; John Franklin, John Closson, Robert Skillen, trustees.

October, 1862—John Closson, L. L. Tutter, justices; James Franklin, Lyman Chapin, constables; J. G. Closson, Matthias Wuest, John Franklin, trustees; J. O. Bucknam, clerk; John Chapin, assessor.

October, 1863—Albert Sykes, assessor; Erastus Warner, justice; Otis Clark, Jacob Chapin, Hiram Lester, trustees; J. H. Martin, clerk; Charles Davis, W. B. Hale, constables.

November, 1864—John Chapin, supervisor; Jacob Chapin, J. J. Cooke, P. P. Newell, trustees; J. A. Hale, H. O. Walker, justices; L. O. Bucknam, clerk; J. H. Martin, assessor; James Blake, Frank Kelsey, constables.

October, 1865—Jacob Chapin, J. J. Cooke, Robert Skillen, trustees; E. A. Churchill, Henry Simon, justices; Monroe Chapin, Wm. Moody, constables; J. H. Martin, assessor; J. O. Bucknam, clerk.

October, 1866—Robert Skillen supervisor; John Clark. A. Countryman, John Fritz, trustees; John H. Dwyer, clerk; E. A. Churchill, assessor; E. A. Churchill, John Kasemeier, justices; John Kline, Fred. Moehling, constables.

October, 1867—H. Lester, T. Warner, J. Fritz, trustees; C. C. Cooke, clerk; J. M. Jarvis, assessor; John Chapin, supervisor; Hugh Hazlett, John Franklin, justices; Charles Stitger, J. Harnburg, constables.

November, 1868—Hiram Lester, supervisor; A. E. Sweet, J. O. Bucknam, Jacob Chapin, trustees; Asa T. Martin, justice; Henry Sweet, Franklin Rust, constables; J. H. Martin, clerk; J. O. Bucknam, assessor.

October, 1869—C. C. Cooke, James Skillen, C. Schuknecht, trustees; Hugh Hazlett, justice; Adolph Kock, constable; J. H. Martin, clerk; J. O. Bucknam, assessor.

October, 1870—A. E. Sweet, Jacob Chapin, James A. Skillen, trustees; S. Fitts, justice; Asa T. Martin, constable; J. H. Martin, clerk; Christoph Rohlwing, assessor.

October, 1871—Hugh Hazlett, John Fritz, justices; Andrew Carstensen, Hugh Hazlett, H. W. Lobdell, trustees; D. Warner, Hubert Wynhoff, constables; J. H. Martin, clerk; C. Rohlwing, assessor.

October, 1872—John Wynhoff, justice; James Brown, A. E. Sweet, C. F. Davis, trustees; Hubert Wynhoff, Jehu Jensen, constables; John Moehling, clerk; H. W. Lobdell, assessor.

October, 1873—John Franklin, justice; Hugh Hazlett, assessor; John Moehling, clerk; W. G. Hazlett, Christopher Koch, John Kasemeier, trustees; P. M. Trobridge, James C. Franklin, constables.

October, 1874—John Wynhoff, Christoph Rohlwing, justices; Andrew Carstensen, assessor; John Moehling, clerk; Wm. G. Hazlett, A. E. Sweet, John Bunger, trustees; P. Trowbridge, John Bunger, constables.

October, 1875—Thomas Martin, C. S. Vincent, justices; Andrew Carstensen, assessor; John Moehling, clerk; A. E. Sweet, Mathias Wuest, Hubert Wynhoff, trustees; A. E. Kelsey, B. Lobdell, constables.

November, 1876—John B. Jordan, H. W. Lobdell, justices; Asa T. Martin, assessor; John Moehling, clerk; Andrew Carstensen, Wm. Feghtmeier, Matthias Wuest, O. C. Vaughn, A. Warner, trustees.

October, 1877—C. Rolhwing, assessor; John Moehling, clerk; John Franklin, C. Schuknecht and Rober Skillen.

October, 1878—Hugh Hazlett and Asa T. Martin, justices; Mathias Wuest, assessor; John Moehling, clerk; C. Schuknecht, James A. Skillen, J. H. Martin, trustees; O. C. Vaughn and James Churches, constables.

October, 1879—Aldoph Kock, assessor; John Moehling, clerk; Wm. G. Hazlett, trustee.

October, 1880.—Adolph Koch, trustee; John Moehling, clerk; Christopher Wilharm, Hugh Hazlett, justices; Christ. Rohlwing, assessor; F. Gunsalas, C. Laudenboch, constables.

October, 1881.—C. Schuknecht, trustee.

October, 1882.—Wm. G. Hazlett, trustee; Christopher Wilharm and Hugh Hazlett, justices; F. Gunsales, C. Laudenbeck, constables; John Moehling, clerk; L. C. Kock, assessor.

The present township officers are: A. Cook, Wm. Hazlett, C. Schuknecht, trustees; John Moehling, clerk; L. C. Cook, assessor; Hugh Hazlett, Christ. Wilharm, justices; Frank Gunsales, Charles Ludenback, constables.

TRIPOLI.

This town was named by H. J. Wynhoff in honor of the old town of the same name, situated in Frederika township. The land upon which the town now stands was owned by Hiram Lester, Carl Schroeder, Conrad Clansing, Andrew Carstensen and John Jensen. The first house built was by B. Kingsbury. It is now owned by S. M. Ferrow, who occupies it. The next house was built by Marvin Trowbridge, and is now owned and occupied by Noel Slack.

The first wagon shop was established by Otto & Mueller, who are still in the business.

The first blacksmith was Marvin Trowbridge, who opened here in the spring of 1873, and remained until 1880, when he moved to Dakota.

TRIPOLI POSTOFFICE.

This office was moved here from the old town of Tripoli, in February, 1880, and the first postmaster appointed was H. G. Wynhoff. He held this position until June, 1882, when he was succeeded by J. M. Bean, who is the present incumbent.

EDUCATIONAL.

The Tripoli school district was organized as an independent district in the spring of 1882. The terms of school were held in the old school-house of the district, during the summer of that year. The present school building was erected during the summer of 1882, and cost, without furniture, $3,100. The first principal of the independent district was Professor Moore, the first primary teacher was Miss Effie Cook.

RELIGIOUS.

The St. Peter's German Evangelical church was built in 1881 and dedicated the same year, the dedicatory sermon being delivered by Rev. N. Savering. He was assisted by Rev. Off. Among the first members were John Moehling and wife, Andrew Carstensen and wife, Fred Moehling, Christ Kuhart and wife, Carl Schroader and wife, Christ. Koch and wife and Carl Tegtmeier and wife. The church has a membership of 24, with an attendance of 35 families. The first pastor, Rev. Paul Foerster, came here from Missouri in February, 1882. He returned to Missouri, December, 1882. The church at this writing is without a pastor. The building is a frame structure and cost, when erected, $2,010. The society was organized in August, 1880, and services were held in the Tripoli school house until the church was completed. In connection with this church there is a Sabbath School during the summer. The first officers of the church were Fred Schultz, Christ. Kuhrt and Carl Schroeter, trustees; John Moehling, secretary; Andrew Carstensen, treasurer.

BAPTIST CHURCH.

The first members of this organization were, Mrs. Eisenhart, E. A. Kelsey and wife, John Kelsey, George Kelsey, and Mrs. C. C. Cooke. A church building was erected, in the fall of 1881, at a cost of $2,000. In size it is 30x54 feet, and constructed of wood. The first minister was Rev. R. Norton, who is still the pastor. The first services were held in the school house at Tripoli. The dedicatory sermon, when they afterward built a church, was by Elder Moxem, of Cedar Falls, assisted by several others, among whom were Rev. Pierce, of Greene.

TRIPOLI CREAMERY.

The Tripoli creamery was established in November, 1880, by S. H. Kingsley. At the commencement he met with considerable opposition, but determined by honest dealing to convince the people that it was money to them to patronize the creamery. He started two teams gathering cream, but was compelled to withdraw one of them. His first shipment was three tubs, containing 56 pounds each. During the first month he shipped twelve tubs, since this time his business has steadily increased, until it now averages 80 tubs a month, and at some seasons reaches as high as 500 tubs per month. His business now amounts to about 2,320 tubs annually, making a business of $70,000 annually, which is steadily increasing. This is one of the leading industries in this part of the country, and probably has done more than any other branch of business in advancing the interests of Tripoli.

RAILROAD.

The first railroad survey was that of the Dubuque and Dakota Company, during the summer of 1872. The road was built and ready for operation in 1880, and upon January 1st, of that year, a train entered Tripoli.

MERCANTILE.

The first store was started by Wynhoff & Co., in May, 1873, in a building now occupied as a millinery store, opposite Wynhoff & Cook's present location. This firm remained in trade two years, when H. J. Wynhoff succeeded to the business, and in June, 1880, took in, as a partner, G. B. Cook. During the summer of 1880 this firm erected their present store building, which is 24x104, and moved into it the fall of the same year. H. J. Wynhoff, of this firm, was born in Germany, on the river Rhine, January 2, 1843. His education was acquired in the common schools of that country; there, also, he learned the shoemaker's trade. In 1868 he came to America, and followed his trade at West Bend, Wisconsin, for three years, and at Appleton, Wisconsin, one year. He then went to Neenah, Wisconsin, and opened a soda-water factory. After remaining there one year, he came to Iowa, and settled in Tripoli. Soon after his arrival, he opened a store, which was the pioneer one of the town, and at that time it was a great undertaking, as all of his goods had to be brought by team from Waverly, and very often the young merchant found it discouraging work. However, *to succeed* was his aim, and by perseverance and hard work he conquered, and now stands among the leading business men of Bremer county. Mr. Wynhoff was appointed first postmaster of Tripoli, and also first express agent of the place, and still holds that position. He is also a member of the board of education. In 1871 he was married to Miss Lizzie Arneman. They are the parents of five children—Addie, Augusta, Henry, Amanda and an infant.

The second store was a hardware establishment opened by Thomas & Ray, who opened early in the spring of 1880, in a building now occupied by Jacob Berg, with furniture. They remained one year when they failed

Christoph Wilharm established a wagon and blacksmith shop in the old town of Tripoli in the spring of 1867, and in the spring of 1880 removed to his present location on the south side of the track, where he runs a wagon, blacksmith shop and planing mill. He employs six men. Christoph Wilharm was born in Germany, July 31, 1844. When he was about ten years of age, the family came to America, first locating at Chicago, Illinois, where Christoph learned the trade of wagon-making and blacksmithing. In 1861, he enlisted in Company K, One Hundredth Illinois Volunteers, and served until honorably discharged at Nashville, Tennessee, in 1865. Two years later, he came to the old town of Tripoli and opened a shop, and in the spring of 1880, came to Tripoli, where he now does an extensive business. Mr. Wilharm is present justice of the peace and has held that office for the past eight years. He was married in 1867, to Miss Sophia Claus. Ten children have been born to them, of whom seven are now living—Christoph, Henry, August, Christina, Clara, Emma and Louisa. His wife, Sophia, died in the spring of 1881, and he was again married, November 27, 1881, to Mary Kahle.

John Franklin began the importation of English draft horses in the fall of 1880. His first venture consisted of three colts. These colts are "Briton," an iron gray, weight at two years old, 1400 lbs. "Model" a light bay, weight at two years old, 1300 pounds. "George Hill," brown color, weight at the same age, 1200 pounds. His next importation was three stallions, registered as "Drayman," age six years, weight 1800 pounds, color, light bay. "Prince Albert," age, six, weight, 1900 pounds, color, dark brown. "Somerset Hill," color, black, weight, 1700 pounds, age, four years. His barn is 36x56, with box stalls for each horse.

The first hotel built in the village was the Tripoli House, erected in the spring of 1880, by August Bonekhouse. This house has nineteen rooms, with a good barn in connection.

E. J. Bean established a hardware store in March, 1881, in a building on the north side of the track. In November, 1881, he moved to his present location on the south side.

R. R. Ahler's drug store was opened in August, 1881, in his present building on the south side of the track.

Theodore N. Mathes established his harness shop in March, 1881.

Otto & Mueller opened their blacksmith and wagon shop in May, 1880.

M. M. Watkins commenced the sale of lumber in the spring of 1880.

An agricultural implement warehouse was opened by C. H. Moehling, in November, 1880.

C. H. Moehling was born in Germany, August 29, 1849. In 1852 he came to America with his parents, who settled in DuPage county, Illinois. There they remained until 1856, when they came to Iowa, and settled in Jefferson township. In 1870, C. H. settled on a farm in section 15, Dayton township, where he lived until 1880, when he opened his agricultural implement store in Tripoli. Mr. Moehling held the office of trustee of Dayton township, two years. In 1872 he was married to Sophia Oldendorf. They have had three children—Herman, August and Ada.

R. R. Ahlers, druggist, is a son of Sophia (Saniter) and H. C. Ahlers, and was born in Dubuque, Iowa, on the 7th day of July, 1853. He acquired a good education in the city schools of that place, and after leaving the high school, received private instruction in French. Before reaching his twentieth year, he had spent one and one-half years in Germany, studying medicine. In 1873 he went to Independence and clerked in a drug store for a while, and then went to Waverly and clerked for J. C. Pomeroy, druggist. From the last place he moved to Dubuque, and was in the employ of T. W. Ruete, druggist, and then made a trip to Fort Benton, Montana. In 1870 he returned to Waverly and bought out J. C. Pomeroy. There he remained until August, 1881, when he came to Tripoli, and engaged in the same business.

August Bouckhouse, of the Tripoli House, was born in Germany, March 20, 1849. When he was seven years old the family came to America, and settled in Kankakee county, Illinois, where August grew to manhood. During the year 1879 he came to Tripoli, and in the spring of 1880, built the "Tripoli House," and has since been its proprietor. In 1875 he was married to Miss Mary Clausing. They have two children—Henry and Louisa.

Eisenhart & Kline, general merchandise, commenced business in 1880, and have a large increasing trade.

James Gardner has a lumber yard and agricultural implement warehouse, and keeps a good stock, and has a large trade.

Most branches of business are here well represented, and Tripoli seems to be making some advance.

CHAPTER XXII.

JACKSON TOWNSHIP.

This township is located in the southwestern corner of the county, having Washington on the north and Jefferson on the east. It is three miles wide, by eight miles long, containing about 15,360 acres. Two rivers traverse the township. The Shell Rock entering on section 20, flowing through 21, 28, 29 and making exit on 33, and the Cedar flowing from the north crosses the boundary line on section 19, then traversing sections 25, 24, 23 and 26, leaves from 35. There are two railroads; the Illinois Central running through about the center, and the Burlington and Cedar Rapids running diagonally through the western portion of the township. The soil is a dark loam and inclined to sandiness in places. It is well timbered, and contains many excellent farms.

EARLY SETTLEMENT.

There is frequently a difference of opinion as to the first settlement of a township, and we present herewith the date, as near as they can be ascertained, upon which numerous early settlers arrived.

Ezra G. Allen was the first settler in this township, and came from Lynn county in 1848, locating on section 25. Here he remained until January, 1852, when he removed to Horton in this county.

J. T. Barrick was the next settler. He came here with his family in 1849, and was the founder of the village of Janesville. Isaac Barrick, his son, yet remains a citizen of the township.

Isaac Barrick was born in Highland county, Ohio, January 25, 1834. In 1849 he came to Bremer county with his parents, and has since made it his home. During the second year of our late rebellion he enlisted in Company B, Thirty-eighth Iowa Infantry, and served until its close. He participated in the siege and capture of Vicksburg, and also in the charge on Fort Blakesly. During his term of service he crossed the Gulf of Mexico four times. His regiment was consolidated with the Thirty-fourth Iowa before the close of the war. Mr. Barrick was mustered out at Houston, Texas, and discharged at Davenport, Iowa. On the 19th day of December, 1865, he was united in marriage with Miss Elizabeth Wagoner, of La Porte, Indiana. They have three children——Emeline, Georgiana, and Edwin. Mr. Barrick owns 160 acres of land, which is under excellent cultivation, and valued at $50 per acre. He is a member of the Presbyterian Church. His father, John T. Barrick, is a native of Kentucky, but, when a mere child, was taken to Ohio, and reared by an aunt. Upon reaching his majority John returned to the State of his birth, and was there given, by his father, a plantation and ten slaves. The gift he refused, because of his opposition to slavery, which was decidedly marked in consequence of his educa-

tion, having been reared by a Quaker family. Returning to his foster State, he followed the trade of a carpenter and joiner. In 1840 he removed to Muscatine county, Iowa, and while there erected a saw mill. In 1845 he located in Cedar Falls, Black Hawk county, and was the first person to utilize the water power at that place, building its first mill. In 1849 he came to Bremer county, and founded the town of Janesville, naming it for his wife, Jane (McPherson) Barrick. Here he built and operated the first mill in the county, (at the same time carrying on his farm), and also erected the first frame house in the town of Janesville.

Isaac McCaffrey was also a settler of 1849, and selected a home on section 32, where he remained about two years, when he removed to Kansas.

Aaron Moore, James H. McRoberts, Rev. S. W. Ingham, and Rev. S. T. Vail, also came during the same season.

Aaron Moore selected a location on section 21, and remained about three years, when he moved to section 20. He is now living near Shell Rock.

J. H. McRoberts, located on section 25, where he remained until his death, which occurred in October, 1852. The farm was occupied by his sons a number of years. It is now owned by J. St. John and C. K. Loveland.

Rev. S. W. Ingham settled on section 20, where he erected a cabin, and remained a few years, when he removed to Tama county.

William Payne was a settler of 1850, and came from Linn county in the spring of that year, but was formerly from Ohio. He located near the present site of Janesville, on section 36, where he remained until the fall of 1853, when he sold to Judge M. Rowen. The place is now owned by Briden and Sevenson.

Rev. S. T. Vail selected a home in Janesville, being the first preacher in this section of the country.

During 1851, J. H. Martin, Samuel Jennings, Simeon F. Shepard, Wm. McHenry and Abraham Myers arrived.

J. H. Martin located on section 26, remained there a few years, when he sold to Maxfield brothers, and removed to section 22, and thence to Oregon.

Samuel Jennings was born in Muskingum county, Ohio, on the 13th day of May, 1823. His father, Samuel Jennings, was a native of Pennsylvania, who emigrated to Ohio in 1812, and soon enlisted and participated in the war with Great Britain. After the war he engaged in blacksmithing, which trade he followed for a number of years. In 1832, he removed to Owen county, Indiana, where he engaged in farming, and where he remained until his death. He married Sarah Smock, by whom he had twelve children, six sons and six daughters. The subject of this sketch was reared on a farm, and received his education in the common schools of that State. The seats of the school house were made of slabs hewn from the timber. The light was received by cutting out a log and putting in 8x10 glass. On the 10th day of December, 1848, he married Miss Mary J. McHenry, a daughter of Wm. and Catherine (Ashbough) McHenry, natives of Kentucky, who emigrated to Indiana previous to the War of 1812. She was born in Owen county, Indiana, July 9, 1828. Eight children blessed this union, seven of whom are living—William S., Sarah C., Catherine L., Lucretia J., Elizabeth E., John H. and Edward L. In the spring of 1851, Mr. Jennings, with his family, left Indiana and emigrated to Jones county, Iowa, where he remained until the following fall, when he removed to Bremer county and located on the place where he now resides. Mr. and Mrs Jennings came to the county poor, but by hard work and economy have accumulated a fine property, having 500 acres of land valued at $45 per acre. Mr. Jennings was a member of the first petit jury of Bremer county.

Simeon F. Shepard, one of the earliest settlers of Bremer, was born in Madison county, New York, September 12, 1818. He is a son of Orrin and Electa (Fish) Shepard, natives of the State of Connecticut. Simeon was one of a family of twelve children, nine of whom are now living. About 1836, his parents removed to Alleghany county, New York, and thence to Crawford county, Pennsylvania, where his father died April 16, 1851, and his mother, April 28, 1873. The subject of this sketch was married in Chautauqua county, New York, July 8, 1844, to Miss Susan W. Pitcher, a native of Cataraugus county, born March 6, 1820. Seven children have been born unto them, five of whom are now living—Martha E., George C., Maurice, Homer and Charles M. In 1847, Mr. Shepard emigrated with his family to Du Page county, Illinois, and thence, in 1851, to Bremer county, Iowa. He had previously purchased the claim where he now resides, and on which he has lived for thirty-one years. At the time of his settlement in this county, there was not a house where the present town of Waterloo now stands; the rivers without bridges, and one could ride for miles without meeting any obstruction from fences. But what a change can be seen now in passing over the country. Either thriving towns and villages meet the eye, or beautifully cultivated farms, upon which, are substantial residences and farm buildings. Mr. Shepard at one time owned 520 acres of land, which he has since divided among his children. He is a member of the M. E. Church, and his wife of the Presbyterian. In politics he has always adhered to the principles of the republican party. During 1857 and 1858, he assessed the county.

William McHenry located on section 32, where he remained until his death, which occurred about 1863. The farm is now owned by Samuel Jennings and his son, William.

One of the earliest pioneers of this county was Abraham Myers. He was born May 9, 1810, in Westmoreland county, Pennsylvania. He was one of a family of seven children, four of whom are now living. During his early life, Abraham learned the coopers' trade, and followed that occupation for some years. On the 28th day of March, 1833, he was united in marriage with Miss Hester Ann Shepard. In 1851 they removed to Bremer county, Iowa, locating on section 21, Jackson township. There they lived three years and then settled on their present place. Mr. Myers was in Waverly at the time that city was located. Though not an ordained minister, he occasionally preached at that time, in private houses and school houses. He, with his family, emigrated to this State and county with an ox-team, and drove their cattle along with them. It was a wet spring and the water was very high. At Janesville Mr. Myers lashed two canoes together and ferried his family across the river. He now owns 120 acres of land, valued at $40 per acre, and on which are comfortable farm buildings. Mr. Myers and wife are, and have been for many years, members of the Methodist Episcopal Church.

Frank Coddington, one of the enterprising farmers, and an old settler, of Bremer county, was born in Chautauqua county, New York, June 22, 1830. He was reared on a farm, and educated in the common schools, finishing with the grammar department. In the spring of 1853, he emigrated to Belvidere, Boone county, Illinois, and while there was engaged in railroading. In September of the same year, he came to Bremer county, Iowa, locating on a farm on section 34, where he now resides. Mr. Coddington was married in the town of Belvidere, April 29, 1855, to Miss Harriet R. Stewart, daughter of William Stewart, born in Chautauqua county, New York, July 30, 1835. Four children have blessed this union—Mary E., now the wife of Albert Rowen, son of the late Judge Rowen, of Parker, Dakota; Jessie A., now a student at Osage, Iowa; Alva B., and William S. When Mr. Coddington came to this county, he was the possessor of but a few hundred dollars, but by economy and strict attention to business he has accumulated a fine property, and to-day is one of the "well-to-do" farmers of the county. He owns 120 acres of excellently located land, on which is a fine brick residence, the upright part being 28x32, and the ell 20x26. The building is two stories in height, and was erected at a cost of $3,000. His main barn is 36x40, and the addition 16x64. Mr. Coddington, his wife and two daughters are members of the Baptist Church.

John Bloker was born in Erie county, New York, September 16, 1837. He is a son of Jacob and Hannah (Bowers) Bloker. John remained in his native State until sixteen years old, and then, in company with his parents, removed to Bremer county, Iowa. Upon their arrival, his parents purchased a farm, and continued to live on the same until their death. They were members of the Presbyterian Church. In 1866 John Bloker was united in marriage with Miss Delia Harris, a native of Lake county, Illinois, born in July, 1850. She was a daughter of Jesse Harris. They have a family of three children—Frank, Walter and Edith. Mr. Bloker owns 180 acres of land, valued at $45.00 per acre. The family are members of the Presbyterian Church, of Janesville.

E. W. Fish, a pioneer of Bremer county, was born in Otsego county, New York, May 31, 1825. He is a son of Rev. Abraham Fish, a Methodist minister and pioneer of Otsego county, New York, who is still living, at the advanced age of 88 years. When E. W. was nineteen years old, he removed to Rochester, New York, where he remained until 1849. During his residence there he was united in marriage with Miss Elizabeth M. Predmore, who bore him one child—Elizabeth—and died in 1846. Upon leaving Rochester, Mr. Fish located in Erie county, Pennsylvania, where he married Miss Lorella Taber, who has borne him five children,

Harvey E., Horace G., Alice C., Annette C. and Bertha A. In September, 1853, Mr. Fish settled in Bremer county, Iowa, and during the first four years of his residence here, was engaged in building and contracting. He then embarked in his present business, wagon and carriage making. Mr. Fish came to this county with just eleven dollars and a set of carpenters' tools. To-day he is known as one of Janesville's enterprising business men, having a good business established there, and owning property in the town valued at $3,000. He also owns a farm of 65 acres, valued at $50 an acre, in Black Hawk county. In politics he is a republican, and has held the offices of justice of the peace, township clerk and school treasurer.

B. F. Davis, who ranks among the pioneers of Bremer county, was born in Yates county, New York, August 6, 1826. When seventeen years old, he learned the trade of a carpenter, which occupation he followed until the fall of 1854. His marriage with Miss Jane E. White occurred in 1848. She was born December 10, 1831, in New York State. There, also, three children were born to them—Emily F., Mary J., and Anna E. In 1854, the family left their old home in the Empire State, for Bremer county, Iowa, arriving here on the 15th day of October. They first settled in Janesville, and at the end of two and one-half years, settled on their present place, where three more children were born to them—Catherine R., Lydia M., and Ella C. Mr. Davis owns 115 acres of land, valued at $40 per acre. In politics, he is a republican.

David High, one of the old land marks of Bremer county, is a native of Franklin county, Pennsylvania, born on the 30th day of March, 1823. He is a son of David and Lydia (Bohrer) High. He was one of a family of three sons and six daughters. In 1837 his parents emigrated to Fairfield county, Ohio, where he was reared on a farm, and received his education. He was married in Fairfield county, May 4, 1843, to Miss Margaret Kern. By this union there were six children, all living to be adults; three of whom are now living— Lydia E., wife of F. J. Pattee, of Kansas; Esther C., wife of Amos Garner, of Waverly; and David S., of Dakota. In 1845, Mr. High left Ohio for Clinton county, Indiana, where he remained until 1854, when he came to Bremer county, Iowa, locating on section 18, where he remained a short time, and then removed to the place where he now resides. Mrs. High died March 5, 1861. She was a member of the Baptist Church. December 24, 1862, Mr. High married Miss C. Keeler, a daughter of Rev. James Keeler, who came to the county in April, 1854. She was born in Wallingford, Connecticut, April 9, 1825. One child blessed this union—James. Mr. High is one of the most prosperous citizens of Bremer county, having a farm of 466 acres, worth about $20,000. This property has been accumulated since his arrival here. His portrait is given in this volume.

Among the early settlers of Bremer county we find D. B. Dougherty, who settled here in the spring of 1854. He was born in Washington county, Pennsylvania, January 6, 1808. While a young man he learned the shoemakers' trade, which occupation he continued to follow many years. He was married in Beaver county, Pennsylvania, in 1831, to Miss Eliza Crail, a native of that county, born August 30, 1809. They have five children—Eli M., Edward C., Sarah S., Marion B., and Eliza J. Upon coming to this county Mr. Dougherty and family made the trip to Muscatine, by water, and from there to Jackson township, by team. They first lived for a short time with a family by the name of Pitcher, and then removed into a small cabin 12x14 feet, where they remained two months. While living there Mrs. Dougherty says a storm came up, and the poles of which their dwelling was made, were so small that she could see them bend. As soon as possible Mr. Dougherty erected a cabin on his own place, it being the first one on the prairie. Into this the family moved before the sides were chinked enough to keep the wind from blowing rain clear across the room. Mr. and Mrs. Dougherty have been members of the Methodist Church for many years, and since their settlement in this county have done much toward building up and supporting the same. They own a farm of 80 acres, valued at $50 per acre, and on it are comfortable farm buildings.

William N. Gaines, one of the earliest settlers of Polk township, Bremer county, is a native of Madison county, New York, where he was born November 16, 1825. He is a son of Obed and Lydia (Connable) Gaines, who were born in the State of Vermont. When William N. was eight years of age he was "bound out" to a man by the name of Newcomber. In 1835 he removed with him to Kirkland, Ohio, and thence, in the summer of 1838, to Kane county, Illinois, where he worked at the carpenter's trade. During the fall of 1853, he came to Bremer county, Iowa, locating in Polk township, in the neighborhood of Plainfield. There he opened a farm and subsequently erected the first hotel in the town, and was its proprietor for a number of years. Mr. Gaines was the first postmaster in the township. The office was then known as Polk Precinct, but was afterwards changed to Syracuse, and still later, to Plainfield. In 1854 Mr. Gaines was united in marriage with Miss Sarah A. Swain, a native of Waukegan, Illinois. They have had five children—Mary E., wife of James D. Miller; William H.; Charles E.; Florence L. and Jeannette. Mr. Gaines has a farm of 200 acres of land in Bremer county, also owns 360 acres in Wadena county, Minnesota. On his farm in this county, is a comfortable residence and a barn 38x50, with basement. In 1854 his parents started west, but while on the road his mother died, leaving the father to finish the journey alone. While living here he made his home with Wm. N. and a brother. He died in Polk township and was buried at Plainfield.

William Briden, a native of Yorkshire, England, and an early settler of Bremer county, was born January 6, 1808. In 1831 he left his native country for the United States. Upon landing in New York City, he immediately proceeded to Livingston county, on the Hudson river, where he was engaged as gardener. One year later he removed to Westchester county, New York, where he had charge of a stable of thoroughbred horses. During the fall of 1834 he removed to Chicago, Illinois, and the following spring made a claim at Des Plaines, Cook county, which he immediately began improving. January 8, 1837, his marriage with Miss Elizabeth Curtis, a native of England, occurred in that country. They have had two children—H. T. and Henry W. She died in England, January 25, 1842; she was a member of the Methodist Episcopal Church. In 1843 Mr. Briden removed to White Pigeon, Michigan, where he married Mrs. Mary Burnan, a native of Yorkshire, England. They had one child—John. She died January 28, 1852; and was, also, a member of the Methodist Church. May 18, 1854, Mr. Briden was married to Mary Ann Cleaver, who was born February 9, 1826, in Columbia county, Pennsylvania. They have had one child—Mary E., now the wife of George E. Sevison, of Janesville, Iowa. The same year of Mr. Briden's last marriage, he came to Bremer county, Iowa, and settled in Jefferson township, where he continued to reside until 1868, when he removed to his present place in the town of Janesville. He came to this country a poor man, but by economy and good management, has accumulated a very comfortable property, and has also been able to give each of his children a good start in life. At one time Mr. Briden owned 1440 acres of land in the central part of Iowa.

Others came during the years of 1853 and 1854, and the township then filled up with a good class of people; sketches of some are here presented.

Amos D. Cooper was born in Lancaster county, Pennsylvania, April 3, 1827. He is the son of Amos and Jane (Downing) Cooper, who emigrated in the spring of 1836, to Highland county, Ohio. The subject of this sketch was reared on a farm, and educated in the primitive schools of that day. His mother died in Ohio, and father in Muscatine county, Iowa. In 1855 Mr. Cooper was married in Poweshiek county, Iowa, to Miss Rachael A. Larkins, who was born in Harrison county, Ohio, in 1829. In 1854 he removed to Cedar Falls, and in 1857 came to Bremer county, where he has since resided. The wild prairie land upon which he settled, has been transformed into a highly cultivated farm, and to his original possession he has from time to time added more land, until he has now 359 acres, of which 284 is under cultivation. In politics Mr. Cooper is a republican. The family are members of the Presbyterian Church.

C. K. Loveland was born in St. Lawrence county, New York, on the 31st day of August, 1837. When nineteen years of age he came to Bremer county, Iowa, where he spent three years—a portion of the time teaching school. In the mean time he pre-empted a piece of land, which he afterward sold, and then returned to his home in New York State; he there remained until 1862, then again came to Bremer county, and has since made it his home. May 23, 1867, he was joined in wedlock with Miss J. L. St. Johns, who was born in Cataraugus county, New York, January 1, 1851. She is a daughter of James St. Johns, who came to Bremer county in 1855, and is a native of Saratoga county, New York. Five children blessed their marriage—Cora E., Annie A., Vinnie, Julia A., and Mary L. Mr. Loveland's farm consists of 180 acres of land, valued at $45 per acre. On it is a fine residence, erected at a cost of $1,500, and a barn that cost $1,000. In politics he is a republican. The family are members of the M. E. Church of Janesville.

Enos F. Shaw, an enterprising farmer of Jackson township, is a native of Northfield, Vermont, born on the 20th day of March, 1828. There he was reared on a farm and obtained a common school education. During 1854 he went to California, where he remained eight years, working in the mines. In 1862 he returned to Vermont, and the same year came to Iowa, settling in Bremer county. He enlisted in Company B, Thirty-Eighth Iowa Infantry, in January, 1864, and served until the close of the war. He participated in the capture of Fort Morgan, and also in the charge on Fort Blakesly, his regiment being the first to plant the colors on those walls. Mr. Shaw was mustered out at Houston, Texas, and discharged at Davenport, Iowa. He then returned to Bremer county, where he was united in marriage with Miss Ellen Cadwallader, a native of Henry county, Indiana, born October 23, 1825. He owns 20 acres of timber and also 160 acres of farm land, on which he has a beautiful residence and a large and commodious barn 36x72, built at a cost of $1,200.

Daniel Pierce, an enterprising farmer of Bremer county, is a native of St. Lawrence county, New York, born December 22, 1824. He is a son of Amasa and Alma (Baldwin) Pierce, whose married life was of sixty years duration. His mother died in 1880, but his father is still living in St. Lawrence county, at the advanced age of eighty-two years. Daniel was reared and educated in his native State. In 1851, he was united in marriage with Maria Loveland, also a native of that county, born in 1833. They have a family of six children —Royal A., Mary E., Lilly M., Amasa L., Matthew E. and Hattie M. In 1865, Mr. Pierce left his home in New York for Iowa, and upon reaching Bremer county, purchased his present farm in Jackson township. He owns 140 acres of land which is well cultivated and valued at $50 per acre. In 1882, he built a fine residence at a cost of $2,000. The family are members of the M. E. Church of Janesville.

William H. H. Youngs, a dairyman of Jackson township, settled in Bremer county, on his present place, in 1864. He owns a beautiful farm of 212½ acres, which is under excellent cultivation, and valued at $50 per acre. In 1865 he turned his attention to cheese-making, building the first cheese factory in the county. He now keeps an average of thirty head of cows, from which he manufactures 1,000 pounds of cheese monthly. He also buys milk enough to make another 1,000 pounds. Mr. Youngs is a native of St. Lawrence county, New York, where he was born July 22, 1840. He is a son of Amasa and Sibyl (Hutchins) Youngs. His mother was born in Middletown, Vermont, June 28, 1801, and his father in Pownall, Vermont, October 10, 1799. They were married September 14, 1821, and have been members of the Methodist church for over fifty years. Their home is now in Jackson township, where they expect to pass the remaining years of life. William H. H. was reared and educated in his native State. During 1860 he was joined in wedlock with Miss Jane Steele, who was born in 1841, and is a daughter of Joseph Steele, of St. Lawrence county, New York. Four children have blessed their marriage—Cora, Dora, Anson and Charlie.

In June, 1867, Thomas Mickley settled in Bremer county. He is a son of Henry and Mary (Burcolter) Mickley, natives of Pennsylvania, and is one of a family of ten children, five brothers and four sisters. His birth place was Lehigh county, Pennsylvania, where he was born April 5, 1820. While still a boy, Thomas learned the tailor's trade, which occupation he followed for fifteen years. In 1838 he removed to Seneca county, New York, and there worked in a distillery for a number of years, and then became proprietor of the same, and operated it for five years. January 7, 1840, he was married to Miss Margaret Miller, a native of Seneca county, born February 2, 1823. Six children have been born to them, five of whom are now living—Stephen E., William H., Cornelia F., wife of Adrian Van Nordstrand; Mary E. wife of Daniel Newell; Jennie V., wife of Homer Healey. Since his settlement in this county, Mr. Mickley has been engaged in farming. He and his wife are members of the M. E. church, of Janesville.

Israel Freeman, farmer and stock-raiser, was born in Franklin county, Vermont, November, 1829. He is a son of Mitchell and Mary (Post) Freeman. The former was a native of France, but reared in Canada and the latter a native of the last named country. When Israel was six years old, he removed with his parents to Chittenden county, Vermont, there remained until he reached his majority, and then went to the State of Massachusetts, where he was engaged in getting out ship timber. In 1856, he follwed Horace Greeley's advice by coming west. He first located in Fillmore county, Minnesota, and while living there became acquainted with and married Miss Mary E. Lamb, December 16, 1857. They have had a family of eight children —Stewart, Angie, Frank, Delia, Cora, Belle, Ella M., May and Maud. In November, 1865, Mr. Freeman removed to Bremer county, purchasing a farm in Jefferson township, upon which he lived for eleven years. He then sold it and came to his present place in Jackson township. His land in this county consists of 113 acres, which is valued at $45 per acre. He votes the republican ticket and has held local offices of trust.

John C. Hand, a son of Dr. Wm. R. and Phoebe (Annin) Hand, born September 29, 1827, in Bedminster township, Somerset county, New Jersey. When he was a small lad, his parents removed to Hunterdon county, New Jersey, where his father followed his profession for a number of years, and then located in Nottaway county, Virginia, where he shortly afterwards died. During John C's younger life he thought of becoming a physician, and therefore began reading medicine, preparatory to entering college. After a few months' study, however, he abandoned the idea, and determined instead, to devote his life to farming. In 1853, he was married to Miss Mary Rittenhouse, born November 1, 1832. Six children have been born to them, five of whom are living— Emeline, William, Silas, Fannie and Frank. During the month of April, 1864, Mr. Hand came to Bremer county, Iowa, and settled on his present farm in Jackson township, where he owns $187\frac{1}{4}$ acres of land, valued at $45 per acre. The family

are members of the Presbyterian Church of Janesville.

Chester Cadwallader, one of the enterprising farmers of Jackson township, came to Bremer county in the fall of 1861, and moved his family here in 1862. He was born in LaPorte county, Indiana, December 3, 1836, and is a son of Byron and Sarah (Hague) Cadwallader, who were born in the State of Virginia. Chester was one of a family of eight children, six of whom are now living. His youth was passed in his native State, where he also obtained his education. The first school he ever attended was held in a log cabin, with slabs for seats, and pins drove into the wall and slabs laid across them for writing desks. In 1858 he was married in Indiana, to Miss Laura Shaw, a native of Vermont, born in 1826. They have three children—Eva, Minnie and Martha. For some years after coming to Bremer county Mr. Cadwallader taught school during the winter season, and farmed in the summer time. He owns a beautiful farm of 130 acres, valued at $50 per acre. In early life he was an abolitionist, but at the time of the organization of the republican party, he joined it. He represented Jackson and Washington townships in the board of supervisors for three years. At one time, his father lived in Bremer county, but at the end of three years, removed to the State of Wisconsin, where he died. His mother is living in Bremer county, at the advanced age of 82 years.

S. N. Jones, a son of Francis Jones, was born and reared in Columbia county, Georgia. About 1807 he, in company with six families of friends, emigrated to Miami county, Ohio. At that date that section of the State was one vast wilderness, and our new settlers were obliged, among other hardships of pioneer life, to burn and dig out mortars in stumps, with which to grind their corn. The subject of this sketch was born in Miami county, Ohio, January 7, 1821. During 1857 he removed to Indiana, and while in that State was married to Miss Elizabeth Foor, who died soon after. He was again married, this time choosing for a helpmeet Elizabeth Beals, who bore him two children—George W. and Adelia A. In 1857 Mr. Jones came to Bremer county, Iowa, and the following year removed to Franklin county, where he continued to live until 1863. At that date he returned to this county, locating on his present place in Jackson township. He owns 90 acres of good land, valued at $40 per acre.

E. M. Dougherty, an enterprising merchant of Janesville, and also an early settler of the county, was born in Jefferson county, Ohio, July 7, 1832. When fifteen years of age he learned the shoemakers' trade, which occupation he followed for a number of years. In 1853 he, in company with his father, came west for the purpose of securing a good location for settlement. During their trip his father purchased the land upon which he now resides. In 1854 they settled permanently in Bremer county, and the subject of this sketch employed his time in helping his father open up his farm, and by working at his trade. In 1862 he enlisted in Company B, Thirty-eighth Iowa Infantry, and served until the close of the war. He participated in the siege and capture of Vicksburg, the capture of Fort Morgan, and was color-bearer at the charge on Fort Blakesly, planting the first colors on those walls. In the fall of 1863, while crossing the Gulf of Mexico, their ship was caught in a terrific storm, which disabled it to such an extent that they were forced to return to Galveston, and then by rail to New Orleans, where they re-shipped, and proceeded to Texas. While in that State Mr. Dougherty was taken sick, and sent home on a furlough. While recuperating his health he was married, in this county, May 11, 1864, to Miss Mary J. Pattee, a daughter of Colonel Pattee, who was also a pioneer of Bremer county. During the fall he returned to his regiment, which was stationed at Donaldsonville, Louisiana. After being mustered out, he returned to his home and worked at carpentering for one year, and then engaged in buying produce and stock. Later, he embarked in the mercantile trade, which business he has since followed with good success. Mr. and Mrs. Dougherty are members of the M. E. Church. Kate, Fred, Marion C., and Lucy L. are their children.

R. W. Clewell, a merchant of Janesville, and an old settler of the township, is a son of David and Hannah (Gross) Clewell, who were married in the State of Pennsylvania, and removed to Seneca county, New York, in 1831. They had a family of eight children, who lived to reach majority. Their son, R. W., was born in Seneca county on the 4th day of February, 1831. When he was seventeen years old he learned the shoemakers' trade, which occupation he followed for many years. In 1856 he settled in Janesville, where he worked at his trade for some time, and then added a stock of ready-made boots and shoes. In 1879 he added dry goods, and in 1881, groceries. Mr. Clewell now carries a large stock, and is doing a lucrative business. In 1854 he was united in marriage with Miss E. M. Leddick, a daughter of Jacob and Harriet (Bigelow) Leddick. She was born in Seneca county, New York, March 27, 1835. One child blessed their union—William M., now book-keeper for a mercantile firm, of Dubuque, Iowa.

Hugh Ballantine, farmer and stock-raiser; is a native of county Antrim, Ireland. At the age of seventeen he came to the United States, and settled in St. Lawrence county, New York. In 1861 he enlisted in company G, Sixteenth New York Infantry, but shortly after was taken sick and discharged. In the spring of 1862, he re-enlisted in company C., 106th New York Infantry, and was a participant in the following engagements—battles of Martinsburg, Mine Run or Locust Grove, Culpepper Court House, Manassas Gap, the Wilderness, Spotsylvania, North Ann River and Coal Harbor, where he was wounded in the right arm, breast and left thigh. He was then taken to a hospital at Philadelphia, where he remained until the close of the war, and then returned to St. Lawrence county. Shortly afterward he turned his face westward, tarrying not, until he reached Janesville, Bremer county, Iowa. There he spent a few years, engaged in a flouring mill. In 1867 he returned to St. Lawrence county, where his marriage with Miss Margaret Wallace occurred. He brought his wife to his western home and in 1872 purchased his present farm of 176 acres, which is under excellent cultivation and valued at $50 per acre. His wife has borne him two children—Wallace A. and Frank E. Mr. and Mrs. Ballentine are members of the Presbyterian church.

ORGANIC.

The first township election was held in April, 1854, at the house of Charles N. Martin, on section 13, now in Washington township, at which election sixty-one votes were cast. The following persons were chosen to hold said election: James Queen, E. W. Fish, clerks; S. F. Shepard, Samuel Clayton and Thomas J. Sewell, judges; and the officers elected were: Matthew Rowen, and R. J. Elsworth, justices; P. B. King and Wm. B. Hamilton, constables; T. J. Sewell, James Boyd and James Queen, trustees; E. W. Fish, township clerk.

The present officers are William Briden, Samuel Jennings and R. Simpson, trustees; W. W. Wyant, clerk; D. Smalling, assessor; W. H. Rich, justice; Edward Pitkins, constable.

EDUCATIONAL.

The first school taught in the township was at Janesville by Rev. S. T. Vail. This was a subscription school. The first regular district school was taught by Dr. Loveland in a log school house on section 35, about eighty rods north of the present school building. This was the first school building erected in the township. There are now seven districts in the township, not including the Janesville independent district. These seven districts have good substantial buildings, five of which are constructed of stone, and all well furnished. The present school property of the township is valued at about $7,000, and the school facilities compare favorably with other localities.

CEMETERIES.

There are two cemeteries in this township—"Janesville Cemetery" and "Wuest Burying Ground"—the former is located one-half mile north of Janesville—the first interments were two sons of V. Thomas, who were drowned in a lake near the Cedar river, in 1850. The latter is located on section 19, and the remains of Miss Dryer were the first interred, in 1853.

FIRST THINGS.

The first religious services were held at the house of William Payne, by Rev. S. T. Vail, during the fall of 1850.

The first marriage ceremony united Joseph Thornbrew and Miss Kane.

The first birth was a son to John and Jane Barrick, January 2, 1853.

The first girl baby was "Ada," a daughter of Asbury and Hannah Leverick.

POSTOFFICE.

The first postoffice in this township was Janesville, established in 1853, with John Hunter as postmaster. He was followed by G. W. Maxfield, F. A. Morton, Wm. Morehouse, F. A. Hotchkiss, J. M. Leslie, H. Morehouse, W. H. H. Gable, W. H. Rich, W. B. Mallory, and the present incumbent, Miss Loretta Mallory. It was made a money order office in August, 1870.

TOWN OF JANESVILLE.

This is the only town in the township. It is located on the Cedar river, six miles south of Waverly, and is the oldest town in the county. The first settler was John

T. Barrick, who was born in Campbell, Virginia, November 20, 1808. In 1809 he went to Highland county, Ohio, where he remained until March, 1849, when he located in what is now Janesville. His only neighbors were the Indians. In the immediate vicinity there were camped at one time, 1,700 warriors. Mr. Barrick's first trading points were Cedar Rapids and Dubuque; the journey to the latter place being long, tedious and dangerous. While he was gone Mrs. Barrick remained at home, surrounded by dusky warriors, who were liable to become dangerous on the least provocation. It was no enviable position for a timid woman to be placed in, but Mrs. Barrick was not one of the kind to exhibit fear. To the noble pioneer women, much is due from those now enjoying the results of their sacrifices.

Among the first settlers of Janesville, were William Payne, Aaron Moore, Philip King, Charles Martin and wife with three sons, John, Samuel and William, who located here in 1850. The first store was opened by Hunter & Leverich, they kept a general assortment, including whisky. Keeler & Olmstead soon after established a business as dealers in general merchandise. The first postmaster was John Hunter, who held the office two years, when George Maxfield was appointed in his place, then Elder Morehouse succeeded him. The first death was a child of William Payne, and the second that of Rev. Solomon T. Vail, a Methodist preacher.

The first school was taught by this same minister, and was a subscription school. The next school was taught by Mr. Knapp. The first regular district school was taught in 1854.

RELIGIOUS.

The regular Baptist church, of Janesville, was organized April 17, 1858, by representatives from the churches at Dubuque, Waterloo, Cedar Falls and Waverly. The sermon on that occasion was preached by Rev. A. G. Eberhart.

The first members of the church were as follows: Robert Bisby and wife, William Fairburn and wife, M. L. Stuart and wife, William Stuart and wife, Isaac Creighton, Frank Coddington and wife, L. Stewart and Randall Churchill. At a business meeting, held June 12, William Fairburn and Frank Coddington were chosen deacons and Robert Bisby, church clerk. The first religous services of the denomination were held at the school house. The church has been in charge of the following pastors: A. D. Bush, for one year, H. H. Burrington for four years and Samuel Sill for two years. In February, 1866, the organization decided to build a house of worship, which was erected during the following summer. It is 34x26 feet, was completed and furnished at a cost of $4,500, and was dedicated, free from debt, on the 3d day of February, 1867. The dedicatory sermon being preached by G. J. Johnson, of Burlington. About this time a Sabbath School was organized with H. L. Crosby as superintendent, having an average attendance of one hundred. T. H. Judson was pastor at the time of dedication, and George Morehouse was clerk. The present officers of the church are—F. Coddington, William Fairburn, M. L. Stewart, R. W. Clewell and B. F. Davis, Trustees; F. Coddington, Secretary. The church, at the present writing, (January, 1883,) is without a pastor. Seventy-seven persons have united with this church since its organization, but its present membership is much reduced by death and removal.

THE PRESBYTERIAN CHURCH OF JANESVILLE.

This church was organized at the residence of Matthew Rowen, December 17, 1853. Its corporate members were J. Ackeson Taylor, of the Presbyterian Church of Peru, Indiana; Mrs. Abbe Ann Taylor, of the Presbyterian Church of Logansport, Indiana; Matthew Rowen, Mrs. Lucy Jane Rowen, Miss Susan Rowen, of the Presbyterian Church of White Pigeon, Michigan; Amelia A. Hunter, of the Presbyterian Church of Cedar Rapids, Iowa; Mrs. Moranda Pitcher, of the Presbyterian Church of Jamestown, New York; and Mrs. Susan W. Shepard, of the Presbyterian Church of Janesville, Iowa. J. A. Taylor and Matthew Rowen were elected ruling elders of the church.

The first religious services of the denomination were held at the residence of Matthew Rowen, by Rev. N. C. Robinson, of Vinton, who supplied the church for one year. He was succeeded by Rev. J. M. Phillips, in January, 1855, who continued his services for two years, services still being held in Matthew Rowen's house. Rev. William J. Harrison, of Waterloo, took charge of the church in July, 1858, and held services alternately with the Methodist Church, in the stone schoolhouse, until July, 1860, when Rev. John Glass became pastor of the church. The services were continued in the stone schoolhouse and the hall building during the entire period, five years, of Mr. Glass' labors.

In February, 1866, the church being without a minister, Rev. John B. Clinton was employed as supply for a few months. During the summer of 1866 the church edifice was erected. The dedication services was held on Thanksgiving day. The building is of wood structure, in size, forty by sixty feet, and is surmounted with a tower. The expense of construction was about $6,000.

Rev. G. H. Chatterton took charge of the church in October, 1866, before the building was dedicated, and supplied the church one year.

Rev. James Agnew was his successor, and continued his services until April, 1869. During the summer, from May to September, the church was supplied by Charles M. Howe, a theological student from Auburn Seminary. In November 1869, Rev. Stephen Phelps, from Waterloo, took charge of the church but was obliged to relinquish it, after eight months of service, on account of impaired health. Rev. A. R. Olney, of Waterloo, became pastor in July, 1870, and continued his ministrations until November, 1874. The church was without regular supply for a few months, until June, 1875, when Rev. W. W. Whipple, of Illinois, became its pastor. His term of service continued until April, 1880, when failing health necessitated entire relief from all responsibility, and his work was given up.

Rev. Charles M. Howe, of Eldora, Iowa, who had formerly supplied the church when a student, was engaged to take charge of the church, April, 1880, and is the present pastor.

Since the organization of the church there has been several revival seasons of particular interest. Those deserving special mention occurred: The first in 1858; the second, under Rev. John J. Glass' ministry, in 1861; the third, under Rev. A. R. Olney's ministry, in 1871; the fourth, under Rev. W. W. Whipple's ministry, in 1876; the fifth under Rev. Charles M. Howe's ministry, in 1881.

The present officers are, Elders, J. A. Taylor, T. V. Axtel, A. D. Cooper and S. N. Byram; Trustees, H. R. Paul, Ira Smalling and Robert Simpson.

Total membership since organization, 239; present membership, 102; and the present condition of the church is prosperous.

The Sunday School was organized in 1853, at Matthew Rowen's house, and Matthew Rowen was its first superintendent.

Its present officers are H. R. Paul, superintendent; Rev. C. M. Howe, assistant superintendent; John Wyant, chorister; and Frank Wetherel, treasurer and librarian. Its enrollment is 110; average attendance, 60.

This church has connected with it, a Ladies' Mite Society, a Ladies' Missionary Society, and a society called the Whipple Sunday School Missionary Society, all organized, and doing efficient work.

Rev. Charles M. Howe, pastor of the Presbyterian Church of Janesville, was born in Girard, Erie county, Pennsylvania, March 21, 1842. He is a son of Jonah and Harriet (Boynton) Howe, who settled in Erie county about the year 1838. When the subject of this sketch was fourteen years of age his parents emigrated to Benton county, Iowa, and there his father shortly afterward died. Charles then turned his attention to farming, which occupation he followed until twenty years old, and then attended the Iowa State University, of Iowa City. In 1867 he entered Dartmouth College, graduating therefrom in 1868. Subsequently he spent two years at Auburn Theological Seminary, and one year at the Theological University of Chicago, completing his course in 1871. His first pastoral work was in Eldora, Hardin county, Iowa, where he labored eight years and nine months. During the spring of 1880 he came to Janesville, Bremer county, and assumed his present charge. In 1870 he was joined in matrimony with Miss Mary O. Dennis, of Johnson county, Iowa. Four children have been born unto them, three of whom are now living—Lucius E., Charles B., and Helen E.

The first quarterly conference of the First Methodist Episcopal Church of Janesville, was held December 18, 1852, at the house of William Payne. The work was then known as the "Big Woods Mission." Rev. A. Young was presiding elder. At this quarterly conference, Solomon W. Ingham (local deacon) was appointed, by the presiding elder, preacher in charge for the ensuing quarter.

After the annual conference of 1853, the work was divided, and Janesville appointment fell into the "Upper Cedar Mission," which was composed of the following appointments: Waverly, Moore Class, Janesville, and Waterloo, with Andrew Coleman as presiding elder, and Solomon W. Ingham, preacher in charge.

At the fourth quarterly conference, June 17, 1854, T. Pattee, S. F. Shepard and Andrew Daily were appointed as a board of trustees for the church and parsonage at Janesville. There appears to have been a board of trustees prior to this, but their names and no trace of their appointment can be found.

Janesville circuit was organized in 1854, and the first quarterly conference was held at the house of Mr. Burleigh, November 4, 1854. Andrew J. Coleman was presiding elder. Rev. Hiram J. Burleigh, preacher in charge, and E. Kendall junior preacher. The circuit consisted of the following appointments: Janesville, Waverly, Waterloo, Cedar Falls, Shell Rock and Moore's Class.

At the fourth quarterly conference, in 1855, the trustees report a deed secured for lots at Janesville for a house of worship and parsonage. The expense of the deed and recording was paid by the quarterly conference.

In 1856, H. Morehouse, S. F. Shepard and Elias Pattee were chosen as a committee to make arrangements to build a church at Janesville. Rev. Edwin D. Lamb died at Janesville, August 20, 1857, while preacher in charge. He was appointed to this charge in 1855, and was serving his second year. During the conference years of 1856-7, Janesville and Cedar Falls were connected as one work. Janesville was set off in 1857 as a station, with an appointment four and a half miles east, then known as Briden's School House, but soon after changed to East Janesville.

The village of Janesville was founded by John T. Barrick, by whom lots 3 and 4, in block 4, were donated to the M. E. Church. When and by whom the first appointment and class was formed, cannot now be ascertained, but must have been in 1851, or 1852. The first class leader of whom any authentic account can be obtained was William Payne. H. Morehouse, James Boyd, Wm. Briden, S. F. Shepard and W. H. Rich constituted the first board of trustees. This board of trustees held several meetings during 1856 and 1857, with the view of building a church, but after canvassing the ground, it was found at a meeting held September 30, 1857, that it would not be prudent to attempt to build, and the matter was postponed indefinitely. In 1861, it was found that the church and board of trustees were not properly incorporated under the laws of Iowa, consequently on August 19, 1861, an article of incorporation was properly made out and recorded in the recorder's office of Bremer county, in which article, H. Morehouse, S. F. Shepard, D. B. Dougherty, H. Weygandt and W. H. Reck were named as trustees until their successors was elected or appointed.

In 1864, a meeting was held for the purpose of arranging to build a church, when a subscription was raised, a portion of which was collected that year and invested in material, but the building was not commenced until April, 1865, and completed in February, 1866. Owing to having enlarged the original design and adding a tower and bell, besides the large rise in material and labor, the society found itself in debt about $1,900, but at the dedication, the sum of $2,300 was secured in pledges.

In 1867 the present parsonage was built, which action left the society much embarrassed. In September, 1872, the pledges had shrunk to such an extent that there was still a debt of $400, with about $60 in pledges, which was considered reliable. The church at this time was in need of repairs, that would require about $250, which was at once undertaken. A new subscription was taken to cover the expense of repairs and indebtedness. So small a margin was obtained, however, that care had to be taken to collect, and the last dollar of indebtedness for the original building was paid October 20, 1879.

Prior to 1869 the society experienced several gracious revivals, notably in 1857, by Rev. A. W. Odell. In 1861-63, under Rev. Wm. Smith; 1864, 1866, under Rev. F. X. Miller; 1868, under Rev. J. W. Clinton. The Rev. Samuel W. Heald was pastor of the church from January 6, 1870 to 1871; Rev. Thomas Moore from 1871 to 1873; Rev. R. Norton, 1873 to 1876; Thomas Moore, 1876 to 1877; Rev. W. S. Skinner, 1877 to 1880; Rev. H. H. Green has been pastor since 1880.

MILL.

The foundation for the Janesville flouring mill was laid in the fall of 1857—the projectors designing to erect a building of stone, but concluding the quality of stone was not such as they desired, work was temporarily suspended, and the mill was not built until 1859, and not in running order until 1860. Ransom Moorehouse was proprietor. The building was 36x50, two and one-half stories above the basement, and had three run of stone. An addition was made 20x50 in 1866. The mill is now owned by J. I. Case, of Racine, and is rented by Laur and Duke. It has five run of burrs.

SOCIETIES.

Equity Lodge No. 131, A. F. & A. M., of Janesville, was organized June 2, 1858. The charter members were James Keeler, Asbury Leverick, S. T. Hotchkiss. The first officers were as follows: Jas. Keeler, W. M.; A. Leverick, S. W., and S. T. Hotchkiss, J. W. The present officers are, B. F. Brown, W. M.; Clark Chase, S. W., and E. W. Fish, J. W.; Howard Sewell, treasurer; D. K. Smalling, secretary; J. H. Rowen, S. D.; Wm. H. Young, J. D. The lodge is in good working order, with about thirty members in good standing.

JANESVILLE IN 1883.

Janesville is the oldest town in the county, and is very pleasantly located—having at this time, six stores, two blacksmith shops, two wagon shops, three doctors, one saw and grist mill, a tin shop, stock dealers, grain buyers, meat market, two livery stables, three churches, two hotels, and a good graded school.

RETROSPECT.

As one looks upon the well tilled acres and comfortable homes in this township, it is difficult to realize the change wrought during the last thirty years. The credit and honor for work and sacrifice, producing this desirable transformation, certainly belongs to early settlers—men and women, who are as truly heroes and heroines, as he who marches, unfalteringly, through the storm of battle, and stands, unflinchingly before the cannon's mouth. Many things which in an early day served a good purpose, would now be considered a curiosity. The plow, the harrow, and

Samuel Jennings.

various utensils of agriculture, have undergone great changes. Marvellous improvements have been made in every department. The necessities of the case brought into play the inventive genius of these hardy pioneers, and many a rudely-constructed "pestle and mortar" has performed the work of the more complicated machinery of the grist mill. In consequence of the scarcity of teams, the beasts of the forest and prairie were utilized. In one instance, Isaac Barrick, son of the founder of Janesville, became the possessor of two buffaloes, two deer and two elk, and soon demonstrated that buffalo made good work teams, and the elk a speedy animal, outstripping the best horse, when harnessed to a buggy. This young man, athletic, strong, square built and fearless, had under his subjection not only buffalo, deer and elk, but bears, wild cats, coons, beaver, and the various beasts of the forest, and it was not an unusual thing to see him spinning along the trail, in his buggy, driving an elk of speed and bottom, or in the field, behind the plow, making the buffalo useful in turning the sod. At one time he made sale to an eastern man, of his buffalo, deer and elk for $600, which in those days was a considerable amount of money. This same young man, some time afterward, went to the City of New York, with an uncle, and in "taking in the sights," visited P. T. Barnum's great show. A familiar call from a certain part of the building, attracted his attention, and, upon investigation, proved to be the voice of recognition from one of these elk. There the pair stood, and their joy in meeting their former master was expressed in the strongest language and action, known to the brute creation. Now, in place of trail and ford, they have roads and bridges; in place of buffalo and rudely-constructed breaker, the blooded horse and sulky plow, and this community is one of thrift, enterprise and intelligence, occupying a portion of land second to none in the county.

CHAPTER XXIII.

JEFFERSON TOWNSHIP.

This territory lies in the southern tier of townships of Bremer county, with Maxfield on the east, Warren on the north, and Washington and Jackson on the west. It consists of about 15,360 acres, and is watered by a creek called Quarter-section Run, which flows from the north through the eastern and southern portion, and Dry

Run, flowing through the western part, and making confluence with Quarter-section Run within the limits of the township.

At the time of early settlement this township was about one-half covered with timber; but it has been reduced to about one-quarter. Unlike many other townships, the supply of wood here, although abundant years ago, is being rapidly reduced, from the fact that when cut off the land is put immediately under cultivation. There is very little, if any, waste land. Different classes of people are represented, but the population is mainly American. The soil of timber lands is a light clay, mixed with a vegetable mould, except upon the bottoms, and has a clay sub-soil. On the prairies the soil is a rich, dark, sandy loam, very productive, and desirable for agricultural purposes.

EARLY SETTLEMENT.

To Charles McCaffree belongs the honor of being the first settler in Jefferson township. He was without a family, and came from Lee county, Iowa, in the spring of 1845. Locating on section 34, he went to work, and broke about fifty acres. He made this his home until 1858, when he sold out, and, after a time, went to Missouri, where he lived until the outbreak of the rebellion. Being a strong Union man, he was compelled to leave that locality, he therefore returned to Jackson township, where he died in 1871.

The next settler was an Irishman, by the name of Jerry O'Conner. He came from Lee county, and settled near McCaffree, on section 33, near where Henry D. Gould now lives.

During the fall of the same year Jacob Beelah, Isaac Samples, his son-in-law, and Isaac McCaffree located in the township. Jacob Beelah, a native of Ohio, settled on section 35, where was built the first log cabin in the county, on the premises now owned by J. E. Berlin. Mr. Beelah removed to Floyd county. Isaac McCaffree now lives in Missouri, and Andrew Sample removed in 1851, to Bradford, Chickasaw county, and there improved the water power, where he remained about four years, failed in business and removed to Missouri.

In 1846 John H. Messinger, with his family, and his two brothers and their families, Wesley and Henry Tibbits, were added to the settlement. Mr. Messinger selected a farm on section 35. Wesley Tibbits located on section 15, his brother Henry selecting a place on section 16. The Tibbits brothers removed to Kansas, where Wesley still remains. Henry, at last accounts, was living in southern California.

E. J. Messinger came about the same time and located on section 25, where he remained until 1870, when he went to Waterloo, engaged in milling and where he still resides. When Mr. Messinger first came to this township quite a number of Indians made this their hunting ground. The Winnebago tribe having a village near by of about 500. They were generally peaceable and friendly, however, and left the township in 1849. Womanokaker, or Woman-taker, was war chief of this tribe, and lived on section 23, near the creek, where is now the residence of H. C. Krech. There were also some other Indians in this vicinity, representatives of other tribes and they were, as before stated, generally friendly, but occasionally they would secure horses belonging to the settlers and demand meal or flour for their redemption.

Robert P. Messinger still lives on the old homestead, and is the earliest male settler now living within the county limits. About the same time came T. Fisher and P. Miller from Marion county, Indiana. They did not remain long, and but little is known concerning them.

During the year 1847, Joseph and James Fee settled near the Tibbits, where they remained a short time and then went to Chickasaw county.

These are all the earliest settlers that can be remembered. Among those who came in soon after were: Moses Mishler with a numerous family, consisting of a wife and nine children—Jonas, Michael, John, Moses, David, Washington, Susanna, Catherine and Fannie. Mr. Mishler died in 1863. The widow, now seventy-three years old, lives on the old homestead.

With the Mishlers came Dan and Jacob Winklepeck, and about the same time or a little later, P. McGeehee and Johnson Eveland arrived.

William Tharp settled on section 34, in 1849. Afterward he moved to Franklin county, then to Kansas, and finally to Arkansas. Tharp settled on the farm where John Stears now resides, he having located about 600 acres of land in that vicinity, which in 1853 was purchased by John Stears and his brother Henry, in company with a brother-in-law, Richard Holton. John Stears still resides on a portion of that tract; his brother, Henry, who was postmaster in this township for a number of years, now resides in Black Hawk county.

Mr. Holton, who was a speculator, never lived on his land, but disposed of it some years after. He now resides in Michigan.

John M. Bennett came the year following, and selected a home on section 33. He now lives in Waterloo, and the place is owned by John Schunemann.

Israel Trumbo, from Ohio, this season, settled on section 16. He was the first county surveyor, and moved to Dakota where he died.

James Bevard, from Illinois, also came in 1850, and located on section 15, where he remained until his death, in 1862.

Eli Roberts occupied a portion of this same section, where he remained a few years, and left the county. E. H. Bartells now owns the land.

John Hurst, in 1850, settled on section 14, and remained about two years.

This year and the year following, came Matthew Farrington, Wm. Smith, Judge J. Farris, John W. Dean, Walter Farrington, James Michael, Julian Webster, Joseph Farris, Austin Farris, John Oaks, Elijah Smith, Calvin Tuttle, H. Robinson, J. T. Thomas, Humphrey Hogan, L. Tatum, Sam. Armstrong, Levi Bevard, Jacob Bevard, S. Cooper, William Staagee, Fred Bruntz, and others. Still later came John and Henry Stears, Alexander J. Flemming and family, Devillo Holmes, David Phillips, and others. The settlement of this township was identical with the early settlement of the county, and a more extended history may be found in that connection. Many of these men were quite prominent in the affairs of the county and

SETTLERS' PROTECTION SOCIETY.

At an early day there was an organization for the protection of land claims of the settlers. This was designed to operate against speculators, "land sharks" and claim jumpers, and in favor of actual settlers; consequently strangers could not ascertain anything concerning desirable lands, unless holding proper credentials. This society had its desired effect, and through its influence actual settlers were protected. It remained in existence until the organization of the county, and the appointment of a school commissioner, when it was discontinued.

FIRST THINGS.

The first matrimonial alliance was formed by the union of Isaac McCaffree with Rebecca Beelah, in December, 1845. There being no one in the township qualified to perform the ceremony, they made a trip to Independence, where the twain were made one flesh, returned to Jefferson township, and dwelt in peace and happiness a number of years, then removing to the State of Missouri.

The first birth in the township was a daughter to Isaac and Rebecca McCaffree, born in 1846. The child died when two years old, and was the first death in Jefferson. It was buried on section 35.

The first religious service was held at the house of John H. Messinger, in the winter of 1845-46, by Rev. Mr. Collins, a Methodist Episcopal minister, from Marion, Linn county. He held services twice during that winter.

EDUCATIONAL.

The first school was held at the house of Aaron Dow, on section 25, in the winter of 1850, and was taught by Richard Miles, a young man who had a claim in that vicinity. There was an attendance of six scholars. Mr. Miles was formerly from Connecticut. He remained here a number of years and then went to St. Paul, Minnesota.

There are now six school districts in the township, all having good buildings, well furnished. Educational facilities compare favorably with other localities. School property is valued at $3,000.

ORGANIC.

The first township election was held at the house of James Bevard, on section 15, in April, 1855. Those appointed to hold said election were as follows: Judges, William Westervelt, J. H. Messinger, and J. S. Jenkins; clerks, John Pattee, and M. Farrington. There were 64 votes cast at this election. The following persons were elected:

Humphrey Hogan and William P. Harris, justices; H. B. Boyd and W. Hogan, constables; William Kern and E. J. Messinger, trustees; G. A. Michael, township clerk.

The present officers are: Trustees, R. P. Messinger, H. D. Gould, Christian Bodeker; clerk, John Wilder; assessor, Matthew Farrington; justices, J. B. George, Fred Barlets; constables, John Calease, Fred Heidemann.

POSTOFFICE.

The first postoffice established in the township was in 1849. It was also the

HISTORY OF BREMER COUNTY.

first in Bremer county. John H. Messinger was the first postmaster. It was called Neutral postoffice, from the fact of its location on neutral land. In 1851 Mr. Farrington consented to attend to the business, and the office was moved to his house, on section 35. Mr. Messinger was succeeded by Henry Stears, who removed the office to his residence on section 34, where it remained until it was removed to the residence of Robert Shannon, in Black Hawk county. Thomas Fitch was the next postmaster, and remained in charge until it was discontinued.

The first mail route was a special from Cedar Falls to this point, mail being transferred on horseback or on foot once each week. Elijah Smith was mail carrier, and always announced his near approach by vigorously blowing a large horn, which he carried with him. This proceeding not only gave the postmaster an abundant opportunity to prepare himself, but added a certain dignity and importance to the occasion.

An office was established in Jefferson City, in 1856 or 1857, called "Breckenridge". Alexander J. Flemming was first postmaster. About 1863, its name was changed to "Denver", the present name. Guy Farnsworth is the present postmaster.

CEMETERY.

There is but one cemetery in this township, located on section 25. It was never regularly laid out. It consists of about one-half acre of land, and was deeded to the township by E. J. Messinger. The first burial here was that of a stranger found by Andrew Daley, in a dying condition, on the road from Independence to Janesville, in Black Hawk county.

JEFFERSON CITY.

This village was laid out in 1855, by Jeremiah Farris, the surveying and platting being done by M. Farrington. During the year 1856, a blacksmith shop was opened by John B. Ackerson. Powell & Farris commenced a general merchandising business; Sabin Cooper opened a cabinet shop; J. Schucker engaged in wagon making; and David Briggs began shoemaking.

Notwithstanding it is surrounded by a rich farming country, Jefferson City has not increased in population since the first year, and the business transacted yearly is not as great as in 1856.

BIOGRAPHICAL.

We here append sketches of a number of the old settlers and representative men of Jefferson township.

Hon. M. Farrington, a pioneer of Jefferson township, was born on the 18th day of September, 1822, in Poughkeepsie, New York, and his early life was passed on a farm. He received an academic education, and when eighteen years old began teaching school, which profession he followed for a number of years. In 1850 Mr. Farrington moved to Delaware county, Iowa, and one year later came to Bremer county, and settled on section 35, Jefferson township, where he has since resided. He was formerly a William Lloyd Garrison Abolitionist, and would not accept any office offered him until after the Emancipation Proclamation. It is said of Mr. Farrington that at the first convention called to nominate candidates for local offices in Bremer county, he received the nomination for county surveyor, but upon hearing of the honor conferred upon him, he made a speech, respectfully declining, at the same time stating that he would never take an oath to support the Constitution of the United States so long as that Constitution allowed slavery. During the years 1871-2, he held the office of county supervisor. On the 19th day of March, 1851, he was united in wedlock to Miss Ann L. Willis, who was born in Hanover, Grafton county, New Hampshire, April 13, 1827. They are blessed with three children living—Delia J., Edgar L. and Ianthe A. Mr. Farrington is president of the Iowa State League, and is also serving his third term as president of the Liberal League of Northern Iowa. He was also elected the first president of the Farmers' Mutual Fire Insurance Company, and has been annually re-elected to that office until their last meeting, when he was made secretary. When the Emancipation Proclamation was issued, Mr. Farrington felt that he was released from his vow not to vote while slavery was recognized. He then allied himself with the republican party, with which he co-operated until the organization of the National Greenback party, since which time he has advocated the principles enunciated by that party. He is an effective speaker, and has held joint discussions with some of the ablest men of the State, upon political and religious subjects.

H. B. Boyd was born in Kentucky in 1823. When he was fifteen years old, the family moved to Fulton county, Illinois, where he grew to manhood and acquired a limited education. In 1849 Mr. Boyd came to Bremer county, Iowa, and subsequently married Percilla Jenkins, a native of Illinois. She bore him one child—George W., who at present is a resident of Waverly—and died during the year 1852. Two years after her death, Mr. Boyd was married to Lucinda Carberry, who was born in the State of Indiana. They have had three children—Margaret, wife of George F. Leland; Martha Alice; and Mary (deceased.) Mr. Boyd is a greenbacker, and has held the office of constable for seven years.

William Baskins, another early settler, was born in Richland county, Ohio, December 26, 1826. He obtained his education in the district schools of that county, and passed his youth on his father's farm. In 1850 he packed his worldly goods and turned his face to the setting sun. Upon reaching Iowa, he determined to make this State his home and finally settled on a piece of land in Jefferson township, Bremer county. Three years later he was married to Miss Mary Clark, a native of Delaware county, Ohio. They have had two children—Francis, who is a resident of this county; and Sherman, who is now living in Oregon. His wife dying, Mr. Baskins married Mrs. Mary Coats, who was born in Indiana. They have had three children—John, Margaret and Charles. Mr. Baskins belongs to the democratic party, and has held several offices of trust, among which should be chronicled that he was one of the first marshals in Bremer county. His step children are William H. and Silas Coates.

One of the pioneer settlers of Jefferson township is John Stears, who was born in

Yorkshire, England, in 1819. When he was sixteen years old the family emigrated to America, and, upon their arrival, settled in White Pigeon, Michigan, where he obtained his education and reached manhood's estate. In 1850 he was married to Miss Mary Scobie, who is also a native of England. Three years later, with his family, he came to Bremer county, Iowa, and settled in Jefferson township, where he has since resided. Mr. Stears has held several of the local offices, and has been trustee of the Methodist Episcopal church, to which he and his wife have belonged for the past fifteen years. They are the parents of four children—Elinor, Charlotte E., Antoinette and Elizabeth.

John J. Foutch is also an old settler of Jefferson township. He was born in Fulton county, Illinois, December 28, 1833. His youth was passed in his native county, and his school attendance consisted of about sixty days only. Since his marriage, however, by diligent application, he has acquired a fair business education. In 1849, he, in company with Judge Farris, made a tour of the west, their object being to find a good location for settlement, and in the spring of 1850 he claimed the land where he now resides. The following year he was married to Charlotte Jane, a daughter of Judge Farris. They have six children—Rosanna, Hugh, Debby, William J., Hiram, and Nancy C. In 1857 Mr. Foutch went to Kansas with the renowned John Brown, and while there took an active part in the political fight, then waging in that State. In 1861 he returned to Bremer county. Mr. and Mrs. Foutch were the third couple married from this county, and had to go to Independence to secure the license. In those days it was necessary to have both a license and—whisky, upon such occasions. The groom experienced some difficulty in obtaining the former, but none in getting the latter; however, his troubles did not end upon finding the beverage, as he could get no bottle to carry it in. Finally, he succeeded in putting together the pieces of one, which he bound together with twine, and thus carried the fire water and was happy. The distance from their home to Independence was thirty miles, but they made the round trip, on horseback, in twenty-four hours. While at home, John's father always kept (as was the custom in those days) a bottle on the side-board, and the son early acquired a strong appetite for the beverage. However, after marriage, seeing the wrong he was committing, a reformation took place, and he has since been one of the strongest advocates of temperance. About that time he also experienced religion, and is an active worker in the cause of Christ.

E. H. Bartels was born in Germany, July 27, 1814. He was reared on a farm, and received a good common school education in the German Language. In 1843, he came to America, and after spending a few months in the cities of Baltimore, Pittsburg and Cincinnati, came to the territory of Iowa and began trading with the Indians, not far from the present city of Burlington. Eighteen months later he went to Chicago, Illinois, and engaged in carpentering and farming. During the year 1853, he moved to Bremer county, Iowa, and settled on section 15, Jefferson township, where, by economy and strict attention to business, he has accumulated a fine farm of 260 acres, valued at $45 per acre. August 9, 1847, he was united in marriage with Miss Mary Nirge, who was born in Hessen, December 26, 1822. They are the parents of nine children—Frederick W., Ernst F., John H., Sophia M. J., William, Mary S., John F., Herman and August. The family are members of the Evangelical Lutheran Church. Mr. Bartels is a republican, and has held the office of town trustee.

Henry D. Gould, one of the early settlers of Jefferson township, and one of Jefferson's most trusted and enterprising citizens, was born in Morristown, New Jersey, January 13, 1829. He was the son of Z. S. and H. L. (Day) Gould. His father died in 1868; but his mother is still living on the old homestead, in New Jersey, where she has lived for over sixty years, at the advanced age of eighty years. Henry D. is the third of a family of seven children, all of whom are living, excepting one sister. When sixteen years of age, he left the parental roof, going to Brooklyn, Long Island, where he learned the confectioner's trade, following the same, as a journeyman, for something over nine years. Having a thorough knowledge of the business, he determined to embark in this branch for himself; but this proved to be a disastrous move, as in it he lost nearly all of the hard earnings of his early life. Nothing daunted by his misfortune, he resolved to seek his fortune in the West, and in March, 1856, landed in Jefferson township, Bremer county, where he bought land on section 33, on which he has resided ever since. In 1852, he was married to Miss Eliza J. Miller, a native of Brooklyn, born July 18, 1830. The change from city to country life, upon the western prairie, was a great one, and it is no wonder that Mrs. Gould often sighed for the old home. But many changes have been wrought in the years that are gone. The little log cabin in which they first lived has long since been replaced by a more elegant structure. The farm has been improved, and they are now surrounded by all the comforts obtainable in the older countries. Mr. Gould has always been active in township affairs, holding at all times some one or more of the various local offices. Mr. and Mrs. Gould are the parents of four children, three of whom are living—Mary Louisa, living at home; Julietta A., wife of A. Montrouse; Josephine F., wife of John Vincent; Joseph D., who died in 1879, at the age of sixteen years. The family are active members of the M. E. Church. Mr. Gould has been one of the trustees of the church for many years.

Alonzo Gleason, a native of Burrillville, Rhode Island, was born in 1817. He received his education in the common schools of that place and remained there until 1850. In that year he was married to Miss Lydia A. Wood, who, also, was born there. After their marriage the couple went to Providence, where Mr. Gleason was employed in spindle forging. In the fall of 1854, with his family, he came to Bremer county, Iowa, and settled on section 24, Jefferson township, where he now owns a well improved farm of 240 acres, valued at $40 per acre. Mr. and Mrs. Gleason have been blessed with six children—Earlville, Isabel, Lydia E., Leepha, Celia and Herbert O. Mr. Gleason is a

Republican and has held several of the local offices.

S. B. Phillips was born July 16, 1845, in the State of Rhode Island. Nine years after his birth the family moved to Bremer county, Iowa, and settled on a farm on section 14, Jefferson township, where they have since resided. Mr. Phillips received a good common school education, and followed farming until August, 1862, when he enlisted in Company B, Fourteenth Iowa Infantry, and served until honorably discharged in December, 1864. Upon again entering civil life, he returned to his home and, on the 17th day of October, 1871, was married to Miss S. B. McClure, a native of Indiana. Three children have been born to them—Roy J., Ralph W. and Martha D. Mr. Phillips is a republican, and has held the office of director of school board, and is at present township clerk. He is superintendent of the Bethel Sabbath School, held in sub-district, number four.

H. T. Briden, son of William Briden, now of Janesville, was born in Cook county, Illinois, in 1837. When he was four years of age his parents returned to England, their native country, but the subject of this sketch remained in America with friends, and as his mother died during their stay in England, he has no recollection of seeing her. His father returned to America in 1843, and settled in St. Joseph county, Michigan; there H. T. was reared on a farm and received but a limited education. In 1854, he came to Bremer county with his father and brothers, making the entire trip by them, being something over five weeks on the way. They settled in Jefferson township near where Mr. Briden now lives. He remained with his father until he was twenty-three years of age, after which he rented land for some time, and in about 1861, his father presented him with the farm where he now resides. Mr. Briden has been a member of the school board for some time, and has held other minor offices in the town. He was married in 1860, to Miss Susannah Gish, a native of Marion county, Ohio. She came to Bremer county with her parents in 1855, and settled in Waverly. They are the parents of six children—William M., residing at home; Edward U., attending college at Cedar Rapids; Lulu Belle, Jacob A., Charles H. and Mary B. Mr. and Mrs. Briden and their oldest son are active members of the Methodist Church.

The present postmaster of Denver post-office—Guy Farnsworth—was born in the State of Pennsylvania, in 1837. Shortly after his birth, the family moved to Cleveland, Ohio, and later to Liverpool, Medina county, where Guy obtained his education. He first attended the common schools and then spent two terms at Baldwin's Institute, Barea, Ohio. Upon leaving school, he learned the machinists' trade, of his father, and followed this occupation at different points until 1857, when he came to Bremer county, landing in Janesville on the 15th day of September. On the 14th day of December (same year), he entered the employ of Holmes, Kelly & Kay, who, at that time were building a steam saw mill, remaining with this company, working at his trade, until 1861. During the fall of that year he opened a blacksmith shop, in a building erected by himself for that purpose. In September, 1862, he enlisted in Company B, 14th Iowa Infantry, and served until honorably discharged, in December, 1865. Upon receiving his dismissal from service, he returned to Jefferson City, and engaged in his present business. He was united in wedlock June 6, 1866, to Miss Elizabeth McHenry, who was born in Indiana. Four children have blessed this union, three of whom are now living. Mr. Farnsworth is a member of the Liberal League of Northern Iowa. In the year 1877 he was appointed postmaster of Denver postoffice, and still holds that office with great credit.

Henry Otto Meier is a native of Germany, and was born December 5, 1844. When he was thirteen years old, the family came to America, and soon after their arrival, settled in Jefferson township, Bremer county, where they have since resided. Henry received a good common school education, in both the German and English languages. On the 4th of April, 1869, he was married to Miss Mina Bodeker, a native of Germany, born in 1848. They have had three children—Herman, Henry and Anna. The family are members of the Lutheran Church. Mr. Meier is a democrat, and has held nearly all of the local offices.

H. W. Briden, one of Jefferson's enterprising and much respected farmers, is a son of William and Mary Briden, both natives of England, and was born in Illinois, about sixty miles from Chicago, in 1840. Soon after his birth his parents returned to England, where his mother died. After a short stay he returned to America with his father and was reared on a farm in St. Joseph county, Michigan, where he received a common school education. In 1854 he came to Iowa with his father and settled in Jefferson township. Mr. Briden attended school in the primitive log school house, for about three years, after coming to this county. He has always kept out of politics, and has never accepted any of the offices of the town, excepting serving as a member of the school board, which position he held for some time. He has, since 1854, lived on the farm where his father first settled, and, since that date, has never been out of the town, except on short visits to friends in the east. A portion of his extensive farm, which consists of 430 acres, is the piece of land on which Charles McCaffree settled, it being the first claim taken by any white man in Bremer county. Mr. Briden is one of those unassuming, retiring men that are always respected, and rarely, if ever, make an enemy. By hard work and good management, supported by his most excellent wife, he has accumulated a large competency, and is probably the wealthiest man in Jefferson township. He was married in 1864 to Miss Marian Spencer, a native of Michigan. She came to Janesville with her parents in 1855, where her father died in 1861, after which she returned to Michigan, where she remained until 1863. They are the parents of nine children, seven of whom are living—George William, Adell, Francis A., Gertrude, Jennie, Pearle and Earle, (the latter died in infancy) and DeWitt.

Worthy J. Tibbetts, a native of Bremer county, was born in Jefferson township on the 4th day of February, 1857. When fourteen years old, he went to Oswego, Kansas, where he received a good common school education, and afterwards took a commercial course at Crawford Commercial College, Fort Scott, Kansas, graduating therefrom in 1877. The year succeeding his graduation, he returned to Bremer county, and has since resided in Jefferson township. April 7th, 1880, he was married to Miss Alice Winner, born in Belvidere, Illinois. They have one child—Gertrude B. Mr. Tibbetts is a staunch Republican, and has held several of the town offices.

C. L. Bodeker, whose parents were pioneers of Jefferson township, is a native of Germany, born in 1842. When he was ten years old, the family came to America, and settled in Cook county, Illinois, where they remained four years, and then removed to Bremer county, Iowa, settling in Jefferson township. The son received an excellent education in the German language. During the year 1866, he was married to Sophia Meier, who was also born in Germany, in the year 1845. She came to America, with her parents, when thirteen years of age, and grew to womanhood in Bremer county. Six children have been born to them—Henry, Lorence, Sophia, Herman, Anna and William. The family are members of the Evangelical Lutheran Church. Mr. Bodeker is a Republican, and has held nearly all of the town offices.

Henry C. Krech, who is a native of the Prussian Province of Saxony, was born in 1819. He received a good common school education in his native language, and when twenty years old went to France, and during his residence there, mastered that language. In 1844 he returned to Prussia, and entered the army, as a private, in the artillery service; and, after some time, was promoted to the Assistant Surgeon's school, where he remained until he left the army, in 1847. The following year he was recalled to the army, and again served for some months. Upon receiving his dismissal, he immediately enlisted in the war of the rebellion, known as the rebellion of 1848. In the spring of 1849, he left his native country for the "Land of Liberty," and upon arriving here, settled in Westchester county, New York, where he remained nine years, and then emigrated to Bremer county, Iowa. He settled in Jefferson township, and engaged in the occupation of painting and carpentering. In 1867 he purchased a steam saw mill, moved it to Jefferson City, and has since been engaged in the lumber business. Mr. Krech has been married four times. His first marriage was in 1853, to Rachel Grenning, a native of Germany, who bore him six children. His second wife was Katie McDonald, born in Scotland; the third, Lizzie A. Miller, born in Ohio. Mr. Krech's last marriage took place July 22, 1880, his wife's maiden name being Susannah Miller. He has held several of the local offices, and in politics is a greenbacker.

John Oltrogge, one of Bremer county's pioneers, was born in Germany, in 1827. There he grew to manhood and received a good common school education. He came to America in 1856, and after spending one year in Illinois, came to Bremer county, Iowa, first locating in Maxfield township, where he remained twelve years, and then removed to Jefferson township, where he lived until his death, which occurred on the 3d of January, 1882. During the year 1855, he was married to Miss Minnie Grupe, who still survives him.

They have had three children—John, who now carries on the farm; Minnie and Henry. The family are members of the Evangelical Lutheran Church.

Wm. Bayer, one of the enterprising men of Jefferson township, was born in Germany, August 14, 1829. He remained in his native country until nineteen years old and while there learned the trade of blacksmithing. In 1848 he came to America, and the three succeeding years, followed his trade in Boston, Massachusetts. He then came as far west as Chicago, and in 1864, came to Bremer county and opened a blacksmith shop in Jefferson township, where he has since been engaged in business. Mr. Bayer is a republican, casting his first presidential vote for Abraham Lincoln. At present he is a member of the town board. On the 19th of May, 1856, he was married to Miss Mary Peter, a native of Germany. They have had twelve children—William, Rudolph, Louisa, Johanna, Lina, Mary, Anna, Sophia, Lizzie, John, Frederick and Amelia. Mr. Bayer and family are members of the Evangelical Lutheran Church.

Ernst G. Brandt, one of the leading farmers of Jefferson township, was born in Germany, in 1837. He came to America in 1855, and soon after his arrival settled in Cook county, Illinois. Five years later he came to Bremer county, Iowa, locating in Maxfield township, where he lived until 1868, and then settled in Jefferson township, where he now resides, and owns one of the finest farms in the county. It contains 545 acres, and is valued at $30 per acre. In 1860 he was united in marriage to Miss Caroline Nirge, born in Germany, in 1834, but who came to this country with her parents when a small child. Ten children have blessed this marriage, eight of whom are now living—Henry, Sophia, Ernst, Emma, Herman, Bertha, Louis and Theodore. Mr. and Mrs. Brandt are members of the Evangelical Lutheran Church. Mr. Brandt believes in democracy, and has held nearly all of the town offices.

J. W. Calease, a native of Germany, was born in 1841. Five years after his birth, the family came to America and located in Wisconsin, where they lived for eight years, and then moved to LeSueur county, Minnesota. At seventeen years of age J. W. left home for Illinois, remaining there until the first year of our late rebellion, when he enlisted in Company B, Eighth Illinois Cavalry, and served until honorably discharged, in August, 1865. Upon receiving his dismissal he returned to Illinois, but after remaining there a short time, came to Bremer county, Iowa, where he has since resided, with the exception of four years spent in Franklin and Butler counties. He was married in 1870, to Martitia Messinger, who was born in Jefferson township, in 1852. They have five children—Olive, Lydia, Bertha, Harley and Phoebe. Mr. Calease is a republican, and at present holds the office of constable. Both he and his wife belong to the Christian Church.

John Homrighaus was born in Ohio, in 1844. Six years after his birth, the family moved to Illinois, and there John obtained his education and reached manhood's estate. In 1863 he came to Bremer county, Iowa, and settled in Jefferson township, where he has since resided. His principal business has been farming, but he also learned carpentering and wagon-making, following those occupations for a number of years, in Jefferson City. During the year 1872, Mr. Homrighaus crossed the ocean and traveled through the countries of Germany and France. He is a staunch republican, and has held the office of justice of the peace, six years. In 1880, he read law with H. Bezold, of Waterloo. He also took the census of his township, during the same year. He was united in marriage to Miss Eliza Ottman, a native of Illinois, in 1873. In 1882, Mr. Homrighaus was elected county supervisor from the second district, which office he now holds.

Heinrich Braun was born in Hanover. Germany, in 1830. He obtained a common school education in his native country, and followed the occupation of farming until 1857, when he came to America, locating in Kane county, Illinois, where he passed the following eight years. At the expiration of that time, he came to Iowa, and settled in Jefferson township, Bremer county, and embarked in the grocery business, which branch of trade he has since followed. He was married in March, 1859, to Miss Minnie Haase, also born in Hanover, but who, when a child, came to America, with her parents, and settled in Illinois, where she lived until 1865. Nine children have blessed this union, eight of whom are now living—Lewis, Caroline (wife of Charles Moehling), Louisa, Henry, Mina, Frank, William (deceased), Herman and Anna. Mr. Braun's family are members of the Evangelical Lutheran Church.

Lewis Becker is a native of Germany, born in 1843. His early life was passed on his father's farm, in the country of his birth; but when seventeen years old, he came to America, and soon after landing located in Chicago, Illinois. One year was spent in that city, and then he enlisted in Company H, 4th Missouri Cavalry, and after serving three years and three months, he was honorably discharged, because of sickness. Upon receiving his dismissal from service, he returned to Chicago, and in 1866 came to Bremer county, settling in Jefferson township, where he has since lived. During the year 1866 he was married to Caroline Bearsterfield, who also was born in Germany. Five children have been born to them—Henry, Fred, Mina, Anna and John.

Samuel Saylor was born in Pennsylvania, in 1823. He received a common school education and remained on the homestead until he had reached his majority. At that time he began working at the carpenter trade, and continued to follow that occupation for twenty-seven years. In 1848 he was married to Miss Sarah Dull, a native of Somerset county, Pennsylvania. During the year 1860, with his family, he moved to Waterloo, Iowa, where he lived and followed his trade, for eleven years, at the expiration of which time, he came to Jefferson township, and engaged in farming. Mr. and Mrs. Saylor are members of the Methodist church. Nine children have been born to them, of whom six are now living—Amanda, Anna, Mabel, William, Charles and Albert.

Hermann Baumann was born in Germany, on the 7th day of July, 1846. He received a common school education in his native country, and there grew to manhood. At fourteen years of age he began learning the shoe-maker's trade, and after serving his apprenticeship, followed that occupation while in that country. In 1868 he emigrated to America, and settled in the city of Chicago, where he worked at carpentering. About three months after his arrival in Chicago, he made a short visit to Michigan, and upon his return (in the fall of 1868) was married to Miss Matilda Wendorf, who is a native of Germany, born in 1843. Soon after their marriage the young couple moved to Oswego, Illinois, where Mr. Baumann entered the employ of H. Helle, boot and shoe dealer, where he remained until 1874, and then moved, with his family, to Jefferson city, Bremer county, Iowa, and became engaged in his present business. Mr. Baumann is a republican. He is at present assistant postmaster of Denver post-office. Both he and his wife belong to the German Lutheran Church. Six children have blessed this union—Emma, Otto, Herman, Caroline, Lewis and Martha.

CHAPTER XXIV.

LAFAYETTE TOWNSHIP.

This district comprises all of township 92, north of range 14, west of the fifth principal meridian, except the south tier of sections. It is bounded on the north by Polk township, on the south by Washington, on the east by Warren, and on the west by Butler county. It is watered by the Cedar river, which enters on section 4, running thence in a southerly course through sections 9, 17, 16, 21, 22 and 27, leaving the township from the latter sections. Along the banks on either side of this stream is found the only timber in the township. Back from the stream on both sides the land is a rolling prairie. The soil is generally a dark sandy loam. The population is somewhat mixed, Americans largely predominating.

EARLY SETTLEMENT.

The first settler in this township was James Collier, who located on the northwest quarter of section 15, in 1850, where he opened a blacksmith shop. He remained until sometime in 1852, when he removed to Minnesota.

Shortly after J. G. Baker settled on section 26, where he died.

During the next year, James Estep, W. O. Edgington, John R. Buckmaster, Daniel Walters, Isaac Null, Samuel Armstrong and William Wilsey effected settlements.

James Estep settled on section 17, where he remained about one year, and then left the county. The place is now owned by Geo. R. Rayner.

HISTORY OF BREMER COUNTY.

W. O. Edgington made selection on section 16, remained a few years, and then moved from the county.

John R. Buckmaster came from Indiana, and located on section 17. Here he remained until about 1859, when he went to Missouri.

Wm. Wilsey settled on section 16, but removed to Sioux City during the fall of 1853. The land is now owned by J. Andrews.

Daniel Watters settled on section 10, where he remained until his death in 1866.

In 1852 came William Powell, Samuel Beelah, E. M. Wright, Nathan Payton, Nathaniel Harris and brother, with their cousin, M. Sumner.

William Powell selected a place in section 27, on land now owned by William Scudder. He moved to Jefferson township in 1855.

E. M. Wright was from Wisconsin and settled on section 15, where he remained until 1865, when he removed to Linn county and thence to Nebraska.

Nathan Payton came from Ohio and located on section 3, where he lived about two years and then moved to Waverly.

Nathaniel Payton, with his brother and cousin, settled on section 4, where the brother died. Nathaniel, with his cousin, returned to Massachusetts, from whence they came.

Mason Eveland, the oldest living settler in LaFayette township, and son of John and Elizabeth (Jones) Eveland was born in Calhoun county, Illinois, January 18, 1817. His father was a native of Virginia, while his mother was born in New York State. In 1823 his father moved to Fulton county, Illinois, and was the second white settler in that county. His father died in 1832 and his mother followed in 1851. As his father was constantly in advance of civilization, young Mason had but very few advantages of education. In September, 1851, soon after the death of his mother, he came to Bremer county, arriving here October 3. He located in Jackson township on land now owned by J. K. L. Maynard, where he entered a farm, but in 1852 sold it and took a claim of 320 acres in LaFayette township, and in January, 1853, located on this farm, 237 acres of which he still owns. February 5, 1836, he was married to Miss Lucinda Stuffle-beam, a native of Kentucky. Of the ten children, Henry, Charles, John, James, Austin, Lucinda, now Mrs. John W. Ferguson, and Robert Boone, are living. Mr. Eveland was the first white child born on the military tract in Illinois, between the Mississippi and Illinois rivers.

William A. Pelton made a selection on section 10, during the same year. He is still a resident of the township. He is a native of New York State, born in Chatauqua county, June 26, 1828. He is a son of Ransom and Mary B. (Waggoner) Pelton. In 1842 his parents came west to McHenry county, Illinois, and settled on a farm, W. A. remaining with his father until he had helped him to get a home of eighty acres. He then engaged in railroading and working by the month until 1853, when he turned his steps westward, coming to Bremer county, where he entered his present farm of 160 acres, on section 10; but he made no improvements until after the war. At the breaking out of the rebellion he was among the first to answer the Nation's call, from this county. Enlisting, July 10, 1861, in Company G, Ninth Iowa, as a private, he was soon afterward promoted to Corporal, in which capacity he was honorably discharged, at Louisville, Kentucky, in July, 1865. He immediately returned to his farm, in Lafayette township, which he began to improve, and, in 1866, built his present residence. He held, previous to the war, the office of township clerk. In politics he is a republican. He has been a member of the Baptist Church for some time. In 1867 he was united in wedlock with Miss Permelia Wright, a native of Wisconsin. She bore him two sons—Ransom D., and Willie Wright—and died, in 1877, at the age of twenty-nine years. In February, 1882, Mr. Pelton married Calista G. Cutler, who was born at Peoria, Illinois.

Among those who came this season and soon after, were John Miles, Heman Miles, Horace Wallace, John Worthington, Edward Tyrrell, William Vandiver, Justus Hall and Isaac Null. Then others came in more rapidly. Sketches of a few prominent citizens are here given, indicating the general character of the settlement.

Jacob M. Eveland, second son of Henry and Aurenna (Miller) Eveland, was born in Fulton county, Ill., April 21, 1841. In 1854, his parents moved to Bremer county, and settled in Lafayette township, where Jacob has since resided, excepting two and one-half years spent in Davis County, Iowa. His educational advantages were very limited, as he had to assist his father in preparing their future home. In 1875, he bought his present farm, on section 10, on which he has since resided. In January, 1868, he was married to Miss Angeline Stufflebeam, daughter of Joshua and Polly Stufflebeam, one of the pioneers of Bremer county. Seven children have been born to them, four of whom are now living—Nellie Alavanda, Jacob Clarence, Bertha Aveline Aurora, Elfie.

Parker Lucas, one of the pioneers of Bremer county, is a native of Ohio, born in Montgomery county, July 26, 1814. His parents were David and Rachel (Yount) Lucas; his father was a native of Germany, and his mother of Virginia. In 1816 his parents moved to Darke county, Ohio, and in 1823, to Vigo county, Indiana, and in 1826, to Carroll county, Indiana, where they were among the early settlers of that part of the State. His father arrived in that county, a poor man; his entire worldly possessions being one hundred dollars, which he paid for eighty acres of land, he settled twenty-five miles from a store or mill, and even had they been nearer, they were without money to buy. The old proverb, "Necessity is the mother of invention," was practically proven in their case. The family were almost destitute as regards clothing. One day while the father was out, he picked up some nettle stalks and brought them home; upon an examination of them, the mother concluded she could use the "tow" to clothe the family. Accordingly a large amount was collected and woven into cloth, and from this thirty-two yards of "nettle" linen was made, enough to clothe the entire family. Here the subject of this sketch grew to manhood, and in 1833, was married to Nancy Moore, also a native of Ohio. In 1856 they came west to Bremer county, and soon after settled on section 18, Lafayette township, where he now owns a farm of 107 acres. Seven

N. A. Reeves.

children have been born to them—William V., now State Auditor; John T., now living in Oregon; Christal David, now living in Pocahontas county, Iowa; James A., a resident of Dakota; Isaac E., cashier of Allison Bank; Litia, wife of L. L. Lush, cashier of Bremer County Bank; and Martha Ann, now the wife of Lawrence Reed, this town.

Henry Eveland was born in Ohio, in 1814. His parents soon after moved to Fulton county, Illinois, where his father was one of the pioneer settlers. In 1854 he came to Bremer county, and located on section 28, Lafayette township. In September, 1835, he was married to Lorena Miller. Eight children were born to them, seven of whom are still living—Samuel, Jacob, John Mason, James Duncan, Harriett, wife of John Scott, living in Nebraska; Anna, now the wife of Thomas McRoberts; Indiana, now the wife of George Elliott. His wife died March, 1870. He was married in the spring of 1873, to Martha Bingham, born in Greene county, Indiana, January 31, 1832, and daughter of John and Levisa (Bays) Burch. She was married to Wm. Bingham in February, 1850. One daughter was the result of this union—Nancy Jane, now the wife of Nelson Ross, of Lafayette township. Mr. Eveland died May 12, 1878. Nelson Ross and Nancy Jane Bingham were married in 1865; he is a native of Indiana, born in 1843. They have seven children living—James, Henry, Albert, Alva, Loraine and Mabel.

Norman A. Reeves, one of the enterprising farmers of Lafayette township, was born January 30, 1833, in Cayuga county, New York. His father was Mannassah Reeves, a native of Long Island, and his mother, Esther (Perry) Reeves, a native of Vermont. In 1852, the family moved to Buchanan county, Iowa, where Norman remained until he attained his majority. He then came to Waverly, and for one year worked in a saw mill, and then worked one year helping to build a grist mill for W. P. Harmon. He then purchased a half interest in the saw mill, and ran it two years, when he traded his interest for a farm in Jackson township, on which he resided seven years. He then located on section 20, Lafayette township, and now owns 105 acres of land. Mr. Reeves has given a great deal of attention to fruit and shrubbery culture, and has on his farm a grove of about fifty thousand trees, of the European larch, soft maple, white ash, black-walnut, and the different varieties of evergreens. He is a member of the State Horticultural Society, and has given much time and attention to experimenting in fruits, and has written several instructive articles on fruit culture. Mr. Reeves is a member of the society of Knights of Honor, of Waverly. He has been a member of the Baptist Church for some years, and was one of the prime movers of the Spring Lake Sabbath School, and has been its superintendent since its organization. He was married March 30, 1856, to Miss Rhoda Willey, daughter of Tallman and Mary (Bush) Willey, of Tompkins county, New York. Five children have blessed this union—Elsie, now the wife of Byron J. Butler, of Floyd county; Elmer M., James E., and Charles and Minnie, twins. Mr. Reeves has the largest artificial grove in Bremer county, containing over 50,000 trees, of different varieties, all of which have been planted by his own hands. He is also more extensively engaged in horticultural pursuits than any other person in Bremer county.

James Andrews, son of James and Anna (Barnes) Andrews, is a native of Chautauqua county, New York, born August 24, 1822. His father was born in Connecticut, and his mother in New York. His educational advantages were limited to the district schools of that day. In 1845 his parents came west, to McHenry county, Illinois, and settled on a farm, where his mother died, in August, 1873, and his father one month later. James remained at home until 1856, when he came to Bremer county, and settled on a farm on section 15, which he had purchased in 1854, and on which he built a log house in 1855. In 1856, just previous to coming to his new home, he was married to Miss Sarah E. Pelton, daughter of Ransom and Mary B. (Waggoner) Pelton, formerly of Chautauqua county, New York; but then residents of McHenry county, Illinois. Together they came to Bremer county. In 1866 he built his present handsome residence, and now owns and cultivates a fine farm of 158¼ acres. In politics Mr. Andrews is a republican, and has always taken an active part in the political interests of his township, having held, at different times, nearly all of the township offices. Of the five children born to them, four are living— Charles, Anna, Elva, and Nellie. He has been a member of the Baptist Church for thirteen years, and his wife has been a member since her seventeenth year.

Wm. M. Colton, one of the leading farmers of Lafayette township, and the oldest son of Calvin S. and Harriet (Hatch) Colton, is a native of Vermont, born in Bennington county, May 18, 1832. In 1849, his parents moved to DeKalb county, Illinois, his father being one of the pioneers of that county. Here Wm. grew to manhood, and in 1856, came west and located in Lafayette township on a farm on section 20, where he has since resided, on land he had entered in 1853. He now owns a fine farm of 220 acres. Mr. Colton has held various town offices, and is at present one of the township trustees. He is a member of the Methodist Episcopal Church, and was one of the founders of the M. E. class in this township. In 1865, he was joined in wedlock with Miss Nettie Evans, a native of Canada. Eight children have blessed this union—Grant, Hattie, James Evans, Charles, Lida, Cora, Roy and Mortimer.

S. C. Krieger, a native of Northumberland county, Pennsylvania, was born June 21, 1836. He is the second son of Samuel and Mary Magdaline (Conrad) Krieger, both natives of that State. He was reared on a farm, receiving but a limited education. In the spring of 1857, the family came west and settled on section 5, Lafayette township. Here his mother died April 2, 1861, and his father March 25, 1872. In 1864, he was married to Matilda Wilson, a native of Ireland, and soon after settled on his present farm of 190 acres, which is one of the best in Bremer county. Their children are Grant, Ida, Willie, Mary, Gilbert and Lewtie.

Joshua Stufflebeam is a Kentuckian by birth, and was born October 10, 1821. In 1829 his parents moved to Fulton county, Illinois, and in 1852 he came to Bremer county and settled on section 34, Lafayette township, where he entered 320 acres of land. In 1861 he moved to his present location on section 23. He has held the office of trustee one term. He was married in 1840 to Polly Allsbury, a native of Indiana. They have seven children living—Thomas, Jeremiah, Charles Newton, Joshua, Joseph Lee, Angeline and Priscilla.

Jonathan Freeman, who is a native of New York State, was born in Ulster county, July 9, 1843. He is a son of Elijah and Sarah M. (Longyear) Freeman, both natives of that State. The son remained at home on his father's farm until twelve years of age, and then moved, with the family, to Camillus, New York, where he grew to manhood, attending and teaching school. At twenty-one years of age his health failed him to such an extent that he was compelled to give up his former pursuits. He then engaged as book-keeper in a manufacturing establishment at Southington, Connecticut. In 1866 he was united in wedlock to Miss Aurelia L. Hotchkiss, who was born in Southington, Connecticut, and is a daughter of Alfred and Laura Ann (Plant) Hotchkiss, both natives of that State. In 1869 the young couple came west and settled in Lafayette township, where they have since resided. Mr. Freeman is a greenbacker, and has taken quite an active part in the politics of the township, having held, at different times, several of the town offices. He held the office of Secretary of the Farmer's Insurance Company until 1881, at which time he was compelled to resign on account of ill-health. Mr. and Mrs. Freeman are both members of the Baptist church of Waverly. They have been blessed with two children, of whom Lena May is the only one now living.

Daniel H. Chambers is a native of Starkey county, New York, born December 23, 1821. He is the eldest son of Christopher and Phœbe (Alden) Chambers. He was reared on a farm, and received but a limited education; remaining at home until he attained his majority; he came west in 1842 to Belvidere, Boone county, Illinois, where he remained about eight years, and then began farming in that county, which occupation he followed until 1856, when he came to Iowa, settling at Turkey Grove, three miles east of Clarksville, on a farm. Here he remained seven years, then traded farms and located at Janesville, where he was engaged in farming for seven years. He then settled on section 14, Lafayette township. Mr. Chambers has always taken an active part in the politics of the township, and has held, at different times, the offices of trustee, president of the school board, and is at present director of his school district. In 1844 he was joined in wedlock with Miss Mary L. Lawrence, a native of New York State. Seven children have been born to them—Joseph S., who died June 4, 1882; Lauren L., who died during the spring of 1875; Lydia J., now the wife of Ralph Watkins, of Waverly; Noel Rew, Charles L. and George Avery.

N. B. Marsh was born in Victor, Ontario county, New York, February 23, 1841. He is the third son of Isaac and Esther (Rawson) Marsh, both natives of New York. In 1845 his parents moved to Lockport, New York, and in 1859 he came west to Chicago. His educational advantages were attained at the Union school of

Lockport, and Sloan's Commercial College, Chicago, graduating from that institution. In the spring of 1861, at the first call for troops, he enlisted in the Nineteenth Illinois Infantry, afterward known as the "Bloody Nineteenth," but through the interposition of friends, was not allowed to go. Early in 1862, he enlisted in Sturgess' Riflemen, afterward McClellan's body guard; he was once more detained. Upon attaining his majority, he enlisted, May, 1862, in Company E, Sixty-fifth Illinois Infantry, and was honorably discharged at Camp Douglas, on account of disability, four months afterward. He then returned to Lockport, where he was appointed assistant postmaster, which position he held until 1868, when he came to Bremer county, and engaged in farming on section 22, Lafayette township. For the past seven years, Mr. Marsh has held the office of school director. He was married in 1865, to Ellen H. Taylor, a native of Niagara county, New York. They have two sons living—Burton T. and Norman Rawson.

D. E. Loveland was born in Niagara county, New York, April 22, 1824. He is a son of Thomas and Betsy Loveland, of that county. The family afterward lived in Cataraugus county, New York, then in McHenry county, Illinois, and Greene county, Wisconsin. In 1865 D. E. came to Bremer county, and has since lived on section 13, Lafayette township. He now owns a fine farm of 200 acres, all under cultivation. He was married in 1847, to Adeline Johnson, a native of New York State. They have five children living— Thomas, William, Robert, Cyrus, Martha, and an adopted son, Theodore.

Benjamin Bennett was born in Lancashire, England, July 7, 1833. He is son of James and Sarah (Higgenbotham) Bennett, both natives of England. In 1849 the family came to America, and settled in Marquette county, Wisconsin, where he was engaged in farming until 1864. He then came to Lafayette township, and located on section 8, where he remained three years, and then located on section 20, where he now resides, and owns a fine farm of 240 acres. In 1858 he was married, at Portage, Wisconsin, to Elizabeth Ann Slater. Of the fourteen children born to them, thirteen are now living—James Howard, Ainsworth Avelock, Sarah Alberta, Robert Henry, Edward Allen, Zela Ada, William Herbert, Oscar Horace, Rupert Wilson, Willard Melvin, Clarence Eugene, Vivian Bell, and Guy. His father died in 1861, and his mother in 1870.

John Curtis was born in Kent, England, January 17, 1813. He is a son of William and Charlotte (Gibbs) Curtis, both natives of England. In 1828 the family came to America, and settled in Madison county, New York. John afterward came west to Dodge county, Wisconsin, and in the spring of 1857 settled in Douglas township, Bremer county, where he remained until 1860, when he settled on his present farm of 175 acres, two and a half miles northeast of Waverly. In 1858 he married Ruby Ann Harris, a native of New York State. Their children are—Ida May, Fred, Ruby A., Nettie E. and Lorinda— all living at home.

Willard S. Grover, born in Cataraugus county, New York, July 25, 1831, is a son of John and Sarah (Burbank) Grover.

His father was a native of New Jersey, and his mother of Massachusetts. In 1840 his parents moved to Winnebago county, Illinois, where Willard grew to manhood. After the death of his father in 1864, (his mother having died October 9, 1858) he came west to Bremer county, and settled on section 2, where he now owns a fine farm of 180 acres, which is one of the best improved in the county. Although Mr. Grover has never taken a very active part in the politics of the county, he has held several of the minor town offices. In 1858 he was joined in wedlock with Miss Caroline Knapp, of Orleans county, New York. They have been blessed with two children—Elmer and Clara, both living.

Abraham Wade was born in Cambridgeshire, England, April 29, 1823. His father was John Wade, and his mother, Elizabeth (Budge) Wade, both natives of England. His father died in 1830, and his mother in 1843. In 1851, Abraham determined to seek his fortune in the New World, and accordingly arrived in New York during the fall of that year, and in the spring of 1852, located in Cook county, Illinois, where he engaged in ditching on the low lands near Chicago for two years, when he came to Bremer county and entered land, which he owned until 1864, when he enlisted in Company H, of the Fifteenth Iowa Infantry, and served until honorably discharged at Davenport, at the close of the war. He then returned to Waverly and was engaged in running a vineyard and sorghum mill, until 1870, when he settled on his present location on section 3, of Lafayette township, and now owns 310 acres of fine farming land. Mr. Wade has held the office of township trustee, and is the present treasurer of the township. He was married in 1854, to Miss Martha Ingersoll, a native of Illinois. They have been blessed with six children—Edith, Emma, Abraham Lincoln, William, Ralph and Nellie.

Harvey Fuller was born in Cayuga county, New York, May 29, 1847. He is the eldest son of Charles and Lois (Cox) Fuller, both natives of New York. In 1849, the family moved to Onondaga county, New York, and, in 1856, to Moline, Illinois, where his father was engaged in mercantile pursuits. Harvey received a good common school education, and a commercial course at Davenport, Iowa, and, in 1862, although scarcely fifteen years of age, he enlisted in Company H, Sixty-ninth Illinois Volunteer Infantry, as a drummer boy. He was honorably discharged therefrom, and afterwards enlisted, in 1865, in Company I, Twenty-eighth Illinois Infantry, and was honorably discharged, at Brownsville, Texas, at the close of the war. In the early part of 1866, he came to Lafayette township, where his father had settled in 1865. His father died in 1869, and his mother in 1855. In December, 1868, Mr. Fuller was married to Miss Maggie Wright. She died in October, 1869. He married December 24, 1870, Miss Nettie Fritcher, a native of Wisconsin. Mr. Fuller has one of the finest orchards in the county, and is now engaged in horticultural pursuits, on an extensive scale. He was clerk of the township for one year, and was elected justice of the peace at the last election. He is correspondent for various newspapers in the State.

HISTORY OF BREMER COUNTY.

James Kelly, born in Orange county, Indiana, Feb. 14, 1819, is a son of James and Ailsil (Liston) Kelly, both natives of Kentucky. His father was a soldier in the Revolution. In 1826 the family moved to Coles county, Illinois, where his father died in 1849, his mother in 1828. Here he remained and in 1845 was married to Elizabeth Sullivan, a native of Virginia, born February 12, 1827. He afterward moved to Wisconsin, and in 1865 settled in Lafayette township, where he has since resided. His wife died May 8, 1866, and is buried in the Spring Lake cemetery. They were blessed with eight children, seven of whom are still living—Cordelia, born in Coles county, Illinois, April 7, 1849, now the wife of Theodore Holmes, of Polk county, Minnesota; Mary A., born in Coles county, Illinois, in 1847, died in November, 1848; Larabia, born in Coles county, November 14, 1851, is now the wife of James Kelly, living in Dakota; Lucina, born in Coles county, March 10, 1855, now the wife of Charles Kellogg of Butler county; Noah, born November 17, 1857, in Lafayette county, Wisconsin; James P., born July 10, 1860, in the same county, died December 5, 1862; William, born March 23, 1863, in the same county; Josephine, born in Bremer county, January 13, 1866, and is now living at home.

D. B. Fox, son of Benjamin and Melinda Fox, was born in Fulton county, Illinois, December 7, 1842. Losing his parents when a child, he was reared in the family of James Bevard, who came to Bremer county, in 1851, and died here in 1863. His wife, Margaret Bevard, died December 29, 1881. In 1851, they settled in Jefferson township, where young Fox grew to manhood's estate. In 1862 he enlisted in Company B, Fourteenth Iowa Volunteer Infantry, and served in the cause of the Union, until honorably discharged, November 16, 1864. He then returned to Jefferson, and in 1868, moved to section 18, Lafayette township, where he has since resided. September 17, 1868, he was married to Matilda L. Weller, a native of Cook county, Illinois, daughter of John and Hester Weller, of that county. They have had four children—Hattie E., Verner D., Olive May and Lettie E.

Thomas McRoberts was born in Fleming county, Kentucky, August 3, 1834. He is a son of James Henry and Martha (Rollins) McRoberts, his father was a native of Ireland and his mother of Scotland. In 1838 his parents moved to Calloway county, Missouri, and in the spring of 1849, to Linn county, Iowa, and in the fall of that year came to Jefferson township, Bremer county, and in the spring of 1850, moved to Janesville, where his father died soon after. In 1861 Thomas moved to Lafayette township, and in 1869 to his present location on section 19. In 1862 he was married to Miss Margaret Anna Eveland, daughter of Henry Eveland, a pioneer of this township. Six children have been born to them, of which Angelina, James, Hattie and Edward are living. Two died when children—Blanche, nine years of age; and Martha Francis, six and a half years of age.

Jacob Cagley was born in Johnson county, Indiana, July 15, 1845. He is a son of Michael and Elizabeth (Keosling) Cagley. His father was a native of Virginia, and his mother of Tennessee. In 1856, his parents went to Chickasaw county, Iowa, and settled on a farm where his father became one of the largest land owners of that county. In 1866, Jacob settled on section 3, Lafayette township, where he now owns 460 acres, He was married in 1867, to Miss Martha Ann Cuffel, a native of Indiana. They have four children living—John H., Lucia V., Fred E. and Roy L. His father died in Chickasaw, in 1881. His mother is still living.

John R. Foster was born in Maine, February 13, 1836. He is the eldest son of Leighton and Clarissa (Ricker) Foster, both natives of Maine. In 1839, his parents moved to Boone county, Illinois. In 1857, John settled in Nodaway county, Missouri, and in August, 1862, enlisted in Company B, Thirty-fifth Missouri, and served the Union honorably until discharged at the close of the war, in 1865, he then returned to Nodaway county, and in 1866, disposed of his interest there and came to Bremer county, and has since been a resident of Lafayette township. Mr. Foster has taken an active part in the educational interests of his township, and has held the office of school director. In 1861, he was joined in wedlock with Miss Carrie Wagor, a native of New York State. They have five children living—Mamie, Clara, Mabel, Frank, and an infant, Roy.

Seth L. Foster was born in Piscatiquis county, Maine, June 20, 1842. He is the youngest son of Leighton and Clarissa (Ricker) Foster, who are still living, and both natives of Maine. He lived with the family in Maine and Boone county, Illinois, until 1866, when he settled on section 30, Lafayette township, and now owns a farm of 124 acres, all under improvement.

In 1868 he married Miss Sarah S. Conner, a native of Kentucky. They have three children—Arthur L., Effie R. and Jesse A., all living.

Patrick Boylson, one of the pioneers of Bremer county, is a native of Tipperary county, Ireland, and was born in 1831. In 1848 he came to America, and settled on a farm in Rensselaer county, New York, on which he remained four years; he then spent two years in Ohio, and in 1855 settled in Waverly, and in 1860 settled on his present farm on section 30, where he now owns 300 acres of land. In 1854 he was married to Mary Coleman, a native of Cork county, Ireland, born October 10, 1832. Of the six children born to them—William, Mary, Anna, James and George, are living.

P. Oberdorf was born in Northumberland county, Pennsylvania, July 17, 1817. He is a son of John and Mary (Strow) Oberdorf, both natives of that State. His mother died when he was a child, and his father, in 1870. He was reared on a farm, receiving a limited education. In 1857 he came to Waverly, and bought a third interest in a saw mill, which he retained for six years, but misfortune overtook him, a freshet came, and destroyed the earnings of a life time. He then rented a farm three miles south of Waverly, on which he lived three years, he then lived one mile north of Waverly, four years, then settled on section 24, where he now owns 131 acres of land. Mr. Oberdorf has held the office of road supervisor and school director, and is at present, treasurer of District No. 8. He was married, in 1844, to Miss Amasa Dawson, a native of Pennsylvania. They have nine children living—Mary Alice, now the wife of Charles Miller, of Osceola county,

Iowa; Lewis Cass, a resident of Bremer county; Rosanna, wife of Joseph E. Jewell, of Butler county; Alexander, living at home; Sarah Jane, wife of Alaskis Eisenhart, a merchant of Tripoli; Laura Melissa, John, Minerva, and William Henry.

A. B. Wilson, born in Niagara county, New York, July 27, 1830, is a son of Calvin and Hannah (Sherwood) Wilson. He was reared on a farm, and remained in his native county until July, 1864, when he came to Lafayette township, and settled on section 26, where he remained until 1872, when he bought his present farm of eighty acres, on section 13, where he has since resided. Mr. Wilson held the office of school director for eight years. His father died in New York State, in September, 1877. His mother is still living. He was married in 1854 to Miss Angeline Taylor, a native of New York. They have four children living—Carrie, Nettie, Whitten Taylor and Maud.

Joseph Bowen, one of the leading farmers of Lafayette township, was born in Wethersfield, Trumbull county, Ohio, February 5, 1832. He is a son of Peleg and Rachel (Bennett) Bowen, both natives of the Buckeye State. His father died in Butler county, in 1879; and his mother still lives in Shell Rock. In 1846, the family moved to Pennsylvania, where Joseph remained until 1855, when he came to Butler county, Iowa, and worked at his trade (carpenter's) until 1865. He then settled on section 22, Lafayette township, and now owns a fine farm of 195 acres. Mr. Bowen has held the office of township trustee, several times. He was married in October, 1852, to Miss Merilla Bussey, a native of Trumbull county, Ohio. Of their four children, James H., Elmer S., and Sarah Alice are living. His wife died April 7, 1865. In October, 1865, he was married to Sarah A. Miller, a native of Ohio. Four children have blessed this union—Nettie May, Minnie Florence, Edith L., and Lelland P., who died March 1, 1871.

Eri Terry, son of David and Elinor (Wells) Terry, was born in Otsego county, New York, March 3, 1827. The family soon after removed to Courtland county, and in 1840 to McHenry county, Illinois; here Eri remained until 1855, when he came to Bremer county, and settled in Polk township the following fall, residing there until 1880, when he moved to section 2, Lafayette township, although he still retains the ownership of his first farm, and has 230 acres in the county. Mr. Tery held the office of justice, several years, was twice elected supervisor, beside several of the minor town offices. In 1850 he was married to Miss Cornelia Madole, a native of New York State, who bore him four children—Arthur Hugh, Elsie Adelle, Mina Estelle and David Orr. Mrs. Terry died November 27, 1871. Mr. Terry's father is still living, at a very advanced age, 83.

ORGANIC.

The first election held in this township, as organized, with its present boundaries, was at Stephenson and Dudgeon's Mill, December 25, 1858. The officers appointed to hold said election were as follows:—Judges of election, Jas. Andrews, W. V. Lucas and Samuel Pratt; clerks, S. B. Ostrander and W. A. Pelton. The follow-

ing persons were made township officers: Justices of the peace, W. W. Norris and L. B. Ostrander; constables, N. A. Millet and Henry Eveland; trustees, Thomas Dudgeon, Samuel Lease, William Vandever; clerk, W. V. Lucas. The list of officers from that time to the present, are as follows:

1860—James Skillen, justice of the peace; H. H. Cave and W. P. Stephenson, constables; Scoville Shattuck, John Wiles and Daniel Briggs, trustees; W. V. Lucas, clerk, and James Andrews, assessor.

1861—Robert J. Stephenson, township supervisor; Scoville Shattuck and L. B. Ostrander, justices; Wm. Vandever, Wm. Norris and Thomas Dudgeon, trustees; H. H. Cave, assessor; Samuel Pratt, clerk; Wm. Vandever and James Skillen, constables.

1862—Thomas Downing, supervisor; Geo. B. Miller, assessor; H. H. Cave, clerk, but failed to qualify, and Samuel Pratt was appointed in his stead; W. A. Miller and John F. Lees, constables; Samuel Wilson, Daniel Walters and James Skillen, trustees.

1863—Philander Ingersoll, supervisor, Samuel Pratt, clerk; John Will, assessor; he afterwards resigned, and Samuel Pratt was appointed to fill the vacancy; Scoville Shattuck and A. H. Fleischer, justices; Thomas Dudgeon and John F. Lees, constables; Samuel K. Eveland, N. A. Miller and Farman Dudgeon, trustees; the two last resigned, and Henry Eveland and John F. Lees were appointed.

1864—Philander Ingersoll, supervisor; John Cockman, clerk; James Skillen, assessor; Wm. Vandever, Joshua Stufflebeam and Solomon Renn, trustees.

1865—G. W. Leap and John F. Lees, justices; Joshua Stufflebeam, John Wile and Daniel Walters, trustees; John Cockman, clerk; S. C. Krieger, assessor; Jacob M. Eveland and Thomas C. Stephenson, constables.

1866—Norman Reeves, supervisor; James Andrews, clerk; James M. Deyoe, assessor; Wm. Westervelt, justice; Norman Sherman, Edward Fairhurst and Daniel Hurlbut, trustees.

1867—James Andrews, clerk; Edward Fairhurst, assessor; James S. Conner, S. Grover and Joseph Bowen, trustees; Wm. Somberger and Norman Sherman, justices; P. H. Cave and Mason F. Spaulding, constables.

1868—James Andrews, clerk; S. Terry, assessor; James S. Conner, justice; George C. Stephenson, supervisor; Thomas Monogue and John Abraham, constables; James S. Conner, Sanford Vosseler, and G. D. Russell, trustees.

1869—Seth L. Foster, Calvin Kingsley, and Amos Hurlbut, trustees; Sanford Vosseler, and James Andrews, justices; John Vosseler, and William A. Pelton, constables; Otis Clark, clerk, and Stillman Terry, assessor.

1870—Otis Clark, supervisor; D. H. Chambers, S. G. Miller, and N. B. Marsh, trustees; Norman Sherman, justice; C. D. Russell, and J. E. Lucas, constables; James Andrews, clerk, and James S. Conner, assessor.

1872—William H. Jones, and Jonathan Freeman, justices; John Vosseler and H. H. Cave, trustees; John Cockman, clerk; William H. Jones, assessor; D. C. Jones, constable.

1873—William C. Colton, and M. M. Watkins, justices; S. G. Miller, N. F. Bowen, and Noel Rew, trustees; John Cockman, clerk; Joseph Jewell, assessor; Calvin S. Colton, and J. S. Chambers, constables.

1874—Daniel Platt, and M. M. Watkins, justices; George R. Haner, assessor; Jonathan Freeman, clerk; P. H. Caves, Calvin Kingsley, and G. C. Stephenson, trustees; James Andrews, and J. S. Chambers, constables.

1875—G. C. Stephenson, and D. B. Fox, justices; N. L. Shaw, assessor; John Cockman, clerk; G. R. Haner, P. H. Cave, and Joseph Bowen, trustees; H. H. Cave, and Joseph Chambers, constables.

1876—G. C. Stephenson, and H. H. Cave, justices; G. R. Haner, assessor; Harvey Fuller, clerk; G. S. Miller, N. B. Marsh, and H. H. Cave, trustees; G. C. Chambers, and N. R. Haner, constables.

1877—Parker Lucas, justice; H. B. Miller, assessor; John Cockman, clerk; G. R. Haner, Joseph Chambers, and Lawrence Rew, trustees.

1878—George C. Stephenson and Charles Schlaberg, justices; William B. Brown, assessor; John Cockman, clerk; Jonathan Freeman, James M. Deyoe and Marvin Hurlbert, trustees; Charles Pratt and John Mott, constables.

1879—M. M. VanDorn, justice; N. A. Reeves, assessor; John Cockman, clerk; trustee for three years, William Colton.

1880—Trustee for three years, A. H. Sheldon; John Cockman, clerk for three years; J. M. Deyoe, assessor; J. C. Stephenson and G. R. Haner, justices; John Mott and Charles L. Pratt, constables.

The present officers are as follows: Trustees: H. H. Cave, Solomon Renn and A. H. Shelden; clerk, John Cockman; assessor, H. B. Miller; justices, G. C. Stevenson, George R. Haner; constables, Charles Chambers and John Barrick.

EDUCATIONAL.

The first school taught on the west side of the river, was in a log house owned by William R. Lucas, on section 17, during the winter of 1856-7, by the widow Fisher. The first school taught on the east side of the river was in a frame building on land now owned by Joseph Bowen, on section 22, during the winter of 1857-8 by Mr. Brewer. This house was burned in 1864. There are now nine schoolhouses in the township, built at an average cost of $600 each.

FIRST THINGS.

The first religious service was held at the house of Mason Eveland, during the spring of 1853, by Rev. Andrew Goforth, a Baptist minister.

The first marriage was that of Ariel Rima to Miss Harriet Freeman, at the residence of H. Waters, on section 15, in 1855. These parties now live in California.

The first birth was a son to E. M. Wright, in 1852. This child died in about three months, and was the first death in the township. He was buried in the woods on section 15, but the remains were afterward moved to section 22.

Another early death was that of Miss W. O. Edgington, January, 1855. She was buried in the Spring Lake Cemetery. This was the first interment on those grounds. This burial place was not laid out until some years later.

RELIGIOUS.

Services of this character had been held from time to time, at the dwellings of different early settlers, but in 1858, an organization was effected, with Rev. Jas. Skillen as leader. Among the first members were Wm. R. Lucas and wife, Parker Lucas and wife, Scoville Shattuck and wife, John Nile and wife, Wm. V. Lucas and wife, and John Gilmore and wife. The first meetings were held in the Spring Lake Schoolhouse. In 1862 the organization was discontinued.

SPRING LAKE POSTOFFICE.

This office was established in 1857, and Edward Fairhurst was appointed postmaster. It was located on section 17, at the residence of Mr. Fairhurst. He was succeeded by H. H. Cave; he, in turn, by John Cockman. It was discontinued May 3, 1873. Each of the postmasters kept the office at his residence.

CEMETERIES.

There are two cemeteries in this township—one located on the southeast corner of section 17, in which Mrs. W. O. Edgington was the first to receive burial. The other is known as "Andrew's Cemetery," and is located on the southeast quarter of section 15, and was platted in 1865. The first interment was Emma, infant daughter of Joseph Brown, who died December 30, 1865, aged three months and fifteen days.

GENERAL MATTERS.

A saw-mill was built in this township in 1858, by Dr. Burbanks, Mr. Foster, Thomas Downing and Alfred Godridge, on section 28, on land entered by Mason Eveland, and now owned by Calvin S. Colton. The machinery was taken away and the site abandoned, in 1867.

The Stephenson steam saw-mill was built in 1857, by William and William P. Stephenson. It was a thirty horse-power, of Woodbury & Company's patent. It was first located on the west side of the Cedar river, on section 8, where it remained six months, and was then moved to the east side, on section 16. This occurred during the spring of 1858, which was an extremely wet season. The Cedar river was very high, and to move so large a mill was a great undertaking. But William Stephenson was equal to the occasion. The wood-work was removed without much difficulty, but the removal of the boiler seemed to be an impossibility. The river was so high that the water backed up in the slough on which the mill stood, and surrounded it, up to the top of the bed on which the boiler rested. He corked the boiler, made it air tight, rolled it from its bed into the water, and floated it down, about a mile and one-half, to a point opposite its present location, where it was pulled out. The settlers turned out to see Stephenson's boiler sink when committed to the water, but their feelings can be better imagined than described, when it glided smoothly on the water, like so much wood. It was owned by the parties named for the greater part of the time, and in 1879, was torn down and moved to Wisconsin.

CHAPTER XXV.

LEROY TOWNSHIP.

This township lies near the northeast corner of the county, Sumner intervening on the east; on the north is Chickasaw county; on the west, Frederika township; on the south, Fremont and Dayton. It has an area of twenty-one and one-half sections of land, or about 13,760 acres. It is watered by two small creeks, having their source in Chickasaw county, and making confluence near the south line of section 23, and passing out in one stream on the east half of section 34.

The soil is a dark, sandy loam, underlain with clay. About eighteen inches from the surface is a "hard-pan," generally about four inches thick.

The township was originally about one-half covered with timber; but much of this has now been cut away. The surface is gently undulating, though there is some waste land, too wet for cultivation, not being sufficiently drained. The inhabitants are of a mixed class, mostly Germans and Irish.

EARLY SETTLEMENT.

The first settlement was made in June, 1854, by Patrick O'Day, locating on section 2, where he yet lives; W. A. Moulton, Emmor Flood and Nelson Long, on section 13.

Patrick O'Day was born February 15, 1824, in the Parish of Parteen, county Clare, Ireland. He is the son of P. O'Day and Kate Frost, natives of the county Clare. In 1849, he emigrated with his family to America, landing in New York July 4, and without waiting any time started for the west, remaining in Chicago about three months, then went south and worked for Captain J. B. Eads upon a wrecking boat on the Mississippi river, making his home at St. Louis and New Orleans. He was married in Chicago in August, 1850, to Miss Mary Foley, daughter of Hugh F. and Bridget Foley, a native of county Clare, Ireland, by whom he has had ten children—Robert, Hattie Kate, Mary, William and Anne. About two years after marriage, Mr. O'Day came with his family to Bremer county, and settled on the land in Leroy township, where he has since resided. At the time of his coming to the township he found only one family. Mr. O'Day is one of the leading farmers of his township, has at the present time 613 acres of prairie, and 120 of timber. The year after Mr. O'Day came to America he was followed by his father, mother and three brothers, who came to Illinois, where his mother died, when they all came to Bremer county, his father dying April 16, 1876. Mr. O'Day has held several local offices; has always worked with the democratic party, but is now a greenbacker. Himself and family are members of the Catholic Church.

W. A. Moulton remained here until 1865 when he removed to Missouri. The place is now owned by W. B. Barnes, who occupies it. Emmor Flood still remains on the old homestead, and Nelson Long also remains on section 13. In September, 1854, J. N. Fowle, Nathaniel J. Perry, D. C. Thompson and Stephen Parkhurst arrived. Fowle located on section 1, where he remained about one year, when he left for parts unknown, having platted a town on another man's land, and sold lots to different parties. This place was called Leroy.

Perry made his selection on the same section, where he remained a number of years, when he went to Missouri. Mr. Pelton now occupies the land. Thompson located on the same section, but left years ago.

Stephen Parkhurst settled on section 12, remained a number of years, went to Oscaloosa, where he has since died.

Later in the fall, Abram Watenpaugh, from Illinois, with his family, located on section 25, where he remained until his death, which occurred in 1858. Cyrus Odivene settled on the same section, remained a number of years, and removed to Kansas.

Robert Brodie, who came in 1854, was born in the Parish of Peeble, Peebleshire, Scotland, May 25, 1827. He is a son of Charles B. and Christina (Lockie) Brodie, natives of Scotland. His mother died, in her native land, in 1828, and the following year the family emigrated to Canada, and settled near New Market, in Upper Canada. When about seven years of age he left Canada to reside with an elder sister, then married, and living at Buffalo, New York, where he grew up, received a common school education, and learned the trade of stone-cutting, after which he traveled through Virginia and the Middle States, working at his trade. Mr. Brodie was married, April 27, 1850, to Miss Isabella J. Napier, born November 4, 1828, in Scotland. They are the parents of three children, two of whom are living—Margaret, born October 19, 1871; Isabella J., born August 30, 1853, and died January 23, 1856; Charles J., born August 24, 1862. October 6, 1855, he came to Bremer county, and located on the farm where he now resides. In the spring of the following year he returned to New York, to bring out his family. Coming right back, he began breaking his land and building his house. At that time there were only about ten buildings in the township. He has 800 acres of land. Mrs. Brodie is a member of the Presbyterian Church. In politics Mr. Brodie is a republican.

Mr. Stein arrived in this township in 1854, from Illinois, and settled on section 24, where he remained a few years, and then went to Kansas.

John Bingham came in the spring of 1855, from Waukegan, Illinois, and made selection in section 24, afterward moved to Sumner, and is now dead.

A. S. Funston was a settler of 1854, from Illinois. He made a selection on section 13, where he remained many years, but finally removed to Washington Territory.

Patrick Griffin came from Illinois, in 1854, and took a claim on section 11, where he still remains. He spent the first winter in a hay-stack, digging out a hole sufficiently large for himself and family.

E. Watenpaugh settled, in 1855, on section 24, where he yet lives.

Joseph Reddington, from Indiana, settled on section 25, where he remained a few years, and then went to Benton county.

During the summer of 1854, Isaac Gard and family came from Illinois, and settled on section 36. Here he remained until fall, then removed to section 25, having sold his original claim to Robert Brodie. He remained on section 25 about two or three years, when he, with William Willey, who had settled also on section 25, were arrested and sent to the penitentiary, having been connected with a famous band of horse thieves, which gave much trouble in an early day through this part of Iowa. When arrested, these parties were taken to Independence, and, after the preliminary examination, they both broke jail, but did not succeed in making escape, but were captured in Winnesheik county, and again placed in jail. Mr. Gard died in the penitentiary, and Mr. Willey was released before his time expired, and died very soon afterward.

James Wilson came from Ohio with a family, with teams, in the spring of 1854, and located on section 19, where he remained until 1865, and then removed to Missouri. The place is now owned by Joseph Dilley.

Joseph Carter came at that time, from the same State, and located on the same section. He removed to Missouri in 1865.

Peter H. Wilson arrived from Lowell, Massachusetts, in the fall of 1854, with his family, and located on section 19, where he continued until 1864, when he moved to Waverly, remained one year, and then went to New Hampshire, where he died.

C. C. Sweet was a settler on section 18, in the fall of 1865. He was from Ohio, and remained on this place until about 1867, when he became insane, and was removed to the asylum at Mt. Pleasant, and thence to Independence, where he yet remains.

Section 1 received a settler in the summer of 1854, in the person of H. C. Moore, who remained thereon about ten years, when he went to Waverly, stayed a few years, and then removed to Oskaloosa, where he now resides.

Adam Brodie came from Illinois, and settled on section 30, in 1854; he remained until 1865, when he went to Waverly, where he has a blacksmith shop.

The settlement of this township was slow, and it was many years before the land was fully occupied.

At the date of its first settlement, the nearest postoffice was Auburn, Fayette county. The people used to take turns going for the mails. In many instances the trip was made on foot, requiring two days.

E. Watenpaugh was born in Cataraugus county, New York, February 22d, 1835. He is a son of Isaac and Zoa (Thrall) Watenpaugh. When five years of age he came with his parents to Illinois and settled in Kane county, where his parents entered land and turned their attention to farming. In 1856 he left home and came to Bremer county, where his brother had preceeded him about two years. For the next two years his time was fully occupied in breaking his land and getting his house in order. September 23, 1859, he was married to Mrs. Elizabeth Watenpaugh, widow of A. A. Watenpaugh, by whom he has had four children—Fields A., Clara E., now the wife of John Dawson, Jr., Della M., and Zoa M. Mr. Watenpaugh has 297 acres of land in Leroy township. His present handsome residence, he built in 1866. He enlisted October 1st, 1864, in Company B, Fifteenth Iowa Infantry, and served until July of the following year, when he was mustered out at Louisville, Kentucky. Mr. Watenpaugh served as township trustee, assessor and justice of the peace for four years. In politics Mr. Watenpugh is a staunch republican. Robie J., now the wife of Matthew Taylor, is the daughter of Mrs. Watenpaugh, by her first husband.

Nelson Long, son of Philip and Mary (Flood) Long, was born September 19th, 1828, in Hampshire county, Virginia. His education was obtained in his native county, where he lived until 1850, when he came to Iowa and located in Washington county, where he remained until the fall of 1854. In February of the following year, he entered 120 acres of land on section 18, Leroy township, where he now lives, but at the present date, owns 92½ acres. Mr. Long was married to Mrs. Anna Husband, in 1871, and they have one child—Herbert.

Charles Brodie was born in Scotland, March 17, 1818. When he was thirteen years old, the family left their home, and crossing the Atlantic, settled in Upper Canada. Charles remained with his parents but one year, then went to Buffalo, New York, and learned the trade of masonry. He spent a number of years in that city, and afterward was engaged in building railroads. During the year 1854, he in company with Mr. Napier, began building the first bridge across the Mississippi river at St. Paul, Minnesota. He did much of the mason work on the Lake Shore railroad, and also was engaged in bridge building, in the State of Indiana. For some time he had charge of the stone work on the new Illinois State penitentiary. During the year 1869, he came to Bremer county, and settled on section 31, Leroy township, where he now owns 320 acres of land, all of which is under cultivation. Mr. Brodie was married in 1838, to Miss Giselda Napier, whose place of birth was Nova Scotia. They have three children living—Ray, Zella and Frances E.

FIRST THINGS.

The first marriage in the township was J. N. Fowle to Miss Nannie Page; the ceremony was performed by Judge J. Farris.

The first birth was a son to Mr. and Mrs. Isaac Gard, in January, 1855, on section 36.

The second person born in the township was Hattie O'Day, daughter of P. O'Day, April, 1855.

The first death was that of Mrs. Isaac Gard, in January, 1855; her remains were buried on section 25.

The first school taught in the township was in district No. 1, by Mrs. Perkins, of Waverly. The school was closed suddenly, after teaching about two weeks—number of scholars in attendance, eight.

The first postoffice was Leroy.

The first saw-mill was built by N. J. Fowle and others, and was in operation in the spring of 1855. Another saw-mill was in running order soon afterward, at Pinhook, and was erected by Thomas and William Riley.

The first school-house was built during the summer of 1856, on the southeast corner of section 13.

The second death was Norman B. Rogers, in July, 1855.

The first store was opened at Leroy; the two next at Pinhook; the last by Sweet and Hatch.

The first blacksmith shop was opened by Adam Brodie, on land now owned by Mr. Cameron.

EDUCATIONAL.

There are now four school houses in this township, located on sections 12, 24, 36 and 15, the latter being controlled by Frederika township. The school houses are all good frame buildings well furnished. Its educational facilities compare favorably with other localities.

POSTOFFICE.

The postoffice is located at Leroy. Daniel Hatch was the first postmaster; he was succeeded by A. S. Funston, E. Fay, Henry Dunn, John Bingham, W. B. Barnes, Joel Clingensmith, and the present incumbent, Mrs. Charles Countryman.

RELIGIOUS.

Services were held at the school house on southeast corner of section 13, by the Methodists, at an early day. Rev. Moulton, a Baptist minister, came to the township in 1855. The United Brethern held some services about the same time.

St. Mary's Catholic Church was established in 1869, and the congregation erected a building on section 13, at a cost of about $1,000. Services are held once a month, the priest coming from Fairbank. The membership is one hundred and fifty, with an average attendance of eighty. The house has a seating capacity for one hundred and twenty-five.

St. John German Lutheran Church was organized in 1875. The first pastor was Theodore Hanshke, who is still in charge. This society erected a building, in 1879, on section 30, at a cost of $1,500. Services are regularly held every Sabbath, and there is a membership of fifty families. In connection with this organization a day school is taught by the pastor, having an attendance of twenty-five scholars. Henry Keding and August Kirkchmann are trustees, and Henry Stager, treasurer.

VILLAGE OF BREMER CENTRE.

This place was located on land belonging to W. A. Moulton, who caused the village to be platted about 1857. Some business was transacted here about that time. A store was opened by Mr. Pratt, who only remained a short time. Another store was established by Hatch & Sweet, who remained in business about two years. There was also a blacksmith shop. The place is now entirely deserted

BREMER CENTRE CLASS UNITED BRETHEREN IN CHRIST.

This organization was effected during the summer of 1857 by Rev. B. Allen, with the following membership: M. T. Baker, Henry Lease, Jr., Mary Lease,

John Hall, Sarah Hall and others. M. T. Baker was the first class-leader and steward. Services were held at the house of D. R. Hatch and C. C. Sweet, in Bremer Centre. The following named persons have administered to the spiritual wants of this people for the time named: Rev. B. Allen, four months; James Murphy, two years; John Dollarhide, six months; J. S. Brown, six months; O. R. Robbins, one year; John Rowen, one year; John Buckmaster, one year; J. W. Young, six months; E. A. Howe, eighteen months; H. C. Baker, one year; E. A. Howe, again one year; E. P. Mead, two years; D. Bolster, one year; Simon George, one year; D. M. Harvey, one year; M. M. Taylor, one year; R. D. McCormack, one year; George Harding, one year; W. H. Wagoner, three years; J. Baskerville, six months, and W. H. Wagoner, again one year, and he is the present pastor. During the autumn of 1857, under the labors of Rev. James Murphy, quite an interesting revival was experienced by this church, much interest was manifested and about sixty additions to the society were made. There is no regular house of worship. The present officers are—John F. Smith, class-leader; Henry Lease, Jr., class-steward. There is a membership at the present time, of twenty-four, and the church is in a fairly prosperous condition. There was a Sunday School organized during the summer of 1858, with M. T. Baker as superintendent.

CHAPTER XXVI.

MAXFIELD TOWNSHIP.

This is a full Congressional township, having thirty-six sections of land, or about 23,040 acres. It is strictly an agricultural township, having within its boundaries no town or railroad. It is watered by Crane Creek, which flows from the north, through the centre, leaving on section 34. The soil is a very rich, dark loam.

The inhabitants are almost exclusively German, noted for thrift, and as being successful farmers. Houses and barns, of goodly proportions, farms well tilled, and granaries well filled, are noticeable features in this community.

EARLY SETTLEMENT.

The first settlements made in this township was in 1855. With few exceptions, the first settlers were from Cook county, Illinois, but of German birth or descent. The following named were among the number arriving here between the years 1855 and 1860:

Christian Neverman, deceased; Christ Wente, Sr., deceased; Chr. Engelbecht, deceased; J. Griese, deceased; Christoph Kebe, T. Moltger, moved to Black Hawk county; Fr. Koelling, Chr. Kierk, deceased; W. Wente, John Kebe, moved to

HISTORY OF BREMER COUNTY.

Black Hawk county; W. Blasberg, Henry Graening, John Moehling, moved to Fremont township; J. W. Matthias, W. Matthias, deceased; Fr. Oltrogge, A. Fegtmeyer, H. Fegtmeyer, H. Meier, H. Burges, deceased, J. P. Burgess, deceased; John Huchnerberg, N. Leroy, Jr., H. Wilkening, Fremont township; H. Heine, moved to Warren township; C. Pighs, H. Schumacher, Ph. Knief, moved to Fayette county; H. Risck, deceased; Fr. Hagemann, John Oltrogge, deceased; Conrad Oltrogge, Philip Oltrogge, deceased; Christian Buhr, Sr.; Christoph Rohlering, Fremont township; Henry Boedester, moved to Kansas; Conrad Bentrott, deceased; Henry Pook, H. H. Leegers, Henry Schroeder, John Grupe, deceased; John Helle, deceased; H. Steege, deceased; Edward Huebner, H. Roever, Geo. Knief, Joach Wittenburg, John Graf, moved to Cedar Falls; Henry Bivauk, deceased; John Schoof, Fred. Westendorf, Ernst Brandt, moved to Jefferson township; J. H. Leegers, F. Kelling. All these settled, from 1855 to 1860, in the township, and with a few exceptions, they came from Cook county, Illinois.

FIRST THINGS.

Caroline Wente, daughter of W. and Frederika (Clausing) Wente, was born on the 9th of June, 1855, and baptized in the presence of godfather Engel, Mary Bruns, Sophie Wente and Mary Nevermann, and lives on section 18.

The first marriage was that of Fred Hageman and Dorothea King, on the 11th day of April, 1857, the ceremony being performed by Rev. Graetsel.

The second marriage was that of John Bruns and Elenore Grupe, who were united by Rev. Ch. Kessler, June 10, 1859.

The first creamery was established in the spring of 1880, and was built by Little & Huebner. In 1881 Mr. Little bought the interest of his partner, and is now the exclusive owner of the factory. An average of 1,400 pounds of butter is made per week.

The second creamery was established in the spring of 1881 by Huebner & Leehase. Two thousand pounds of butter is made each week.

EDUCATIONAL.

The first school house in the township was built, in connection with the church building, in the spring of 1857, [See history of the St. John's Congregation, German Lutheran Church,] and school was taught by the Rev. Graetsel. In 1865 a school house was erected on the southwest quarter of section 17, for the purpose of holding an English and German school combined. In 1866 this building was moved to the church lot, on section 19. At present there are six public, and three private school buildings, and one church which is used, during the winter, for school purposes.

POSTOFFICE.

A postoffice was established in the township in April, 1873, under the name of Maxfield postoffice. H. Baumteath was the first postmaster. He resigned, in the spring of 1875, and Rev. P. Bredow took charge of the office. He was succeeded, in 1877, by the present postmistress, Mrs. Emily Bredow.

CEMETERIES.

There are four cemeteries in the township. The first is located on the grounds of the St. John's Congregation, German Evangelical Lutheran Church, on section 19.

The second is located on the church grounds of the Evangelical United German, St. Paul's Congregation.

The third is located on the church grounds of the Evangelical Lutheran, Emanuel's Congregation, on section 26.

The fourth is located on the church grounds of the Evangelical Lutheran, St. Matthew's Congregation.

ST. JOHN'S CONGREGATION GERMAN EVANGELICAL LUTHERAN CHURCH.

By Rev. P. Bredow.

The first religious meeting for the early settlers, was held in a private building, section 18, owned by John Moehling, and was conducted by Rev. N. Volkert, who was called from Schaumburg, Cook county, Illinois, for a special service. He was the pastor of the early settlers when they lived in Cook county. He preached on Sunday April 24, 1856, baptized ten children and celebrated the Lord's Supper. Fifty persons were admitted: Christoph Kebe and wife, H. Graening and wife, H. Moeller and wife, F. Noettger and wife, Christ Wente and wife, Christ Neverman and wife, Char. Riech, Char. Engelbreths and wife, W. Wente and wife, Joh. Kehe, John Griese and wife, F. Kolling, H. Meier and wife, W. Blasberg and wife, C. Braus, wife and son, J. Moehling and wife, A. Burgess, J. Wolfrath, W. Matthias, F. Bruns and wife, W. Matthias, Henry Rietk, A. Tegtmeyer and wife, H. Tegtmeyer and wife, Joh. Huehnerberg and wife, Fr. Ottrogge and wife, N. Burgess, H. Wilkening and wife.

Before Christmas, 1856, they called Rev. Graetsel for their own minister. The meetings were held in different private buildings up to spring of 1857, when they built a house, 16x24 and 14 feet high, on southeast side of section 19, where Mr. Charles Bruns, one of the members, made a donation of five acres of land for church property. The upper part of the building was used for church meetings and school, and the lower for parsonage. The house was torn down in the spring of 1879.

Rev. Graetsel, a member of the Evangelical Lutheran Synod of Missouri, Ohio, after finding the work and trouble of a minister in starting a new congregation, too hard, resigned in 1858, promising the congregation to send a successor, but failed to do it. The congregation therefore wrote to the president of the Evangelical Lutheran Synod, of Iowa, Rev. E. Grossman, that time in Clayton county, Iowa, in order to get a minister from this Synod. He sent there in fall, 1859, Rev. P. Kleinlein, whom they called for their own minister. One half year before Mr. Kleinlein came, Rev. G. Grossman, Professors Rev. Sigmund and Gottfried Fritschee, served. In the year 1860, the parsonage was enlarged by a brick building 16x18, and a new church was built, a frame building 30x50, 14 feet high, with a little steeple on the roof, where meetings are held at present.

The congregation grew larger and larger every year, by those coming in from Cook county, Illinois, and from the old country. The highest number of members was in 1869, being about 125 families. In the fall of 1865, Rev. P. Kleinlein resigned, in regard to family circumstances, and Rev. Schieferderke, from Altenburg, Perry county, Missouri, was called and arrived here in April, 1866, the vacancy in the meantime was filled by Rev. Flachenerker, a missionary who came from the Indian Territory. Rev. Schieferderke, who was sixty years of age, could not stand the cold and icy prairie winds and therefore moved, in the winter of 1867, to La Salle county, Illinois. The congregation united in the calling of the Rev. L. Schorr, of McGregor, Iowa, who arrived at the beginning of the year 1868. He was an excellent pastor and a gifted orator, but suffered much from his liver and lungs, his disease finally ending with consumption and death, December 25, 1870. The congregation called Rev. A. Preller, professor of the college at Galena, Illinois. He, after staying ten months, went back to the college, and Rev. P. Bredow, from Dubuque, Iowa, was called, who arrived January 1, 1872, and is at present pastor of the congregation. In the summer of 1872, the congregation built a new parsonage, 24x36, and 18 feet high; also, in 1878, a house for their teacher, 16x26, 14 feet high, with an addition of 12x14 for a kitchen. In the summer of 1881, a new school house was built, 24x36, and 12 feet high, and the old school house was sold and moved away. A new organ for the church was bought in 1877, at a cost of $380, and a new bell weighing 800 pounds, in place of the old one.

The teaching of the youths was at first done by the ministers of the congregation, up to the year 1862, when Mr. G. Jaukel became teacher. He was followed by Mr. John Hopke, and he by Mr. Koehler. They did not have any extra teacher until the fall of 1871, when A. Brumbach was called and took charge of the school October 1, 1871, remaining until the spring of 1875, when he went to the Theological Seminary at Mendota, Illinois, to prepare himself for the holy ministry. His successor was A. Brandenburg, a regular educated German teacher, who is in his position at present. The number of children of the school ranged from sixty to eighty, during the term of eleven months per year. The present number of church members, after establishing several other Lutheran churches in the neighborhood, is about eighty families

The present officers of the congregation are: President, Christ. Wente; secretary, William Ottrogge; treasurer, H. C. Wente; trustees, E. Brandt, H. Bruns, W. Milins; deacons, J. Bruns, J. Schoof, H. Selgers, H. Meier.

The United Evangelical, St. Paul's Church, on section 18, was organized January 22, 1862, by Fred. Bruns, H. Pook, H. Steege and others. The church and parsonage combined was built in the summer of 1863, and dedicated October 25, 1863, by Rev. S. Hartman, of Chicago. The first minister was Rev. G. Geckler. His successors were, Revs. Weidbrecht, Israel, Rausch, Hafenbrack, Hagemann and Severinger, the present pastor of the church. The church now has fifty-six members. Its present officers are: President, C. Clausing; Secretary, H. Pook; Treasurer, H. Schumache; deacons, H. Bauman, H. Haase; trustees, H. Moehling, George M. Eyer, J. Homrighaus.

St. Matthew Congregation, Evangelical Lutheran Church, was organized by Rev. P. Bredow, in 1878. The first members were Henry Buhr, W. Buhr, W. Stroffman, John Tieds, Henry Tieds and others. The church, 20x30 feet, and the parsonage, 16x22 feet, were built in the summer of 1878. The first and present minister is Rev. L. Loberk. The church now has a membership of 40, and is connected with the Evangelical Lutheran Synod of Iowa, and other States.

BIOGRAPHICAL.

Rev. Paul Bredow, a native of Guelzon, Russia, was born in 1839. He attended the higher schools in his native place and afterwards graduated from the Lutheran College, at Nenendettels, Bavaria. In 1861 he came to the United States, and, upon his arrival here, located in Portage City, Wisconsin, where he began preaching the Gospel. Shortly after, he removed to Germantown, Wisconsin, engaging in missionary work. In October, 1862, he located in Ottumwa, Iowa, where he served seven congregations, which were within a circle of one hundred and fifty miles, and spread over five counties. At the end of one and a half years, he received, and accepted, a call from St. John's Congregation, at Dubuque, Iowa. There he continued for eight years and then accepted a call from the St. John's Congregation, in Maxfield township, Bremer county, where he has since remained. During his residence here, Mr. Bredow has organized six congregations, five in this county and one in Black Hawk county. He is a tireless worker in the cause of Christ, and is greatly beloved by all his people. In May, 1864, he was joined in the holy bonds of matrimony with Miss Emily Grassmann, a native of Hesse, Germany, and the eldest daughter of the president of the Evangelical Lutheran Synod, of Iowa and other States. Nine children have blessed this union, seven of whom are now living—Herman, Julius, Agnes, Sophia, Gustof, Otto and Clara.

H. C. Wente was born December 6, 1848, in Cook county, Illinois. When he was but six years old, the family removed to Bremer county, Iowa, settling on section 18, Maxfield township. The son received a good education in the German language, and also obtained a common school education in the English tongue. He was married in 1872 to Miss Sophia Schroeder, who was born in Germany, but during her childhood, came with her parents to the United States, and when eight years old, settled with them in Maxfield township. They have one child—Sarah. Mr. and Mrs. Wente are members of, and earnest workers in, the St. John's Evangelical Lutheran Church. In politics he is a republican, and has several of the local offices.

CHAPTER XXVII.

POLK TOWNSHIP.

This is a full Congresional township, containing an area of thirty-six sections of land. It is the northwestern township in Bremer county, township 93, range 14 west, and bounded on the north by Chickasaw county, on the west by Butler, on the south by Lafayette township, and on the east by Douglas. The Cedar river traverses this township, running through the western portion. Entering on section 5, it pursues a meandering course southward through sections 6, 7, 8, 18, 17, 20, 29, and leaving on section 33. One railroad, a branch of the Illinois Central, passes through this territory, from north to south, nearly parallel with, and running on the west side of the stream. There are also two small creeks running diagonally through the township, from northeast to southwest, making confluence with the Cedar river on section 33. The soil is generally a sandy loam, and along the main ridge, passing through the township, is underlain with limestone. On the bottom lands, the sub-soil is generally mixed with clay. While the soil generally presents an appearance of sandiness, upon closer observation it appears there is no more in most places than is necessary to render the land suitable for cultivation. It takes a good, bright, well-polished plow to scour. It is of the quick productive kind, and nearly everything planted, makes active, vigorous growth. The surface is neither level or rolling, but gently undulating, just enough to secure adequate drainage, consequently there is but little waste land in the township.

Along the Cedar river, mostly on the east side, is found an abundant supply of timber, consisting of hickory elm, rock elm, water elm, sugar maple, hackberry, jack oak, shellbark hickory, and black walnut, although the latter is now scarce. The woodman's axe has seemed to make, at times, sad havoc with this bountiful natural supply, but other trees spring up, rapidly assume goodly proportions, as if in defiance at man's attempt toward extermination. This strip of forest extends back from the river from one to two miles. Polk township is, therefore, well supplied with timber. The population is mixed, Americans predominating, and they are generally an enterprising, thrifty people.

EARLY SETTLEMENT.

The first settlement made in this township was in 1851, by Allen Smith, Lloyd Smith, Stephen D. Jackson, Ezra Allen and their families, on the east side of the river—Allen Smith, on section 21, Stephen Jackson, on section 9, Ezra Allen, where the village of Horton now stands.

HISTORY OF BREMER COUNTY.

Lloyd Smith was born in Virginia, in 1814. When he was quite young, the family left their old home for Illinois, and soon afterwards removed to Indiana, where he received a limited education in the log school house of that day, and grew to manhood. In 1842, he was married to Miss Sarah Allen, a native of North Carolina. In 1850, he came to the "Hawkeye" State, and remained in Dubuque county with his father and brother, who had preceeded him, until the spring of the following year, when he came to Polk township and settled on section 16, where he now has a comfortable house. Nine children blessed this union, of whom Elizabeth Susan, Joseph L., Lucinda, James William, Milton, Jefferson, Rhoda Emeline and Mathew Allen, are living. In politics, Mr. Smith is a democrat.

One of the pioneers of Bremer county, was Alexis Jackson, who was born in Guernsey county, Ohio, February 4, 1824. Ten years later the family removed to McHenry county, Illinois, where Allen received a good common school education, and reached manhood's estate. February 3, 1848, he was united in wedlock with Miss Mary Hammer, a native of the State of Indiana, born April 12, 1828. In 1851, they came to Bremer county, Iowa, and in November of that year, settled on section 9, Polk township, where they lived, honored citizens, until their deaths. Mr. Jackson died December 27, 1878, and his wife followed him, May 12, 1882. They were the parents of three children— Lucretia J., Elmira E. and Sylvester S. The daughters were born in McHenry county, Illinois, and the son, in Polk township, March 15, 1859, where he has always resided. He obtained a good education, having attended the schools of Plainfield, Bradford and Nashua. September 15, 1881, he was married to Miss Genevra M. Jordan, who was born in Ohio, in 1862.

Allen Smith remains on his original claim.

S. D. Jackson sold out and moved to Missouri about twenty years ago. Afterward he returned to this State, and died in Greene county.

Ezra Allen moved to Kansas in June, 1856.

Gideon Phelps selected a home here on section 15, in 1853. His brother, Addison Phelps, came here a short time previous and secured a place on section 23, where he remained about two years and then removed to Minnesota, where he now lives.

Mr. Hosetuttles was a settler of 1852, and located about a mile from what is now Horton.

Section 14 received a settler in 1853, by the name of John Tyler. He remained about twenty years, and went to Minnesota where he died.

J. J. Corlett, a pioneer of Polk township, was born on the Isle of Man, in 1830. In 1847 he crossed the Atlantic, to America, and after spending some time in Milwaukee, removed to Kenosha county, Wisconsin, and thence to McHenry county, Illinois. In 1851 he removed to Fayette county, Iowa, and two years later took the claim where he now resides. Mr. Corlett was married to Miss Ellen Crane, in 1853. Six children have blessed their union, three of whom are now living—Alvaro, Enos and Millie. His wife died in 1871, and two years later he was married to

Miss Margaret Jackson. They have one child—Jane.

Joseph Smith, who is one of Polk township's old settlers, was born in Virginia in 1819. When Joseph was a child the family moved, first to Illinois, then to Ohio, and afterwards to Indiana, where they lived for a number of years. In 1843 he came to Iowa, and settled in Dubuque county, where he engaged in farming for ten years. At the expiration of that time he came to Bremer county, and settled in Polk township, where he has since lived, and now owns a fine farm of 320 acres, valued at $30 an acre. Mr. Smith was married in 1840 to Miss Rhoda Garner, who was born in Tennessee. Twelve children have been born to them, eleven of whom are now living—Mary A., Sarah, Amanda, Melinda, Gilbert, Eliza J., deceased; Charles, Alfred, George W., Caroline, Robert A. and James H.

J. L. Smith, also an early settler, was born in Indiana, April 11, 1847. Three years after his birth, the family moved to Dubuque county, Iowa, and one year later, to Polk township, Bremer county, where the son obtained his education, and still resides. In 1868 he was united in marriage with Miss Catharine D. Cook, who was born in Pennsylvania. Four children—Mollie, Lloyd F., Henry Allen and Sarah, have blessed their union. Mr. Smith is a democrat, and takes a deep interest in the politics of his county and town.

George Bowser came from the "Sucker" State, with his family, in 1854, and made a claim on section 22, where he remained fifteen years, then moved to Missouri, where he died.

The same year, and from the same State, came George Richey. He located on section 15, where he remained a few years, then moved about from place to place, and finally went to Kansas.

The same season, also, and from the same State, came Charles Woodcock, with his family, and settled on section 6. He remained here until his death, which occurred in the spring of 1882. A part of the old homestead is now occupied by his son. At the same time, and settling on the same section, came his brother-in-law, Mr. Hopkins. He afterward removed to Missouri. The claim is now occupied by Mr. Burgess.

William and Obed Gaines arrived in 1854, and located on section 7. Obed is now in Minnesota. William is yet a resident of Bremer county.

Louis Wheeler, from Illinois, put in an appearance this same season, with his family, and established a home on section 18. He sold out and returned about twenty years ago. The place is now owned by Wesley Allen.

Section 27 received a settler the same year, in the person of Mr. Buckmaster, who died in a few years. A. Mr. Orth, of Ohio, jumped his claim, and it was transferred to other parties.

After this time settlers came in rapidly, and the township secured a class of citizens that will compare favorably with other early settlements of the county. Among the arrivals soon after the foregoing, were Nutting, Lane, Eldridge, Tape, Lease Brothers, and Cagley. Quite a number of sketches of representative men are appended. It is impossible to mention all, but a sufficient number are given

to indicate the character of the settlement.

Robert Farnsworth, a native of Pennsylvania, was born in 1822. He grew to manhood in the State of his nativity, where he received but a limited education. When seventeen months old, his father died, and, one month later, his mother also died. After the death of his parents, Robert lived with his grandfather until he was eight years old, at which time the grandfather also died. Robert was then "bound out" to learn the cabinet-maker's trade. At sixteen years of age, he turned his attention to farming, and afterwards was engaged in the iron works, in his native place. In 1855, he came to Bremer county, Iowa, and located in section 7, Washington township. There he remained until 1875, when he sold that farm and removed to Polk township, where he now owns 155 acres of well cultivated land. In 1846, he was married to Miss Mary Wolverton, a native of Pennsylvania. Seven children blessed this union —Teressa J., Harriet L., Martha P., Ella, Isaac W., Robert F. and Joseph Monroe. Mr. Farnsworth's wife died May 12, 1868, and, in 1877, he was married to Miss Sarah Hurlbut, a native of New York.

John K. Head, an early settler of Polk township, was born in New Hampshire in 1823. When he was quite young the family moved to Vermont, where they settled on a farm, and the son spent his time until seventeen years of age, attending school and helping his parents with the farm work. At that age he learned the carpenters' trade, and followed that occupation until 1850, when he spent two years in California, then returned to Vermont, and a few months afterward went to Pennsylvania, where he remained about three years. In 1855 he came to Bremer county, Iowa, settled on section 6, Polk township, and soon after his arrival built the first frame house erected in the township. During the years 1866-67 Mr. Head was a member of the board of county supervisors, and has also held other local offices. He was married in 1854 to Miss Sarah Dunham, a native of New York State, who has borne him five children, two of whom are living. Mr. Head's parents were of Scotch descent; his mother being a descendent of the celebrated John Knox, and also a niece of Mr. Dunham, of Illinois, the great importer of Norman Percheron horses.

W. H. George, born in Richland county, Ohio, February 26, 1843, is a son of John and Eliza (Hittle) George. He remained in his native county until 1856, when he came, with his grandparents, to Bremer county, Iowa, settling in Polk township. In 1861 Mr. George enlisted in the Union army, serving three years. Upon leaving the army he returned to Iowa and, after living a year and a half in Marshall county came to Polk township the second time, and settled on his farm, where he now lives, and owns 320 acres of excellent land.

Thomas Harris, one of the pioneers of Polk township, is a native of Pennsylvania, born on the 10th day of April, 1811. His parents were also natives of that State. His father was a soldier of the war of 1812, and died in 1814, while in the service. Shortly after his death, Thomas was left in the charge of a friend of the family, with whom he remained until seventeen years of age, receiving, during the time, a limited education. In 1832 he was married to Miss Emeline Steward, who was born in Scipio, New York, May 31, 1811. In 1842 they removed to Illinois, residing in that State until 1856, when they came to Bremer county, Iowa, settling on section 10, Polk township, where they have since lived. They are the parents of nine children—Lydia, Lucy S., Nancy, Adeline and Emeline (twins), Lucretia, Mary, William M. and Rosalia A. The latter died April 15, 1866. Mrs. Harris died March 3, 1868. She was a devout christian and a devoted mother.

C. R. Hastings, one of Bremer county's pioneers, and one of the enterprising farmers of Polk township, is a native of New York, and was born in Franklin county, on the 4th of December, 1824. He remained at home on his father's farm, attending the district schools, until twenty-one years of age, at which time he began life for himself. Two years later he came as far west as Illinois, and spent the following ten years in different parts of that State and Wisconsin, at one time being in the employ of the Frink & Walker stage line. During the spring of 1857, he came to Bremer county, and settled on section 22, Polk township, where, by hard work and economy, he has succeeded in accumulating a fine property, having a farm of 162 acres, under a high state of cultivation, and valued at $40 per acre. Mr. Hastings is a staunch republican and has held several offices of trust. He has been one of the directors of the Bremer County Farmers' Mutual Insurance Company for several years, and was elected President at their last meeting. He is also Vice-president of the Bremer county Old Settlers' Association. In 1853 he was joined in wedlock with Miss Dianah Jones, who was born in Wales, in 1830. Four children blest this union—Mary A., Charles H., Clark M. and Dora E. Mr. Hastings is a genial, whole-souled man, and one who is greatly beloved and respected by all his acquaintances. He has always taken an interest in everything pertaining to the welfare of the community in which he lives, and was an active worker in the White Oak Grange, of his township. He was sent by that organization, in 1872, to Minnesota, to purchase seed wheat, and secured two car loads. Another grange near by was so much pleased with his transaction, that they insisted on his making another trip on a like errand, which he did and purchased 1500 bushels, making a judicious selection, to the entire satisfaction of all parties concerned.

E. A. Granger was born in Vermont, in 1835. When he was seven years old the family moved to DeKalb county, Illinois, and there he received a common school education, and passed his youth. In 1855 he came to Bremer county, Iowa, purchased land in Polk township, and then returned to Illinois, where he was married to Miss Olive Marsh, a native of that State, February 22, 1855. The following fall he brought his young wife to their new western home, where they have since lived, and by industry and perseverence, now own 320 acres of well-improved land, valued at $30 per acre. Mr. Granger is a republican, and has held several of the local offices. They have four children—W. A., Adolphus, Ella, and Lester A. Mr. Granger is one of the most enterprising and successful farmers in Polk township. He is engaged extensively in raising stock, and seems to be rapidly accumulating a fortune.

Barnes Thompson, one of the early settlers of Bremer county, was born in Chenango county, New York, in 1825. Ten years after his birth the family moved westward, locating in Delaware county, Ohio, where he grew to manhood, and obtained an excellent common school education. In 1855 Mr. Thompson removed to Illinois, and one year later came to Bremer county, Iowa, locating in Douglas township. The following year he settled in Polk township, where he has since resided. October 19, 1852, he was married, choosing for a helpmeet, Miss Eveline Gardner, a native of New York State. Eight children have been born to them, five of whom are now living—Florence A., Ernest C., Ozem G., Frank L., and Leon L. Mr. Thompson and wife, are members of the Methodist Episcopal Church. In politics Mr. Thompson is a republican.

John F. Spalding was born in Cayuga county, New York, in 1838. His father died when he was but three years old, and, consequently, young John began helping his mother with the farm work, at a very early age. In 1858, he, in company with his mother, came to Bremer county, Iowa, and, after spending about two years at Horton, determined to go to Illinois. As there were no railroads in this section of the country at that time, John, in company with another man, embarked in a skiff on the Cedar river, near where Plainfield now stands, and floated down the stream to Moscow, and there boarded the ars for Henry county, Illinois. After spending the summer in that county, he returned to Polk township, and purchased a farm, upon which he resided about nine years, and then bought his present farm. Mr. Spalding spent three years in the State of California, and, after his return to Iowa, was proprietor of the Centennial Hotel at Waverly, for two years. He is a staunch republican, and has held several of the township offices. In 1863, he was joined in wedlock with Miss Olive Patridge, a native of St. Lawrence county, New York. They have four children—Charlie C., Clyde W., Myrtie M. and Minnie L.

One of the old settlers of Polk township is William Farr, who was born on the 3d day of December, 1826, in Madison county, New York. Nine years after his birth, the family moved to Illinois, and there William obtained his education, and lived for many years. During the year 1857 he came to Bremer county, Iowa, and settled on a farm on section 19, where he lived eight years, and then settled on his present farm. In 1854 Mr. Farr was united in wedlock to Miss Sophia E. Boardman, who is a native of Vermont. They have four children—Willis C., Walker A., Maurice B. and Warren. Mr. Farr has frequently held places of trust in his township, and deservedly has the respect and esteem of the community in which he lives. His reputation for honesty and integrity being second to none. In politics he is a staunch republican, and a hard worker in everything calculated to advance the interests of that party,

E. H. Tyler, a native of New York State, was born in St. Lawrence county in 1835. Four years later the family removed to Ohio, and in 1854 located in Illinois.

During the year 1858 E. H. came to Bremer county, locating on section 19, Douglas township, where he continued to reside until 1880, when he bought an addition to his farm on section 25, Polk township, and settled there. During the second year of our late rebellion, he enlisted in Company B, 14th Iowa, and served until honorably discharged in 1864. At Leesburg, Missouri, he received a wound, from which he has never recovered, and therefore draws a pension. Mr. Tyler was married in 1859, choosing for a helpmeet Miss Mary Rickel, a native of Pennsylvania. They have two children living—Edmund and George.

Adin Terry, an early settler of Polk township, was born in the State of New York, in 1829. When he was sixteen years old, the family moved to McHenry county, Illinois, and there resided until 1855, when they came to Bremer county and settled on section 35, Polk township. Mr. Terry arrived here in the spring, and during the first summer lived in a wagon box. In the fall he erected a log cabin, which made them a good home for a number of years. At the present date he owns a well stocked farm which contains comfortable buildings. In his younger days, school advantages were not what they are at the present time, still, by diligence and perseverence, he acquired a good common school education. Mr. Terry is a republican, and has held several of the local offices. During the year 1862, he was married to Miss Malvina Terry, a native of New York State. Ten children have been born to them, eight of whom are now living—Frank M., Ethèl B., Nellie A., Wallace A., Mason M., Dudley O., Lulu and Robert H. Mr. Terry's mother died in 1872, at the age of sixty-six; his father still survives her, and is now eighty-two years of age. During the war for the Union, he took an active part in raising men to fill the quota of his township, and in this connection some years after, there were charges of wrong doing preferred against him, and it is but just to say, that after a thorough investigation by an impartial committee, he was fully exonerated from any wrong. The proof presented by Mr. Terry as to the disposal of every dollar placed in his hands was sufficient to dispel all belief or prejudice against him.

David Beebe, a native of New York State, was born in 1809. He obtained an education in the common schools of that section and reached manhood's estate in the place of his birth. In 1835 he was joined in wedlock with Miss Nancy Heaton, and two years later emigrated to Boone county, Illinois, where he engaged in farming for ten years, he then came to Bremer county, and settled on section 35, Polk township, where he now lives and owns 380 acres of well improved land; he also owns forty acres in Franklin township. In politics Mr. Beebe acknowledges no allegiance to any party, but always tries to vote for the best man. Five children have been born to this couple, four of whom are now living—Sarah D., James H. Y., Mary J. and David B. Their oldest child, Chester A., enlisted in the army in 1862, and while stationed at Dubuque, was taken sick and died at his home, in 1863.

Lewis E. Branch, a native of France, was born in 1828. Three years after his birth, the family came to America, locating at Watertown, New York, where Lewis grew to manhood. In 1853 he went to California, but, after making a short visit, he returned to New York, and was joined in wedlock. Subsequently he removed to Bremer county, Iowa, locating in Douglas township, where he remained some time and then, in company with his wife, again visited the Pacific coast, this time remaining two years. During their visit, his wife died. Upon his return he again settled in Bremer county, and in 1860 was married to Mrs. Cornelia Andrews, born in Washtenaw county, Michigan, in 1837. This lady had one child, Nelson, by her first husband, and two by the latter, Fred and Dollie. Mr. Branch died on the 3d day of August, 1880.

Samuel Sewell, born in Marion county, Indiana, March 11th, 1836, is a son of Thomas Jefferson Sewell, who died in Waverly, November 19, 1882. Samuel remained in his native State until 1852, wken the family came to Janesville, Bremer county, settling on a farm. August 12, 1862, he enlisted in Company B, Thirty-eighth Iowa Volunteers, and served until honorably discharged, September 7, 1865. Upon being mustered out of service, he returned to Bremer county, and located in Jackson township, where he continued to reside until June, 1874, at which time he settled on his present farm, in Polk township. Mr. Sewell was married December 9, 1860, to Miss Sarah C. McElhaney, a native of Indiana county, Pennsylvania. They have five children living—Margaret Ann, Samuel Allen, Elmira, Hattie L., and Sarah Susan. He was married the first time, in 1856, to Anna Catherine Hursh, who bore him one son, and died in January, 1860.

A. W. Emily was born in Watertown, New York, in 1844. When he was ten years old, the family moved to Dane county, Wisconsin, where he received a liberal education, and lived until the opening of the late rebellion. September 27, 1861, he enlisted in Company A, Eleventh Wisconsin Infantry, and served until January, 1863, when he re-enlisted in the same company and regiment, and served until honorably discharged, September 27, 1865. Upon leaving the army, he returned to Wisconsin, and in 1868 came to Bremer county, Iowa, and settled in Polk township. Mr. Emily is a republican, and has held several of the local offices. In 1868 he was married to Miss Susannah Wightman, who was born in England, and came to this country when ten years old. They have four children—Hattie B., Gertrude L., Sadie and Walter D.

W. M. Davis was born in Genesee county, New York, in 1819. He received a good common school education in his native county, and when twenty years of age learned the painter's trade. During the year 1838, he removed to Racine, Wisconsin, and engaged in house and sign painting until 1840, when he went to Chicago; and, while there, became agent for Van Amburgh & Company's circus and menagerie. With that company he remained seven years, after which he traveled with other companies ten years. In 1857, he settled on his farm, in Wisconsin, and some years later came to Bremer county, Iowa, and settled on sections 26 and 27, Polk township, and now owns one of the finest farms in the county. Mr.

Davis was married February 27, 1854, to Sarah A. Emily, a native of Canada. She removed to New York State, with her parents, when a child, and grew to womanhood there. They are the parents of three children—Walter M., Jr., Susan E. and Stephen H.

W. W. Lynes was born in the year 1842, in New York State. When he was nine years old, the family left their old home, for Wisconsin, and, after spending some years in Walworth county, Rock Prairie and Beloit, they came to Iowa, and settled in Buchanan county. Shortly after, W. W. left the parental roof, for the purpose of seeking his fortune. He passed some years in different parts of the State, and, finally, in 1863, came to Bremer county, and located in Polk township. October 21, 1866, he was married to Miss Ella A. Hutchins, a native of Wisconsin. She bore him two children, and died June 1, 1872. Mr. Lynes afterward married Miss Ella A. Ketchum, by whom he has had three children.

J. Furrow is a native of Pennsylvania, born in 1828. He grew to manhood in the State of his birth, receiving a limited education in the log school house of that day. When of sufficient age, he learned the trade of cabinet-making, and followed that occupation for a number of years. In 1851 he moved to Winnebago county, Illinois, and during the fall of 1861 came to Bremer county, Iowa, locating near Tripoli. Fifteen years later he settled in Polk township, where he lived until 1880, when he moved to Waterloo, Iowa, where he now resides. He was married, in 1852, to Miss Julia Fish, a native of New York State. They are the parents of three children—Sanford M., William H., and Sarah M. William H. was born in Illinois, on the 4th day of September, 1835, and was married, in 1880, to Miss Alice Eisenhart, a native of Iowa, born in 1861. They have one child—Grace. William now lives on the old homestead, in Polk township. In his youth he received an excellent common school education, and for a number of years has followed the profession of teaching. He is a republican.

J. P. Fritcher was born on the 21st day of June, 1811, in Sharon, Schoharie county, New York. Shortly after his birth the family removed to Oneida county, where he grew to manhood, and obtained a good common school education. He also learned the tailors' trade in that county. In January, 1832, he was united in marriage with Miss Melvina M. Avery, a native of New York State. In 1844 he settled in Walworth county, Wisconsin, where he worked at his trade, and farmed, until 1864. At that time he came to Bremer county, Iowa, and settled on section 1, Polk township, where he has since resided. They are the parents of five children—Susan, Elizabeth, Sarah, Denison, and Nettie, all of whom are married. Denison was married January 2, 1869, to Amanda M. Gibson, a native of Indiana. They have two children—Clarence, and John. Mr. and Mrs. Fritcher, and also their son Denison's wife, are members of the Free-Will Baptist Church.

F. H. Bunth is a native of Sweeden, and was born in 1842. Two years after his birth, the family emigrated to America, and upon their arrival in this country settled in Kenosha county, Wisconsin. There the son obtained a common school education and reached manhood's estate. June 14, 1861, he enlisted in Company F, Fourth Wisconsin Infantry, and served until honorably discharged, January 1, 1863. As soon as discharged he immediately re-enlisted, and continued serving until June 19, 1866. He received two wounds during the Siege of Port Hudson, from the effects of which he has never recovered, and therefore draws a pension. Upon leaving "Uncle Sam's" service, Mr. Bunth returned to Wisconsin, and remained there until the spring of 1870, when he came to Bremer county, and settled on section 24, Polk township, where he now owns a well improved farm of ninety acres, valued at $30 per acre. Mr. Bunth was married in October, 1866, to Miss Mary Jane Dyer, born in Kenosha county, Wisconsin. He is an advocate of republicanism, and has held local offices.

One of the pioneers of Polk township, is G. W. Nafus, born in Tompkins county, New York, in 1829. Four years later, his parents removed to Delaware county, Ohio, where they remained nine years, then spent seven years in Wyandotte county, when they located in Monroe county, Michigan, where the subject of this sketch was married, December 25, 1851, to Miss Sarah Southwick, a native of Ohio, born in 1832. In 1854 he removed to Kenosha county, Wisconsin, where he remained until 1861, and then came to Bremer county, Iowa, settling on section 15, Polk township, where he now owns 230 acres of land. Mr. Nafus is a republican, and has held several offices of trust. Their children are, Flora, Jane, George, Charles and William. The family are members of the Free Will Baptist Church. During our late rebellion, Mr. Nafus took an active part in looking after the families of soldiers, living in his neighborhood.

H. S. Bunth was born in Kenosha county, Wisconsin, January 5, 1850. He received a common school education in his native county, and passed his early life there. When twenty years old, he made a short visit in Bremer county, and upon his return home, was married to Miss Carrie E. Hoffman, who was born in Walworth county, Wisconsin. In 1874 he moved to Bremer county, and purchased a farm in Fremont township. There he resided four years, and then sold it and bought the farm in Polk township, where he now lives. Mr. Bunth is a republican, and has held several local offices. They have three children—Minnie, May and an infant.

J. M. Roberts, one of Polk township's most popular men, was born in Ripley county, Indiana, on the 7th day of March, 1837. When he was eleven years of age his parents emigrated to Grant county, Wisconsin, where he grew to manhood, and received a good common school education. At the outbreak of our late rebellion he was among the first to take up arms in defense of his country; enlisting August 19, 1861, in Company F, 7th Wisconsin Infantry. December 30, 1863, he re-enlisted with his regiment, and in December of the following year was promoted to the First Lieutenancy, and to the command of his company. At the battle of Five Forks, Virginia, on the 1st day of April, 1865, he received a wound from which he has never fully recovered, and now draws a pension. June 29, 1865, he was honorably discharged, after which he returned to his home in Wisconsin, and October 1, of the same year, was married to Miss Cornelia L. Crippen, a native of that State. During the year 1871 Mr. Roberts came to Bremer county, and settled on section 30, Polk township, where he has since resided, and now owns a well improved farm of 120 acres, valued at $30 per acre. Mr. Roberts is a staunch republican, and in 1876 was elected to the office of justice of the peace, which place of trust he continues to hold. In the fall of 1881, Mr. Roberts was the nominee of the republican party for representative—having received the nomination by a majority of *sixty-one votes* out of *seventy-five* cast. He was a very popular candidate, but owing to a certain combination of circumstances, was defeated at the general election, by 128 votes. Mr. and Mrs. Roberts are the parents of four children—Nettie, Anna, William and Alexander.

Albert Harrington, a son of Nicholas W. and Betsey (Spencer) Harrington, was born in Rhode Island, October 2, 1815. In 1821, the family moved to Onondaga county, New York, where the son grew to manhood and received a common school education, completed by an attendance at an academy. He was married October 28, 1840, in Onondaga county, New York, to Miss Sally Ann Coffin, a native of that county, born in 1816. Mr. Harrington and family remained in New York State until 1868, when they came to Bremer county, settling on section 25, Polk township, where he now owns a farm of eighty acres. They have one child living—Mary Eliza, who now resides in New York, and is a graduate of the Normal School at Albany.

John Roach is a native of the Emerald Isle, born March 16, 1848. When he was five years of age, his parents came to America and settled in New York City, where they remained for two years, after which they emigrated to Chicago, Illinois, where his mother died soon after their arrival. The family having been broken up by the death of his mother, John was adopted into the family of an Englishman named Ainsworth, and was brought up on a farm, receiving but a limited education. He remained in this family until fifteen years of age, when he enlisted in Company B, Eighth Illinois Cavalry. He participated in many engagements, and was wounded in a skirmish at Rector, Virginia, from the effects of which he now draws a pension; after serving his country true and faithfully, until the close of the war, he was honorably discharged June 5, 1865, after which he returned to Illinois and remained in McHenry county until the fall of 1866, when he came to Waverly, Bremer county, Iowa, where he resided four years, when he came to Plainfield and engaged in the grain and general produce trade, which is constantly increasing, and the name of "Johnnie Roach" is well and favorably known by every farmer in the surrounding country. Mr. Roach is owner of the finest residence in Plainfield, and here, surrounded by his family, he enjoys many pleasant hours not devoted to his business. He has been twice married, the first time, November 27, 1873, to Miss Mary Wanemaker, a native of Wisconsin, who died January 20, 1880, leaving two children—Lewis and Edwin. He was married again in October, 1880, to Miss Dora Wire, who is also a native of Wis-

Adin Terry.

consin. They are the parents of one child, an infant.

H. S. Ingham was born in Herkimer county, New York, in 1838. Five years after his birth, the family moved to Walworth county, Wisconsin. He obtained his education at the district school, near his home, and grew to manhood on his father's farm. During the year 1861, he started west in search of a home, and, liking this section of the country, determined to settle here. Therefore, in November, he purchased his farm, on section 36, and has since resided there. In 1863, he was united in marriage with Miss S. T. Gibson, who is a native of Crawford county, Pennsylvania. Three children bless this union—Winnie B., Lulu Maud and Mabel Laverne.

Thomas Burgess, a native of New York State, was born April 9, 1831. When sixteen years old, he removed to the city of Buffalo, where he was "bound out" to learn the trade of a machinist. Upon reaching his majority, he removed to Illinois, and settled in Chicago, where he became master-machinist of the Galena Railroad. Subsequently, he came to Bremer county. During the year 1850, Mr. Burgess was joined in wedlock with Miss Sarah J. Lay, who was born in Detroit, Michigan, but, when nine years old, removed to Buffalo, New York. They are the parents of six children—Frank C., Anna, Thomas, Cora J., Carrie J., and Freddy.

Charles Lay, the father of Mrs. Burgess, is a native of New York, born in 1812. There he grew to manhood, receiving his education in the district schools. In 1836 he came west to Detroit, Michigan, where he lived a short time, and then, after spending some time in various parts of the State, returned to Buffalo, New York, where he continued to reside until 1856, when he turned his steps westward. After spending six years in Chicago, Illinois, he came to Polk township, where he has since resided, In 1833 Mr. Lay was married to Cynthia Hoag, a native of New York State. Five children were born to them—Mary Ann, Sarah Jane, Harriet, Angeline, and Maria. His wife departed this life, June 23, 1879.

Riley Pierce, one of the early settlers of Bremer county, was born in Chautauqua county, New York, September 4, 1835. He is a son of Luther and Clarissa (Wells) Pierce. His father is a native of Vermont, and his mother of New York. Three years after his birth, the family came west, and settled in DuPage county, Illinois, where Riley grew to manhood, receiving a common school education, finished by an attendance of several terms at a seminary in Elgin. While making a short visit to Bremer county, in 1853, Mr. Pierce took a claim on section 19, Polk township, and in March, 1862, settled on his farm, where he still continues to reside, and now owns 314 acres of land, all of which is under cultivation, and valued at $30 per acre. In September, 1862, he was joined in wedlock with Miss Vernilia Panton, a native of Michigan. Three children have blessed this union—William, Frank, and Vernon. They have, also, an adopted daughter—Ella. In politics Mr. Pierce is a greenbacker. He has held the office of assessor four terms. Mr. Pierce has an enviable local reputation for honesty and integrity, those who know him best, speaking in strongest terms of his uprightness and character.

C. O. Smith was born in New York March 6, 1824. He received a common school education in his native State, and there grew to manhood. When four years old his father died, and at eight years of age he began life for himself, working where he could until fourteen, when he began working for his board in the family of a Mr. Chauncey Wilmoth. He continued with that gentlemen until twenty-one years of age, after which he spent three years in the State of Michigan, and upon returning to his native State, engaged in carpentering. In 1852 he was married to Miss Electa H. Clark, also a native of that State. Some years after his marriage, he turned his steps towards the setting sun, and in October, 1863, settled on section 11, Polk township, where he has since resided. Mr. Smith is a staunch republican, and takes quite an interest in the politics of his town. Two children—Brohelia Estella and Ora Clarence—have been born to this couple.

ORGANIC.

The first election in this township was held at the house of Lloyd Smith, in April, 1854. The following persons were appointed to hold said election:—Judges, Allen Smith, Gideon G. Phelps, Alexes Jackson; clerks, Addison Phelps and J. S. Tylar. At this time the following persons were elected:—Trustees, John S. Tylar, Allen Smith, Gideon G. Phelps; clerk, Addison Phelps; justices of the peace, Gideon G. Phelps and S. D. Jackson; constables, Lavinus Phelps and Spencer Jackson.

The following is a list of persons elected in the township, at the dates named:

1862—Trustees, J. K. Head, Eri Terry, William H. Brooks; clerk, Adin Terry; assessor, O. C. Harrington; justices of the peace, Barnes Thompson, J. K. Head; constables, William H. Fish, Riley Pierce.

1863—Trustees, W. W. Gray, C. R. Hastings, J. K. Head; constables, A. B. Nutting, Wesley Allen; clerk, Adin Terry; township supervisor, Eri Terry.

1864—Trustees, William Farr, B. C. French, A. Dustin; clerk, Moses Littlefield; assessor, Robert Taylor; justices, Barnes Thompson, Riley Pierce; constables, G. W. Nafus, M. L. Jackman.

1865—Trustees, James Gibson, B. C. French; clerk, M. S. Littlefield; assessor, J. E. Callender; justices, Orrin West, J. P. Newell; constables, Wesley Allen, Obijah Lovejoy. At this election, J. K. Head was elected township supervisor.

1866—Trustees, Calvin Githel, Charles Lay, Joseph Shelden; clerk, J. J. Merrill; assessor, Barnes Thompson; justices, John Chapman, Charles Folks; constables, John Sanders, J. Y. Spalding.

1867—Trustees, W. A. Ladd, M. Currier, C. R. Hastings; clerk, J. J. Merrill; assessor, O. C. Harrington; justice, C. A. Brown; constables, Charles Morris, John Sanders. At this election Adin Terry was elected township supervisor.

1868—Trustees, J. P. Sanford, John Colony, Nelson Bement; clerk, J. J. Merrill; assessor, B. Thompson; justices, C. A. Brown, Charles Folks; constables, John Sanders, W. H. Williams.

1869—Trustees, S. F. Spalding, David Beebe, Riley Pierce; clerk, M. S. Littlefield; assessor, John K. Head; constables, John Sanders, A. W. Emily.

1870—Trustees, Orrin West, Walter M. Davis, John K. Head; clerk, M. S. Littlefield; assessor, Barnes Thompson; justices, Warren Jones, David Brainard; constables, A. W. Emily, Foster Flowers.

1871—Trustees, Simon George, Orrin West, Joseph Harding; clerk, Henry Brainard; assessor, Riley Pierce; constabels, William Williams, John Sanders.

1872—Trustees, Adin Terry, W. B. Natton, C. R. Hastings; clerk, M. S. Littlefield; assessor, A. Larkin; justices, A. H. Fleisher, Charles Folks.

1873—Trustees, A. Larkin, C. R. Hastings, William Farr; clerk, Charles Folks; assessor, Allen Showalter; Justice, Joseph Harding; constables, Alfred Fuller, Osman Dana.

1874—Trustees, A. Larkin, William Farr, David Beebe; clerk, [at this election M. S. Littlefield, W. M. Davis and Charles Runyan were candidates for clerk. The vote between Littlefield and Davis being a tie, they received notices to meet at the town clerk's office and draw lots for the office. Mr. Littlefield not appearing, Mr. Davis was declared elected]; assessor, Barnes Thompson; justices, Joseph Hardin, Charles Folke; constable, A. Fuller.

1875—Trustees, A. Larkin, William Farr, David Beebe; clerk, William M. Davis; assessor, Barnes Thompson; justices, Charles Folks, James Harding; constables, A. Fuller, George Orchard.

1876—Trustees, William Farr, E. A. Granger, W. B. Natton; clerk, J. M. Roberts; assessor, C. P. Trescott; justices, J. M. Roberts, Joseph Harding; constables, W. H. Haviland, George Orchard.

1878—Trustees, A. B. Natton, E. A. Granger, A. Larkin; clerk, W. M. Davis; assessor, C. P. Trescott; justices, J. M. Roberts, Joseph Harding; constables, W. H. Haviland, George Orchard.

1877—Trustees, William Farr, E. A. Granger, W. B. Natton; clerk, Walter M. Davis; assessor, C. P. Trescott.

1878—Trustees, Adin Terry, C. P. Trescott, E. A. Granger; clerk, W. M. Davis; assessor, Riley Pierce; justices, J. M. Roberts, George Orchard; constables, A. O. Nutting, Charles Shields.

1879—Trustees, Adin Terry, Allen Showalter; clerk, J. M. Roberts.

1880—Trustees, Adin Terry, Orrin West, A. Larkin; clerk, W. M. Davis; assessor, A. W. Emily; justices, J. M. Roberts, George Orchard; constables, A. O. Nutting, E. S. Newcomb.

1881—Trustees, Orrin West, A. Larkin, John Cunningham; clerk, W. M. Davis; assessor, A. W. Emily; justices, J. M. Roberts, George Orchard; constables, A. O. Nutting, E. S. Newcomb.

1882—Trustees, John Cunningham, C. R. Hastings and Orrin West; clerk, W. M. Davis; assessor, A. W. Emily; constables, A. O. Nutting, O. S. Newcomb; justices, George Orchard, J. M. Roberts.

HISTORICAL ITEMS.

The first postoffice established was Polk, in 1854, with S. D. Jackson as postmaster. It was moved, in 1855, to the west side of the river, and Obed Gaines succeeded Mr. Jackson.

HISTORY OF BREMER COUNTY.

Horton postoffice was established in 1857, Lyman Nutting being the first postmaster.

The first church organization in the township was Methodist, and was formed in 1854.

The first frame school house in the township was at Horton, in 1859.

The first church building was that of the Free-Will Baptist, in 1869.

The first school in this township was held in a log cabin built gratuitously for the purpose by the people. The doors and windows being furnished by the district, for which a tax was assessed. The building was completed and a summer school taught in 1854, by Mrs. Louisa Nutting. There was an attendance of about fifteen scholars. Mrs. Nutting is a daughter of J. H. Eldridge, who came from Illinois with her husband in 1854. She now lives at Sioux Falls, Dakota. This building was used for various purposes—educational, social, religious and political—until 1860, when a new building was erected. The old building was used after this for a residence, and subsequently burned.

A saw mill was built at Horton in the winter of 1855–56, was in running order in March. It had a fifteen horse power engine. The proprietors were C. A. Brown, C. A. Lease & Lyman Nutting. They did a good business until 1876, when it was removed to Bradford, Chickasaw county, where it now remains.

Woodcock and Hopkins erected a saw mill in 1855, on the Cedar river, on section 6. They run it three or four years, but not proving a financial success, it was abandoned.

A steam saw mill was built by Silas Farr in 1855. He run it as a saw mill for three or four years, then remodeled it for a grist mill and distillery. It was finally sold and removed.

The first marriage united the destinies of Mr. Elliott and Miss Ellen Buckmaster, the ceremony being performed by Judge Farris. This occurred in 1853. Elliott left his wife in about one year. She remained with her mother for some time, went finally to Kansas with another man, whom she had married in Waterloo.

The first death was that of Thomas Hawkins, at the house of Ezra Allen, during the spring of 1853; he was buried on section 22.

The first birth was that of Mary E. Smith, daughter to Allen and Elizabeth Smith, on the 19th day of September, 1852. She is now the wife of Barney Thompson, and lives on section 21.

The second birth was a son to Mr. and Mrs. Lloyd Smith; this happy event transpired in November, 1853; he is yet living near the old place, on section 16.

There are two cemeteries in this township, "Horton Cemetery," located near the town of Horton, and "Mitzger's Burying Ground," located on section 8.

The first interment in the former was the remains of Mr. Curtiss, in 1857.

Lloyd Smith is the oldest living settler in the township, and his brother Allen the next.

ROBBERY.

During the years of 1853, and 1854, some hard characters had settled in and about the towns of Chickasaw and Bradford. These men had been members of a secret organization to protect their claims. During the spring of 1855, Thomas Harris came from Winnebago county, Illinois, and settled on a farm in the northern part of Polk township, about six miles from Bradford, which was his trading point. At that time the old gentleman was somewhat addicted to strong drink, and it was known that he had some money left after paying for his place. Early in the winter of 1855, he hitched his ox team to a sled, and went to Bradford to purchase supplies for his family. Quite a number of these men were there, drinking and carousing, and they pursuaded Mr. Harris to drink, from time to time, until the day was well spent, and darkness near at hand, by which time he was considerably under the influence of numerous potations. When he started for home, and had proceeded one or two miles, four or five of the gang overtook him and demanded his money, at the same time striking at him with a club, which broke one of the old gentleman's fingers, as he attempted to ward it off. As he was badly frightened, he threw down his purse, which contained but a few shillings, and "took to his heels" across the prairie, running about four miles to his home, where, summoning his wife to his assistance, they barricaded the doors and windows, loaded with plenty of ammunition the old, rusty gun, and made general preparations for battle. But no enemy came. His ox team strayed into the barn-yard of Mr. Jackson, where it was heard during the night, and one of his boys got up and drove it home to Mr. Harris. The light of morning revealed coffee, sugar, flour, rice, etc., scattered in profusion around the barn-yard. A short time afterward, one of the gang proposed to settle the matter; but Mr. Harris refused, and said if the necessary proof could be had, he would prosecute them to the extent of the law. The outcome was, a number of the gang left the country. The men committing this outrage were commonly known as the "Jones gang." The old gentleman was so thoroughly frightened he did not dare to go to Bradford for years afterward without company.

PATRONS OF HUSBANDRY.

Polk township shared in the general excitement which spread so generally over this section of the State, in reference to the so-called "disadvantage" under which the farmers were placed. The plan proposed seemed feasible; a great saving was promised, by enabling the farmers to pocket the earnings of the "middle men," and consequently realize better prices for their products. Amid considerable enthusiasm "White Oak Grange" No. 143, was organized January 29, 1872, by David High, deputy from the State Grange, with the following named persons as charter members:—Adin Terry, Malvina Terry, Marvin Potter, J. P. Sanborn, Ann Sanborn, Albert Austin, Huldah Austin, Edith Nutting, David Beebe, J. H. T. Beebe, Benjamin Beebe, Warren Potter, C. O. Smith, G. D. Thomas, A. H. Gates, Annie Gates, R. Cronk, Albert Nutting, A. P. Collins, M. S. Littlefield, O. C. Harrington, Joseph Smith, J. J. Ede, George Siebert, Charles Hastings and N. Hastings.

The first meeting was held at Horton, and the following officers were elected:—Marvin Potter, Master; Adin Terry, Overseer; A. P. Collins, Lecturer; M. S. Littlefield, Steward; C. O. Smith, Chaplain, David Beebe, Treasurer; O. C. Harrington, Secretary; Charles Hastings, Assistant Steward; Warren Potter, Gatekeeper; Mrs. Ann Sanborn, Assistant Steward; Mrs. Annie Gates, Pomona; Mrs. H. Austin, Flora; and Edith Nutting, Ceres. A. H. Gates, N. Hastings and G. D. Thomas, finance committee; M. Potter, J. Smith, A. Austin, J. P. Sanborn, Mrs. M. Potter, Mrs. A. Terry, Mrs. A. Austin, Mrs. O. C. Harrington, relief committee.

At this meeting there was paid into the treasury, $67. At a regular meeting held December 31, 1873, the following named persons were elected: M. Potter, Master; A. Terry, Overseer; A. P. Collins, Lecturer; Charles Hastings, Steward; D. Beebe, Treasurer; O. C. Harrington, Secretary; W. Potter, Gatekeeper; M. E. Terry, Eva Littlefield, Rosa Sawyer, Mrs. Harrington, Lady Assistant Stewards.

Many pleasant meetings were held, and the prospect seemed for a time, flattering.

The farmers were congratulating themselves on having perfected an organization, which would meet their wants and save them money.

This Grange was successfully managed for years, and proved quite a saving in many instances to many of its patrons. A warehouse was built and operated for some time, but was finally sold to E. P. Day.

The organization numbered, at one time, over one hundred persons, but it has ceased to exist.

THE IOWA DETECTIVE FORCE.

During the years 1864-5 there was a regularly organized band of horse-thieves taking in, on one of their routes, this part of Iowa, and many horses had been stolen by them. The citizens of Polk township, always awake to every matter of public interest, concluded that they would protect themselves, and formed an organization with the above name. No horse-thieves were caught and hung by them, but the efficiency of the society was demonstrated by the fact that no horses were stolen in this vicinity after they were in working order. The thieves apparently had a wholesome dread of such institutions, and gave the township a wide berth, preferring not to risk themselves under such watchful eyes, or take the chances of the possible results. This organization was effected on the 5th day of May, 1866, when the following temporary officers were elected: A. Terry, president; Mason Spalding, vice-president; J. K. Head, secretary; A. Showalter, treasurer; William Farr, captain; R. Cronk, first-lieutenant; O. Nutting, second lieutenant; John Spalding, third lieutenant; Benjamin Beebe, fourth lieutenant; A. Nutting, C. Lease, W. S. Grover, Joseph Smith and David Beebe; detective committee. To these, on the 12th of May, a standing committee was added as follows: C. A. Brown, O. C. Harrington, Marvin Potter, J. P. Austin and William Farr.

In a short time the organization was made permanent by the election by ballot, of the following named officers:

J. J. Merrill, captain; James Wilson, first lieutenant; C. R. Hastings, second lieutenant; G. M. Lease, third lieutenant; W. S. Grover, fourth lieutenant; C. A. Lease, Joseph Smith, R. Cronk, John Crane and O. Nutting, detective committee; J. F. Spalding, R. C. French and O. Nutting, committee on claims. The place of meeting was at Hastings' School House, and the society was soon in good working order, with fifty-five members. The society continued in existence until 1873, when it disbanded. The following were the last officers: A. H. Fleisher, president; Eri Terry, vice-president; J. H. Eldridge, secretary; J. P. Sanborn, assistant secretary; A. Showalter, treasurer; A. Terry, captain; A. Gates, first lieutenant; C. R. Hastings, second lieutenant; M. Spalding, third lieutenant; J. E. Callinder, fourth lieutenant.

VILLAGE OF HORTON.

In the midst of a gently undulating plain, skirted near by with timber, and surrounded with an intelligent class of farmers, lies the little village of Horton. Although a small place, and the various branches of trade not numerously represented, yet a considerable business is done. It is located on parts of sections 26 and 27, and was platted by C. A. Lease, in 1856.

The first house built after the place was laid out was by Carlton Brown.

The first store was opened by Anson Nutting, and about the same time a blacksmith shop was built by C. A. Lease, who employed a man by name of Brower to run it.

The first preaching in the place was by Elder David Terry, a regular Baptist, in 1857, in a hall over what is now Eldridge's store. This reverend gentleman also performed the first marriage ceremony in the village, which united the destinies of W. W. Gray and Miss Lucinda Nutting, in the summer of 1857.

The first death was an infant, daughter of Chauncey Lease, and the first birth was a son to the same parties.

There is now one blacksmith shop, one blacksmith and wagon shop, two stores, a Free-Will Baptist Church building, and a brick school house, within its limits.

The blacksmith and wagon shop is owned by Potter & Crooks. They have a rapidly increasing trade, and are pushed to the utmost to meet the demand. They have an annual trade of about $6,000.

Warren Potter, of this firm, was born in 1836, and is a native of New York State. While there he received a common school education and learned the wagon-maker's trade. In August, 1862, he enlisted in Company F, One Hundred and Forty-second New York Volunteers, and, while at Chapin's farm, in front of Richmond, received a gun-shot wound, from which he has never recovered, and therefore draws a pension. He was honorably discharged from service in the month of May, 1865, and returned to his home in New York. The year following, he came to Horton, Bremer county, and opened his wagon-making establishment, in which trade he has since continued. Mr. Potter was married, in 1857, to Miss Sarah J. Maxam, a native of New York. Three children—Carrie, Hattie and Frankie—have been born to them.

The blacksmith shop is conducted by C. M. Hastings, a good and accommodating mechanic.

W. J. Pierson is the proprietor of one of the stores, and carries a general stock. He commenced business in the spring of 1881, has a stock of about $4,000, and his sales amount to about $20,000 per annum, with a steady increasing trade. He was born in the town of Walton, Delaware county, New York, on the 10th of March, 1852. After becoming proficient in the branches taught in the district schools, near his home, he attended the Delaware Library Institute, where he obtained an excellent education. Upon leaving school, Mr. Pierson followed the profession of teaching for several years—taught three terms in the State of New York, and six in Iowa. In 1875 he went to Floyd county, Iowa, was traveling salesman for a nursery firm. After remaining in their employment five years, he went to Tripoli, Bremer county, and engaged in the agricultural implement business one summer, then came to Horton, Polk township, and opened his present business. He was married to Miss Ida Fish, a native of Floyd county, Iowa, in 1880.

W. Eldridge, dealer in general merchandise does a good business.

The shoemaking trade is represented by Mr. Brainard.

HORTON POSTOFFICE.

This office was started, as stated, in 1857. The general character of the citizens of this section is largely indicated by the fact that more mail, more newspapers, are received at this office than any other in the vicinity. Stamps are annually cancelled amounting to a large sum. The present postmaster is Albert Austin. W. J. Pierson, as deputy, has full control.

Albert Austin, postmaster at Horton, was born in 1828, in Cayuga county, New York, and there he passed his youth and obtained his education. In the fall of 1857, he came to Bremer county, Iowa, and settled on section 22, Polk township, where he has since lived, with the exception of six years spent in the town of Waverly. Mr. Austin is an advocate of republicanism, and during his residence in the county has held several of the local offices. In March, 1881, he was appointed postmaster of the Horton postoffice, and fills that position at the present date. On the 8th day of October, 1850, he was married to Miss Huldah E. Spalding, who also was born in Cayuga county, New York, in 1831. Two children—Charles A. and Hattie A.—bless their union. Their son is engaged in the mercantile trade at Sumner.

RELIGIOUS.

The First Free-Will Baptist Church in Horton was organized at the house of C. A. Lease, in the village of Horton, by the Rev. A. K. Moulton, on the 28th day of March, 1858, with twenty members, comprising the following named persons: Lyman Nutting; Lydia Nutting, James Lynes, Sarah Lynes, O. C. Harrington, Ellen Harrington, C. A. Brown, Ama Brown, C. A. Lease, Jenett A. Lease, G. M. Lease, Jenett Lease, Worlin Gray, Lucinda Gray, Edgar Nutting, Edmund Nutting, Mary A. George, Jane Adams, John P. Leape, Mrs. J. P. Leape. C. A. Brown and Worlin Gray were appointed the first deacons of the church, and O. C. Harrington first clerk. The present membership is about thirty-five. The officers are: M. S. Littlefield and F. H. Bunth, deacons, and O. C. Harrington, clerk.

The first pastor of the church, Rev. A. K. Moulton, was recognized as one of the most intellectual men in the county. He

was the first school superintendent elected in the county; he also ranked among the first as a pulpit orator. He came to Bremer county from Massachusetts, in 1854, and located on a large tract of land in Sumner township, where he continued to reside until he left the county, in 1859. Before coming west he had been pastor of churches in some of the largest towns in the New England States, among them Lowell, Massachusetts; Portland and Lewiston, Maine; Manchester and Dover, New Hampshire. He was also associate editor of the *Morning Star*, for a number of years, the denominational organ of the Free-Will Baptists. He was born in Lower Canada about 1810, and was killed June, 1873, in Cleveland, Ohio, while returning home with his wife and child, from a festival, by stepping from a railroad bridge. He had been residing in Cleveland some years, engaged in missionary work. The second pastor of the church was Rev. N. R. George, a young man from Ohio, of more than ordinary ability. He attended school one term with President Garfield. He is now residing in Nebraska.

The third pastor was Charles Pierce, a native of New York, and a graduate of Oberlin College, Ohio; a good man and a polished speaker. He is now an old man, but much of the fire of his younger days still remains. He is now living and preaching in Marble Rock, Floyd county, Iowa.

F. P. Newell, the fourth pastor, was born in Boston, Massachusetts; educated at Whitestown Seminary, New York; he is an able man and preacher. Is now living in Smith county, Kansas.

Rufus Hayden, the fifth pastor of the church, is a native of Massachusetts, and an excellent preacher, always commanding a full house, and eminently successful in revival work; under his labors a fine church edifice and parsonage were erected. He is now living and preaching in Sac county, Iowa.

J. W. Drew, the sixth pastor, is a native of Canada; a man of dignified and commanding presence, and a fair preacher; is now pastor of a church at Oelwein, Fayette county, Iowa.

S. S. Summerlin, the seventh pastor, is a native of Ohio; has had some success as a preacher; is now living and preaching in Mitchell county, Iowa.

A. Palmer, the eighth pastor, was born in Madison county, New York, over forty years ago; came west when a young man. He was married to Chloe Larrabee, a highly respected young lady of Delaware county, Iowa. Some eighteen or twenty years ago, was converted to christianity, and commenced preaching a few years after his marriage, in the same county. He was fluent and sympathetic as a speaker, his discourses being characterized by great spirituality and power. The church was greatly prospered under his ministrations. Being a good mechanic he kept everything about the church and parsonage in good repair. It could be said of him in truth, he was one of nature's noblemen—an honest christian and a faithful pastor. His death was caused by his falling from a platform while assisting to calcimine the church, in November, 1879, surviving his injuries only ten hours from the time of the accident. A general gloom settled over the whole community, as he was loved and respected by all who knew him.

Rev. D. N. Thompson, a licentiate and member of the church, a young man who is highly respected in the community, is now occasionally supplying the church, with preaching.

TOWN OF PLAINFIELD.

Plainfield, a town on the Iowa division of the Illinois Central Railroad, is located on the west half of the northwest quarter of section 29, and the east half of the northeast quarter of section 30, in township 93, range 14, west. The town was platted October 16, 1866, by H. S. Hoover, county surveyor, upon the request of Charles Folks, E. J. Dean, Riley Pierce, and George Ketchum, on land owned by George Ketchum.

Charles Folks was born on the 15th day of March, 1821, in Columbiana county, Ohio. Shortly after his birth the family moved to Wisconsin, and located in Grant county. When Fort Sumter was fired upon, his loyal heart was stirred to its depths, and he was among the first to take up arms in defense of his country. He enlisted in Company H, Seventh Wisconsin Infantry, when he was made First Sergeant. In the course of time, he became First Lieutenant, and, just before his company was discharged, was promoted to the Captaincy. At the battle of Gettysburg he was severely wounded, but recovered sufficiently to re-enlist with his regiment. After three and one-half years of service, however, he was obliged to be discharged because of that wound. In 1865 he came to Bremer county, Iowa, and laid out the original town site of Plainfield. During his residence there he was engaged in the mercantile trade. He built the first business house in the place, and was the first postmaster. He held the office of justice of the peace, several years. Mr. Folks was a member of the Methodist Episcopal Church, and always took a deep interest in its progress. He was married in 1840, to Miss Rebecca Laughman, who was born in Pennsylvania, but moved to Ohio, with her parents, when nine years of age. Mr. Folks died April 9th, 1879, leaving a widow and five children—William, Emma, Amanda, Charles, and Elmer.

Quite a number of the old settlers were from Plainfield, Illinois, and consequently the place was named in remembrance of the country from whence they came. Previous to the platting of the town site, Mr. Folks had built a frame building, 16x32, for a dwelling and storeroom, and put therein a stock of goods. This was the first store in the town, and the building was the first erected on what is now the town of Plainfield. The postoffice was kept in this building a number of years. Mr. Folks sold out to another party, who moved the building across the street, where he remained in business a short time, when the building was purchased by a third party, who moved it to Main street. It is now used for a storeroom. In 1867 an addition was made to the town adjoining the old plat on the west, by George Ketchum. Upon this addition, the business portion of Plainfield is now located.

In 1867 another addition was made on the south, by E. J. Dean, and called Deanville. On this plat the railroad company built their depot. In 1869 another plat was made on the west of Deanville, known as Pike's addition.

PLAINFIELD POSTOFFICE.

During the administration of President Buchanan a postoffice was established called Polk, and S. W. Jackson was appointed postmaster. In his first quarterly report to the department we find he had received for postage forty-five cents, and there was postage unpaid on books, pamphlets, etc., twenty-seven cents, which indicates the amount of business transacted at that early day. Mr. Jackson remained in charge of this office until he sold his farm in the spring of 1858. He was succeeded by the purchaser, Amos Head, who received his commission August 13, 1858. Mr. Head remained in charge of the office until August 13, 1861, when he was succeeded by W. N. Gaines, and the office was moved to his residence on section 18, and the name changed to "Syracuse." Mr. Gaines discharged the duties of the office until 1863, when his brother, Obed, received the appointment, and the office again removed to his house on the same section. Mr. Anson Leonard received the appointment in June, 1865, but the business was done by Mr. Gaines until Mr. Hutchins took charge. The next postmaster was H. Hutchins, who assumed the duties of the office in 1866. Mr. Hutchins was relieved in October, 1866, and Charles Folks received the appointment, when the office was moved to Plainfield. In February, 1868, the name of the office was again changed, and has since been called Plainfield.

Mr. Folks was succeeded by Mr. M. A. Gordon, who remained in charge until September, 1877, when Elias C. Walker was appointed. This was made a money order office, July 1, 1878, and the first order was issued to Conrad Ditmore, for $10.00, dated July 1, 1878, in favor of S. P. Farley & Son, Dubuque, Iowa, and during the first quarter there were issued 142 money orders, amounting to $2,313.20. During this quarter, also, there was received for postage stamps and stamped envelopes, $239.86, and stamps cancelled to the amount of $187.74. The present postmaster is J. M. Boardman, who received his commission about January 1, 1883.

Amos Head, one of the early postmasters of the Plainfield postoffice, was born in Pembroke, New Hampshire, in 1810. While in his native town, he received an academic education, and also learned the printer's trade. During the year 1841, he removed to Charleston, South Carolina, engaging in the book and stationery business, and, while there, he originated the express business, which has since grown to be one of the leading enterprises of the world. Upon leaving Charleston, Mr. Head spent six years in the State of Massachusetts, and, in 1858, came to Bremer county, Iowa, settling in Polk township. He belonged to the Democratic party, and was one of the early postmasters of Polk Precinct postoffice, now Plainfield. In 1842, he was married, choosing for a helpmeet Miss Laura L. Whitney, a native of Massachusetts. Three children—Elizabeth, John K. and George W.—blessed this union. June 29, 1869, Mr. Head died, as he had lived, respected and beloved by all, who were honored with his acquaintance. His wife still survives him.

Elias C. Walker was born in St. Charles, Illinois, in 1847. Four years after his birth, the family moved to Hainesville, where they resided five years, and then came to Iowa, locating on a farm in Chickasaw county. October 4, 1863, when only sixteen years old, Elias enlisted in Company B, Fifteenth Iowa Infantry, and served until honorably discharged in July, 1865. He received a bayonet wound, while upon duty, at Savannah, Georgia, but was fortunate enough to recover from its effects. Upon quitting "Uncle Sam's" service, he returned to Chickasaw county, and during his residence there, learned the tinner's trade. In October, 1875, he came to Plainfield, Bremer county, and opened a hardware store, in which business he continued until January, 1882, when he sold the stock to his brother, and purchased an interest in the Plainfield hotel. In the fall of 1877, Mr. Walker received the appointment of postmaster of the Plainfield post office. He has also held other local offices. During the year 1867, he was united in marriage with Miss Sarah L. Bolton, born in the State of New York, but when ten years of age, moved with her parents to Fredericksburg, Chickasaw county, and still later, to Jacksonville, same county. Four children have been born to them, of whom Addie and George are now living; Cora May and Floyd L. being deceased. Mr. Walker is a strictly honest and reliable business man, besides being the possessor of those pleasing qualities that win him hosts of friends, wherever he may be.

SOCIETIES.

Lodge No. 354, I. O. O. F., was organized in August, 1876, with the following charter members: Henry Robinson, Elias C. Walker, H. Nichols, N. H. Larkin and E. F. Temple. The first officers were—H. Robinson, N. G.; Elias C. Walker, V. G.; H. Nichols, secretary; William Denning, treasurer. The lodge seemed to be in a flourishing condition until January, 1882, when it surrendered its charter for want of a suitable room in which to hold meetings. The last officers were—E. Wuthy, N. G; James Cooper, V. G.; J. M. Roberts, secretary; H. Nichols, treasurer.

A lodge of the Independent Order of Good Templars was organized September 17, 1881, by Francis J. Norton, State Deputy. The first meeting was held in Sullivan's hall, and the following persons installed for the first quarter: George F. Harwood, W. C. T.; Miss Edna M. Nichols, W. V. T.; Irving Moody, W. S.; Elmer Folks, W. F. S.; Henry Eckert, W. T.; Albert Taylor, W. I. G.; F. H. Nichols, W. O. G.; Albert Farr, W. M.; Mrs. William Hograbe, W. D. M.; H. Nichols, W. C.; B. A. Folks, L. D. At the close of the second quarter, the membership numbered 64. Francis J. Norton, the State deputy, has held office in the order for fifteen consecutive years, and has been representative to the grand lodge of Iowa eight years in succession. He is now chairman of the State committee. The lodge was named Frances Willard, in honor of the great lady apostle of prohibition. Public sentiment in Plainfield is very strongly in favor of temperance.

WOMAN'S CHRISTIAN TEMPERANCE UNION.

At a meeting held in the Methodist Episcopal Church, in Plainfield, November 19,

1879, the Woman's Christian Temperance Union was organized. After an address by Mrs. M. F. Goode, a constitution was adopted, and the following officers were duly elected:—Mrs. D. Battin, president; Mrs. William Lynes, vice-president; Mrs. Olive Logan, vice-president; Mrs. V. M. Hall, treasurer; Miss N. Williams, secretary.

Their first preamble declares their object to be "to plan and carry forward measures which will result in the suppression of intemperance in our midst."

An executive committee was appointed, and twenty-eight members were enrolled. This union has been the banner one in the county since its organization. It took the law into its own hands, and wiped out two saloons, the trial lasting for several days, and creating great sensation. The meetings are held on Thursday, at 3 o'clock P. M., every two weeks. The present officers are: Mrs. S. Harwood, president; Mrs. Dr. Nichols, vice-president; Mrs. S. W. Putney, secretary; Mrs. M. Walker, treasurer. This society did most effectual work during the amendment campaign.

METHODIST EPISCOPAL CHURCH.

The Plainfield circuit was formed in the fall of 1870. Rev. W. Ward Smith was pastor, and Rev. Dr. William Brush, presiding elder. In 1869 and 1870, Plainfield formed a part of the Horton and Prairie Valley charge, having but few members—ten in all—under the pastorate of Rev. H. Warner, of whom it may be said: "He planted the church of Plainfield."

On the 24th day of January, 1869, the first class of the Methodist Episcopal Church, of Plainfield, was organized in the Plainfield school house, by Rev. H. Warner, at the request of Rev. S. A. Lee, presiding elder of Cedar Falls district, Upper Iowa conference. J. M. Boardman was appointed class leader. The following persons composed the membership: J. M. Boardman, Emma R. Boardman, Sabron Temple, Lucinda B. Temple, Ada T. Temple, Harriet Ketchum, Nancy Warner, Fanny Hovey, Sarah A. Pike, and Almira M. Robinson. This class met every Sabbath for religious worship. At the first quarterly conference following the organization of the class, a board of trustees were elected, consisting of J. M. Boardman, George Eck, C. P. Trescott, W. B. Notton, Charles Folks, and John Cunningham.

During the summer of 1874, the society and friends of the congregation erected a house of worship, at an expense of $3,500, and on November 29, 1874, it was dedicated by Rev. Dr. A. B. Kendig and Rev. Dr. R. W. Keeler, presiding elder of Charles City District, Upper Iowa Conference, at 11 a. m.

Soon after, a Ladies' Aid Society was organized as follows: Rev. Mrs. William Gibson, president; Amanda Folks, vice-president; Emma Jackman, secretary; Mrs. Emma R. Boardman, treasurer. This society took upon itself $200 of the church indebtedness, and employed Revs. A. B. Kendig, S. W. Ingham, J. T. Crippen and R. W. Keeler, D. D., to deliver a series of lectures to raise the amount.

The Methodist Episcopal Sunday School was first organized December 6, 1874, with the following officers: B. M. Lillabridge, superintendent; Emma R. Boardman, assistant superintendent; James

Dunlap, secretary and treasurer; Orrin West, chorister. The Sabbath School met at 10 a. m., and had twenty-two members. It has grown in interest and increased in numbers, until it now numbers, with officers, teachers, scholars and contributing members, 110 in all. The present officers are: Mrs. Hattie Eddy, superintendent; J. M. Boardman, assistant superintendent; Prof. C. W. Van Dorn, secretary; Orrin West, treasurer. The school is well officered and wisely conducted.

The school was organized as a missionary society, auxiliary to the missionary society of the Methodist Episcopal Church, by the present pastor, Rev. Francis J. Norton, September 15, 1881. During the conference year it has contributed $38 to the cause of missions, besides paying one year in advance for Sunday School literature, books, papers, cards, and all Sunday School requisites, and has money in the treasury to defray expenses for another year. The Sunday School gives public concerts once a quarter; thirteen teachers are employed, and teacher's meetings are held on Wednesday evening of each week. Mrs. S. M. Harwood occupied the office of superintendent for one year and a half, and was the most efficient officer the school has ever had. The plan of the work for the present year has been carefully arranged, and the Sunday School is destined to grand results.

In 1877 the appointment at Horton was dropped, and the appointment at Kingsley school house, in Warren township, with Plainfield, constituted the Plainfield charge. The following great revivals have taken place under the pastorate of Rev. Wm. Gibson:

In 1872, scores were converted, and the reinforcement to Methodism in Plainfield was the occasion of much joy.

In 1881 another most glorious revival took place under the pastoral labors of Rev. Francis J. Norton; there were sixty-five accessions to the church during the year.

The following pastors have served this charge: Rev. H. Warner, 1869 and 1870; Rev. W. Ward Smith, 1870 to 1872; Rev. Wm. Gibson, 1872 to 1875; Rev. J. Baldwin, 1875 to 1876; Rev. S. T. McKim, 1876 to 1877; Rev. A. M. Shimer, 1877 to 1878; Rev. J. N. Blodgett, 1878 to 1879; Rev. Daniel Battin, 1879 to 1880.

The present pastor, Rev. Francis J. Norton, was appointed to this charge, October 6, 1880, and was re-appointed September 26, 1881, and again September 25, 1882. He is, therefore, now serving his third year, and is greatly beloved by his church, and is very popular among all the people. He was born in the city of Utica, Oneida county, New York, December 16, 1857. His parents removed to Iowa, in 1858, and settled at Koszta, in Iowa county, where they have resided for nearly a quarter of a century. His father, Arowit R. Norton, died August 18, 1874. He was an early pioneer of Iowa county, and was foremost in the progressive movements of the country. Mr. Norton's mother, Mrs. Olive D. Norton, lives at the old home with her son. She is a lady beloved by all, and sincerely endeared to her children. She is one of those noble and true women who have done much for society and the general good. Mr. Norton's parents have been members of the Methodist Episcopal Church for many years. Mr. Norton, after leaving the district school, took the high school course, after which he took the normal course, and then engaged in teaching for five years. He was converted at the Koszta Methodist camp meeting, August 27, 1869, and united with the Methodist Episcopal Church, and at once began to prepare for the ministry. He was licensed to preach by Rev. Banner Mark, presiding elder of Newton District, Iowa Conference. He entered the itinerant ministry after serving Montour charge, under the elder, Rev. F. C. Wolfe, for five months, at the Twenty-fourth Session of the Upper Iowa Conference, held in Davenport, Iowa, September 24, 1879, and received his appointment, as pastor of the Methodist Episcopal Church of Northwood, county seat of North county, Iowa, which he served with perfect acceptability for one year. He was successful in liquidating the church debt of $1,350, and at the urgent calls of duty, he was appointed to Plainfield charge, where he not only provided for a heavy debt, but built a new church in Warren township, which he dedicated October 22, 1882.

Mr. Norton identifies himself with every worthy and commendable enterprise, and pushes his work as if the universe were depending. He was a leader in the temperance campaign of 1881 and '82; he was a delegate to the State Prohibition Convention, which met in DesMoines in 1882; he was also a delegate to the Republican State Convention, where he voted for Governor Buren R. Sherman. In 1882, he represented the Third Congressional District of Iowa in the National Prohibitory Home Protection Convention, held in Chicago, August 23. The home, the church, the school, and the government, are to him the safe-guards of a higher civilization. During the summer of 1880, his health, being broken, he, in company with his most esteemed friend, Mr. N. W. Egleston, now of Chamberlain, Dakota Territory, took a tour through the south and east, attending the General Conference of his church in Cincinnati, and spending some time in Washington, District Columbia. Mr. Norton is a natural orator, commands universal respect, is greatly beloved by the people, and has a future of great usefulness before him. The present membership of his church is one hundred and four. He has a committee on missions, Sunday Schools, temperance and education, each composed of three members. The weekly prayer meeting is held on Thursday evenings of each week. The present board of trustees are, J. M. Boardman, Mrs. Hattie Eddy, Mrs. M. Walker, Mrs. M. Denning, Mrs. E. P. Day and Mr. Orrin West.

The Ladies' Aid Society is a valuable aid to the social and financial interests of the church. The present officers are, Mrs. Ada Folks, president; Mrs. H. White, vice-president; Mrs. M. Denning, treasurer; Mrs. M. L. Jackman, secretary. The choir, under the leadership of Mr. Oliver Powers, with Mrs. Libbie Burgess organist, is among the fine attractions, and forms a most helpful part of the church service.

A former pastor, Rev. J. Baldwin, departed this life in great peace, in 1877.

EDUCATIONAL.

The first school in Plainfield was taught by H. M. Swan, a local Methodist preacher, in the store room of Charles Folks. Mr. Swan had taught a term of school, the previous winter, in a house belonging to George Ketchum, about one mile north of this place. Before the close of his school in Plainfield, the district commenced building a school house, which was so far completed, that upon the last day of school an exhibition was held in it. Mr. Swan now lives a short distance east from Clarksville, in Butler county. He was at one time candidate for county superintendent of schools.

Plainfield originally was included in the territory of a sub-district, and the district school house was erected during the winter of 1868, at a cost of $600.

The independent district of Plainfield was set off in 1872; but the old building was used until 1881, when a school building was erected at a cost of $3,400, which would be a credit to a much larger town than Plainfield. It is constructed for a graded school of four departments. Up to the present time there has been occasion to use but three. The first term of school in this building was during the winter of 1881–2. Mr. George Harwood was the first principal, with Mrs. Harwood in charge of the intermediate department, and Miss E. Nichols, of the primary. There were enrolled upward of 120 scholars. At the present time, C. W. VanDorn is principal, and Mrs. I. W. Moody has charge of the primary department.

The old school building was sold to J. C. Garner, and is used for an office and store room, for agricultural impliments.

DRIVE-WELL EXCITEMENT.

Good water is a necessity in any country, and the supply here has been secured by means of drive-wells. In 1880, there was considerable excitement in many States in reference to these wells, and means of securing water, particularly in Butler and Bremer counties, Iowa. There were parties who unjustly claimed the "patent right" of these wells, or methods of securing them, and they were collecting a royalty of $10 on each well. If parties refused to pay, an action was at once instituted against them in the courts. This seemed to have the desired effect, and many persons paid the amount asked, fearing the expense and uncertainty of litigation. The citizens of Plainfield, however, with a determination not to be thus swindled, pursued another course. Notices had been received by the postmaster and justice of the peace, stating the day the agent would be on hand to collect, and advising all parties to meet him promptly, and settle the matter by paying $10, and, unless they complied with this request, an action would be immediately commenced in the courts, against them. This plan had worked very well heretofore, and, was expected to be successful here, but the citizens, justly incensed by the action of this set of swindlers, concluded to give the agent a warm reception. To perfect a plan of operation, a meeting was called, the situation discussed and a committee appointed to confer with the gentlemen. The nature of this conference appears hereafter.

Upon the day selected as the one when money would liberally pour in, and ten dollar bills flow like a river, into the insatiable craws of these swindling rascals, this representative approached the town with confidence. Arriving at the

depot he thought there was a funeral in town, that usually busy place at train time seemed deserted, and contemplating upon the uncertainty of life and the certainty of death—from dust we came, to dust we must return—and many other thoughts, suggested by the mournful desolate appearance of things, he wended his way toward the business part of the village. At the postoffice he was informed that a committee had been appointed to confer with him in reference to the drive-well business. This information, together with a glimpse he had caught of a rope with a noose at one end dangling from something suggestive of the gallows, and a large crowd congregated near by, led him to the conclusion, that his supposition when at the depot was premature, that the funeral was one in contemplation, and in which he might be personally interested. In consideration of all these things, he had very urgent business elsewhere, did not care to remain in Plainfield, his thoughts reverted to the days when the good advice of his mother was given; his sins appeared before him in glowing light, especially his connection with the drive-well business. But every other consideration was swallowed up in this one desire to leave the town, and leave he did, the first opportunity. Since which time the citizens of this place have never been troubled by any agents for this worst of all swindles.

HOTELS.

The Plainfield House, a frame structure, was the first hotel. It was moved from the country by George Ketchum and rebuilt. He was the first landlord and remained in the business a number of years. Afterward it was rented to different parties until 1877, when it was purchased by John Smith, who, having rebuilt and remodelled it, sold it to Edward Temple, and in 1882 it was again transferred. It afterward, was purchased by a company consisting of the following gentlemen: Elias J. Walker, John Roach, J. M. Roberts, G. M. Harker and E. J. Huff. Mr. E. J. Walker now has charge.

SHOEMAKER.

Mr. Henry Flint was the first to engage in this business. He came from Freeport, Illinois, and had a shop where Dr. Nichols now has his office. He afterward went to Oregon, where he still lives.

SAW-MILL.

The first saw-mill was built by Bement and Boorom, and was located a little northeast of where J. M. Boardman's store now stands. A good business was done at this mill until the fall of 1869, when the boiler exploded, damaging the building and machinery to such an extent that it was abandoned. The proprietors now live in Minnesota.

PHYSICIAN.

Dr. H. Nichols was the first practicing physician to locate here. He was from Illinois and came in 1869. He has since resided here, except one year in Osage, Mitchell county.

HARDWARE.

E. F. Temple commenced business here in 1873, in the building now occupied by the postoffice. He remained until the spring of 1877, when he sold the stock and the building to E. J. Walker, who remained in the business until the spring of 1882, when he sold his stock to his brother, who is now engaged in the same business.

DRUGS.

The first drug store was established in 1870 by Warren Connor, a young man from Clayton county; he remained in the business until 1873, when he went to Manchester, Delaware county.

LEGAL.

A. A. Stewart was the first to enter upon the practice of the legal profession here; he removed to Cedar Rapids. In the winter of 1874-5, S. B. Patterson, from Mason City, opened a law office in the building now occupied for a justices office; it stood at that time where the meat market now stands. Mr. Patterson remained here until the spring of 1876, when he removed to Iowa City.

BLACKSMITH.

William Ryan, from Indiana, came to the village in the fall of 1876, and early the following spring erected a store building and put in a stock of goods. He also built a blacksmith shop, and hired a man by the name of Peter Fisher to do the work, who was the first blacksmith, and the building was the first blacksmith shop in Plainfield.

PRESENT BUSINESS OF PLAINFIELD.

Plainfield House—E. J. Walker, proprietor. A hotel creditable to the place.

J. M. Boardman, the oldest merchant in the town, occupies a new building, 24x46 feet, erected to accommodate his rapidly increasing business. He carries a large stock of general merchandise.

Fulton Brothers commenced business January 22, 1880, with a stock of drugs, groceries, boots, shoes, hats, caps, etc., of about $1,300. Their trade has increased until they now carry a stock of $2,500. They occupy a building, on Main street, 20x30 feet. This is a live and energetic firm.

Joseph W. Empson engaged in his present business in 1880, previous to which time he was engaged in the shoe trade. He carries a full line of groceries, confectioneries, tobacco and cigars, and in connection with his trade, carries on a barber shop.

D. Farnsworth built his shop, 22x40 feet, and commenced blacksmithing in 1872, since which time the business has increased until it reaches $2,000 per year.

The Plainfield creamery was established by a joint stock company. They use a building 30x84 feet, erected for the purpose. It was run as a cheese factory until January, 1880, when C. A. Kingsley purchased the property, and the creamery has since been in operation. The machinery is worked by a six-horse power steam engine.

Harness shop—U. C. Newcomb commenced this business in the fall of 1878. He carries a full line of harness, saddlery, etc., and has a trade of about $1,500 per year. A. J. Newcomb has charge of the business.

Meat market—A. J. Newcomb opened a shop in September, 1881, and furnishes everything necessary in his line.

Railroads—The Cedar Falls and Minnesota Railroad Company erected a depot, 36x54 feet, in the spring of 1868. The road was completed the following July. John D. Eddy was the first agent. In October the road was leased to the Illinois Central Company, and is now called by that name. In 1870 Mr. Eddy was relieved here and sent to Storm Lake. He returned in 1875, and again took charge of the office, which position he still holds. A telegraph station was established the year after the completion of the road.

Feed-mill.—One was built in 1876 by Foster Flowers, a wind-mill power.

John Roach, handling grain and seeds, commenced trade in 1877.

Blacksmith.—H. B. Annis commenced business March 15, 1882. He manufactures wagons and does a general business.

Lumber.—J. C. Garner, dealer in lumber and agricultural implements, pumps, coal, &c., carries a stock of $8,000. C. P. Collins, superintendent.

Justice of the peace, J. M. Roberts, does an insurance business, makes collections, &c. He has held the office since 1876.

P. N. Walker succeeded E. J. Walker in the hardware trade, February, 1882. He carries a stock of about $2,500.

J. M. Boardman, a leading merchant of Plainfield, was born in Napoli, Cataraugus county, New York, in 1840. His youth was passed on his father's farm, and at the age of twenty, he began teaching school. At the opening of our late war, he was continuing his studies at the academy, in Randolph, Cataraugus county; however, on the 17th of August, 1861, he forsook a student's quiet life, for a soldier's more daring career. Enlisting in Company B, Sixty-fourth New York Infantry, he served until the 7th of December, 1862, when he was honorably discharged on account of disability. Upon receiving his dismissal, Mr. Boardman returned to his home, but after remaining there six months and fourteen days, again enlisted, this time in Company B, One Hundred and Forty-seventh New York Infantry. He was taken prisoner at the battle of the Wilderness, on the 5th of May, 1863, and was sent, with others, to Andersonville, where he arrived June 4th. He remained in that prison until fall, and was then transferred to Florence prison, South Carolina, where he stayed until the close of the war, being one of the last to leave. He was sent through the Union lines to Wilmington, and then by sea to Annapolis, Maryland, where he received his dismissal, June 13, 1865. He then returned to his home, and after spending some time visiting the oil region of Pennsylvania, came, in the spring of 1867, to Iowa, and settled in Fremont township, Butler county, engaging in farming and teaching. Mr. Boardman continued to live there until May, 1872, when he came to Plainfield, Bremer county, and engaged in company with his brother-in-law, S. E. Preston, in the mercantile trade. They remained in partnership until the spring of 1873, when Mr. Boardman bought out Mr. Preston's interest, thus becoming sole proprietor. On the 17th of October, 1868, he was joined in wedlock with Miss Emma Rhodes, who was born at St. Louis, Missouri, March 28, 1845, her parents being temporarily located there. When she was three years old, her parents returned to their native place, Sullivan county, New York, and at the age of sixteen, the daughter attended Randolph academy, and before her marriage, had taught several terms of school. She and her husband are members of the Methodist Episcopal church. Mr. Boardman is a republican, and while a resident of Butler county, held several local offices. At the present time he holds the office of school treasurer. He is an upright, honest, industrious business man, and is held in high esteem by his large circle of friends and acquaintainces.

P. N. Walker, a hardware merchant of Plainfield, was born in the town of Avon, Kane county, Illinois, in 1850. Six years after his birth, the family emigrated to Iowa, and located in Jacksonville, Chickasaw county, where his father engaged in the hotel business. P. N. remained at home until twenty-one years old, then went to Murray county, Minnesota, and took a homestead, which he lived on until 1874. At that time he returned to Iowa, settling in Plainfield, Bremer county, engaging in the rag and iron trade, until February, 1882, when he purchased the hardware store owned by his brother, Elias C., and since then has followed that business. In 1875, he was united in marriage with Miss Eva Ingalls, a native of Wisconsin, but who resided in the State of Minnesota at the time of her marriage. They have two children—Guy and Pearl. Mr. Walker is an advocate of republicanism.

Albert D. Fulton, of the firm of Fulton Brothers, is a native of McHenry county, Illinois, born December 15, 1855. When he was twelve years old, his parents emigrated to Shell Rock, Iowa, and there the son obtained his education. At the age of eighteen he became clerk in the drug house of A. S. Clark, of Shell Rock, and afterwards spent several years clerking for the firm of J. S. Hummer, George Farrer & Dr. Thorpe. During the year 1878, he made a trip to Kansas, and upon his return to this State, settled in Plainfield, and engaged in the drug trade with his brother. They opened their busines on the 22d day of January, 1880, and two days succeeding, he was married to Miss Susie Delanah, who was born in Providence, Rhode Island.

Carlos P. Collins, a lumber dealer of Plainfield, is a native of Vermont, and was born in 1851. When he was fourteen years old the family emigrated to Dane county, Wisconsin, where they remained two years, and then moved to Bremer county and settled on section 18, Douglas township, where his father still lives, his mother dying in the fall of 1880. After learning what he could in the district school at his home, Carlos spent two terms at the Bradford Academy, and thus obtained an excellent business education. In 1871, he was joined in wedlock with Miss Susan Dyer, who was born in Wisconsin. Three children—Willie, Ettie and Roy—gather around their hearth. Mr. Collins is a republican, and has held several of the local offices.

E. S. Newcomb is a native of Pennsylvania, born in 1844. He received a common school education in the State of his birth, and grew to manhood on his father's farm. When twenty years of age he came west, and settled in Earlville, Delaware county, Iowa, where he learned the harness-maker's trade. After following it for two years in that place, he moved to Manchester, and worked at it until 1872, then went to Traer, Tama county, and engaged in the same business for six years. At the end of that time he came to Plainfield, where he has since resided, and at present is engaged in harness-making, and also owns the meat-market of the town. Mr. Newcomb is a republican, and now holds the office of constable. In 1865 he was joined in the holy bonds of matrimony with Miss Jennie Trentor, who was born in the State of Virginia. Five children— Willie E., Lulu May, Nettie E., Clarence and Lloyd E.—have been born to them.

One of Plainfield's leading merchants is Joseph W. Empson, who was born in Orleans county, New York, September 9, 1847. He remained at home until the second year of our late rebellion, when he enlisted August 26, in Company C, 21st New York Cavalry, and served until honorably discharged, June 14, 1865. While on battalion drill at Washington, he accidentally received a severe wound in the knee, from which he has never recovered, and since leaving the army has drawn a pension. Upon receiving his dismissal from the service he returned to New York, and there lived until October, 1867, when he came to Bremer county, and settled in Polk township. In 1874 he embarked in the boot and shoe trade, continuing to follow that business until 1880, when he became engaged in mercantile pursuits; he is now a notary public also. Mr. Empson was married in 1873 to Miss Lucretia J. Jackson, born in Illinois, but when a child came to Bremer county with her parents, and settled in Polk township. One child —now deceased—has been born to them.

Mr. Empson is a member of the Methodist Episcopal Church.

H. B. Annis, a blacksmith of Plainfield, was born in Michigan in 1859. While he was a child, his parents moved to Will county, Illinois, where they remained three years, and then came to Iowa, locating in Bremer county. However, after living in this State one year, they returned to Illinois, and the son continued living at home until 1882, when he again came to Bremer county, this time settling in Plainfield, and in the same year opened his present business. While a resident of Illinois, H. B. attended the Lockport High School, graduating from it in 1873. Mr. Annis was married November 23, 1881, to Miss B. A. Beltorf, who is a native of Lockport, Illinois. One child has blessed their union—Eva.

D. Farnsworth, an old settler of Plainfield, was born in New York State in 1842. When ten years of age, his parents came west, and settled in Delaware county, Iowa, and lived until 1862, then came to Bremer county, and settled in Plainfield. Soon after his arrival, he opened a blacksmith shop—which trade he had learned of his father—and has since followed that business. Mr. Farnsworth was married to Miss Elizabeth Lynes, a native of New York State, on the 21st day of April, 1866. Four children have blessed this union— Charles W., Cora E., Addie M., and Allie.

Henry Eckert, a shoe-maker of Polk township, was born in 1830, in Pennsylvania, and there he received a liberal education and grew to manhood. When seventeen years of age, he learned the shoe-maker's trade, at Williamsport, Lycoming county, Pennsylvania. In 1855, he moved to Strawberry Point, Clayton county, Iowa, and engaged in the shoe and harness making business; and, in the fall of 1880, came to Bremer county, and settled in Plainfield. Immediately upon his arrival, he opened a shoe making establishment, and still continues in that business. In 1853, he was married to Miss Elizabeth Ames, who died in the spring of 1856. Mr. Eckert was married to Miss Emily Logan, a native of Michigan, in 1857, and she has borne him thirteen children, seven of whom are now living.

CHAPTER XXVIII

SUMNER TOWNSHIP.

This township lies in the extreme northeastern corner of Bremer county and consists of thirty-two sections of land, or about 20,480 acres. The soil is a rich dark sandy loam. The surface is gently undulating, and in some sections nearly level. It is well drained by natural depressions and water courses, and there is very little if any waste land. There are two streams passing through the township: Buck creek and the Little Wapsipinicon river. The former having source near the northern boundary line on section 4, and flowing south through sections 8, 17, 20, the northeast corner of 29, 28, and leaving on 33. The latter has its source in Chickasaw county and in two streams, enters this township, making confluence on section 2, passing thence through the southwest corner of section 1, it flows through sections 12, 13 and passes out toward the east. on the northeast corner of 24, entering again from the east on section 25, it flows toward the northwest and curves again southward on the northwest quarter, passing thence through section 26, it makes its final exit on 35. There is one railroad passing diagonally through the southern portion of the township, called the Dubuque and Dakota, entering on section 32 and leaving on 24. Sumner is the only town in the township. This is an excellent agricultural township and consists mostly of prairie, although there is a considerable supply of timber along the Wapsipinicon river. The land is occupied mainly by actual settlers, there being but very little land unimproved.

EARLY SETTLEMENT.

The first settlement made in this township was by E. P. Bemis, J. N. Bemis and Allen Rowe, in June, 1854. The Messrs. Bemis settled on section 12, and Rowe on section 24. J. N. Bemis erected the first house. He is now a resident of Fayette county. E. P. Bemis now lives in Kansas. Allen Rowe also removed to that State. In the fall of the same year came Chas. Rowe and A. L. Stevenson.

Chas. Rowe, son of Anthony and Martha Rowe, was born in Windsor, Windsor county, Vermont, September 24, 1824. His parents are both dead, his father dying in Illinois, and his mother in the town of Sumner, in 1877. Mr. Rowe lived in Vermont, until 1844, when he went to Illinois, where he remained ten years. In 1854, he came to Sumner and settled on section 24, on the farm, where he now lives. He first built a log house, but in 1855, put up a small frame house, to which, he has since built an addition. He was justice of the peace for two years, has been constable for a number of years, and one of the trustees of the town for five years. Mr. Rowe has been connected with the school interests of the town for a good many years; was one of the first school board, and assisted in building the first school house in the town, also engaged the first teacher. He was married in 1848, to Miss Jane A. Riley, a native of Henrietta county, New York. Her father, William, and mother, Euphemia Riley, came to Sumner in 1856, and both died there, the former in 1867, and the latter in 1880. Mr. and Mrs. Rowe have ten children—Mary J., George H., Eddie W., Alphonso, Susan E., Esther, Augusta, Frank, Martha Ellen and Euphemia A. Frank Rowe was born January 28, 1856. This was probably the first birth in the township.

A. L. Stevenson was born in Plattsburg, Christian county, New York, January 5, 1830. He was the son of David and Hannah Stevenson, who were also natives of New York. When he was four years old his parents moved to Huron county, Ohio, where A. L. grew to manhood. He received a liberal common school education, and at the age of eighteen went into the mercantile business, in company with his father, in Clarksfield, Ohio, remaining with him until 1852, when he went to California, going overland with an ox team, making the trip in about five months. On arriving there he engaged as clerk in a mill for about six months, and then formed a partnership with James Bullock, in the wood business, they having a wood ranche on the Sacramento river, where they engaged in selling wood to steamboats. He remained in California until the fall of 1853, and on his way home met with an accident, which made him a cripple for life. Returning to Huron county, Ohio, he engaged in the grocery business, continuing there about one year, when he started for Iowa, making the trip by team, being four weeks on the way. This was his wedding trip, as he was married just before starting, to Miss Cynthia Jane Carpenter, a native of Duchess county, New York. They settled in October of that year in Sumner, on a farm, on the southwest quarter of section 6. Mr. Stevenson has improved four farms in this township. At two or three different times he has been a member of the county board of supervisors, the last time serving from 1875 to 1878. He has also been town clerk, trustee, assessor, justice of the peace, and in fact, has held every office in the gift of the people of the township. He has built about 130 bridges in Bremer county, in the past twelve years, some of them while a member of the county board, and the remainder under contract. He has been engaged in farming ever since he came to the county, even while he was in the bridge building business. Mr. Stevenson was one of the men that carried the returns from the first election to Waverly. Mr. and Mrs. Stevenson have had eight children, five living—Alta Belle, who has taught school in this district twelve terms, and in others six months; Charles Lincoln, Susan May, Erwin and Elwin, twins.

Rev. A. K. Moulton purchased land and settled in 1855.

The next year Albert Rowe, son of Anthony and Martha Rowe, arrived. He was born in Windsor, Windsor county, Vermont, July 31, 1831. He remained in his native town until he was sixteen years of age, when he went to Will county, Illinois, near Joliet, where he lived five years, engaged in painting. In 1852, during the gold excitement, he packed up his worldly effects, and, with an ox team, started overland for the "golden land," with the hope of making an independent fortune. He made the entire trip in six months, and after arriving there engaged in mining, and worked faithfully for four years. Although his brightest hopes were not realized, yet he met with fair success. In 1856 he returned, by water, via New York, and during that winter came to Bremer county, and settled on a farm in Sumner township, where he still lives. He has been identified with the school interests ever since he came to this place. He was one of the school directors for some time, and for a number of years was chairman of the school board. He has also been constable for about six years. He was married, in 1851, to Miss Mary A. Wilkins, a native of Vermont. She died in September, 1880, at the age of forty-six. They had two children—Isabella and Eugene.

In 1857 came George Wheaton and D. R. Hatch.

George W. Wheaton, son of Henry and Sarah Wheaton, was born in Oneida county, New York, March 15, 1817. When he was about ten years of age his parents moved to Detroit, Michigan, in which place he learned the book-binding trade, following that branch of business, in different places, upward of forty years. In the spring of 1857 he came to Sumner township, and settled on the farm where he now lives. He was appointed postmaster in 1862, and held the office for about eight years. He was justice of the peace for a number of years; assessor, and has held many other offices. He was married, in 1844, to Miss Julia Fitzpatrick, a native of Canada. They have had five children, two of whom are living—Andrew, who died when a child; Charles, died in the army, in 1862, at the age of sixteen; George Alfred, and Samuel Albert, (twins), Samuel A. died at the age of five; Philip Milton, who was among the first born in the town, and who married, in 1880, Miss Edith Belle Marsh.

D. R. Hatch, son of Benjamin and Naomi Hatch, natives of Vermont, was born in St. Lawrence county, New York, February 24, 1829. He grew to manhood on a farm in New York, receiving a common school education. In 1849 he went to Janesville, Wisconsin, and engaged in farming for two years, and then for five years was in the book business.

HISTORY OF BREMER COUNTY.

In 1856 he came to Iowa, stopping at Fort Dodge to buy land, but not being satisfied with the outlook, concluded to come to Sumner, when he bought the farm where he now lives. He opened a small store in Leroy township, which was the first in that place, and kept it for one year. At one time he was a member of the board of county supervisors; has held all the offices in the gift of the people, in the township where he resides; has taken an active part in the developement of the township, has been identified with the educational interests of the township from its earliest day, up to the present time. He is a member of the present school board. Mr. Hatch's parents are both dead, his father dying in St. Lawrence county, New York, in 1843, at the age of fifty-three, and his mother in Sumner, in 1872, at the age of seventy-eight. He was married April 15, 1858, to Miss Mary Davis, a native of New Hampshire. This was the first marriage ceremony performed in Sumner, Rev. A. K. Moulton officiating. Mrs. Hatch taught school in Leroy township, in 1857, and taught one of the first schools in this township. They have three children—David, May and Anson.

The settlement of Henry Lease, Jr., and George H. French, dates from this same year.

Henry Lease, Jr., son of Henry and Lydia (Cadwallader) Lease, was born in Hampshire county, Virginia, on the 5th day of March, 1827. He acquired his education in his native county and lived there until twenty-three years of age. At that time he came west and located in Washington county, Iowa, where he remained seven years and then moved to Bremer county, locating on section 17, on land entered for him by his brother. At the present time he owns 230 acres under a good state of cultivation. Mr. Lease is the present town clerk, and has held that office for twelve years; and has also held the office of assessor, several years. In politics he is a republican. He was married in the year 1848 to Miss Mary Baker, who was also born in the State of Virginia. They have eleven children living—Lydia M., wife of S. P. Madden of Cherokee county; John W., who lives in Cherokee county; Henry B., also living in Cherokee county; Mary W. V., wife of W. J. Beightol, living at West Union; Nimrod M., living in Cherokee county; Wesley H., Hiram M., Myria E., Martha A., Robert E. and J. Amos. Mr. and Mrs. Lease are members of the United Bretheren in Christ.

Geo. H. French, born in Tewksbury, Massachusetts, February 5, 1825, is a son of Benjamin and Alice S. (Sanders) French, who were also natives of Massachusetts. His grandfather, Benjamin French, was a soldier in the Revolutionary War, and served as Washington's body guard for three years, and during the time was wounded in attempting to save the General's life. George H. passed the first ten years of his life in his native town, and the next twenty-two years in Lowell, Massachusetts, working for the Middlesex Corporation, which is the largest woolen manufacturing establishment in the world. During 1857, he came west, arriving in Sumner in December of that year. He settled on section 22, on a farm of forty acres, which he had entered two years previously. Shortly after his arrival he purchased 80 acres more, and still owns the farm. He is a republican, and has held the office of township trustee, besides other minor offices. Mr. French was married on the 6th day of February, 1847, to Miss Miriam S. Holt, who was born in Andover, New Hampshire, and there lived until fifteen years of age, then moving to Lowell, Massachusetts. Five children have been born to them, of whom three are now living—Isora A. L., wife of Charles Follansbee, of Morrison, Rice county, Minnesota; George O. B. and Eddie B.

These are all the first settlers that can be remembered. The township did not settle very rapidly for a number of years. Among those who came in later, and are now residents outside the town of Sumner, may be found several sketches of whom are here given:

David Caswell, son of Timothy and Mercy (Short) Caswell, was born on the 14th day of May, 1806, in the town of Warren, Herkimer county, New York. When he was twelve years old, the family moved to Broome county, New York, where he grew to manhood, and, when old enough to do business for himself, engaged in farming and lumbering. In 1835, he moved to Winnebago county, Illinois, forming one of the very first settlers of that county, having none but the Indians for neighbors. During Mr. Caswell's residence there, he improved a farm, and was the first in that county to cast a vote. In the year 1863, he came to Bremer county, Iowa, and settled on section 20, Summer township, where he now resides, and owns 160 acres of land. He has filled the office of justice of the peace five years. March 19, 1832, he was united in marriage to Miss Irene Rairden, who was born in Broome county, New York, and is a daughter of John and Rebecca (Atwater) Rairden, who were natives of New York. Mr. and Mrs. Caswell have three children living—Lydia Elvira, wife of George N. Gardner, and living in Kansas; John David, who lives in Kansas; Roxy C., wife of James N. Doty, and living in Nebraska.

S. N. Orvis, son of Timothy B. and Rachel Orvis, was born in Pennsylvania in 1835. His father died in 1876, at the age of 86; his mother, who is now 82 years old, is a member of Mr. Orvis' family. In 1841 his parents moved to Madison county, New York, where they remained until 1850, when they went to Boone county, Illinois. Mr. Orvis was reared on a farm, receiving but a limited education. In 1861 he came to this State and settled in Clayton county, remaining, however, but three years, when he came to Sumner and bought the farm where he now lives. He has been trustee of the town, and trustee of the schools for a number of years. Mr. Orvis is one of those quiet, unassuming men who always make friends and never enemies. He was married, in 1870, to Miss Anna Lowe, a native of Delaware county, Iowa. They have had five children, one died—Edith, Millicent, Alma and Bruce.

J. Dawson was born in Yorkshire, England, August 15, 1836. During the year 1857, he came to America, and first settled on a farm, near the city of Chicago, where he worked two and one-half years, then moved to Missouri and entered the Missouri Home Guards. After remaining in that State two and one-half years, he came to Bremer county, Iowa, and located on a farm in Leroy township. In December, 1869, he sold that farm and purchased 160 acres on section 16, Sumner township. He now owns 400 acres of land, all of which is under cultivation. Mr. Dawson has held the office of town clerk two years and is present assessor. In the year 1860, he was united in marriage to Miss Mary Harrington, who, also, was born in England. They have eight children living—William, John, Annie E., Mary J., Thomas, Samuel, Charles W. and Henry.

Isaac Taft was born in Lewis county, New York, July 2, 1822. When he was five years of age he went to St. Lawrence county, where he lived until he was thirteen, and moved to Loraine county, Ohio, where he grew to manhood on a farm. He went to Michigan, remained a short time, and then went to Illinois, remaining four years. He again returned to Michigan and engaged in farming for sixteen years, when he came to Iowa, and bought the farm where he now lives. Mr. Taft has had charge of the Wilson Grove Cemetery for the past twelve years. He was married in 1849, to Miss Mary Hopkins, a native of New York; they were married in Lucas county, Ohio. They have had three children, one died when an infant—Fannie, the wife of Ed. Wentworth, of Sumner, and Frank, who lives at home. He was married in 1875, to Miss Martha Parker, who died, leaving twin babies and son, Guy H., seven years of age. They are the possessors of a bureau which was brought to the United States in the Mayflower, in the Baker family, and was at that time, a chest of drawers. They also have a piece of the boat cut from the Mayflower.

William C. Husband, son of John and Margaret (Tarr) Husband, was born January 12, 1827, in Westmoreland county, Pennsylvania. He obtained his education in his native county, and, when of sufficient years, learned the trade of blacksmithing. When nineteen years old, he came as far west as Ohio, and located in the town of Akron, where he was employed in the machine shops. During the year 1866, he came to Bremer county, and settled on a farm in section 17, where he now resides, and owns 130 acres of land. In January, 1870, he was married to Miss Harriet E. Parshall. Mr. Husband has two sons—John and Charles A.—by a former wife.

Frederick Krause, born in Germany in 1828, came to America in 1857, and settled in Wisconsin, where he engaged in farming. He remained there for ten years, when he came to Iowa and settled on a farm in Sumner, where he still lives. He has made all the improvements on his farm, and has 285 acres of land. Mr. Krause was a school director for two years, and was largely instrumental in the building of the German Church. He was the first class leader and first superintendent of the Sunday School. He was married in Germany to Miss Wilhemina Ludwig. They have seven children—Louisa, Will, Emma, Augusta, John, Fred and Nettie.

Anton Miller, son of John and Effie Barbara Miller, was born in Germany, in 1848. He came to America in 1851, when he was but three years of age, and lived in Jefferson county, Wisconsin, where he grew to manhood on a farm, receiving a common school education. In 1871 he came to Sumner and settled on the farm where he now lives. He is at present one of the school board of Pleasant Valley Independent district. Mr. Miller was married in 1871, to Miss Anna Rockdaschel, a native of Wisconsin. They have four children—Emma, Arthur, Aaron and Louisa Almira.

HISTORICAL ITEMS.

The first marriage in the township was that of D. R. Hatch to Miss Mary A. Davis, in April, 1858, by Rev. A. K. Moulton.

The example of this couple was soon followed by Charles Sweet and Nancy Moulton, who promised to each other to ever be true, and following very soon came Dwight Mabb and Miss Levina Drake, who had concluded to make the journey of life together.

The first birth in the township was a child to Mr. and Mrs. A. L. Stevenson, born in May, 1855. It only remained a few weeks when it was numbered among the dead.

Frank Rowe, son of Charles Rowe, is the oldest living inhabitant in Sumner township.

The first death was Hattie, wife of Andrew Parkhurst, who died October, 1856, and was buried in Mentor Cemetery, Leroy township.

There are two cemeteries in the township, "Wilson Grove," located on the east line, and the "German Evangelical," situated on section 17.

The first school taught in Sumner was by Mary Ann Hart, on the premises of J. N. Bemis, in a little building used by him as a granary, during the fall of 1857.

The first school house was built in 1858, in what is now known as Rowe Independent district. The first school board was: A. L. Stevenson, secretary; J. Hubbard, president, and Luther Hubbard, treasurer. There are now five school houses in the township, outside of Sumner village. The total valuation of school property is estimated at $7,500; the total number of school children, about 400.

The first religious services were held by Rev. A. K. Moulton, near Wilson's Grove. There are now three churches in the township: Presbyterian, Methodist Episcopal, and German Evangelical.

During the early days mail had to be carried from Douglas postoffice, Fayette county, a distance of twenty-five miles. Afterward a postoffice was established at Wilson's Grove, J. N. Bemis postmaster.

ORGANIC.

In the summer of 1858 the following notice was served:

To Charles Rowe:

You are hereby notified that the County Court of Bremer county has, this 27th day of July, A. D. 1858, formed and erected into a new civil township the territory embraced in Congressional township No 93, range 11, west, in said county, to be known by the name of Sumner township, and you are required to post up notices in the most public places thereof, embracing the following, to-wit: That a special election will be held in said Sumner township, on the 16th day of August, at the house of Rev. A. K. Moulton, at which the following officers will be elected: Two justices of the peace, one township clerk, three township trustees, and two constables. Notice of the same shall be given

HISTORY OF BREMER COUNTY.

at least fifteen days before the day of holding the same. You are also required to return this warrant to the presiding officer of the meeting, with your return thereon, as required by law.

Given under my hand and seal of office, at Waverly, this 27th day of July, A. D. 1858.

[SIGNED]   GEORGE W. MAXFIELD,
                                            County Judge.

I hereby certify the above to be a true copy of the original warrant.

H. W. GRIFFITH,
Township Clerk.

The election was held accordingly, at which time George H. French was elected chairman; E. P. Bemis, J. N. Bemis and H. W. Griffith, judges; H. E. Jaggar and George Wheaton, clerks. The following officers were elected: J. N. Bemis and J. E. Wilson, justices; H. E. Jaggar, Geo. H. French and L. N. Sholes, trustees; H. W. Griffith clerk; Charles Rowen, M. Baker, constables.

The following comprises the township officers from 1858, to date:

October 12, 1858.—H. E. Jaggar, J. E. Wilson, justices; H. E. Jaggar, Geo. H. French, David Stevenson, trustees; L. M. Sholes, clerk; H. W. Griffith, assessor; Charles Rowe, A. Stevenson, constables.

October 11, 1859—At the house of John Hall.—D. R. Hatch, C. Rowe, F. Mabb, trustees; L. M. Scholes, clerk; Abel Perkins, Jr., assessor; A. L. Stevenson, C. I. Thorp, constables.

November 6, 1860—At the house of John Hall.—L. M. Sholes, supervisor; H. S. Munger, clerk; J. O. Huddatt, Chas. Rowe, justices; Abel Perkins, Jr., assessor; Allen Rowe, George Wheaton, B. Webster, trustees; A. Stoddard, Albert Rowe, constables.

October 6, 1861—At the house of John Hall.—Abel Perkins, Jr., supervisor; Elias Congdon, justice; U. B. Webster, assessor; H. S. Munger, clerk; Chester Miller, E. P. Bemis, L. M. Sholes, trustees; N. Bogart, J. W. Hart, constables.

October 14, 1862—At the school house in sub-district No. 5.—N. E. Jaggar, justice; L. M. Sholes, assessor; D. R. Hatch, clerk; Calvin Miller, John M. Lombard, U. B. Webster, trustee; David Whitney, Henry L. Dunn, constables.

October 13, 1863—At a school house.—D. R. Hatch, justice; D. R. Hatch, supervisor; O. S. Wright, assessor; S. B. Hatch, clerk; Elias Congdon, Allen Rowe, D. Berkstresser, trustees; John Lombard, Nelson Bogart, constables.

October 10, 1865—At the school house in District No. 3—Elias Condon, supervisor; David Caswell, justice; R. H. Reynolds, John Caswell, constables; H. S. Munger, clerk; D. R. Hatch, assessor; Allen Rowe, Walter Tabor, H. Witney, trustees.

October 9, 1866—At the school house in sub-district No. 3—D. R. Hatch, supervisor; L. M. Sholes, clerk; Myron Condon, assessor; H. B. Bixby, Charles Rowe, S. N. Orvis, trustees; David Caswell, justice; M. F. Watenpaugh, O. L. Farrand, constables. The trustees elected did not qualify according to law, and April 13, 1867, J. A. Barnes, H. B. Bixby and S. N. Orvis were appointed, who qualified.

STATE OF IOWA, } ss.
BREMER COUNTY.

To the township clerk of Sumner township, Bremer county, Iowa:

"You are hereby notified that on the 5th day of June, A. D., 1867, sections 6 and

7, in township 93, range 11, west of the 5th principal meridian, was by the board of supervisors of said county, detached from Leroy township, and attached to Sumner township, for all civil and political purposes. In witness whereof, I have hereunto written my name and affixed the seal of my office, at Waverly, the 12th day of June, 1867.

H. C. MOORE,
Clerk of the Board of Supervisors
of Bremer county."

Tuesday, October 8, 1867—At the school house in sub-district No. 3—S. N. Orvis, Myron Congdon, Allen Rowe, trustees; Henry Lease, Jr., clerk; G. H. Hinkley, G. H. French, constables; L. M. Sholes, county supervisor; A. L. Stevenson, justice; J. O. Barnes, assessor.

Tuesday, November 3, 1868—School house No. 3—David Caswell, Alonzo O. Ketchum, S. N. Orvis, trustees; Chester Dymond, David Caswell, justices; Geo. W. Tabor, O. Farrand, constables; Henry Lease, Jr., clerk; J. A. Barnes, assessor.

Tuesday, October 12, 1869—At school house District No. 3—A. L. Stevenson, supervisor; Lester Congdon, Charles Rowe, D. Berkstresser, trustees; Philip Callahan, George Hinkley, constables; Henry Lease, Jr., clerk; Geo. Wheaton, assessor.

Tuesday, October 11, 1870—At school house No. 3—Charles Rowe, D. Berkstresser, Lester Congdon, trustees; D. Berkstresser, George Wheaton, justices; U. D. Smith, L. A. Munger, constables; Henry Lease, Jr., clerk; S. F. Cass, assessor.

August 5, 1871—At Cass's store, in Sumner.—For taxation or no taxation, to aid the Iowa Pacific Railroad—For, 60; against, 29.

Tuesday, October 10, 1871—At Cass Hall, Sumner.—John A. Haag, David Berkstresser, Myron Congdon, trustees; Henry Lease, Jr., clerk; A. J. Lowe, assessor; Lester Congdon, M. F. Watenpaugh, constables.

Tuesday, November 5, 1872—At Cass' store.—David Berkstresser, Myron Congdon, Charles Rowe, trustees; Henry Lease, Jr., clerk; S. F. Cass, assessor; George Wheaton, David Berkstresser, justices; John Brown, M. F. Watenpaugh, constables.

Tuesday, October 14, 1873—At Cass' store.—S. N. Orvis, assessor; Henry Lease, Jr., clerk; Myron Congdon, Charles Rowe, John A. Haag, trustees; M. F. Watenpaugh, Alfred Wheaton, constables.

Tuesday, October 13, 1874—At Cass' store—E. Brooks, David Berkstresser, justices; S. F. Cass, assessor; Henry Lease, Jr., clerk; John A. Haag, Myron Congdon, Charles Rowe, trustees; C. C. Parsons, M. F. Watenpaugh, constables.

Tuesday, October 12, 1875—At the Sumner House.—S. F. Cass, assessor; Henry Lease, Jr., clerk; Myron Congdon, Orris Wescott, John A. Haag, trustees; H. H. Horton, F. N. Steen, constables.

November 7, 1876—At the Sumner House.—James Muffley, D. R. Littell, justices; A. F. Thull, assessor; Henry Lease, Jr., clerk; Myron Congdon, John A. Haag, Orris Wescott, trustees; A. H. Jarvis, E. B. Carroll, constables.

October 9, 1877—At the Sumner House.—O. O. Tibbits, assessor; John Dawson, clerk; Myron Congdon, Orris Wescott, George Baumgartner, trustees.

October 8, 1878.—D. R. Littell, David Berkstresser, justices; Henry Lease, Jr., assessor; John Dawson, clerk; Myron Congdon, F. Ladwig, B. J. Allen, trustees; A. H. Jarvis, M. F. Watenpaugh, constables.

October 14, 1879.—Henry Lease, Jr., assessor; John Dawson, clerk; F. Ladwig, trustee.

November 2, 1880—At Carpenter's Hall. —Myron Congdon, trustee; D. R. Hatch, assessor; Henry Lease, Jr., clerk; D. R. Littell, J. Lowe, justices; A. H. Jarvis, William Winn, constables.

October 11, 1881—At the restaurant of D. H. Robinson.—B. J. Allen, trustee.

November 7, 1882—At King's Hotel.— T. W. Tower, H. C. Alger, justices; Henry Lease, Jr., clerk; John Dawson, Sr., assessor; F. Ladwig, trustee; A. H. Jarvis, D. H. Robinson, constables.

HORSES.

In every community where the people are as prosperous as in the vicinity of Sumner, there is a constantly increasing demand for good horses. This demand is fully met by Tower & Tibbits. They have many good animals of the best strains of imported stock. Among recent purchases may be found the following: "Young Scotland's Glory," a jet black, 17 hands high, weight 1815 pounds, age four years. A stallion imported from Glasgow. He is the best bred horse in this part of the State, and is valued at $2,000. "Young Clyde," three years old, weighs 1435 pounds, is 16½ hands high, was imported from Scotland in 1881. He is a blood-bay and a fine animal. Another horse deserving of mention is Mohawk Hambletonian, a blood-bay, sixteen hands high, sired by Mohawk, Jr., with a record of 2.25.

Thomas W. Tower was born in Underhill, Chittenden county, Vermont, April 21, 1824. He was the son of Hon. John H. Tower, one of the first settlers of Underhill, who was between thirty and forty years, a leading merchant of that place; associate judge of that district for two terms; also one of the board of commissioners of the Vermont Central Railroad. He died at the age of sixty-two. Thomas was brought up in the mercantile business, but having a desire to become an attorney, he supplied himself with law books and commenced to read law while attending to his duties about the store, continuing for three years, or until he was twenty, when he went to Morrisville, Vermont, into the law office of Judge Poland. Mr. Tower continued in his office study, however, but one year, when at the urgent solicitation of his aged father, he gave up his chosen profession and returned to Underhill to take charge of the extensive mercantile business his father had built up. He remained in Vermont until 1854, when he moved to Wisconsin and settled in Crawford county. There he built a flouring mill and in the same year surveyed and platted the village of Towerville. He also engaged in the mercantile business, and in 1865, built and operated a woolen mill. He built up a prosperous business in each branch he undertook, and also made a thriving little village which grew to be quite a business and manufacturing place. He continued the mercantile business in Towerville until he came to Sumner, in 1879, and engaged in business with Tibbetts, Reimler & Co. Mr. Tower was a member of the county board of Crawford county for a number of years, and a member of the State Legislature of Wisconsin in 1858, for one term, elected by the Whig party. He continued in business in Sumner, until August, 1882, when he sold out and engaged with his son-in-law, O. O. Tibbetts, in the horse business. Mr. Tower was married, in 1846, to Miss H. Maria Livingston, (a distant relative of Dr. Livingston, of African fame,) a native of Chittenden county, Vermont. She died in 1855, leaving three children. Mr. Tower married again in 1856, and in 1872 married for his third wife, Miss Rasallie R. McAuley a native of Wisconsin. They have five children living—Ida M., Eva E., May L., John H., Pearl E. Dewitt C. died at the age of twenty-five years.

O. O. Tibbitts, son of Chauncey and Hannah Tibbitts, born in Canada, in 1853, came to the States with his parents, settling in Fremont county, Michigan, until 1861; they then went to Towerville, Wisconsin, where they remained seven years, then came to Sumner.* Mr. Tibbitts being then fifteen years of age, went into the store of his brother-in-law, S. S. Cass, as clerk, remaining until he went in company with him, in 1877, under the firm name of S. F. Cass & Co. In 1879, in company with C. Reimler and T. W. Tower, he bought out the Cass interest, and continued the business under the firm name of Tibbits, Reimler & Co., and continued under that name until the firm was succeeded by S. F. Cass & Co. In the fall of 1879 he, with his father-in-law, T. W. Tower, platted what is known as Tibbitts' and Tower's addition to Sumner. In 1879 and 1880, Mr. Tibbitts built one of the finest residences in the village. He was postmaster from 1878 to 1882, also express agent from the time the railroad came through, until 1882. He was married in 1878 to Miss Mary L. Tower, daughter of T. W. Tower. They have one child—Mattie, aged three years.

TOWN OF SUMNER.

In the midst of a gentle, rolling prairie, bordered on the northeast by a ridge, on the east by timber, and on the southeast by the meandering course of a small river, is a still more gently undulating plain of several hundred acres extent, from which rises the flourishing little town of Sumner. "Forty years ago the plain where Sumner now stands was a vast, howling wilderness," does the embryo orator credit; but does not do justice to the town or the wilderness. Ffteen years ago this was one wide expanse of prairie, except here and there a lonely farm, but the virgin soil of the present town plat was then unbroken. The large portion of this plat, which was owned by Chauncy Carpenter, before the railroad or town were even thought of, was broken up in 1869, and annually presented waving fields of grain thereafter, till its agricultural worth gave place to a town site, and possible future greatness. Sumner, in Sumner township, Bremer county, Iowa, is principally located on the southwest quarter of the southwest quarter of section 24, township 93, range 11, west of the fifth principal meridian. At a distance of one-half mile east of town is Wilson's Grove, extending from one mile south to three miles north, making a total length of four miles, and having an average width of about one mile. Rising far to the north of Wilson's Grove, extending through its entire length, and then

taking a huge bend to the northwest, with a gradual return to its southerly direction, is the Little Wapsipinicon.

In June, 1871, a company of engineers made the first survey, coming in from the east of what is now the railroad. The company employing them was styled the Iowa & Pacific Railroad Company, and the proposed road was to form a juncture on the prairie, this side of Randalia, with a Minnesota line, that was to make Dubuque connections. When the surveyors struck this plain they found the surface to be on grade, and, after due consideration, thought it a suitable location for a town, so in the fall of 1871 they returned and, assisted by Chauncey Carpenter, owner of the land, staked off the southwest quarter of the southwest quarter of section 24, consisting of forty acres, into town lots, and called it Sumner, at the instance of the proprietor. This was the original town of Sumner.

As the locating of stations is at the option of railroad companies, the Iowa and Pacific very naturally exacted of Mr. Carpenter a consideration for the location of a depot on his land. In compliance Mr. Carpenter donated the company for depot grounds a strip of fine land eighteen rods wide and ninety rods long, amounting to ten and one-eighth acres. In addition to this he also gave to the company ten acres in town lots. So, that of the original plat of forty acres, the railroad company secured half. Mr. Carpenter's donation was not all. In the fall of 1871, Sumner township voted a five per cent tax in aid of the road, as did a few other townships on the line. Banks township voted down the tax. About $400 of the tax voted by Sumner township, was paid into the company treasury, and drawn by the Iowa & Pacific Railroad.

In June, 1872, work was commenced all along the line, from the junction this side of Randalia to Belmont, twenty-five miles beyond Hampton, and was vigorously prosecuted till toward winter, when operations ceased, and were not resumed for some years. Meantime, the proposed road was very nearly graded and bridged over the entire extent, and the track laid from Waverly to Clarksville. Work on the road with which it was to form a junction was also abandoned. There were many along this line, who lost work, material or board furnished; but the greatest disappointment came to those who built their hopes on Sumner. Every winter and spring, hope would build on what the next summer would bring forth, only to fall and die with the leaves of autumn. In the season of 1872, during which the road was graded, Sumner was a field of waving grain, the stakes having been driven down so as to interfere with nothing except plowing; but the next year the demands for a town in the vicinity, railroad or no railroad, became so apparent and imperative that Mr. Carpenter gave up farming in the streets of Sumner, and threw open the site for future developments already begun. In 1878 a new company was organized on the ruins of the old, styled the Dubuque and Dakota, and the road was soon in operation from Waverly to Hampton. The company proposed to the people along the line, from Waverly east, to complete the road, if a five per cent. tax was voted in their aid. Sumner township voted the tax, on the additional proviso that the company would connect Sumner by rail to some road to the east of it. The completion advanced, in 1879, from Waverly eastward till Tripoli was reached; but the company concluded to forfeit Sumner's aid rather than try to reach Randalia, and thus Sumner endured another year of hope deferred.

To the original town plat has been added Carpenter's Addition, consisting of twenty-four acres in the southwestern part of the southeast quarter of the southwest quarter of section 24. Carpenter's Addition of six acres along the north side of the northeast quarter of the northwest quarter of section 25; Wescott's Addition of fourteen acres along the entire north side of the northwest quarter of the northwest quarter of section 25; Wescott's Addition of two acres in the northeast corner of section 26; Tower and Tibbett's Addition of ten acres on the southeast corner of section 23; Koerth's Addition of three acres immediately north of Tower and Tibbett's Addition. This gives a total in the town plat of ninety-nine acres, nearly all of which is fit for building lots without any preparation. The main street runs east and west between sections 24 and 25, and is called on the plat, First street. The parallel streets to the north of this are numbered in their order, 2d, 3d and 4th streets. There is one street south of First street with the romantic name of Wapsie street. Of the north and south streets, the one running by the M. E. Church is called Pleasant street; by the postoffice, Carpenter street; by the depot, Railroad street; east side of stock yards, Guilford street. The streets are uniformly sixty-six feet wide. The lots are each sixty-six feet wide by one hundred and thirty-two deep, and eight lots constitute a block. Each block is divided by a sixteen and one-half foot east and west ally, with four lots abutting each side. The first house built on the present plat of Sumner is the residence of Chauncey Carpenter, built in 1871.

Mr. Parsons built the second house, which is still his residence. The first erected on the original plat, was built in 1872, by Ebed Brooks, it being his present residence. He waded into wheat up to his elbows to choose his lots, and the deed he received was the first title given to Sumner property, except that given to the railroad company. A. S. Beels built the next house, in 1873. The next building erected was I. N. Kepler's house, in the summer of 1873, by John Borland, for a hotel, and known for several years thereafter as the "Sumner House." D. B. Hatch, who had for a time previously, been running a store on his farm near town, moved to town in the summer of 1873; this was the first store in Sumner. The building now stands where Mr. Hatch placed it, and is occupied by F. N. Norman for a saloon. Mr. Hatch was soon succeeded by Brown & Ward, who opened up in Chauncey Carpenter's building, the one now occupied by Clarke & Austin; this was the second house built in the fall of 1873. The above firm was soon succeeded by Green & Lovejoy, of Lawler, who occupied Carpenter's building during the spring of 1874, while their fine building, now owned and occupied by William King for a hotel, was being erected. Stephen Todd put up, in 1874, the next business place, and occupied it for a while as a furniture store; this building is now occupied by Mrs. Woodring for millinery.

Sumner has several natural advantages. The surrounding country is of the greatest fertility, producing corn, oats, flax, barley, garden products, timothy, clover, and many other products, in abundance, commensurate only with their cultivation. The town is adjacent to timber on the east, of about four sections, consisting principally of hard woods, and furnishing large quantities of fence-posts and fire wood.

An important factor in the growth of Sumner, has been the hand and enterprise of S. F. Cass. Mr. Cass came to Sumner township, from Wisconsin, in 1866, with a few dollars, at most a few hundred dollars ready cash, and set about at once to find a suitable location for a country store. He finally bought a few acres of land, about four miles northwest of the present town site, and built a residence thereon, using the front room of the same for a store room. This trade soon became extensive, and his improvements and facilities kept pace with his ever-increasing business. In 1867, he received the postoffice. As a result of the large trade centering here, two blacksmiths, Samuel Koerth and John Blair; a physician, Dr. J. N. Wilson, and a large competing store, by G. R. Edmonds, became established here. So that "Cassville" became a place of considerable notoriety and importance, and all prospered, except Edmonds, who yielded up his stock to his creditors, and his store building to Cass. Finally, notwithstanding Sumner's dubious prospects, the whole crowd, in 1875, concluded to cast in their lot with those who had built here in the hope of the final advent of the railroad. Accordingly, the winter of 1875-6 saw all Cassville on runners. Mr. Cass moved seven buildings, including the building opposite the bank, and the two-story portion of the building occupied by Cass & Co. The latter building was drawn by a team of forty horses, and two yoke of oxen were attached to the rear for a "pull back," while going down hill. Mr. Koerth also moved his shop. This was an addition to Sumner, quite equal to her former self, an addition that gave a new impetus to her growth, and a firmer prospect of permanency. The next summer the present school house, consisting of two stories, well finished and furnished, was built at an expense of $3,000.

In 1882 the growth of the place and rapid increase of pupils demanded an addition to this building, which was erected at a cost of $1,000. The first building was ready for occupancy in the fall of 1876, and W. W. Quivey, formerly superintendent of Fayette county, was installed as principal in the higher department, and his wife as teacher in the lower department. Mr. and Mrs. Quivey had charge of the school during the first two years. Mrs. Quivey's successors have been Miss Isadore Warner, (now Mrs. C. D. Hallett), Miss Mary Hatch and the present teacher, Miss Maggie Mitchell. Mr. Quivey's successors have been George Harwood, Miss Isadora Warner, Dr. G. B. Thompson, Miss Coryell and G. P. Linn, who has had charge of the school from September 1881, until November 30, 1882, when he resigned.

Chauncey Carpenter, the father of the town, has done as much, if not more, than any citizen here toward making Sumner the thriving and enterprising town that it is, neither sparing time or money where it would further the general advantage of the town, often sacrificing his own financial interests for the purpose of encouraging and aiding the prosperity of Sumner.

Chauncy Carpenter was born in Bradford county, Pennsylvania, December 11, 1830. When he was about five years of age, his parents moved to DuPage county, Illinois; there he lived until he was twenty years of age, receiving but a limited education. In 1850 he went to Will county, Illinois, and in 1851, during the gold excitement in California, Mr. Carpenter was seized with the desire to go to the mountains, to make a fortune, but was obliged to borrow money to make the trip. He went overland with a team, making the trip in ninety days, a remarkably short time. After arriving there, he was engaged in mining for three years, and was very successful, returning with quite a little fortune. He has quite a collection of photographs of gold nuggets that he dug himself, ranging from $15 to $3,000; he also has kept as a memento, a nugget in the rough state, which he wears as a scarf pin, valued at $11. On his return from California, coming by water, via New York, he went to Will county, Illinois, where he engaged in farming until the spring of 1872, when he moved to Sumner having bought the present site of the village, in 1869. He has quite a number of lots yet unsold; owns a large farm and a fine residence in the village, which he occupies; also a store 20x70, two stories high, occupied by Clarke & Austin; the hardware store occupied by Copeland & Langmier; and several other buildings in the village. Mr. Carpenter is justly proud of the town he has been so instrumental in creating and building up; and well he may, for he has spared neither time nor money in making this a lively and progressive town. He has been identified with the educational interests of the town from the start; has taken an active part in the building of the fine school house, and has been, and is now, a member of the school board. In politics, a staunch republican; in religion, a Free-Will Baptist; a man of high moral standing, respected by all, disliked by none. Such a man as Mr. Carpenter is a credit to any community. He married, the first time, in 1854, to Miss Nancy Merwin, a native of Ohio. She died in October, 1863, leaving two children—Cordelia, who died when she was sixteen, and Alice, who was nineteen years of age the 23d of October. In July, 1864, Mr. Carpenter married Miss Agnes Parsons, a native of Ohio. They have four children —Hattie, Ella, Lottie and Guy.

Orris Wescott, son of George and Olivia Wescott, was also identified with the interests of the town. He was born in Chautauqua county, New York, in March, 1830. His father died in 1870, at the age of 77; his mother is still living, and is 83 years old. The subject of this sketch received a common school education. He remained in New York until 1851, when he went to Erie county, Pennsylvania, and there lived for about fourteen years, when he again returned to New York, buying a farm adjoining the one where he was born. He there continued to live until 1870, when he came to Sumner, and settled on a farm, a portion of which is now included in the plat of the town. Some years after the village of Sumner was started, seeing that a portion of his farm could be utilized as building lots, he platted about twelve acres, known as Wescott's addition to Sumner. Mr. Wescott, for a number of years, was engaged in the general hardware business, in company with Mr. Thull. He has been one of the trustees of the town for a number of years, is a member of the A.O.U.W., and is one of the officers of that organization. He was married in 1856 to Miss Mary M. Carroll, a native of Pennsylvania. They have five children—Eugene M., Franklin R., Harley, Orris, Edna Maud.

At the present writing the town of Sumner has a population of about 500, and about fifty places of business, which are now briefly mentioned.

The firm of Clark & Austin has been doing business here since September, 1880, and have built up a good trade. With the beginning of the year 1883, they inaugurated a new feature in Sumner business—"Strictly Cash." The business is in the personal charge of C. A. Austin. A. H. Clark is traveling for Reid, Murdock & Fisher, a grocery house, of Chicago.

C. A. Austin, of this firm, was born in Onondaga county, New York, November 1, 1851. In 1865, his parents, Albert and H. E. Austin, moved to Iowa, and settled in Horton, Bremer county, being among the first settlers in that town. Mr. Austin received his education at the High School in Charles City, and at the Bradford Academy. At the age of twenty, he engaged in the mercantile business, in company with Mr. Terry, continuing for one year. He then engaged in business, in Horton, for himself, until the spring of 1878, when he and his father formed partnership. In 1880, Mr. Austin formed a partnership, at Sumner, with Clarke Brothers. He still retained his interest in the store at Horton, but devoted his time and attention to the Sumner store, leaving the other in care of his partner. On March 8, he sold out his share of the business in Horton. Out of a comparatively small beginning in Sumner, through the push, energy and integrity of this wide-awake young business man, the business gradually increased, until now they are doing a cash business upwards of $50,000 a year. Mr. Austin was married in 1871 to Miss Eva Mary Watkins, a native of Illinois. They have four children—Fannie, Vina C., Katie and Mattie.

S. F. CASS & CO.

The members constituting this firm are S. F. Cass, Myron Congdon, C. E. Reimler and M. S. Wright, and, through a line of succession, might be considered the pioneer firm of Sumner. They own and operate the two large stores, one formerly occupied by Tibbits, Reimler & Co., the other by Cass Brothers & Littell.

S. F. Cass, banker and merchant, was born in Prescott county, Canada, January 31, 1839, and is a son of S. C. and J. Cass, natives of Vermont. His father is still living in Wisconsin. His mother died in 1872, at the age of sixty-six years. The subject of this sketch was brought up on a farm until he was twenty-one years of age, receiving up to that time, but a common school education. But after receiving his majority he entered Bryant and

Stratton's Commercial College, at Ogdensburg, New York, from which he graduated in 1864, after which he taught in the same College for one term. Previous to this, or in 1860, he with his parents removed to Vernon county, Wisconsin, where he worked on the farm at different intervals, between 1860 and 1864, while he was pursuing his studies at Ogdensburg. In 1865, he severed his connection, as teacher, in Bryant and Stratton's Commercial College, after which he made a visit to his former home in Wisconsin; and then in the same year came to Iowa and settled in Sumner township, buying five acres of land on the southeast of section 9. Here he erected a small building in which he opened a country store on a very small scale. At this point it may be stated, the real career of S. F. Cass' life began. Commencing here as he did with a few dollars, or at most a few hundred dollars capital; out of this small beginning, a great and prosperous business has been built up. Year after year his business increases, demanding additions to his former small building, in which he not only kept a general store and postoffice, but also a hotel. Other buildings were erected on his land, until the place assumed the proportions of a lively village, in which Mr. Cass was the leading spirit, and which was known as Cassville. Here he remained until the present village of Sumner was underway, and he saw that business was bound to center there, so in 1875, he removed here his entire business interests, including several buildings, and soon came to the front as the leading merchant. His business has gradually increased until he is now at the head of two immense stores, both being under the firm name of S. F. Cass & Company. Aside from these two large stores, Mr. Cass is the owner of several small buildings and the large grain warehouse, in addition to which he has agricultural warehouses etc., etc. Although Mr. Cass has done a general banking and exchange business ever since he has been in business, he did not engage in banking as a separate business until January 1, 1881, when he started the Bank of Sumner, of which he is sole proprietor. The large building in which the bank is located, was built by him in 1878–9 and '80. In this building is located his private dwelling, Masonic Lodge, and on the first floor is located the banking room, which is a large and spacious room, fitted up with one of the best substantial vaults in the State, inside of which is located a time-locking safe that cost $1,200. On the west of the banking room, and connected with, is the general business office of the bank; opening out of this is the elegant private office of Mr. Cass. Aside from his business interests he has held various offices in the town; was appointed postmaster in 1866, while he was a British subject. Some of his neighbors tried to have the office taken away from him on that account, but he made application for citizenship, and was retained in the office. He was for a number of years, assessor of Sumner; he was one of the charter members of "Lookout" Masonic Lodge, No. 395, and was Master of the lodge for one year. He was married in the fall of 1861, in Wisconsin, to Miss M. J. Wilcox, a native of New York. They have had six children, four living—Joseph, Louis,

Eugene and Claude. Dwight H. died in 1862, at the age of three months; Ernest died May, 1878, at the age of four and a half years.

Myron Congdon, born in Broome county, New York, June 23, 1831, is a son of Elias and Rosamond Congdon. His father was a native of Vermont, and his mother of New York. His father was a farmer, but devoted a part of his time to railroad building; he died in 1867 at the age of 68. His mother is still living and a member of his family; she is 78 years old and in good health. When he was six years of age his parents moved to Belvidere, Boone county, Illinois. There he was brought up on a farm, receiving but a limited education. There he continued to live until 1861, when he came to Iowa, and settled in the northwest quarter of sec. 3, Sumner township. There he lived, following farming, until March 1, 1882, when he came to this village; and in August of the same year formed a partnership with S. F. Cass, M. S. Wright and C. F. Reimler, under the firm name of S. F. Cass & Company, having an interest in both stores. Mr. Congdon has been township trustee for eleven years, was one of the charter members of Sumner Lodge, Number 88, A. O. U. W., of which he is the financier. He still owns his farm in Sumner township. Was married to Miss Gertrude Orvis, a native of New York. They have two children, H. W. and Alice.

C. F. Reimler was born in Hille, Minden county, Germany, November 24, 1849. At the age of fifteen he came to America and settled in Schenectady, New York, where he went to work on a farm. He received a good German education, and attended school awhile after coming to this country. He remained in New York for two years, then went to Wisconsin, where he settled at Madison and was engaged in a store as clerk for two years. In 1872 he came to Sumner, Iowa, and worked on a farm about nine months, after which he worked on S. F. Cass's farm for two years, when he was taken into the store as clerk. Afterwards he, in company with others, bought Mr. Cass out, the firm name being Tibbitts, Reimler & Co. This firm continued business until August, 1882, when it was succeeded by S. F. Cass & Co., Mr. Reimler remaining in the firm. About this time he was appointed postmaster and express agent of the American Express Company, which offices he still continues to hold. Mr. Reimler is a young man with fine business abilities, honest and upright in all his dealings and will undoubtedly make a mark in the financial world. He was married in 1880 to Miss Rosa Hagg, a native of Wisconsin.

M. S. Wright was born in Littleton, Massachusetts, July 19, 1838. When quite young his parents went to Lowell, where he received an academical education. At the age of nineteen, he went into the produce business with his brother, A. F. Wright, under the firm name of A. S. & M. S. Wright. In this he continued until 1870, when he came to Iowa, and settled in Sumner township. He was on a farm four years, then went to Lafayette township, where he remained one year, and then returned to Sumner, and formed a partnership with Mr. Cass, in the mercantile business, under the firm name of Cass & Wright. In this business he continued one year, and then returned to his farm in

Lafayette township, where he remained until August, 1882; he then formed a partnership with Mr. Cass and others, under the firm name of S. F. Cass & Co. He has the management of one of the stores, and keeps the books for both of the large stores owned by this firm. Mr. Wright is a member of the Masonic Lodge, Knight Templar, and also of Pilgrim Commandery, of Lowell, Massachusetts, and is, also, a member of the A. O. U. W., of this place. He was married, in 1871, to Mrs. Lizzie French, a native of New Hampshire. She had one child, a daughter, named Ida M.

Hardware.—Copeland & Langmier are successors to Hoffman & Foster and came in possession in November, 1882. Joseph Copeland has charge of the business and is making many friends.

One of the oldest dealers in this town is M. Robish, having been in business here eight years. He deals in hardware and machinery, besides having a tin-shop in connection with his store. By close application to business, Mr. Robish has become one of the growing and prosperous men of the town.

Boots and Shoes.—The store of J. F. Fassel is filled with a good stock of boots, shoes and groceries. He has a store-room 18x56 and a good cellar. He is a practical shoemaker and has a good, increasing trade.

Meat-market.—The first meat-market in the town was started by D. R. Littell in 1875, and continued until 1880, when he sold to Fred Frank, who continues in the business, and has a well appointed market, for a town of this size.

D. R. Littell, son of David and Almira Littell, was born in New Jersey, October 30, 1843. In 1850 his parents moved to Illinois, making the trip by water, in the steamer "Belle of the West." They met with a severe loss in the burning of the steamer, losing all of their goods, and $2,000 in money. There were fifty-three lives lost, Mr. Littell and his parents barely escaping the tragic death of burning or drowning. After reaching Illinois they remained there only nine months, and then went to Fairchild county, Wisconsin, where they engaged in farming for four years, when they moved to Monroe county, where Mr. Littell lived until 1869, when he came to Bremer county, Iowa, settled in Sumner township, and engaged in farming for two years. In 1875 he started the first meat-market in the town, which he kept for five years. He was in the harness business one year, and then went into general mercantile business with the Cass Brothers, under the firm name of Cass Brothers & Littell. He continued in this until August, 1882, when he retired from business. He has been justice of the peace for six years. He was made a Mason in 1881, and was elected Junior Warden at the last election. He is, also, a member of the A. O. U. W., of which he is a charter member. He was Recorder of the lodge for three years. Mr. Littell's father is still living with him, and is seventy-seven years old. His mother died in Wisconsin in 1868. He was married, in 1867, to Miss Laura C. Davis. They have three children—William O., Franklin D., and Ezra B.

Fred H. Frank, the present proprietor of the meat market, was born in Germany in 1850. He is the son of Henry and Dora Frank, both living near Charles City. They came to America in 1866.

John Honnighaus

Fred lived in Indiana one year, and then went to Chicago, where he remained seven years, engaged in a meat-market. From there he went to Charles City, on a farm, where he stayed four years, and then lived in Waverly one year, where he again engaged in the meat business. In the fall of 1880, he came to this place and bought the market belonging to D. R. Littell, in which business he has been since engaged. It is the only one in the place. He bought the building in which he has his market, and owns four lots in the village. Mr. Frank is a member of the German Lutheran Church. He was married, in 1874, to Miss Dora Scheffel, a native of Germany. They have two children—Henry and Johnnie.

HARNESS SHOP.

The first business of this kind was established by Mr. Baumgartner, in 1873. From a small beginning, his trade has continued to increase, and, by strict integrity and hard work, he has built up a good and paying business.

A. Baumgartner was born in Jefferson county, Wisconsin, in 1854, and is the son of Henry and Elizabeth (Rubracht) Baumgartner. He was reared on a farm until twelve years of age, receiving a common school education. When he was fourteen years old he commenced to learn the harness trade, in Jefferson, Wisconsin, there he lived until he came to this place, in 1873, and commenced business for himself. He first commenced in a little shop in the upper part of town. In 1874 he built his present shop. Mr. Baumgartner was one of the charter members of the A. O. U. W., and is the present Master of the lodge. He was married in 1877, to Miss Mary Gada. They have had two children —George and Ferdinand.

FURNITURE.

This business was first established by S. T. Todd, in 1874, who continued until 1876, when he sold out to the presnt proprietor, P. Woodring, who soon after making the purchase, erected a large and commodious building suitable for this branch of trade. He is a practical cabinet maker, and thoroughly understands his business in all its branches. In addition to general furniture, he carries a large stock of school furniture, organs, sewing machines and clocks. He is also undertaker for the town, and deals in tombstones and monuments. He has in a large measure, the respect of the community and has built up a large and constantly increasing business.

He was born in Northampton county, Pennsylvania, in 1844. He was the son of Peter and Elizabeth Woodring. The former died in 1858 and the latter in 1856. When Peter was six years old his parents moved to Stephenson county, Illinois, where he lived until 1861, when he enlisted in the Thirty-seventh Illinois Volunteers, remaining until the close of the war in 1866. When he returned from the army he went to Waverly and worked for Woodring Brothers, until the fall of 1868. Then he went to Plainfield, where he went into business for himself, but remained only a short time. In the spring of 1869 he went to Clarksville, Butler county, where he remained one year, and then returned again to work for Woodring Bros., in Waverly. There he remained until 1876, when he came to this place and engaged in business, meeting with good success. Here S. T. Todd purchased the establishment of the first furniture store in this place. His present store building was erected in 1880. It is 32x36, and two stories high. He is connected by telephone with Woodring Bros., of Waverly. Mr. Woodring spends a portion of his time on the road. He is a member of the United Brethren in Christ, and is licensed to preach. He married May 18, 1868, Miss Mary J. Fague, a native of Woodford county, Illinois. They have seven children, Clara E., Alberto J., Amy L., Lila A., Ada S., Gertie P. and Henry E. They lost one, Marietta, at the age of one year and five months.

MILLINERY.

This business is well represented by Mrs. Peter Woodring, who carries a choice and well selected stock of everything in that line.

DRUGS.

The pioneer drug store of the town was started in 1874 by Dr. J. N. Wilson, in company with J. H. Muffly, the Doctor the same year erecting the fine store building now occupied by Frank A. Lee. Dr. Wilson continued in the drug business until his practice became so extensive he was obliged to give up his interest and devote his time to the profession. This was in 1876, since which time the store has changed hands a number of times, and is now owned by Frank A. Lee, of Waverly, and is under the management of Asa K. Leonard, a capable and popular young man. There is another drug store, which was established some years later, now controlled by Dr. Z. Z. Bryant, who has a stock of drugs, and M. Robish, who has a stock of hardware. They commenced business in May, 1882.

J. H. Muffly, son of C. T. and Jemima Muffly, was born in Stephenson county, Illinois, January 15, 1851. In 1868, his parents moved to Hardin county, Iowa, where they remained, however, but two years, and then went back to Illinois. At the age of nineteen, having received a liberal education, he taught school for two years, then went to Fayette county, where he was engaged in farming for two years. In the year 1875, he came to Sumner, and became connected with Dr. Wilson, in the drug business. In this he continued until 1879, when he went to work for Hunt, Holt & Co., in the grain business. Mr. Muffly was justice of the peace for two years. He was married, in 1873, to Miss Minerva Baker, a native of Stephenson county, Illinois. They have one child—Louisa May.

BANKS.

S. F. Cass, in connection with his mercantile trade, did a general exchange and banking business, which increased to such an extent that in January, 1881, he established a bank as a separate business. The bank building is 56x58, two stories, and was built at an expense of about $5,000. It contains the bank and residence of S. F. Cass and a Masonic hall. In addition to the general banking room, there is a commodious general business office, for the use of those connected with the institution, and, opening from this is the private office of the proprietor. The main banking room is the best appointed in the county. The vault is 10x12, fire-proof, having heavy, double, steel doors, with combination lock, within which is a burglar-proof safe, weighng 4,550 pounds, valued at $1,300. The safe is Diebold's latest improved pattern and has a time lock. Mr. Cass has worked up a banking business which requires all his time and the assistance of an efficient cashier.

Frank Thull, born in Ozaukee, Wisconsin, April 15, 1854. He is a son of Peter and Doratha (Weaver) Thull, the former still living in Wisconsin, the latter dying in February, 1874, at the age of 62 years. Frank was educated in the common school, receiving a liberal education. He was engaged as clerk in a store, until 1877 when he came to this place as clerk for his brother, in the hardware store, remaining with him two and a half years. He then engaged with Cass & Co., in the store, but in July, 1881, went into the bank as cashier. He is an honest, upright young man, and has won the respect and esteem of all that have come in contact with him. Was married May 20, 1882, Miss Sadie E. West, a native of Linn county, Iowa.

HOTELS.

The first regular hotel started in this town was the "Pacific House," which for a long time did a flourishing business under the management of Charley Spears, but for some reason was closed in the fall of 1882, for the winter. There has been quite a number of hotels started, of various grades, from time to time, but the only one running in December, 1882, was "King's Hotel," owned and managed by William King, who came here from Lawler in the fall of 1880, purchased the building which had heretofore been used for a general store, remodeled the same and made a good hotel building, 22x100 feet, two stories high, it contains a commodious office, 24x24, a dining room 24x24, and accommodations for forty guests. William King, the gentlemanly and accommodating proprietor, was born in Saratoga county, New York, January 31, 1816. He was the son of Ebenezer and Martha Sarah King. His father was in the boot and shoe business, but died when William was but nine years old. When four years old his parents moved to Oneida county, New York, where he lived until he was twenty years of age. In early life he learned the shoemaker's trade. In 1845 he removed to St. Charles, Illinois, where he worked at his trade, until his health failed him, when he became engaged in peddling through the county with a team. In 1869 he came to Iowa and settled in Lawler, where he engaged in the hotel business, continuing until February, 1879, when his house was burned, causing the loss of nearly everything he had. While he was in Illinois, he was postmaster for four years, under James Buchanan. Mr. King tells quite a laughable incident in connection with his getting the appointment of postmaster in Illinois. Having been a life-long republican, and the town being almost unanimously democratic, there being only three republican voters beside himself, he was asked by the people to accept the appointment of postmaster under James Buchanan's democratic administration. The petition sent to Washington stated, that there was not a democrat in the town that they dare trust, and of the four republicans, Mr. King was set forth as being the only honest one among them. The result was, James Buchanan appointed him postmaster, which office he held during the entire administration. Mr. King was married in 1840, to Miss Matilda Rosa, a native of New York. They had an adopted son, John, who was killed by accident on the Northern Pacific Railroad, on the 24th of May, 1882, age twenty-seven.

LIVERY STABLE.

Mr. Jarvis is proprietor of a livery, feed and sale stable. He located here in 1876 and engaged in this business, being the first in town, and is now the only one in this line. His barn is 56x60, with an addition, 12x24, for an office, which is designed to be increased by an addition, 40x50. He keeps eighteen horses, and has as good turnouts as will be found anywhere in the county. He has generally carried the mail between Sumner and West Union, Randalia and Henry's Mill, during the last ten years, and from here to Waverly until the route was established by rail. He now runs to Plainfield and the points named. He is one of the pioneer men of Sumner, is public-spirited, enterprising and prosperous, and has a host of friends. A. H. Jarvis, son of J. M. and Catherine Jarvis, was born in Paynesville, Ohio, in June, 1846. His parents are both living in Nebraska. Mr. Jarvis lived in Ohio until he was nine years of age, when his parents moved to Illinois, remaining six years, and then moved to Waterloo, Black Hawk county, Iowa. He was brought up on a farm, receiving but a common school education. In 1870 he came to Bremer county, and settled on a farm in Warren township, where he remained for five years. From there he went to Waverly, and was in the stage line business, but came to Sumner in 1876, where he has since been in business. In the meantime, in 1863, at the age of seventeen, he went into the army and went "from Atlanta to the sea," with Sherman. He remained in the army until the close of the war in 1865. Mr. Jarvis has been deputy sheriff for five years, and constable for the past six years. Was one of the charter members of the Masonic lodge. He was married in 1870 to Miss May Cook, a native of New York.

SUMNER CREAMERY.

The business was established in May, 1880, by Tibbets & Tower, who continued the business until October, when they sold to A. O. Kingsley and H. G. Fairchild. Soon after it passed into the hands of A. O. Kingsley, who continued to run it until August, 1881, when Gardner, Murphy & Company, of Boston, became the proprietors. They installed H. C. Alger as superintendent, who at once commenced to refit it and put it into first class shape. The main building is 24x65 with ice house 24x36. The machines are operated by a six horse power steam engine, with eight horse power boiler. This establishment has all the modern improvements for the manufacture of butter, and is one of the most thriving and progressive branches of business in Sumner. During the season of 1882, they manufactured on an average one thousand pounds of butter per day.

H. C. Alger, the son of E. A. and A. M. Alger, was born in Lowell, Massachusetts, April 15, 1857. There he lived until 1861, when his parents moved to Cambridge, Massachusetts, where he attended the High School, until he entered Harvard College, graduating in the class of 1879. He entered the Harvard Medical College, but did not take the full course; between the years 1880 and 1881, he took a vacation. In the summer of 1881, he was sent to this place by Gardner, Murphy & Company as, superintendent of their creamery. Mr. Alger was elected justice of the peace at the last election, for one year. He is a member of Lookout Lodge, of which he is S. D. He is a young man of fine education, excellent business ability, and is fast winning the respect and esteem of the citizens in his adopted home.

STEAM FEED MILL.

Owen & Son, proprietors of this mill, came to Sumner from Black Hawk county, in May, 1882. They at once secured a location, and commenced building a steam feed mill. The size of the building is 16x33 feet, two stories high, run by a six and one-half horse-power steam engine. They do a general milling business. This is the first mill of any description started in Sumner. The present capacity is one hundred bushels per day, which is hardly sufficient to meet the demand.

C. Owen was born in Steuben county, New York, in 1817. His father, J. R. Owen, was a miller by trade, and was one of the first settlers of Black Hawk county, locating there at the same time with his son, C. Owen, in 1857. Mr. Owen lived in New York until 1852, when he went to Illinois, remained five years, and then went to Lester, Black Hawk county, where he became engaged in farming and working in a flouring mill. There he remained until 1882, when he sold his farm and came to Sumner, built a mill, and, in connection with his son, became engaged in the milling business. Mr. Owen was one of the trustees of the town in which he lived, in Black Hawk county, and his father for a number of years was justice of the peace. The entire family are members of the Free-Will Baptist Church. Mr. Owen was married, in 1840, to Miss Sophrona Smith, a native of New York. They have two children living—L. S., and Parley.

L. S. Owen was born in Black Hawk county, Iowa, in 1857, his father being one of the first settlers of that county. He was educated in Lester and Waterloo, and commenced teaching in 1876, in the district schools of that county, continuing teaching until he came to Sumner in 1882. He is a member of the Free-Will Baptist Church, of which society he is an officer. He was married, in 1879, to Miss Katie Miller, a native of Pennsylvania. They have two children—Earl, and Ralph.

CARRIAGE SHOPS.

There are three carriage and repair shops here, prominent among which is the one owned by McMeekin & Co., who, in addition to the general blacksmith and carriage business, manufacture different vehicles for the trade. Mr. McMeekin established in business during the season of 1876, and has since continued.

William McMeekin, son of Thomas and Rhoda McMeekin, was born in Delhi, Delaware county, Iowa, December 28, 1855. His parents lived in Delhi but a short time after his birth, when they moved to Bremer county, and settled in Leroy township. William received a common school education, was brought up on a farm, where he worked until he was twenty-one years of age, when he commenced to learn the blacksmith business. He soon settled in this place, and went in business on his own account. He was married, in 1879, to Miss Ella Kellogg, a native of New York State. They have one child—Eugenie.

LUMBER YARDS.

The Minneapolis lumber yard, managed by T. P. Emmons, was established November 1, 1880. The stock for the same came on the first train that entered Sumner, and was located on railroad land, on the north side. They carry a full and complete stock. Mr. Emmons also deals in farm machinery, wood and coal.

T. P. Emmons, son of Morton and Eliza Emmons, was born in Delaware county, New York, in 1842. After attaining his majority, he moved to Oneanta, Otsego county, where he grew to manhood, receiving an excellent business education, which was completed at Eastman's Business College, receiving his diploma in 1865. The same year he came west, and settled in Waverly, where he was engaged in the grain business for one year. Returning then to his old home, in New York, he engaged in the grocery, dry goods, boot and shoe business, remaining nine years. Returning again to Waverly, he engaged in farming until he was made agent for the Minneapolis lumber yard, November 1, 1880. The firm carry about $7,000 worth of stock, deal extensively in window sash, doors and blinds. The firm have been doing a good business ever since they first started. Mr. Emmons still owns his farm near Waverly. His father and mother are both dead, the former dying in 1866, and the latter in 1865. He was married, in 1865, to Miss Mary Martin, a native of Maine. They have two children—Lillian and Willie. Mr. Emmons is a member of the Masonic Lodge No. 466, Oneanta, N. Y.

J. C. Garner's lumber yard does a mammoth business, immense quantities of lumber passing through this yard every year. He carries a stock, including farm machinery, coal, &c., of about $10,000, and does a business of upwards of $25,000 a year. This yard is in charge of A. J. Curtiss, assisted by Willie Carpenter.

O. O. Tibbitts also carries on a lumber yard on a smaller scale.

PHOTOGRAPHY.

The photograph gallery now owned by S. M. Goodall was established in the spring of 1881 by J. F. Davis, who continued in the business until May, 1882, when he was succeeded by S. M. Goodall.

GRAIN DEALERS.

There are two extensive warehouses in Sumner, one built in 1879 by Hunt, Hall & Co., and the other in 1880, by S. F. Cass. One is operated by the Waverly Board of Trade, with J. H. Muffly as manager and the other by A. Fortner & Co., of Waverly, with C. Fortner as manager.

HISTORY OF BREMER COUNTY.

Both are doing a flourishing business, handling all kinds of farm produce.

JEWELER.

J. C. Rand, practical jeweler, watchmaker, engraver, &c., was born in Grant county, Wisconsin, in 1846. He is the son of Nathaniel Allen and Mary Rand. He lived in Wisconsin until 1865, when he came to Iowa, but soon left and went to Illinois, where he lived ten years. He commenced to learn his trade when he was fifteen, and has kept steadily at it ever since, working in the Elgin watch factory for a short time. He located here in the spring of 1882, coming from Lena, Illinois. He has been doing a good business since he started and intends to make this his permanent home. Mr. Rand must surely succeed, for he does his work in a thorough and reliable way. His father went to California in 1852, and on his way home, the next year, was taken sick coming across the Isthmus and died. His mother still lives in Alouez, Keweenaw county, Michigan.

STOCK YARDS.

The shipment of live stock here indicates a remarkable degree of prosperity among the farmers, and the showing will compare favorably with any place of this size. There are quite a number of local buyers who make it a business at this point, furnishing a ready market for cattle and hogs.

OTHER INTERESTS.

Besides the business mentioned, there is a barber shop, gun shop, shoe shop, three saloons, three dressmakers, one milliner store with hair store combined, restaurant, two dray lines, etc. There are telephone connections with Waverly, which prove a great convenience. To guard against fire two wells have been dug on First street. There is a hand engine owned by S. F. Cass, and hose and cart owned by the town. The business men also employ a night watchman.

PROFESSIONAL.

Z. Z. Bryant, M. D., read medicine three years under Z. A. Bryant, attending one course of lectures in Humboldt College, St. Louis. He became a member of the Hahneman Medical Association, of Iowa, in 1877. He is a graduate of the Hahneman Medical College, of Chicago, Illinois. He also attended a full course of lectures on the diseases of women, by R. Lualam, a specialist, of Chicago. Dr. Bryant has been a resident physician in this locality for about nine years, and has an extensive practice.

J. N. Wilson, M. D., is a graduate of the school of Physicians and Surgeons, Keokuk, Iowa. He also attended the medical department of the Iowa State University two years. Besides the practice of medicine, he is also a practical Surgeon. He has a certificate of pharmacy. Dr. Wilson has had thirteen years practice, ten of which have been in Sumner and vicinity. He was the first regular physician to locate in Sumner.

The legal profession is represented by Josiah Carpenter, he being the only attorney ever locating in Sumner. He also deals in real estate and insurance.

Frank K. White represents the fire insurance interests, and is agent for the following companies: Phœnix, of Hartford, German, of Freeport, Illinois, Life and Equitable, of Waterloo, and others. Mr White is an energetic man, and has built up a considerable business in this line.

Frank K. White was born in Greene county, Wisconsin, July 8, 1846. At the age of four years his parents moved to Rock county, remaining there until he was nine years of age, when they came to Iowa and settled in Chickasaw county. There Frank was reared on a farm until he was eighteen years of age, receiving a liberal education. In 1864 he engaged in the mercantile business, in Jacksonville, afterwards in New Hampton, where he continued until 1869. Unfortunately his experience in the mercantile world was not all that he could have hoped for. When he retired from the business, the firm succeeding him, soon after, made a financial failure, which involved him to quite an extent, leaving him badly in debt. But to his credit, let it be said, that every dollar of the indebtedness, whether it justly belonged to him or not, has been liquidated, dollar for dollar. Nothing daunted by the misfortunes of the past, Mr. White, with a strong determination, stronger, if possible, than at the start, set out to build himself up in the financial world. At that time he became connected with some of the most prominent insurance companies of the state, as special agent, slowly but surely working his way upward and onward. He has continued to follow the insurance business from that time up to the present. In May, 1881, he came to Sumner, where he located permanently, as special agent for the State Insurance Company of Des Moines. By strict attention to business, hard work, and a determination to succeed, he has built up a large and profitable business, not only this, but he has won the entire confidence of the company in whose employ he is, to such an extent that they have appointed him general agent for the northeast part of the State, including twenty-one counties, and having in his charge upwards of forty men. With the push and enterprise for which he is noted, it is safe to predict that he will yet make his mark in the world. In politics, an independent, having identified himself with the greenback movement, he still clings to the principles of that party. In religion he is a liberalist, being at this time chairman of the Liberal League Association, of Northwestern Iowa. He is a member of the Masonic fraternity, to which he is much attached. He was married September 4, 1870, to Miss Mary C. Shepard. They have three children, J. Edsall, Gene C., Pearl E.

RELIGIOUS.

Wilson Grove Presbyterian Church was organized November 9, 1859, by Rev. J. M. Boggs and J. D. Caldwell, who were constituted a committee appointed by the Dubuque Presbytery. The first members were: Levi Williams and wife, William T. Wade, Agnes C. Wade, Miss H. J. Wade, B. M. Savage, Mary A. Savage, Mrs. S. T. Bent, John Black, Jane Black, John Husband, and Mrs. Husband. The first officers of the Church were: William T. Wade and B. M. Savage, elders; Levi Williams, and John Black, deacons. The first services were held at the residence of

Henry Heine.

William T. Wade. The first pastor was L. R. Lockwood, who remained two years. He was followed by J. D. Caldwell, who supplied the church at different times; then Jacob Swarth, two years; then J. D. Caldwell, from 1875 to 1878; E. Sayre, June, 1878, to 1880, who was succeeded by the present pastor, W. H. Jennings, in July, 1880. This organization erected a church at Sumner in 1875-6, 32x60 feet, at an expense of $2,500. The present officers of the church are: William T. Wade and David Caswell, elders; John Black, deacon. The congregation now numbers about one hundred. Here a Union Sabbath School was organized, with A. Beels as superintendent. The present officers of this school are: William T. Wade, superintendent; L. P. Owens, assistant superintendent; Peter Smith, secretary and treasurer. It has an enrollment of 70, with an average attendance of 55.

Rev. W. H. Jennings, the present pastor, is the son of Henry and Catherine Jennings, born in Fayette county, Pennsylvania, June 28, 1849, where the family lived until he was fourteen years of age, when they came to Iowa and settled in Delaware county. Here the subject of this sketch grew to manhood, prepared for college at Cedar Rapids, and in 1870 entered the Wabash college, of Indiana, graduating in 1874. He then entered the Lena Theological Seminary and graduated in 1877. In the same year he was stationed at Houston, Iowa, where he remained one year. He then took a vacation of a year, after which he spent a term supplying churches in Marion county. In the summer of 1881 he came to Sumner, to assume the pastoral duties of the Presbyterian church. He also has charge of a society at Maynard, Fayette county, and in Dayton township, Union schoolhouse. Mr. Jennings took an active part in the temperance movement for prohibition, in 1882. He is a young man, of fine education and good ability, and is much beloved by the members of his congregation, is honest and upright in all his dealings, a true and faithful christian. He was married in 1877, to Miss Mary H. Kemper, a native of Cincinnati, Ohio. They have two children—Lillie May and John Lewis.

GERMAN EVANGELICAL CHURCH.

This society was organized about 1870, by Fred Krause, J. A. Haag, F. Ludwig, J. F. Schaiphorster, Adam Lang, Fred Miller, Henry Pinoe, George Hammetter, and Fred Reimler. The first meetings of this organization were held in Buck Creek school house, Lang's residence, and other places until the church was built, in 1875. In 1875, they purchased a building lot for $100, on the northeast corner of section 17, Sumner township, and at once commenced the erection of a comfortable church. They have a membership of seventy-five, with a large and flourishing Sabbath School. The first superintendent was Fred Krause. The present superintendent is George Debercimer; assistant superintendent, Fred Reimler; secretary, Herman Wattke; treasurer, John Maller; librarian, August Wattke. The society is free from debt, and in a prosperous condition. Besides these churches herein mentioned, are the following organizations, which have services occasionally, but are without buildings or regular pastors: United Brethren, German Lutheran, Seven-Day Advents, and Baptists.

A. F. AND A. M.

Lookout Lodge, No. 395, A. F. and A. M., was organized in 1879, Dr. J. N. Wilson, Dr. Z. Z. Bryant and S. F. Cass taking an active part. The following are the charter members: J. N. Wilson, George F. Harwood, S. F. Cass, Nathan Bent, E. E. Fay, Z. Z. Bryant, A. J. Lowe, Martin Robish, Alex. Carman, E. Fay, David Littell and Nathan Reynolds. At the first meeting, the following officers were elected: J. N. Wilson, W. M.; George F. Harwood, S. W.; S. F. Cass, J. W.; Nathan Bent, Treasurer; E. E. Fay, Secretary; Z. Z. Bryant, S. D.; A. J. Lowe, J. D.; Charles Seeley, J. S.; C. M. Reed, Tyler. The present officers are: Z. Z. Bryant, W. M.; C. A. Seeley, S. W.; C. Kaimanska, J. W.; M. Robish, Secretary; J. F. Fasil, Treasurer; H. C. Alger, S. D.; A. J. Lowe, J. D.; L. C. Head, S. S.; A. Countryman, J. S.; John Reynolds, Tyler. They have a commodious hall in Cass' building, 20x40 feet, which is furnished in good shape. The lodge is in excellent condition, having a membership of forty-two. There has not been a death in the society since its organization.

A. O. U. W.

Sumner Lodge, A. O. U. W., No. 88, was organized December 11, 1876, by W. H. Burford, with the following as charter members: R. M. Carrol, S. E. Conner, R. L. Fox, I. N. Kepler, C. M. Reed, S. E. McNaul, A. Baumgartner, S. F. Fisher, E. L. Fitch, A. C. Wilkins, C. G. Spears, W. T. Wade, J. N. Wilson, D. R. Littell, M. S. Wright, J. D. Blair, A. P. Fowler, D. M. Meeker, C. C. Parsons, S. N. Orvis, A. Mc-Meekin, W. W. Quirey, M. Congdon. The first officers of this organization were: E. L. Fitch, P. M. W; W. W. Quirey, M. W; S. E. McNaul, G. F.; R. L. Fox, O; S. E. Cowner, Recorder; M. S. Wright, Financier; W. L. Wade, Receiver; D. R. Littell, Inside Watch; I. N. Kepler, Outside Watch. The present membership is twenty-four. There has been one death since the organization, that of William Wade. The present condition of the lodge is prosperous.

OPERA HOUSE.

In the spring of 1882, Sumner, not having a suitable place for entertainments, Peter Forssman determined to erect an opera house and commenced at once to build. He completed the building in a short time. It is 80x34 feet, 28 feet high. The stage is 16x34 feet. It has a seating capacity of 600, and and cost nearly $2,-500. It is a good building and would do credit to a much large town than Sumner.

Peter Forssman, proprietor of "Sumner Opera House," was born in Stockholm, Sweden, in 1843. He was the son of Magmus and Anna Forssman, who are both living in Sweden. He was reared in the mines, and had charge of one mine for seven years, following this business until 1871, when he came to America and settled in Hartford, Connecticut, where he was engaged in a stone quarry and in brick making. In 1873, he came to Iowa and settled in Buchanan county, near Independence, engaged in fancy stock-raising on an extensive scale. This he followed for several years, after which he spent one year in Independence, where he kept a saloon and billiard hall. In 1881, he came to Sumner and opened a billiard hall, where he continued until the fall of 1882, when he sold out. In the spring of 1882, realizing the necessity of a public hall for entertainments, and receiving sufficient encouragement from the citizens, he purchased a lot and commenced the erection of a commodious building, to be used for such purchases. Mr. Forssman was married in 1872, to Miss Louisa Larson, a native of Sweden. They have three children, two girls and one boy—Ellen, Martha and Peter.

BUSINESS DIRECTORY OF SUMNER.

S. F. Cass & Co.—General merchandise—S. F. Cass, Myron Congdon, M. S. Wright and C. F. Reimler.

Clark & Austin—General merchandise—A. H. Clark and C. A. Austin.

Copeland & Longmier—General hardware.

Martin Robish—General hardware.

J. F. Fasel—Groceries, boots and shoes.

Bryant & Robish—Druggists.

Frank A. Lee—Druggist.

Peter Woodring—Furniture, sewing machines, organs, clocks, etc.

J. C. Rand—Jeweler.

Eugene Ellsworth—Gunsmith.

William Turner—Barber.

A. Baumgartner—Harness shop.

Fred. Frank—Meat-market.

A. H. Jarvis—Livery stable.

J. H. Muffly—Grain buyer.

E. P. Emmons—Lumber yard.

J. C. Garner—Lumber yard.

A. J. Curtis—Depot agent.

William King—Hotel.

Mrs. Peter Woodring—Milliner.

Miss Priffer—Milliner.

S. F. Cass—Banker.

Frank Shull—Cashier of Bank.

Josiah Carpenter—Attorney at law.

Tower & Tibbits—Horses.

Chauncy Carpenter—Capitalist.

G. P. Linn & Co.—Printing office.

Telephone exchange—A. J. Curtis.

Peter Forssman—Manager opera house.

Gardner, Murphy & Co.—Creamery.

Frank White—Insurance agent.

Josiah Carpenter—Insurance agent.

S. M. Goodall—artist.

A. H. Jarvis—Dray line.

McMeekin & Co.—Blacksmiths.

S. Koerth—Blacksmith.

J. N. Wilson and W. E. Whiting—Physicians.

Z. Z. Bryant—Physician.

Al. Wemple—Saloon.

F. A. Nounan—Saloon.

CHAPTER XXIX.

WARREN TOWNSHIP.

This township comprises all of township 92, range 13, west of the fifth principal meridian, and is bounded on the north by Douglas, on the south by Washington and Jefferson, on the east by Fremont and on the west by Lafayette. The surface of the township is rolling prairie, except where it is crossed by small streams. There are three groves of timber, "Wumbo's" grove, located on sections 34, 27 and 26, and is about one and one-half miles long by one mile wide. The timber is principally burr oak, jack oak, and shell-bark hickory. Quarter-section Grove is located on section 15 and contains sixty acres of timber, the greater part of which is burr oak. "Sturtevant's" Grove is located in the southwestern part of the township, and is covered with the same kinds of timber as the others.

The territory now comprising this township is a subdivision of what was once Washington township. It assumed its present boundaries and was organized as a township in 1859.

EARLY SETTLEMENT.

Among the early settlers were Israel Trumbo and family, who came here from Ohio in 1853 and located on section 34, where he lived until 1860, when he moved to Dakota, where he has since died.

William Ogden and family came here from Kentucky in 1853 and located on section 26, remaining until 1856, when he moved to Mitchell county, Iowa, where he has since died. Nelson M. Smith came in the same year and selected a farm on section 31. Claudius Albee arrived the same year and established a home on section 32.

Clarence Tyrrell, who is a son of Edward and Elizabeth (Canada) Tyrrell, was born in McHenry county, Illinois, on the 20th day of January, 1850. In the year 1853, he, in company with his parents, came west and settled in Bremer county, where he has since resided. During the years of his youth he received a good common school education. Mr. Tyrrell lived with his mother until the spring of 1882, when he bought 80 acres of land in section 18, and has since resided there. He has held the office of trustee of the township. In the year of 1876, he was married to Miss Susan Garrity, who was born in the State of New York. They have two sons living—Guy E., born October 12, 1877; Jerry H., in the year 1882.

W. B. Ingersoll was born in Syracuse, New York, December 18, 1818, and is a son of Hiram and Sarah (Smith) Ingersoll. He remained in his native town until nine years of age, when the family moved to Chicago, Illinois, where he remained until October, 1853, when he came to Bremer county, and, shortly after his arrival, settled on section 7, Warren township, where he has since resided. He now owns 242 acres of land in Bremer county. In 1842 he was married to Miss Eliza Tyrrell, who is a native of Troy, New York. Nine children have been born to them—William, Nicholas, Albert, Ann, Charles, Lee, Sarah, Ann and Eunice L. Mr. Ingersoll's father died in Bremer county in the year 1870. His mother is still living.

James M. Sturdevant, the third son of Ira H. and Acenath (Lilly) Sturdevant, was born on the 5th day of May, 1820. Five years later the family moved to Chautauqua county, where they lived until 1834, when they removed to Erie county, Pennsylvania. Here James grew to manhood, and his life up to this period, was passed upon his father's farm. He received but a limited education, because of his parents constantly living on the frontier where schools were few and of short duration. In 1844, he came west to McHenry county, Illinois, where he remained for the succeeding ten years. In 1854, he moved to Waverly, Bremer county, where he passed the winter; and the following spring located at Trumbo's Grove, where he entered 160 acres of land on section 26, and also bought 40 acres of Isarel Trumbo. At the present date Mr. Sturdevant owns 46 acres; having disposed of the rest of his landed property. He has held the office of township trustee several terms. In December, 1841, he was married to Miss Phila E. Hart, who is a native of Chautauqua county, New York. Ten children have been born to them, seven of whom are now living—Henry Alonzo, who lives at Otter Tail, Minnesota; Martha M., wife of William Webber, of Waverly; Laura E., wife of Edward Keller, of Otter Tail county, Minnesota; Addie E., wife of Royal Pierce, of Otter Tail county, Minnesota; James M., who is now engaged in railroading in Minnesota; Mary E. and Flora A. Harvey B. died at Keokuk hospital from diseases contracted while in the army; Horace E. died in November, 1852, and Charles J. died in 1854.

Henry Heine was born in Hanover, Germany, August 12, 1826. He came to America in 1848, and after residing in New Orleans for five months, went to Cook county, Illinois, where he engaged in farming for about six years. In 1854 he moved to Iowa, and settled in Bremer county, entering 160 acres of land on section 12, Jefferson township, where he lived until November, 1867, when he disposed of his place and bought 720 acres of land on sections 15, 21 and 22, Warren township. At the present date, he and his sons own 600 acres, and on their place is a fine grove of trees, known as the "quarter section grove." Mr. Heine has held several of the town offices at different times. He was married in 1852, to Miss Mary Stegge, who was born in Germany. Eight children have been born to them, seven of whom are now living—Henry, Hermann, William, John, Mary, Flora, Hulda and Emma. The last two were twins; Emma died December 25, 1879.

Nelson Prue was born in Lower Canada, near Montreal, July 15, 1820. He is the third son of Nicholas and Mary (Dizotel) Prue. At the age of sixteen, he went to Worcester, Massachusetts, where he engaged in farming twelve years, and then went to Rhode Island and spent seven years. In 1855, he came to Bremer county, and settled on section 19, Warren township, where he now owns ninety-two acres of land. When Mr. Prue first came to this county, he purchased 120 acres of land, and brought with him $600 worth of furniture. This furniture, with his comfortable dwelling, was completely destroyed by fire June 1, 1857. This misfortune to the new settler left him almost destitute, and he was compelled to dispose of a part of his land, in order to raise means for the erection of another house. In 1848, he was married to Miss Elizabeth Brickhell, who was born in England, and is a daughter of Rev. Samuel Brickhell, a Methodist divine. One son was born to them—Charles, now living in Kansas. This wife died in September, 1872, and Mr. Prue was again married January 5, 1874, to Miss Anna Royer, who is a native of France. They have been blessed with four children—Esther May, Jennie Dora, Ann Elizabeth and Wesley Xavier.

Daniel Chittenden was born in Columbia, New York, on the 3d day of October, 1814, and is a son of Benjamin and Fanny (Loper) Chittenden. His father was born in New York, and his mother on Long Island. In 1816 his parents moved to Wayne county, New York, and remained until 1831, when they settled in Cataraugus county. Here Daniel grew to manhood, and remained at home until about 28 years of age, when he came west and located in St. Joseph county, Michigan, where he remained thirteen years. In 1855 he came to Bremer county, Iowa, and first located near the big woods in Washington township. Here he lived on a rented farm for two and one-half years and then settled on his present farm in section 21, Warren township. He had traded for this land while in Michigan, and previous to moving on it had had fifteen acres of the eighty broken. Mr. Chittenden was married on the 8th day of June, 1837, to Miss Phœbe Ray, who is a native of Ontario county, New York. Ten children have been born to them, six of whom are now living—Fernando, a resident of Warren township; Benjamin, also a resident of this township; Eliza, now the wife of B. F. Banks, of Rockford, Illinois; Mark Eugene, Daniel Arthur and Tina.

James Cruthers was born in county Down, Ireland, in 1828. When about fifteen years of age he went to Scotland, where he spent three years, and while there was engaged in farming. He then came to America and passed the next five years in Buffalo. In 1856 he came to Bremer county and settled in Warren township. Here he bought 45 acres of land on section 32, and at the present date owns about 100 acres. Mr. Cruthers was married in 1856 to Miss Eliza McCortney, who is also a native of Ireland. Of nine children born to them, six are now living—Belle, now the wife of Isaac Lemmon; George, Elizabeth, Margaret, Effie and Edwin.

Homer H. Case, one of the pioneers of Bremer county, was born in Genesee county, New York, June 7, 1820, and is the third son of Nathan G. and Harriet (Scoville) Case. In 1824 his mother died and in 1829 the family moved to Rutland county, Vermont, and in 1830 to Chautauqua county, New York. Here his father died in 1866. In the spring of 1856 Homer came west and passed the summer in Illinois, and in the fall, came on to Bremer county and remained through the winter in Horton. During this time, he purchased his present farm on section 8, Warren township. In the spring of 1857, he moved his family to the township, and rented a house in which they lived during the summer, while building on his farm. Mr. Case has always taken a great interest in the politics of his county. He has held the office of township trustee and secretary of the school board, and has also been justice of the peace for the past seventeen years. In politics he is a staunch Republican, casting his first presidential vote for Henry Clay. He was married in Chautauqua county in 1850 to Miss Ellen Phinney, who is a native of Vermont. Five children have blessed this union, of whom Harriet, Daniel, Julien and Hudson are now living. Stella died in January, 1875. Mr. and Mrs. Case are members of the Baptist church in Waverly.

Moses H. Robinson, who was born in Canada East, on the 17th day of May, 1834, is a son of William and Catherine (Moore) Robinson. His father and mother were of Scotch descent. Moses remained in the town of his birth until 1851, at which time he left for Clinton county, New York, where he remained for two years, when he came west, and located in DeKalb county, Illinois, where he engaged in brick-making, and here spent the following six years. Upon leaving Illinois he moved still farther west, taking up his residence in Buchanan county, Iowa, and followed his old occupation in the town of Independence. He then enlisted in Company E, Fifth Iowa Infantry, and served in this company until mustered out at Chattanooga. Here, also, he was mustered into Company G, Fifth Iowa Cavalry, and served until honorably discharged, at Clinton, Iowa, at the close of the rebellion, August, 1865. During the year 1857 he visited Bremer county, and entered 80 acres of land on section 6, Warren township, and while in the war, had 40 acres of it improved. Upon returning to civil life he settled on his farm, where he still resides. He was married at Independence, Iowa, in 1861, to Miss Sarah J. Wright, who is a native of New York. Seven children have been born to them, six of whom are now living—Ella A., Mary E., William E., Ida E., Clara Bertha, and Pearl Edna. Satie J. died in 1878.

Gould Nichols was born in Connecticut, and there grew to manhood, and was married to Philena Barnum. Five sons were born to this couple, of whom Levi was the second, and was born in Connecticut April 1, 1819. While Levi was quite young, the family moved to New York, and, several years after their settlement there, his mother died in Clyde county, in 1829, at thirty-seven years of age. The family still continued to reside there, and Levi made that his home for fifteen years, and then came west to McHenry county, Illinois, where he was married December 10, 1846, to Clarisa A. Couse, who was born in Otsego county, New York, August 25, 1828. They remained in Illinois until 1856, and during their residence there, two sons and one daughter were born to them. Frank L., their first child, was born August 14, 1848; Esther G., was born on the 15th day of April, 1851, and their third child, Henry Gould, was born November

6, 1854. In 1856, the family moved westward, and settled in Dodge county, Minnesota, where Edward K. was born, on the 28th day of February, 1857. In 1864, the family came to Iowa, and settled on section 31, Warren township, where they have since resided. Frank L. was married November 20, 1873, to Helen M. Case, who was born at Monroe, Greene county, Wisconsin, November 15, 1851. They are now residents of Warren township. Esther G. was married to Isaac Hazlett, on the 3d day of December, 1875, and they now live in Nashua, Iowa. Henry Gould married Sarah A. Caulfield, who was born at at Belvidere, Illinois, June 15, 1854; she is a daughter of James G. Caulfield, who was born October 11, 1818. At the beginning of our late rebellion, he enlisted in Company C, Fourty-fourth Illinois Volunteers, and was killed in the battle of Mission Ridge, November 25, 1863. Mr. Caulfield's wife died while Sarah was a child. Henry and his family are residents of this township. The fourth child, Edward K., now lives at Nashua, Iowa.

John Hanner, a son of Alexander and Jane (Morrison) Hanner, was born in Canada, in April, 1835. He remained in his native country until 1854, when the family emigrated to the United States and located in Stephenson county, Illinois. Here John remained until 1866, when he came to Iowa, and settled on a farm on section 9, Warren township. He now owns 240 acres of fine land, all under cultivation. Mr. Hanner has held the office of trustee and school director. On the 1st day of March, 1860, he was married to Miss Margaret Jewell, who is a native of Illinois. They have seven children—Joseph R. A., John William, Martha Jane, Lillie May, Charles B, Robert Edward and Ellen.

Jasper Wylam was born in England, on the 11th day of May, 1830. When he was seven years of age, his parents came to America, and settled in West Virginia, where they lived six years, and then moved to Illinois and settled in Jo Daviess county, where Jasper grew to manhood and engaged in farming and mining. He was married in 1854, to Miss Barbara March, who was born in England, but when seven years of age, with her parents, came to America and settled in Shellsburg, Wisconsin. In the spring of 1855, Mr. Wylam moved to Grant county, Wisconsin, and engaged in merchandising. He continued in business until 1862, when he left his home for Montana, where he pursued mining for the three following years, and then went back to his home, remaining there until September, 1868, when he came to Bremer county, and settled in Warren township, on a farm which he had bought the July previous. He died here on the 2d day of January, 1877. Eight children were born to them, all of whom are living—Sarah J., now the wife of W. J. Nicholson, Amelia F., Dorothea E., Ellen B., George T., William J., Edward J. and Francis E.

Edward Bullock was born in Cornwall, England, in July, 1832. In 1846, in company with his parents, he came to America and settled in Lafayette county, Wisconsin. Here his father engaged in mining and Edward remained at home, until he reached the age of nineteen, when he went to California, where he remained for seven years and then returned to Lafayette county. He again made this his home

EDWARD TYRRELL.

until November, 1868, when he came to Bremer county, and settled in Warren township, in section 5, where he now owns a fine farm of 200 acres. He was married in 1859 to Miss Eliza J. Gribble, who is a native of England. They have seven children living—Eliza, Ella, William, Edward A., Minnie, Grace and Edith.

S. H. Kingsley was born in Courtland county, New York, on the 24th day of July, 1824. He is a son of A. C. and Cloe B. (Leonard) Kingsley, who were both natives of the State of Connecticut. The family remained in Courtland county until 1835, when they moved to Manchester, New York, where they lived for five years, and then located in Monroe county, where S. H. lived until twenty-three years of age, when he was married to Miss Elinor J. Demarest, a native of New York City. After their marriage the young couple came west to Wisconsin, and located in Walworth county, where they lived until 1850. During that year they returned to the east, where they remained for five years, and then again moved west, and settled in Sycamore, DeKalb county, Illinois, where they lived for eight years. In 1863 they came to Bremer county, and lived in the town of Waverly for one year, and then settled on their farm of 160 acres, on section 8, Warren township, which farm Mr. Kingsley had purchased three years previous to his settlement in this county. He now owns 170 acres of land, and is also engaged in the creamery business at Tripoli, where he turns out some of the finest butter made in this section of the country. Mr. Kingsley held the office of assessor for three years—from 1868 until 1871. They have eight children now living—Albert F., who is now in the Pension Department, at Washington, D. C.; Charles A., who resides at Plainfield; Henry M., of Strawberry Point; Hiram A., who is in the Department of the Interior; Erwin, now attending Orchard City Business College, at Burlington, Iowa; William S., now teaching school; Bertie S., on the farm, and Eldora, now at home.

W. A. Rice, born in Seneca county, New York, May 2, 1821, is a son of David and Hannah (Stearns) Rice, who were both natives of Massachusetts. W. A. was reared on a farm, and during his minority received a good education in the common schools of that section of the State. He lived in the county of his birth, and Monroe county until 25 years of age. In the year 1848, he came west and settled in Wisconsin, first locating near Janesville, and afterwards near Madison. Here he remained until March, 1857, when he came to Iowa and settled on a farm of 120 acres in section 16, Butler township, Butler county. He lived in Butler county until 1871, when he removed to LaFayette township, where he followed farming until the year of 1880. Having been appointed overseer of the county poor farm, in February, of this year, he entered upon his duties there. Mr. Rice was married in the year 1846, to Miss Miriam Garrison, who was born in Orleans county, New York. Eight children have been born to them, five of whom are now living—William, Lottie, Charles Herbert, Medora, Lenora.

William Nicholson, eldest son of James and Sarah (Ball) Nicholson, was born in Nottingham, England, May 31, 1818. While in his native country, he learned the trade of carpenter and joiner, and for years followed that occupation. In 1848, he came to America and located in the city of Rochester, where he remained eighteen months, and then removed to Livingston county where he took up his residence and worked at his trade six years, when he moved west to Belvidere, Illinois, where he remained until he came to Bremer county, in the fall of 1867. He settled on section 18, Warren township, where he now owns a farm of 120 acres. In politics, Mr. Nicholson is a republican. He was married in 1848 to Miss Hannah Briggs, who is also a native of Nottingham, England. They have been blessed with six children, five of whom are now living—Sarah, now the wife of Charles Banks; William J., Mary Jane, Stephen, Frederick D.

W. J. Nicholson, a son of William and Anna (Briggs) Nicholson, was born in Rochester, New York, January 9, 1849. The family remained in that State until 1856 when they came west to Boone county, Illinois, and located in Belvidere, the son receiving his education in the public schools of that town. In 1867, with his parents, he came west and settled in Warren township. He was married in 1876 to Miss Sarah Jane Wylam, born in Grant county, Wisconsin. During the first year of their marriage, the young couple settled on their farm of forty acres, on section 17. They have one child—Maud.

John Simmons, a native of Cornwall county, England, and a son of Joseph and Mary (Gomnan) Simmons, was born October 20, 1841. He came to this country with his parents when only six years of age, and lived in Grant county, Wisconsin, on a farm, and received his education in the common schools of said county, after which he pursued farming as his avocation. In 1874 he came to Warren township, and, in the spring of 1875, settled on section 5, where he now resides and owns a farm of 184 acres of prairie and 5 acres of timber. He was united in marriage in February, 1865, with Miss Jemima Bullock, a daughter of William Bullock of Grant county, Wisconsin. By this union there are five children—Jennie, born January 16, 1866; Eliza, April 25, 1869; John, July 29, 1872; May, October 27, 1874; Elmer, January 18, 1880. Mr. Simmons is a member of Tyrrell Lodge, No. 116, of A. F. & A. M., of Waverly, Iowa, and a republican in politics.

Christian Thoren, born in Brakelsiek, Lippe-Detmold, Germany, on the 8th day of February, 1831, is the youngest son of Frederick and Amelia (Beinemeier) Thoren. He resided in his native country until 1857, when he emigrated to the United States, settling in Stephenson county, Illinois, where he resided until 1864, when he came to Warren township and bought a farm on section 28, where he has since resided and now owns a farm of 240 acres, and 11 acres of timber. In 1864, he was drafted into the army, serving one year in the Twelfth Iowa Infantry; took part in the battle of Spanish Fort, Alabama, and was discharged at Mobile, in December, 1865. He was married in 1857, to Miss Amelia Sickmeier. By this union there are six children living—Amelia, born January 15, 1858, wife of Rev. J. Knoche; Henry, February 6, 1860; Charley, July 25, 1862; Mary, March 28, 1867; Franklin, February 23, 1870, and Minnie, October, 1877. In politics Mr. Thoren is a republican, which he has been ever since becoming a citizen. He is a member of the Evangelical Church of Warren township, in which he has served as Sunday School superintendent.

ORGANIC.

On the 28th day of February, 1859, the first election of Warren township was held at the house of N. M. Smith. The following officers were appointed to hold said election: H. W. Perry, N. W. Perry and Horace Smith, trustees; H. D. Perry and H. D. Smith, clerks. The following persons were elected: Justices of the peace, N. W. Perry and Horace Smith; constables, E. N. Perry and O. Skillen; trustees, B. W. Ingersoll, H. D. Perry and N. W. Perry; town clerk, H. W. Perry. The officers since elected, have been as follows:

1861—Assessor, Orville McGinnies, supervisor, A. M. Smith; constables, E. N. Berry and P. Skillen; justices, A. M. Winner and A. J. Stroat; clerk, H. D. Perry; trustees, P. Smith, G. A. Michael and A. J. Stroat.

1862—Justices of the peace, N. W. Perry and John Buckmaster; constables, William Berry and Calvin Kingsley; assessor, James Murphey; town clerk, N. M. Smith; trustees, Duncan Berry, Proctor Smith and John Buckmaster.

1863—Supervisor, D. Winrech; justice, H. M. Wood; trustees, John Buckmaster, A. J. Buck and A. Kinney; clerk, Calvin Kingsley; assessor, Geo. Custer.

1864—Supervisor, John Buckmaster; justices, H. H. Case and James Sturdevant; trustees, Amos Kinney, Charles Stocking and Daniel Chittenden; clerk, Calvin Kingsley; assessor, S. Hammon; constables, Isaac Trumfair, W. B. Case.

1865—Trustees, Amos Kinney, James Murphy, John Fauver; justices, James Murphy, Jno. Buckmaster; supervisor, John Smalley; constables, H. H. Timblin, W. B. Ingersoll; assessor, S. H. Kingsley.

1866—Clerk, T. Caswell; assessor, S. H. Kingsley; trustees, H. H. Case, John Woodruff, A. Kinney; justices, H. H. Case, Charles Stocking; constables, John Stocking, H. H. Timblin.

1868—Supervisor, J. D. Woodruff; trustees, Amos Kinney, T. Caswell, G. H. Wiggins; justices, H. H. Case, C. Sheduede; constables, W. J. Stevens, C. Thorne; clerk, J. K. Stocking; assessor, George Luce.

1869—Trustees, Amos Kinney, G. H. Wiggins, John Hanner; constables, C. Thorne, W. P. Stevens; clerk, J. K. Stocking; assessor, E. Thompson.

1871—Supervisor, John Chapin; justice, Ch. Mohling; trustees, S. H. Kingsley, Henry Heine, Amos Kinney; assessor, Edward Thompson; constables, John Hanner, C. Thorne; clerk, B. Chittenden.

1872—Supervisor, S. H. Curtis; trustees, C. Mohling, Amos Kinney, S. H. Kingsley; clerk, C. M. Kingsley; constables, John Allbright, James Bocker.

1874—Justices, C. Thorne, H. H. Case; Assessor, C. Mohling; clerk, George Gors, trustees, John Albright, Henry Kaiser, M. H. Robinson; constables, Fred Werdman, Fred Platte.

1875—Justices, H. H. Case, Charles Stocking; assessor, C. A. Mohling; clerk, Charles Gors; trustees, Amos Kinney,

George Curtis, John Albright; constables, M. Shaver, Charles McCormack.

1877—Justices, H. H. Case, C. Thorne; assessor, Henry Klages; clerk, Charles Gors; trustees, Clarence Tyrrell, Henry Kaiser, William Arns; constables, Daniel Case, Henry Kaiser.

1878—Justice, H. H. Case; assessor, C. A. Mohling; clerk, Charles Gors; trustees, William Arns, C. A. Mohling, Henry Heine; constable, D. G. Case.

1880—Trustee, H. Kaiser; clerk, Charles Tyrrell; assessor, H. Klages; justice H. H. Case; constables, L. Rust, D. Case.

1881—Trustee, William Arns; justice, H. H. Case.

1882—Trustee, Thomas Loveland; justices, Homer Case, Andrew Pitcher; assessor, Eugene Chittenden; constables, Louis Rust, J. W. Case.

EDUCATIONAL.

The first school was taught on section 34, in a log school house built by the neighborhood, during the winter of 1854-5, by Miss Lottie Crawford, now a resident of Philadelphia, Pennsylvania. There are now nine school houses in the township, all frame buildings, and erected at an average cost of $600.

A school was taught by Jessie Berry, during the summer of 1855, in the log school house on section 34.

FIRST THINGS.

The first marriage was George Michael to Miss Elizabeth Trumbo, at the residence of Israel Trumbo, on section 34, by 'Squire Ellsworth, in 1854.

The first death was a child of W. B. Ingersoll and wife.

The first birth was a son (Abner) to William Ogden and wife, in 1854. He is now living in Mitchell county, Iowa.

The first house was built by Israel Trumbo, on section 34. It has since been torn down.

CEMETERIES.

There are three cemeteries in this township. One is located on the northeast corner of the northwest quarter of section 33, and was laid out in 1875. The first interment was the wife of John Yojrs, during the same year. Another is located on the northeast quarter of section 26, and was laid out in 1871. The first burial was John Frederick, a son of J. Shaver and wife, December 24, 1871. The other is located in the southwest corner of section 30. The first burial here was a son of Proctor Smith, who was drowned during the summer of 1856.

RELIGIOUS.

The first services of this character were held in 1858 in a school house on section 27, by Rev. Sessions, a Methodist Episcopal minister from Waverly. Afterwards services were held by Elder Wright, in January, 1863, in the school house on section 31. He soon after changed the place of worship to Case School House, where services were held for one year, once every four weeks. A Presbyterian minister by the name of Sheeley, also held services here every four weeks. Meetings have been held regularly from that time to the present.

In May, 1868, a Union Sabbath School was organized at this school house. The first superintendent was William Nicholson; he was succeeded by B. S. Wales, and he by William Brown, and Brown in turn by N. L. Shaw. There were twenty scholars at the time of organization. There is now an average attendance of about sixty, and the school is in a very prosperous condition. It has had a very healthy growth ever since first established, and has been the means of accomplishing much good. A Methodist Episcopal Church has been organized, a building erected at a cost of $1,700, and dedicated free from debt, as among the legitimate fruits of this organization. The influence for good has been widespread. The death of its estimable superintendent, Wm. Brown, in December, 1882; the death of Jasper Wylam, teacher of the bible class, six years ago, are among the sad incidents of the school. During all these years only three other members have been called hence—Stella Case, in 1877, Frankie Brown, in March, 1882, and Mrs. Joseph Simmons, in June, 1882.

The German Evangelical church erected a building of logs in 1864. It was located on section 34, in Trumbo's Grove. Their first pastor was Rev. Geiper. Their present church edifice was built on the southeast corner of the southeast quarter of section 28, in 1872. It is a frame structure and cost $3,300. The first pastor was Rev. Jacob Nuhn, afterward came Rev. Fritz Belser, Rev. Jacob Knotoka, Rev. Ulthouse, Rev. Henry Lescholt and the present pastor is Rev. Beamer. Their first members were Fred Bohmeir and wife, Fred Schroedeneir and wife, Fred Clagas and wife, Christian Dorn and wife, Charles Meader and wife, William Meader and wife, Fred Roeker and wife, Henry Armsbud and wife, William Eickman and wife and Conrad Schrodemeir and wife. The present officers of the church are Henry Walthagen, president, Fred Bohmeir, treasurer, Fred Schroedemeyer, secretary. Their Sabbath school was organized in 1864. The first superintendent was William Eickman; the present one is Henry Arns. They have a membership of about eighty. Another German Evangelical Lutheran church is located on the northeast quarter of section 26. It is a frame structure, built in 1871, and cost $1,500.

Their first pastor was Rev. L. J. Cramer, then came the present pastor, Rev. M. Stephan. The first members were Henry Heine and wife, Henry Platte and wife, Frederick Clansing and wife, Fred Groepper and wife, and Fred Dueck and wife.

The church has a membership of 250. A neat and commodious parsonage was built in connection with the church. A day school is taught by the pastor.

Rev. John Buckmaster, a United Brethren minister, was the first to hold religious service in the township, of that denomination, during the summer of 1865, at his house on section 29. Among his sermons was one on the subject of "The influence of woman," in which the ladies suffered considerably.

METHODIST EPISCOPAL CHURCH.

This organization built a house of worship in 1882, and dedicated it in November of that year. The sermon on that occasion was preached by Rev. Elliott, from Charles City, assisted by Elder Crippin. The building is 26x40 feet, located on section 6, and cost $1,700. Rev. Francis Norton now has charge, this being his third year. There is a membership of about forty.

The present officers are: N. L. Shaw, Edward Bullock, Charles Kelly, John Hanner, H. Robinson, C. E. Banks and W. J. Nicholson, trusteees; William Nicholson, class-leader; W. J. Nicholson, N. L. Shaw, stewards; W. J. Nicholson, secretary; Edward Bullock, treasurer.

CHAPTER XXX.

WASHINGTON TOWNSHIP.

This territory lies in the western tier of townships in Bremer county, and is bounded on the north by Warren and Lafayette, on the west by Butler county, on the south by Jackson township, and on the east by Jefferson and Warren. Embraced within these limits is the city of Waverly, which receives due attention. Including this city, which occupies sections 2, 3, the south half of 34 and 35, and the north half of 10 and 11, there are about 19,200 acres of land within its boundaries. The Cedar river traverses this township, entering from the north on section 34, running thence through sections 35, 2, a portion of 11, then 12, 13, and leaving on the south half of 18. The Shell Rock river flows through the southwestern corner, entering from the west on section 18 and making exit on 17. The Illinois Central and Dubuque and Dakota railroads pass through this township and make junction near the east line of section 33. The Burlington and Cedar Rapids road, running toward the southeast, crosses the extreme southwestern corner.

In an early day there was an abundance of timber in this township, but the woodman's axe has considerably diminished the supply. The soil is a dark, sandy loam in general, but in some sections it is composed of light clay and vegetable mould. There are many desirable farms. The surface is gently rolling, back from the river bottoms, drainage good, and the land fully occupied by an industrious class of people.

ORGANIC.

Washington township was organized by holding an election at the house formerly occupied by Heman A. Miles, on Monday, the 3d day of April, 1854, when the following officers were elected:

Justices of the peace, Nelson M. Smith, and John B. Buckmaster; constables, Joseph G. Ellis, and Jonathan Goforth; drainage commissioner, E. Tyrrell; township clerk, Nelson M. Smith; trustees, Edward Tyrrell, Horace Wallace, James Estep; assessor, Edward Tyrrell; supervisor of roads, William Powell.

The judges at this election were Haywood Howell, William A. Pelton, William Powell. The clerks were, Nelson M. Smith and Edward Tyrrell.

The following named are the officers elected in 1882:

Justices of the peace, A. H. McCracken, J. W. Rowray, A. J. Tanner; township clerk, S. H. Morse; assessor, J. S. Connor; trustee, S. Goodspeed; trustee to fill vacancy, A. S. Lawrence; constables, John L. Leonard, F. W. Foster, H. B. Ellsworth; supervisor road district No 1, Willard Chandler; No. 2, J. S. Connor; No. 3, Louis Buering; No. 4, Fred C. Meyer; No. 5, J. K. Meyers; No. 6, A. Adams; No. 7, W. D. Lashbrook; No. 8, R. W. Egleston; No. 9, Joseph Baskins; No. 10, E. O. Fairbanks; No. 11, Joseph Boylson; No. 12, E. Conley.

EARLY SETTLEMENT.

The earliest settlement of this township, and the events connected with it, are in a great measure identical with those of the city of Waverly.

Biographies are here presented which will show the general character of this settlement.

Abner Baskins, a son of one of Bremer county's earliest settlers, was born in Richland county, Ohio, February 15, 1836. He is a son of Abner B. and Mary (Kerr) Baskins, who left their home in Ohio for Bremer county, Iowa, May 27, 1852. Their journey was made with teams. Arriving here on the 22d day of June, they immediately located on section 4, Jefferson township, where the husband and father made a claim, subsequently purchasing it. Their first house was a log cabin covered with clapboards, and having a puncheon floor. They were obliged to go to Dubuque for groceries. The subject of this sketch was reared on a farm, and educated in the subscription schools. In 1861 he was married to Miss A. Ross, who came to this county in 1858. She was born May 29, 1842. Five children bless their home —Edna, Clark, Minnie, Nellie and Abner. Mr. Baskins owns 85 acres of land, which is under cultivation and valued at $40 per acre. He had two brothers who served in the Union army, one in the Thirty-Eighth Iowa Infantry, who died at Port Hudson, and the other in the Ninth Iowa.

Joseph Baskins, a pioneer of Bremer county, emigrated with his father, Abner B. Baskins, to this county, June 22, 1852. They located on what is now known as Baskins' creek (the creek deriving its name from them). There the father entered some land, which he improved, and continued to live upon until his death, which occurred in 1864. The journey from Ohio here, was made by team. Dubuque was their nearest trading post. Game, such as bear, deer, wild turkeys, wolves, etc., was in great abundance. Joseph was born in Rockland county, Ohio, on the 27th day of February, 1834. In 1861, he was married to Miss Phœbe Miner, who was born in Fulton county, Illinois, December 6, 1838. They have two children—Miner and Maggie.

William P. Harris was a settler of 1853, and is an enterprising farmer. He was born in Allegheny county, Pennsylvania, September 27, 1811. A few years after his birth, the family emigrated to Nicholas county, Kentucky, and there his father died. During his youth, William P. learned the trade of brick-maker and mason. In 1839, he was joined in wedlock with Miss Julia Ann Crosby, who shortly after died. He was again married, February 14, 1844, to Miss Sarah A. F. Fritts, who is a native of Kentucky, and was born April 22, 1828. In 1850, he removed to Burlington, Iowa, and thence, by team to Linn county, where he had friends. Leaving his family in the town of Marion, Mr. Harris set out for the purpose of finding a good location for settlement. He finally purchased land in Buchanan county, and there removed his family. During the first winter of their residence there, they occupied a log cabin, with another family, being separated from them by a thin board partition. The succeeding spring he erected a cabin of his own, 14x14, making it of poplar poles, and moving into it before it had either floor or door. In February, 1853, he came to Bremer county, and in his house, in April, was held the first election, there being sixty-three votes. Mr. Harris now owns 116 acres of land within the corporation, and on it is his fine residence, the whole being valued at $10,000. The family are members of the M. E. church, of Waverly.

Moses Lehman, an enterprising man and an early settler, was born in Dauphin county, Pennsylvania, February 9, 1824. He is a son of Samuel and Mary (Romberg) Lehman, who were blessed with ten children, six sons and four daughters. Moses was reared on his father's farm, and obtained his education in the old time subscription schools. At the age of eighteen he started out in life for himself. During the spring of 1847, he emigrated to Stephenson county, Illinois, making it his home for seven years. June 6, 1854, he removed to Waverly, Bremer county, Iowa. Mr. Lehman says he remembers well how he passed the first night after his arrival here. He stopped with a brother who lived in a pole shanty, through the roof of which the rain poured down upon them all night long. At that time lumber was not to be had for love or money. April 28, 1859, Mr. Lehman was married to Miss Electa Miles, who was born in Sheffield, Vermont, July 2, 1822, and a daughter of Masten M. and Mary (Jenness) Miles. They have two children—Elva M. and Sidney M. Mr. Lehman came to this State comparatively a poor man, but by industry and economy, is to-day the happy owner of 124 acres of land, valued at $50 per acre, and containing all that the best farm life requires. In politics he is a republican. Mrs. Lehman is a member of the Episcopal Church, of Waverly.

Nicholas Cavanaugh, who may be ranked among the early settlers of the county, is a native of Ireland, and was born on the 3d day of July, 1825. In June, 1853, he emigrated to the United States, landing in Philadelphia, Pennsylvania, where he was employed in a grocery store. During the spring of 1855, in company with John J. Smith, who afterwards built the Bremer House, he came to Waverly, Iowa. For some time after his settlement here, he worked in a hotel, but later, was employed as clerk in Mr. Hullman's store. He was married in 1861, to Miss Mary Tyrrell, a native of Quebec, Canada, and a daughter of Nicholas Tyrrell. They have three children—John E., Francis J., and Mary

Ann. During Mr. Cavanaugh's twenty-seven years of life in the county, he has been out of it but once. At the time of his settlement, the town and surrounding country seemed one vast wilderness, with wolves, deer, and all kinds of game, in great abundance.

One of Bremer county's most enterprising men, Thomas Lashbrook, was born in Devonshire, England, November 5, 1819. He is the son of Richard Lashbrook, and one of fourteen children. In 1831, the family emigrated to Quebec, Canada, and thence to Clinton county, New York. During the year 1836, they came west, locating in McHenry county, Illinois, near Harvard Junction, where they entered land and settled, the father dying on the old homestead in December, 1881. Thomas passed his youth on a farm, and although his school days were few in number, he yet, by his own exertions in later years, has obtained a fair business education. In February, 1849, his marriage with Miss Hannah R. Wilson occurred, she being a native of Essex county, New York, and born June 4, 1820. They have five children living—Cordell D., Watson D., Thomas W., Clarence E. and Ulysses L. July 4, 1856, Mr. Lashbrook and family embarked in prairie schooners, for Bremer county, Iowa, and upon their arrival, settled on land in Frederika township, which he had purchased two years previous. Their first house was a log cabin 13x13. Mr. Lashbrook owned, at one time, 1,740 acres of land, at present he owns 412 acres, with much valuable town property in Waverly, consisting in part of a fine brick residence valued at $6,000, three stores valued at $3,000, one frame building valued at $2,000, one shoe-shop valued at $1,000, two drug stores valued at $1,800, four lots on Main street valued at $400, besides other property valued at $1,000, making the total valuation of his town property about $20,000. Mr. Lashbrook has held the offices of supervisor, school treasurer and director. He is a staunch democrat.

Frank Bulckins, a native of France, was born April 18, 1824. When fourteen years of age he entered the navy as midshipman, but after serving some time he had a difficulty with one of the officers, which closed his career as a sailor for the time, when he located in New Orleans, Louisiana. From there he again "took ship," and followed the sea for eight years, during which time he sailed into nearly every port on the globe. Upon again becoming a landsman, Mr. Bulckins returned to the States, and shortly after his arrival, was appointed surgeon at Washington, D. C. From that city he removed to New Orleans, where he opened an intelligence office, and thence, after some time, to Boston, Massachusetts, where he took passage for California, by way of Cape Horn. At the expiration of a few years he returned to the east, after which he made a trip to Liverpool. In 1856 Mr. Bulckins removed to the city of Chicago, where he was employed on the lakes for a couple of years. Subsequently he embarked in the commission business. His marriage with Miss Julia Wheeler occurred in 1860. Three children—Grace, Bell and Lou—have blessed their home.

Thomas J. Sewell, one of the pioneers, was born in Botetourt county, Virginia, March 11, 1808. He is the son of William and Sarah (Dallard) Sewell, who were the parents of twelve children, ten of whom lived to mature years. William Sewell emigrated in 1826, with his family, to Pike county, Ohio, where he remained about one year, then removed to Hamilton county, near Cincinnati, where he engaged in farming. A few years later he removed to Wabash county, Indiana, purchasing land where Jamestown now stands. Here he died, in 1838, and Mrs. Sewell, in 1856. Thomas J. Sewell was reared and educated in West Virginia. In 1829 he was married, in Pike county, Ohio, to Miss Margaret Henry, daughter of Judge Samuel Henry, of the same county. Mr. and Mrs. Sewell lived together more than half a century, and have been blessed with eight children, six of whom are living—Allen, William, Samuel, Mary, James M., and Sylvester. April 27, 1853, he left his home in Indiana, and with teams came to Bremer county, arriving May 27th, 1853. He located in Jackson township, spending one year in a log cabin, on the place where Thomas Axlet now resides. He sold his claim, and purchased land of Abraham Myers, section 21, where he made a home, and resided until the spring of 1882, when he removed to Waverly. Mr. Sewell was in Waverly before there was a stake driven, or the town laid out. For his milling he went to Cedar Falls, and for groceries to Dubuque, with teams. In politics he was an old Jacksonian democrat, his first vote being cast for Andrew Jackson. Mr. Sewell had three sons, (one an adopted son), and a son-in-law in the Union army. Mr. Sewell died late in the fall of 1882.

Charles Leverich, a pioneer of Bremer county, is a native of Richland county, Ohio, born March 24, 1813. When he was nineteen years old his parents emigrated to LaGrange county, Indiana, and thence in 1838, to Cedar county, Iowa. Subsequently they removed to Linn county, and afterwards to Butler, where the father died. Charles was reared on a farm, and obtained his education in the pioneer district schools. The first school he attended being taught in an old log cabin, whose windows were simply holes cut through for the purpose of light and air. At the age of twenty-one he learned the cooper's trade. He was married in Indiana, to Miss Lucy Heam, who died in less than a year after becoming his wife. In 1838, he removed to Muscatine county, Iowa, where he became acquainted with and married Miss Jane E. Adair, who bore him ten children, three of whom are now living— George, Martha and Julia. In 1841, he removed to Linn county, Iowa, and thence, in 1854, to Butler county, where he remained about one year, and then settled on his present place in Washington township.

John Wile, one of the pioneers, was born in the Province of Bavaria, on the 4th day of June, 1828. In 1844 he left his native country for America, and, upon his arrival, located in Lycoming county, Pennsylvania, working as a laborer in the timber. During 1856 he removed to Bremer county, Iowa, and purchased land in Lafayette township, which he immediately began improving. There he continued to live until 1872, at which date he settled near Waverly, where he now has a beautiful home. In 1851 he was joined in wedlock with Judith Leas, a native of Lycoming county, Pennsylvania, born in 1830. Two children blessed the marriage—A. J.

and Frederick. Mr. Wile came to this county a poor man, but since his residence here has, by hard work and close attention to business, accumulated a fine property. His land consists of 290 acres, valued at $40 per acre. In politics he is a republican. The family are members of the Evangelical Association.

E. I. Bussey, born in Trumbull county, Ohio, May 22, 1825, is a son of Edward and Dorcas (Parish) Bussey. He remained on the old homestead, assisting his father with the farm work, until 1856, when he came to Bremer county, Iowa, and settled on section 18, of Washington township, where he now owns 130 acres of land. In 1853, he was united in marriage, in his native county, with Miss Sarah Jane Sinclair, who also was born there. They have three children living—Martin, Jarett F. and Elizabeth. Mrs. Bussey died in August, 1860. In April, 1862, he was again married, choosing for a companion Elizabeth Sinclair, a sister of his first wife. Of eight children born to them, William, Edward, Sarah, Nealie and Cyrus McClellan, are living. His father died at his (E. I's) residence on the 19th day of August, 1864, and his mother, during the year of 1869.

A. M. Winner, an excellent farmer of Bremer county, was born on the 2d day of February, 1827, in Courtland county, New York. He is a son of Frederick and Anna (Keator) Winner, who are natives of New York. He remained in his native State until eighteen years of age, and then came west with his parents, settling in Belvidere, Boone county, Illinois, where he spent twelve years, engaged in merchandising and buying grain. In the year 1858 he came to Iowa, locating in Bremer county, near the town of Waverly. Previous to his settlement here, Mr. Winner had purchased 640 acres of land in the county; of this, he improved 160 acres and disposed of the balance; afterwards, he disposed of the improved 160 acres. At the present date he owns 150 acres one mile northeast of Waverly. In politics, Mr. Winner is a staunch Republican. He has held several of the town and school offices, and always did all in his power to further the interests of education. On his farm are a large number of fine fruit trees, in the care of which he spends much time and labor. During the season of 1882 he marketed about 1,000 bushels of fruit. In 1854 he was joined in matrimony with Miss Miranda Campbell, a native of Lockport, New York. Ten children have been born to them, eight of whom are now living: Alice, now the wife of J. W. Tibbetts, of this county; Effie E., Earl, Kittie, Herman, Florain, Carl and Max. Frank died in the year 1858, and Leslie in 1868.

Edward N. Perry, an early settler of Bremer county, was born in Orleans county, New York, April 9, 1830. He is a son of Nathaniel W. and Lockey (Ferguson) Perry, who removed to Fulton county, Illinois, in 1840, and in July, 1858, came to Bremer county, Iowa, where the husband and father had previously entered land. He died in 1875. His wife is still living at the advanced age of 81 years. Edward N., one of the family of five children, who lived to be adults, was united in marriage with Miss Martha J. Miner, a daughter of James Miner, who was a pioneer of Fulton county, Illinois. She was born in Jefferson county, Indiana, October 3, 1827. They have one child living—Clara. Mr. Perry owns 75 acres of land valued at $40 per acre.

Orlando Babcock, born in Onondago county, New York, January 13, 1837, is a son of Russell and Susan (Ouderkirk) Babcock. His youth was passed on his father's farm, while he obtained his education in the common schools of the county. In 1856 he removed to Ogle county, Illinois, where he worked as a laborer for two years and then engaged in stock dealing. His marriage with Miss C. L. Taylor occurred in 1866. They have five children—Landy B., Charles, Guy, Emma and Ollie. The year of Mr. Babcock's marriage he came to Bremer county and settled in Washington township on a part of his present farm of 85 acres, which he purchased at that time. Since then he has added many acres to it, owning to-day, 557 acres, which, being under such excellent cultivation and containing so many comfortable farm buildings, may be called a model farm. Mr. Babcock is extensively engaged in stock raising, and owns at the present time, 260 head of horned cattle, 150 head of hogs and a large number of horses. His cattle are grades from a blooded short horn bull, and his horses are the Abe Downing, the Membrino and the Clydesdale. His barns are large and well arranged and of the following dimensions. The main building of his cow stable is 38x84, and the ell 28x80, his shedding and henery 18x180; his corn-crib and feedstable 22x150, and another corn-crib and pig-pen 36x50.

One of the enterprising farmers of Bremer county, Willard Chandler, was born in Canada East, May 15, 1827. When he was seventeen years old, his mother died, and he was left alone. Subsequently he removed to Vermont, and there resided for some time. In 1849 he settled in Potter county, Pennsylvania, where he engaged in lumbering for the space of nineteen years. He came to Bremer county, Iowa, in 1867, and purchased his present farm, in Washington township. In 1847 Mr. Chandler was joined in wedlock with Miss Lovina Briggs, who bore him three children, two of whom are now living—Edwin, and Willard W. He owns 100 acres of land in this county, and 320 acres in Floyd county, in connection with his sons.

H. R. Wells was born in Stockton, Chautauqua county, New York, October 4, 1828. He is a son of Jesse and Acenith (Bennett) Wells, both natives of New York. In 1836, his parents came west to Geauga county, Ohio, where they remained until 1842, when they moved to Stephenson county, Illinois. In 1854, he came west to Floyd county, Iowa, and remained two years at Marble Rock engaged in milling. In 1856, he traded his mill for a farm near Waverly; on this farm he remained eleven years, and then settled on section 36, Washington township, where he now owns 95 acres, and is engaged quite extensively in stock-raising. In 1853, he was married to Miss Lavina Price, a native of Canada, who came to Illinois with her parents when four years of age. They have nine children living—Mettie, wife of Bennett Youmans; Wayne W., Addie, Jesse, Grant, Delia and Frank Olah.

W. L. Stockwell was born in Windom county, Vermont, December 28, 1827. He is the second son of Lot and Nancy (Talbot) Stockwell, both natives of Vermont. In 1835, his parents moved to Livingston county, New York, where they remained eight years, and thence to Boone county, Illinois, where his father died in June, 1863, his mother in November, 1858. His educational advantages were common school, with an attendance one year at the Belvidere Academy. He was married at that place May 3, 1854, to Miss Tripp, who was born in De Ruyter, Madison county, New York, July 16, 1830, and eldest daughter of James D. and Angeline (Moxon) Tripp, both natives of that State. They are still living in Belvidere, Illinois, where they settled in 1850. In 1868, W. L. moved his family to one mile north of Waverly, where he now resides, and owns a fine farm of 200 acres. Five children have blessed this union—William Whilford, Carrie C., May A., Katie and Stephen.

John Rosencrans, born in Sussex county, New Jersey, January 1, 1809, is the fourth son of Simeon and Sarah (Shoemaker) Rosencrans. His father was a practicing physician in that county. Until 16 years of age, John attended the common schools. He then engaged in clerking and followed it for three years, then went to Vermont, and at the age of 21 engaged in mercantile pursuits at Burlington. He remained six years, when, in company with his brother Chadwick, he moved to Cleveland, Ohio, and was engaged in the dry goods trade three years. He then came to Troy, Walworth county, Wis., and engaged in trade, remaining a few years, when he moved to Beloit, Wisconsin, to educate his family. In 1865 he removed to Butler county, Iowa, but located only temporarily, and the following year he settled on section 34, Washington township. He was married in Dover, Ohio, in 1838, to Mary Johnson, who bore him seven children: Helen, now the wife of D. W. C. Duncan, of Charles City; Florana, now the wife of Frank Sterling, of Helena, Montana; Henry J., now engaged in stock raising in Texas; Lucia and Lucien, twins; Milo, now at Fort Benton, Montana, and Amelia, now the wife of Calvin Smalley, of Waverly. His wife died in 1848. In 1850 he married Mary M. Perkins, who died in 1854. In 1866, he married his present wife, then Mary Ann Stewart.

Daniel A. Long, born in Woodford county, Kentucky, March 13, 1825, is a son of William Long, a native of Pennsylvania, who emigrated to Virginia in an early day, where he became acquainted and subsequently married Miss M. Wheat. He afterwards moved to Kentucky, where Mrs. Long died, and he married Susannah Martin. Mr. Long subsequently removed to Lawrence county, Indiana, where he died. Daniel A., the youngest of the two families, was reared in a new country, attending his first school in the primitive log cabins. He afterward attended an academy, receiving a good academic education. Daniel remained in Indiana with his parents until he was twenty-one years old, when he went to Howard county, Indiana, where he purchased land and commenced farming, remaining there four years. March 12, 1848, he married Margaret Darraugh. She was born in Harrison county, Kentucky, February 22, 1832. By this union there was a family of seven children who lived to be of mature age.

In the fall of 1852, Mr. Long purchased land in Buchanan county, Iowa, and in the spring of 1853, he moved his family to that county. The same year he came to Bremer county and purchased land in Jackson township, where he remained until 1855. He then returned to Buchanan county, making it his home until 1865, when he again removed to Bremer, and in 1869, moved to his present place. Mr. Long has 940 acres of land near the city of Waverly under a high state of cultivation, valued at $75 per acre. He has a beautiful brick residence with plenty of choice fruits.

Jeremiah C. Messenger, superintendent of J. H. & W. R. Bowman's stock farm, born in Northumberland county, Pennsylvania, November 3, 1842, is a son of Peter and Ann M. (Miller) Messenger. In 1852 his parents emigrated to Winnebago county Illinois, where they took up government land, and made a home. His father still resides there. His mother died in 1858. J. C., in August, 1861, enlisted in the Twenty-sixth Illinois Volunteer Infantry, Company B, and participated in the following engagements: New Madrid, Island No. 10, second battle of Corinth, Iuka, siege and capture of Vicksburg, Sherman's march to the sea, and Jackson, Mississippi. He was in the Grand Review at Washington, D. C. Mr. Messenger never had a sick day; but was always ready to do his duty. After the war he returned to Winnebago county, and in 1868 came to Waverly, where his time has been occupied in handling fine horses. He broke and fitted Abe Downing, who has made his record in 2:20¾. In 1869 Mr. Messenger married Miss Sarah E. Fobbs, who was born in Sangamon county, Illinois.

John Carey, farmer and fruit grower, was born in Quebec, Canada, September 15, 1842. When he was nine years old, his parents died, in the city of Quebec, and shortly after, in company with his brothers and sisters, he removed to Toronto. There John worked on a farm a couple of years, and then concluded he would try his fortune in "York State." He went by way of Niagara Falls, to the city of Rochester, and there continued to live for a number of years. In 1859, he removed to Evansville, Missouri, where he attended school for five years. In 1866, he was joined in wedlock with Miss Emma L. Palmer, a daughter of Stephen Palmer, of Allegheny county, New York, where she was born February 24, 1847. Three children were born unto them, one of whom, Stephen E., is now living. In 1870, Mr. Carey came to Bremer county, Iowa, locating in Washington township, where he has since resided. He owns 50 acres of land, under a high state of cultivation, and worth $60 per acre. In politics, he is a republican, and cast his first presidential vote for Abraham Lincoln.

C. E. Egleston owns 400 acres of cultivated land in Washington township, Bremer county. He settled here in 1872. His birth took place April 2, 1811, in Rensselaer county, New York. When a young man he removed to Columbia county, New York, where he became acquainted with and married Miss Betsey Barden, who was born in Massachusetts, December 1, 1818. Eleven children have been born to them, of whom the following ten are now living—George H., Lucretia D., Roswell W., Alpheus C., Abbie J., William E., Nancy M., Charles A., Silas M. and Sarah A. In 1857, Mr. Egleston and family left the State of New York, for Boone county, Illinois, where he engaged in farming until his settlement in Bremer county. Mrs. Egleston is a botanic physician, having followed her profession for the past thirty years.

H. W. Goodsell was born September 12, 1809, in Wayne county, Pennsylvania. He is a son of Amasa and Experience (West) Goodsell, who emigrated to Pennsylvania from Hartford county, Connecticut, their birth place, in 1805. In 1836 they removed to Lycoming county, New York, and thence, in 1841, to McHenry county, Illinois, where Mr. Goodsell afterward died. The subject of this sketch early learned the trade of carpenter and joiner, his father being a carpenter and joiner before him. In December of 1839, he was joined in the holy bands of matrimony with Miss Sarah Sherwood, a native of Livingston county, New York, born August 29, 1819. Three children—Marquis, James Earl and Hiram H. were born to them. The wife and mother died in Walworth county, Wisconsin, September 16, 1863. During July, 1864, Mr. Goodsell came to Bremer county, Iowa, and purchased a farm in section 7, Washington township, where he now resides. He owns 274 acres of land in the counties of Butler and Bremer. In politics, he is a greenbacker.

Jesse Leverich was born in Onondago county, New York, March 15, 1818. He is a son of Richard B. Leverich, who was born in the State of Connecticut, but when quite young removed with his parents to Long Island. In 1816, he shipped on board a sloop to Albany, and thence by team to Onondago county, where he purchased land and embarked in farming. There he continued to reside until his death. The subject of this sketch was reared in a new country and obtained his education in the district schools, which were at a distance of two and a half miles from his home. During 1843, he was united in marriage with Miss Mary Case, who was born during 1812, in Onondago county, New York. She is a daughter of Rufus Case, who was born in Berkshire county, Massachusetts, and lived to be nearly one hundred years old. Mr. and Mrs. Leverich are the parents of six children—Mary, wife of Levi B. Raymond, now editor of the Hampton *Recorder*, Homer, Ella, Adelle, wife of John Haskett, Bayard T. and Willie. In 1840, Mr. Leverich removed from New York State to Racine, Wisconsin, and thence, after a short time, to Clinton Junction, where he purchased land and soon had a comfortable home. He belongs to the republican party, and while living in Wisconsin, held several offices of trust. For the past forty years he has lived in the west, and many and rapid have been the changes he has witnessed. In 1867, he came to Bremer county, Iowa, purchasing property in the town of Waverly, where he now lives a retired life.

H. B. Harriman was born in Merrimac county, New Hampshire, on the 5th day of July, 1819. When 20 years of age he went to Lowell, Mass. In 1843 he was married to Miss Hannah Q. Bailey, a daughter of Thomas Bailey, a native of Hopkinton, New Hampshire. She was born in Hopkinton in 1821. By this union there was a family of two daughters, viz.: Margaret, now the wife of Dr. Z. Z. Bryant, of Sumner; and Helen, wife of George Ellis, one of the prominent merchants of Waverly. In 1863, Mr. Harriman was elected to the State Legislature, where he proved a useful member. Besides holding this honorable position, he served in several local offices in his own town. In 1868, Mr. Harriman turned his face westward, locating in Bremer county, where he purchased property and has since remained.

Charles McCormack was born in Washington county, Virginia, on the 14th day of May, 1811. He is a son of John and Margaret (Stapleton) McCormack. His parents were married in Virginia, and there twelve children were born to them—six sons and six daughters. Charles passed his early life on a farm, and during his young manhood was married to Miss Mary Hamilton, a daughter of James Hamilton, of South Carolina. Eleven children blessed their union, eight of whom are now living. In 1855 Mr. McCormack left the State of Indiana, where he had resided for some years, emigrating to Dane county, Wisconsin, where he continued to live for ten years. At the expiration of that time, he came to Bremer county, Iowa, locating on a farm in Washington township. In 1877 he removed to Waverly, where he still resides. Mrs. McCormack died in 1867, leaving a large family to mourn her loss. The subject of this sketch again married, choosing for a wife Mrs. Emily Buckmaster, widow of Alexander Buckmaster, who came to the county in 1855. One child has been born to them. Mr. McCormack has always taken a deep interest in the politics of the county, aud was one of the prime movers in the organization of the republican party, to which he adhered until the passage of the resumption act. He is now a staunch greenbacker.

Seymour Goodspeed, a farmer and nurseryman, came from Niagara county, New York, to Bremer county, Iowa, in 1866. Upon his arrival here, he settled on a farm in Washington township, where he now does a good business, and is known as an enterprising nurseryman and farmer. His land consists of 75 acres, which is under an excellent state of cultivation, being valued at $50 per acre. He was born in Niagara county, March 1, 1834, and is a son of Herman and Louisa (Albright) Goodspeed. His mother's father emigrated to Niagara county with one horse, which carried all his worldly effects; and for six weeks the family had nothing to eat but different kinds of roots. His daughter, Louisa, was the first white child born in that county. Seymour's early life was passed on a farm, and he obtained his education in the district schools of his native county. During the year of 1862, he was married to Miss Mary J. Furguson, who has born him nine children, seven of whom are living Luella, Bertha, Jennie, Nellie, Nettie, Almeda and Ray.

Henry A. Thies, a son of Frederick and Elizabeth (Schild) Thies, natives of Lippe-Detmold, Germany, was born on the 9th day of February, 1855. His parents moved to Benton county, Iowa, when he was one year old, and lived on a farm near Belle Plain until 1867, when they came to Washington township, Bremer county, Iowa.

His parents both died in 1873, leaving Henry A. with six younger sisters and brothers, on a farm, and the management of both farm and the younger children was chiefly left to him. At the age of 21 years he became the owner of the valuable farm, consisting now of 260 acres of land and timber. In 1877 he was married to Miss Hattie S. Weber, daughter of Andrew Weber, of Warren township, now Waverly, Iowa. In politics he is a republican. He is a member of the Evangelical church of Warren township.

STOCK FARM.

Among the many farms and enterprises worthy of special mention, is the stock farm of J. H. and W. R. Bowman. It is called "Willow Lawn Stock Farm." An adequate idea of this farm and the stock upon it, can only be gained by personal visit and inspection. Among the fine animals to be there found, may be mentioned "Abe Downing," a magnificent horse, sired by Joe Downing; dam by Hattison. He has a trotting record, made at Buffalo, New York, of 2:20¾. This animal possesses not only speed, but is a well formed creature, of many excellent points, and a breeder of rare merit. The proprietors not only have this remarkable horse, but also about one hundred head more, together with six hundred head of hogs and five hundred head of cattle.

Among other horses may also be found, "Membrino Paris," number 1,337, sired by "Membrino Patchen;" roadster brood mares by "George Wilkes," "Almont Harrold," "Membrino," "Abdallah," etc.

Norman Horses—"Arcola," number 850, weight, 1,650 pounds; "Boobdil," number 852, weight, 1,760 pounds; "Black Prince," number 52, weight, 1,650 pounds; and others.

Roadsters—"Tennant," number 1968, two years old; by Abe Downing. "Phantom," number 1969; sired by Membrino Paris. "Alphonso," number 1970; by Abe Downing. "Ensign;" by Abe Downing. All these mentioned are well-bred and from desirable strains. Among the cattle may be found well formed representatives of the best blooded strains. The buildings on this farm are numerous, extensive and well adapted to the work of successfully handling stock.

Benjamin Archer, superintendent of Bowman Lone Tree Farm, was born in Middlesex county, Connecticut, on the 18th day of November, 1828. He was reared on his father's farm, and received a common school education. In 1855, he was married to Miss Mary J. Stevens, a daughter of Samuel Stevens of Hartford county, Connecticut. Two children blessed this union—Bell and Fannie. In 1867, Mr. Archer emigrated to Clayton county, remaining one year, when he removed to Bremer county, purchased a farm in Lafayette and Warren townships, where he remained until the spring of 1880, when he was employed by the Bowman Brothers to superintend their Lone Tree Farm. Mr. Archer is a practical farmer, and thoroughly understands his business.

CHAPTER XXXI

CITY OF WAVERLY.

This beautiful and enterprising city originated about a third of a century ago, when the beautiful valley of the Ceder river was just beginning to attract the attention of those in search of homes, and the surroundings were as free and wild as the time when the stars of the morning sang anthems of joy at nature's dawn. The changes from the primitive to the developed state have been constant and rapid. It has been one continual change from the moment of its projection, until Waverly of to-day stands forth one of the brightest jewels in the diadem of a noble State. While there may have been nothing really remarkable in the development of the past, or nothing peculiarly striking in the present, still there is much that cannot fail to be of interest to those who have been closely connected and identified with the city in all the various changes that have occurred from year to year. To those who have watched its progress from its earliest origin—when Bremer county was a wilderness—until the present time, the accomplishment of by-gone days would seem now like a herculean task, but are in reality the sure and legitimate results of an advanced state of civilization. Endowed with many natural advantages aided by the strong arm of enterprising husbandry, Bremer county has assumed a position among the best and wealthier of her sister counties throughout the State; and Waverly, as the first town within her boundaries, has kept pace with the improvements and advancement.

Waverly is situated in the southwestern part of Bremer county, on the banks of the Cedar river, and is about eighty miles from the Mississippi at the nearest point of landing. Two lines of railway pass through the city limits, connecting it with the leading markets; they are the Illinois Central and the Dubuque and Dakota, the former from north to south, the latter from east to west, affording excellent marketing facilities. The city is surrounded by some of the finest and most productive agricultural and stock raising lands in the State, which is a guarantee of a permanent and ever increasing trade. In addition to these advantages, the Cedar River, upon the banks of which the city rests, is one of the finest streams in the west, often being termed the "Gem of Iowa Waters." It furnishes a most desirable water power which, although it has already been improved to a certain extent, is not fully utilized, for the power is capable of propelling a vast amount of machinery. A substantial iron bridge spans the river, uniting the eastern and western divisions of the city.

There are many fine and substantial brick and stone blocks to be seen upon the business thoroughfares, and a stroll through the city discloses many elegant and costly dwellings. There are a number of fine church edifices, and elegant buildings for educational purposes. An abundance of shade trees adorn the streets, which in summer add greatly to the beauty of the place. The location is exceedingly healthy; the inhabitants are possessed of intelligence, and the society is of the most refined and desirable character.

RECORDED PLATS.

The various town plats of Waverly were filed for record as follows:

Waverly proper by William P. Harmon, recorded in 1854.

Cretzmeyer's addition was recorded on the 14th of April, 1855; also May 2, 1856.

Hess' addition, March 7, 1856.

Gothard's addition, March 7, 1856.

Gothard's addition, July 3, 1857.

Harmon and Le Valley's addition, November 4, 1857.

William Sturdevant's addition, December 14, 1857.

Ira H. Sturdevant's addition, February 29, 1860.

J. J. Smith's addition, May 7, 1858.

EARLY DAYS.

The initiatory step toward the development of this locality was taken in 1852. The settlement of the county had been progressing slowly since 1845, but mostly in the region of what has since been organized as Jefferson township. The site of Waverly was covered with heavy timber. In 1852 Frederick Cretzmeyer made his appearance and was the first settler upon the site. He was a native of Germany and brought his family, consisting of two girls, his wife being dead. He located a soldiers' warrant upon 160 acres of land, which has since been platted and become a part of the city. His land is described as part of section two, township 91, range 14, lying just east of the court house. He put up the first building, a little log hut which stood between the present site of the court house and Catholic church. He remained here until after Waverly began to be quite a place, when he and his family removed to Missouri where he has since died. Before leaving this place he was again married, but after reaching his Missouri home separated from his second wife.

About the same time or possibly a little later, Wendeline Cretzmeyer a brother of Frederick, came accompanied by his family and a sister of Mrs. Cretzmeyer. Ten acres were secured from Frederick, upon which the family erected a log shanty and settled. This land is yet in the possession of the boys and widow who yet live upon it, engaged in the manufacture of brick. The old shanty was torn down a few years ago to make room for the present comfortable structures. The old gentleman lived there until his death.

Wendeline Cretzmeyer was born in the city of Baden, Germany, in 1803. His wife was Miss Catherine Ludwig, who was born in 1809. Three children, Stephen, Franklin and Henry, blessed their marriage. In 1847 they left their native country for America and, upon their arrival, located in Columbia county, New York. During the year of 1852 they came to Bremer county, Iowa, and settled in what is now the city of Waverly. Mr. Cretzmeyer landed in the county as a poor man, and, during the first years of his settlement here, worked as a day laborer. However, by industry and perseverance he was afterwards enabled to open a business of his own. He died in 1867, leaving his wife and children to survive him. Franklin was born in Germany. In 1870 he was married to Miss Annie Struble, who was born in 1848. Stephen is also a native of Germany, and was born November 14, 1839. His wife was Miss Lizzie Gishbert. Henry was born in Columbia county, New York, January 16, 1848, and was joined in wedlock with Miss Margaret Mooney, who was born August 7, 1855, and was a native of Baltimore, Maryland. As has already been stated, the sons mentioned are still citizens of Waverly and are engaged in the manufacture of brick. The mother, Catherine Cretzmeyer, still lives with members of her family.

The real founder of the city was William P. Harmon. Early in the spring of 1853, he took a trip from the point at which he had located, to Bremer county, and in passing over the ground which is now crowned by the city, was struck with the great advantages of the good solid rock bottom, good banks and ample fall in the river, and decided that the location was just the place to begin a town; the river running due north and south from the proper place to put a water power. He at once set the project on foot, by using all the influence he could bring to bear to have the county seat of Bremer county—which was then organized—located at this point, and at the same time, after securing the land, hired O. H. P. Roszell, county judge of Buchanan county, to survey the same into lots. This survey, which made, the foundation of Waverly, began with Court street and extended westward to the river. Mr. Harmon then returned to Independence and made arrangements to have his brother-in-law, R. J. Ellsworth, move with him to the new town and help in the erection of a mill.

In July he went down to Cedar Rapids and met Mr. Ellsworth, and together with Mr. Ellsworth's family, consisting of a wife and two boys—Gorham E., now deceased, and Henry Byron, who were aged respectively 10 and 15, they came to Independence, arriving there upon Thursday, July 28, 1853. In the evening, Mr. Harmon was married to Miss Alzina Reeves, and the following morning with his bride and the Ellsworth party, he took an early start for Bremer county, arriving in the evening of the same day. Here they found Frederick and Wendeline Cretzmeyer safely housed in their log huts just east of the court house, and on the other side of the river, Elder Goforth and Jacob Hess had also taken up farms. The two latter were about a mile west of the Cretzmeyer's. Where to stop that night was at first a puzzler, but finally it was arranged that all sleep at the cabin of Fred Cretzmeyer. The bed was taken down, and as there was only one room in the cabin, the bedding was laid upon the floor so as to accommodate as many as possible, and when time for retiring came, the entire settlement went to bed in this room, there being Mr. and Mrs. Ellsworth and their two boys, Mr. [Cretzmeyer and his two girls, two teamsters and the newly married couple, Mr. and Mrs. Harmon.

HISTORY OF BREMER COUNTY.

In this manner they lived until the new comers had erected their log cabin which was complete and ready for occupancy early in August, 1853. The log cabin erected by Harmon and Ellsworth was somewhat better than the pioneers generally had; it was about 18x18 feet, one story and a half, although Mr. Ellsworth says he never could get anyone to sleep in the "half." The logs were plastered together and the holes chinked with mud; on the inside sheets were hung around the walls, to make it look more home-like. A door was not to be thought of and until October a blanket was hung up in lieu thereof. This hut stood directly in the center of Bremer Avenue, a few rods east of the river, a little nearer the river than the Bremer County Bank. The forest was just as dense at that time as it was anywhere in the Big Woods, and about the house there was no more "clearing" than was made in getting logs for the cabin. A crooked, winding trail alone afforded means of communication between the settlers. The women, however, insisted that a clearing be made about the house that they might see the sun now and then; so Harmon and Ellsworth pushed their way down to the bank of the river and from the bottom of the hill commenced cutting the trees on the side next the river. They treated a whole swath in this way until they came to the little clearing about the cabin. The upper trees were then felled, and falling, carried the whole swath to the ground like ten pins. After this the setting sun and the beautiful Cedar could be seen from the cabin.

These things accomplished, the saw mill was the next matter to receive attention. A dam was thrown across the river, logs, stone and other material being used in its construction, and on the east side of the river a building was erected, about 20x40 feet in size. The machinery was hauled from Rock Island, Illinois, by R. J. Ellsworth, and an old fashioned "sash" or "up and down" saw was placed in the mill. All this took time and much hard work, there being other workmen beside Harmon and Ellsworth engaged. About the 1st of March, 1854, everything being in readiness, it was announced that the saw mill would commence operation. Quite a crowd of interested settlers from various parts of the county had collected to see its inauguration, and the water was turned on. The mill had been built back from the river, and when the water came rushing in about the basement, the frost was taken from the ground, and but a few moments elapsed before it was discovered that water which went under above looking clear, came out below looking dirty and riley.

This produced the greatest excitement as it indicated that the water had cut into the foundation and would soon wash out the underpinning of the mill. The hole through which the water had found its way, was at first small, but soon washed out and became a whirlpool or a minature maelstrom. The settlers at once set to work with a will and hay, stones, logs and other material was thrown in to stop the hole, but all sucked through in an instant. Finally when hope had almost failed Mrs. R. J. Ellsworth, who was also at work with the rest, suggested that straw beds be thrown in. It was adopted and all the straw ticks in town were called for. They were forthcoming and in a few moments eleven beds were piled up by the mill. Then all prepared, a tick was thrown in and the bystanders threw rocks upon it. This served the purpose and saved the mill although it took about every bed in town. The damage was repaired and the mill began operations with a capacity of sawing about 2500 feet of lumber per day. The first lumber was sold to Heman A. Miles. In a few years a lath machine and edger were added to the mill and circular saws put in and for many years it continued its busy hum. A few years ago it was torn down and the crib filled with stone, a few rods north of the bridge.

R. J. Ellsworth was born in Cumberland county, Maine, March 22, 1809. His youth was passed on a farm and he received his education in the pioneer schools of his native State. At the age of fifteen he was apprenticed to a cabinet-maker, remaining with him five years, and during the time, receiving as wages, his clothes, which were estimated at $25 per year. December 2, 1832, he was joined in the holy bands of matrimony with Miss Elizabeth M. Harmon, a native of St. Stephens, New Brunswick, and born February 14, 1814. Five children were born to them, one of whom is now living. In 1852 Mr. Ellsworth turned his face westward, making his way to Linn county, Iowa, and locating for a short time in the town of Cedar Rapids. During the month of July, 1853, he removed to Bremer county, Iowa, settling in Waverly as one of its pioneers.

Their first dwelling consisted of a cabin 16x20 feet and made out of rough logs. There they lived until Christmas eve and then moved into a building standing on the site where the new Bremer county bank now is. The following September they removed to their present place of residence. A few years ago Mr. Ellsworth built a large and commodious brick dwelling in which himself and wife expect to spend the remaining years of their life. In politics he was formerly a whig, but for many years has allied himself with the republican party. He was Waverly's first justice of the peace. The family are members of the M. E. Church.

In a few weeks after the arrival of the mill party, Samuel Henderson and family moved to the spot, and he commenced work on the mill, which was in course of erection. Cutting a space in the forest, he put up a little log cabin upon the same lot that is now occupied by the *Independent* office, and from his door he could just barely see—through the timber—the cabin of his neighbors, which stood in the middle of the street near the bridge. He was followed shortly afterward by James Null, who came with his family and erected a little log house near where Mooney's blacksmith shop now stands, on Water street. This was torn down many years ago. Henderson remained for a few years, when he removed to Missouri.

William B. Hamilton came from Independence early in 1853, and after making arrangements for erecting a building and starting a store, returned. About the last of August, Porter W. Earle made his appearance. He had been, and was at the time, peddling goods for Green & Brother, of Cedar Rapids, and chanced to stop at the river—just where Knott's livery stable stands—to water his horses. Ellsworth saw him from the opposite side, and having known him, called "come over." Earle crossed the river, and going to Ellsworth's cabin received a hearty welcome.

The next morning he unloaded his goods, and, having decided to start a store, commenced the erection of a building, and began selling goods. While he was engaged in building he piled his goods beside the Harmon and Ellsworth house, and it is a good illustration of the brotherly feeling existing among the settlers, that any-one who wished went and helped themselves. If a plug of tobacco or pound of sugar was taken while Earle was up by the Cretzmeyer's getting out timber, the money was paid when they met. Earle put up a log cabin 18x24 feet, upon the lot now occupied by J. P. Olds' stone store, the latter being put up by Earle a few years later. He remained until about 1855, when he returned to Cedar Rapids. This was the first store started in Waverly.

In a few months W. B. Hamilton returned, and purchased the lot now occupied by the offices of the *Independent* and *Republican*, 8x4 rods, for $25. He had brought lumber with him from Independence, and erected the first frame building in the town, in which he kept store and lived. He had a fair stock of goods, and commenced selling early in the winter. He held the office of treasurer and recorder, and is noticed at length in that connection. He remained until about 1861.

During the fall of 1853, Ellsworth and Harmon erected another house which stood where the elegant Bremer County Bank block now stands. It was a frame building of fair size. They moved into it on Christmas eve, 1853, and remained there until the following June, when it was turned over to John J. Smith, who opened it as a hotel. Mr. Ellsworth then moved to the little building which they had erected just back of the Bremer house, on the same lot where his present fine brick house now stands. This building is still standing in a dilapidated condition, and is undoubtedly the oldest in the city.

The house into which J. J. Smith moved, remained with many additions until about 1881, when it was torn down. He at once commenced the erection of the Bremer House, which, when half finished, was occupied by the carpenter, James G. Burnett, who used it partially as a hotel.

When the spring of 1854 opened, nothing marked the site of Waverly except the blue smoke curling heavenward from the few cabins among the timber. No roads were cut except a zig-zag trail through the settlement and paths from clearing to clearing. During the year 1854, however, there were many arrivals, and Main street or what is known as Bremer avenue was partially cleared.

Court was to be held this year and preparations were made for it. The red cedar stake which had been driven to mark the county seat location, was in a lot just north of the court house, west of where the school house now stands. On this lot, early in the spring of 1854, a little board building was thrown together in which to hold court. It was about 20x30 feet, one story high, and boards were thrown upon the ground for a floor. The jury was sent to a neighboring house or were corraled in the brush.

Among those who are remembered as coming this year, are the following named:

John C. Hazlett, Dr. Fisher, Jeremiah Farris, William Sturdevant, Anson A. Case, Samuel, Hamilton and Horatio Geddis, Nelson and Samuel Flynn, Hayward Howell, Nelson L. Turner, James W. Wood, Charles Ensign, Philip and Elijah Smith, the Hinton family, Demus Buckingham, David Millburn, William Reeves, P. B. Foster, Henry Harmon, Dr. Burbank, Heman A. Miles, and others who came only to remain a short time. This years advancement made Waverly appear something like a village, the forest began to melt away before the woodman's axe, and all classes of trade were represented.

John C Hazlett, an early arrival of this year was a native of Ohio, but came here from Comanche, Iowa. He brought his family with him, and hewing down the trees erected a dwelling and store building over the stumps upon the lot now occupied by Dr. J. C. Pomeroy's drug store. He put in a small stock of general merchandise and commenced trade. He was a good business man, but unfortunate. A few years after the close of the war he removed to Shell Rock and from there went to Nashua where he was living when last heard from.

Dr. Fisher, who is mentioned as coming this year, was the first doctor to locate at Waverly. He is noticed at length in the medical chapter.

Jeremiah Farris, moved into town this year from his farm in Jefferson township, for the purpose of filling the office of County Judge to which he had been elected. He left this place in 1857, and went to Kansas where he died.

William Sturdevant, settled upon the west side of the river and lived in the old tumble down building still standing on Water street. He owned 80 acres of land extending from the river nearly to the depot on the south side of Bremer avenue. This tract has since been recorded as an addition to Waverly. When the war broke out Mr. Sturdevant enlisted and died on the Mississippi river.

Anson A. Case came this year and erected a frame story and a half house on the west side of the river, which is yet standing. He was the first county coroner and a brother of Louis Case.

The Geddis brothers came here from Indiana, although originally from Ohio. Samuel, the oldest, was a carpenter by trade, and brought a family. He put up the house in which Mayor Kinne lives and also the one in which Jack Hoffman lives. He was a good workman and a jolly fellow, but would now and then drink too much, and, when under its influence, would show the Indian blood which courses through his veins by yelling, jumping and being as noisy as possible. He remained here many years and finally went to Mason City and from there to Cedar Falls, where he still remains. Horatio Geddis, or, as he was usually called, "Rash," had a wife and one child. He erected the building in which Mr. Kothe now lives, and opened a shop for the sale of liquor. One day, accompanied by his brother, he left his family to go a short distance for hay, but they never came back. Mrs. Geddis still lives in the city. Hamilton Geddis erected the building which is now used as an office by J. C. Garner, opposite the Centennial house.

Nelson and Samuel Flinn were brothers, coming from Illinois, the former married, and the latter an unmarried man. At once they commenced the erection of a house upon the site now occupied by the magnificent dwelling of Thomas Lashbrook. While their building was in course of erection, they placed a pole in the crotch of a tree, and spreading a carpet over it, made a kind of tent in which they camped until their dwelling was completed. The brothers engaged in the manufacture of shingles, and remained for a number of years. Finally they removed to the eastern part of the county, and from thence to Denver.

Hayward Howell was here only for a short time, but long enough to get in debt to many persons. He then "slid out" to avoid paying them. He went from here to Missouri, and has never since been heard from.

Charles Ensign was a native of Ohio, and a splendid good fellow. He taught the first school in the city, and soon removed to New Hartford, Butler county, where he still lives.

The Hinton family came here in 1854, were very wealthy, owning 600 acres of land adjoining the city plat. The family consisted of the mother and a number of children. The mother and several of the children removed to Kansas a number of years ago, where she died. Two of her sons now live in Waverly.

Dennis Buckingham, a native of Ohio, also came here in 1854. He erected a building upon the lot now occupied by Mooney's blacksmith shop, and started the first blacksmithing business in the city. It is said that after he got started he knew almost nothing about the trade. He was a queer genius, and was of that disposition which inclined to believe all that was told him. To illustrate this, the anecdote is related that upon one occasion soon after he arrived here, he was obliged to sleep one night between heavy copperplate flannel blankets. He perspired a great deal, and as a consequence, in the morning he found that he had changed color, his neck, face and hands were tinted with a blueish hue. He sought several of his friends to find what ailed him. He was told that "mortification had set in," and that something should at once be done. Accordingly he poulticed his arms, neck and jaws, and for several days tramped around all bound up. All he needed was a good wash as it was merely the color from the blankets that ailed him. He left here years ago for Indiana.

Nick Cavanaugh came this year and is yet here.

David Millburn, a native of New Brunswick, came here with his family in the winter of 1854. He was a carpenter and a cabinet maker, and at once commenced work at his trade.

P. B. Foster came here from Illinois with his family, and erected a building upon the site now occupied by Beebe & Loomer's store building. For a time he was in company with Thomas Downing, in the mercantile trade.

Henry Harmon was a brother of William P. Harmon, the founder of the city, and a native of Maine. For the first few years after his arrival in Bremer County he was engaged in the saw mill, but afterward removed to the country and engaged in farming. A few years ago he removed to Dakota.

Heman A. Miles moved into town this year. He is noted elsewhere in this volume.

In June, 1854, Dr. Oscar Burbank, accompanied by David Millburn, drove to Waverly from Cedar Rapids, in a buggy, for the purpose of examining matters with a view to locating. He made up his mind to locate, and after stopping one night with R. J. Ellsworth, returned to Cedar Rapids. In September he again arrived, this time with his wife and baby (the latter now being Mrs. Frank A. Lee), and permanently settled. Their first few weeks were spent in boarding with the family of R. J. Ellsworth, and as the house was very small, many disadvantages were undergone. Several of the hands engaged in the mill were stopping with Mr. Ellsworth, and there were only two rooms in the house—one on the first floor and the other overhead. The little girl was boosted up through the trap door and the older folks got into their room by the aid of a chair. Sometimes the light would be blown out and again, when the moon was full, a blanket was stretched in front of the bed. Dr. Burbank is still a citizen of the city.

Hallmann and Lenkuhl also came in 1854. They erected a building east of the present residence of Louis Case, and opened a store of general merchandise. It was known as the "dutch store." These parties are both dead. Mr. Hallman's family, consisting of a wife and four children, are still residents of the city.

Daniel Lehman also came during this year. He was a plasterer by trade, and after working a number of years, removed to Jackson township.

Alexander Buckmaster opened a cabinet shop here about this time. The machinery was propelled by water power. The building was one and one-half stories high, and 16x30 feet.

INCORPORATION.

Waverly was incorporated as a town in 1859. In 1868 it was incorporated as a city of the second class. Under both town and city government business has generally been transacted in a satisfactory manner to the people.

ITEMS CHRONOLOGICALLY ARRANGED.

The first death in Waverly occurred in the winter of 1853–4, a sister of Mrs. Wendeline Cretzmeyer. She was buried upon the bluffs south of town.

The next death was that of Mrs. Scarf, in 1854. She was buried on the west side of the river.

The first birth was a son to Mr. and Mrs. James Null. He was christened William Waverly—the first name in honor of William P. Harmon, and the latter in honor of the place. This occurred early in 1854. When last heard from, William Waverly Null was in Missouri.

The first marriage in Waverly was that of Norman A. Reeves to Miss Rhoda Willis.

The first school taught was by Charles Ensign, now of Butler county, in the old log house of Ellsworth and Harmon's, near the bridge.

The first religious services were held in the old log cabin erected by R. J. Ellsworth, the preacher being Rev. James Burley, a Methodist Episcopal circuit rider.

HISTORY OF BREMER COUNTY.

The first store started in Waverly was by Porter Earle, who also sold the first goods.

The first election in Waverly was held at the house of Frederick Cretzmeyer.

Dr. Fisher was the first doctor, and Dr. O. Burbank was the first regular graduate.

Porter Earle erected the first stone store in Waverly, in 1854.

William B. Hamilton erected the first frame building in the fall and winter of 1853, hauling the lumber from Independence.

Fred Cretzmeyer erected the first log cabin on the site.

A man named Barclay was the first circuit preacher to locate in Waverly.

P. W. Earle was the first postmaster.

The first school building in town was a stone one erected in 1855.

P. B. Foster erected the first brick store in town, in 1855.

The first hotel in the town was erected by Harmon and Ellsworth, in 1853, and stood where the Bremer county bank now stands. It was first run as such by John J. Smith.

The first bridge across the Cedar was erected in 1857, by subscription. It was a free bridge.

In 1855 P. B. Foster erected a brick block on Bremer avenue which was the first in the city. About the same time the stone school house in the first ward was built.

The contract was let this year to George LeValley and H. F. Beebe for building the court house, and in the same year the walls went up.

A safe belonging to S. H. Curtis, was blown open during this year and a considerable amount of money was taken from it. The burglars escaped.

In 1858—on the 26th of January—the free bridge was swept away by a freshet. In July another freshet created havoc through this region. The Waverly Republican described it as follows:

"Early in the morning the quiet town was startled with the cry that the river was overflowing its banks and rising rapidly. Not much rain had fallen for a few days in the town, and no one thought of a freshet, and at first the news was scarcely credited. A sight of the raging Cedar, however, confirmed all, and more. Before sunrise the water had risen nearly to the second floor in the large flouring mill of Messrs. Harmon & Reeves. Large quantities of wheat were stored on this floor, and a crowd of willing men soon were there hurrying everything perishable and movable to the third story and on shore. Men went in boats, or swam, as the only means of reaching the mill. Very little flour was injured, but quite a quantity of wheat got wet before it could be removed. By 8 o'clock A. M., the water was two feet deep on the second floor. Meanwhile, Mores Bros., with their cabinet shops, were in trouble. Messrs. Harmon, Reeves & Ellsworth had a saw mill, lumber and logs to look after. Messrs. Carr and Neff were in a similar fix. Messrs. Brownell & Oberdorf's mill had been swept clean by the freshet of 1st and 2d of July, hence there was but an empty mill for them to care for. At 10 A. M. the carding machine of W. P. Harmon was under water. The houses of J. C. Hazlett, H. J. Hoffman, S. Geddis, Hopkins, Buckmaster and McClure, (Jack and Queen of

Clubs) were in water from one to three feet deep, and by 12 o'clock M., four feet four inches above the second floor in the flouring mill. At 12 o'clock A. M., we crossed Bremer avenue in a boat, from the stone store to Hazlett's grocery. East and West Water street were nearly submerged. Cellars were filled, wells overflowed, and many houses were in water to the windows. Damages to the amount of hundreds of dollars was experienced, and it was some time before people could recover their equilibrium from the effects of the terrible freshet."

THE LOST CHILD.
By a Local Writer.

On Wednesday evening, May 1, 1856, a little boy five years old, the son of George Case, of Waverly, went out to play with his dog, as he was accustomed to do, and not returning at supper time, his parents commenced searching for him and returned unsuccessful.

The shades of night were approaching and they became alarmed, and the cry of "Lost Child" immediately spread through the town, and our citizens turned out to prosecute the search, in which I participated until about 11 o'clock, when we found his foot-prints in the sand along the creek, about 100 rods from his father's house, where we traced them in different directions to the bank of the river, when they could be traced no farther.

The bank bearing his foot-prints plain and fresh, as well as being disturbed by the scratching of the dog, led us to believe that he had found a watery grave, and, as the dog had returned home an hour or two before, it confirmed our belief. The night was dark, it thundered and lightened and while we were preparing to search the river, the rain commenced falling in torrents and continued to pour very hard during the night. After searching for some time along the bank and edge of the river, we returned to the house of Mr. Case. It was a little past 12 o'clock when, after relating discoveries, the child's parents sank in despair. After fixing the residence of Mr. Case as the place to meet next morning, to renew our search, we returned home to await daylight.

As soon as light the next morning I returned to the place which I left but a few hours before, when I saw the foot-prints of the boy's mother to and fro along the bank and heard her exclaim, "Oh, my child, my child!" which called forth our strongest sympathies.

Before they had collected at the place agreed upon to resume the search, in a moment of quietness, when the family were all seated in the house, they were suddenly aroused by the well known foot steps of their lost boy, at the door, who was affectionately welcomed by his father's embrace, when the boy said, "Oh, Pa, didn't you know that I was out all night in the rain?" It would be useless for me to undertake to describe the feelings of the family. They were too much for the mother to undergo. She sank down senseless. After the child was stripped of wet and muddy clothes, and partially recovered from his chill from the cold and wet during the night, I sat down by his bed side and he related to me how he got lost, and how he managed up to the time he returned home, which was as follows:

He said when he went out to play with Fido, Fido found a rabbitt, and he set him on, and followed Fido to catch the rabbit, and when he tried to come home he could not find the way, and he went back. Then he tried again and went back and had a great mind to cry, but did not. He called his Pa and Ma, but they did not come, and then he called the Lord, and asked him why he did not take him home. He then sat down on some dry grass by two large trees, and laid his head on Fido, and Fido wanted to get away but he held onto his legs and kept him as long as he could, but when Fido left, he laid his head on the ground and pulled his cap over his face, and put one hand in his pocket and one under him to keep them warm. He saw the lightning and heard it thunder, but was not afraid because the Lord knew where he was and he would take care of him, and he was not going to try to go home till the Lord made it light in the morning. He said he did not sleep very well, and was cold and shook in the night, and in the morning when he got rested a little, he started home.

The first church was built by a Baptist organization in 1856. It is now occupied by J. B. Barber for a residence.

In July, 1856, three men waiting in the old log pen for the next term of the district court, concluded to save Officer Hayden and his deputies the trouble of any further watching, and accordingly, one Saturday night they broke up the old floor, that had been very insecure for some time past, and dug out. It appears that they had some kind friends out side to assist them in making a start in the world, as two iron bars were found in the jail. They objected somewhat to their boarding house arrangments, as appears from the following letter they left by way of explanation for their absence:

"Mr. Hayden:—We, the undersigned, do not consider ourselves guilty of any crime whatever, and we are losing our health and liberty by staying in this dungeon, besides getting the leavings of a Dutch boarding house, which not a dog in Dubuque would eat unless starved to it. It is our intention to appear at the next term of court, if not before.

C. F. FOSTER,
JACKSON MORGAN,
JAMES FAY."

In October, 1856, the citizens constructed a foot bridge across the river, and a ferry was run to accomodate teams.

In June, 1859, Waverly was incorporated as a town, and officers were elected. October 30, 1859, the first teachers' institute convened at the court house, under the auspices of the county superintendent, Rev. A. K. Moulton. The lecturers were Rev. A. K. Moulton, Dr. O. Burbank, L. W. Thickstun, and E. C. Moulton.

In 1860 the second bridge was constructed across the Cedar river.

In 1861, the war broke out, and a military company was organized at Waverly on the 22d of April. There were about forty men, the officers being, G. W. Ruddick, Captain, and H. F. Beebe, First Lieutenant. For names of volunteers see war chapter.

On the 29th of December, 1861, the post office and *Republican* office were destroyed by fire. This caused the suspension of the newspaper for several months.

The brick school house in the second ward was erected in 1861.

In August, 1864, the depot of the Cedar Falls and Minnesota Railroad was located.

Another church building in Waverly was erected in 1864, the St. Andrews Protestant Episcopal. Rev. H. Townsend was the rector in charge of the Parish. In 1865, the church was ready for use. About this time the Congregational, Baptist, Methodist Episcopal and Presbyterian Churches were built.

In December, 1864, the first train of cars ran into Waverly and from this time the city grew rapidly.

The bank of Johnson & Leavitt was established this year, being opened in November.

In 1866, the Cedar Falls and Minnesota R. R. was extended to Charles City.

In 1868, the school houses in third and fourth wards were built.

In June, 1870, the Bremer County Bank was organized and in a short time the fire proof county offices were erected.

In August the Bank of Waverly, then known as the bank of Bowman & Burr, was opened.

Thomas Lashbrook and Aldrich & Goes, erected brick blocks.

The school house in the first ward was erected in 1870.

On the 26th of February, 1871, the second bridge across the Cedar was swept away by ice and high water. The present iron bridge was erected the same fall.

The High school building was commenced this year, and finished, costing $22,000.

In 1872, H. K. Swett, David Clark and the Hermann Brothers erected commodious brick stores.

In 1873, J. B. Barber, erected his brick store on the corner opposite the Bremer County Bank.

BUSINESS DEVELOPMENTS.

In 1853 the first step was taken in the direction of mercantile trade. Porter W. Earle was the first merchant, erecting his little log store building upon the corner now occupied by the stone store of J. P. Olds. Earle put in a stock of general merchandise. William B. Hamilton opened the next general merchandise store upon the corner now occupied by the brick block in which is the *Independent* office. Hamilton died about 1861. The next general merchandise dealer was John Hazlett, who is now of Nashua. His brother, Theodore Hazlett, succeeded him in the trade. He enlarged the business and kept a general variety store. For a number of years this was the principal store in the village. Hazlett, or, as he was usually called, "Thede," after remaining a few years, went to Cedar Falls. H. J. and Samuel E. Hoffman were about the next in the field. H. J. is now in the hardware trade, in partnership with Mr. Foster. Jeremiah Farris was in the general mercantile trade for a few years in early days and there are others whose names have been forgotten.

As trade increased and the business of Waverly began to assume city proportions, the general merchandising began to separate, and the various stores handled one line exclusively. The dry goods branch has passed into the hands of George P. Ellis, upon the south side of Bremer avenue, who also handles boots and shoes, hats and caps, etc.; Rogers & Riner, who occupy the next door, and handle about the same line of goods; John and Henry Eifert, in the store opposite the *Independent* office; Herman Brothers, R. A. Busby, on the west side of the river, and H. L. Ware, upon the north side of Bremer avenue, on the east side of the river. Mr. Ware is one of the most extensive dealers in the place.

H. L. Ware was born in Castleton, Rutland county, Vermont, November 21, 1845, and is a son of Henry and Sarah A. (Gould) Ware. When he was eight years of age, his parents emigrated to Grant county, Wisconsin, where he was raised and received a liberal education. In 1861, having developed a taste for newspaper life, he entered the office of the Grant county *Herald* as an apprentice. He remained however but a short time, when he removed to Waverly, Bremer county, Iowa, where he was employed in the *Republican* office, under J. K. L. Maynard. He remained in this occupation until 1865, when he entered the general mercantile establishment of C. B. Parson, as salesman. With him, however, he remained but one year, when he decided to embark in the mercantile business on his own account. Starting as he did with a very small capital, he has by strict attention to business, honest and upright dealings, steadily increased until he now stands at the head of the dry goods trade, having the largest and most extensive business in that line, of any house in Bremer county. Mr. Ware is truly a self made man, having by his own energy and integrity, worked himself up from very limited circumstances, until he is now one of the leading and most influential men of this county, and a business man in whom Waverly takes a just pride. He was married in 1863, to Miss Eudora C. Downing, a daughter of Thomas Downing, Esq., one of Waverly's pioneer merchants. They have one child, Minnie. Mr. and Mrs. Ware are both members of the Methodist Episcopal church of Waverly.

Among the first to establish a store exclusively devoted to groceries, was James F. Brown. He erected a two story building of brick, upon the corner where now stands Thomas Downing & Sons store. Raymond Brothers were also in the same building with a grocery store, and it was finally destroyed by fire. The present dealers in groceries and provisions are the following named: Thomas Downing & Son, who occupy a building where formerly stood the Brown building; J. B. Barber, on the corner, one block further west; William Fritz, who succeeded the Raymond Brothers; Mr. Waite and R. A. Busby.

Thomas S. Downing, one of the pioneer business men of Waverly, was born on the 7th day of March, 1821, in Bartholomew County Indiana. When eight years of age his parents emigrated to Mercer County, Kentucky, where he was educated in the common schools. In 1838 he returned to Indiana, remaining there until 1840, when he removed to Linn county, Iowa, locating at Marion, where he embarked in the tailoring business, with a brother. He was afterwards employed as a clerk in a store. In February, 1843, he married Miss Caroline Keys, by whom there was one child. Eudora C., now the wife of H. L. Ware, of Waverly. Mrs. Downing died in Marion, in 1845. She was a member of the

Congregational church and highly respected by all who knew her. Mr. Downing afterwards married Jane Morton, of Ohio. By this union there were four children—two of whom are living—Fred and Willie. Mr. Downing came to this county in limited circumstances, but went to work to make a home and to-day is one of the prosperous business men of the county. Mr. Downing, in politics, is a republican, has held the office of school fund commissioner for two terms, with other local offices of trust.

The first hardware dealer in Waverly was Sidney H. Curtis, who is yet in the trade. He erected a two story frame building on the same spot now occupied by his three story brick block, and used the lower part for his store; the upper story was used as a newspaper office, and also by George W. Ruddick, as a law office. Theodore Hazlett also handled a little hardware in his general store. David Clark, about 1872, erected the brick block at present occupied by Herman Brothers' store, and opened a large stock of hardware. For a time he was in company with another gentleman under the firm name of Clark & Morgan. They finally went out of business. In 1861, H. J. Hoffman became a hardware dealer, and is still in the trade in company with Mr. Foster. At present the hardware firms are S. H. Curtis; Hoffman & Foster, and D. S. Sitger; the latter being on the west side of the river.

S. H. Curtis, one of the pioneer business men of Bremer county, was born in Oneida county, New York, October 19, 1829. He is a son of Ezra and Lucy Ann (French) Curtis, natives of Connecticut. When S. H. was fifteen years old he was apprenticed to the trade of a tinner, in North East, Erie county, Pennsylvania. He was married in Westfield, Chautauqua county, New York, in 1853, to Miss Harriet N. Dean, a daughter of Samuel Dean. Mrs. Curtis died the same year. In 1854 Mr. Curtis came west in search of a location. He finally returned to New York, and in the following July came to Waverly, where he embarked in the hardware trade, and to-day has one of the largest establishments of the kind in this section of the country. In 1856 he married Miss Sarah A. Crouse. She was born in Otsego county, New York. By this union there are ten children—Harriet D., now the wife of H. L. Mosher; Millard H., Charles H., Edward H., Ezra H., George F., Lucy L., Peter C., Abbie B., and Martha W. In politics Mr. Curtis is one of the staunch republicans, who has always stood by the old ship. He was elected to the office of county supervisor, and served with credit for eight years. He has also held other local offices of trust in the gift of the people. Mr. Curtis is not a member of any church, but has always donated liberally in building up the different churches of Waverly. He has been identified with the business interests of Waverly for over twenty-seven years, and is one of the representative men of the county.

H. J. Hoffman, an enterprising hardware dealer of Waverly, was born in Union county, Pennsylvania, September 21, 1828. When he was fifteen years old, the family removed to Stephenson county, Illinois, and there he received a part of his education. It was, however, completed at an academy in the city of Freeport. During

HISTORY OF BREMER COUNTY.

a visit to Bremer county in the spring of 1854, Mr. Hoffman purchased some property in Waverly, and two years later settled here. The same year he opened a store of general merchandise, in company with a brother, S. E. Hoffman, who is now President of the Valley National Bank, of St. Louis, Missouri. The succeeding summer Mr. Hoffman "sold out," and became proprietor of the Bremer House. There he continued for a few years, and then embarked in the grocery business. In 1861, he became a hardware dealer, and to-day is the owner of an extensive and complete line of heavy and shelf hardware. Mr. Hoffman's first wife was Miss C. Denio, of Beloit, Wisconsin, who bore him five children; four of whom are now living—Alice, Kate, Frank and George E. The latter being a teller in the Valley National Bank, of St. Louis. Mrs. Hoffman died February 20, 1866, and the following year Mr. Hoffman was joined in wedlock with Mrs. Peter B. Foster, of Waverly.

The first drugs sold in town were probably from the store of Porter Earle. The first regular drug store was started by Richard Currier, who erected a little frame building just east of the court house, upon Bremer avenue, and remained in the business for a couple of years. He also erected the building which is now known as Bodeker's saloon, although it has since been moved to its present location. E. H. Woodruff succeeded him, and kept the store in a little building which stood where Frank A. Lee's store now stands, and then in the little stone building.

A man named Kissell, from Dubuque, was also in the drug trade here, and was succeeded by Dr. Samuel Jones, upon whose death, was succeeded by his son, Samuel Jones.

The next drug store was started by Dr. J. C. Pomeroy and Philip Rudemann, in the east side of the building now occupied by Hoffman & Foster. Dr. Pomeroy now runs the store alone.

Sidney Covert erected a building on the west side of the river, and is still in the drug business.

Frank Ball opened a drug store where G. P. Ellis is now. He married a daughter of John Goes, and a partnership was formed, as Ball & Goes. Before it was discontinued, John Wiedemann had charge of it for a time.

About 1872, Dr. Oscar Burbank started a drug store, and was succeeded by Burbank & Lee, and finally, Frank A. Lee purchased the entire store. The building now occupied was erected by Dr. Burbank.

H. K. Sweat was about the first merchant to deal exclusively in boots and shoes. About two years after Sweat opened his store, Louis Case had a boot and shoe establishment in a building now a part of the Centennial hotel. It then stood where Frank A. Lee's drug store now stands. At present this line is represented by Julius Goodman and C. N. Morse.

The confectionery line at present is represented by Billy Martin and Barber Brothers.

The first bakery was opened by August Miller.

The first clothing store was opened by M. S. Graham.

The second clothing store in Waverly was started by Mr. Israel, about 1858, and stood where George P. Ellis' store now stands, but afterward removed to the

Smith & Shepard building. He finally left for Waterloo. A brother-in-law of his, Mr. Geismar, was also in the clothing business here for a time. The line at present is represented by Smith & Shepard, who succeeded Israel; Levi & Hiller, Herman Brothers, L. S. Hanchett and H. L. Ware.

About the first shoe shop started in Waverly was by Lorenz Selbig, and was kept near where the Bremer county bank stands. He is now engaged in running the cigar factory. A. Starr was among the first to start, and he is still in the business. There are others who have, at different times, had shops. The present shoemakers are: William Quimby, Mr. Fosselmann, Mr. Cummings, Mr. Colby, Ludwig & Buesing and A. Starr. Starr is among the oldest business men of Waverly, and the oldest in his business. A sketch of him is subjoined:

A. Starr, one of the pioneers of Bremer county, was born in Berks county, Pennsylvania, on the 29th day of October, 1812. He is a son of Anthony and Christina (Wortz) Starr, and one of the three surviving children from a family of eight. He was educated in the district schools of his native State, and had to travel three miles, morning and evening, in going to and from school. In 1838 he was married to Miss Mary Smith, who bore him six children, two of whom are now living— William L. and John H. During the fall of 1855 he removed, with his family, to Waverly, Bremer county, Iowa, which, at that time, was a small village of twenty-seven houses. Mr. Starr came here without money, furniture or even a cup to drink coffee from, but, by hard work and perseverance, he is to-day one of Waverly's well-to-do business men. Mrs. Starr died in September of 1882. She was a member of the M. E. church, and had lived the life of a christian woman for many years. Mr. Starr has been a life-long democrat, and cast his first vote at the re-election of President Andrew Jackson.

The first harness shop was opened by James W. Wood.

The second harness maker was Gilbert Hamilton, who came at an early day and opened a shop near where the Waverly Bank stands. He was a brother of William B. Hamilton, and long since went to California. Another early harness maker was Cyrus Blossom, who is still here, and in the business. This industry is at present represented by D. W. Bigelow, U. C. Newcomb and Cyrus Blossom.

The first tailor in Waverly was Amoa Behman. About the next to make it his sole business was J. R. Smith. J. R. Smith and Wm. Cody are at present in this business.

The first blacksmith shop was started by Demus Buckingham, in 1854, as stated elsewhere. He remained about twelve years. Among those who have at various times since been in this business here, are the following: M. J. Neilsen, Shane Brothers and Hiram Lampson. The present ones are: William Mooney, Adam Broadie, Bigelow, Henry Christiern and Hill Brothers.

Adam Broadie, one of the pioneers of Bremer county, was born in Chatham, Province of Quebec, May 24th, 1824. When eighteen years old, he was apprenticed to a blacksmith, and served three years. In 1850, he emigrated to Winnebago county, Illinois, and thence, after a short time, to LaSalle county, where he was employed on the Illinois Central railroad. His marriage with Miss Jane Steen took place in Winnebago county. In 1855, he removed to Bremer county, Iowa, locating in Leroy township, where he worked at his trade and also engaged in farming. Mr. Broadie was the first blacksmith to settle in that portion of the county, the nearest shops to him being in Waverly and West Union. Ten years later, he settled in Waverly, and has since followed his trade. He votes the republican ticket, and has held offices of trust, being at the present time a member of the council.

A good blacksmith of Waverly is William Mooney, who was born in County Antrim, Ireland, during 1836. His father, Alexander Mooney, was by occupation a blacksmith, and William partially learned the trade in early life. When sixteen years old, he came to the United States, locating in New York City, where he completed his apprenticeship. In March, of 1856, he removed to Chicago, and thence, after a short time, to Independence, Buchanan county, Iowa. The following spring he settled in Waverly, Bremer county, and immediately began working at his trade. Mr. Mooney is to-day the oldest smith doing business in the town. He was united in marriage with Miss Mary Smith, a daughter of William O. Smith, who is a pioneer of Bremer county. Five children were born to them, two of whom, Nellie and Bessie, are now living. The family are members of the Catholic church.

J. H. Christiern, a blacksmith of Waverly, was born in Rochester, New York, September 13, 1827. When fourteen years of age he was apprenticed to a carriage-maker, with whom he spent three years. When eighteen years of age, he shipped on board the old frigate "United States," which was commanded by Commodore Reed and Captain Smoot. He visited the coast of Africa, and then sailed to the Mediterranean Sea. He was in France in 1848, at the time that country was declared a Republic, and Napoleon elected President. About the year 1852, Mr. Christiern returned to Rochester, and three years later removed to Madison, Wisconsin, where he was employed in the carriage shops of Bird & Baird. During the war he was employed by the government, being stationed at Chattanooga, and, a part of the time, at Marshville. In 1868 he came to Bremer county, Iowa, and was employed by R. S. Bently, carriage-maker. While working for that gentleman he ironed the first sulky and buggy that ever took a premium in a Bremer county fair. He married Miss Annie Melone. Two children—William and Harriet—blessed this union.

It is claimed that the first wagon shop was started by Stephen Pelton, in 1856. He opened a shop on West Water street. Horton Holbrook, Miles Comstock and Charles B. Taylor, were early engaged in this business. The present representatives of this branch of industry are Peter Neilsen, who established in 1878; John H. Hollenbeck, 1877; B. Schmitt, 1874, and Henry Christiern, 1882.

The first millinery shop was opened by a Miss Woodruff, who was also a dress-maker. Mrs. R. J. Ellsworth handled this line of goods for many years, and Mrs. Andrews was among the first in the busi-

HISTORY OF BREMER COUNTY.

ness. At present the following represent the trade: Mrs. Kohn, Mrs. Mary Bocquet and Mrs. Clark, who is a dressmaker also.

Among the first barbers were Frank Kiernan and Jake Long, who are still here. John Dickinson was also here a few years. At present writing, there are three shops, by Reiter & Smith, Mr. and Mrs. Lines and J. Long.

The first furniture dealer was Jack Hoffman, who brought in a few cane bottom chairs and exposed them for sale in 1856. Anson Case was also in this trade at an early day, as was David Milburn. The present representatives of this line are John Wagner and the Woodring Brothers, who also manufacture furniture.

J. F. Woodring, of the firm of Woodring Brothers, was born in Northampton county, Pennsylvania, in February, 1837, where he lived until the age of nine years. In 1846, he left his native county with his parents and settled in Union county, the same State, where he resided until 1851, when he emigrated to Stephenson county, Ill. His education was confined to the common schools of the day, attending them the greater part of the time until he was sixteen years of age. His father being a cabinet-maker, J. F. took a liking to that business; accordingly, at the age of sixteen, he commenced to learn the trade, working at it in Stephenson county four years, after which he spent one year in Kansas, during the border troubles, then returned to Illinois, where he was engaged in the furniture and cabinet business in Winnebago county, until 1862, when he entered the army in the Seventy-fourth Illinois Volunteer Infantry, as corporal. He was detailed as color guard, serving as such the entire length of time he was in the army—one year. The only battle he was in of importance was the battle of Perryville. After receiving his discharge, he again returned to Winnebago county, where he was engaged in the furniture business until 1865, when he came to Iowa, settling in Waverly, where, in company with his brother Henry, he purchased the furniture establishment, owned and operated at the time by Mores Bros. Their principal place of business was then located on East Water street, back of the present postoffice, and in the building now occupied by them for manufacturing purposes. There they continued until 1877, when they moved into the fine store on Main street, now occupied by them. The business conducted by this enterprising firm, is the largest in this or any of the surrounding counties. The building on Main street, where their salesroom is located, is 132 feet in depth, 23 in width, two stories high, with basement, all of which is packed full of every article known to the trade, the greater part of which is turned out of their extensive manufactory on East Water street, where they keep ten men constantly employed in turning out goods for their rapidly increasing trade. In connection with the furniture trade, Mr. Woodring does a general undertaking business, and for the accommodation of the public, has one of the finest hearses in the west, the cost of which was about $900. We also find in their main salesroom, a large variety of musical instruments, such as pianos, organs, violins, etc. This department is under the management of Thomas Woodring, another brother, who thoroughly understands this branch of the business. Aside from this, they also own a furniture store at Sumner, under the management of Peter Woodring, also a brother of the subject of this sketch. Mr. Woodring was married in 1860 to Miss Mary E. McKinley, a native of Illinois; they are the parents of three children—Laura, Nettie and William. Mr. Woodring is a member of Tyrrell Lodge, No. 116, A. F. and A. M., also of the United Workmen, and of the Legion of Honor; he is one of the trustees of the Workmen lodge. He is a member of the Methodist church, being the oldest member of the choir of that church.

John Wagner, a furniture dealer of Waverly, is a native of Prussia. When he was twenty years old the family emigrated to the United States, locating in Freeport, Illinois, where John followed the trade of a cabinet maker for seven years. He was also married in that city, in 1865, to Miss Caroline Marshall, who was born in Prussia during 1843. Five children—Eddie, Willie, Mary, John and Annie—have been born to them. In 1867, Mr. Wagner removed with his family to Waverly, Bremer county, where, soon after his settlement, he opened a furniture store, and now carries a stock worth about $2,000. He is a fair and square business man, and enjoys a liberal trade. The family are members of the Evangelical Association, and Mr. Wagner is a member of the A. O. U. W.

The first hotel was kept by J. J. Smith, as is stated elsewhere. He moved into the house which had been erected by W. P. Harmon and R. J. Ellsworth, in June, 1854, and thereafter kept all travelers who chanced this way. Previous to this, Frederick Cretzmeyer had lodged such travelers as could find no other accommodations. Smith at once commenced the erection of what is now the Bremer House. It was finished in 1855, and M. J. Burnett, the carpenter, first occupied it and kept boarders. This hotel is still standing, and is run in good shape by A. Fortner. The other hotels are the Waverly House, kept by Charles Kinnie, erected about 1865, by Andrew Dailey; Centennial Hotel, kept by A. VanOrdstrand and Mickley, erected several years ago by John Acken. The Ida House was kept by E. F. Tabor. It is now closed. There are several boarding houses, among which are Mrs. Margaret Broughton and Mrs. Frank Woodring. The principal hotel, however, is the Bremer House. It stands near the center of the business portion of the city.

A. Fortner, proprietor of the Bremer House, was born August 9, 1835, in Alleghany county, New York. He is a son of Thomas and Margaret (Hill) Fortner, who emigrated to Bremer county in 1854, locating in Franklin township, which was then a wild and unbroken country. Their son, of whom we write, started in life as a pioneer. In 1858 he was joined in wedlock with Miss Clarissa J. Wilson, a daughter of Samuel Wilson, of Buchanan county, Iowa. She was born in Clarion, Pennsylvania, September 15, 1840. Five children have been born to them, three of whom are now living—Elbert, who is a graduate of the Iowa State Agricultural College at Ames, and now attending his first course of lectures at the Chicago Medical College; Elroy B., and Frank Ellis. Shortly after his marriage Mr. Fortner became a tiller of the soil, and continued to pursue that occupation until 1865, when he came to Waverly and became proprietor of the Cedar Valley Hotel. In 1878 he purchased the Bremer House, where he still continues "mine genial host." For many years he has been a member of the Masonic Order.

The first bank in Waverly was established by the Hon. Emmons Johnson, aided by Messrs. Leavitt & Lush, of Waterloo. It was in a building where Rogers & Viner's dry goods store is, and was afterward removed to where the Bremer county block now stands. Emmons Johnson is now in Waterloo. The present banking institutions are the Bank of Waverly, and Bremer County Bank.

The Bank of Waverly, successors of Bowman Bros. & Burr, was established in 1870, and reorganized under existing State laws in March, 1876. The institution was reorganized with a subscribed capital of $200,000, of which $50,000 was paid up. The official management of the concern is vested as follows: President, J. H. Bowman; vice-president, S. R. Hunt; cashier, H. S. Burr. The officers and stockholders are all residents of this vicinity, and the representatives of property interests aggregating more than a million dollars. The gentlemen comprising the official head of the institution are known throughout this section of the State for reliability and probity of character, as well as men of wealth and extensive business experience. The president, Mr. Bowman, is of the firm of Bowman Bros., stock men. Mr. Hunt and Mr. Burr have been identified with Waverly business interests for many years. As regards the transaction of all business pertaining to banks and banking, no establishment in the State is better facilitated for doing business. Briefly, this institution is regarded as one of the staunch and reliable fixtures of Bremer's business interests, and entitled to the unlimited confidence of the public.

J. H. Bowman, one of the enterprising business men of Waverly, was born in Fayette county, Pennsylvania, on the 23d day of October, 1848. He is the son of Goodloe H. and Jane C. (Smith) Bowman. His father was a native of Fayette county, Pennsylvania, and mother of Berks county, Pennsylvania. There were five children, all of whom were born in the same county. His grandfather was the first president of the Monongahela Bank, chartered in 1812. James L. Bowman was second president. His father was president up to the time of his death, in January, 1865. His mother died in August, 1867. J. H. Bowman's education was completed by three years' attendance at the military academy at West Chester, Pennsylvania. When nineteen years old, his father's health failed and he was called home to take charge of the outside business. Mr. Bowman came to this State in 1866, and in 1869 located in Bremer county, where he has since resided. In November, 1872, he married Miss Caroline Snowden Jacobs, a daughter of Adam and Ann Jacobs, of Brownsville, Fayette county, Pennsylvania. By this union there are five children—Jane, Vaughan, Goodloe H., Ann Jacobs, Margaretta Vaughn. The following sketch of G. H. Bowman is from the History of Fayette County, Pennsylvania.

"The late Mr. Goodloe H. Bowman, of Brownsville, who died January 30th, 1876, was of German and Irish extraction. His father, Jacob Bowman, was born in Washington county, then Frederick county, Maryland, near Hagerstown, June, 1763. In 1787, he married Isabella Lowry, who was of Scotch descent and was born in Donegal, Ireland, and came to America when seventeen years old. Goodloe Harper Bowman, was the seventh child and the third son of this union, and was born April 20th, 1803. He was reared and educated in Brownsville, and entered upon active business life as a merchant about the age of twenty years, and continued in merchandising, in partnership with his brother, until 1855, when he relinquished the business and gave his attention principally to the affairs of the Monongahela Bank, of Brownsville, of which bank he was elected president in 1857, and continued such to the time of his death, immediately succeeding his elder brother, James L. Bowman, in the presidency thereof, as the latter had succeeded his father Jacob Bowman, who was the first president of the bank. January 9, 1840, Mr. Bowman married Miss Jane Correy Smith, of Reading, Berks county, Pennsylvania, by whom he had five children, Isabel Lowry, James Lowry, John Howard, Ann Sweitzer and William Robert. Mr. Bowman, like his father, was an active member and supporter of the Protestant Episcopal church, and for many years senior warden of Christ church, Brownsville. He was, in politics a whig, in early life, and became an ardent republican and contributed liberally to the support of the union cause during the late rebellion."

Henry S. Burr, cashier of the Bank of Waverly, Iowa, was born in Berkshire county, Massachusetts, on the 26th day of May, 1839. He was educated in the schools of his native State, his business education being attained at Eastman's Commercial College, where he graduated in 1864. His early life was spent on a farm in Massachusetts until he came to Iowa, in 1864, locating at Waterloo, where he was employed in the county clerk's office, his brother-in-law being clerk. He remained there but four months, and about the 1st of January, 1865, came to Waverly, where he entered the bank of Johnson, Leavitt & Company, as book-keeper, remaining in their employ for five years. In August, 1870, J. B. Bowman and H. S. Burr opened a private bank under the name of Bowman & Burr, operating as such until 1876, when they organized a stock company as the bank of Waverly, since which time Mr. Burr has held the position of cashier. He is also one of the stockholders. He married Fannie A. Smilie, of Cambridge, LaMoille county, Vermont, born in 1848. She is a daughter of Francis Smilie and a niece of Henry Smilie, both of Cambridge, Vermont, the latter one of the leading men of that city. By this union there were five children, three of whom are living—Mary A., born October 8, 1873; Henry S., Jr., born December 9, 1875; Clarence B., born May 21, 1881. In 1874, Mr. Burr lost his mother, but his father still lives in Berkshire county, Massachusetts, on the old homestead where Mr. Burr was born. Mr. Burr is, and always has been, identified with the republican party. He has been treasurer of the city school for about eight years. He is a member of the Masonic Fraternity, Tyrrell Lodge, No. 116, of Waverly.

The Bremer County Bank was organized under existing State laws, in 1870, and at once assumed, and still maintains a permanent place in the banking interests in this section, and is a most valuable adjunct to commercial interest.

The subscribed capital stock of the institution is $100,000, paid-up capital $50,000. The facilities for transacting all business pertaining to the banking system are unsurpassed, and in its construction and organization, everything has been considered calculated to enhance the interest and security of those so fortunate as to be numbered among its patrons. The official management of the institution is vested as follows: President, N. B. Ridgeway, Vice President, N. P. Ellis, Cashier, L. L. Lush. The officers, directors and stockholders are nearly all residents of the county, many of them men of large property connections and well known throughout this section of the country for reliability and integrity of character. A general banking business is transacted, as in National banks, except in the mere matter of the issue of money. They deal in foreign and domestic exchange, and have most excellent facilities for making collections, which is a prominent feature.

The incorporators of the Bremer county bank, were D. P. Holt, A. Slimmer, Joe Rosenbaum, William Trowbridge, S. R. Hunt, Clark Fairfield, William C. Holt and N. P. Ellis.

The first officers were D. P. Holt, president, N. P. Ellis, vice-president, Joe Rosenbaum, cashier.

Abram Slimmers was born in Germany in September, 1835. He came to America in 1850, landing in New York, where he remained but a short time. He followed different occupations until the fall of 1860, when he came to Iowa from Arkansas. He first settled at Jessup, Buchanan county, where he associated himself with S. F. Searles in the buying and shipping of cattle, which continued until the fall of 1861, when he went to Cedar Falls, where he became associated with a firm in Wisconsin for the purpose of buying furs in this State and in the northwestern Territories, with headquarters at Fort Dodge. In this he continued until the following spring, and then engaged in his former occupation, with headquarters at Cedar Falls; at the same time operating largely in Nebraska, Dakota, Minnesota, Wisconsin and Missouri, through different parties. There he remained until the fall of 1863, when he removed to Waverly, where he became associated with Morris & Rosenbaum, formerly of Cedar Falls, Iowa, for the purpose of carrying on the stock business on a larger scale. He remained in partnership with them several years, in that business, and in 1867 he formed a business connection with A. V. Bass, of Dixon; Illinois, for the purpose of opening and improving farms in southwestern Iowa; Mr. Bass superintending the same and Mr. Slimmer furnishing the capital. They at once opened a farm of 1280 acres in Fremont county, and about the same time opened several other farms in different parts of Iowa. No other man in this part of the State has been so largely interested in the opening and developing of the farming interests in the State. While he was en-

gaged in the stock trade he did as much or more business than any man in the State. He was instrumental in organizing the Bremer County Bank, of Waverly, in 1870, of which he was one of the largest stockholders, and at his suggestion, D. P. Holt was elected as president, but soon after resigned and Mr. Slimmer was elected in his place, and continued to hold that office until he resigned. In August, 1872, Mr. Slimmer was instrumental in incorporating the Bank of Nashua, Iowa, of which he was one of the principal stockholders and vice-president, continuing until it was consolidated with the First National Bank of the same place, of which he is a large stockholder. In June, 1871, he was instrumental in organizing the Butler County Bank, of Clarksville, Iowa, of which he was a director and a large stockholder; continued until the entire stock of the bank was purchased by himself and his nephew, Louis Slimmer, of Clarksville, and which is now run under the name of Butler County Bank, Louis Slimmer & Company, proprietors. In February, 1875, he bought the bank of C. V. McClure, of Greene, at which time he was instrumental in incorporating the Shell Rock Valley Bank, of Shell Rock, with a capital of $50,000, and of which he is the largest stockholder. Soon after the bank was organized he was elected president, which office he still continues to hold. In 1881 he was instrumental in starting the bank of Allison, Iowa, of which he is at present one of the principal owners. In 1876 Mr. Slimmer started an extensive lumber yard in Waverly, in company with others, and about the same time engaged in the manufacturing of lumber at Wausau, Wisconsin, large quantities of which was shipped to their distributing yard at Waverly, and the balance to different parts of this and other States. He is also associated with the Bremer County Horse Importing Company, in which he owns a one-fourth interest. It would seem by the many business interests above mentioned, that there would be no ground for enlarging upon the business capacity of the subject of this sketch; but it is nevertheless true that these are but a few of the business enterprises in which he has been, and is still engaged. In fact, it would be hard to find a business enterprise of any great importance, in either Bremer or Butler counties, in which the hand and heart of this self-made man has not been prominent. In politics Mr. Slimmer was a strong republican, up to the Greeley movement, in 1872, when he joined the Greeley party, and has since been independent in politics, voting for the best man. Bitterly opposed to caucuses and jobbery in politics, of any kind, he has never been known to hold, or even accept, a political office. Having been born under a monarchical form of government, he appreciates the government like the one he finds in his adopted country. In 1872 he was appointed trustee of the Dubuque and Dakota Railroad, which office he held until 1874. In religion he is a strong Liberal; desiring each to worship God according to the dictates of his own conscience, and respecting him for so doing. He is a liberal in more than one sense of the word, giving largely to the support of religious denominations of different kinds; indeed, his liberality is seen in every public enterprise; no one asks of him, but receives, none are turned away empty-handed. In 1873, Mr. Slimmer took a trip to Europe in company with his sister, traveling through Italy, Switzerland, Germany and France, returning in November, 1874. In this trip of over a year he spent $13,200, giving $6,000 to the poor. Though an active business man, Mr. Slimmer is a lover of the beautiful, whether it be produced by the hand of nature or man. In fine art he takes great pleasure; this can be plainly seen by visiting his elegant residence, which was erected in 1878, regardless of money consideration. From the exterior, one forms an opinion that the resident there, is a man of culture and taste, but not until he passes to the interior does he obtain a correct idea of the true taste of the builder. The residence is furnished with all the modern improvements and decorated with the finest work of art, Mr. Slimmer often paying exorbitant prices for works that pleased the eye. The beautiful ground of fourteen acres surrounding this elegant residence is decorated with every conceivable kind of shrubbery and foliage. Such a home as this, is one of which any man might be proud.

L. L. Lush, Cashier of the Bremer County Bank, was born in Erie county, New York, July 14, 1842, and is the son of Hiram and Jane Thompson Lush, who also were natives of New York. He spent his boyhood on his father's farm in McHenry county, Illinois, where the family emigrated when he was about two years of age. His early education was received in the common schools of that county, under great difficulties, the family living about two miles from the nearest school house. He was obliged to walk that distance every day during the winter, to and from school. During the winter of his fourteenth, fifteenth and sixteenth years, he was not only compelled to walk that distance, but in order to pay his way did chores for his board. Aside from that, during the winter term, he chopped wood enough to supply the family for a year. He first came to Iowa in 1859, settling in Butler county, near Parkersburg; afterwhich he completed his education at Cedar Valley Seminary, at Osage, Iowa, about 1864, where he also did chores to pay his way. It will thus be seen that his education was received under great difficulties. In 1862, he came to Bremer county and settled in Washington township, where after completing his education, he continued to farm until 1867, when he received the appointment of deputy county treasurer of Bremer county, which position he held until 1872. In February of that year he accepted the position of assistant cashier of Bremer County Bank, which office he held until January 1, 1880, when he was elected cashier of the same institution, which position he has faithfully filled to the present time. Aside from this, Mr. Lush has held various local offices, such as city clerk, city treasurer, etc. He is a member of Tyrell lodge, No. 116, of which he has been treasurer about five years. Previous to this, he was secretary for about the same length of time. He is also a member of Royal Arch Chapter, No. 24, of which he was secretary for three or four years, and has been treasurer for the past five years. He is a member of the A. O. U. W., of which he has been treasurer since its organization; also a member of the Iowa Legion of Honor, and been treasurer since its organization in 1874. Mr. Lush was married October 4, 1864, to Miss M. A. Lucas, daughter of Parker Lucas, and sister to Captain W. V. Lucas, now auditor of the State of Iowa, also sister of J. E. Lucas, cashier of bank at Allison. They have three children, Estella, Ethel and Pearl.

D. P. Holt, the first president of the Bremer County Bank, was born in Brandon, Rutland county, Vermont, February 17, 1806. His father was Lieutenant Seth Holt, a soldier of the War of 1812. His mother was Abigail (Cheney) Holt. His father died in Cayuga county, New York, when D. P. was about one year old. After his father's death his mother removed to Brandon, Vermont, where she married Daniel Galusha. By the first marriage there were three children—D. P., Elijah H. and Phylancy. By the second marriage there was one child—Lucien. In 1840 the family removed to Carroll county, Illinois, locating in Fair Haven Township where his mother died in 1866. When seven years old, D. P. was thrown on his own resources. His first undertaking was to learn the tanner and currier trade, which he followed for a couple of years. His mother removed at that time to Lyons, where he accompanied her. They remained here a short time, when she removed to Cayuga county, New York, and from there to Sodus, Wayne county, New York. His first work here was on the Erie Canal; his business was the distribution of whisky rations to a large body of men employed on the work, receiving six dollars per month, with privilege of keeping crackers and cheese for sale to the laborers, making about as much money out of the sales as he received for his labor. From this labor he saved his first one hundred dollars. From there he went to Leroy, Greene county, New York, where he was employed by an uncle on a farm, at six dollars per month. The following year he went to Batavia, New York, where he worked in a brick-yard. Two years later he took the yard on shares, and married Miss Sarah Huntington, a daughter of G. Huntington, the owner of the yard. By this union there were six children—five of whom are living—Julia, Mary Ann, Susan, Frances, and Sarah O. After marrying, he remained in the brick business one year, when he turned his attention to farming, taking a place on shares with his uncle, who was to receive one-third, himself one-third and the landlord the same. At this time he was not worth a cent, and had to get trusted for his household goods, which amounted to five dollars, giving security for that amount. The next year he bought a yoke of oxen, for which he ran in debt, and rented land another year. Meeting with good success, he paid for his oxen and wagon and some other things for the house. The following year he traded his oxen for a horse team, and moved to Niagara county, New York, where he purchased a claim of Elijah Cheeney of 100 acres, with heavy birch and maple timber standing upon it. With his axe he cleared this 100 acres, and a few years later he purchased 50 acres more adjoining, making a farm of 150 acres. He then entered into the land speculation with a man in Batavia by the name of Mix, which proved a financial success. He rented his farm for five years at $500 per year, taking a mortgage on another farm for the rent. He then embarked in the mercantile business with a man by the name of Knup, for one year, when he purchased Knup's interest, remaining in the business for three years. Selling out, he went to St. Louis, where he embarked in the steamboat business, engaging first as a hand at $40 per month, loaning his captain $500. He worked one year and lost his wages and $500. The following year he still kept in the business, loaning his captain $500 as before and did the collecting of freight bills at New Orleans. He again lost his money which he had earned but made it out of the freight bills. The following year he moved to St. Louis, where he engaged in the tobacco trade, buying and shipping. He afterwards purchased a boat running between St. Louis and Cairo, having as a partner Mr. Douglas. In 1840 he went to Carroll county, Illinois, with Mr. Galusha, when he became infatuated with the country, and purchased a large tract of land in Fair Haven township. In 1848 he moved to Carroll county, where he improved his land. In the fall of 1849 he purchased a stock of goods and embarked in the mercantile business, in Savanna, which business he prosecuted for eighteen years. In the mean time he was director of the old Racine & Mississippi Railroad. Mrs. Holt died in Wisconsin. He afterward married Mrs. Coy, by whom he had five children—Josephine, Frank, Albert, Emma and Edward. Mrs. Holt died and he then married Mrs. Mary Bowker. One child blessed this union. In 1870 Mr. Holt sold his interest, in Savanna, Illinois, and came to Waverly; embarked in the banking business in company with Joseph Rosenbaum and A. Slimmer, purchasing the Bremer County Bank, Mr. Holt being chosen president, Joseph Rosenbaum cashier. He afterward established a bank in Grundy Centre, and Steam Boat Rock. Mr. Holt is a large land owner in Grundy county, possessing 2,563 acres of land. He has 100 acres in Bremer county. His landed property and real estate is valued at $108,000. In 1881 he sold his banking interest in Grundy county and Steam Boat Rock for $32,000. Mr. Holt was the first supervisor of Fair Haven township, being elected on the democratic ticket.

N. P. Ellis, a native of Fairfield county, Connecticut, was born October 4, 1847. He was reared on a farm and received his education in subscription schools of that day. When four years old his parents moved to Seneca Co., New York. When 21 years old, he entered a mercantile establishment, where he remained ten years. In 1831, he married Esther Bailey, by whom he had one child—George P., now of Waverly. After living with her for about twenty years, she died, and he afterward married Cindirella Bailey, by whom there was one child—Lillie. Mr. Ellis has retired from the mercantile business, leaving that in the hands of his son, George P. Ellis, now one of the leading merchants in the city. He has 200 acres of Bremer county land, valued at $35 per acre. Mr. Ellis is a temperance man in all which the name implies. He has never used any intoxicating liquors or tobacco in any form. He was one of the prime movers in organizing the temperance movement in the county.

HISTORY OF BREMER COUNTY.

INDUSTRIAL ENTERPRISES.

The first saw mill in the city was erected in 1853, by William P. Harmon and R. J. Ellsworth.

The next saw mill was erected in 1858, by Eben Martin. It stood on the west side of the river upon the site now occupied by the grist mill. It was a financial success, and was kept in operation until after the war, when it was torn down to make room for the grist mill. Eben Martin, the founder of the saw mill, was a native of Maine, and came here from Independence.

About the time the mill was torn down, a steam saw mill was erected on the east side of the river by Carr & Hoppins, the latter an ingenious Scotchman, who was for a number of years a partner of Mr. Mooney in the blacksmith business. The mill was well equipped with circular saws and the necessary machinery. It is yet in operation, at present owned by Mr. Boattcher.

The Waverly Woolen Mills were established by William P. Harmon, in 1861. The building is 30x40 feet in size, and is three stories in height. Carding machines were placed in it, and all the necessary apparatus to make a complete establishment. It is now owned by G. D. Stowell. Connected with the woolen mills Mr. Stowell operates a feed mill, which has a capacity for grinding about three hundred bushels of feed per day.

The flouring mills of Waverly are two in number—the Waverly City mill, on the west side of the river, and the White Swan mill on the east side. The White Swan mill was the first in this section of the State. It was erected by William P. Harmon. The Waverly City mill was constructed about 1866, and for the past twelve years has been under the management of Ridgeway & Coy, having been put up by Joseph Kidd.

In the fall of 1876 the White Swan mill, then belonging to the Harmon estate, was also purchased by the above gentlemen, since which time both mills have been under one management. Both mills have recently been overhauled, and new machinery substituted, being with the latest improvements made, the equipments are not inferior to any mills in the State. The two mills contain ten run of burrs, affording an extended capacity, and while their facilities enable them to grind corn, rye, etc., the manufacture of wheat flour is a specialty, and the patent, or improved process flour made here occupies a foremost place in the various markets of the country. In the arrangement and construction of the establishments, nothing has been omitted that tends to better the process of flour making, and with the aid of the best and most experienced millers that can be procured, the great disideratum has been accomplished. Mr. Coy, of the firm, is a practical miller of many years' experience, and under his personal supervision both establishments are operated. They do both merchant and custom work. The Waverly City mill contains six run of burrs, which are kept continually on merchant grinding. The market for their productions is wide spread, and wherever introduced the Waverly mills' flour has achieved a leading reputation. Ridgeway & Coy are also owners of the water power here, and their combined interests form one of the most important features in the industrial or business affairs.

In 1854, Alexander Buckmaster put up a building about 20x40 feet in size, just north of the Harmon grist mill, and established a furniture factory. A lathe, circular saw and some other machinery was put in. It was run by water power, Buckmaster owning 100 inches of water. This was in a short time after sold to Shores & Keith, who subsequently enlisted in the army. It came to the possession of William and Alfred Mores, who equipped the mill with the necessary machinery, and employing eight or ten men, did a large business for a number of years. Lyman Tondro was the next possessor of the property, and finally the work was discontinued.

Woodring Brothers next started their furniture factory near the river. They still own and operate it, doing an extensive business. They also have a store on Bremer avenue.

Among the leading business interests of Waverly is the cigar manufactory of Selbig & Son. The fact that one of the firm, Charles Selbig, is a practical and experienced cigarmaker, warrants success. L. Selbig has been a resident and identified with the county in various ways for the past twenty-seven years, and is one of the pioneer business men of Bremer county. By honorable and fair dealing they have built up a lucrative business which is a credit to themselves and the city in which they live.

Lawrence Selbig, a cigar manufacturer, of Waverly, was born in the Rhine Province of Bavaria, February 12, 1825. In 1848, he emigrated to the United States, locating in Rochester, New York, where he learned the trade of boot and shoe making. March 10, 1855, he settled in Waverly, Bremer county, Iowa, and immediately opened a shoe shop. At that date there were but four buildings on the west side of the town, and about fifteen on the east side. Many were the times, after working late in the evening, that Mr. Selbig stumbled over stumps and logs, in picking his way home. In May of 1856, he, in company with Mr. Michael Caspes, opened the first brick yard in Bremer county. Subsequently he sold out and embarked in the saloon business, with Peter Fosselmann. During September of 1878, he began manufacturing cigars, and also wholesaling and retailing tobacco. The firm is now known as Selbig & Son. They carry a $2,000 stock, and some of their favorite brands are Diploma, Young Tar and Young America. Mr. Selbig was married in 1853, to Johanna Casper, a native of France, and born in 1835. Thirteen children were born to them—seven sons and six daughters.

The Waverly Canning Company was effected under the general incorporation laws of Iowa, December 1, 1882, with a capital stock of $20,000, with the following named officers: Louis Case, president; H. L. Ware, vice-president; S. H. Morse, secretary; W. R. Bowman, treasurer. This enterprise is yet in its infancy, but bids fair to soon become one of the main industries of the city.

Arrangements are perfected for the erection of a factory in the spring of 1883, for the purpose of canning fruits, vegetables, etc., 64x80 feet, two stories. During the season it will furnish employment to over one hundred persons.

WAVERLY PRODUCE ASSOCIATION.

The advent of the railroad dates the commencement of Waverly as a shipping point. O. A. Strong shipped the first car load of wheat and the first car load of dressed hogs from this place in the latter part of December, 1864. During the year 1865, the town enjoyed the distinction of being one of the best shipping points in northern Iowa. The shipments for the year were over 500,000 bushels, requiring over 1250 cars for transportation.

The vast amount of shipments brought into the field a large number of buyers, who, in their anxiety to purchase, often gave more for grain than the market price would warrant. This necessitated the withdrawal of some from the trade and the organization of the Waverly Produce Association, which has since, to some extent, regulated the market. The Association sprang into existence in 1873, and was composed of W. C. Holt, president; O. A. Strong, secretary; Edward Knott, Clark Fairfield, S. R. Hunt, Amon Fortner and Samuel Beswick. During the first year the Association shipped over 300,000 bushels of wheat in addition to other grain and live stock, and expended between $800,000 and $900,000.

The shipments at present are not so large as formerly, there being many competing points surrounding, and farmers receiving the same price for grain and stock, sell to dealers nearest their place of residence. Mr. Holt still retains the presidency of the Association, and Mr. Strong is yet its secretary.

Orrin A. Strong, secretary of the Association, was born in Summit county, Ohio, May 3, 1829. He is the son of L. M. and Nancy (Griswold) Strong. In 1838 his parents emigrated to Iowa, locating at Marion, Linn county, where his father was elected a member of the first constitutional convention. In 1850 his parents removed to Dodgeville, Iowa county, Wisconsin, from which place, in 1856, his father was elected county judge, which office he held until his death, which occurred in 1868. Orrin came west with his parents, and was educated in the common schools of Iowa. In 1844 he went to Iowa county, Wisconsin, and while there was employed by a company at Chippewa Falls, scaling logs. While in the latter place he did not see but one white woman for one and one-half years. In the spring of 1851 he went down the Mississippi river on a raft. At that time there was but one dwelling at Reed's landing. In 1852 Mr. Strong removed to Cedar Rapids, where he engaged in the lumber trade. In 1854 he went to Clarksville, where he built a saw mill, and in 1857, built a grist mill, the first on the Shell Rock river, north of Black Hawk county. In 1862 he removed to Cedar Falls, where he engaged in the produce trade. In December, 1864, he came to Waverly, engaging in the same business. In 1852 Mr. Strong was united in marriage with Emily A. Doolittle, a cousin of the renowned P. P. Bliss. They have had four children, one son and three daughters —Addie B., Emma T., L. E., and Nellie B.

PHOTOGRAPHY.

Waverly, in 1883, is represented by two first class photographic establishments. A superior class of work is made. A. Garner is proprietor of one gallery and N. E. Pierce of the other.

A. Garner, is a native of Howard county, Indiana, and was born March 4, 1848. He is a son of Samuel and Charity (Moon) Garner, natives of Ohio. Eight children, five sons and three daughters, blessed their home. In 1851 Mr. Garner turned his steps westward, emigrating with an ox team, to Franklin county, Iowa, and locating near Hampton, where he entered a large tract of land, which is now known as Maine's Grove. After remaining there about twelve years, he removed to Bremer county, and thence to Black Hawk county, where he at present resides. He built the first log cabin in Franklin county. J. O. Garner, a grandfather of A's., was the founder of the town of Hampton, giving to that place forty acres of land, on which is now the business portion of the city. Isaac, a brother of Mr. Garner, was the first white child born in the county. The subject of this sketch was reared on a farm and obtained his education in the common schools of the county. When nineteen years of age, he embarked in the photographic business, working in various localities until 1878, when he came to Waverly, where he has since continued his business. By close attention to the same, and by fair dealing, he has become the possessor of a trade which is a credit not only to himself but to the city. His marriage with Mrs. Esther C. Sewell (widow of Thomas J. Sewell, Jr.), occurred in 1868. One child, Birdie, brightens their home.

N. E. Pierce, was born in New York State, June, 1848. He is the son of H. N. and Olive Pierce, who are both natives of Vermont; he is the oldest of a family of five children. In early life he received a common school education; also took a course at Eastman's Commercial College. When he was seventeen years of age, in company with his parents, he came west and settled at Janesville, in Bremer county. There he worked at the painter's trade for a time. In 1874 he commenced to learn the photographer's trade, working in Chicago and Dubuque, until he had thoroughly mastered his business, after which he followed his trade in different places until 1881, when he returned to Bremer county and settled at Waverly. In September, 1882, he fitted up his fine gallery in Burbank's building, where he is building up a large and constantly increasing business. His pleasant and agreeable manner and his superiority as an artist, is making him very popular with the public. Some of his pictures are said by good judges to equal, if not surpass, many of the noted artists of the east. Mr. Pierce is something of an inventive genius, having invented various machines used in his business. In 1876, he invented and patented a re-touching machine, which for the time proved to be quite a success. He was married in 1869 to Miss Honor D. Lehman, of Janesville. She died November 16, 1882, leaving three children, aged respectively eight, ten and twelve—Willie, Herbie and Charlie.

POSTOFFICE.

This office was established in the winter of 1853-4, or early in the spring following. Porter Earle was the first postmaster appointed. He kept the office in a little log building, which stood on the corner now occupied by the stone corner belonging to J. P. Olds. After a few years the little

D. A. Long.

log building was torn down, the stone store now standing was erected, and into this the office was removed. The first mail was carried from Independence, through the woods, and consisted of less than a dozen letters.

The postoffice has been moved at various times, to different places about town, and has changed hands many times. Early in the seventies, Daniel Fichthorn was appointed and held the office for nearly four years.

In 1876, Edward Knott was appointed postmaster, and is the present incumbent, making a gentlemanly, courteous and efficient official. The deputy postmaster is L. M. Sholes.

Edward Knott, the present postmaster of Waverly, was born in the city of London, England, March 4, 1842. He is the son of Alfred and Jane (Blondon) Knott, who emigrated to this country in 1855, and located in Boone county, Illinois. Edward received his education in his native country. He came to Boone county with his parents, and thence to Richmond, McHenry county, Illinois. In 1863, he came to Bremer county and settled in Janesville, where he engaged in working by the month. Here he became acquainted with Eliza Egleston, and was married January 31, 1865. He then went on a farm, which he carried on for one year, meeting with success. He then engaged in buying grain, at Janesville, shipping the first car load from that place. In the spring of 1866, he came to Waverly, where he embarked in the livery and grain business. In connection with the livery business, he is also engaged in buying and shipping horses. In 1882, he paid out $35,000 for horses alone. Mr. Knott has, for the last few years, taken an active interest in the politics of the county. In 1876, he was appointed postmaster of Waverly, which position he holds at the present time. He has also held other local offices of trust in the gift of the people. Mr. Knott came to the county in limited circumstances, but went to work with a will, and by judicious management and close attention to business, has accumulated a comfortable property, and to-day ranks with the well-to-do business men of the county. Mr. and Mrs. Knott are the parents of four children—John, Carrie, Marion and Alfred. Mr. Knott is a member of the Masonic fraternity, of Waverly.

Lewis M. Sholes, deputy postmaster and express agent, was born in Otsego county, New York, May 24, 1828. He is the son of Miner and Mary (Sheldon) Sholes. Lewis was educated in the common schools. In 1852, he married Miss Euphemia Tyler. In the spring of 1857, he left New York, with his family, for Bremer county, Iowa, and located in what is known as Summer township, where he engaged in farming. In January, 1867, he removed to Waverly. In May, 1870, he was appointed agent of the American Express Company. November, 1874, he was appointed as assistant postmaster, which offices he holds at the present time. Mr. and Mrs. Sholes are the parents of four children, three sons and one daughter. Mr. Sholes is a member of Tyrrell Lodge, No. 116. In politics, he is a republican.

RELIGIOUS.

There are nine regular churches in the city, in addition to which other denominations occasionally hold services.

HISTORY OF BREMER COUNTY.

THE FIRST SUNDAY SCHOOL.
By a Local Writer.

The first Sunday School in Waverly was organized May 1, 1854; the settlement then contained about fifteen families. Three small stores, kept by Messrs. Wm. B. Hamilton, John Hazlett and Thomas Downing, were of ample capacity for the business of the place; the last named gentleman, who also kept the postoffice, has a vivid recollection of the interests and excitement usually manifested by the company seen together around the office when it was known that the mail had come, especially when it had been delayed a month or so, as was sometimes the case. Preaching services were usually held every Sabbath, alternating between Rev. Burley, Methodist; Terry, Baptist, and Blakely, Presbyterian. The place of meeting had been, until about this time, a small log house, built by R. J. Ellsworth and Wm. P. Harmon, and used successively as a dwelling, meeting house, school house, lunatic asylum, jail, cooper shop, etc. It stood in the center of what is now Bremer avenue, near the east end of the present bridge. A Good Templar's Society was also organized about this time, showing the anxieties of the fathers at that early day upon the subject of intemperance. Another enterprise creating much interest in the community, was building the first school house, commenced in the autumn of 1855, and (Mr. Hullman says) finishing ever since, and not done yet. But the grand movement was the organization of the first Sunday School. The meeting was held in the old court house, then new, being simply a covered frame with an oak floor of green boards, not nailed. Said meeting was called to order by Mr. Buckingham. Mr. R. J. Ellsworth offered the opening prayer, after which Mr. Geo. A. Brown was appointed superintendent, and Miss Agelia Wordsworth assistant; Mr. Hegley, secretary; O. M. Reeves, treasurer, and J. W. Low, librarian. The teachers were Miss Augusta Morse, Mrs. Ellsworth, Miss Martin, O. M. Reeves and Oliver P. Haughawout. D. Patterson was chosen bible class teacher. The average attendance was about twenty-five, nearly all the children in the settlement. The Misses Ada Downing, Rosa Foster, Clara and Abner Harmon, Harry Hazlett, H. B. and G. E. Ellsworth were among the first scholars. The school started out with an eighteen dollar library, partly the gift of the Sunday School Union. Deacon O. M. Reeves purchased and brought it from Dubuque, arriving here on Saturday evening; busy hands, until a late hour, got the books properly marked and ready for the next days use. The school was kept up through the summer, and made a source of much interest, most of the citizens taking an active part. This school, with change of officers, was kept up for three summers, when two schools were organized.

ST. ANDREW'S EPISCOPAL CHURCH.

The first regular services of the Episcopal church, held in Bremer county, were established in 1854, by the Rev. James Keeler, residing in Janesville.

St. Andrew's Parish, in Waverly, was formally organized in December of 1863, under the ministry of Rev. Hale Townsend. Services had been held for some time in the court house and at halls. At the time of organizing, there were eleven families, representing forty souls, (adults and children) recorded in the register, as follows: J. E. Burke, Daniel Ellis, John P. Ellis, H. S. Hoover, Thompson Houser, Dr. Samuel Jones, Charles Parsons, Moses Lehman, William Tallet, Edward Tyrrell, A. J. Tanner and Joseph Wade, with their families.

The church building, a brick edifice, seating 125 persons, was erected in 1854, being the first church built in Waverly. It measures 24x40 feet, and cost $2,000.

The first vestry consisted of Dr. Samuel Jones and H. S. Hoover, (wardens) William Tallet, Charles R. Beardsley and A. J. Tanner.

The present officers are Rev. S. R. J. Hoyt, rector; H. S. Hoover, senior warden; Henry Christiern, junior warden; William R. Bowman, secretary and treasurer; Geo. Franklin, Edward Wearne and J. H. Bowman.

There have been 107 communicants since the organization of the parish, 150 baptisms, 75 confirmed and 31 burials.

The present membership is 55 communicants, 32 families and 128 individuals.

The present condition of the parish is desirable. It has no indebtedness, has a handsome sum in hand for the erection of a new church edifice, owns a very fine rectory, and keeps its current expenses paid up promptly. It has a good Sunday School, organized in 1863, by Rev. Hale Townsend, its first superintendent. Its present officers are Rev. S. R. J. Hoyt, (the rector) superintendent; H. S. Hoover, assistant superintendent, and E. E. Hoover, secretary and treasurer. It has ten teachers, four males and six females. There are 107 scholars enrolled, and the average attendance is about 60. The school is self-supporting, and contributes to benevolent objects more than one hundred dollars annually.

There have been five different rectors in charge of the parish since its beginning. Rev. Hale Townsend came in 1863, and resigned in 1865. Rev. Charles Stewart succeeded him in the fall of 1865, and left in April, 1866. The next rector was Rev. William Wright, who began his work in April, 1866, and resigned in 1869. He was followed by the Rev. F. Humphrey, in 1873, who held the rectorship until Easter, of 1877. Rev. S. R. J. Hoyt, the present rector took charge of the parish July 1, 1877.

Rev. Hale Townsend is the second son of Richard and Jeannett Townsend, both natives of New York State. He was born in Detroit, Michigan. He spent his early years in some half a dozen States of the Union. He graduated at Hobart Free College, Geneva, New York, in 1856, and at the Theological Seminary, of Virginia, three years later. He worked as a deacon in Bradford and Sullivan counties, Pennsylvania, and Columbia county, New York. He was ordained a Presbyter in Dubuque, May, 1862, and before coming to Waverly secured the building of churches in Worthington and Independence. He was afterward an assistant minister of the Bishop's Church, at Davenport, while teaching in Griswold College there. He then resumed missionary work, and has been engaged in building churches at Decorah, Emmettsburg, and Sheldon, in Northern Iowa. He is now in the East, seeking recovery from severe illness. He was married, September 1, 1870, to Miss Harriet Boardman

Lane, daughter of the Rev. A. D. Lane, of Waterloo, New York.

Rev. Charles Stewart was born in Scotland. He studied divinity at the Bishop Seabury Seminary, in Minnesota, and Griswold Seminary, Davenport, Iowa. He remained in Waverly but a few months.

Rev. William Wright was born in London, England. He studied divinity at the Theological Seminary near Alexandria, Virginia, and was ordained in 1853. He at once went as missionary to the then "Colony of Maryland in Liberia," in Africa, remaining there until the spring of 1855. He afterward had charges in the States of Delaware and Pennsylvania and at Boston. He assumed charge of St. Andrews church, Waverly, in April 1866, resigning that charge in the year 1869. Mr. Wright was a faithful, untiring worker and won the love of the poor, and the respect of all, during the term of his ministry in Waverly. He now has charge of the work in East DesMoines, and at Ames, Iowa.

Rev. Frederick Humphrey succeeded the last named in charge of St. Andrews Parish, in 1873. He was a man of about fifty years of age, of fine presence and of extended knowledge. He was for some years a professor in schools of learning, and entered the work of the ministry late in life. His labors in Waverly were rewarded by large additions to the church membership, and he held the esteem of the whole community at the time of his resignation in April, 1877. He at present has a parish at Fairmount, Minnesota.

The present rector of St. Andrew's Parish, the Rev. Samuel Roosevelt Johnson Hoyt, is the son of Rev. Melancthon Hoyt, D. D., well known in the Episcopal Church, as the great pioneer of the church. Dr. Hoyt, a native of Connecticut, and a graduate of Yale College, completed first a course of study for the practice of law, and afterwards studied for the ministry of the Episcopal Church. He was one of two to join the first Missionary Bishop (Bishop Kemper), and to penetrate the "great west" of that day. S. R. J. Hoyt was born in Meriden, Connecticut, on the 9th day of December, 1839. He came with his father into Iowa, from Wisconsin, in 1858, and settled in Sioux City. In 1861, he entered Griswold College, Davenport, Iowa, where he completed both the collegiate and seminary courses of study. In 1866, he became assistant tutor in the preparatory department of the college, and in the following year, was made principal of that department and a member of the faculty of the college, which position he held for two years. While in this position he held mission services in West Davenport, where in 1867 he built Christ Church. He was ordained to the Diaconate in 1868, and to the office of priest in 1869. A few weeks after his second ordination, he married the daughter of Rev. Dr. W. H. Barris, one of the professors in the Theological Seminary, and in October sailed from San Francisco, California, in the steamship "China," en route for China, to which country he had accepted an appointment as missionary. Landing at Shanghai, Mr. and Mrs. Hoyt went from that place six hundred miles into the interior, up the Yang Tze Kiang, and entered upon their new life at a point about as far removed from their home and friends as this mundane sphere will permit—at Wu

Chang, the capital of the province of Hu-Pêh. Their first work was to acquire a knowledge of the language. They entered upon untried ground, and watched year after year the growth of the seed of their planting. With nothing to begin with, they finally saw two churches, two boarding schools, a day school, and a hospital, in full working order. After a residence of nearly eight years, Mr. Hoyt was obliged to resign his work in China, on account of his wife's failing health. He entered upon his duties as rector of St. Andrew's Church, on the 1st of July, 1877; but in April, 1878, returned alone to China, to hold the work of the church in WuChang until new men could reach the field and prepare themselves for their peculiarly difficult labor. St. Andrew's parish granted him a leave of absence for two years, and hence, after being gone a little more than two years, he resumed work in Waverly, in June, 1880. During Mr. Hoyt's travels, he crossed the Pacific Ocean five times, and once made the entire circuit of the earth. He visited the most important parts of Japan, both upon the coasts and in the interior, and while in China, went once as United States interpreter, with General Isaac F. Shepard, American Consul at Han How, a thousand miles up the river Yang Tze, through its magnificent gorges, over its terrific rapids, and among the peated mountains of Tze Chwän. At other times he visited the great tea fields, and the principal marts for China and porcelain ware, and, being something of an antiquarian in his tastes, spent much of his time of recreation in delving among the stores of curio shops. Some of the oldest works in bronze, copper and Chinaware in the United States were brought here by him, and he owns probably the largest and most complete collection of ancient and modern coins of China and its neighboring States, to be found in this country. In his travels, Mr. Hoyt has visited many points on the coasts of Southern China, and in India. He has seen the old cities and wonderful antiquities of Egypt, as well as the most famous cities of Italy, France and England. He has in his possession some most flattering letters of thanks and commendation from the Board of Foreign Missions, for his services during his long term of years in their field. In his present position he enjoys the confidence and hearty support of his people, and the parish, at this time of writing, is enthusiastically at work preparing to build a new and larger church edifice.

The first Methodist sermon preached on the ground where Waverly now stands, was by Rev. S. W. Ingham, Sr., at a spot a few rods northwest of where the court house now stands. This was in 1853. It is not now recalled by any one here, what the name of the circuit to which it then belonged, was. The appointments were eight weeks apart. In 1854, Rev. J. Burleigh succeeded to the charge, and during that, or the year following, the first organization was effected, being a class of which R. J. Ellsworth was the leader, the members being Mrs. Elizabeth M. Ellsworth, Alexander Buckmaster, Demas Buckingham, George Kerr, Rachel Kerr, Emily Buckmaster, William Sturdevant, George W. Baskins, Sr., Bettie Baskins, and a few others whose residences were remote. Meetings were then held in a log house which stood at a spot about two rods east of the east end of the bridge, and in the middle of what is now the street; subsequently, in the original court house building. In 1855, William Gough succeeded to the charge, and in 1856, Rev. E. D. Lamb became the pastor. The circuit appears as Janesville and Cedar Falls. During the year 1857, Rev. Mr. Lamb died at Janesville. In 1858, Rev. C. M. Sessions became the preacher in charge, while in 1859 A. N. Odell had charge, and in 1860 C. M. Sessions was re-appointed, and in 1861 and 1862 William Smith was the pastor. It was during this pastorate that the legal incorporation of the society took place, the date being April 23, 1862. The incorporate name chosen was "First Methodist Episcopal Church, in Waverly, Bremer County, Iowa." The first, or original board of trustees was Reuben J. Ellsworth, George W. Baskins, Sr., Andrew Dailey, John Glassford and Hiram Lamson. These articles of incorporation were acknowledged before E. C. Moulton, justice of the peace, May 3, 1862, and filed for record June 27th, of that year.

In 1863-4, H. S. Church was in charge. In 1865-6, F. X. Miller was pastor. At this time the charge came to be called Waverly, and had attached an out appointment or two. It was during this pastorate also that the erection of a church building began. A brick building, Romanesque, two towers, a basement, and an audience chamber.

In 1867, J. S. Anderson was appointed as the pastor. Meetings were then held in the court house, now in use.

The new building was not ready for occupancy until January 12, 1868, at which time the basement was opened for use. At that date Rev. T. M. Eddy, D. D., then editor of the *Northwestern Christian Advocate*, Chicago, Ill., preached an eloquent sermon, and with the dash and zeal for which he was characteristic, led in the work of raising funds for the enterprise. The total cost of the building to that date was $11,000, of which the people of Waverly had payed about $3,000, and the Church Extension Society of the Upper Iowa Conference $1,000, leaving over $6,000 to be raised that day. By the morning and evening effort, Dr. Eddy raised, with a subscription or two, one-half the amount believed to be adequate to liquidate all indebtedness. The outlook at that time was very hopeful.

In 1869, E. W. Jefferies became the pastor; during the year the bell was procured and placed in the tower.

In 1870, R. D. Parsons was placed in charge, and remained during that year, as also 1871 and 1872, who directed affairs towards the collecting of subscription and applying on the debtedness.

1873-4, W. A. Allen was in the pastoral charge, and at the first official meeting, steps were taken to complete the audience room; with L. M. Stephenson, E. C. Dougherty, James Jewell, Ezra White, and Roswell Allen, as the building committee, it was accomplished, much to the astonishment of all. In 1875-6, F. M. Robertson was in charge.

During the years 1877-8-9, B. C. Hammond was the pastor, and by personal effort and solicitation, he succeeded in raising *bone fide* subscriptions to pay the church indebtedness, which, for many reasons, had become a large amount—something over $3000. In 1880, J. C. Magee was assigned to the work, and is, at this writing, December, 1882, in the third year of his pastorate. During the time, the obligations pledged on the church indebtedness have been met, the Ladies Mite Society having raised over $200, to pay on a loan from the Church Extension Society, which was the last of the old debt. During this pastorate, the church steeple, which had become very frail and dangerous, was taken down, and a new and strong belfry erected, at a cost of over $500. Trustee Allen Sewell directing the matter to a successful termination. Also, an attractive fence was erected about the church lots, and a park of beautiful trees set out. This was very largely due to the energy of S. F. Baker.

The trustees of the church at present are L. L. Lush, S. H. Curtis, B. DuBois, W. P. Harris, J. C. Garner, Allen Sewell, L. M. Stephenson. Messrs. Curtis and Garner, while not members of the church, have consented for several years to act.

The board of stewards are H. S. Munger, J. F. Woodring, Allen Sewell, E. L. Smalley, Jay J. Morton, J. H. Cummins, I. S. C. Gorham, L. M. Stephenson, W. M. Barber, M. D.

Class leaders, Jos. Brown and I. S. C. Gorham.

The present membership of the church is about one hundred and eighty.

The Sabbath School numbers about one hundred and forty pupils, teachers and officers. S. F. Baker, superintendent; I. S. C. Gorham, assistant superintendent and chorister; Miss Libbie Sholes, secretary, Mrs. M. M. Faville, treasurer; J. F. Woodring, librarian; W. O. Clark, M. D., assistant librarian; Miss Nettie Woodring, organist; Miss Hattie Seaman, assistant organist.

A review of the history of the church, and a study of the causes of success, or the embarassing hindrances to greater success, would be interesting, but space forbids. Upon these historic pages there ought to appear many names of persons who have contributed to the results obtained, but who must be content with the consciousness of having performed well their part, in which it is said all the honor lies. It would be unjust, however, to omit the mention of the name of the now deceased, but highly honored William P. Harmon, the founder of the city of Waverly, who did so much in his life time to promote the interests of this society. His name appears on the memorial window of the church building, as does also that of Governor Oran Faville, a much honored member of the church, who, being deceased, is a precious memory, he having been a lifelong Methodist, and widely known in the educational circles of the church at large. His widow, Mrs. M. M. Faville, has continued to reside here, and in all ways has contributed most steadily, through the last seventeen years, to promote the interests of this church.

The following is a list of the ministers who have served the charge as presiding elders: Andrew Coleman, P. E. Brown, John T. Coleman, John Gould, D. N. Holmes, Elias Skinner, S. A. Lee, William Brush, D. D.; R. W. Keeler, D. D.; S. W. Ingham, Jr.; J. T. Crippen, and Daniel Sheffer, present incumbent.

Rev. John Calvin Magee, A. M., the present pastor of the church, was born in Centre county, Pennsylvania, October 31,

1845. His parents, David F. and Abigail Rankin Magee, removing subsequently to the western part of the State of Pennsylvania, and in the spring of 1855, they came to Iowa. Mr. Magee is of Scotish descent, from both sides of the house, though he is of the third generation, born on American soil. He is the eldest of eleven children, most of whom are living. His ancestors of both the Magee and Rankin families were strong adherents of the Presbyterian faith, though after removing to the west his parents became members of the Methodist Episcopal Church, and at the age of fifteen he also identified himself with that body, although at the time a member of a Presbyterian Sunday School (old school), uninfluenced in his choice by his parents, they leaving the matter wholly with himself. His father's family settled on a new farm in Scotch Grove, Jones county, in 1858, where he remained working on the farm in the summer and attending the district school in winter. During these years he was restless to procure as liberal an education as possible, preparatory to the christian ministry, to which he had felt himself called from earliest life. At the outbreak of the war of the rebellion, his father (true to the military instinct of the family, the great-grandfather of this sketch having died in camp as a soldier for the colonies in the Revolutionary War), was among the first to enlist to fight for the Union, and served for nearly a year and a half as a commissioned officer. John being the eldest of the family, though not yet sixteen years old, took charge of the farm with his younger brother. On the return of the father to the home, being free from the cares of the farm, he entered as a student in Lenox Collegiate Institute, at Hopkinton, Iowa, a school under the care of the Presbyterian denomination. After an academic year there, he began teaching a country school, and at the close of the term, having arrived at a suitable age, he was seized with the "war fever," and enlisted as a private soldier in Company D, Ninth Regiment, Iowa Volunteer Infantry, doing active service in the Atlanta campaign, on the march to the sea, under Sherman, and in the campaigns of the Carolinas. And, immediately after the war, was with his company on the march from Raleigh, North Carolina, to Washington, District of Columbia, where he participated in the grand review, in May 1865. Being mustered out and discharged from the service that summer, he re-entered Lenox Collegiate Institute, and remained there for a time. He afterwards attended the Upper Iowa University, at Fayette, where he formally graduated, having procured his education almost wholly by his own efforts. He subsequently received the degree of Master of Arts from this institution. He also studied theology for a time at Garrett Biblical Institute, Evanston, Illinois, He was first licensed to preach when about twenty-one years old, and did much work gratuitously as a local preacher, while a student in school and while teaching in the public schools, which he did for three years, being one year principal of a graded school. He was married in June, 1870, to Miss Jennie Cole at Fayette, Iowa, who has proven a most worthy helpmeet for him. He was admitted on trial as a traveling preacher in the Upper Iowa

Annual Conference of the M. E. Church, in September, 1870, and was in due time admitted to full connection and ordained, and has since been in pastoral charge of churches in his conference at Rockford, New Hartford, LaPorte City, Grundy Centre, Maquoketa, and, at the time of procuring the data for this sketch, is in the third year of his pastorate of the Methodist Episcopal church at Waverly, Bremer county, Iowa.

The Baptist church in Waverly, Bremer County, Iowa, was organized September 9, 1855. A preliminary meeting was held at the court house, September 8th. At this meeting, Rev. David Terry was chosen moderator, and Nathan Payton, clerk. The moderator read the article of faith and the covenant, together with a resolution on temperance and one on slavery. After a full conference and consultation, it was resolved to meet the next day and complete the organization of the church. Accordingly, the next day Elder Terry preached a sermon; text, First Timothy, 3: 15. The church, the pillar and ground of truth. Brother Beckwell made an address to the church, and gave them the hand of fellowship. The original members were seven in number—Rev. David Terry, Nathan Payton, Jane Payton, Samuel Patterson, Catherine Patterson, R. Churchill and Mrs. Oscar Burbank. Brother Coddington and wife, Miss Mary Coddington, Mrs. Emeline Stewart, were present at this meeting, and expressed their intention of uniting as soon as they could get their letters. A few meetings only were held that fall, at private houses. In March, 1856, a covenant meeting was held in the new stone school house; afterwards, they met in the court house. Brother A. S. Lawrence was the first clerk and one of the first deacons. At the same meeting, Giles Mabie was elected one of the deacons. Elder Terry was the first minister, and Rev. Austin D. Bush, first pastor, called in June, 1857, serving one year and eight months. Rev. H. H. Burrington, was called April 2, 1859, serving five years and four months. Rev. Thomas F. Thickston, called August, 1862, served two years and eight months. Rev. Alvin T. Cole, called November, 1868, served three years and one month. Rev. J. Hall was next called, and served about two years. Rev. F. A. Marsh, called September, 1872, served one year and five months. Rev. Thomas T. Thickston, re-called in 1874, remained three months. Rev. Robert Leslie, called November, 1874, served four years, nine months. Rev. Thomas Keith, called September, 1879, served one year, eight months. Rev. W. C. Pratt, called January, 1882, remained three months. Rev. William M. Simons is the present pastor.

In the fall and winter of 1857 and 1858, a house was built, which answered the double purpose of place of worship and a dwelling place for the minister. Mr. Burrington says he can speak with authority.

The church outgrew the house, and in 1867, the present house was built, 40x70 feet, costing $7,000.

The church has had, in twenty-six years, seven different pastors; 161 persons have been baptized; 265 received by letter; 426 additions; 166 dismissals by letter; 41 excluded, and 36 have died. Present membership, 171.

The First Presbyterian church of Waverly, Iowa, was organized September 15,

1856, by the Rev. S. F. Wells, missionary agent of the Presbytery of Dubuque. The organization consisted of six members—O. P. Houghawout, Harriet N. Houghawout, William G. Houghawout, George S. Mathews, Elizabeth Mathews, Esther Mathews.

Eighty-two in all, have since been added to the original number. The present membership of the church is about twenty.

The first ruling elder of this church was O. P. Houghawout. Those who have subsequently filled the office are John Elliott, George S. Dawes, Robert B. Shannon, John Findley and James P. McCord. The two last named being now the ruling elders, and also trustees by virtue of their office.

The ministers of the church have been J. D. Caldwell, 1857; John Smalley, 1858-1866; Virgil G. Sheeley, 1867-1869; James G. Patterson, 1870-1871. Since the resignation of Mr. Patterson, the pulpit has been vacant.

For a time the church held its meetings in a stone school house, standing near the court house square. The next place of meeting was Union hall, a room in the second story of a building diagonally across the street from the Bremer House. In 1866, the congregation resolved to erect a house of worship. Some money has been raised for this purpose, at a fair held in the court house. The building, which is of brick, 28 feet by 42, cost about $2,000, in addition to the labor and materials contributed by the people.

A Sabbath School was established and kept up for two or three years, during the earlier part of Mr. Smalley's ministry. Its sessions were held in the stone school house. J. P. McCord was the superintendent.

A Presbyterian Sabbath School was established again, soon after the settlement of Mr. Sheeley, and he was its first superintendent. It grew to a membership of more than a hundred. It was discontinued after the resignation of Mr. Patterson.

The Sabbath School now in existence in this church, was organized in December, 1879. Mrs. Mary B. Smalley is the superintendent, and J. P. McCord, assistant superintendent. There are on its roll about forty names.

On Sunday, January 15, 1865, a meeting of persons desirous of forming a Congregational Church was held at the court house in Waverly, Dr. Guernsey, of Dubuque, presiding as chairman. It was resolved, that, in the opinion of the meeting, the time had come when a Congregational Church should be organized in the community, and that several persons had expressed themselves as desirous of uniting in such an organization. W. H. Jay, W. B. Goodhue and Thomas Downing were appointed a committee to prepare rules for the church. The following resolution was adopted:

Resolved, That we engage in this enterprise with feeling of entire kindness towards existing churches in this place, and with the simple purpose and desire to do our part in what *seems* to *us* the best and most efficient way for the furtherance of the Redeemer's Kingdom.

The council called to recognize this church, met May 5, 1865, at the Episcopal Church. There were present from Congregational Church in Dubuque, Rev. J. Guernsey, delegate; Waterloo, Bro. J. A.

Cobb; Cedar Falls, Rev. I. B. Fifield, pastor, and Bro. J. Porter, delegate; Bradford, Rev. J. K. Nutting, pastor, and J. Smith, delegate; Charles City, Rev. D. Bodwell, pastor.

The services were held at the court house, at 7:30 P. M., when the council proceeded to recognize the church. The sermon was preached by Rev. J. Guernsey, D. D., of Dubuque. W. H. Jay and G. H. Curtis were subsequently elected deacons.

Steps were taken to erect a house of worship, which was completed and dedicated February 4, 1866, Rev. Lyman Whiting, of Dubuque, officiating.

Rev. E. L. Palmer was called as the first pastor, by unanimous vote of the church, March 2, 1865. He was succeeded by Rev. M. K. Cross, who began his labors October 24, 1867, remaining until December 31, 1870, when he resigned. Rev. W. H. Rice was then called, July 24, 1871, and served until May 5, 1872, when he resigned, on account of failing health. September 2, 1872, Rev. J. G. Spencer was called. He remained until July 5, 1874. Rev. R. M. O'Neil was his successor, beginning his labors November 3, 1874. He was succeeded by Rev. G. R. Ransom, who remained about four years, when Rev. S. M. Case, the present pastor, was called.

The original members of the church were: Sarah Jay, James W. Jay, Sarah B. Morse, George H. Curtis, Eliza W. Williams, Lydia Briggs, William B. Goodhue, Mary H. Goodhue, Thomas Downing, Jane Downing, Louisa M. Fiske, Laura M. Riggs, Emmons Johnson, Lucy Johnson, Emily A. Strong, Rev. E. S. Palmer, Maria B. Palmer, Mrs. E. A. Brown, Emma Case, Mrs. A. C. Moulton, Mary Williams, Addie Williams and H. C. S. Weldon.

The present officers of the church are: Thomas Downing, Caleb Morse, H. N Dubois, deacons; H. S. Burr, Mr. Marsh and O. A. Strong, trustees; M. F. Spalding, treasurer; O. A. Strong, secretary. The Sabbath School has a general attendance of eighty-five.

The first meetings of the Evangelical Association were held at private houses and in the court house. The first sermon was preached by Rev. John Schmidt, now of Minnesota. In 1871, the congregation built a house of worship on the west side of the river, at a cost of $2,000. The church will seat, comfortably, 200. There is at present a membership of about forty-five. The trustees are: John Wile, James Bucher; steward, John Schmidt. Their present pastor is Rev. J. F. Berner; class leader, James Ebly. The original members of this congregation were: F. Nidemeir and wife, J. Wagner and wife, J. Haase and wife, C. Stamm and wife, T. Pattas and wife, Jacob Appley and wife, and a Mrs. Miller.

The first Catholic families who settled in the vicinity of Waverly were: John J. Smith, W. O. Smith and family, L. Selbig and family, Charles Fosselmann and family, Mrs. Tyrrell, mother of Mrs. Cavanaugh; Nicholas Cavanaugh and family, and Fred Cretzmeyer. The first priest was Father Tracy. The church was organized in October, 1856, and soon after arrangements were made for the erection of a church edifice. Some time in the fall of 1868, their brick church building was completed. at a cost of $6,000.

The first regular priest was Father John Shields, who took an active interest in building up the church.

There is at present a membership of forty families, who support the church.

Father Coyle has charge of the congregation at present.

They have a Sabbath School in connection with the church, Father Coyle superintendent, with an average attendance of about forty.

EDUCATIONAL.

The first school taught in Waverly was in 1854, by Charles Ensign, now of Butler county.

The first school house was erected in Ward No. 1, in 1855, and was a two story stone building. It was torn down years ago.

In the spring of 1858, the township of Washington was organized as a district, and on the 15th of May of that year, the first meeting of directors was held. The board was called to order by Edward Tyrrell, president, and roll shows that the following directors were present: Butler S. Freeman, S. H. Curtis, Samuel Patterson and Thomas Glenn. It was ordered that B. S. Freeman be authorized to hire Miss H. F. Curtis as teacher. B. F. Perkins was clerk of the board at this time.

At the next meeting, B. W. Johnson was appointed secretary, to fill the vacancy occasioned by the resignation of Perkins, and E. C. Moulton was chosen permanent secretary.

Waverly continued as a part of the district township until 1866, when it was organized as an independent district. The first meeting of the board of directors for the independent district was held on the 16th day of April, 1866. There were present, Rev. T. F. Thickston, in the chair; Rev. John Stone, David Clark and J. K. L. Maynard. On motion, George W. Ruddick was appointed secretary in place of Louis Case, who refused to qualify. The members who were not present were N. P. Ellis, president, and E. Johnson, treasurer. At a meeting held shortly afterwards, it was resolved that "the directors be appointed a committee to employ teachers, grade the schools, and to introduce such text books as they might think for the best interest of the schools." Also, that the wages of male teachers be $45 per month, and female, $35, for the primary schools.

In 1868, the school houses in the Third and Fourth Wards were erected, and orders were drawn to the amount of $3,500.

In the spring of 1871 the city was divided into five wards, and in this shape it still remains. Wards No. 1 and 4 are on the east side of the river, the former on the north, and the latter on the south side of Bremer Avenue. On the west side of the river are wards No. 2 and 3, the former on the north, and the latter on south side of the same avenue. No. 5 is beyond these, near the depot. There are now five buildings for school purposes, one in each of the wards, except No. 5, and including the high school building. The latter was erected in ward 3, in 1872-3, at a cost of $22,000. It is an elegant, three-story brick.

In the five buildings there are twelve schools, named as follows: First Ward, lower room, Washington school; upper room, Jefferson school; Second Ward, lower room, Franklin school; upper room,

Garfield school; Third Ward, lower room, Webster school; upper room, Sumner school; Fourth Ward, lower room, Lincoln school; upper room, Adams school; first grammar room, Whittier school; second grammar room, Longfellow school; third grammar room, Taylor school; fourth grammar room, Bryant school; High school, Irving school.

There are fifteen teachers employed, three males, and twelve females. The number of pupils in the city school, exclusive of High school, is 621.

The total number of children attending all the schools in September, 1882, was 811, of which 349 were boys and 417 girls. The average cost of tuition per month, for each scholar, is $1.28. The total value of school property in the city is $40.000. The number of volumes in the library is 340. Three terms, of thirteen weeks, are held each year. In January, 1883, the following named comprise the corps of teachers: W. F. Cramer, superintendent of city schools, and principal of High school; G. G. Sampson, assistant principal; grammar grades, Miss Kate Webster, Miss Lottie Smilie, Miss Sarah Cadwallader, Mrs. Maggie J. White; primary, Miss Emma Smith, Miss Anna Smith, Miss Julia Cooper, Miss Jennie Barker, Miss Clara Hazlet, Miss Mary L. Barker and Miss Ettie Palmer. The city superintendents have been, in order: W. B. Waterbury, C. C. Kuepper, D. C. Chamberlin, H. L. Grant and W. F. Cramer. The present superintendent, Mr. Cramer, came to Waverly, in 1880, resigning his position as principal of the High school in Cedar Falls, where he had been for a year.

The present school board is composed of the following named gentleman: W. R. Bowman, president, term expires in March, 1883; W. R. Knight, term expires March, 1883; C. H. Cooper, term expires March, 1884; H. H. Gray, term expires March, 1884; H. S. Munger, term expires March, 1885; L. L. Lush, term expires March, 1885. secretary, A. H. McCracken; treasurer, H. S. Burr.

Non-resident children may be admitted to the Waverly public schools, when there are vacant seats, by paying the following rates, in advance, to the treasurer: ward schools and grammar school, per term, four dollars; high school, five dollars.

There was also established, some years since, a German Lutheran College. They have a good building, and the institution promises something for the future; but, as yet, is in its infancy.

F. Eichler, a teacher in the German college of Waverly, was born on the 22d day of January, 1855, in Hungary, Austria. When he was twelve years old his parents emigrated to the United States, locating in Cairo, Illinois. Two years later, they removed to St. Louis, Missouri, and, at the expiration of eight years, to San Francisco, California, where they at present reside. The subject of this sketch attended, and was confirmed at the German Evangelical School, of Cario. Subsequently, he removed to Clayton county, Iowa, and thence to Galena, Illinois, where, for four years, he attended an Evangelical Lutheran College. He then returned to Clayton county, and afterwards, attended a theological seminary, and in 1875, was ordained. His first call was from Dixon, Illinois, and there he preached to a small congregation and also taught school. In 1878, he located in Jackson county, Iowa, where he taught music and English for about one year, and then settled in Waverly, Bremer county, being employed in the German college. Mr. Eichler was married in 1879, to Anna E. Schwarz, born in Buffalo, New York. One child—Alfred—brightens their home.

HARLINGTON CEMETERY.

This city of the dead is situated on the south half of the southwest quarter of section 2, township 91, range 14, west of the fifth principal meridian, the west line being a direct continuation of West Water street. The south line being the section line between section 2 and 11 in said township. It is beautifully laid out, with circular drives fourteen feet wide. The work of platting was done by Mr. H. S. Hoover, by direction of H. H. Conse and Caroline Conse, his wife, who were the owners of the property, and was recorded on the 30th day of October, 1865.

SOCIETIES.

Tyrrell Lodge, No. 116, A. F. and A. M., was instituted June 2, 1858, with the following named officers and Master Masons: Thos. Downing, W. M.; G. C. Wright, S. W.; W. W. Brown, J. W.; Theodore Hazlett, Treasurer; Geo. W. Maxfield, Secretary; L. B. Ostrander, Sen. D.; Edward Tyrrell, Jr. D.; Nicholas Tyrrell, Tyler. J. S. Harris, Wm. Battams, John Tyrrell, H. F. Beebe, Wm. B. Hamilton, Geo. W. Briggs, Walter Wood, W. P. Harmon, Theodore Hullman, Jas. P. Olds, S. H. Curtis, A. P. Goddard, John Ranyan, Geo. W. LeValley, P. B. Foster, S. F. Beebe, D. M. Cool. No lodge in the State has probably had a more prosperous existence than Tyrrell Lodge. Composed, as it has been, of the best men in Waverly, it has experienced none of the difficulties encountered by many societies. The members of the order here are earnest and enthusiastic in the work, and know how to extend a brotherly hand to those needing assistance. The following named have served as Masters of the lodge since its organization: Thomas Downing, 1858 –1865; G. W. Ruddick, 1866; W. V. Lucas, 1867–1873; J. K. L. Maynard, 1874; D. C. Chamberlin, 1875 ; W. V. Lucas, 1876 ; C. H. Cooper, 1877, to the present time. Its present officers are: C. H. Cooper, W. M.; A. H. McCracken, S. W.; A. J. Bessmer, J. W.; L. L. Lush, Treasurer; F .H. Schlutsmeyer, Secretary; Wm. Hathaway, S. D.; Benjamin Speaker, J. D.; J. M. Andrews, Tyler. The present membership of the lodge is 113.

Nicholas Tyrrell, to honor whom the lodge was named, was born in Westmeade county, Ireland, in 1776, where he grew to manhood, learning the trade of a mason. He followed this business, in his native county, until he was 22 years of age, when he came to America, and settled in New York. Here he continued at his trade until 1841, when he removed to McHenry county, Illinois, where he resided until 1857, when he came to Iowa, and settled in Washington township, buying a large tract of land. He lived on his land, a greater part of the time, until the death of his wife, in 1862. When not engaged in farm work, he worked at his trade of mason. Mr. Tyrrell was married about 1805, to Miss Ann Highland. When quite a young man, he joined the Masonic fraternity, and was strongly attached to the order. When the lodge was started at Waverly, Mr. Tyrrell being the oldest of the charter members, was honored by having it named after him, and probably no man in Bremer county, did more for Tyrrell lodge than did Nicholas Tyrrell. His whole heart and soul was wrapped up in Free-masonry, and he spent much of his time and money for the advancement of the cause, and at the time of his death, he willed to the lodge a tract of land near Waverly, valued at about $1,600, for the purpose of building a lodge room. Mr. Tyrrell died in 1872, at the ripe old age of 96 years. Three score years and ten of that time he was a member of the Masonic fraternity, and a truer or more faithful man than "Father Tyrrell" never bowed at the altar of Free-masonry; and when, by old age, he was taken away, he was buried with Masonic honors, and probably the largest Masonic funeral ever held in Bremer county, was held over the remains of "Father Tyrrell."

There is also a flourishing Chapter in Waverly—Jethro Chapter, No. 24. It was first organized under dispensation, with the following named officers:

T. Downing, H. P.; G. C. Wright, K.; N. Tyrrell, S.; G. W. Maxfield, Sec.; G. W. Maxfield, C. H.; W. P. Harmon, P. S.; H. F. Beebe, R. A. C.; S. B. Wheeler, M. 3d V.; J. P. Harris, M. 2d V.; J. Gould, M. 1st V.; J. Tyrrell, G.

The following named were the first officers under the charter:

T. Downing, H. P.; G. C. Wright, K.; N. Tyrrell, S.; H. F. Beebe, Treasurer; G. W. Maxfield, Secretary; W. P. Harmon, C. of H.; G. W. Maxfield, P. S.; H. F. Beebe, R. A. C.; L. J. Thomas, M. 3d V.; J. Gould, M. 2d V.; J. Tyrrell, M. 1st V.; W. Wood, Guard.

Herdman Lodge, No. 74, K. of P., was instituted April 27, 1882, by E. H. Hibben, G. C., with the following named as charter members:

J. M. Andrews, J. B. Barber, C. H. Cooper, E. C. Cooper, G. N. Cooke, W. H. Coats, W. S. Chapman, F. M. Downing, W. A. Douglas, E. A. Dawson, E. C. Dennis, Henry Eifert, G. M. Foster, W. R. Knight, Henry Kessler, Ephraim Kinne, Frank A. Lee, H. L. Mosher, C. W. Mantor, C. Neuhaus, W. T. Rogers, W. E. Spencer, Adolf Schwarz, John Sager, C. D. B. Sitzer, W. H. Tyrrell, H. O. Thies, John Warner, Ed. Wearne, C. H. Wilcox, and J. B. York.

The officers for the first term were: Henry Eifert, P. C., and Rep. Grand Lodge; Ephraim Kinne, C.C.; H. L. Mosher, V. C.; W. R. Knight, P.; F. M. Downing, M. of F.; G. M. Foster, M. of E.; Frank A. Lee, K. of R. and S.; W. E. Spencer, M. at A.; Henry Kessler, I. G.; J. M. Andrews, O. G.

Ephraim Kinne served as C. C., from April 27, 1882, to July 1, 1882; H. L. Mosher, from July 1, 1882, to January 1, 1883.

There have been no deaths since organization.

Thirty-two is the total membership since organization, which is also the present membership.

The lodge has been successful, and its present condition is flourishing.

For a number of years there was an organization of Odd Fellows in Waverly, but, from lack of interest, it was finally abandoned.

OPERA HOUSE.

A local paper thus speaks of the Opera House: "The enterprise of a town is manifest in various ways. When we see a city with fine residences, beautiful lawns, substantial churches and school edifices, handsome business houses, shaded streets and numerous industries, we are led to believe, and truly, that it is peopled with an enterprising class of citizens.

"In Waverly there are many beautiful and commendable fixtures, many evidences of thrift and progress, but, in nothing is the element more clearly defined than in the presence of its magnificent Opera House. That *is* magnificent for a town of this size.

"Many of the first-class cities of the country cannot boast of so good a one. This house belongs to a joint stock company, and is largely the property of the city. The official management of the house is vested as follows: President, S. R. Hunt; secretary, J. H. Bowman. The building is of brick, 110 feet in length by 44 in width, embracing an auditorium, with gallery, capable of accommodating 800 people.

"In the basement is a large hall, suitable for festivals or dancing parties, and this department is supplied with a kitchen and all the desirable appliances for a complete cookery. The front basement is used by the city as council room, &c. The interior is neatly frescoed and ornamented; the stage is 22x44, is supplied with two elegant drop curtains, sliding scenery, and large enough for the presentation of any ordinary drama. Dressing-rooms, cloak-rooms, &c., are all provided. The entire building is illuminated with gas, and all the modern improvements found in the best halls of the country, are utilized here. This is a feature of which Waverly may well feel proud, and, to the notice of the amusement fraternity we would especially commend it. The location is favorable and the terms of the hall of the most reasonable character."

BIOGRAPHICAL.

Following will be found sketches of many of the prominent citizens of Waverly:

Among the early settlers of Bremer county we find Thomas Tyrrell, who was born in Montreal, Canada, September 25, 1833. Shortly after his birth, the family removed to Albany county, New York, and seven or eight years later, to McHenry county, Illinois. At the time of their settlement in the last named State, it was one vast prairie, without a single railroad traversing it, nor a bridge spanning any of its streams. In 1853 Mr. Tyrrell, senior, came to Bremer county, Iowa, where he purchased 360 acres of land and settled. Thomas learned the trade of a stone-mason from his father, and has continued to follow that occupation through life. In 1853 he removed to Cedar Rapids, Iowa, and while there, became acquainted with, and married Miss Mary J. Babbitt, who was born in Madison county, New York, June 24, 1836. Their marriage took place in 1855, and the same year they came to Bremer county, where they have since resided. Four children blessed the union, three of whom are now living—Alice, Emma and

NICHOLAS TYRRELL.

David. Mr. Tyrrell's father organized the Masonic lodge that bears his name.

A. J. Case, one of Bremer county's pioneers, was born in Chautauqua county, New York, September 2, 1824. When a boy of fourteen years, he, with his parents' consent, started in life for himself, by working out at so much a month, and upon reaching his majority, had twenty-five dollars in his pocket. In 1845, he emigrated to Kane county, Illinois, where he acted in a capacity of traveling agent for a wholesale house. He was joined in wedlock, in January of the year 1848, with Miss Julia A. Morris, of Brooklyn, who was born June 15, 1828. Five children have blessed the marriage, three of whom are now living—Oscar F., Prentice A. and W. G. During the spring of 1855, Mr. Case and family came through by team, to Butler county, where he entered 160 acres of government land, which he immediately began improving. In 1857, the water became so high that it submerged his farm, and therefore, the following year he removed to Waverly and embarked in the sewing machine business, during the first few years traveling on foot, and selling a hand machine. Canvassing the machine business over in his own mind, he came to the conclusion that the "Singer" was the best machine. He therefore, in 1861, made arrangements for handling that make, since which time, over five thousand have passed through his hands, and he has paid out to that company over $305,000. In 1878, the Singer Sewing Machine Company appointed him manager of a branch office, and he, at the present time, has five counties under his charge. Mr. Case has had many of the county and town offices offered him, but has never accepted any, excepting that of councilman for one term.

J. Q. A. Russell, a native of Chautauqua county, New York, was born February 17, 1824. He was married in 1855, to Miss Emity J. Stroud, who was born in Geauga county, Ohio, in 1835. Seven children were born to them, six of whom are now living: George H., Hiram J., Sarah J., Arthur W., Walter J. and Laura A. In 1862, Mr. Russell removed from Ohio to Hardin county, Iowa, and in the spring of the following year located in Waterloo, thence, in the fall to Waverly, Bremer county, where he erected his present foundry building, and let us add, that it is the only one in the town. He has followed that business since 1855, first embarking in it at Bloomfield, Trumbull county, Ohio. Mr. Russell's father was one of the pioneers of Sheboygan county, Wisconsin.

Keeler Norris, one of Waverly's enterprising business men, was born in Orange county, New York, August 23, 1820, and is a son of Stephen and Nancy (Hottslander) Norris. His mother was a native of Orange county, and was born in 1792. His father was born in the State of Connecticut, June 20, 1793, and was a soldier in the War of 1812, participating in the siege of New York. Two years after Keeler's birth, the family removed to Tompkins county, New York, and there his mother died, a few years later. When a young man, Mr. Norris, senior, was very anxious to possess a certain beautiful farm in Orange county, therefore, in later years, he returned to that county and became its owner. His second marriage was with Sarah Burr, who has borne him three children, two of whom are now living. He was a member of the Congregational Church, and was the leading spirit in the building of Grotton Seminary, of which he was a stockholder and also a trustee, for many years. The subject of this sketch was married December 23, 1847, to Miss C. J. Schoonmaker, a native of Orange county, New York, born March 5, 1824. Seven children have blessed the union, six of whom are now living—Arabella, wife of John Norman, train dispatcher of Waterloo; Henrietta, Fannie, Lizzie, William and Charles A. Mr. Norris removed to Kane county, Illinois, in 1855, and thence, in 1861, to Cedar Falls, Iowa. In 1863, he settled in Waverly, where he has been engaged in contracting. In politics he is a greenbacker, and since coming west, has held several local offices.

A. S. Mores was born in Oneida county, New York, July 13, 1826. He was left an orphan when but a mere boy, both of his parents dying in his native county. But being left alone in the world, at this tender age, he was by no means discouraged, for, having a strong will, he determined to succeed in the world, let what might come. He at once commenced to work on a farm, at the same time struggling to gain an education. But advantages for education, in those days, were so meagre that he could supply himself with only a limited common school education, but this, with his natural ability for business, has made him a thorough-going business man. He continued to reside in his native county until 1855, following farming, carpenter work, and, in fact, anything that he could lay his hands on, to earn an honest dollar, and when he turned his face westward, he was possessed of a snug little property, all earned by the sweat of his own brow. In the spring of 1855, he came to Iowa and settled in Waverly, and commenced a business career that has proved to be very successful. Mr. Mores was first engaged in the saw mill business, and in 1856, engaged in the cabinet business, his being the first business of the kind ever established in the county; this he continued to run, in connection with his saw mill, until 1863. In 1870, he bought and remodeled the steam saw mill, which he continued to run until 1879, when he sold out. Previous to this, or in 1863, he commenced to buy land in Bremer county; his first purchase was 181 acres adjoining the plat, to this he has added from time to time, until now, he, in connection with his brother, owns 1,500 acres in this county, much of which is under a good state of cultivation. Since he sold his business interest in Waverly, he has devoted much of his time to superintending his large farm; aside from his landed interests, he owns a large amount of valuable property in the city of Waverly, including his pleasant home "on the hill." Truly it may be said of Mr. Mores, that he has been identified with the interest of Wavely, in Bremer county, from its infancy to the present time, and is considered as one of its most prosperous and trusted citizens. In politics, Mr. Mores has always been a strong democrat; he has also always been a strong supporter of the temperance cause, having taken an active part in the prohibitory question during the campaign of 1882. In 1861, he was married to Miss Jane Crieghton, who was born in Franklin county, Ohio, in 1830. They have seven children—Effie, Rosa, Hattie, Alta, Dacy, Jason and Willie. Mr. and Mrs. Mores are both active members of the Baptist Church.

E. F. Taber, one of the pioneers of Bremer county, was born in Cayuga county, New York, June 16, 1822. His early life was passed on a farm; but, at the age of seventeen, he clerked for a short time in a store of general merchandise. In 1844, he removed to Jackson, Michigan, and thence, the following spring, to the town of Marshall. He was married, in Branch county, in 1847, to Lydia A. Jeffery, a native of Spencerport, New York. Shortly after, he emigrated to Port Washington, Wisconsin, where he engaged in hotel-keeping and farming. During his residence in Wisconsin, Mr. Taber was postmaster for eight years, receiving his appointment in 1848. In 1855, he came to Bremer county, Iowa, and entered some land. Three years later—in 1858—he removed his family to this county. At the time of his settlement here, the country schools were so few in number, and situated so far from his residence, that he finally traded his farm for town property, in order that his children might have better educational advantages. Mr. Taber was elected the first city treasurer of Waverly. He is one of the oldest Odd Fellows in the northwest, having been a member for thirty-five years. He is a brewer, and has been in that business for the past sixteen years. His wife bore him six children, four of whom are now living —Albert W., George E., Frank S., and Mary. Mrs. Taber died, March 1, 1863..

Austin S. Lawrence, who ranks among the old settlers of Bremer county, is a native of Onondago county, New York, born March 16, 1814. He is a son of John and Lydia (Sweet) Lawrence, the former being of English descent, and the latter, a native of New York. Austin S. was the fourth child of a family of eleven children. His early life was passed on a farm, and his education was obtained in the public schools. When eighteen years of age, he learned the tailors' trade and continued to follow that occupation until his health failed to such an extent that he was obliged to abandon it for some branch of trade less confining. In January, of 1836, his marriage with Miss Betsy Hamilton occurred. She was born June 22, 1812. Five children were given them, three of whom are now living. In 1842 the family emigrated to Boone county, Illinois, and there remained until 1856. During the spring of that year, they removed to Waverly, Bremer county, Iowa, which still continues to be their home. Mr. Lawrence brought with him a sack of goods, which he placed in a store-room, and began selling. In the spring of 1856, he, in company with Giles Mabie, purchased a stock of goods of Harmon & Hamilton; continuing business under the firm name of Lawrence & Mabie, until the following winter. The subject of this sketch has been a member of the Baptist Church since 1831, nearly fifty-two years. Their youngest son, John H., was killed in Texas, in 1876, by a band of desperadoes, because of his northern birth and politics.

Daniel Dean, a liveryman of Waverly, was born in Otsego county, New York, July 7, 1836. He was reared, and also received his education in his native county. In 1852, he emigrated to McHenry county, Illinois. Four years later, he came to

Waverly, but did not immediately locate; first, spending some time looking over the northwest. Subsequently, he engaged in speculating in land and horses. He brought the first plows to the county that were sold in this market. In 1875, he was married to Miss Lucretia D., daughter of Eli Eggleston, who bore him three children—Harry, William and Silas. Mr. Dean is at present engaged in the livery business, the firm being Dean & Jewell, and they keep a stable of twelve horses, with first class turn-outs. He takes an active part in the politics of his county, always supporting the best man. During the years of 1856-7-8, he was deputy sheriff under James Ellis.

George W. LeVally, was born in Waterbury, Connecticut, in 1818. In 1822, he removed with his family to Lockport, New York, where he resided until 1850. At that date he removed to the state of Illinois, and three years later, went to California, where he was engaged in the nursery business. In 1856, he returned to New York, and in the same year, settled in Waverly, Bremer county, Iowa, where he became one of the founders of the town. He visited California three times during his life, principally for the sake of his health. Mr. LeVally was married in 1845, to Miss M. Norris, a daughter of Samuel Norris, of Connecticut. She was born in Steuben county, New York, during October, of 1820. Four children were born to them—George W., Winfield Scott, Eva J., wife of S. F. Baker, of Waverly, and Vacenia J., wife of Benjamin Chrisley, of Batavia, New York. He departed this life March 7, 1877.

James P. McCord, an early settler of Bremer county, is a native of Duchess county, New York, and was born October 25, 1812. He is a son of John I. and Maria (Voorhees) McCord, the latter being a native of Duchess county, and of Scotch-Irish descent. James P. obtained his education in the common schools, finishing it with a three years' course at the Whitesborough High school. In 1848, he was united in marriage with Miss Julia Woodworth, who was born in Rockland county, New York, on the 9th day of April, 1816, and is a daughter of John and Elnore Woodworth. One child blessed the union—Dr. Eugene W. McCord, who is now practicing medicine in Nebraska, and is also associated with the Jasper County *News*. In the spring of 1857, the subject of this sketch emigrated to Bremer county, Iowa, locating in Polk township, where he remained one year engaged in farming, and then settled in Waverly, where he has since resided. His life has been passed almost wholly in teaching and farming. Mr. McCord has written many articles for publication in various papers and magazines, and both his prose and poetry contain some very fine thoughts which are expressed in beautiful and graceful language.

E. A. Woodruff, an early settler of Bremer county, was born in Duchess county, New York, July 16, 1820. When he was five years old, the family removed to Bradford county, Pennsylvania. In 1845, his parents emigrated to Illinois, or rather they started, but his father died on the way, leaving his mother to enter that state alone. The subject of this sketch obtained his education in the common schools, and when eighteen years old, removed to the State of Illinois. During the winters of 1839 and 1840, he formed one of a corps of engineers, who were surveying out railroads. In 1843 he was united in marriage with Miss Cynthia A. Hammond, a native of Jefferson county, New York. Nine children were born unto them, eight of whom lived to reach their majority. In 1854, Mr. Woodruff came to Bremer county, Iowa, and after spending some time in looking up a good location, finally settled in Waverly, and in 1856, removed his family here. During the same year, he opened a drug store, which was the first one in the place. In the fall of 1881, he made a trip to the Pacific coast, returning, the following spring.

William Smith, one of Bremer county's enterprising business men, was born in Oneida county, New York, April 18, 1809. His education was partially obtained in the common schools; but principally, he owes the knowledge he possesses to his own efforts, during his leisure moments through life. When twenty-one years of age his health failed to such an extent that he was obliged to give up occupations requiring hard manual labor. He therefore embarked in the mercantile trade, and at the same time operated an ashery. At the end of three years, Mr. Smith sold out and became engaged in farming. In 1836, he married Miss Rhoda Ward, a native of New York State, who bore him one child,—William W., now located at Hartford, Butler county, Iowa,—and died in January, 1838. He again married, choosing as a helpmeet, Miss Eliza C. Frost. In 1853 the subject of this sketch came to Bremer county, Iowa, and purchased a large tract of land. He, however, did not move his family here until the spring of 1860. At present he owns 1,522 acres of land in the counties of Butler and Bremer, besides his town property.

M. S. Spalding was born in Cayuga county, New York, October 30, 1832, and is a son of David and Harriet (Fuller) Spalding. He was reared on a farm, and received an education in the public schools of his native State. In 1857 he removed his family to Bremer county, Iowa, settling in Waverly, where he has since resided. During 1860, he was joined in wedlock with Miss Mary Terry, a native of Wisconsin. She bore him three children—Florence, Farry and Mary—and died in 1869. Subsequently, Mr. Spalding married Miss Lucia Rhodes, a native of New York. One child, a son, has been born to them. Mr. and Mrs. Spalding are members of, and earnest workers in, the Congregational church.

Francis Smilie, a respected citizen of Waverly, was born in Cambridge, Lamoille county, Vermont, on the 20th day of November, 1817. He received an excellent education in the different institutions of learning in that section of the country, and was married June 1, 1845; to Miss Mary A. Perry, a daughter of Uri and Aroxa (Reynolds) Perry. Eight children were born to them, four of whom are now living—Fannie A., wife of H. S. Burr of Waverly, Clara L., Annie Laurie and Earl M. In the fall of 1868, the family removed from their home in Vermont, to Waverly, Iowa, where they at present reside. Mr. Smilie's father, the Honorable Nathan Smilie, was born in Harrisville, Massachusetts, January 29, 1787. He received an academic education at Atkinson Academy, and when twenty-five years of age, removed to Galaway, in Northern New York, and thence, the following year to Cambridge Vermont. October 31, 1815, he was joined in the holy bonds of matrimony with Miss Esther Green, of Cambridge. After his marriage Mr. Smilie turned his attention to mercantile pursuits, following that branch of business for many years with good success. Later in life he devoted his time to agriculture, having become, during his business career, an extensive land owner. In 1825 he was elected to the State legislature, and for fourteen years, with the exception of two, continued a member of that body, being nine years in the House and three years in the Senate. It was there that he distinguished himself as an able debater, as a clear, original and profound thinker, and, as a statesman of incorruptible integrity. The claims of education always engaged his most earnest attention and he never failed in using his power to promote its advancement. In 1839 he was the democratic candidate for governor of Vermont, and was again nominated the following year. In 1840 there was no election of the people, consequently Mr. Smilie was defeated in the legislature. He died in Cambridge, Vermont, August 12, 1862.

William H. Mores was born in Oneida county, New York, on the 8th day of April, 1824. His parents being poor, he was bound out to a man by the name of Hale, who nearly starved him. When ten years old, he went to Oraskiny, New York, where he was employed in a woolen mill, receiving twelve shillings per week, the first year, and in the meantime worked over time to earn his clothing. The second year he went into the weave room, where he received three dollars per week, and was afterwards promoted to superintendent of the weave room, having charge of 800 employes. His health failing, he left the mill and went into a grist mill, remaining one year. About this time he commenced to learn the carpenter trade. He continued in this business about one year and a half, when he went to Cleveland, Ohio. He then went to work for John Remington, and afterwards formed a partnership with him and built the large railroad shops at Rome. After finishing the shop he went to Williamsburg, New York, where he had charge of a gang of men for F. B. Furguson, where he remained two years. In 1853, he went to Indiana, to erect some buildings for Alexander Kent, who there owned a large tract of land. The men under his charge took the fever so that he was compelled to return to Rome. In the spring of 1855, he came to Waverly, where he followed his trade a short time, and soon after embarked in the manufacture of furniture, which business he followed for nine years. In the meantime, in company with his brother, he purchased the saw mill. He sold his furniture business and purchased a large tract of land near Waverly. He and his brother have 1,840 acres of land. In 1875, he married Miss S. S. Couch, the widow of Henry Curtis, of Waverly.

Allen Sewell, an early settler of Bremer county, is a native of Pike county, Ohio, and was born May 9, 1830. His early education was obtained in a log school house, and to reach it, he was obliged to travel three miles through the forest. At a later period he attended the Asbury University, and gained while there, an excellent education. March 18, 1852, he was joined in the holy bonds of matrimony with Miss Lydia E Mullens, a daughter of John H. Mullens, of Indiana. They have one son, R. H. During the summer of 1852, Mr. Sewell came to Bremer county, Iowa, locating in Jackson township. After remaining here some little time, he returned to his home in the State of Indiana, and the following year, removed his family here. The subject of this sketch, came to Jackson township in limited circumstances, but instead of sitting down to build air castles, he went to work, and is now the possessor of a fine property, and is looked upon as one of Bremer county's good business men. For the past twenty-two years he has bought and shipped stock, in connection with farming. Himself and wife are members of the Methodist church of Waverly.

James W. Wood was born in Athol, Warren county, New York, August 29, 1824. When a young man he emigrated west, and while on his way, fell in company with Joseph W. Willis and family, who were on their way to Iowa. He continued with the family, and upon reaching Delaware county was married, July 4, 1851, to Miss Alma Willis, the daughter of his fellow traveler. Shortly after, he with his bride, located in Janesville, Bremer county. One day while working on a building in that town, he fell, breaking his ankle, which afterwards necessitated the amputation of his foot. In 1854, he settled in Waverly and began manufacturing shingles. Later, he engaged in various pursuits. Mr. Wood was one of the first county commissioners of Bremer county, serving with Judge Russell and W. P. Harmon. He died at his residence, in Waverly, September 26, 1862, and was missed and mourned by a large circle of friends. Of the four children born to Mr. and Mrs. Wood, but one—Theon W.—is now living.

Austin Runyard, one of the early settlers of Bremer county, was born in Dorsetshire, England, July 4, 1831. He emigrated to the United States, and soon after landing upon this soil, located in Rockford, Winnebago county, Illinois, and began working at his trade—wagon-making. He afterward came to Bremer county, Iowa, and settled in Waverly, opening the second wagon shop in the town. In 1852, he was united in marriage with Miss Jane Simmondson, who bore him eight children, seven of whom are now living—Edwin J., Clement, Austin, Elizabeth, Emily, Alice, and Mary. Mr. Runyard has been identified with the county for a number of years, and has taken a great interest in its settlement, and the building up of its towns and villages.

J. F. Brown was born in Nicholas, Tioga county, New York, December 20, 1830. He was united in marriage with Miss Elizabeth A. Goodyear, of Cayuga county, New York, August 23, 1855, and the same year, removed to the State of Illinois. During the spring of 1861, he came, with his family, to Waverly, Iowa, and continued to reside here, with the exception of seven years spent in Huntsville, Alabama, until his death. He erected, on what is known as "cheap corner," one of the first brick buildings of Waverly, and, at its completion, opened a grocery store in it. In 1863 he was superintendent of the erection of the brick school house in the Second ward. In the spring of 1866, he removed to Huntsville, Alabama, where he dealt in cotton, as a broker, until his return to Waverly, in 1872. Mr. Brown then engaged in various branches of trade until the time of his death, which occurred July 1, 1882. The funeral took place at the family residence, the Rev. A. M. Case, of the Congregational church, officiating, assisted by Rev. H. H. Burrington. By his death, Waverly lost one of her most respected citizens, and one, whose genial disposition won the admiration and love of all who came in contact with him, either socially or in a business way. Charles W., the only surviving child of J. F. and Elizabeth Brown, was born in Cayuga county, New York, July 15, 1859. He received a liberal education, completing the same at Bryant & Stratton's Commercial College, Chicago, in 1877. Immediately upon leaving school, he entered his father's store as book-keeper, and, in 1879, embarked in the wood and coal business for himself. During the fall of 1879, he was joined in wedlock with Miss Lilla B. Clark, who was born in Racine, Wisconsin, April 6, 1861, and is a daughter of Hon. R. B. Clarke, (deceased) of Waverly. One child—Luella Dixie—brightens their home.

William Hurley, is a native of Miami county, Ohio, and was born September 10, 1810. He is a son of Zachariah and Mary (Manning) Hurley. The father was a native of Virginia, and through life, followed the occupation of " a tiller of the soil." He emigrated to the State of Ohio in 1808, being one of its pioneers. In 1831 he removed to Grant county, Indiana. William was reared on his father's farm, in the wilds of a new country, and consequently his education was sadly neglected. In 1847 he was married to Miss Mary Boots, who was born in Ross county, Ohio, November 29, 1817. Ten children blessed the union, six of whom are now living: Francis M., Lydia A., wife of Charles Parminter, Jasper., Mary, wife of Homer Daily, William N. and George. April 26, 1853, Mr. Hurly took up his line of march for the far west, locating in Bradford, Chickasaw county, Iowa. In 1858 he removed to Pearl Rock, and two years later came to his present home, in Waverly. He now owns 111 acres of land, under good cultivation, and valued at $45.00 per acre. He has been identified with the State for twenty-nine years, and many and rapid have been the changes he has witnessed. The family are members of the Baptist church.

John Voight, one of the oldest meat-market men of Waverly, was born in Sondershousen, Germany, March 14, 1829. He left his native country for America in 1850, landing in the city of New York, on the 4th day of July. Shortly after, he removed to Syracuse, New York, engaging in the butcher business. He was married in that city, in 1856, to Miss Emma Wusthoff, a native of Germany, and born May 11, 1834. Five children have been born to them, four of whom are now living—Mary, born June 7, 1857; John, born January 1, 1859; Charlie, born March 2, 1867, and Emma, whose birth occurred September 8, 1874. During 1854, he removed to Waterloo, New York, and there resided twelve years. In 1867, they settled in Waverly, Bremer county, Iowa, and Mr. Voight immediately launched in his former business. To-day, he has an

D. T. Gibson.

excellent trade, doing from $8,000 to $10,000 worth of business per year. He is a member of the Masonic Fraternity, and also of the I. O. O. F. The family belong to the Congregational church.

F. H. Schlutsmeyer was born in the Principality of Lippe-Detmold, Germany, on the 26th day of May, 1853. He is a son of F. and Mina (Thoren) Schlutsmeyer. His parents had nine children born to them—four sons, and five daughters—of whom three sons and one daughter are now living. The subject of this sketch was educated in the Gymnasium of Lemgo, Germany. At the age of seventeen he entered the counting room of F. W. Wippermann, of Lemgo, remaining an apprentice two and one-half years. In 1872, he came to this country, and, shortly after landing on American soil, settled in Waverly, Iowa, finding employment in the dry goods establishment of Bringmann & Schmidt—afterward F. W. Schmidt—where he remained three and one-half years. At the expiration of that time, Mr Schlutsmeyer was employed by J. F. Brown, and took charge of the dry goods department of said house. Three years later he was appointed deputy clerk of courts, which position he filled for over a year, and was then engaged by H. L. Ware, as salesman in his dry goods establishment. During the year 1876 he was united in marriage with Miss Amelia S. Klages, daughter of Fred Klages, of Warren township, Bremer county. She was born on the 12th day of July, 1855, at Milwaukee, Wisconsin. They are blessed with two children—Carl W, a boy of five years, and Minnie A., four months of age.

Harvey Sullivan was born in Otsego county, New York, September 6, 1837. When a boy of fifteen years, he left his home to battle for himself. He has spent more or less of his life on the race track, first riding running horses and afterwards driving and selling horses. He was married in 1860, to Miss Lucinda Wright, a daughter of Wise Wright, a native of New York State. Three children—Carrie, Charlie and Wilbur—have been born to them. Mr. Sullivan enlisted in Company "G," Twenty-second Ohio Infantry, and participated in the following engagements: First, in the Battle of Williamsburg, Seven Pines; second, Battle of Bull Run and Gettysburg, thence to the Shenandoah Valley, where he engaged in the battles of Lynchburg, Walnut Hill, Cedar Creek, and others. He was mustered out at the close of the war. In the fall of 1865, he came to Bremer county, Iowa, locating at Waverly, where he has since been engaged in buying and selling horses. Among the horses owned and handled by Mr. Sullivan are, Hate Lakeaway, whose record is 2:38; Wahoo, with a record of 2:45, and New Hampton Girl, whose record is 2:23½; St. Louis, for which he paid $500, has made his mile in 2:22, and was sold for the neat little sum of $2,300. He also owns other good horses, which are now in training.

B. M. Reeves was born in Cayuga county, New York, February 21, 1825. He is a son of Manassah and Estherl (Perry) Reeves, who were married in Cayuga county, New York, March 27, 1817, and were the parents of eight children, seven of whom are living. His parents were poor, and his father had to work by the month to support a large family. For six years he worked for $13 per month, and in that time, with the help of his wife and older children, had accumulated $600. When B. M. was thirteen years of age, his father purchased a tract of land in the wilderness, which B. M. was active in helping to clear. When twenty-two years of age he left home without a cent in his pocket, having given his last penny to his father. In the fall of 1848, he came west, locating in Boone county, Illinois, where he was soon after employed in a mill, where he remained for six years. He again started west, stopping at Manchester until the fall of the same year, when he came to Waverly, where he soon after embarked in the milling business. September 30, 1856, he married Miss Eliza H. Sellens. She was born November 25, 1834, in Oneida county, New York. Three children blessed this union—Kittie E., Hubert H. and Edward M. Mr. and Mrs. Reeves have a beautiful farm in the limits of Waverly, on which he has one of the finest orchards with the choicest fruit in the county. Mr. Reeves has taken an active interest in the county, holding several important offices. He has also always taken an active part in educational matters, his own opportunities being very limited, he saw the necessity of giving his children a good education. During the war for the Union, Mr. Reeves was a member of the board of supervisors, and it is doubtful if any man in Bremer county, did more towards raising soldiers to fill the quota of this county; and certainly none did more towards looking after the families of the soldiers, and alleviating their sufferings. During the entire war he had charge of all the soldiers' families in this vicinity, and such was the great confidence placed in his integrity and ability, that he was asked by the three companies, raised in this county, through their captain's, Captain Beebe, Captain Tinkham and Captain Avery, to take charge of, and pay over to the several families of these companies, all of the money paid to them by the government. This request was made by these companies without a single dissenting voice. Although crowded with business, private and public, Mr. Reeves accepted this trust, and faithfully distributed to all of these families, during the war, over $10,000, in money, and, let it be said to his credit, that he did it without receiving one cent for his trouble, and never received an unkind word from any of the families, save one. During the sanitary fair, held at Dubuque, for the benefit of the sanitary commission, Mr. Reeves donated twenty-one barrels of flour, together with a premium of $40.00, which was paid him by the fair, for the largest amount of flour furnished by any one firm in the State, making upwards of $400, donated by him at that time, to the sanitary commission. Mr. Reeves has a stack of letters and papers, all of them complimentary to him, which if compiled, would make a volume the size of the one before you. But time and space does not admit of more, but suffice it to say, that Mr. Reeves has a war record that he and his friends may be justly proud of.

C. H. Barrows, Superintendent of the Waverly Telephone Exchange, was born in Rockford, Winnebago county, Illinois, on the 6th day of November, 1843, and is a son of Hamilton W. and Lucy (Marsh) Barrows. His father removed to Winnebago county, Illinois, in 1841, making the journey on foot. At his arrival in Chicago, he purchased a ham and some crackers, and started for Rockford. After his settlement there, he built and operated the first ferry on Rock river. Subsequently he entered so ne land, which he improved and built upon, and it still remains in the possession of the family. Mr. Barrows died in Rockford, at an advanced age. His wife was born in Canada, but came by team to Rockford, when quite young. She, with her people, living in their wagon for many weeks. The subject of this sketch was reared and educated in Winnebago county. During the first year of our late Rebellion, he enlisted in Company "G," Forty-fifth Illinois Infantry—commonly known as Washburn's Lead-mine regiment, and under Gen. Smith. The regiment participated in the attacks on Forts Henry and Donelson. Also the siege and capture of Vicksburg, Big Platt and Jacksonville, and one battle at Corinth. He served until the close of the war, and during the time was in twenty-two engagements. After being mustered out of the service, he returned to Rockford, and engaged in the livery business. In 1865, he was joined in wedlock with Miss Emogene Buchanan, a daughter of Alexander Buchanan, and a native of Beloit, Wisconsin. Mr. Barrows is a member of the G. A. R., Post 124; also, a member of the Soldiers' Reunion of Bremer county.

Patrick Byrnes—section boss—is a native of County Tipperary, Ireland, and was born in 1831. In 1850, he left his native country for the purpose of finding a new home and building up his fortune on American soil. He first located in Kane county, Illinois, where he was employed on a farm. Two years later he began railroading, and for the last thirty years, has been in charge of a corps of railroad hands. His first experience was on the Beloit and Madison branch, thence to the Racine and Mississippi railroad, where he continued until 1869. His marriage with Miss Sarah McClossen, a daughter of John McClossen, of Elkhorn, Wisconsin, occurred in 1859. Eight children bless the marriage—Michael, John, Thomas, Ellen, Maggie, Joseph, Willie and Sadie. Mr. Byrnes owns a fine residence in Waverly. The family are members of the Catholic Church.

L. C. Haase, son of L. F. and Caroline (Steinwarth) Haase, was born on the 3d of May, 1850, at Dundee, Kane county, Illinois. His parents came from Hannover, Germany, to the United States, in 1848. They lived at Chicago about two years, when they moved to Dundee, engaging in the milling business. In 1865 they came to Iowa, settling in Jefferson township, Bremer county, where they resided on a farm until 1870. The subject of this sketch received a common school education. He moved to Waterloo, Iowa in 1870, where he engaged as a miller, forming a partnership with his father. In 1873 he came to Waverly, Iowa, buying an interest in the East Side grist mill, which he run, with his father, until 1878, when they sold the mill, and he bought an interest in the grocery firm of John Eifert, under the firm name of Eifert & Haase, buying the interest of John Eifert the year following, and is now engaged in the grocery, and boot and shoe business. In 1873 he was married to Miss Pauline Rodeck, a native of Saxony, Germany. They have three children—Herman, Fred, and Edwin. Mr. Haase is a member of the board of trustees for Washington township.

Frank A. Lee, druggist, was born in New York, October 3, 1854. He is a son of Spencer and Mary (Fortner) Lee, and removed to Illinois with his parents, when two years of age. His mother was a daughter of Thomas Fortner, an early settler of Bremer county, Iowa. In the fall of 1856, Spencer Lee, with the family, removed to Iowa, and settled in Franklin township, Bremer county, where he purchased a farm of 250 acres. For sixteen or seventeen years, Mr. Lee, Sr., made this farm his home, then removed to Oldwine, Fayette county, and, in 1878, removed to DesMoines, where he still resides. He had a family of eight children, six sons and two daughters, all of whom are still living. Frank A. was brought up on a farm, and accustomed to hard work. He was educated at the Upper Iowa University, and at the Hopkinton Lenox Collegiate Institute; also, attending the Ames Agricultural College, where he graduated, and then returned to Waverly. During his attendance at the Agricultural College, his principal study was chemistry. In the meantime, he had kept books for T. C. Aldrich for sometime. In the fall of 1878, he became a partner of Dr. O. Burbank, in the drug business, under the firm name of Burbank & Lee, and they shortly afterward erected the building which Mr. Lee now occupies. In the fall of 1879 he purchased Dr. Burbank's interest, and still owns and conducts the establishment. F. A. Lee was married to Miss Carrie L. Burbank, daughter of Dr. O. Burbank, his former partner, December 31, 1879. They have one child—Edward B., born July 6, 1881. Mr. Lee is a member of the Knights of Pythias, and is secretary of the Bremer County Old Settlers' Association. Politically, he is a republican.

The following sketch should have appeared in connection with the history of Albion township, in Butler county, but was received by the historian after Albion had been printed:

Rev. Oliver H. Sproul was born in Cornwall, Canada, March 19, 1846, and was educated in Dundas. The early years of his life were devoted to teaching. He was converted October 15, 1869, joined the Wesleyan Methodist church, and came to Iowa the same year. He entered the ministry of the M. E. Church in the fall of 1872. He married Miss Chole A. McNairn, of Canada, June 11, 1873. Mr. Sproul was ordained Elder in 1876. In 1873, he was appointed to Parkersburg, and, for eight years, was a resident of Butler county. At present he is pastor of the church in Geneva, Franklin county, Iowa.

CHAPTER XXXII.

MISCELLANEOUS.

"Gather up the fragments that nothing be lost," is a divine injunction. In this chapter are presented several matters of more or less interest to the general readers, and worthy a place in this volume.

BREMER COUNTY BIBLE SOCIETY.

This society was organized in 1857. The Waverly *Republican* gave the following account of its organization:

"Our citizens were favored on Sunday, October 25, 1857, by a very able sermon from the Rev. R. W. Keeler, President of Cornell College, Mt. Vernon, after which the agent of the American Bible Society, Mr. S. P. Crawford, made a brief address on the subject of his agency, and proceeded to organize an Auxiliary County Bible Society, by the adoption of a constitution and the election of the following officers: Giles Mabie, President; J. Glassford and Thomas Downing, Vice-Presidents; H. S. Hoover, Secretary; A. S. Lawrence, Treasurer; G. S. Hamilton and H. K. Swett, Executive Committee.

COUNTY TEMPERANCE SOCIETY.

A county Temperance society was organized Monday evening, April 26, 1858. The society adopted the following pledge:

"I solemnly promise, on my sacred word and honor, that I will not use intoxicating liquors, henceforth and forever, as a beverage; and I further promise that I will use my best efforts to discourage the manufacture, sale and use of alcoholic beverages."

The first officers elected were as follows: W. P. Harmon, president; O. Burbank, M. D., vice-president; H. S. Hoover, recording secretary; C. T. Smeed, corresponding secretary; Giles Mabie, D. P. Daniel, John Glassford, Matthew Rowen, S. D. Bryant and Lyman Nutting, executive committee.

The society, for some time continued to do active work, but was finally abandoned. Temperance efforts were not, however, abandoned, and, during the exciting canvass in 1882, for the prohibatory amendment, a strong effort was put forth in its behalf, and a large vote was given for it.

It is said that men will drink, and that all efforts for the suppression of the drinking custom will be without avail. The following is said to have taken place in Waverly some years ago.

A drunken "bummer" in Waverly was once arrested by a German saloon keeper and sued for unpaid drinks. He scorned the advice of council or assistance of attorneys, and delivered himself for the edification of the court, of the following ingenious plea:

"May it please your honor! To borrow is the first principle of nature. Does not the river borrow from the brook, and the ocean from the river? Does not the clouds borrow from the air, and the earth from the clouds? Does not the moon borrow her light from the sun, and the night borrow it again from the moon? Was not man taken from the earth, and his frau formed from his side? Since then all nature has established this grand system of universal credit, why should not man made in the image of God, have a natural claim on the credit system. And since the mighty ocean is not ashamed to borrow of the running river, why then should not a lean "bummer" borrow from a fat bar keeper? Now, your honor knows the feeble sighted moon never returns the borrowed light of the sun? Why then should a poor beer drinker pay a rich beer seller? It is contrary to national laws— it is an absurdity. But what does the river do when it has borrowed too much from the brooks and streams? It runs away. Nature, then, has set me an example. I will follow it and run away." And before the officer could reach him he had cleared the court room and was out of reach.

HONORED DEAD.

Jacob Chapin was born in the town of Heath, Franklin county, Massachusetts, on the 29th day of May, 1828, and was therefore over fifty-three years of age at the time of his death. In the fall of 1828, he removed, with his parents, to Nunda, Livingston county, New York, and from there, in the fall of 1838, to Geneva, Walworth county, Wisconsin. He was married, to Annie Hudson, March 9, 1846. In 1855, in company with his brother, John, he went to California, returning in 1854. In 1855 he came to Bremer county, bought a farm, and moved his family to it in 1860. In the spring of 1861 he experienced religion, united with the Baptist Church, and was a devoted, faithful and consistant christian, always ready to give a reason for the hope within him, which he felt to be an anchor to the soul, both sure and steadfast. He died, at his residence, in Freemont township, March 4, 1875.

Oran Faville was born October 13, 1817, at Manhein, Herkimer county, New York. He was brought up on a farm and educated at the district schools, but having access to a small library he was enabled to gratify a taste for reading, and was prompted to higher things. He commenced teaching in 1834–5, and was engaged the following winters, until 183², when he removed to Ohio, here he spent two years in teaching and in preparatory study at Granville College. He afterwards studied two years at the Fairfield Academy, in his native county, with intervals of teaching, and entered the junior class in Wesleyan University, at Middletown, Connecticut, in 1842. After graduating, he taught two years in the Oneida Conference Seminary, at Cazenovia, New York, six years in the Troy Conference Seminary, at West Poultney, Vermont, and the next year in McKendree College, at Lebanon, Illinois. In 1853, he took charge of the Wesleyan Female College, at Delaware, Ohio, but ill-health compelling him to resign his profession, he removed, in 1855, to Iowa, and commenced frontier life as a farmer in Mitchell county. Subsequently was elected county judge of the same county. In October, 1857, Mr. Faville was elected Lieutenant-Governor and *ex officio* President of the State Board of Education, then newly organized. At its first session, in December, 1858, the board adopted the main fixtures of the present system of public instruction. In April, 1863, he became the acting secretary of the board, and in January following was appointed its secretary, by the Governor. In March, 1864, he was elected by the legislature, Superintendent of Public Instruction, the board of education being abolished. He was re-elected by the people in October, 1865. In 1867, he resigned on account of ill-health. From 1863 to 1867, was editor of the Iowa School *Journal*. In 1868, he removed to Waverly, Iowa, where he lived a retired life. He was married July 24, 1845, to Miss Maria Peck, of DeWitt, New York. In addition to his educational labors in the schools and in public office, Mr. Faville delivered various addresses at teachers institutes and associations, several of which have been published. Oran Faville died some years ago.

Edward Tyrrell was born in Westmeathe county, Ireland, April 20, 1819. In 1825 his parents came to America. He was a son of Nicholas and Ann (Highland) Tyrrell, both natives of Ireland. Upon arriving in America, they settled in Lower Canada, and afterward moved to Albany county, New York, where he grew to manhood, receiving a good common school education. He was married in August, 1839, at Rochester, New York, to Elizabeth Worthington, who was born in Ireland, December 21, 1822. She came to America with an uncle, John Worthington, and wife, in 1824, they settling in Renssellaer county, New York. After marriage, Mr. and Mrs. Tyrrell remained in that State one year, and then came west to McHenry county, Illinois, where they settled on a farm and remained until 1854, when they came to Bremer county, first settling in Lafayette township, on a farm which he improved. Six years later they moved into Waverly, where he was elected justice of the peace. In 1861 he enlisted in Company "G," Ninth Iowa Infantry, as a private. At the Battle of Pea Ridge, he was promoted to first lieutenant of that company, and was shot at the Battle of Vicksburg, May 22, 1862, dying on the battle field. Mrs. Tyrrell has since been a resident of the county, and now lives in section 31, Warren township. They were blessed with seven children—Frank, now engaged in farming in California; George, engaged in mining in Montana; Jane, wife of James S. Conner; William, editor of the *Republican*; Clarence, now a resident of Warren township; Charles, who is teaching school in their home district, and Effie, who was married November 19, 1882, to Dr. H. S. Strickland, of Kirksville, Missouri. Mrs. Tyrrell's father's name was Thomas Kennedy, and John Worthington was a brother of Mrs. Tyrrell's mother, but she was named Worthington, and, until her marriage, always bore that name. Her father died when she was a child. Her mother died in this county, in 1875, at the age of seventy-six. Frank Tyrrell, their oldest son, went into the army in 1861, in Company K, Third Iowa Volunteer Infantry, and was wounded at the battle of Shiloh, and taken prisoner at the same time. He remained in prison for about three years. After that long time he made his escape to Little Rock, Arkansas. All this time he was thought, by the family, to be dead, but returned home and is now in California. Edward Tyrrell was a member of the Masonic Lodge and was one of the officers of the lodge for several years.

Henry Morehouse was born in Saratoga county, New York, and was about sixty-eight years old when he died. About 1840, he went south and spent several years teaching writing school in Alabama. While in the south he was converted, and in 1848, moved to Plato, Kane county, Illinois, and entered actively upon the work of the ministry, in which he continued for about seven years. In the summer of 1855, he removed to Janesville, Bremer county. His first few years in Janesville was buying and selling land. He afterward embarked in merchandizing. A few years later misfortune over took him and he failed. His immense weight prevented him from active duties of any kind. For several years his standing weight was 350 pounds. After coming to Janesville he did not preach regularly, and as far as can be learned, did not attach himself to any conference. He would often fill appointments for others. In the pulpit, Elder Morehouse was a host. Few men surpassed him in powers of eloquence and scope of knowledge of scripture. Elder Morehouse was always highly esteemed by a very large circle of acquaintances. His strength and clearness of mind made him a formidable opponent in a discussion of any kind. His piety was unquestioned at all times and under all circumstances. He died at Janesville, Tuesday, February 3, 1875, leaving a wife and two daughters to mourn his loss.— *Waverly Republican.*

John Elliott, one of the pioneers of Bremer county, some years ago with his family, settled on the prairie about four miles north east of Waverly. By patient toil he had made for himself a home there, of which any man might feel proud. Just as he was beginning to enjoy the comforts of prosperity, he was stricken down, and passed away from the contemplated joys forever. Mr. Elliott was widely known and respected in the county. Of late years he had paid considerable attention to the improvement of fine stock in the county, and with good success. The farming community lost a valuable worker, the county a good citizen, and his wife and family a husband and father, whom they revered and loved, and mourn as only a good man can be mourned. He died at his home in Lafayette township, October 16, 1876.

James F. Lyman was born in Southport, Chemung county, New York, October 8, 1845. When he was a year old, his parents moved to Warren, Bradford county, Pennsylvania. There he lived the greater part of the time until he was nineteen, when he came west to Bonus Prairie, Boone county, Illinois, where he worked at farming. He was married in Boone county, May 28, 1856, to Miss Lydia E. Case, and moved to Bremer county, November 17, 1856, and settled near Horton, where Mrs. Lyman died, December 5, 1860. Mr. Lyman enlisted soon after the war broke out, and served with his company until after the taking of Vicksburg, when he was taken sick and died, October 4, 1863, at Carrolton, Louisiana, where his body lies buried. His wife was born at French creek, Chautauqua county, New York, October 6, 1835, and moved, with her parents to Illinois in the fall of 1854. They had but one child, a daughter, Ella M.

BREMER COUNTY IN 1858.

The following interesting review was published in *The Republican*, at the date mentioned:

This county lies in about the same latitude as Rochester and Buffalo, and about one hundred miles west from Dubuque. Waverly, the county seat, and principal town, is about eighty miles from the Mississippi river, at the nearest point of landing, there being but little difference in distance between this and Guttenburg or McGregor.

The business of the county is principally done at Dubuque.

The county includes twelve townships of land, which, for fertility of soil, if equalled, is unsurpassed by the same number of acres in any one body in the west.

WATERS.

The county is watered by the Cedar river, which traverses the western tier of townships from north to south.

This river rises in Minnesota, and, with its tributaries, which are all fed by constant springs, drains one of the finest valleys on the globe.

Its waters are always, with the exception of freshets, clear, bright and silvery, running over a sandy, pebbled bottom. Its banks are high, but seldom bluffy, and the bottom lands are generally so elevated as to be above the highest rise of water.

This river and its tributaries furnish an immense amount of water power, which is constant, never-failing in the dryest season, and seldom interfered with by the water rising and backing upon the mills.

The next stream in importance, is the main Wapsipinicon, which rises also in Minnesota. The eastern portion of Mitchell, the Western portion of Howard, and the central part of Chickasaw counties, are drained by branches of this stream, which unite in the north tier of townships of this county, from which it pursues a southeasterly course, crossing the southern line of the county some three miles west of the southeastern corner. This, as well as the Cedar and all other streams of the county, being fed by springs, never run dry or fail of having a constant flow of water. The banks of the Wapsipinicon, are not so high, and the bottom lands are more subject to being overflowed, than those of the Cedar. This stream furnishes considerable water power, which is constant and reliable. Five, of the twelve townships, are intersected and watered by it. The little Wapsipinicon rises in Chickasaw county, crosses the northeastern township of Bremer county, into Fayette county, but soon recrosses into Bremer, and again into Fayette, continuing near the line, and falling into the main Wapsipinicon, in Buchanan county.

Buck creek takes its rise in Chickasaw county, running southwardly through the eastern tier of townships, falls into the little Wapsipinicon.

Cam creek rises near the north line of the county, west of the main Wapsipinicon, and runs nearly parallel with it across

HISTORY OF BREMER COUNTY.

the county, uniting with it in Black Hawk county, and at the same time giving a speedy drainage for all surplus. The southwestern township is crossed by the Shell Rock river, as beautiful a mill stream as ever was run, and on which, in the edge of Butler county, is the beautiful town of Shell Rock, at which there is an excellent flouring mill, hotels, stores, etc. Excellent water is obtained every where in the county, by digging at an average depth of about twelve feet.

TIMBER.

Equal to the soil and water is timber. Few counties in Prairie countries, possess so much and so excellent timber as well distributed as this.

The lower big woods which contain twenty-six thousand acres of heavy oak, ash, maple, elm, linn, locust, Kentucky coffee, black walnut, butter nut, aspen, etc., each variety of the best quality, and the largest growth lies entirely in the county on the east side of the Cedar river, near to the south line. From this body north, the cedar is skirted on either side nearly all the way to the north line, by large groves of fine timber. The Wapsi is skirted with timber the entire breadth of the county, and at some points extends to several miles in width, which will supply the prairies east and west with fuel, lumber and timber. Wilson's grove lies on the little Wapsi, and is partly in this and partly in Fayette county, and contains several hundred acres of timber. Between the Wapsi timber and the big woods on Crane creek, are several groves.

A fine grove, called quarter section, lies near the center of the county.

Trumbo grove also occupies a central position.

Near the cedar timber is Smith grove, which contains about 320 acres of splendid timber. This grove is intersected by a small, never-failing stream, which runs so circuitous as to water every one of the several farms surrounding the grove.

Several communities of beavers still hold possession of the artificial ponds, created by dams erected across the Cedar by these ingenious and persevering artificers. During the autumn these animals lay away their winter store of food by felling the aspen trees, and cutting them into logs which they carry or roll into their ponds and sink. Great ingenuity is displayed by them in cutting such only as will fall towards the pond, and then such parts only are cut up as they can roll into the water. They often cut trees two feet in diameter.

Six mile grove, a very extensive one, lies further north, and two miles from the Cedar timber.

The Shell Rock has much good timber on its banks. Thus it will be seen that every portion of the county has timber at convenient distances within its own limits.

FACE OF THE COUNTRY.

From what has already been written, it will be seen that the county has a southern declivity, as all the streams run south. The country along the Cedar is perhaps rather too rolling at some points, but no where so rough or broken as not to be susceptable of cultivation, if we except some very limited spots where the rock lies too near the surface. In all other portions of the county the land lies as fair as

HISTORY OF BREMER COUNTY.

land can lie. Just sufficiently undulating to drain handsomely.

SOIL.

The county possesses every variety of good soil, from the sandy river bottom to the rich clay sub-soil grass land of the Wapsi; which, while it is admirably adapted to grass, and pasturage is equally well adapted to the cultivation of corn and the cereals. The rolling clay sub-soil upland is deemed the best for all purposes.

PRODUCTS.

Every kind of farm product which is cultivated in this latitude, grows to perfection here—wheat, corn, oats, beans, peas, millet, timothy and clover grow remarkably well. Potatoes, turnips, onions and all the esculent roots make very heavy crops of the finest quality.

FRUIT.

Too little attention has been paid to the cultivation of fruit. As is generally the case in all new countries far removed from nurseries, trees, without reference to adaptability, are procured and carelessly, and often negligently planted, and then left to care for themselves, are the first abortive attempts at fruit raising.

CLIMATE.

Being in the same latitude as the interior of New York, the climate would be the same if there were no modifying causes. The absence of great bodies of water, or high elevation of land, is also an absence of the cause of great and sudden atmospheric changes.

That the winter of 1857, was severe is too true, but the severity was only general, and cannot be urged against this locality. The present winter, 1882–83, which is said by those best acquainted with the matter, to be an usual Iowa winter, has been as favorable as could be desired for comfort or business.

A little more snow at times would have been acceptable, there having been not more than three inches at one time. The cold weather here is steady, the air bracing and invigorating, producing an exuberance of muscular energy and activity seldom or never experienced in low latitudes. The prevailing northwest winds, from the vast expanse of unbroken country north and west, although in the winter they bring cold, or rather they carry off the caloric, are full of life and health, and in summer time, modify the temperature. The atmosphere is as pure as can be had in any lattitude. Fogs or excessive humidity in the atmosphere rarely happens. The absence of great irregularities of surface secures a uniformity of atmospheric currents, and as a legitimate consequence an equal distribution of rain. Severe drouths are seldom experienced.

HEALTH.

This is usually conceded to be a remarkably healthy region, entirely free—with very limited exceptions—from any local disturbing causes. The entire absence of miasmatic poison, leaves it entirely free from billious diseases, and consequent debility.

SETTLEMENT.

It is thirteen years since C. McCaffree, the first white-face, located himself in the county. Its present population is from seven to ten thousand, well distributed. The western portion, near the Cedar, being the more densely settled. In northeastern and southeastern portions, along the Wapsipinicon, are fine settlements.

SOCIETY.

The settlers are mostly from New England, New York, Pennsylvania, and Ohio, with representatives from various other States, and are an enterprising, intelligent, and reading people. Religious societies and schools are established in almost every neighborhood throughout the county.

LANDS.

Very little or no land remains unentered, but large scopes are in the hands of non-residents, and can now be purchased at rates far preferable to settlers, taking into consideration the advantages of settlements, schools, roads, bridges, mills, etc., to any wild land now offered by the Government. The purchaser, with cash, can buy at a very trifling advance above Government price, and, sometimes, for even less.

TOWNS.

Waverly is the county seat and principal town. It is in the southwest corner township, on both sides of the Cedar, in the western skirts of the Big Woods.

The county seat was located here in June, 1853. The county was organized in August of the same year. Waverly was laid out the following fall, when it contained two houses and a saw mill. It now contains from nine hundred to a thousand inhabitants.

Sixty-six substantial buildings were erected in 1857, among which was an elegant court house, 43x73 feet on the ground, and three stories high, mounted by a handsome dome. The basement or lower story is of stone, and is designed for a jail and dwelling for the jailor. The other stories are of brick. The second appropriated to county offices, in which there is a fire proof vault, for the preservation of the records in case of fire. The court room is on the upper floor, and is 40x50 feet in the clear.

The building was commenced in June, and is now nearly completed, Its cost was about $24,000. The timber, the lumber, the stone, the lime, the sand and bricks with which the court house was erected, could have been obtained within one mile of its site. Among the business establishments are three large general stores, one hardware, tin and agricultural implement store, one grocery store and several less trading places. A good flouring mill with three run of burrs; two saw mills with siding and lath mills attached; one cabinet and chair manufactory, in which a number of hands are constantly employed, and a carding machine, all driven by water. Only a portion of the available water power is yet employed. A rotary steam saw and siding mill has recently been added to the lumbering facilities. A shingle cutting machine, driven by horse power, furnishes roofing material.

The mechanical pursuits are represented by four smith shops, two wagon shops, a reaper shop, a cooper shop, a jeweler, a milliner, saddle and harness shop, a boot and shoe shop, news and job printing office, besides carpenter and joiner shops. There are two good hotels here. A large two

HISTORY OF BREMER COUNTY:

story stone school house is occupied most of the time with a good school.

The religious societies, the Episcopal Methodist, the Baptist and New School Presbyterian, are organized and hold stated meetings.

Two brick yards, three lime kilns and five stone quarries, are among the facilities for furnishing building materials.

Janesville, is located on the east side of the Cedar river, near the south line of the county. It has four hundred inhabitants, and some very fine residences.

A large flouring mill, at this date, November, 1882, is in process of erection on the Cedar river. A good hotel and three or four stores and a smith shop, etc., are among the business places.

Horton is located on the east side of the Cedar river, ten miles north of Waverly. It has a good hotel, a store and steam saw mill.

Syracuse is on the west side of the Cedar, two miles above Horton. It has a hotel and water power saw mill.

Martinsburg is on the west side of the Wapsipinicon river, about twelve miles from Waverly. It has a store, a hotel and steam saw mill, a siding and shingle mill, smith shop, etc.

Bremer is east of the Wapsipinicon, about sixteen miles from Waverly. There is a store and a steam saw mill, located at that place.

Jefferson is at the eastern point of the Big Woods, eight miles from Waverly. It has a steam saw mill.

BREMER COUNTY OF TO-DAY.

It has been but a little over a third of a century since Charles McCaffree erected his rude log cabin in Bremer county. Then all was a vast wilderness. To-day cities and villages are upon every hand. The railroad crosses its borders in different directions, the shrill whistle of the engine giving its warning of approach, where once the trail of the red men passed, and their wild yells were repeated in a thousand echoes. In schools, churches manufactories, public and private edifices, Bremer county shows unexcelled enterprise and remarkable greatness. Newspapers make their way into every home, giving information of the thousand and one events of daily and weekly occurrence. Change is written upon every hand, and changes are daily being made, and the end is not yet.

Surname Index

ABBEY, 1033
ABBOTT, 1043
ABERNETHY, 907-909
ABRAHAM, 1121
ACKEN, 820 898 901 921 932 1000
    1013 1027-1028 1265
ACKERSON, 1095
ADAIR, 908 911-912 930 1001
    1232 James 930
ADAMS, 850 909 912 917 969 971
    997 1013 1027 1052 1158 1227
ADICKS, 1035-1036
ADKINS, 1053
AGER, 1051
AGNEW, 1085
AHLER, 1066
AHLERS, 1067 R R 1067
AIKEN, 1001
AINSWORTH, 850 899 915 1148
AKEN, 818
AKERS, 912 986
ALBEE, 849 1214
ALBERT, 1029
ALBRIGHT, 1223-1224 1238
ALCOCK, 1022 1028 1046
    Charles 1022
ALDEN, 1113
ALDRICH, 921 1256 1314
ALEXANDER, 918
ALGER, 1187 1204-1205 1205 1212
ALLBRIGHT, 1223
ALLEN, 790 796 839 845 856 860
    860 898 901 911 954 958 969-970
    989 1031-1032 1032 1034-1036
    1068 1128 1131 1136-1137 1137-
    1138 1152 1154 1187 1286 A D
    1032 C C 860
ALLISON, 900-903 914

ALLSBURY, 1113
ALNEY, 1028
ALSHOUSE, 1030
ALTON, 1023
AMBROSE, 1034-1035
AMES, 1176
ANDERSON, 856 861 903 951 953
    1286 W W 861
ANDREWS, 794 830 856 863 965 1004
    1107 1112 1118 1121-1122 1145
    1263 1296-1297 James 1112 W W
    863
ANNIN, 1078
ANNIS, 1173 1175 H B 1175
APPLEY, 1293
ARCHER, 910 993-994 1241 Benj
    1241
ARMSBUD, 1225
ARMSTRONG, 792-793 796 837 952
    1093 1106
ARNAL, 961
ARNEMAN, 1066
ARNS, 1224-1225
ASHBOUGH, 1071
ASHLAND, 966
ATWATER, 1182
AUNER, 961
AUNEY, 830
AUSTIN, 1051 1056 1155-1156 1158
    1192 1194-1195 1213 Albert 1158
    C A 1195
AVERY, 853-854 856 858 867 874
    878 902-903 919 921 966-967
    1146 1312 O F 858
AXILE, 956
AXLET, 1232
AXTEL, 1086
AXTELL, 818 820 899

AYERS, 830
AYRES, 1027
BABBIT, 899
BABBITT, 1298
BABCOCK, 1234 Orlando 1234
BACHER, 966-967
BACON, 855 1039
BAGLSTON, 999
BAHER, 898
BAILEY, 908 917 1030 1051 1237 1274
BAIRD, 1263
BAKER, 837 862 907 911-912 925 925-926 1106 1128 1131 1181 1183 1185 1202 1287 1304 S F 925
BALDWIN, 1077 1167
BALL, 907-908 933 1221 1261
BALLANTINE, 1082 Hugh 1082
BALLARD, 910
BALLENTINE, 1083
BALLINGER, 902
BANE, 904
BANKS, 844 1216 1222 1226
BARBER, 875 883 910-911 913 992 1255-1257 1261 1287 1297
BARCLAY, 961 1253
BARDELL, 856
BARDEN, 1236
BARDWELL, 910
BARKER, 853 903 1042 1295
BARLETS, 1094
BARNARD, 975 1029-1030 1051
BARNES, 908 1041 1048 1112 1125 1128 1185-1186 Eli 1048
BARNHOUSE, 970
BARNUM, 1217
BARR, 1055
BARRICK, 792 794-796 799 820 839 845-846 848 936 956 966-967 1000 1007 1068 1068-1069 1071 1083-1084 1084 1087 1091 1122 Isaac 1068 John T 1084
BARRINGER, 1020
BARRIS, 1284
BARROWS, 1312 1312-1313 C H 1312
BARTELLS, 1093
BARTELS, 1068-1097 1097-1098 E H 1068-1097

BARTLETT, 820 829 966
BASELEY, 961
BASKEINS, 956
BASKERVILLE, 1131
BASKIN, 829 875
BASKINS, 793-794 796 820-821 831 849 875 885 897 931 966 971 1000 1096 1227 1285-1286 Abner 1227 Joseph 1227 Wm 1096
BASS, 1268
BATEMAN, 975
BATES, 890 1058
BATTAMS, 1296
BATTIN, 1165-1166
BAUM, 966 971
BAUMAN, 1134
BAUMANN, 1105 1105-1106 Hermann 1105
BAUMGARTNER, 1186 1201 1212-1213 A 1201
BAUMIBACH, 1029
BAUMTEATH, 1132
BAXTER, 1051
BAYER, 913 1104 Wm 1104
BAYS, 1111
BEAL, 993-994 1000 1038 1040 W W 1040
BEALL, 1030
BEALS, 1081
BEAMER, 1225
BEAN, 1064 1066
BEARD, 969
BEARDSLEY, 1283
BEARS, 907
BEARSTERFIELD, 1105
BEATH, 830
BECK, 903 908 911 1019 Joseph 1019
BECKER, 1029 1105 Lewis 1105
BECKWELL, 1291
BEEBE, 819-820 898 932 954 956 966-967 971 1001-1002 1144 1152-1153 1155-1156 1156 1251 1253 1255 1296-1297 1312 David 1144
BEEBEE, 971
BEEKER, 961
BEELAH, 789 794-796 801 1092 1094 1107

BEELER, 840
BEELS, 1192 1211
BEHERENT, 1061
BEHMAN, 1262
BEIGHTOL, 1181
BEINEMEIER, 1222
BELDEN, 830
BELL, 890 951 966 971 1051
BELLKERRYS, 829
BELLOWS, 1038
BELSER, 1225
BELT, 969
BELTORF, 1175
BEMENT, 901 1050 1152
BEMERMAN, 913
BEMIS, 899 909-910 922 933 1176-1177 1184-1185 1185
BENARD, 849
BENJAMIN, 966 971
BENNETT, 795 830 894 907 909 986 1012 1093 1114 1118 1234 Benj 1114
BENT, 1208 1212
BENTLEY, 992 1039
BENTLY, 1263
BENTON, 902
BENTROTT, 1132
BERG, 1066
BERGER, 1039
BERGMAN, 1028-1029
BERIE, 1000
BERKSTRESSER, 1185-1186
BERLIN, 1092
BERNER, 1293
BERRINGTON, 999
BERRY, 846 1039 1223-1224
BERZMAN, 1029
BESSEMAR, 1054
BESSMER, 1296
BESWICK, 1277
BEVARD, 961 989 1093-1094 1116
BEVEND, 961 971
BEZOLD, 1036
BICE, 911
BIEDERMAN, 904
BIGELOW, 914 927 1049 1082 1262
BILLINGS, 863 865 865-866 931 N E 865

BINGHAM, 822 970-971 1111 1125 1128
BIRD, 1263
BISBY, 1084
BISSELL, 902
BITHNER, 883
BIVAUK, 1132
BIXBY, 1185
BLACK, 1208 1211
BLACKWELL, 967 1007 1013 1027
BLAINE, 897
BLAIR, 890 893 1193 1212
BLAKE, 965 1063
BLAKELY, 1282
BLASBERG, 1132-1133
BLAZIER, 1007
BLESSIN, 1061
BLIM, 911
BLISS, 1277
BLOCKER, 966-967
BLOCKEY, 829
BLODGETT, 1034 1166
BLOKER, 971 1073 John 1073
BLONDON, 1281
BLOSSOM, 1262
BOARDMAN, 910 1143 1163 1165 1165-1167 1171-1173 1173-1174 J M 1173
BOARDMORE, 829
BOATTCHER, 1275
BOCKER, 1223
BOCKHERT, 830
BOCQUET, 1264
BODECKER, 961
BODEKER, 1094 1102-1103 1103 C L 1103
BODWELL, 1293
BOEDESTER, 1132
BOGART, 967 971 1185
BOGG, 872
BOGGS, 1208
BOHMEIR, 1225
BOHRER, 1074
BOLSTER, 1131
BOLTER, 1038
BOND, 1040
BONEKHOUSE, 1066
BOODIE, 999-1000
BOOK, 1030 1035 1042

BOOTH, 1062
BOOTS, 1308
BORLAND, 1192
BORP, 1051
BOSTWICK, 898 927 1001 1044-1045 1050 W R 1045
BOUCKHOUSE, 1067 A 1067
BOUTWELL, 975
BOWEN, 1118 1121-1122 Joseph 1118
BOWERS, 794 1051-1052 1073
BOWKER, 1274
BOWMAN, 908 969 992 1236 1241 1256 1266 1266-1267 1276 1283 1295 1298 J H 1266
BOWSER, 1138
BOWSTITCH, 965
BOYCE, 1050 1052
BOYD, 790 829 1004 1083 1087 1094 1096 H B 1096
BOYED, 830
BOYER, 1049 1052 M L 1049
BOYLSON, 1117 1227 Patrick 1117
BOYS, 875 877-883-884 1059 Wm 877
BRADFORD, 867 882 882-883 D S 882
BRAINARD, 876 1027 1153 1158 T H 1027
BRANCH, 1013 1055 1144 1144-1145 L E 1144
BRANDENBURG, 909 1134
BRANDT, 1030 1104 1132 1134 E G 1104
BRANT, 967 970
BRAUM, 1105 Heinrich 1105
BRAUN, 1105
BRAUS, 1133
BRECHNER, 1039 1042
BRECKENRIDGE, 886 890 899 951
BREDOW, 794 1132-1135 1135 Paul 1135
BREMER, 800 1044
BRENNAN, 904
BREWER, 1122
BRICKHELL, 1216
BRIDEN, 788 941 1071 1075 1075-1076 1083 1087 1101 1101-1102 H T 1101 H W 1102 Wm 1075
BRIDGES, 882
BRIGGS, 830 955 1027 1095 1121 1222 1234 1293 1296

BRIN, 1001
BRINGMANN, 1311
BRISTOL, 970
BROADIE, 1262 1262-1263 Adam 1262
BROCLAN, 844
BRODIE, 794 821 909 1001 1125 1125-1127 1127-1128 Charles 1127 Robert 1125
BRONSON, 913
BROOKS, 966 1014 1034 1036 1046 1152 1186 1192
BROUGHTON, 1265
BROWER, 966-967 1157
BROWN, 820 831 850 856 862-863 868 871-872 889 893 898-899 904 907 909 912 914-915 955-956 961 965-967 971 1001 1004 1054 1062-1063 1088 1097 1122-1123 1131 1152 1154 1156-1158 1186 1192 1225 1257 1269 1282 1287 1293 1296 1307 1307-1308 1311 A F 868 J F 1307 James 1054
BROWNE, 900
BROWNELL, 1253
BROWNING, 862
BRUMBACH, 1134
BRUNS, 1132 1132-1134
BRUNTZ, 794 1093
BRUSH, 1165 1287
BRYANS, 969
BRYANT, 875 877 880-881 881 912 1007 1202 1207 1212-1213 1213 1238 1308 1315 Z A 877 Z Z 881
BUCHANAN, 857 886 951 1163 1203-1204 1313
BUCHER, 1293
BUCK, 1018 1223
BUCKHOLT, 1037 1042
BUCKINGHAM, 1001 1248 1251 1262 1282 1285
BUCKMAN, 1001
BUCKMASTER, 821 829-830 956 961 967 1106-1107 1131 1138 1154 1223 1225-1226 1238 1252-1253 1276 1285
BUCKNAM, 1056 1062-1063 J O 1056
BUDGE, 1115
BUELL, 963
BUERING, 1227

BUESING, 1262
BUHR, 1035 1132 1135
BULCKENS, 992
BULCKINS, 1231 Frank 1231
BULIS, 907
BULLOCK, 1177 1218 1222 1226
   Edward 1218
BULS, 1029
BUNGER, 1063
BUNTH, 1146 1146-1147 1147 1158 F
   H 1146 H S 1147
BURBANK, 817 875-876 876 878 883-
   884 985 999 1003-1004 1114 1248
   1252-1253 1255 1261 1291 1314-
   1315 Jerome 878 Oscar 876
BURBANKS, 998 1002 1007 1012 1123
BURCOLTER, 1078
BURFORD, 1212
BURGES, 1132
BURGESS, 794 1028 1132-1133 1138
   1151 1167 Thomas 1151
BURKE, 850 856 859 861 861-862
   867 901-902 907 915 917 955
   966-967 1283 John E 861
BURLEIGH, 1087 1285
BURLEY, 1252 1282
BURLINGAME, 967
BURNAN, 1076
BURNETT, 1247 1265
BURR, 992 1256 1259 1266-1267
   1267 1293 1295 1301 1305 H S
   1267
BURRINGTON, 894 899 907-909 980
   983 986 999 1001 1084 1291 1308
   H H 980
BURRIS, 970
BUSBY, 904 1257
BUSH, 1084 1111 1291
BUSSEY, 1118 1233 E I 1233
BUSSY, 830
BUTLER, 820 826 839 877 907-908
   912 939 966 971 1039 1111
BUTTS, 1052
BYRAM, 1086
BYRNES, 1313 Patrick 1313
BYRON, 1244
BYWATER, 970
CADWALLADER, 825-826 1025 1077
   1081 1181 1295 C 1081

CAGLEY, 849 1116 1138 Jacob 1116
CALDWELL, 867 1208 1211 1292
CALEASE, 1094 1104 J W 1104
CALHOUN, 997
CALL, 822 856 863 868 1043 O A
   863
CALLAHAN, 1186
CALLENDER, 1152
CALLIINDER, 1157
CAMERON, 1128
CAMPBELL, 830 895 910-911 969
   1233
CANADA, 1214
CANBY, 968
CANFIELD, 1046
CAPEN, 958
CARBERRY, 829 961 1096
CARD, 850 903
CAREY, 1236 John 1236
CARKADDON, 957
CARKSADDEN, 958
CARMACK, 1047
CARMAN, 1212
CARPENTER, 863 873 895 902-903
   907-908 1020 1177 1188 1191-
   1192 1194 1206-1207 1213
   Chauncey 1194 Josiah 873 Philip
   1020
CARR, 856 862-863 868 910 956 958
   1253 1275 Ezra 862
CARROL, 1212
CARROLL, 1186 1195
CARSTENSEN, 794 825-826 994 1063-
   1065
CARTER, 1053 1126
CASE, 794 818 823 854 864 885 889
   891 897 899-902 904 907-909
   917-918 918-919 921 926-927 932
   938-940 943 948 969-971 998
   1000-1003 1088 1216 1216-1218
   1223 1223-1225 1229 1237 1248
   1252 1254 1261 1264 1276 1293
   1293-1294 1301 1308 1318 A J
   1301 Homer H 1216 Louis 918
CASPER, 1276
CASPES, 1276
CASS, 794 1033 1033-1034 1036
   1186 1188 1193 1195 1195-1198

CASS (cont.)
    1202-1203 1206-1207 1212-1213
    1213 E M 1033 S F 1195
CASSADY, 907
CASWELL, 1182 1185-1186 1211 1223
    David 1182
CATTELL, 899-900
CAULFIELD, 1218
CAVANAUGH, 998 1228 1231 1251
    1293 N 1228
CAVE, 956 1121-1123
CAVERN, 1040
CAVES, 1122
CELSEY, 966
CHADWICK, 821 961 967-968 1035
CHAMBERLIN, 879 895 910-912 980-981 981 986 1295-1296 D C 981
CHAMBERS, 853 956 1113 1121-1122 D H 1113
CHANDLER, 969-971 1227 1234
    Williard 1234
CHAPIN, 794 821 824 907 993 1012
    1056 1058 1062-1063 1223 1316
    John 1056
CHAPMAN, 1152 1297
CHASE, 890 1088
CHATTERTON, 1085
CHEENEY, 1273
CHEEVER, 925
CHENEY, 1273
CHESLEY, 966
CHETTENDEN, 970
CHILD, 932
CHITTENDEN, 1000-1001 1004 1216
    1223-1224 D 1216
CHRISLEY, 1304
CHRISTIERN, 1262-1263 1263 1283 J H 1263
CHRISTY, 907-908
CHURCH, 1072
CHURCHES, 1063
CHURCHILL, 961 993 1062-1063 1084 1291
CLAGAS, 1225
CLANSING, 1064 1225
CLAREY, 794
CLARK, 791 791-792 794-796 799
    818 820 823 839-840 853 875

CLARK (cont.)
    878-879 879 912 916 930 961 971
    998 1000 1004 1007 1024 1042
    1062-1063 1096 1121 1152 1174
    1195 1213 1256 1258 1264 1287
    1294 1308 David 791 John 791 W
    O 879
CLARKE, 904 1018 1192 1194-1195 1308
CLAUS, 1066
CLAUSING, 1067 1132 1134
CLAY, 997 1217
CLAYTON, 830 1083
CLEARG, 1014
CLEARY, 1014 Timothy 1014
CLEAVER, 1076
CLEAVEY, 830
CLELAND, 910 912
CLEWELL, 1082 1084 R W 1082
CLIGGETT, 910 912
CLINGENSMITH, 1128
CLINTON, 1085 1088
CLOAN, 861
CLOSSON, 1062
COAN, 856 861 D W 861
COATES, 1096
COATS, 1096 1297
COBB, 1292-1293
COCKMAN, 1121-1123
CODDINGTON, 794-795 823 1002 1004
    1015 1073 1084 1291 Frank 1073
CODNER, 830
CODY, 1262
COFFIN, 1148
COLBY, 967 1262
COLE, 899 901 909 1288 1291
COLEMAN, 1040 1087 1117 1287
COLFAX, 893
COLLIER, 840 1043 1106
COLLINS, 795 902 969-970 1018
    1094 1155-1156 1173-1174 1174 C P 1174
COLONY, 1152
COLTON, 1112 1119 1122-1123 Wm M 1112
COMINS, 853
COMSTOCK, 814 817 1263
CONDON, 1185

CONGDON, 822 1185-1187 1195 1197 1212-1213 Myron 1197
CONGER, 911 913
CONLEY, 1227
CONNABLE, 1075
CONNER, 790 826 907-908 930 961 1001 1117 1121 1212 1317 James A 930
CONNON, 1119 James 1119
CONNOR, 1019 1172 1227
CONRAD, 1112
CONSE, 1296
CONVERSE, 958 1033 C W 1033
CONWAY, 1040
COOK, 913-914 967 1001-1002 1035 1057 1062 1064-1065 1138 1204 D W 876 J J 1057
COOKE, 1063 1065 1297
COOL, 875-876 876 884 1296
COOPER, 831 895 909 911-913 928 1005 1076 1086 1093 1095 1164 1295 1295-1297 A D 1076 C H 928
COPELAND, 1040 1194 1198 1213
CORLETT, 1137 J J 1137
CORMACK, 1057
CORNELL, 876
CORNFORTH, 994
CORSE, 899
CORY, 878
CORYELL, 1193
COSTELLO, 1019
COUCH, 1306
COUNTRYMAN, 1063 1128 1212
COUSE, 831 877 1217
COVERT, 1261
COWEN, 903
COWN, 929
COWNER, 1212
COX, 1115
COY, 1274-1275
COYLE, 956 1294
CRAIG, 903
CRAIL, 866 966-967 1075
CRAMER, 1225 1295
CRANE, 1002 1035 1137 1156
CRAWFORD, 1224 1315
CREIGHTON, 1084 1302
CRETZMEIER, 1000

CRETZMEYER, 792 799 829 838 885 936 1243 1243-1244 1247 1252-1253 1265 1293 Fred 1243 W 1243
CREYTON, 830
CRIPPEN, 1148 1165 1287
CRIPPIN, 1226
CROCKER, 840
CRONK, 1155-1156
CROOKS, 1157
CROSBY, 1084 1228
CROSS, 902 1293
CROUSE, 1258
CRUTHERS, 1216 James 1216
CUFFEL, 1117
CULLESON, 910
CUMMINGS, 1262
CUMMINS, 1287
CUNNINGHAM, 1153 1165
CURRIER, 813 820 958 961 963 1152 1261
CURTIS, 818 820-821 824-825 831 904 956 958 966-967 1001 1031 1034 1076 1114 1213 1223-1224 1253 1258 1287 1293-1294 1296 1306 John 1114 S H 1258 W V 1031
CURTISS, 843 899 908 1034-1035 1154 1206
CUSHING, 925
CUSTER, 1223
CUTLER, 1108
CUTTS, 907-908 956
DAGGETT, 876
DAILEY, 1265 1286
DAILY, 898 1003 1086 1308
DALEY, 1095
DALLARD, 1231
DALLEN, 1031
DANA, 1153
DANIEL, 1315
DANIELS, 794 935
DARRAUGH, 1235
DAUGHERTY, 966
DAVIDSON, 961 971
DAVIS, 882 898 914 952 966-967 981 1003 1036 1038 1062-1063 1074 1084 1145 1145-1146 1153 1181 1184 1198 1206 B F 1074 W M 1145

DAWES, 1292
DAWSON, 863 867 867-868 1117 1127 1182 1182-1183 1186-1187 1187 1297 E A 867 J 1182
DAY, 907 910 1039 1098 1156 1167
DAYTON, 904
DEAN, 793 829 895-897 900-901 910-912 917 947-948 948 961 979 986 1002-1003 1007 1012 1093 1162 1258 1303 Daniel 1303 E J 948 Geo R 979
DEBEREIMER, 1211
DECAMP, 969
DECKMEYER, 830
DEERING, 840 909 911-912 914
DELANAH, 1174
DEMAREST, 1221
DEMENT, 878
DENIO, 1261
DENNING, 1164 1167
DENNIS, 1297
DERE, 913
DERMENDEN, 875
DETRICK, 821
DEVELIN, 1031
DEVIN, 910
DEVOE, 1122
DEWEY, 829 900
DEXTER, 1038
DEYOE, 907 1121-1122
DIBBLE, 794 1032 1041 R V 1041
DICK, 1046
DICKEN, 830 961
DICKEY, 1035
DICKINSON, 1027 1264 A A 1027
DIETRICH, 822
DIFFEE, 1022
DILDINE, 961
DILLEY, 1126
DILLON, 901 904
DINGMAN, 967
DITMORE, 1163
DIXEY, 966
DIZOTEL, 1215
DOANE, 909
DODGE, 889 899 966-967 969 971 1031
DOERR, 904
DOLLARHIDE, 1131

DONAN, 903-904 914-915
DOOLITTLE, 912 1277
DORN, 1225
DORSON, 1051
DOTY, 1182
DOUGHERTY, 820 863 866 868 874 903-904 911 926 966-967 1074 1074-1075 1081 1081-1082 1087 1286 D B 1074 E C 926 E M 1081 M B 866
DOUGLAS, 862 890 899 951 997 1274 1297
DOVE, 821-822
DOW, 793-794 796 839-840 911 1094
DOWN, 830
DOWNER, 967
DOWNING, 886 889 898-899 979 1076 1121 1123 1241 1251 1257 1257-1258 1282 1292-1293 1296 1296-1297 1315 Thomas S 1257
DOWNS, 820 966 971
DOWNU, 1001
DRAKE, 1184
DREW, 1161
DRUNKENMOLLER, 1042
DRYER, 949 1083
DUBOIS, 916 1033 1287 1293
DUDGEON, 829 966-967 1121
DUECK, 1225
DUKE, 1088
DULL, 1105
DUNBAR, 901
DUNCAN, 1235
DUNCOMB, 901
DUNCOMBE, 907
DUNGAN, 895 911
DUNHAM, 1141
DUNKAVEY, 903
DUNKELBERG, 883 883-884 R A 883
DUNLAP, 1166
DUNN, 1128 1185
DURHAM, 913
DUSTIN, 1152
DUTCHER, 961
DWYER, 1063
DYER, 1147 1174
DYMOND, 1186
DYRE, 969
DYSART, 908

EAD, 1212
EADS, 848 897 1124
EARL, 849
EARLE, 1246-1247 1253 1256 1261 1278
EARLY, 1024 Wm 1024
EASTMAN, 901
EBEL, 926
EBERHART, 1084
EBEY, 830
EBLY, 1293
ECK, 1165
ECKERT, 1164 1175 1175-1176 Henry 1175
EDDY, 1166-1167 1173 1286
EDE, 1155
EDGINGTON, 830 849 967 971 1106-1107 1122-1123
EDMONDS, 1193
EDSON, 980
EDWARDS, 1050
EGGLESTON, 878 1236 1304 Betsy 878 C E 1236
EGLESTON, 875 878 1167 1227 1236-1237 1281
EIBOECK, 910
EICHLER, 1295 1295-1296 F 1295
EICKMAN, 1225
EIFERT, 1257 1297 1313
EISENHART, 1001 1046 1046-1047 1065 1067 1118 1146 Eli 1046
ELDER, 910
ELDREDGE, 969
ELDRIDGE, 831 854 900 902 929 956 989 1002 1013 1138 1154 1157 1157-1158 J H 929
ELLES, 1001
ELLIOT, 829
ELLIOTT, 901-903 911 1000-1001 1111 1154 1226 1292 1318
ELLIS, 817-818 824 850 885-886 894 898-899 901 908-909 929 952 956 999-1000 1039 1043 1226 1238 1256 1261 1268 1274 1283 1294 1304 N P 1274
ELLSWORTH, 794 904 955 1213 1224 1227 1244 1244-1246 1246-1247 1252 1252-1253 1263 1265 1275 1282 1285-1286 R J 1246

ELSWORTH, 1083
ELWOOD, 900
EMILY, 1145 1145-1146 1153 A W 1145
EMMONS, 1206 1213 T P 1206
EMPSON, 1172 1175 J W 1175
ENGEL, 1132
ENGELBRECHT, 1131
ENGELBRETHS, 1133
ENGELKE, 1029
ENGLISH, 897
ENSIGN, 1248 1251-1252 1294
ERNST, 1041
ESTEP, 1106 1227
EVANS, 868 921 967 971 1112
EVELAND, 793-794 845-846 849 1093 1107 1107-1108 1108 1111 1116 1121 1123 Henry 1111 Jacob M 1108 Mason 1107
EVERDENG, 1061
EVERETT, 890 1038-1039
EVERSON, 1041
EWING, 844 965
EYER, 1134
FAGUE, 1202
FAIRBANKS, 969 1227
FAIRBROTHER, 965
FAIRBURN, 1046 1084
FAIRCHILD, 1204
FAIRFIELD, 850 902-903 992 1268 1277
FAIRHURST, 1121 1123
FARLEY, 1163
FARNER, 1034
FARNSWORTH, 910 961 1095 1101 1101-1102 1141 1172 1175 D 1175 Guy 1101 Robert 1141
FARNUM, 969
FARR, 1143 1152-1153 1153-1154 1156 1164 Wm 1143
FARRAND, 1185-1186
FARRER, 1174
FARRING, 796
FARRINGTON, 792-795 799 824 839 893 895 902 904 910-911 986 992-995 1004 1007 1010 1093-1095 1095-1096 M 1095
FARRIS, 795 799 811 820 829-830 849 854 885 898 920 928 966-967

FARRIS (cont.)
   1093 1095 1097 1127 1154 1248
   1256 Jeremiah 920
FASEL, 1213
FASIL, 1212
FASSEL, 1198
FAUVER, 1223
FAVIES, 1007
FAVILLE, 889 899 902 980 1287
   1316-1317
FAY, 1128 1212 1255
FEE, 790-791 795 839-840 1093
FEGHTMEIER, 1063
FEGTMEYER, 1132
FELT, 908 1002 1020 1050
FERGUSON, 1107 1233
FERRIS, 910
FERRO, 1062
FERROR, 1054
FERROW, 1064
FERRY, 908
FICHTHORN, 896 940 945-947 949
   1012 1281
FIFIELD, 1293
FIGG, 956
FINCH, 1048
FINDLEY, 1292
FINLEY, 1045
FISH, 969 1072-1073 1073-1074
   1083 1088 1146 1152 1158 E W
   1073
FISHER, 790 839 875 903 914 970
   974 1013 1093 1172 1195 1212
   1248 1253 Dr 875
FISK, 919
FISKE, 1293
FITCH, 1095 1212
FITCHTHORN, 946 Daniel 946
FITTS, 1063
FITZPATRICK, 890 1178
FLACHENERKER, 1134
FLEISCHER, 1121
FLEISHER, 820 966 1153 1157
FLEMMING, 1093 1095
FLESHER, 967
FLETCHER, 943-944 944 1002 1052-
   1053 1062 James 944
FLINN, 1251
FLINT, 1171

FLOOD, 794 1001 1124-1125 1127
FLOWERS, 1153 1173
FLOYD, 951
FLYNN, 1248
FOBBS, 1236
FOERSTER, 1064
FOLEY, 913 1124
FOLKE, 1153
FOLKS, 1152-1153 1153 1162 1162-
   1165 1167-1168 Charles 1162
FOLLANSBEE, 1182
FOOR, 1081
FOOT, 864
FORD, 1056
FORDNEY, 970
FOREMAN, 902-903 909 912
FORSSMAN, 1212 1212-1213 1213
   Peter 1212
FORTNER, 894 909 970 992 1039
   1043 1206 1265 1277 1314 A 1265
FORTUN, 1000
FOSSELMANN, 992 1262 1276 1293
FOSTER, 1117 1121 1123 1198 1227
   1248 John R 1117 Seth L 1117
GASAWAY, 866
GASS, 989
GASTON, 912
GATES, 897 933 967 969 971 1155-
   1157
GEAR, 895 911
GECKLER, 1134
GEDDES, 901
GEDDIS, 1248 1253
GEER, 910
GEIPER, 1225
GEISMAR, 1262
GEORGE, 1002 1013 1027 1131 1141
   1153 1158 1161 W H 1141
GEORGEGTON, 1094
GERBERT, 1029
GERRY, 823
GIBBONS, 910
GIBBS, 1030 1034 1114
GIBSON, 829 863 867 867-868 874
   1146 1151-1152 1165-1166 1309 D
   T 867
GILBERT, 792 967
GILLASPIE, 889 899 904

GILLETT, 794 830 853 893 898 902 904 912 915 927 955 989 999-1001 1010 1044-1046 1046 1049-1051 David 1046 M F 927
GILLETTE, 823-824
GILLILAN, 1044 1050
GILMORE, 961 971 1123
GISH, 1101
GISHBERT, 1244
GITHEL, 1152
GLASS, 967 1085-1086
GLASSFORD, 1286 1315
GLATTLEY, 911 1031 1034 1036
GLEASON, 1007 1098 1098-1099 Alonzo 1098
GLENN, 1294
GODDARD, 1296
GODRIDGE, 1123
GODWIN, 901
GOES, 1256 1261
GOFORTH, 830 1122 1226 1244
GOMNAN, 1222
GOODALL, 1206 1213
GOODE, 1165
GOODENOW, 898 969 971
GOODHUE, 1292-1293
GOODLOE, 1267
GOODMAN, 1261
GOODSELL, 1237 H W 1237
GOODSPEED, 1227 1238 Seymour 1238
GOODWIN, 892 899 901 910-911 933 985 1013-1014 1027-1029
GOODYEAR, 1307
GORDON, 1163
GORHAM, 1287
GORS, 1223-1224
GOSTING, 955
GOTHARD, 838 1243
GOTTSCHALK, 900 902
GOUGH, 850 1286
GOULD, 789 795 977 1092 1094 1098 1217 1217-1218 1257 1287 1297 H D 1098 Nichols 1217
GRAENING, 1132-1133
GRAETSEL, 1132 1132-1133
GRAF, 1132
GRAHAM, 970 1057 1261
GRANGER, 958 1142 1153 E A 1142

GRANT, 893-894 903 907 964 1295
GRASSMANN, 1135
GRAVES, 961 971
GRAY, 859 863 867-868 873 873-874 955 1152 1157-1158 1289 1295 H H 873
GREELEY, 862 893-894 907 1043 1078
GREEN, 956 969-970 1088 1192 1246 1306
GREGORY, 975
GRENNING, 1103
GREY, 1010
GRIBBLE, 1221
GRIESE, 1131 1133
GRIEVER, 961
GRIFFIN, 966 1125
GRIFFING, 830
GRIFFITH, 899-900 971 1185
GRIMES, 975
GRINNELL, 1011-1012 1032 1034-1035
GRISWOLD, 1277
GROEPPER, 1225
GRONEWIG, 909
GROSS, 878 878-879 1001 1082 J N 878
GROSSMAN, 1133
GROVE, 901 955
GROVER, 1114 1114-1115 1121 1156 W S 1114
GRUPE, 1103 1132
GUARD, 1030 1042
GUE, 902
GUERNSEY, 1292-1293
GUILBERT, 907
GULEN, 1013
GUNSABRIS, 955
GUNSALAS, 1064
GUNSALES, 1064
HAAG, 1186 1211
HAASE, 912 1105 1134 1293 1313 1313-1314 L C 1313
HAFENBRACK, 1134
HAGEMAN, 1029 1132
HAGEMANN, 1132 1134
HAGG, 1197
HAGUE, 1081

HAHN, 1061
HAIRIMAN, 881
HALBERT, 907 939
HALE, 845 966 1062-1063 1306
HALL, 840 867 900 903 908 961 969 980 1061 1108 1131 1165 1185 1206 1291
HALLETT, 1193
HALLMANN, 1252
HALSEY, 864
HALT, 865
HAM, 907
HAMBLIN, 853
HAMILTON, 819 838 885 898 902 914 922 970 1035 1083 1238 1246-1248 1253 1256 1262 1282 1296 1303 1315 W B 922
HAMLIN, 890
HAMMER, 903 1137
HAMMETTER, 1211
HAMMON, 1223
HAMMOND, 955 1286 1305
HAMORY, 829
HANADON, 873
HANCHETT, 894-895 897 909-912 917 917-918 930 1054 1262 L S 917
HANCOCK, 896-897 911
HAND, 1078 John C 1078
HANEBUTH, 921
HANER, 1122
HANNER, 1218 1223 1226 John 1218
HANSHKE, 1128
HARDIN, 1153
HARDING, 1131 1153
HARGES, 908
HARKER, 902 969-970 1022 1027-1028 1171 John 1022
HARMON, 811 817-818 838 849 856 885 889 897 899-900 915 931 933 936 955 959 961 989-990 1001 1007 1111 1243 1243-1248 1251-1252 1252-1253 1265 1275 1275-1276 1282 1287 1296-1297 1303 1307 1315 W P 856
HARNBURG, 1063
HARRIMAN, 1237 1237-1238 H B 1237
HARRINGTON, 794 820 904 907 916 994 1001-1002 1007 1011-1012 1037 1042 1139 1148 1152 1155-

HARRINGTON (cont.)
 1156 1156 1158 1183 Albert 1148 O C 916
HARRIS, 1003-1004 1007 1010-1011 1073 1094 1107 1114 1141 1141-1142 1155 1227 Thomas 1141 Wm E 1227
HEAD, 822 998-999
HEALD, 1088
HEALEY, 1078
HEAM, 1232
HEATON, 1144
HEERY, 829
HEGLEY, 1282
HEIDEMANN, 1094
HEINE, 992 1132 1209 1215 1223-1225 Henry 1215
HELLE, 1132
HEMMING, 1061
HEMPSTEAD, 800
HENDERSHOTT, 901 912
HENDERSON, 830 913-914 1246
HENDRICKS, 894
HENRY, 822 967 971 997 1048 1051-1052 1232
HENSTON, 820
HERBERT, 1041
HERDY, 830
HERMAN, 1257-1258 1262
HERMANN, 1256
HERRON, 956 968
HESS, 792-793 796 838 1243-1244
HEWETT, 1051
HEWITT, 847-848
HIBBEN, 1297
HIGGENBOTHAM, 1114
HIGGINS, 961 971 1061
HIGH, 896 908 910-911 985 992-993 1007 1074 1155 1189 David 1074
HIGHLAND, 1296 1317
HILDEBRAND, 794 1029
HILL, 903 911 1031-1032 1040 1262 1265
HILLER, 1262
HILMER, 949
HILTON, 873
HINKLEY, 956 1051 1186
HINTON, 792-793 796 821 830 966-967 1248 1251

HITCHCOCK, 958
HITTLE, 1141
HOAG, 1151
HODNETT, 968
HOFFMAN, 856 861 865 999 1147
    1198 1248 1253 1256 1258 1261
    1264 H J 1258 S E 861
HOGAN, 1093-1094
HOGRABE, 1164
HOHYNER, 796
HOLBROOK, 1263
HOLLAND, 912
HOLLENBECK, 1263
HOLLIS, 1027
HOLMES, 893 900-902 908 911 915
    958 1093 1101 1116 1287
HOLT, 1182 1202 1268 1271 1273
    1273-1274 1277 D P 1273
HOLTOM, 838
HOLTON, 1093
HOLWAY, 986
HOMRIGHAUS, 826 913 1104 1104-
    1105 1134 1199 John 1104
HOOD, 958
HOOKER, 908 911 957 979
HOOVER, 893 898-903 907-912 931
    1004 1052 1162 1283 1296 1315 H
    S 931
HOPKE, 1134
HOPKINS, 969-970 1138 1154 1183
    1253
HOPPENWORTH, 1029
HOPPER, 1029
HOPPINS, 1275
HOPPINWORTH, 1028
HORTON, 969 1186
HOSETUTTLES, 1137

HOTTSLANDER, 1301
HOUGH, 1027
HOUGHAWOUT, 1292
HOUGHTON, 967
HOUSER, 1283
HOVEY, 1165
HOWARD, 918
HOWE, 1085-1086 1086 1131 Chas M
    1086
HOWELL, 1052 1227 1248 1251

HOYT, 1283-1284 1284-1285 S R J
    1284
HUBBARD, 1184
HUBBELL, 853
HUCHNERBRG, 1132
HUDDATT, 1185
HUDNOTT, 967
HUDNUT, 915
HUDNUTT, 900
HUDSON, 955 1316
HUEBNER, 1132
HUEHNERBERG, 1133
HUFF, 1171
HUGH, 999
HUGHES, 967-968
HULL, 878 910-912
HULLMAN, 1228 1282 1296
HUMMELL, 981
HUMMER, 1174
HUMPHREY, 1283-1284
HUNSOCKER, 1061
HUNT, 901 903 992 1202 1206 1266
    1268 1277 1298
HUNTER, 799 830 838 922 936 1083-
    1085 John 922
HUNTINGTON, 1273
HURD, 969 971
HURLBERT, 1122
HURLBUT, 1002 1121 1141
HURLEY, 1308 Wm 1308
HURLY, 1308
HURMON, 1000
HURSH, 966 970-971 1145
HURST, 830 1093
HUSBAND, 1127 1183 1208 Wm C 1183
HUSTON, 966
HUTCHINS, 1077 1146 1163
HUTCHINSON, 830 1040
INGALLS, 1174
INGERSOLL, 794 812-813 1000 1115
    1121 1214 1223 1223-1224 W B
    1214
INGHAM, 829 1071 1086 1151 1165
    1285 1287 H S 1151
INGRSOLL, 821
IRISH, 910
IRSEP, 838
ISRAEL, 1261-1262
JACKMAN, 1152 1165 1167

JACKSON, 829 849 877 1136-1137
    1137-1138 1152-1153 1155 1163
    1175 1232 1262 Alexis 1137
JACOBS, 1266
JAGGAR, 1185
JAMES, 839 904 910
JAMIESON, 1019
JARVIS, 1063 1187 1204 1213 A H
    1204
JAUKEL, 1134
JAY, 989 991 1007 1292-1293
JEFFERO, 967
JEFFERS, 966 1023 1027 J F 1023
JEFFERSON, 969 997
JEFFREY, 1303
JEFFRIES, 1286
JENKINS, 811 849 900 933 1007
    1050 1094 1096
JENNESS, 1228
JENNINGS, 840 847 849 1036 1071
    1071-1072 1083 1089 1211 Samuel
    1071
JENNINS, W H 1211
JENSEN, 1063-1064
JESSUP, 910
JEWELL, 1118 1122 1218 1286 1304
JOHNSON, 794 826 830 890 892 916
    957 969 971 1007 1040 1049 1084
    1114 1235 1256 1266-1267 1293-
    1294
JOHNSTON, 823 907 1050-1051
JOLLY, 1056 Robert 1056
JONES, 820 899 909 911 913 955
    966 972 1023 1040 1081 1107
    1121 1142 1153 1261 1283 S N
    1081
JORDAN, 956 991 1063 1137
JUDSON, 1084
KAHLE, 1066
KAIMANSKA, 1212
KAISER, 1223-1224
KALLOCK, 875
KANE, 1083
KAPPINYER, 1029
KARKER, 956 972
KASEMEIER, 895 910-913 926 994
    1063 Henry 926
KAUN, 1043
KAY, 1101

KEATH, 911
KEATLY, 908
KEATOR, 1233
KEBE, 1131 1133
KEDING, 1128
KEELER, 1074 1084 1088 1165 1282
    1287 1315
KEENEY, 992
KEER, 971
KEHE, 823 907 1133
KEITH, 961 972 1276 1291
KELLER, 966 1215
KELLEY, 958
KELLING, 1132
KELLOGG, 853 898 1116 1206
KELLY, 1101 1116 1226 James 1116
KELSEY, 966 972 1062-1063 1065
KEMPER, 1211 1284
KENDALL, 849 1087
KENDIG, 956 1165
KENNECOTT, 880
KENNEDY, 1317
KENNY, 987
KENT, 1306
KENYON, 966
KEOSLING, 1116
KEPLER, 1192 1212
KERN, 966 972 1074 1094
KERR, 793-794 796 821 849 931 961
    966-967 999 1001 1037 1042-1043
    1227 1285
KESSLER, 1132 1297
KETCH, 839
KETCHUM, 1146 1162 1165 1168 1171
    1186
KEYS, 1257
KIDD, 1275
KIERCHHOFF, 1021 1027 1029
    Diedrich 1021
KIERCHOFF, 1021
KIERK, 1131
KIERNAN, 1264
KIMBAL, 1052-1053 1053 1062
    George 1053
KIMBALL, 910 917 1001
KIMPTON, 864
KING, 882 908 966 972 1083-1084
    1132 1192 1203 1203-1204 1213
    Wm 1203

KINGSBURY, 1064
KINGSLEY, 853 903-904 929 1001
    1065 1121-1122 1172 1204 1221
    1223 S H 1221
KINNE, 912 1248 1297
KINNEY, 1223
KINNIE, 863-864 864-865 1265 Eph
    864
KINSEY, 956
KINYON, 820
KIRKCHMANN, 1128
KIRKWOOD, 843 889 894 899-900 909
KISSELL, 904 975 1261
KLAGES, 993 1224 1311
KLEINLEIN, 1133-1134
KLINE, 831 1063 1067
KLINGEMSMITH, 1047
KNAPP, 907 910 1084 1115
KNIEF, 1132
KNIFFKEN, 1037 1042
KNIGHT, 909 1295 1297
KNITTLE, 1042
KNOCHE, 1222
KNOLTE, 1029
KNOTOKA, 1225
KNOTT, 967 992 1239 1246 1277
    1281 E 1281
KNOWLES, 922
KNUP, 1274
KOCH, 1031 1042 1063-1064
KOCK, 1063-1064
KOEHLER, 1134
KOELLING, 1131
KOERTH, 1192-1193 1213
KOHN, 1264
KOLLING, 1133
KOLLOCK, 878 Harriet M 878
KOOP, 830
KOPP, 1054
KOTHE, 1248
KOUKLE, 812
KRAUSE, 1183 1211 Frederick 1183
KRECH, 788 1007 1092 1103 H C
    1103
KRIEGER, 1112 1121 S C 1112
KUEPPER, 1295
KUHART, 1064
KUHRT, 1050 1065
KUNG, 1001

KURZ, 1029
KUTHE, 1029
LADD, 856 862 998 1152
LADWIG, 1187
LAMB, 831 903 1078 1087 1286
LAMPSON, 956 986 1017 1262
LAMSON, 961 1286
LANE, 890 1138 1283-1284
LANG, 1211
LANGMIER, 1194 1198
LARAH, 900
LARKIN, 1153 1164
LARKINS, 1076
LARRABEE, 1161
LARSON, 1213
LASH, 901
LASHBROOK, 900 908 961 966 970
    994 1013 1027 1047 1227 1231
    1251 1256 Thomas 1231
LASO, 1001
LATHROP, 907
LAUDENBECK, 1064
LAUDENBOCH, 1064
LAUGHMAN, 1162
LAUMAN, 964
LAUR, 1088
LAWRENCE, 929 955 1007 1113 1227
    1291 1303 1315 A S 1303
LAWTON, 1034
LAY, 1151 1151-1152 Charles 1151
LAYMAN, 812
LAYTON, 958
LE, Valley 1243
LEAMAN, 794 1014 J S 1014
LEAP, 1121
LEAPE, 1158
LEAS, 1232
LEASE, 823 907 1121 1128 1131
    1138 1154 1156 1156-1158 1181
    1186-1187 Henry Jr 1181
LEAVITT, 1256 1266-1267
LEDDICK, 1082
LEE, 849-850 876 918 948 999-1000
    1010-1011 1165 1202 1213 1249
    1252 1261 1297 1314 F A 1314
LEEGE, 820
LEEGERS, 1132
LEEHASE, 1132
LEES, 1121

LEFLER, 894 898 909
LEGGE, 961
LEHMAN, 794 885-886 898 928 1046-1047 1228 1252 1278 1283 Daniel 928 Moses 1228
LEHMANN, 994
LELAND, 1096
LEMMON, 1216
LENKUHL, 1252
LEONARD, 912 963 1042 1163 1202 1221 1227
LEROY, 1132
LESCHOLT, 1225
LESLIE, 966 972 1083 1291
LESTER, 794 823 907 1053 1054 1062-1064 Hiram 1053
LEVALLEY, 819 838 1253 1296 1304 Geo 1304
LEVALLY, 926 1304
LEVERICH, 795 817 956 971 1084 1232 1237 Charles 1232 Jesse 1237
LEVERICK, 936 966 972 1083 1088
LEVI, 1262
LEWIS, 849 914 966-967 972
LIEBERT, 1041 Charles 1041
LILLABRIDGE, 1165
LILLY, 1215
LINCOLN, 862 890-892 899 901 916 930 951-954 997 1104 1236
LINDEMAN, 902
LINDLEY, 903 945
LINES, 1264
LINK, 1027 1031 1035 1040 1042
LINN, 912 948-949 949 1193 1213 G P 949
LINSEY, 956 972
LISTON, 1116
LITTELL, 1186 1195 1198 1201 1212 D R 1198
LITTLE, 902 1132
LITTLEFIELD, 1017 1017-1018 1152 1152-1153 1155-1156 1158 M S 1017
LIVINGSTON, 1188
LOBDELL, 1055 1057 1063
LOBERK, 1135
LOCKEBER, 831
LOCKIE, 1125

LOCKWOOD, 1211
LOFTUS, 969
LOGAN, 1165 1176
LOMBARD, 1185
LONG, 794 1124-1127 1235 1236 1264 1279 D A 1235 Nelson 1127
LONGMIER, 1213
LONGYEAR, 1113
LOOMER, 1251
LOPER, 1216
LORD, 945
LOSEE, 1022 1022-1023 L E 1022
LOVEJOY, 969-970 1152 1192
LOVELAND, 794 882 898 1071 1076 1076-1077 1083 1114 1224 C K 1076 D E 1114 J 822
LOVELL, 850
LOW, 1282
LOWE, 820 889 899-900 909 966-967 1182 1186-1187 1212
LOWELL, 879
LOWRY, 1267
LOZIER, 894 909
LUALAM, 1207
LUCAS, 844 892 902-904 911 918 925 943 945 947 958 961 963 972-973 998-1001 1108 1118 1121 1121-1123 1273 1296 Parker 1108
LUCE, 1223
LUCUS, 956
LUDENBACK, 1064
LUDWIG, 1183 1211 1243 1262
LUMAN, 966
LUSH, 907 992 1111 1159 1266 1268 1272 1272-1273 1287 1295-1296 L L 1272
LUTHER, 830
LYMAN, 792 972 1318
LYNES, 1146 1158 1165 1175 W W 1146
LYON, 843 1034 1036 1058 Wm T 1034
LYONS, 909
LYTLE 1048 Henry 1048
MABB, 961 1184-1185
MABEE, 989
MABIE, 1291 1303 1315
MACOMBER, 794
MADDEN, 1181

HISTORY OF BREMER COUNTY 1341

MADIGAN, 948
MADOLE, 1118
MAGEE, 1286-1287 1287-1288 John C 1287
MAHONEY, 900
MAIN, 1051
MALLAHAN, 939-940
MALLER, 1211
MALLERY, 967
MALLORY, 864 956 969 1083
MANN, 975
MANNING, 912 1308
MANSFIELD, 855
MANTOR, 1297
MARCH, 1218
MARK, 1167
MARKELL, 1054
MARQUIS, 789 818 820
MARSH, 879 955 1024 1113 1113-1114 1121-1122 1142 1178 1291 1293 1312 N B 1113
MARSHALL, 855 912 917 1265
MARTIN, 792-794 796 799 846-847 875 885 894 897 904 909 920 966 976 979 1001 1012 1047 1050-1051 1055 1057 1062-1063 1071 1083-1084 1206 1235 1261 1275 1282 A T 1055 Asa T 1047 Betsy 875 J H 1057
MARVIN, 1037
MASON, 899 901 903
MATHES, 1066
MATHEWS, 903 1292
MATHIAS, 818 820
MATTHEWS, 874 886 898-901 904 1052
MATTHIAS, 1132-1133
MATTIX, 966-967
MAXAM, 1157
MAXFIELD, 814 817 854 886 889 898-901 920 920-921 1071 1083-1084 1185 1296-1297 Geo M 920
MAXON, 876
MAXWELL, 917
MAYDOLE, 1032
MAYNARD, 857 863 863-864 896 910-911 917 938-939 945 1107 1257 1294 1296 J K L 863
MCALESTER, 879

MCAULEY, 1188
MCCAFFRE, 839
MCCAFFREE, 788 788-790 794-795 799 801 909 1004 1007 1092 1094 1102 1321 1323 C 788
MCCAFFREY, 1071
MCCALL, 872
MCCARTY, 903
MCCLELLAN, 892 901 1114
MCCLINTOCK, 900
MCCLOSSEN, 1313
MCCLURE, 947 956 1101 1253 1271
MCCOOL, 875
MCCORD, 1292 1304 J P 1304
MCCORMACK, 903 1131 1224 1238 Charles 1238
MCCORMICK, 853 1014
MCCORTNEY, 1216
MCCRACKEN, 863 865 908-910 928 1013 1023 1227 1295-1296 A H 865 Thomas 1023
MCCRAY, 1035 1039
MCCREA, 1042
MCCREADY, 909-910
MCCUMBER, 1031 1034-1036 Albert 1031
MCDONALD, 929 969 972 1013-1014 1014 1017 1103 R G 1014
MCDOWELL, 1032
MCELHANEY, 1145
MCGEE, 829
MCGEEHEE, 1093
MCGINNIES, 1223
MCGINNIS, 971 1028
MCGLATHERY, 900
MCGOWAN, 1040
MCHENRY, 820 829-830 838 847-848 966-967 1071-1072 1102
MCHUE, 1040
MCINTYRE, 1057
MCJUNKIN, 910
MCJUNKINS, 909
MCKAY, 946
MCKIM, 1166
MCKINLEY, 1039 1265
MCKINLY, 850
MCKINNIE, 902
MCKNOWN, 1057
MCLANE, 970

MCMEEKIN, 1205-1206 1206 1212-
    1213 Wm 1206
MCMULLEN, 867
MCNAIRN, 1314
MCNAUL, 1212
MCPHERSON, 912-913 1071
MCRAE, 794 994 1037 1037-1038
    John 1037
MCREA, 1000-1001 1042
MCROBERTS, 792-793 795-796 799
    839 845-846 955-956 966-967 972
    1071 1111 1116 Thomas 1116
MEACHAN, 858
MEAD, 822 1131
MEADER, 1225
MEEDER, 831
MEEIR, 961
MEEKER, 961 1212
MEIER, 961 1036 1102-1103 1132-
    1134 H O 1102
MELONE, 1263
MERCHANT, 1040
MERRILL, 902-904 933 1003 1152
    1156
MERRITT, 900
MERWIN, 1194
MESSENGER, 790 1092 1236 E J 1092
    J C 1236 J H 790
MESSINGER, 789-790 792 794-796
    799 821 830 839-840 885 898 902
    933 961 972 1007 1092-1095 1104
MEYER, 1227
MEYERS, 1227
MICHAEL, 795 820 829-830 849 966-
    967 1001 1093-1094 1224
MICHNER, 1051
MICKEL, 910
MICKLE, 911 933
MICKLEY, 1078 1265 Thomas 1078
MILBURN, 1003 1264
MILES, 792 795-796 799 812 830
    839-840 845 849-850 853 856-857
    885-886 897-898 926-927 935-938
    961 1094 1108 1226 1228 1246
    1248 1252
MILINS, 1134
MILLBURN, 1248 1251-1252
MILLER, 790 830 839 880 900-901
    967 1004 1020 1029 1031 1036

MILLER (cont.)
    1075 1078 1088 1093 1098 1103
    1108 1111 1117-1118 1121-1122
    1183-1185 1205 1211 1236 1261
    1286 1293 Anton 1183
MILLET, 1121
MILLS, 817 903
MINER, 1227 1233
MINKLER, 1036 1038
MISCHLER, 902
MISHLER, 795 829-830 1093
MITCHEL, 970
MITCHELL, 899 1013 1051 1193
MOEHLING, 1036 1054 1054-1055
    1062-1065 1067 1105 1132-1134
    H 1067 John 1054
MOELLER, 1133
MOHLING, 822-823 899 933 961 993
    994 1223-1224
MOHLIS, 1030 1036
MOLLER, 1029
MOLTGER, 1131
MONOGUE, 1121
MONROE, 901
MONTROUSE, 1098
MOODY, 879-880 880 883 970 1057
    1063 1164 1168 W J 880 Wm 1057
MOON, 927 970 1278
MOONEY, 1244 1251 1262-1263 1263
    1275 Wm 1263
MOORE, 822-823 828-830 848 892
    900-903 911 927 966-967 972
    1007 1027 1064 1071 1084 1088
    1108 1126 1186 1217
MOOREHOUSE, 898 1088
MORE, 956
MOREHOUSE, 817 823 825 885 898
    907-909 925 1083-1084 1087 1311
    Geo 925
MORES, 1253 1264 1276 1302 1303
    1306 A S 1302 Wm H 1306
MORGAN, 908 961 1255 1258
MORRILL, 972
MORRILLE, 971-972
MORRIS, 898 1152 1268 1301
MORRISON, 1218
MORROW, 958
MORSE, 822 900-901 907-909 921
    925 969 999 1227 1261 1276 1282

MORSE (cont.)
  1293 Caleb 925
MORTON, 940 956 969-970 1083 1258 1287
MOSER, 961
MOSHER, 1258 1297
MOSS, 795 848
MOTT, 1122
MOULTON, 889 899 902 939 955 978-979 985 1124-1125 1128 1158 1178 1181 1184 1255 1286 1293-1294 A K 978
MOXEM, 1065
MOXON, 1235
MUELLER, 1064 1066
MUFFLEY, 1186
MUFFLY, 912 1202 1206 1213 J H 1202
MULLARKEY, 847
MULLENS, 1307
MULLIN, 830
MULOCK, 1048 1057
MUMM, 907
MUMMEALTIE, 1021
MUNGER, 909-911 926 1185-1186 1287 1295
MURDOCK, 850 1195
MURPHEY, 1223
MURPHY, 1131 1204-1205 1213 1223
MUSCH, 877
MYERS, 956 972 1071-1072 1073 1232 Abraham 1072
MYGATT, 867
NAFUS, 1056 1147 1152 G W 1147
NAPIER, 1125 1127
NASH, 903 909-911 925-926 933 992
NATTON, 1153
NEAL, 1040 1042
NEEDHAM, 900
NEFF, 956 1253
NEGUS, 909
NEIDERT, 908
NEILSEN, 1262-1263
NERGO, 961
NETTLOCH, 1046
NEUHAUS, 1297
NEVERMAN, 1131 1133
NEVERMANN, 1132
NEWBOLD, 909

NEWCOMB, 1153 1172 1174 1174-1175 1262 E S 1174
NEWELL, 966-967 1029 1063 1078 1152 1161
NICHOL, 961
NICHOLLS, 908
NICHOLS, 879 879-880 883-884 904 909-910 933 966 1164-1165 1168 1171 1217 Horace 879
NICHOLSON, 1218 1221 1221-1222 1222 1224-1226 W J 1222 Wm 1221
NICOLS, Gould 1217
NIDEMEIR, 1293
NIRGE, 1098 1104
NIVEN, 850
NOBLE, 902 911 914 969
NOETTGER, 1133
NORMAN, 1192 1302
NORRIS, 818 889 899 922 922-925 925-933 933-966 966-979 979 1121 1301 1301-1302 1304 Keeler 1301 W W 922-979
NORTON, 1012 1065 1088 1164 1166 1166-1167 1226 Frances J 1166
NOTTON, 1165
NOUNAN, 1213
NOURSE, 900
NUHN, 1225
NULL, 830 849 1106 1108 1252
NUTE, 1040
NUTTING, 929 966 972 1138 1152-1156 1156-1158 1293 1315
OAKS, 1093
OBENCHAIN, 967
OBER, 966 972
OBERDORF, 908 911 1117 1253 P 1117
O'BRIEN, 961 972
O'BRYAN, 1055
O'CONNER, 788-789 894 903-904 907 1092
O'CONNOR, 894
O'DAY, 1124 1127 Patrick 1124
O'DEA, 794 823
ODELL, 1088 1286
ODIVENE, 1125
OFF, 1064
OGDEN, 821 829 966 972 1214 1224
OGLESBY, 1034

OLDENDORF, 1067
OLDS, 1247 1256 1278 1296
OLENCHAIN, 972
OLMSTEAD, 838 1084
OLNEY, 1020 1085-1086 J B 1020
OLTROGGE, 1103 1132 John 1103
O'NEIL, 1293
ORCHARD, 1153
ORLEDGE, 1031
ORTH, 1138
ORTHMANN, 820
ORVIS, 1182-1186 1197 1212 S N 1182
OSBORN, 879
OSBORNE, 879
OSTHMAN, 966 972
OSTRANDER, 898 932 1118 1121 1296
OTTMAN, 1105
OTTO, 1064 1066
OTTROGGE, 1133-1134
OUDERKIRK, 1234
OVELERUG, 829
OVERMAN, 847
OWEN, 898 932 1061 1205 C 1205 L S 1205
PACKARD, 1034
PAGE, 830-831 1043 1127
PALMER, 893 1161 1236 1293 1295
PANTON, 1151
PAQUIN, 904 933
PARISH, 1233
PARKER, 822-823 878 961 972 1035-1036 1108 1183 Lucas 1108
PARKHURST, 1125 1184
PARKS, 876
PARMENTER, 958
PARMINTER, 1308
PARSHALL, 1183
PARSON, 1257
PARSONS, 856 863 1186 1192 1194 1212 1283 1286 C B 863
PARTRIDGE, 865
PATRIDGE, 1143
PATTAS, 1293
PATTEE, 811 829 849 891 898 900 904 918 935 955 969-970 989 1074 1082 1086-1087 1094
PATTERSON, 965 1039 1056-1057 1172 1282 1291-1292 1294

PAUL, 898 1086
PAULGER, 949
PAYNE, 792 795-796 1071 1083-1084 1086-1087
PAYSON, 970 972
PAYTON, 849 1107 1291
PEACOCK, 1022
PEAPE, 1002
PECK, 794 970 1030-1031 1034-1035 1038 1042-1043 1317 N C 1038
PEEBLES, 969
PELTON, 794 956 1107 1107-1108 1112 1118 1121 1125 1227 1263 Wm A 1107
PENDLETON, 892
PERKINS, 814 850 856 860 1024 1127 1185 1235 1294 Benj F 860 D E 1024
PERRY, 892 900 904 989 1040 1040-1041 1043 1111 1125 1223 1233 1233-1234 1305 1311 E N 1233 M E 1040
PETER, 1104
PEYTON, 955
PHELPS, 830-831 929 967 1085 1137 1152
PHILLIPS, 961 1085 1093 1101 S B 1101
PHINEY, 1217
PICKEL, 1050
PICKENS, 951
PICKETT, 1046
PICKLE, 1052
PICKWICK, 856
PIERCE, 963 1065 1077 1151 1151-1152 1152-1153 1153 1161-1162 1215 1277-1278 1278 Daniel 1077 N E 1278 Riley 1151
PIERSON, 916 1157 1158 W J 1157
PIGHS, 1132
PIKE, 1165
PINOE, 1211
PITCHER, 845 969 1072 1085 1224
PITKINS, 1083
PITT, 997
PIXLEY, 1053
PLANT, 1113
PLATT, 1122
PLATTE, 1223 1225

POHLER, 1035
POLAND, 1187
POLLARD, 898
POMEROY, 875 883-884 1067 1248 1261
POMROY, 878 J C 878
PONDE, 830
POOK, 1132 1134
POOL, 829 1031
POOR, 849-850 858
PORCH, 1062
PORTER, 910 1035 1037 1042 1293
POST, 1078
POTTER, 824-825 908 965 1018 1049 1155-1156 1156-1157 1157 M 1018 Warren 1157
POUND, 971
POWELL, 811 829 849 970 1095 1107 1227
POWERS, 910-911 1167
PRANTY, 1053
PRATT, 907-908 914 1118 1121-1122 1128 1291
PREDMORE, 1073
PRELLER, 1134
PRESTON, 814 849-850 856 1173
PRICE, 844 956 965 1056 1234
PRIFFER, 1213
PRINCE, 821
PRINDLE, 908
PROP, 1029
PRUE, 1215-1216 Nelson 1215
PUTNEY, 1165
QUEEN, 849 885 898 966 1083
QUIMBY, 1262
QUINN, 989
QUIREY, 1212
QUIVEY, 1193
RAHN, 1061
RAINBOW, 1020
RAIRDEN, 1182
RAND, 1207 1213 J C 1207
RANKIN, 902-904 1288
RANSOM, 1293
RANTOON, 925
RANYAN, 1296
RATHBURN, 1041
RATHE, 912
RATHROCK, 910

RAUSCH, 1056 1134
RAWSON, 1113
RAY, 1066 1216
RAYMOND, 1237 1257
RAYNER, 1106
REARDON, 1035
RECK, 1087
REDDINGTON, 831 1001 1126
REDEMAN, 882 908 P 882
REED, 1022 1111 1212 1263
REEVES, 818 820-822 830 857 892 902 908 991 998 1000 1109 1111 1121-1122 1179 1244 1248 1252-1253 1282 1311 1311-1312 B M 1311 N A 1111
REHERN, 928
REID, 1195
REIDEMAN, 909
REIMLER, 1187-1188 1195 1197 1211 1213 C F 1197
REINEGER, 910 912
REINIGER, 853 907
REITER, 1264
REMINGTON, 1306
RENGORY, 830
RENN, 820 967 1121-1122
RENO, 966
REPP, 1007
REUM, 956
REW, 1122
REYNOLDS, 820 966 972 1185 1212 1305
RHODES, 1173 1305
RICE, 826 898 913 1221 1293 W A 1221
RICH, 958 1083 1087
RICHARDS, 901 1040 1042
RICHARDSON, 904 955 972
RICHEY, 1138
RICHMAN, 961
RICHMOND, 818 820-821 830 989 1037-1038 1042-1043
RICKEL, 1144
RICKER, 1117
RIDEMAN, 910
RIDENOUR, 909
RIDGEWAY, 824 1268 1275
RIECH, 1133
RIED, 1024 C D 1024

RIETK, 1133
RIGGS, 1293
RILEY, 1128 1177
RIMA, 849 927 1044-1045 1045-1046
  1050-1051 1122 Levi 1045
RIMON, 830
RINEHART, 1023
RINER, 1256
RIPLEY, 912
RISCK, 1132
RISDEN, 956
RITTENHOUSE, 1078
ROACH, 1148 1171 1173 John 1148
ROBB, 900
ROBBINS, 821 961 966 972 1031
  1131
ROBERTS, 893 897 902 912 980 1093
  1147 1147-1148 1153 1164 1171
  1173 C B 980 J M 1147
ROBERTSON, 862 1286 And Ladd 862
ROBINSON, 794 856 880 961 1021
  1021-1022 1022 1028 1033 1035
  1038 1050-1051 1053 1085 1093
  1164-1165 1187 1217 1223 1226 M
  H 1217 W A 1022 W S 1021
ROBISH, 881 1198 1202 1212-1213
ROCKDASCHEL, 1184
ROCKWOOD, 961
RODEAMAL, 908
RODECK, 1313
RODGERS, 966 972
ROEKER, 1225
ROEVER, 1132
ROGERS, 1128 1256 1266 1297
ROHLERING, 1132
ROHLFE, 907
ROHLWING, 1061 1063-1064
ROLLINS, 1116
ROMBERG, 1228
RONCO, 1048
ROOD, 1037
ROOP, 969-970
ROOT, 912 965 1057
ROSA, 1204
ROSE, 925 966-967
ROSECRANS, 902 1048
ROSENBAUM, 1268 1274
ROSENCRANS, 1235 John 1235
ROSENTHAL, 1029

ROSS, 955 1048 1111 1227
ROSZELL, 795 799 907 910 1244
ROURAY, 908
ROWE, 1176-1177 1177-1178 1178
  1184-1185 1185-1186 Albert 1178
  Charles 1177
ROWEN, 795 830 847-848 854 898
  900-902 921 933 989 999 1071
  1073 1083 1085-1086 1088 1131
  1185 1315 M 921
ROWRAY, 904 926 1227
ROYER, 1216
RUBRACHT, 1201
RUDDICK, 814 843 850 853-854 856-
  857 859 863-864 867-868 886
  898-899 901 904 907 910 912 915
  921 931 954 961 1000-1001 1003
  1255 1258 1294 1296 G W 850
RUDEMANN, 1261
RUETE, 1067
RUMMELLS, 911
RUMSEY, 847
RUNNELLS, 908
RUNYAN, 903 1153
RUNYARD, 1307 Austin 1307
RUNYON, 911 961 1002
RUSCH, 899
RUSSELL, 904 907 1052-1053 1121
  1301 1307 J Q A 1301
RUSSETT, 967 972
RUST, 895 909-912 921 1063 1224
  Herman 921
RYAN, 1172
SABIN, 1027 1042
SAGER, 1297
SAILES, 1014
SAINTJOHN, 956 966-967
SAINTJOHNS, 1076
SAMPLE, 789 840 1092
SAMPLES, 839 1092
SAMPSON, 844 1295
SAMUELS, 889 899
SANBORN, 1155-1157
SANDERS, 1042 1152-1153 1181
SANFORD, 1027 1152
SANITER, 1067
SANKEY, 1000 1038
SATTERSFIELD, 1053
SAVAGE, 1208

SAVERING, 1064
SAWYER, 1017 1156
SAYERS, 1036
SAYLES, 899 979 1027 1051
SAYLOR, 1105 Samuel 1105
SCARF, 1252
SCHAFFER, 966
SCHAIPHORSTER, 1211
SCHEFFEL, 1201
SCHEUAM, 1027-1029
SCHIEFERDERKE, 1134
SCHILD, 1238
SCHLABERG, 1122
SCHLUTSMEYER, 1296 1311 F H 1311
SCHMIDT, 1293 1311
SCHMITT, 1263
SCHOFIELD, 882
SCHOLES, 1185
SCHOOF, 1132 1134
SCHOONMAKER, 1302
SCHORR, 1134
SCHROADER, 1064
SCHROEDEMEIR, 1225
SCHROEDEMEYER, 1225
SCHROEDER, 1064 1132 1135
SCHROETER, 1065
SCHUCKER, 1095
SCHUKNECHT, 1058 1061 1063-1064 C 1058
SCHULTZ, 1065
SCHUMACHE, 1134
SCHUMACHER, 1132
SCHUNEMANN, 1093
SCHWARTZ, 1029
SCHWARZ, 1296-1297
SCOBIE, 1097
SCOTT, 794 829 903 940 947 951 956 958 1111
SCOVILLE, 1216
SCREBNER, 969
SEAL, 871
SEAMAN, 883 1287
SEARLES, 1268
SECOR, 908-909
SEELEY, 1212
SEEVERS, 913
SELBIG, 1262 1276 1293 L 1276
SELGERS, 1134
SELLENS, 1312
SELLS, 898-899
SEMPLE, 789
SENNETT, 902
SERVICE, 1051
SESSIONS, 1224 1286
SEVAN, 849
SEVENSON, 1071
SEVERINE, 961
SEVERINGER, 1134
SEVERS, 909
SEVISON, 1076
SEWARD, 880 890 954 970
SEWELL, 794 849 896 911 956 966-967 1002-1003 1007 1012 1083 1088 1145 1231 1231-1232 1278 1287 1306 1306-1307 Allen 1306 Samuel 1145 T J 1231
SEYMOUR, 893 903
SHAFFER, 1000
SHANE, 966-967 1262
SHANNEMAN, 1029
SHANNON, 1095 1292
SHARP, 820 930 958 966-967
SHATTUCK, 1121 1123
SHAULTZ, 850
SHAVER, 856 861 904 1224 Hiram 861
SHAW, 820 882 963-964 967 1049 1077 1081 1122 1225-1226 1226 Enos F 1077
SHEDUEDE, 1223
SHEELEY, 1224 1292
SHEFFER, 1287
SHELDEN, 1122 1152
SHELDON, 1281
SHEPARD, 790 794-795 845-847 886 898 966 972 986 994 1071-1072 1072 1079 1083 1085-1087 1208 1262 1285 S F 1072
SHEPHERD, 970
SHEPPARD, 1004
SHERIDAN, 843
SHERLIE, 1027
SHERMAN, 844 908-910 912 957 965 1038 1057 1121 1167 1236 1288
SHERWIN, 970
SHERWOOD, 1118 1237
SHEWARD, 907
SHIELDS, 862 914 1153 1294

SHIMER, 1166
SHIPPY, 830
SHIRLEY, 1019 1020 1028 John W 1019
SHIVLEY, 961
SHOEMAKER, 961 1235
SHOLES, 818 820 1185 1186 1281 1287 L M 1281
SHORES, 966-967 1276
SHORT, 1182
SHOWALTER, 1002 1153 1156-1157
SHULL, 1213
SIEBERT, 1155
SIEKMEIER, 1222
SIGMUND, 1133
SILL, 1084
SIMMONS, 1222 1225 1291 John 1222
SIMON, 1063
SIMONDSON, 1307
SIMPSON, 1083 1086
SINCLAIR, 1233
SINDERSON, 1019 Thomas 1019
SITGER, 1258
SITZER, 1297
SKILLEN, 907 910 917 999 1001-1004 1007 1010 1046 1062-1063 1121 1123 1223
SKILLIN, 917 James A 917
SKINNER, 1088 1287
SLACK, 1022 1064
SLATER, 1114
SLEEPER, 961 967
SLEMMER, 952
SLIMMER, 824 1268 1271-1272 1274
SLIMMERS, 1268 Abram 1268
SMALLEY, 823 863 866 1223 1235 1287 1292 E L 866
SMALLING, 1083 1086 1088
SMEED, 937-939 1315
SMELTZER, 1043
SMILIE, 1267 1295 1305 1306 Francis 1305
SMITH, 814 818-821 830 850 875 878 878-879 885 893 898-899 901-904 917 929 933 949 961 964-967 969-970 972 989 992 999 1019 1032 1048 1052 1061 1088 1093 1095 1131 1136-1137 1137-1138 1138 1152 1154-1156 1156

SMITH (cont.)
1165-1166 1171 1186 1205 1211 1214 1223-1224 1226-1228 1243 1247-1248 1253 1262 1262-1267 1286 1293 1295 1305 1313 C O 1152 J G 878 J L 1138 Joseph 1138 Lloyd 1137 N M 929 Wm 130
SMOCK, 1071
SMOOT, 1263
SNIDER, 831
SNYDER, 898 1058 1062
SOMBERGER, 1121
SOUTHWICK, 1056 1147
SOWERS, 961
SPALDING, 1143 1152 1156 1158 1293 1305 J F 1143 M S 1305
SPAULDING, 1027 1121
SPEAKER, 1296
SPEARS, 1203 1212
SPENCER, 1014 1051 1102 1148 129: 1297
SPROUL, 1314
SPURRIER, 912
STAAGEE, 1093
STAGER, 1128
STAMM, 1293
STANNARD, 794 1013 1027
STANSBURY, 907
STAPLES, 963
STAPLETON, 1238
STARBUCK, 1055
STARR, 1003 1007 1262 A 1262
STEARNS, 821 966 1221
STEARS, 794 830 838 1093 1095-1096 1096-1097 1169 John 1096
STEEGE, 1132 1134
STEELE, 957 1024 1077
STEEN, 1186 1263
STEGGE, 1215
STEIN, 1125
STEINWARTH, 1313
STEPHAN, 1225
STEPHENS, 830 1023 Alex 1023
STEPHENSON, 794 820 823 904 922 992 1121 1121-1123 1286-1287
STERLING, 994 1032 1034 1235 W P 1032
STEUBENRAUCH, 909

STEVENS, 900 918 952 968 1223
    1241
STEVENSON, 818 825 828 909 1122
    1177 1177-1178 1184-1186 A L
    1177
STEWARD, 1142
STEWART, 867 897 930 938 948 961
    981 986 1073 1084 1172 1235
    1283-1284 1291
STILES, 904
STILWELL, 871
STITGER, 1063
STOCKING, 1223
STOCKWELL, 992 1234 1234-1235 W L
    1234
STODDARD, 902 1185
STONE, 901-902 1294
STONEMAN, 864 904
STORY, 855
STOUFFER, 931
STOUNE, O A 1277
STOW, 944
STOWE, 856 861 903 W A 861
STOWELL, 1275
STRATTON, 1308
STREETER, 961
STRICKLAND, 853 1317
STROAT, 1223
STROFFMAN, 1135
STRONG, 1277 1293
STROUD, 1301
STROUNE, 1277
STROW, 956 1117
STRUBLE, 1244
STUART, 1084
STUBBS, 910
STUFFLEBEAM, 885 897 1107-1108
    1112 1121 J 1112
STUMME, 794
STURDEVANT, 794 829 838 849 853
    936 956 966-967 969 972 999
    1001 1004 1010 1215 1223 1243
    1248 1285 J M 1215
STURGESS, 1114
STYLES, 902
SULLIVAN, 1116 1311 Harvey 1311
SUMMERLIN, 1161
SUMNER, 893 1107
SUNDERLIN, 958

SUTHERLAND, 865
SWAIN, 912 1075
SWALE, 1001
SWAN, 812 849-850 856 885-886
    897-898 931 935 1024 1167-1168
    P V 856
SWARTH, 1211
SWEARINGEN, 911
SWEAT, 1261
SWEET, 1057 1057-1058 1058 1063
    1126 1128 1131 1184 1303 A E
    1057 H H 1058
SWETT, 1256 1315
SYKES, 1061-1062
SYLVESTER, 900
TABER, 956 1073 1303 E F 1303
TABOR, 956 1185-1186 1265
TAFT, 1183 Isaac 1183
TALBOT, 1235
TALLET, 1283
TANNER, 823-824 863-864 864 956
    1227 1283 A J 864
TAPE, 1138
TARR, 1183
TATUM, 1093
TAYLOR, 821 863 966 972 992 1038
    1042 1051-1052 1085-1086 1114
    1118 1127 1131 1152 1164 1234
    1263
TEGTMEIER, 1064
TEGTMEYER, 1133
TEMPLE, 911 1164-1165 1171
TENAURE, 961
TERRY, 821 823 853 908 1001 1028-
    1029 1056 1118 1121 1144 1149
    1152 1152-1153 1153 1155-1157
    1195 1282 1291 1305 Adin 1144
    Erl 1118
TERY, 1118
THARP, 1093
THICKSTON, 1291 1294
THICKSTUN, 985 1255
THIES, 792 1035 1238 1297 Henry
    1238
THOMAS, 872 903 1066 1083 1093
    1155-1156 1297
THOMPSON, 818 820 825 883-884 892
    901 912 952 1055 1125 1143 1152
    1154 1162 1193 1223 Barnes 1113

THOREN, 1222 1222-1223 1311
    Christian 1222
THORINGTON, 913-914
THORNBREW, 1083
THORNBRUE, 956
THORNE, 1223-1224
THORNSBREE, 956
THORNTON, 855
THOROMAN, 1044 1050
THOROUGHMAN, 1013
THORP, 792 796 829-830 837 849
    856 961 972 1185
THORPE, 863 1174
THRALL, 1126
THULL, 910 1186 1195 1203 Frank
    1203
THURSTON, 830
TIBBETS, 840 1204
TIBBETTS, 790-791 796 840 849
    1102-1103 1188 1192 1233
TIBBITS, 839 1092 1186-1187 1195
    1197 1213
TIBBITTS, 1102 1188 1206 O O 1188
    W J 1102
TIBBLES, 969
TIEDS, 1135
TILDEN, 894-895 909
TIMBLIN, 1223
TINA, 1000
TINKHAM, 955 966 968-969 1312
TITCOMB, 885 898 932 989 1052-
    1053 1062
TODD, 1192 1201-1202
TOMPKINS, 882
TONDRO, 1276
TOOKSBURY, 1032
TORRENCE, 1040
TOWER, 948 1187 1187-1188 1192
    1204 1213 Thomas W 1187
TOWNSEND, 1256 1282-1283
TRACY, 1293
TRAYNER, 872
TRENTOR, 1175
TRESCOTT, 1153 1165
TRIMBLE, 895 902 911
TRIMBO, 839
TRIPLETT, 1034
TRIPP, 1235
TROWBRIDGE, 1063-1064 1268

TROY, 821
TRUE, 956
TRUMBAUER, 993
TRUMBO, 793-794 796 799 829-830
    837 840 886 898 931 1062 1093
    1214-1215 1224 Israel 831
TRUMBULL, 862 893
TRUMFAIR, 1223
TUCKER, 1019
TURK, 1045 1049-1050
TURNER, 856 862 1213 1248
TUTTER, 1062
TUTTLE, 849 901 1093
TYLAR, 1152
TYLER, 961 1003 1137 1143 1144
    1281 E H 1143
TYNER, 963
TYRELL, 955-956
TYRREL, 944 1007
TYRRELL, 812-813 885 897 930 933
    940 943-945 949 956 971 1108
    1214 1215 1219 1224 1226-1228
    1283 1293-1294 1296 1297 1298-
    1299 1301 1317-1318 Clarence
    1214 N 1296 Thos 1298 Wm H 944
ULTHOUSE, 1225
VAIL, 795 1071 1083-1084
VALE, 908
VANAMBURGH, 1145
VANANDA, 902
VANBERGEN, 1031
VANBUREN, 1054 1057
VANCOELIN, 910
VANCOELLIN, 911
VANDERWALKER, 1042-1043
VANDEVER, 914 1121
VANDEVERE, 899 956-957
VANDIVER, 1108
VANDORN, 1122 1166 1168
VANKLECK, 956
VANNORDSTRAND, 1078
VANORDSTRAND, 1265
VAUGHAN, 1021
VAUGHN, 1063
VINCENT, 1063 1098
VINER, 1266
VOIGHT, 1308 John 1308
VOLKERT, 1133
VONCOELIN, 909

VOORHEES, 1304
VOSSELER, 1121
WADE, 965 999 1004 1115 1208
    1211 1212 1283 Abraham 1115
WAGGONER, 1107 1112
WAGNER, 1264 1265 1293 John 1265
WAGONER, 1068 1131
WAGOR, 1117
WAIT, 876 955 980
WAITE, 1035 1257
WAITING, 1001
WALDEN, 904
WALES, 1225
WALKER, 862-863 872 898 910-912
    933 1021 1021-1022 1028 1043
    1062-1063 1142 1163-1164 1164
    1167 1171 1174 E C 1164 Geo E
    872 P N 1174 R 1021
WALLACE, 901 904 931 1082 1108
    1227
WALLING, 818-820 903 916 927 961
    989 1002 1010-1012 1045-1046
    1048 1049-1051 1054 D P 1049 E
    J 1048
WALTERS, 812 1001 1046 1106 1121
WALTHAGEN, 1225
WANEMAKER, 1148
WARD, 823 875 877 1040 1041 1192
    1305 Jacob 1040 Jesse 877
WARE, 1257 1262 1276 1311 H L
    1257
WARNER, 1061-1063 1165-1166 1193
    1297
WARRING, 904
WASHBURN, 986
WASHINGTON, 997 1181
WATENPAUGH, 794 1125-1126 1127
    1185-1187 E 1126
WATERBURY, 1295
WATERHOUSE, 829
WATERS, 1122
WATKINS, 912 966 972 992 1055
    1056 1067 1113 1122 1195 M M
    1055
WATROUS, 1050
WATSON, 955
WATTENPAUGH, 1001
WATTERS, 1001 1107

WATTKE, 1211
WATTS, 794 912 969-970 1001 1030
    1031 1054 Geo 1030
WAVERLY, 1252
WEARNE, 1283 1297
WEART, 908
WEAVER, 896-897 911 917 1203
WEBB, 917 961 1051
WEBBER, 1215
WEBER, 1241
WEBSTER, 829-830 997 1093 1185
    1295
WEHRMACHER, 1055
WEIDBRECHT, 1134
WEIDMANN, 949
WELDON, 1293
WELLER, 907 910-911 1116
WELLMAN, 823
WELLS, 830 903 958 975 1118 1151
    1234 1292 H R 1234
WEMPLE, 955 1213
WENDORF, 1106
WENRICK, 821
WENTE, 1131-1135 1135 H C 1135
WENTWORTH, 1033 1183
WERDMAN, 1223
WERMACHER, 1042
WESCOTT, 1186 1192 1194-1195
WESEMANN, 1058
WEST, 881 958 966-967 1039 1152
    1153 1166-1167 1203 1237
WESTCOTT, 1194 Orris 1194
WESTENDORF, 1132
WESTERVELDT, 849
WESTERVELT, 961 1094 1121
WETHEREL, 1086
WEYGANDT, 1087
WHEAT, 1235
WHEATON, 1178 1185 1186 Geo W
    1178
WHEELER, 894 1138 1231 1297
WHIPPLE, 1085-1086
WHITCOMB, 903-904
WHITE, 830 872 1032 1035 1042
    1062 1074 1167 1207 1208 1213
    1286 1295 Frank K 1208
WHITING, 908 1024 1027-1028 1213
    1293 Luther 1024

WHITNEY, 872 884 1163 1185
WIEDEMANN, 1261
WIGGINS, 1223
WIGHTMAN, 1145
WILCOX, 919 1196 1297
WILDER, 1094
WILE, 1121 1232 1233 1293 John 1232
WILES, 1121
WILHARM, 1064 1066 C 1066
WILKENING, 1061 1132-1133
WILKINS, 1178 1212
WILL, 1121
WILLARD, 1164
WILLEY, 830 1111 1126
WILLIAMS, 844 850 880 900 902-903 1056 1152-1153 1165 1208 1293
WILLIAMSON, 912 1032 1034-1035
WILLIS, 1096 1252 1307
WILMOTH, 1152
WILSEY, 1106-1107
WILSON, 795 818-820 826 849-850 863 880-884 894 899 911-912 928 933 966-967 1018 1053 1112 1118 1121 1126 1156 1185 1193 1202 1207 1212 1213 1231 1265 A B 1118 J N 880 L P 1018
WINKLEPECK, 1093
WINKLEPLECK, 961
WINN, 1187
WINNE, 794
WINNER, 1103 1223 1233 A M 1233
WINRECH, 1223
WINSLOW, 956
WINTER, 795 882
WIPPERMANN, 1311
WIRE, 1148
WISE, 971
WISNER, 1036
WITNEY, 1185
WITTENBURG, 1132
WOLF, 1035
WOLFE, 1167
WOLFRATH, 1133
WOLLING, 830
WOLVERTON, 1141

WOOD, 794 799 813 862 955 969 1001 1098 1223 1248 1262 1296-1297 1307 J W 1307 James W 862
WOODBURY, 1123
WOODCOCK, 1138 1154
WOODRING, 1193 1201 1202 1213 1264 1264-1265 1276 1287 J F 1264 Peter 1201
WOODRUFF, 823 828 1223 1261 1263 1304 1304-1305 E A 1304
WOODS, 908 999
WOODWARD, 909
WOODWORTH, 929 1304
WORDEN, 1033 John L 1033
WORDSWORTH, 1282
WORTHINGTON, 1108 1317
WORTZ, 1262
WRIGHT, 813 831 850 856 857 859-861 863 885-886 889 897-904 911 931 944 949-950 961 989-990 998-1001 1007 1040 1107-1108 1115 1122 1185 1195 1197-1198 1212-1213 1217 1224 1283-1284 1296-1297 1311 Gancelo C 857 M S 1197
WUEST, 918 1053 1054 1061-1063 1083 Matthias 1054
WUSTHOFF, 1308
WUTHY, 1164
WYANT, 912 1048 1083 1086
WYLAM, 1218 1222 1225 Jasper 1218
WYLE, 850
WYNHOFF, 1063-1065 1066 H J 1065
YAGER, 948
YARGER, 948
YEOMAN, 911
YERTON, 794 1032 1034-1036 J H 1032
YOJRS, 1224
YORK, 1297
YOUMANS, 929 1234
YOUNG, 854 907-909 1057 1086 1088 1131
YOUNGS, 1077 Wm H H 1077
YOUNT, 1108
ZIMMERMAN, 1031 1034-1035 1051
ZOLER, 961

www.ingramcontent.com/pod-product-compliance
Lightning Source LLC
Chambersburg PA
CBHW060907300426
44112CB00011B/1377